Dynamic Disequilibrium Modeling presents some recent surveys and developments in dynamic disequilibrium and continuous time econometric modeling, along with related research from associated fields. Specific areas covered include applications in business cycles and growth, tests for nonlinearity, rationing and disequilibrium dynamics, and demographic and international applications.

The contents of this volume are drawn from the proceedings of the ninth conference in *The International Symposia in Economic Theory and Econometrics* series, under the general editorship of William Barnett. The proceedings volume includes the most important papers presented at a conference held at the University of Munich on August 31 – September 4, 1993. The symposia in the series are sponsored by the IC² Institute at the University of Texas at Austin and are cosponsored by the RGK Foundation. This ninth conference was also cosponsored by the Deutsche Forschungsgemeinschaft (DFG) and the Bavarian Ministry of Education, along with the Seminar for Mathematical Economics (SEMECON), the Center for Economic Studies (CES), and the Economics Department at the University of Munich. The symposium was held at the University of Munich.

The organizers of the ninth symposium, which produced the current proceedings volume, were Claude Hillinger at the University of Munich, Giancarlo Gandolfo at the University of Rome "La Sapienza," A. R. Bergstrom at the University of Essex, and P. C. B. Phillips at Yale University.

T0323719

Dynamic disequilibrium modeling

International Symposia in Economic Theory and Econometrics

Editor
William A. Barnett, *Washington University in St. Louis*

Other books in the series

William A. Barnett and A. Ronald Gallant
*New approaches to modeling, specification selection, and
econometric inference*

William A. Barnett and Kenneth J. Singleton
New approaches to monetary economics

William A. Barnett, Ernst R. Berndt, and Halbert White
Dynamic econometric modeling

William A. Barnett, John Geweke, and Karl Shell
Economic complexity

William A. Barnett, James Powell, and George E. Tauchen
*Nonparametric and semiparametric methods in econometrics
and statistics*

William A. Barnett, Bernard Cornet, Claude D'Aspremont,
Jean Gabszewicz, and Andreu Mas-Colell
Equilibrium theory and applications

William A. Barnett, Melvin J. Hinich, and Norman J. Schofield
Political economy: Institutions, competition, and representation

William A. Barnett, Hervé Moulin, Maurice Salles, and
Norman J. Schofield
Social choice, welfare, and ethics

Dynamic disequilibrium modeling: Theory and applications

Proceedings of the Ninth International Symposium in Economic Theory and Econometrics

Edited by

WILLIAM A. BARNETT
Washington University in St. Louis

GIANCARLO GANDOLFO
University of Rome "La Sapienza"

CLAUDE HILLINGER
University of Munich

CAMBRIDGE
UNIVERSITY PRESS

CAMBRIDGE UNIVERSITY PRESS
Cambridge, New York, Melbourne, Madrid, Cape Town, Singapore,
São Paulo, Delhi, Dubai, Tokyo, Mexico City

Cambridge University Press
The Edinburgh Building, Cambridge CB2 8RU, UK

Published in the United States of America by Cambridge University Press, New York

www.cambridge.org
Information on this title: www.cambridge.org/9780521174978

© Cambridge University Press 1996

First published 1996
First paperback edition 2011

A catalogue record for this publication is available from the British Library

Library of Congress Cataloguing in Publication data
International Symposium in Economic Theory and Econometrics
(9th : 1993 : University of Munich)

Dynamic disequilibrium modeling : theory and applications :
proceedings of the Ninth International Symposium in Economic Theory
and Econometrics / edited by William A. Barnett, Giancarlo Gandolfo,
Claude Hillinger.

p.   cm. – (International symposia in economic theory and
econometrics)

ISBN 0-521-46275-4 (hc)

1. Equilibrium (Economics) – Econometric models – Congresses.
I. Barnett, William A.   II. Gandolfo, Giancarlo.   III. Hillinger,
Claude, 1930–   .   IV. Title.   V. Series.
HB145.I59   1993
330'.01'5195 – dc20   95-47537
                                                                 CIP

ISBN 978-0-521-46275-4 Hardback
ISBN 978-0-521-17497-8 Paperback

Contents

Volume editors' preface

The contents of this volume comprise the proceedings of the conference, "Dynamic Disequilibrium Modeling: Theory and Applications," held at the University of Munich in Munich, Germany, on August 31 – September 4, 1993. This proceedings volume includes 18 of the most important refereed papers presented at that conference.

The purpose of the conference was to document the achievements of dynamic disequilibrium (DDE) modeling, particularly in the construction of theoretical and econometric models. The major effort and greatest progress in DDE modeling has been in the area of continuous time macroeconometrics. That literature is the principal focus of the survey papers in the first section, and the methodology is used in many of the other papers appearing in this volume.

Macroeconomics, by its very nature, is characterized by compromises. These compromises may involve placing emphasis on: partial equilibrium at the expense of general equilibrium; elementary goods and individual agents at the expense of aggregation over goods and economic agents; linearity at the expense of the inherent nonlinearity of microeconomic theory; infinitely rapid adjustment at the expense of rational transient response; perfect memory and complete information at the expense of learning; perfect rationality at the expense of bounded rationality; small models at the expense of real-world explanatory power; perfect certainty modeling at the expense of risk aversion; static modeling at the expense of dynamics; and/or atheoretical time-series methodology at the expense of economic theory. Dynamic disequilibrium theory represents a middle ground, providing the ability to use much structural economic theory in a manner that permits coherent econometric application with existing macroeconomic data.

In its most elegant manifestations, DDE modeling uses continuous time macroeconometric methods, which permit the estimation of the parameters of systems of differential equations in a manner providing accurate inferences about dynamics. The DDE approach is based upon the generation of a stochastically equivalent discrete time analogous model. This methodology is important because the economy itself is a continuous time dynamical system, whereas the data are available only in discrete time as point observations. The common practice of modeling the theory itself in discrete time connects theory with available data in a convenient and immediate manner. However, that greatly simplifying approach is less satisfactory than continuous time macroeconometrics, since discrete time economic theory unreasonably implies that all transactions occur at the boundaries of time intervals. In a measure-theoretic sense, discrete time economic models imply that the economy exists almost nowhere within the time domain – and does not exist almost everywhere within that domain – because the sequence of boundary points of discrete time intervals has Lebesgue measure zero on the real-line time domain.

The estimation of the parameters of difference equation models produced from discrete time economic theory can result in seriously erroneous inferences regarding dynamic response rates in the continuous time real world. The computationally difficult, but very sophisticated, approach of continuous time macroeconometrics addresses these issues directly through the generation and estimation of the parameters of a stochastically equivalent discrete time analogous model. The advantages of continuous time macroeconometrics are important. One reason for those many advantages is that dynamic adjustment disappears only in the steady state, which characterizes no one's views of the real world.

Since the subject of DDE is large and growing, the conference could not include papers representing all constructive areas of research in the DDE tradition. One such important omitted area, which nevertheless merits explicit mention in this introduction, is the research on disequilibrium growth theory begun by Takatoshi Ito in 1980 and extended in many recently published papers by Ito and by other economists.

This volume is divided into six parts, corresponding to the six major topics of the conference. Part I of the volume consists of three survey papers. Part II's topic is continuous time models. Part III consists of two papers on business cycles and growth, and Part IV deals with tests for nonlinearity. Part V introduces rationing into disequilibrium dynamics. Finally, Part VI contains three papers on demographic and international applications.

At the University of Munich the conference benefited from the support of the Economics Department and its Dean, Professor Dr. Klaus Zimmermann, as well as of the Center for Economic Studies (CES), directed by Professor Dr. Hans-Werner Sinn. The organizational work was managed at the Seminar for Mathematical Economics (SEMECON) by

Ulrich Woitek, assisted by Secretaries Anne Kaiser and Christa Rosak as well as an enthusiastic crew of students. The editors thankfully acknowledge the financial support of the IC^2 Institute at the University of Texas at Austin, the RGK Foundation in Austin, Texas, the Deutsche Forschungsgemeinschaft (DFG), and the Bavarian Ministry of Education.

William A. Barnett
Washington University in St. Louis

Giancarlo Gandolfo
University of Rome "La Sapienza"

Claude Hillinger
University of Munich

Series editor's preface

The conference that produced this proceedings volume is the ninth in a conference series entitled *International Symposia in Economic Theory and Econometrics*. The proceedings series is under the general editorship of William Barnett. Individual volumes in the series generally have co-editors, who differ for each volume since the conference topics change each year. The symposia in the series are sponsored by the IC^2 Institute at the University of Texas at Austin and are cosponsored by the RGK Foundation.[1]

The first conference in this Cambridge series was co-organized by William Barnett and Ronald Gallant, who also co-edited the proceedings volume. That volume appeared as the volume 30, October/November 1985 edition of the *Journal of Econometrics* and has been reprinted as a volume in this Cambridge University Press monograph series. The topic was "New Approaches to Modeling, Specification Selection, and Econometric Inference."

Beginning with the second symposium in the series, the proceedings of the symposia appear exclusively as volumes in this Cambridge University Press monograph series. The co-organizers of the second symposium and co-editors of its proceedings volume were William Barnett and Kenneth Singleton. The topic was "New Approaches to Monetary Economics." The co-organizers of the third symposium, "Dynamic Econometric Modeling," were William Barnett and Ernst Berndt; the co-editors of that proceedings volume were William Barnett, Ernst Berndt, and Halbert White. The co-organizers of the fourth symposium and co-editors of its proceedings volume, "Economic Complexity: Chaos, Sunspots, Bubbles, and Nonlinearity," were William Barnett, John Geweke, and Karl Shell. The co-organizers of the fifth symposium and co-editors of its proceedings volume, "Nonparametric and Semiparametric Methods in Econometrics and Statistics," were William Barnett, James Powell, and George Tauchen.

[1] IC^2 stands for Innovation, Creativity, and Capital.

The co-organizers and proceedings co-editors of the sixth symposium, "Equilibrium Theory and Applications," were William Barnett, Bernard Cornet, Claude d'Aspremont, Jean Gabszewicz, and Andreu Mas-Colell. The co-organizers of the seventh symposium, "Political Economy: Institutions, Competition, and Representation," were William Barnett, Melvin Hinich, Douglass North, Howard Rosenthal, and Norman Schofield. The co-editors of that proceedings volume were William Barnett, Melvin Hinich, and Norman Schofield.

The eighth symposium was part of a large-scale conference on "Social Choice, Welfare, and Ethics." That conference was held in Caen, France, on June 9–12, 1993. The organizers of the conference were Maurice Salles and Hervé Moulin. The co-editors of that proceedings volume were William Barnett, Hervé Moulin, Maurice Salles, and Norman Schofield. The ninth symposium, which produced this volume, was organized by Giancarlo Gandolfo, Claude Hillinger, A. R. Bergstrom, and Peter C. B. Phillips.

The tenth volume in the series will be the joint proceedings of a conference held in Florence, Italy, on "Nonlinear Dynamics in Economics" and the invited sessions of the annual meetings of the American Statistical Association held in San Francisco. The editors will be William Barnett, Mark Salmon, and Alan Kirman. The eleventh volume will be produced from the proceedings of a conference to be held at Washington University in St. Louis in September 1995. That conference, co-organized by William Barnett, Andrew Lo, Lars Hansen, and George Tauchen, is on the topic of "Computation and Estimation in Finance and Economics."

The intention of the volumes in the proceedings series is to provide *refereed* journal-quality collections of research papers of unusual importance in areas of currently highly visible activity within the economics profession. Because of the refereeing requirements associated with the editing of the proceedings, the volumes in the series do not necessarily contain all of the papers presented at the corresponding symposia.

William A. Barnett
Washington University in St. Louis

Contributors

William P. Anderson
Department of Geography
McMaster University

Giuseppe De Arcangelis
CIDEI
University of Rome "La Sapienza"

William A. Barnett
Department of Economics
Washington University in St. Louis

A. R. Bergstrom
Department of Economics
University of Essex

B. Dejon
Institute of Applied Mathematics
University of Erlangen–Nürnberg

Steven N. Durlauf
Department of Economics
University of Wisconsin at Madison

A. Ronald Gallant
Department of Economics
University of North Carolina at Chapel Hill

M. Gallegati
Department of Economics
Universita' G. D'Annunzio-Pescara

Giancarlo Gandolfo
CIDEI
University of Rome "La Sapienza"

D. Delli Gatti
Department of Economics
Universita' Cattolica-Milan

F. Graef
Institute of Applied Mathematics
University of Erlangen–Nürnberg

Claude Hillinger
SEMECON
University of Munich

Melvin J. Hinich
Department of Government
University of Texas at Austin

Mark Jensen
Department of Economics
Southern Illinois University at Carbondale

Jochen Jungeilges
Department of Economics
University of Osnabrück

Alfred Maussner
Department of Economics
Universität zu Köln

H.-J. Meier
Institute of Applied Mathematics
University of Erlangen–Nürnberg

J. Novotný
Institute of Applied Mathematics
University of Erlangen–Nürnberg

K. B. Nowman
London

Pier Carlo Padoan
CIDEI
University of Rome "La Sapienza"

Yorgos Y. Papageorgiou
Department of Geography and
   Department of Economics
McMaster University

Michael Reiter
SEMECON
University of Munich

Laura Sabani
CIDEI
University of Rome "La Sapienza"

Werner Smolny
Department of Economics
Universität Konstanz

Claus Weddepohl
Department of Economics
University of Amsterdam

Ulrich Woitek
SEMECON
University of Munich

Clifford R. Wymer
CIDEI
University of Rome "La Sapienza"

Peter A. Zadrozny
Institute on East Central Europe
Columbia University

PART I

Survey papers

CHAPTER 1

Survey of continuous time econometrics

A. R. Bergstrom

1   Introduction

I have, already, published several surveys of the field of continuous time econometrics (1976, 1984a, 1988, 1990). In surveying the field again for this conference, I will emphasize the more recent developments and the importance of continuous time econometrics for dynamic disequilibrium modeling. My survey will cover both the theory of continuous time econometric methods and their empirical applications. It will start, however, with a restatement and discussion of the main arguments for the specification of econometric models in continuous time rather than discrete time.

2   Advantages of continuous time econometric models

I will briefly discuss seven advantages of continuous time econometric models, although the list of advantages could be extended (see e.g. Gandolfo 1993, pp. 2–4).

The first advantage, which is a very general one, is that a continuous time model can take account of the interaction between the variables during the unit observation period. Although the variables in a typical macroeconomic model are measured only at regular discrete intervals (for example, quarterly or annually), we know that they are adjusting at much shorter random intervals as a result of the uncoordinated decisions, at different points of time, of a large number of economic agents. Moreover, we do have information, from economic theory and other sources, concerning the interaction between the variables during the unit observation period. Because of the smallness of the samples with which econometricians must work, it is very important that we should take account of this information in our estimation procedures.

A second advantage, which is closely related to the first one, is that a continuous time model can represent a causal chain or causal system, in

3

which each of the variables responds directly to the stimulus provided by a proper subset only of the other variables in the model, and yet there is interaction between all the variables in the model during the unit observation period. The formulation of econometric models as causal chains was strongly advocated by Herman Wold in his celebrated long-running debate with the Cowles Commission in the 1950s on causal-chain models versus nonrecursive, simultaneous equations models (Wold 1952, 1954, 1956, 1960; Bentzel and Hansen 1954; Strotz and Wold 1960; Strotz 1960). Wold had been brought up in the Stockholm tradition and regarded causal-chain models as more fundamental than nonrecursive simultaneous equations models. Moreover, although the models used in his own work were formulated in discrete time, he recognized the potential importance, for econometrics, of causal-chain models formulated as systems of differential equations (Wold 1956).

From an econometric point of view, an important argument in favor of causal-chain models is that they can take account of a priori information concerning the causal ordering of the variables. When the model is formulated as a system of linear differential equations, most of the coefficients in the system are restricted to zero, and the causal ordering of the variables is represented by the pattern of these zero restrictions. The assumption that the variables can be arranged in a causal chain of this type need not depend on any elaborate or controversial economic theory, but only on our knowledge of the information available to various agents at particular points of time. It is obvious, for example, that aggregate consumer expenditures on a particular day can be influenced by the levels (on that day) of only those variables that are known to consumers – particularly personal income, personal assets, and prices – and not by the levels (on that day) of such variables as exports, imports, and investment. This is very strong information, which can be used to reduce the variances of the parameter estimates. But it can be used efficiently only if the model is formulated in continuous time. For, because of the interaction of all variables during the unit observation period (say a quarter), the conditional expectation of the value of each variable in quarter t, conditional on information up to the end of quarter $t-1$, will be a function of the values in quarter $t-1$ (and, generally, quarters $t-2, t-3, ...$) of all the variables in the model, not just a proper subset of them.

A third advantage of continuous time models is that they permit a more accurate representation of the partial adjustment processes in dynamic disequilibrium models than is possible in a discrete time model. Nearly all of the continuous time macroeconometric models that have been developed during the last twenty years, starting with the disequilibrium neoclassical growth model for the United Kingdom by Bergstrom and Wymer

(1976), have been dynamic disequilibrium models formulated according to a common general pattern. A typical equation in such a model can be formally split into two parts. The first part, which can normally be derived from microeconomic equilibrium theory, is an equation relating the partial equilibrium level of the causally dependent variable to a proper subset of the other variables in the model. The second part is a differential equation of first or higher order, representing the adjustment of the causally dependent variable in response to the deviation of its current level from its partial equilibrium level. Such an equation can be obtained by solving a dynamic optimization problem, taking account of adjustment costs of various orders. (See e.g. Bergstrom and Chambers 1990; Hillinger, Reiter, and Wesser 1992.)

A fourth advantage, which is closely related to the previous one, is that a continuous time model provides the basis for a more accurate estimation of the distributed lags with which each variable depends on the variables on which it is directly causally dependent. Indeed, the distributed lag relation will have the form of a convolution integral that can be derived from the differential equation representing the partial adjustment relation. In this connection, it is worth recalling the important article of Sims (1971) (see also Geweke 1978), which showed that distributed lag relations satisfied by discrete data that have been generated by a continuous time model can give a very misleading impression of the underlying continuous lag distributions.

A fifth advantage is that procedures for estimating continuous time models make a clear distinction between the treatment of stock variables (e.g., the money supply and the stock of capital), which are measured at points of time, and flow variables (e.g., output and consumption), which are measured as integrals. Standard procedures for the estimation of models formulated in discrete time make no distinction between the treatment of stock and flow variables. Consequently, estimates of the parameters can be seriously biased owing to the specification error resulting from the aggregation over time implicit in the definition of the flow variables.

A sixth advantage is that the form of a continuous time model does not depend on the unit observation period. Discrete time models are much less flexible. Indeed, the form of quite simple discrete time models is dependent on the unit observation period. For example, if the monthly observations of a certain variable satisfy a second-order autoregressive model, then the quarterly observations of the same variables satisfy an autoregressive moving-average model. Since the econometrician can seldom choose the observation period but rather must work with the available data, the dependence of the form of the model on the unit observation period is a serious drawback.

A seventh advantage is that a continuous time model can be used to generate forecasts of the continuous time paths of the variables. Such forecasts can be of considerable value, in spite of the fact that the variables are observable only at discrete intervals of time. For example, a forecast of the continuous time path of the gross domestic product could be used by businessmen for sales forecasting or by the government for policy formulation.

3   Econometric methods for continuous time models

The antecedents and early history of continuous time econometrics were discussed in my historical survey (1988; reproduced in Gandolfo 1993), and I will now review them very briefly.

The problem of estimating the parameters of a continuous time stochastic model from discrete data was first discussed by Bartlett (1946). He pointed out that the economy does not cease to exist between observations, and went on to consider the problem of estimating single first- and second-order differential equations from discrete data. His paper was presented at a Meeting of the Royal Statistical Society and stimulated a lively discussion by M. G. Kendall and other leading statisticians, particularly concerning its potential importance for econometrics. But it seems to have been overlooked by econometricians. A possible reason for this is that, three years earlier, Haavelmo (1943) had introduced his simultaneous equations methodology, which became the dominant econometric methodology for the next thirty years.

The first econometrician to recognize the potential importance of continuous time models in econometrics was Koopmans (1950), who had himself played an important role in the development of the simultaneous equations methodology (see Koopmans, Rubin, and Leipnik 1950). But it was A. W. Phillips (1959) who developed the first detailed algorithm for estimating a continuous time model of sufficient generality to be used in applied work. From an econometric point of view, a limiting feature of the algorithm developed by Phillips was that it could not take account of a priori restrictions on the coefficient matrices of the continuous time model, such as the restriction that certain elements of these matrices should be zero.

I commenced work on continuous time econometrics in the early 1960s, and one of my objectives was to develop methods of estimation that could take account of these a priori restrictions. I decided that it would not be practicable, with the computing resources then available, to obtain asymptotically efficient estimates of the parameters of a continuous time model of ten or more equations, taking account of the exact restrictions on the distribution of the discrete data implied by the continuous time model. I decided, therefore, to follow a simpler approach based on the use of an approximate discrete model in the form of a nonrecursive simultaneous equations model. The idea that a nonrecursive simultaneous equations model is best regarded as some sort of approximation to a causal system had already been put forward by Strotz and Wold (1960).

In Bergstrom (1966) I derived the asymptotic bias of estimates obtained by applying the method of three-stage least squares to such an approximate discrete model. It was assumed, for this purpose, that the continuous time paths of the variables were generated by a closed system of first-order differential equations, with white-noise innovations, and that they were observable at equispaced points of time. The type of approximate discrete model used in this study was extended in subsequent articles by Sargan (1974, 1976) and Wymer (1972) to take account of exogenous variables and flow data. Moreover, a computer program for the estimation of the parameters of a continuous time model by applying the method of full-information maximum likelihood to the approximate discrete model was developed by Wymer (1968), and has been used in the estimation of nearly all of the continuous time models produced during the last twenty years.

It will be useful, at this stage, to return to the simpler case discussed in my 1966 article, and consider the relation between the approximate discrete model introduced in that paper and the exact discrete model satisfied by the data. The assumed continuous time model is a first-order system that can be written as

$$dx(t) = A(\theta)x(t)\,dt + \zeta(dt), \tag{1}$$

where $\{x(t), \infty < t < \infty\}$ is an n-dimensional continuous time random process, A is an $n \times n$ matrix whose elements are known functions of a p vector θ of unknown parameters ($p \le n^2$), and $\zeta(dt)$ is a vector of white-noise innovations (see Bergstrom 1984a for a precise interpretation of this system). A sequence of equispaced observations $x(0), x(1), x(2), \dots$ generated by the system (1) satisfies the exact discrete model

$$x(t) = F(\theta)x(t-1) + \epsilon_t, \tag{2}$$

where

$$F = e^A = I + A + \frac{1}{2}A^2 + \frac{1}{3!}A^3 + \cdots \tag{3}$$

and

$$E(\epsilon_s \epsilon_t') = 0, \quad s \ne t. \tag{4}$$

By integrating the system (1) over the interval $(t-1, t)$ and making a trapezoidal approximation to the unobservable integral $\int_{t-1}^{t} x(r)\,dr$, we obtain the approximate discrete model

$$x(t) - x(t-1) = \tfrac{1}{2}A\{x(t) + x(t-1)\} + u_t, \tag{5}$$

which is a simultaneous equations model.

The degree of accuracy of the approximate discrete model can be most easily assessed by considering its reduced form

$$x(t) = \Pi x(t-1) + v_t, \tag{6}$$

where

$$\Pi = [I - \tfrac{1}{2}A]^{-1}[I + \tfrac{1}{2}A]$$
$$= I + A + \tfrac{1}{2}A^2 + \tfrac{1}{4}A^3 + \cdots. \tag{7}$$

Comparing (3) and (7), we see that the difference between F and Π depends only on A^3 and higher powers of A. The model (1) implies that the elements of A have the same dimension as the unit of time, which we are here identifying with the unit observation period. Our comparison of F and Π thus implies that the error in the model (6), regarded as an approximation to the exact discrete model (2), is of the same order as the cube of the unit observation period (as the latter tends to zero).

If the only restrictions on A are that certain elements be zero, in which case θ is just the vector of unknown elements of A, then θ can be estimated by applying standard simultaneous equations estimation procedures to the approximate discrete model (5). Numerical examples considered in my 1966 article showed that the asymptotic bias of such estimates is quite small under realistic assumptions about the speeds of adjustment and the unit observation period. Moreover, it was later shown by Sargan (1974, 1976) that the asymptotic bias of such estimates is of the order of the square of the unit observation period as the latter tends to zero.

In spite of these asymptotic results, an important Monte Carlo study by P. C. B. Phillips (1972) showed that, with finite samples, spectacular gains in efficiency can be obtained by using the exact discrete model (2) rather than the approximate discrete model. Assuming a first-order three-equation model with observations at equispaced points of time, he obtained parameter estimates first by applying three-stage least squares to the approximate discrete model and then by applying the minimum distance estimation procedure of Malinvaud (1980, chap. 9) to the exact discrete model. He found that use of the exact discrete model led to a more than 50-percent reduction in the root-mean-square errors of the estimates of most of the parameters of his model, and that this was mainly due to a reduction in the variance.

The results obtained by Phillips suggested that we should, ultimately, develop methods of estimation based on the exact discrete model. But the use of such methods would not have been practicable with the computing resources available in the 1970s, except for the first-order models with no flow variables. When the variables are a mixture of stocks and flows, then the exact discrete model corresponding to even a first-order system is a vector autoregressive moving-average model with complicated restrictions between the autoregresive and moving-average coefficient matrices. When estimating continuous time models from flow data, the normal procedure (until very recently) has been first to transform the data using an autoregressive transformation introduced by Bergstrom and Wymer (1976) and then to use the transformed data to estimate the approximate discrete model (1) or, in some cases, the discrete model (5). But estimates obtained in this way are not asymptotically efficient, even if the model (5) is used.

During the last decade there have been enormous developments in computing technology, and the latest generation of supercomputers is capable of speeds of several billion floating-point operations per second. Concurrent with these developments in computing technology has been an immense amount of work on the development of algorithms for the computation of asymptotically efficient estimates of the structural parameters of continuous time models. These algorithms are applicable to mixed stock and flow data and take account of the exact restrictions on the distribution of the data implied by the continuous time model. They are also applicable to models formulated as systems of second- or higher-order differential equations. Such models permit a much richer dynamic specification than the predominantly first-order models developed during the last twenty years.

The most general program that has been developed for the computation of asymptotically efficient estimates of the parameters of a continuous time model is that of Nowman (1992). This program is applicable to a second-order system with mixed stock and flow data and yields the exact Gaussian estimates (which are the exact maximum likelihood estimates if the innovations are Brownian motion) when either the model is closed or the exogenous variables are quadratic functions of time.

I will now describe, in some detail, the algorithm implemented by Nowman's program and developed in a series of articles published during the 1980s (see Bergstrom 1983, 1985, 1986, 1989). For various extensions and limiting cases, see Agbeyegbe (1984, 1987, 1988), Chambers (1991a), and Nowman (1991). The basic model to which the algorithm is applicable can be written in the form

$$d[Dx(t)] = [A_1(\theta)Dx(t) + A_2(\theta)x(t) + B(\theta)z(t)]\, dt$$
$$+ \zeta(dt), \quad t \geq 0, \tag{8}$$
$$x(0) = y_1, \quad Dx(0) = y_2,$$

where $x(t)$ is an n-dimensional vector of endogenous variables, $z(t)$ is an m-dimensional vector of exogenous variables, θ is a p-dimensional vector of unknown structural parameters ($p \leq 2n^2 + nm$), A_1, A_2, B are matrices whose elements are known functions of θ, y_1 and y_2 are nonrandom vectors, D is the mean-square differential operator, and $\zeta(dt)$ is a vector of white-noise innovations. The model (8) can be made more general by including the first and second derivatives of $z(t)$; the computer program of Nowman (1992) is directly applicable to the more general model using interpolation formulas for $Dz(t)$ and $D^2z(t)$ given in Nowman (1991). However, for simplicity of exposition, I will confine the discussion to the model (8).

We assume that both the endogenous and exogenous variables are a mixture of stocks and flows, and (without loss of generality) that they are ordered so that the vectors $x(t)$, $z(t)$, y_1, and y_2 can be partitioned as

$$x(t) = \begin{bmatrix} x^s(t) \\ x^f(t) \end{bmatrix}, \qquad z(t) = \begin{bmatrix} z^s(t) \\ z^f(t) \end{bmatrix},$$

$$y_1 = \begin{bmatrix} y_1^s \\ y_1^f \end{bmatrix}, \qquad y_2 = \begin{bmatrix} y_2^s \\ y_2^f \end{bmatrix},$$

where $x^s(t)$ and $z^s(t)$ are vectors of stock variables (which are observable at points of time) while $x^f(t)$ and $z^f(t)$ are vectors of flow variables (which are observable as integrals over the period $(t-1, t)$).

We define the observable vectors $\bar{x}_t$ and $\bar{z}_t$ by

$$\bar{x}_t = \begin{bmatrix} x^s(t) - x^s(t-1) \\ \int_{t-1}^t x^f(r)\,dr \end{bmatrix}, \qquad \bar{z}_t = \begin{bmatrix} \frac{1}{2}\{z^s(t) + z^s(t-1)\} \\ \int_{t-1}^t z^f(r)\,dr \end{bmatrix}.$$

The sample then comprises the set of vectors

$$\bar{x}_1, \bar{x}_2, \ldots, \bar{x}_T, \bar{z}_1, \bar{z}_2, \ldots, \bar{z}_T$$

together with the initial stock vector $y_1^s = x^s(0)$, which is the only part of the initial state vector that is observable.

The remainder of the initial state vector, that is, the vector defined by

$$y_1 = \begin{bmatrix} y_1^f \\ y_2^f \end{bmatrix},$$

is unobservable and must be treated as part of the parameter vector to be estimated. We can also parameterize the covariance matrix of the white-noise innovation vector by writing it in the form

$$E\{\zeta(dt)\zeta'(dt)\} = dt\Sigma(\mu),$$

where Σ is a positive definite matrix whose elements are known functions of a parameter vector μ. The complete vector of parameters to be estimated is then $[\theta, \mu, y']$.

In order to derive the Gaussian likelihood function, we make use of a discrete time dynamic model which is exactly satisfied by the data when the unobservable continuous time paths of the exogenous variables are polynomials in t of degree not exceeding 2 and which is also a very good approximation under much more general conditions. The assumption that the exogenous variables are quadratic functions of time was first used in the derivation of estimates of the parameters of continuous time models by Phillips (1974, 1976). He dealt only with first-order systems, however, and assumed that all variables are observable at equispaced points of time; that is, there are no flow variables.

The exact discrete model derived from the second-order system (8) is, in its most basic form, the following set of equations (9)–(11):

$$\bar{x}_1 = G_{11}y_1 + G_{12}y_2 + E_{11}\bar{z}_1 + E_{12}\bar{z}_2 + E_{13}\bar{z}_3 + \eta_1, \tag{9}$$

$$\bar{x}_2 = C_{11}\bar{x}_1 + G_{21}y_1 + G_{22}y_2 + E_{21}\bar{z}_1 + E_{22}\bar{z}_2 + E_{23}\bar{z}_3 + \eta_2, \tag{10}$$

$$\bar{x}_t = F_1\bar{x}_{t-1} + F_2\bar{x}_{t-2} + E_0\bar{z}_t + E_1\bar{z}_{t-1} + E_2\bar{z}_{t-2} + \eta_t, \quad t = 3, \dots, T, \tag{11}$$

where

$$E(\eta_1\eta_1') = \Omega_{11}, \qquad E(\eta_2\eta_2') = \Omega_{22},$$
$$E(\eta_2\eta_1') = \Omega_{21}, \qquad E(\eta_3\eta_1') = \Omega_{31},$$
$$E(\eta_3\eta_2') = \Omega_{32}, \qquad E(\eta_4\eta_2') = \Omega_{42},$$
$$E(\eta_t\eta_t') = \Omega_0, \quad t = 3, \dots, T,$$
$$E(\eta_t\eta_{t-1}') = \Omega_1, \quad t = 4, \dots, T,$$
$$E(\eta_t\eta_{t-2}') = \Omega_2, \quad t = 5, \dots, T,$$
$$E(\eta_t\eta_{t-r}') = 0, \quad r > 2, \quad t = 3, \dots, T.$$

The matrices of coefficients in (9)–(11) are all functions of θ and whose precise forms are given in Bergstrom (1986); the matrices Ω_{11}, Ω_{22}, Ω_{21}, Ω_{31}, Ω_{32}, Ω_{42}, Ω_0, Ω_1, and Ω_2 are all functions of $[\theta, \mu]$ and whose precise forms are also given in Bergstrom (1986). Moreover, (11) is exactly satisfied for any interval $[t'-3, t']$ over which the elements of $z(t)$ are quadratic functions of t, and the coefficient matrices E_0, E_1, E_2 depend only on θ and not on the parameters of the quadratic functions defining $z(t)$. For this reason, the model represented by equations (9)–(11) is a very good approximation even if the behavior of the exogenous variable varies greatly (as between different parts of the sample period), provided that the paths are sufficiently smooth.

From (9)–(11) and the listed conditions on the covariance matrix of the vector $[\eta_1', \eta_2', \dots, \eta_T']'$, we can derive (see Bergstrom 1990, chap. 7) the exact discrete model in the form of a generalized VARMAX model, which is a very convenient basis for estimation, testing, and forecasting. The generalized VARMAX model is given by equations (12)–(14), in which the matrices M_{tt} ($t = 1, ..., T$) are lower triangular matrices with positive diagonal elements, as follows:

$$\bar{x}_1 - G_{11}(\theta)y_1 - G_{12}(\theta)y_2$$
$$- E_{11}(\theta)\bar{z}_1 - E_{12}(\theta)\bar{z}_2 - E_{13}(\theta)\bar{z}_3 = M_{11}(\theta, \mu)\epsilon_1, \quad (12)$$

$$\bar{x}_2 - C_{11}(\theta)\bar{x}_1 - G_{21}(\theta)y_1 - G_{22}(\theta)y_2$$
$$- E_{21}(\theta)\bar{z}_1 - E_{22}(\theta)\bar{z}_2 - E_{23}(\theta)\bar{z}_3 = M_{21}(\theta, \mu)\epsilon_1 + M_{22}(\theta, \mu)\epsilon_2, \quad (13)$$

$$\bar{x}_t - F_1(\theta)\bar{x}_{t-1} - F_2(\theta)\bar{x}_{t-2} - E_0(\theta)\bar{z}_t - E_1(\theta)\bar{z}_{t-1} - E_2(\theta)\bar{z}_{t-2}$$
$$= M_{tt}(\theta, \mu)\epsilon_t + M_{t,t-1}(\theta, \mu)\epsilon_{t-1} + M_{t,t-2}(\theta, \mu)\epsilon_{t-2}, \quad t = 3, ..., T, \quad (14)$$

where

$$E(\epsilon_t) = 0, \quad t = 1, ..., T,$$
$$E(\epsilon_t \epsilon_t') = I, \quad t = 1, ..., T,$$
$$E(\epsilon_s \epsilon_t') = 0, \quad s \neq t, \; s, t = 1, ..., T.$$

The moving-average coefficient matrices in this model can be computed, recursively, by first using equations (15)–(23) and then, for $t = 5, ..., T$, equations (24)–(26):

$$M_{11}M_{11}' = \Omega_{11}, \tag{15}$$

$$M_{21} = \Omega_{21}[M_{11}']^{-1}, \tag{16}$$

$$M_{22}M_{22}' = \Omega_{22} - M_{21}M_{21}', \tag{17}$$

$$M_{31} = \Omega_{31}[M_{11}']^{-1}, \tag{18}$$

$$M_{32} = \Omega_{32} - [M_{31}M_{21}'][M_{22}']^{-1}, \tag{19}$$

$$M_{33}M_{33}' = \Omega_0 - M_{31}M_{31}' - M_{32}M_{32}', \tag{20}$$

$$M_{42} = \Omega_{42}[M_{22}']^{-1}, \tag{21}$$

$$M_{43} = \Omega_1 - [M_{42}M_{32}'][M_{33}']^{-1}, \tag{22}$$

$$M_{44}M_{44}' = \Omega_0 - M_{42}M_{42}' - M_{43}M_{43}', \tag{23}$$

$$M_{t,t-2} = \Omega_2[M_{t-2,t-2}']^{-1}, \tag{24}$$

$$M_{t,t-1} = \Omega_1 - [M_{t,t-2}M_{t-1,t-2}'][M_{t-1,t-1}']^{-1}, \tag{25}$$

$$M_{tt}M_{tt}' = \Omega_0 - M_{t,t-2}M_{t,t-2}' - M_{t,t-1}M_{t,t-1}'. \tag{26}$$

These computations involve only standard operations on $n \times n$ matrices, with Cholesky factorizations in equations (15), (17), (20), (23), and (26).

It should be noticed that the parameterization of the autoregressive and moving-average coefficient matrices in (12)–(14) implies cross-restrictions between the autoregressive and moving-average coefficient matrices, and it also imposes restrictions on the evolution of the moving-average coefficient matrices over time. It has been shown (see Bergstrom 1990, chap. 7, thm. 1) that the system of nonlinear difference equations (24)–(26) in the matrices $[M_{tt}, M_{t,t-1}, M_{t,t-2}]$ $(t = 5, 6, ...)$ has an asymptotically stable solution $[M_0, M_1, M_2]$, and our experience in computing those matrices is that they have converged up to four decimal places after about twelve unit observation periods.

Let $L(\theta, \mu, y')$ denote "minus twice the logarithm of the Gaussian likelihhod." Then

$$L = \sum_{t=1}^{T} \epsilon_t' \epsilon_t + 2 \sum_{t=1}^{T} \log |M_{tt}|,$$

where $\epsilon_1, \epsilon_2, ..., \epsilon_T$ are functions of $[\theta, \mu, y']$ and the observations. These functions are defined by (12)–(14), and $\epsilon_1, \epsilon_2, ..., \epsilon_T$ can be computed recursively from these equations. It should be noticed that, since M_{tt} is a triangular matrix, $\log |M_{tt}|$ equals the sum of the logarithms of the diagonal elements of M_{tt}.

The exact Gaussian estimates of the parameters are obtained by minimizing L with respect to $[\theta, \mu, y']$. In carrying out this minimization, we can make use of the iterative procedure proposed by Bergstrom (1985) as follows. We first obtain an estimate of y by an interpolation formula, then minimize L with respect to $[\theta, \mu]$ using a numerical optimization procedure, then obtain a new estimate of y using an explicit formula (given in Bergstrom 1985, eq. (37)), and so on.

The system of equations (12)–(14), together with the Gaussian estimates of the parameters, provides a very convenient basis for hypothesis testing and forecasting. A procedure for obtaining forecasts of the post-sample discrete observations is described in Bergstrom (1989), where it is also shown that these forecasts are optimal (see also Chambers 1991b). Hypothesis testing is discussed in Bergstrom (1990, chap. 7), which includes formulas for the implementation of these tests. (See also Chambers 1993b, which deals with nonnested tests.)

The finite sample properties of the exact Gaussian estimates were the subject of a Monte Carlo study by Nowman (1993a), who used his computer program to estimate the parameters of a three-equation second-order model in which both the endogenous and the exogenous variables are a mixture of stocks and flows. The results obtained in this study were very encouraging, and the next step was to use the program in the first major empirical application of the new methodology. This was the exact Gaussian estimation of a fourteen-equation second-order continuous time macroeconometric model of the United Kingdom, described in Bergstrom, Nowman, and Wymer (1992). The complexity of this estimation problem is indicated by the fact that it is equivalent to the estimation of a second-order generalized VARMAX model whose coefficient matrices (for each time period) include 1,477 elements, all of which are very complicated (but known) transcendental functions of 168 unknown parameters of the continuous time model. The exact Gaussian estimates presented by Bergstrom et al. (1992) were obtained on the Cray X-MP/48 supercomputer, after obtaining preliminary estimates (which were used as starting values in the optimization algorithm) on a personal computer using an approximate discrete model. It is remarkable that Nowman (1993b) has been able to obtain revised exact Gaussian estimates (using more recent data and a different measure of the money supply) of the parameters of the same model on a personal notebook computer, using a new version of his program written in GAUSS.

During the last decade, there have been several other important developments in econometric methodology relating to continuous time models. One of these is the development of the Kalman filter algorithm for evaluating the exact Gaussian likelihood for the parameters of a higher-order continuous time dynamic model from discrete data. The Kalman filter was first used for this purpose by Jones (1981), who assumed that all variables are observable at points of time and thus avoided the complications associated with flow data. A more general Kalman filter algorithm that allows for flow data was developed by Harvey and Stock (1985, 1988a,b); further generalizations were made by Zadrozny (1988). The Kalman filter algorithm is particularly useful for taking account of errors in the data and observations at different frequencies. On the other hand, the algorithm based on the exact discrete VARMAX model satisfied by the data has the advantage that this model is of independent interest and provides a very convenient basis for hypothesis testing and forecasting.

Another important contribution to the problem of estimating the parameters of higher-order continuous time dynamic models from discrete data is the further development of Fourier methods of estimation. Robinson (1993) has generalized, in various ways, the Fourier methods that he developed during the 1970s (Robinson 1976a,b,c, 1977, 1980a,b), particularly by allowing for mixed stock and flow data. The Fourier estimates are obtained by maximizing a frequency-domain approximation to the Gaussian likelihood that is similar to those introduced by Whittle (1951, 1953). These approximations are asymptotically efficient, under suitable conditions, and have computational advantages over the exact Gaussian estimates. However, unlike exact Gaussian estimates, their derivation is based on the assumption of stationarity.

The methods discussed so far are directly applicable only to models that are linear in the variables while generally nonlinear in the parameters. In order to apply them to models that are nonlinear in the variables, it is necessary to make a linear approximation – for example, by taking a Taylor series expansion about the sample means. Wymer (1993) has developed an alternative method, which is directly applicable to a system of stochastic differential equations that is nonlinear in both the variables and the parameters. His method makes use of the exact solution of the nonlinear differential equations system (without the innovations) and can be expected to yield considerably better estimates than any that depend on a linear approximation about the sample means if the model is severely nonlinear. Another contribution to the estimation of nonlinear models has been made by Lo (1988) concerning the maximum likelihood estimation of generalized Ito processes.

Finally, I will mention two contributions that are concerned with the estimation of linear continuous time models under rather different circumstance from those assumed in earlier studies. One is the contribution of Phillips (1991), who proposes a method of estimating long-run relations in a continuous time model with some zero eigenvalues. The method yields asymptotically efficient estimates of long-run parameters, even when the innovations are stationary processes of unspecified form. The other contribution is that of Hamerle, Singer, and Nagl (1993), who deal with the estimation of continuous time dynamic models from panel data while assuming that the model contains random individual specific components as well as exogenous variables. The score function and maximum likelihood equations for the continuous time parameters are derived explicitly.

In addition to the contributions to estimation methodology there have been others relating to the more basic problem of identification, particularly the *aliasing* problem – that is, the problem of distinguishing between structures that generate cycles whose frequencies, per unit observation period, differ by integers. Early contributions to the literature on this problem were made by Telser (1967) and Phillips (1973). In a more recent contribution, Hansen and Sargent (1983) showed that there are at most a finite number of structures attributable to aliasing that are indistinguishable (on the basis of the observations) from the true structure. An implication of their theorem is that the true structure will be identifiable if the unit observation period is sufficiently short.

4   Empirical applications

During the last twenty years, continuous time econometric methods have been used in the estimation of a wide variety of dynamic disequilibrium models. These include macroeconometric models of most of the leading industrial countries of the world, as well as models of financial markets, commodity markets, and consumer demand.

The empirical modeling of macroeconomic phenomena in continuous time commenced in the early 1970s. Two early studies were Wymer's (1973) disequilibrium adjustment model of the U.K. financial markets and Hillinger's three-equation model of the U.S. business cycle (Hillinger, Bennet, and Benoit 1973). However, the first economywide continuous time macroeconometric model was that of Bergstrom and Wymer (1976), and this model set the pattern for macroeconometric models of many other countries. Two particular features of the Bergstrom–Wymer model have been widely followed. The first, which I have mentioned earlier, is that the model was formulated as a system of partial adjustment equations in each of which the causally dependent variable is adjusting in response to the deviation of its current level from its partial equilibrium level. The second is that the model is designed in such a way as to permit a rigorous mathematical analysis of its steady-state and asymptotic stability properties. The steady-state and stability analysis follows the general methodology developed in Bergstrom (1967) and has been clearly explained in a more detailed exposition by Gandolfo (1981, chap. 2).

The most intensively tested and used of the continuous time macroeconometric models that were developed following the Bergstrom–Wymer approach are the model of the Australian economy by Jonson, Moses, and Wymer (1977) and the model of the Italian economy by Gandolfo and Padoan (1982, 1984, 1987, 1990). The latter model has also been frequently revised and updated.

Other economywide continuous time macroeconometric models include two early models for the United Kingdom, one by Jonson (1976) and one by Knight and Wymer (1978); two models for Italy, one by Tullio (1981) and one by Fusari (1990); and models for Canada by Knight and Mathieson (1979), for Germany by Kirkpatrick (1987), for the United States by Donaghy (1993), for Sweden by Sjöö (1993), for Iceland by Stefansson (1981), for New Zealand by Bailey, Hall, and Phillips (1987), and for various developing countries by Aghevli and Khan (1977, 1980). Finally, there is the second-order model for the United Kingdom by Bergstrom et al. (1992). This was the first economywide continuous time macroeconometric model to be estimated by the exact Gaussian method. It is, essentially, a development of the model of Bergstrom and Wymer (1976) and retains the basic features of that prototype. However, it is formulated as a system of second-order differential equations, thus providing a more sophisticated and realistic specification of the partial adjustment relations. It also has a more elaborate financial sector and makes systematic use of the assumption of long-run rational expectations.

In addition to the various economywide models, there have been several partial continuous time macroeconometric models developed for particular purposes. These include models by Sassanpour and Sheen (1984) for comparing monetary policy in France and Germany, and a model by Drollas and Greenman (1987) for the investigation of energy demand in the United States. There have also been several small continuous time business cycle models, including an early model for Germany by Hillinger and Schüler (1978) and a more recent one for the United States by Hillinger and Reiter (1992).

Most of the macroeconometric models mentioned here have been used for policy analysis: see Bergstrom (1978, 1984b), Bergstrom, Nowman, and Wandasiewicz (1994), Gandolfo and Padoan (1982, 1984, 1987, 1992), Gandolfo and Petit (1986, 1987), Jonson and Trevor (1981), Jonson, McKibbin, and Trevor (1982), Kirkpatrick (1987), Sassanpour and Sheen (1984), Stefansson (1981), and Tullio (1981). These studies include simulations of the behavior of the model under various policy assumptions, the mathematical analysis of the effects of various types of policy feedback on their stability, and the application of optimal control methods.

As mentioned earlier, continuous time econometric methods have also been used in the estimation of dynamic disequilibrium models of various sectors of the economy. Models of financial markets include models of the U.K. financial markets by Wymer (1973) and the Eurodollar market by Knight (1977), a global adjustment model of exchange and interest rates by Richard (1980), an exchange-rate adjustment model by Armington and Wolford (1984), and a currency substitution model by Donaghy and Richard (1993). Models of commodity markets include models of the sugar market by Wymer (1975), the copper market by Richard (1978), and the oil market by Drollas (1981).

Finally, there have been two more recent studies concerned with dynamic disequilibrium models of consumer demand. In the first of these, Bergstrom and Chambers (1990) estimated separate demand models for several categories of consumer durable goods in the United Kingdom. The form of model used is, essentially, a development of the early model of Houthakker and Taylor (1966), but with a more sophisticated and realistic dynamic specification. In the second study, Chambers (1992) estimated an integrated model with cross-equation restrictions for durable, nondurable, and semidurable consumer goods in the United Kingdom. The models used in these two studies were estimated by the exact Gaussian method for continuous time models, and the articles include further methodological developments to take account of the fact that consumer stocks are not observable.

In addition to the extensive use of continuous time econometric methods in the estimation of dynamic disequilibrium models, there has been some work on the application of these methods in the estimation of rational expectations equilibrium models. In particular, Christiano, Eichenbaum, and Marshall (1991) have estimated some simple continuous time general equilibrium models of the United States in order to test a continuous time martingale hypothesis for aggregate consumption. At a more general level, Hansen and Sargent (1991) have shown how to represent the solution of a rational expectations equilibrium model as a differential equation system, so that its parameters can be estimated by the methods described earlier in this survey.

Many of the empirical models mentioned here have been used to generate postsample forecasts, and these forecasts have been compared with those obtained from structural, naive, and standard time-series models (such as unrestricted VAR or VARMA models). On the whole, the forecasts obtained from the continuous time models have compared very favorably with those obtained from other models. They have been particularly successful in forecasting exchange rates. For example, the continuous time exchange-rate adjustment model developed by Armington and Wolford (1984) was used by the Wharton Econometric Forecasting Association for predicting exchange rates, and an independent study by Levich (1983) showed that their forecasts were better than those obtained from any of the nine other models being used at that time for exchange-rate forecasting in the United States. The Italian continuous time macroeconometric model developed by Gandolfo and Padoan (1990) has also been used for exchange-rate forecasting, and has been shown (Gandolfo et al. 1990) to generate postsample forecasts superior to those obtained, not only from standard structural models, but also from a random-walk model.

A comparison of the forecasting performance of a continuous time dynamic disequilibrium model with that of standard time-series models has been made by Chambers (1993a). He showed that postsample forecasts obtained from his integrated system of demand equations for durable, nondurable, and semidurable consumer goods in the United Kingdom are generally superior to those obtained from an unrestricted VARMAX model. This is as we should expect. For, as I emphasized earlier, one of the main arguments in favor of continuous time econometric modeling is that it enables us to take account of a priori information relating to the interaction of the variables during the unit observation period. Because of the smallness of the samples with which econometricians must work, this information is very important for increasing the efficiency of the parameter estimates and the forecasts based on these estimates.

5   Future developments

As I have shown in this survey, continuous time econometrics is a rapidly growing field. The acceleration of research activity within this field during the last decade has, to a considerable extent, been stimulated by recent developments in computing technology. The immense power of modern computers has made feasible the estimation of more sophisticated models and the use of more efficient estimation methods, avoiding the use of approximations made in earlier continuous time econometric work. These trends will undoubtedly continue.

Some of the theoretical work now in progress is concerned with the development of algorithms for the exact Gaussian estimation of more complex linear (in the variables) models, which are formulated as systems of mixed-order stochastic differential equations and incorporate unobservable stochastic trends. Like the algorithms already in use, these will be applicable to samples of mixed stock and flow data. There is scope, also, for further work on methods of estimation of the parameters of nonlinear (in both the variables and parameters) continuous time stochastic models, avoiding the use of linear approximations.

There will be a growing use of these new methods in future empirical work, and this can be expected to result in further improvements in the forecasting performance of continuous time econometric models. There is likely, also, to be a growing amount of empirical work comparing the performance of continuous time econometric models with that of conventional discrete time models. This work will definitely include comparisons of the ability of the alternative models to explain stylized facts (such as spectral estimates obtained from the data by standard time-series methods) as well as comparisons involving more formal hypothesis testing. The latter type of study will be greatly facilitated by the recent work on the derivation of exact discrete models in VARMA form from the underlying continuous time models generating the data.

REFERENCES

Agbeyegbe, T. D. (1984), "The Exact Discrete Analog to a Closed Linear Mixed-Order System," *Journal of Economic Dynamics and Control* 7: 363–75.

(1987), "An Exact Discrete Analog to a Closed Linear First-Order System with Mixed Sample," *Econometric Theory* 3: 142–9.

(1988), "An Exact Discrete Analog of an Open Linear Non-Stationary First-Order Continuous-Time System with Mixed Sample," *Journal of Econometrics* 39: 237–50.

Aghevli, B. B., and M. S. Khan (1977), "Inflationary Finance and the Dynamics of Inflation: Indonesia 1951–1972," *American Economic Review* 67: 390–403.

(1980), "Credit Policy and the Balance of Payments in Developing Countries," in W. L. Coates and D. R. Khatkhate (eds.), *Money and Monetary Policy in Less Developed Countries*. Oxford: Pergamon.

Armington, P., and C. Wolford (1984), "Exchange Rate Dynamics and Economic Policy," Armington Wolford Associates, Washington, DC.

20   **A. R. Bergstrom**

Bailey, P. W., V. B. Hall, and P. C. B. Phillips (1987), "A Model of Output, Employment, Capital Formation and Inflation," in G. Gandolfo and F. Marzano (eds.), *Keynesian Theory Planning Models and Quantitative Economics: Essays in Memory of Vittorio Marrama*. Milano: Giuffré.

Bartlett, M. S. (1946), "On the Theoretical Specification and Sampling Properties of Autocorrelated Time-Series," *Journal of the Royal Statistical Society Supplement* 8: 27–41.

Bentzel, R., and B. Hansen (1954), "On Recursiveness and Interdependency in Economic Models," *Review of Economic Studies* 22: 153–68.

Bergstrom, A. R. (1966), "Non-Recursive Models as Discrete Approximations to Systems of Stochastic Differential Equations," *Econometrica* 34: 173–82.

(1967), *The Construction and Use of Economic Models*. London: English Universities Press.

(1976), *Statistical Inference in Continuous Time Economic Models*. Amsterdam: North-Holland.

(1978), "Monetary Policy in a Model of the United Kingdom," in A. R. Bergstrom, A. J. L. Catt, M. H. Peston, and B. D. J. Silverstone (eds.), *Stability and Inflation*. New York: Wiley.

(1983), "Gaussian Estimation of Structural Parameters in Higher Order Continuous Time Dynamic Models," *Econometrica* 51: 117–52.

(1984a), "Continuous Time Stochastic Models and Issues of Aggregation over Time," in Z. Griliches and M. D. Intriligator (eds.), *Handbook of Econometrics*. Amsterdam: North-Holland.

(1984b), "Monetary, Fiscal and Exchange Rate Policy in a Continuous Time Model of the United Kingdom," in P. Malgrange and P. Muet (eds.), *Contemporary Macroeconomic Modelling*. Oxford: Blackwell.

(1985), "The Estimation of Parameters in Nonstationary Higher-Order Continuous Time Dynamic Models," *Econometric Theory* 1: 369–85.

(1986), "The Estimation of Open Higher-Order Continuous Time Dynamic Models with Mixed Stock and Flow Data," *Econometric Theory* 2: 350–73.

(1988), "The History of Continuous-Time Econometric Models," *Econometric Theory* 4: 365–83.

(1989), "Optimal Forecasting of Discrete Stock and Flow Data Generated by a Higher Order Continuous Time System," *Computers and Mathematics with Applications* 17: 1203–14.

(1990), *Continuous Time Econometric Modelling*. Oxford University Press.

Bergstrom, A. R., and M. J. Chambers (1990), "Gaussian Estimation of a Continuous Time Model of Demand for Consumer Durable Goods with Applications to Demand in the United Kingdom, 1973–84," in A. R. Bergstrom (ed.), *Continuous Time Econometric Modelling*. Oxford University Press.

Bergstrom, A. R., K. B. Nowman, and S. Wandasiewicz (1994), "Monetary and Fiscal Policy in a Second Order Continuous Time Econometric Model of the United Kingdom," *Journal of Economic Dynamics and Control* 18: 731–61.

Bergstrom, A. R., K. B. Nowman, and C. R. Wymer (1992), "Gaussian Estimation of a Second Order Continuous Time Macroeconometric Model of the UK," *Economic Modelling* 9: 313–51.

Bergstrom, A. R., and C. R. Wymer (1976), "A Model of Disequilibrium Neoclassical Growth and Its Application to the United Kingdom," in A. R. Bergstrom (ed.), *Statistical Inference in Continuous Time Economic Models*. Amsterdam: North-Holland.

Chambers, M. J. (1991a), "Estimating General Linear Continuous Time Systems," *Econometric Theory* 7: 531-42.

(1991b), "Forecasting Discrete Stock and Flow Data Generated by a Second Order Continuous Time System," *Computers and Mathematics with Applications* 10: 107-14.

(1992), "Estimation of a Continuous-Time Dynamic Demand System," *Journal of Applied Econometrics* 7: 53-64.

(1993a), "Forecasting with Continuous-Time and Discrete-Time Models: An Empirical Comparison," in P. C. B. Phillips (ed.), *Models, Methods, and Applications of Econometrics*. Cambridge, MA: Blackwell.

(1993b), "A Nonnested Approach to Testing Continuous Time Models against Discrete Alternatives," *Journal of Econometrics* 57: 319-44.

Christiano, L. J., M. S. Eichenbaum, and D. Marshall (1991), "The Permanent Income Hypothesis Revisited," *Econometrica* 59: 397-423.

Donaghy, K. P. (1993), "A Continuous-Time Model of the United States Economy," in G. Gandolfo (ed.), *Continuous Time Econometrics*. London: Chapman and Hall.

Donaghy, K. P., and D. M. Richard (1993), "Flexible Functional Forms and Generalized Dynamic Adjustment in the Specification of the Demand for Money," in G. Gandolfo (ed.), *Continuous Time Econometrics*. London: Chapman and Hall.

Drollas, L. P. (1981), "An Econometric Model of the Rotterdam Spot Oil Price," in *Proceedings of the European Association of Energy Economists*, pp. 584-605.

Drollas, L. P., and J. V. Greenman (1987), "The Price of Energy and Factor Substitution in the U.S. Economy," *Energy Economics* 6: 159-66.

Fusari, A. (1990), "A Macrodynamic Model Centered on the Interrelationships between the Public and Private Sectors of the Italian Economy," *New York Economic Review* 20: 32-58.

Gandolfo, G. (1981), *Quantitative Analysis and Econometric Estimation of Continuous Time Dynamic Models*. Amsterdam: North-Holland.

(1993), *Continuous Time Econometrics*. London: Chapman and Hall.

Gandolfo, G., and P. C. Padoan (1982), "Policy Simulations with a Continuous Time Macrodynamic Model of the Italian Economy: A Preliminary Analysis," *Journal of Economic Dynamics and Control* 4: 205-24.

(1984), *A Disequilibrium Model of Real and Financial Accumulation in an Open Economy*. Berlin: Springer-Verlag.

(1987), *The Mark V Version of the Italian Continuous Time Model*. Siena: Instituto di Economia della Facolta di Scienze Economiche e Bancarie.

(1990), "The Italian Continuous Time Model, Theory and Empirical Results," *Economic Modelling* 7: 91-132.

Gandolfo, G., P. C. Padoan, and G. Paladino (1990), "Exchange Rate Determination: Single Equation or Economy-Wide Models? A Test against the Random Walk," *Journal of Banking and Finance* 14: 965-92.

Gandolfo, G., and M. L. Petit (1986), "Optimal Control in a Continuous Time Macro-Econometric Model of the Italian Economy," in W. Domschke et al. (eds.), *Methods on Operations Research*. Frankfurt: Athenäum.

(1987), "Dynamic Optimization in Continuous Time and Optimal Policy Design in the Italian Economy," *Annales d'Economie et de Statistique* 5/6: 311-33.

Geweke, J. (1978), "Temporal Aggregation in the Multiple Regression Model," *Econometrica* 46: 643-62.

Haavelmo, T. (1943), "The Statistical Implications of a System of Simultaneous Equations," *Econometrica* 11: 1–12.

Hamerle, A., H. Singer, and W. Nagl (1993), "Identification and Estimation of Continuous Time Dynamic Systems with Exogenous Variables Using Panel Data," *Econometric Theory* 9: 283–95.

Hansen, L. P., and T. J. Sargent (1983), "The Dimensionality of the Aliasing Problem," *Econometrica* 51: 377–88.

(1991), *Rational Expectations Econometrics*. Boulder: Westview.

Harvey, A. C., and J. H. Stock (1985), "The Estimation of Higher-Order Continuous Time Autoregressive Models," *Econometric Theory* 1: 97–117.

(1988a), "Continuous Time Autoregressive Models with Common Stochastic Trends," *Journal of Economic Dynamics and Control* 12: 365–84.

(1988b), "Estimating Integrated Higher-Order Continuous Time Autoregressions with an Application to Money-Income Causality," *Journal of Econometrics* 42: 319–36.

Hillinger, C., J. Bennett, and M. L. Benoit (1973), "Cyclical Fluctuations in the U.S. Economy," *Dynamic Modelling and Control of National Economics* (IEE Conference Publication no. 101).

Hillinger, C., and M. Reiter (1992), "The Quantitative and Qualitative Explanation of Macroeconomic Investment and Production Cycles," in C. Hillinger (ed.), *Cyclical Growth in Market and Planned Economies*. Oxford University Press.

Hillinger, C., M. Reiter, and T. Wesser (1992), "Micro Foundations of the Second-Order Accelerator and of Cyclical Behaviour," in C. Hillinger (ed.), *Cyclical Growth in Market and Planned Economies*. Oxford University Press.

Hillinger, C., and K. W. Schüler (1978), "Cyclical Fluctuations in the German Economy: A Continuous-Time Econometric Model," *Munich Social Science Review*, pp. 75–85.

Houthakker, H. S., and L. D. Taylor (1966), *Consumer Demand in the United States 1929–1970, Analysis and Projections*. Cambridge, MA: Harvard University Press.

Jones, R. H. (1981), "Fitting a Continuous Time Autoregression to Discrete Data," in D. F. Findley (ed.), *Applied Time Series Analysis*. New York: Academic Press.

Jonson, P. D. (1976), "Money and Economic Activity in the Open Economy: The United Kingdom 1880–1970," *Journal of Political Economy* 84: 979–1012.

Jonson, P. D., W. J. McKibbin, and R. G. Trevor (1982), "Exchange Rates and Capital Flows: A Sensitivity Analysis," *Canadian Journal of Economics* 15: 669–92.

Jonson, P. D., E. R. Moses, and C. R. Wymer (1977), "The RBA 76 Model of the Australian Economy," in W. E. Norton (ed.), *Conference in Applied Economic Research*. Sydney: Reserve Bank of Australia.

Jonson, P. D., and R. G. Trevor (1981), "Monetary Rules: A Preliminary Analysis," *Economic Record* 57: 150–67.

Kirkpatrick, G. (1987), *Employment, Growth, and Economic Policy: An Econometric Model of Germany*. Tübingen: Mohr.

Knight, M. D. (1977), "Eurodollars, Capital Mobility and the Monetary Approach to the Balance of Payments," *Economica* 44: 1–21.

Knight, M. D., and D. J. Mathieson (1979), "Model of an Industrial Country under Fixed and Flexible Exchange Rates," in J. S. Bhandari and B. H.

Putman (eds.), *Economic Interdependence and Flexible Exchange Rates*. Cambridge, MA: MIT Press.

Knight, M. D., and C. R. Wymer (1978), "A Macroeconomic Model of the United Kingdom," *IMF Staff Papers* 25: 742-8.

Koopmans, T. C. (1950), "Models Involving a Continuous Time Variable," in T. C. Koopmans (ed.), *Statistical Inference in Dynamic Economic Models*. New York: Wiley.

Koopmans, T. C., H. Rubin, and R. B. Leipnik (1950), "Measuring the Equation Systems of Dynamic Economics," in T. C. Koopmans (ed.), *Statistical Inference in Dynamic Economic Models*. New York: Wiley.

Levich, R. M. (1983), "Currency Forecasters Lose Their Way," *Euromoney* (August): 140-7.

Lo, A. W. (1988), "Maximum Likelihood Estimation of Generalized Ito Processes with Discretely Sampled Data," *Econometric Theory* 4: 231-47.

Malinvaud, E. (1980), *Statistical Methods of Econometrics*. Amsterdam: North-Holland.

Nowman, K. B. (1991), "Open Higher Order Continuous-Time Dynamic Model with Mixed Stock and Flow Data and Derivatives of Exogenous Variables," *Econometric Theory* 7: 404-8.

  (1992), "Computer Program for Estimation of Continuous-Time Dynamic Models with Mixed Stock and Flow Data," *Economic and Financial Computing* 1: 25-38.

  (1993a), "Finite-Sample Properties of the Gaussian Estimation of an Open Higher-Order Continuous-Time Dynamic Model with Mixed Stock and Flow Data," in G. Gandolfo (ed.), *Continuous Time Econometrics*. London: Chapman and Hall.

  (1993b), "A Note on Continuous Time Dynamic Disequilibrium Modeling of the United Kingdom," Chapter 6 in this volume.

Phillips, A. W. (1959), "The Estimation of Parameters in Systems of Stochastic Differential Equations," *Biometrika* 46: 67-76.

Phillips, P. C. B. (1972), "The Structural Estimation of a Stochastic Differential Equation System," *Econometrica* 40: 1021-41.

  (1973), "The Problems of Identification in Finite Parameter Continuous Time Models," *Journal of Econometrics* 1: 351-62.

  (1974), "The Estimation of Some Continuous Time Models," *Econometrica* 42: 803-24.

  (1976), "The Estimation of Linear Stochastic Differential Equations with Exogenous Variables," in A. R. Bergstrom (ed.), *Statistical Inference in Continuous Time Economic Models*. Amsterdam: North-Holland.

  (1991), "Error Correction and Long-Run Equilibrium in Continuous Time," *Econometrica* 59: 967-80.

Richard, D. (1978), "Dynamic Model of the World Copper Industry," *IMF Staff Papers* 25: 779-833.

  (1980), "A Global Adjustment Model of Exchange and Interest Rates," in D. Bigman and T. Taya (eds.), *The Functioning of Floating Exchange Rates: Theory, Evidence and Policy Implications*. Cambridge, MA: Ballinger.

Robinson, P. M. (1976a), "Fourier Estimation of Continuous Time Models," in A. R. Bergstrom (ed.), *Statistical Inference in Continuous Time Economic Models*. Amsterdam: North-Holland.

  (1976b), "The Estimation of Linear Differential Equations with Constant Coefficients," *Econometrica* 44: 751-64.

(1976c), "Instrumental Variables Estimation of Differential Equations," *Econometrica* 44: 765–76.

(1977), "The Construction and Estimation of Continuous Time Models and Discrete Approximations in Econometrics," *Journal of Econometrics* 6: 173–98.

(1980a), "Continuous Model Fitting from Discrete Data," in D. R. Brillinger and G. C. Tiao (eds.), *Directions in Time Series*. East Lansing, MI: Institute of Mathematical Statistics.

(1980b), "The Efficient Estimation of a Rational Spectral Density," in M. Kunt and F. de Coulon (eds.), *Signalling Processing: Theories and Applications*. Amsterdam: North-Holland.

(1993), "Continuous-Time Models in Econometrics: Closed and Open Systems, Stocks and Flows," in P. C. B. Phillips (ed.), *Models, Methods and Applications of Econometrics*. Cambridge, MA: Blackwell.

Sargan, J. D. (1974), "Some Discrete Approximations to Continuous Time Stochastic Models," *Journal of the Royal Statistical Society B* 36: 74–90.

(1976), "Some Discrete Approximations to Continuous Time Stochastic Models," in A. R. Bergstrom (ed.), *Statistical Inference in Continuous Time Economic Models*. Amsterdam: North-Holland.

Sassanpour, C., and J. Sheen (1984), "An Empirical Analysis of the Effect of Monetary Disequilibrium in Open Economies," *Journal of Monetary Economics* 13: 127–63.

Sims, C. A. (1971), "Discrete Approximations to Continuous Time Distributed Lag Models in Econometrics," *Econometrica* 39: 545–63.

Sjöö, B. (1993), "CONTIMOS – A Continuous-Time Econometric Model for Sweden Based on Monthly Data," in G. Gandolfo (ed.), *Continuous Time Econometrics*. London: Chapman and Hall.

Stefansson, S. B. (1981), "Inflation and Economic Policy in a Small Open Economy: Iceland in the Post-War Period," Ph.D. thesis, University of Essex, Colchester, UK.

Strotz, R. H. (1960), "Interdependence as a Specification Error," *Econometrica* 28: 428–42.

Strotz, R. H., and H. Wold (1960), "Recursive vs Non-Recursive Systems," *Econometrica* 28: 417–27.

Telser, L. G. (1967), "Discrete Samples and Moving Sums in Stationary Stochastic Processes," *Journal of the American Statistical Association* 62: 484–99.

Tullio, G. (1981), "Demand Management and Exchange Rate Policy: The Italian Experience," *IMF Staff Papers* 28: 80–117.

Whittle, P. (1951), *Hypothesis Testing in Time Series Analysis*. Stockholm: Almqvist and Wicksell.

(1953), "The Analysis of Multiple Stationary Time Series," *Journal of the Royal Statistical Society B* 15: 125–39.

Wold, H. O. A. (1952), *Demand Analysis*. Stockholm: Almqvist and Wicksell.

(1954), "Causality and Econometrics," *Econometrica* 22: 162–77.

(1956), "Causal Inference from Observational Data, A Review of Ends and Means," *Journal of the Royal Statistical Society A* 199: 28–50.

(1960), "A Generalization of Causal Chain Models," *Econometrica* 28: 442–63.

Wymer, C. R. (1968), "Full Information Maximum Likelihood Estimation with Non-Linear Restrictions; and Computer Programs: Resimul Manual," mimeo, London School of Economics and Political Science.

(1972), "Econometric Estimation of Stochastic Differential Equation Systems," *Econometrica* 40: 565-77.

(1973), "A Continuous Disequilibrium Adjustment Model of the United Kingdom Financial Markets," in A. A. Powell and R. A. Williams (eds.), *Economic Studies of Macro and Monetary Relations*. Amsterdam: North-Holland.

(1975), "Estimation of Continuous Time Models with an Application to the World Sugar Market," in W. C. Labys (ed.), *Quantitative Models of Commodity Markets*. Cambridge, MA: Ballinger.

(1993), "Estimation of Nonlinear Continuous-Time Models from Discrete Data," in P. C. B. Phillips (ed.), *Models, Methods and Applications of Econometrics*. Cambridge, MA: Blackwell.

Zadrozny, P. A. (1988), "Gaussian Likelihood of Continuous Time ARMAX Models When Data Are Stock and Flow at Different Frequencies," *Econometric Theory* 4: 108-24.

CHAPTER 2

Dynamic disequilibrium economics: history, conceptual foundations, possible futures

Claude Hillinger

1   Introduction

Throughout most of its modern history, economics has been divided between the dominant *mainstream,* concerned with the analysis of optimality and equilibrium, and more heterogeneous movements to which I will refer collectively as *alternative* economics. Here another basic division is between *left-wing* economics (most prominently Marxism), concerned primarily with such issues as equality and justice, and *empirical* economics. In the latter category I include such movements as German historicism and American institutionalism. More importantly from the perspective of this paper, I include in empirical economics all of the contributions dealing with *disequilibrium* economics. This category begins with Malthus, and includes the traditional writings on business cycles, New Keynesian economics, and *dynamic disequilibrium* economics, which is the central focus of this paper. These distinctions are indicative of general tendencies; there is no implication that traditions labeled "empirical" are completely atheoretic, or that there is no empirical content in the other traditions.

The foregoing classification is essentially neutral. It accepts the common view of alternative economists that the mainstream is too formalistic and too little concerned with explaining significant observable features of the real world. At the same time, it is also conformable with the mainstream criticism of alternative economics as being insufficiently theoretical.

Disequilibrium economics is part of empirical economics because it is motivated by the intrusion of empirical reality in the form of the recurrent crises, depressions, and milder periodic fluctuations that characterize the history of capitalism. Mainstream economics has been substantially unable or unwilling to expand or modify its central doctrines in order to

For helpful comments I am indebted to D. Colander, M. Reiter, and A. Zellner.

deal with disequilibrium phenomena. Consequently, disequilibrium economics has, through most of its history, been part of the alternative rather than part of the mainstream.

An atypical rapprochement between mainstream and alternative economics characterized the decades of the forties, fifties, and sixties. The cataclysmic events of the first half of the twentieth century, particularly the Great Depression and the influence of the resulting revolutionary or reformist political movements, motivated mainstream economics to adopt some of the ideas and goals of alternative economics. Two economists were the principal architects of the rapprochement. First, Keynes proclaimed that he had created a general theory of disequilibrium of which traditional equilibrium analysis was but a special case. Later, in his enormously successful introductory text, Samuelson propagated the "neoclassical" synthesis in which the market provides efficiency while the government looks after social justice and macroeconomic stability.

The rapprochement was not permanent, because it failed to create a genuine empirical science. The inability of Keynesianism to deal with rising inflation and unemployment became obvious. Subsequently, macroeconomics was characterized by rapid paradigm changes and ultimately by fragmentation.

Keynes had tried to achieve a better understanding of reality, specifically of deviations from equilibrium, by means of a theory that merged elements of mainstream and disequilibrium economics. This effort failed because of the largely static nature of Keynes's thought. Dynamic disequilibrium theory in macroeconomics, while incorporating central Keynesian elements, is free from this defect. I believe that dynamic disequilibrium economics will be successful if it transcends the often sterile disputes between mainstream and alternative economics and moves in the direction of the methodology of the natural sciences.

The main arguments that I elaborate in the course of this paper may be summarized as follows.

The merging of theoretical and empirical approaches, characteristic of modern science, never occurred in economics; their separation is reflected in the split between mainstream and empirical economics. The mainstream has emphasized rational behavior and static equilibrium analysis. Empirical economics allows more room for nonrational and irrational behavior, and focuses on dynamic disequilibrium processes. The history of this split is reviewed in Section 2.

Related to the division of economics is the failure to agree on a satisfactory methodology. Very roughly, it may be said that mainstream economics has adhered to *apriorism* and empirical economics to *descriptive realism*, whereas more recently econometrics has opted for a statistical version of *falsificationism*. In Section 3 I discuss the methodology of the natural sciences and argue that it involves both attention to the realism of assumptions and to the predictive consequences of a theory. I also argue that the methodology of econometrics is flawed because it has failed to realize that predictive testing in science requires that a theory be confronted with *independently ascertained stylized facts*.

Concepts are the building blocks of scientific theories, as of all forms of rational discourse. A basic aspect of scientific concepts is that they evolve along with the theories in which they play a role. Lack of scientific progress in economics is reflected in a failure to converge on clearly defined concepts and to secure agreement on their range of applicability. This applies in particular to the concepts of *rationality* and *equilibrium*, in terms of which mainstream and disequilibrium economists express their most basic disagreements. Unfortunately, these concepts are often employed more as weapons for beating down the intellectual opponent than as tools for understanding. In Section 4 I deal with these fundamental concepts, with how they may reasonably be defined and their possible further evolution.

Science is a social system in which, as in any other profession, most practitioners are primarily interested in optimizing their careers. In Section 5 I look at economics from this point of view and try to devise reasonable strategies for advancing the cause of dynamic disequilibrium economics as an empirical science.

In the following discussion, the classification of the various macroeconomic schools was chosen with a view toward facilitating my arguments while adhering as much as possible to established usage. Any such classification is necessarily somewhat arbitrary and cannot account for a great deal of variation. For example, I do not here distinguish between the "economics of Keynes" and the subsequent "Keynesian economics." The reason is that I stress their common central concern, which is the demonstration of the need for and feasibility of stabilization policy. For a recent, somewhat different classification of macroeconomic schools, see Colander (1992).

My discussion is necessarily wide-ranging and almost any topic could usefully be discussed at much greater length. Also, the focus is generally not coextensive with dynamic disequilibrium economics. Sometimes it is wider, including all of economics or – at an even more general level – appealing to the methodological unity of the sciences. Conversely, the range of examples is narrower, being largely confined to macroeconomics and especially to the modeling of cyclical growth (the area of my own specialization), where I have tried to put into practice the methodological precepts expounded in this paper. I do believe that the discussion is relevant for all of dynamic disequilibrium economics.

2   Notes on the history of mainstream and disequilibrium economics[1]

2.1   *The birth of science and of economics*

Science arose in the course of the sixteenth century as a result of the merging of two traditions: the speculative tradition of natural philosophy, originating in Aristotelianism and attracting the attention of intellectuals in the church, the aristocracy, and the emerging universities; and an empirical tradition involving artisans, particularly glass blowers and lens makers, as well as alchemists, the precursors of the later chemists. Those of the first tradition became the theoreticians while those of the second became the experimentalists of the evolving scientific fields.

An institutional framework for the merger of the two traditions was provided by the first scientific societies: in Italy, the Nuova Scienza of which Galileo Galilei was a member, and in England, the Royal Society. An important function of these societies was to raise the social status of the experimenters to the same level as that of the theoreticians. Also important was the emergence of a new style of discourse, directed against the obscurantism of traditional philosophy. The intellectual ferment and enthusiasm associated with the rise of the natural sciences understandably also had a decisive influence on the emerging discipline of economics.

2.2   *The mainstream and its alternative in economic history*

Much of the subsequent history of economics is understandable in relation to its origin. Adam Smith is usually regarded as the founder of modern economics, but in my judgment William Petty deserves to share this honor.

Petty is generally regarded as the father of economic and demographic statistics.[2] He was a universal genius with multiple additional careers as surgeon, music professor, and estate manager. He was also one of the most active participants in the general scientific activities of his day and one of the founders of the Royal Society. Petty took the decisive step from mercantilism to modern economics with the assumption that the

---

[1] Histories of economic thought tend to be written from the point of view of the mainstream. It is therefore difficult to obtain from such histories any detailed and objective evaluations of the contributions of alternative movements. A considerably more detailed account of the material in this section, along with references to the literature, can be found in Hillinger (1992a).

[2] Most of Petty's writings appeared posthumously and are collected in Petty (1899). Roncaglia (1987) provides a concise discussion of Petty's life and contributions.

contribution of the economy is to be measured in terms of the goods and services produced, not in terms of its effect on the treasury of some reigning monarch. Furthermore, in the true scientific spirit, he operationalized this concept in terms of the market value of the total product and made the first crude attempt at measurement.

With Petty, economics originated in the style of empirical science. Like his fellow scientists in other fields, he broke with the philosophical and theological tradition of purely abstract and often abstruse reasoning, as well as with the descriptive empiricism of human and natural history. Petty's work had no significant direct consequence for economics. Demography, which became a predominantly empirical discipline, unfortunately split off from economics. The reason is probably that the theoretical analysis of populations does not lend itself to the static optimization paradigm of the mainstream.

Adam Smith, like Petty, was interested in and well informed regarding the sciences of his day. The methodology of the natural sciences is, however, less evident in his work. In contrast to Petty, Smith did not directly engage himself in any field of natural science. Smith's work in economics is much more extensive and systematic; it is also more traditional, speculative, and not oriented toward measurement.

Moving from moral philosophy to economics, Smith retained a basic interest in human feelings, motives, and actions. When compared to traditional philosophy, his writings are refreshingly informal and enriched by observation. His work, and that of subsequent generations of economists, did retain a philosophical character in that it was assumed that economics requires no more than an explication of what is already known to a reasonable person. The resulting theories were regarded as obvious and neither capable of, nor in need of, testing. Specialized observations or measurements were deemed unnecessary. While Smith in one passage did cite some statistics on the corn trade, he added apologetically, "I have no great faith in political arithmetic" (Smith 1789, p. 501).

While Smith made many insightful comments on economics, his immortality rests on essentially half a page in the *Wealth of Nations* that contains his argument for the efficiency of a competitive economy, expressed in the famous analogy of the "invisible hand." The subsequent evolution of mainstream economics can be regarded as an elaboration on this theme. It lends itself to the nonempirical style, because the basic elements of what became general equilibrium theory are already implicit in the work of Smith. The evolution of real economies – for example, the substitution of public corporations, with hired managers and interlocking boards of directors, for the individual entrepreneur – had scant impact on the central theory. This evolution was reinforced by the fact that the elaboration of general equilibrium theory, by the nature of the subject matter, called first for formalization and then for mathematization. These features were pointed to as evidence for the increasingly scientific status of economics.

2.3   *Alternative economics*

Throughout the ages of classical and marginalist economics, individual authors and larger movements with a predominantly empiricist orientation remained outside the mainstream. This marginality manifested itself in a number of ways. One is that since England and France were centers of orthodoxy, empirical schools (particularly the German historical school and American institutionalism) were able to flourish only at distances from these centers. Secondly, and this applies particularly to writers on business cycles, alternative economists thrived mostly outside of academe. Their writings were amateur efforts, rather than part of their main careers, and had no significant impact on the academic orthodoxy.

In this section I focus on the history of the business cycle literature for several reasons. One is that, until very recently, business cycle and dynamic disequilibrium analysis were coextensive. Another is that significant stylized facts, discovered by the early business cycle researchers, have lost none of their validity. (This has been a basic finding of SEMECON research.) Finally, these stylized facts have been incorporated into contemporary macroeconomic models in the tradition of the dynamic disequilibrium models of cyclical growth.[3]

The earliest (and arguably the most significant) figure in disequilibrium economics was Thomas Malthus, regarded by Keynes as his principal precursor. Malthus made two major contributions. First, he pointed out that Say's law need not hold in a monetary economy. If individuals can hoard money, aggregate demand can fall short of aggregate supply. Intellectually, Malthus scored on this point against the orthodoxy. Even Say felt compelled to acknowledge the validity of Malthus's arguments. From a practical point of view, the victory was inconsequential because mainstream theorizing continued to ignore disequilibrium phenomena. The second contribution was to demography. Here Malthus continued the empirical tradition of Petty, but his major contribution was the analysis of population dynamics. His famous postulate, that the population will grow until the scarcity of resources forces wages down to the subsistence level, caused economics to be designated the "dismal science." Malthus

---

[3] I am using the term "business cycle" loosely to include writings that antedate the discovery of periodicities and the introduction of the word "cycle."

also considered the complex medium-term dynamics of populations and the possibility of overshooting or even cyclical movements.

Keynes resurrected the first contribution of Malthus and made it a part of the modern mainstream. I believe it is time to do the same for his second contribution. A substantial part of the world population is even now existing under conditions of starvation, chronic and epidemic disease, and endemic warfare over declining resources. These conditions are likely to become worse rather than better. It is hard to see how the alternatives for the human race over the next 50–100 years can be reasonably assessed without modeling the complex and interacting dynamics of population and environment.

Regarding business cycle theory proper, I limit myself to a composite picture of the most significant elements. The origin of the theory was the recognition of the occurrence from time to time of "crises." These were initially viewed as isolated events caused by external factors, but Clement Juglar came to the conclusion that the crises repeated themselves fairly regularly at an interval of about 10 years. Following Schumpeter, these are now referred to as Juglar cycles.[4] He viewed them as being related to the investment behavior of firms. Though with limited success, Juglar tried to explain the cycle as a dynamic phenomenon in which each phase generates the next.

A variety of similar theories were produced subsequently. Common to most of them is the assumption of contagious and excessive optimism in the expansion phase. This leads to an investment boom, fueled by bank lending. Industrial capacity expands faster than demand, leading to excess capacity. Profits decline, and banks become fearful of losses on bad debts and of a general liquidity crisis; they cease lending and try to liquidate their outstanding loans. This in turn worsens the situation of the firms, many of which become insolvent and bankrupt. Now pessimism becomes excessive; investment and the economy go into a downward spin. Eventually, depreciation and obsolescence reduce the capital stock, while firms consolidate their financial positions. At some point, investment, perhaps related to technical innovations, again appears profitable. The next cycle can begin.

The discovery of another set of stylized facts of great importance for understanding cyclical fluctuations had to wait until the twentieth century and the availability of new statistical series. Kitchin discovered the shorter cycle that bears his name. Abramovitz found that for U.S. manufacturing, most of the fluctuations in output over this short cycle can be accounted for by inventory accumulation and decumulation.

---

[4] Other cycles identified subsequently are: the Kondratief or "long wave" cycle; the Kuznets or "building" cycle of about 20 years; and the 3–4-year Kitchin or "inventory" cycle.

By the 1950s and early 1960s, the existence of a short (3–4-year) inventory–output cycle and an 8–10-year cycle in fixed investment was generally accepted. Thereafter, interest in business cycles declined under the illusion that smooth growth would henceforth characterize the world economy. The relevant stylized facts were forgotten.

2.4   *Keynes*

Following the publication of Keynes's (1936) *General Theory,* disequilibrium economics rose for the first time to preeminence and retained this position for two or three decades. To understand Keynesianism it is necessary to understand Keynes's perceptions and motives as well as those of subsequent Keynesians. Keynes was an underconsumptionist – he believed that he was living at the beginning of a new era of capitalism, characterized by excessive savings and inadequate aggregate demand. He thought that the Great Depression was a manifestation of this new constellation and saw the solution in the augmentation of private by public expenditure.

Keynes was primarily an intuitive pragmatist rather than an analytical theorist. He did not write the *General Theory* until *after* he had already developed his policy preferences. The *General Theory* needed a lot of subsequent clarification on the part of more theoretically oriented economists, particularly Hicks. Keynes had astutely realized that, in order to have a major impact, he needed to offer a convincing alternative to the mainstream paradigm of full employment equilibrium. While stressing the revolutionary character of his work, Keynes stayed close to the mainstream tradition from a methodological point of view. He presented a static equilibrium framework, the difference being that the likely equilibrium was at a level of less than full employment.[5] This had the advantage that Keynes could claim his system to be general, with classical full employment as only a very special case.

A great contribution of Keynes was his definition of the major sectors and of the variables to which they react or which they control. He was also instrumental in the creation of the national income and product accounts, which are the empirical correlates to his theoretical constructs. This part of Keynes's contribution is independent of his theoretical model and remains the foundation of empirical macroeconomics.

The economic evolution after the Second World War demonstrated that Keynes's basic assumption of chronically deficient demand did not correspond to reality. The classical patterns of business cycles reasserted themselves. (This is clearly demonstrated by the SEMECON work on

[5] I am using the term "equilibrium" in the sense that each agent has fully adjusted to the constraints encountered.

the stylized facts of cyclical fluctuations.) However, while the increasing instability of the world economy could not be denied, the traditional business cycle patterns were not generally recognized for two reasons. They did not fit the static Keynesian model, and economists refused to recognize a phenomenon that, according to their theory, should not exist. In addition, the concern to establish stylized facts, which had existed at least informally, became lost in the formalisms of econometric practice.

After Keynes, Keynesian macroeconomics flourished for some time, while retreating to the theological style of the mainstream. Economics now had two separate paradigms: general equilibrium theory remained as the interpretation of the Bible of Smith; to this was added macroeconomics, as the Bible of Keynes. These paradigms were the foundations of Samuelson's highly successful neoclassical synthesis.

Keynesianism of the fifties and sixties derived its prestige from the unsubstantiated claim that the relatively smooth and strong growth rates characteristic of most industrialized economies during this period were the consequence of Keynesian demand management. When this period came to its natural end and was replaced by one of low growth, high instability, and inflation, Keynesianism became discredited and was abandoned. This demise was somewhat undeserved, as had been the earlier success. There had simply been no serious, sustained effort to establish macroeconomics as an evolving empirical science on the foundation established by Keynes. The large-scale macroeconometric models were not conceived as tests of basic Keynesian theory. In textbooks, the IS–LM model and its various associated pathologies (such as the liquidity trap) were expounded as pure dogma, unrelated to empirical evidence.

Much of the sterility of textbook Keynesian theory was due to its static character. For this Keynes himself must be assigned some of the blame, because in the *General Theory* he emphasized the static aspects. It is important to realize that in Chapters 5, 12, and 22 of the *General Theory,* Keynes had also presented, though in fragmentary form, a dynamic theory of business cycles. His emphasis in this theory was on two decisions made by firms. One is the output decision, based on short-term expectations of demand and on inventory levels. The other is the investment decision, based on a longer horizon, on the amount of fixed capital available, and on the cost of capital. Unfortunately, Keynes referred to the business cycle as a nineteenth-century phenomenon of merely historical interest. He thereby disqualified his own dynamic analysis, which was subsequently ignored in the textbooks. However, Keynes's thought on the dynamics of business cycles did influence the dynamic disequilibrium models of cyclical growth to be discussed in what follows.[6]

---

[6] An extended discussion of Keynes's views of business cycles is given in Hillinger (1987).

2.5   Macroeconomic dynamics and the rise of the econometric movement

As described in the previous section, Keynes reacted to the Great Depression by creating a static theory that came to dominate economics for the next half century. An immediate consequence of the success of the *General Theory* was that dynamics, which was being studied by other economists, was pushed from center stage and was subsequently largely ignored.

The three authors to be discussed in this section – Frisch, Tinbergen, and Kalecki – possessed a level of mathematical sophistication far above that of other economists of the time. Frisch and Tinbergen are rightly considered to be the founders of the econometric movement. Kalecki was less interested in the development of econometric methods, but along with Frisch and Tinbergen he provided the first quantitative parameter estimates for mathematical economic models. All three may therefore be regarded as pioneers of econometrics.

The models estimated by the three authors were all intended to explain economic cycles. They have some strongly similar features that are related to their common origin in cobweb models of agricultural product cycles. Models of the type now referred to as "cobweb" were elaborated by Tinbergen and by a number of other authors, all of whom published in German in 1930.

In that same year, Tinbergen (1930) published a model of the shipbuilding cycle that proved to be seminal in a number of respects. In the first place, the cobweb model was utilized for the first time to explain investment in a producer's durable good. Secondly, the idea of a gestation lag, covering the time from initiation to completion of an investment project, was introduced. In the case of shipbuilding, this lag is about two years. Finally, the dependent variable was taken to be the rate of investment, regarded as a continuous variable. The consequence is that the investment process is governed by a characteristic mixed difference–differential equation, which became the basic building block also of the models of Frisch and Kalecki.

Both Frisch (1933) and Kalecki (1933, 1935, 1954) took the decisive next step of constructing "business cycle" models for a national economy rather than for an isolated market. The key variable of their models is the volume of fixed business investment. Frisch demonstrated that for plausible parameter values his model produces two cycles, regarding which he wrote:

The primary cycle of 8.57 years corresponds nearly exactly to the well-known long business cycle . . . . Furthermore, the secondary cycle obtained is 3.50 years, which corresponds nearly exactly to the short business cycle. (Frisch 1933, p. 170)

In contrast to Frisch, who made no further contribution to this subject, macroeconomics was the main interest of Kalecki throughout his professional career. Despite his many articles and books on economic cycles, his basic approach and model did not change very much. The basic formulation is contained in his 1933 paper, which was published in Polish. In that paper Kalecki cites no references, and it is likely that he was unaware of the cobweb models mentioned earlier. After moving to England, he published in 1935 a more elaborate paper in which he cited Frisch and Tinbergen and used their solution methods to analyze a highly sophisticated and carefully specified lag structure of the investment process. He showed that, for plausible parameter values, the model generates cycles that lie in the observed range of 8–12 years. In subsequent publications (particularly Kalecki 1954) he tested his model against different data sets and obtained generally plausible results.

Regarding the investment process, Kalecki distinguished between *orders* for investment goods; actual *investment,* which takes place subsequently for the duration of the gestation lag; and *additions to the capital stock,* which occur at the end of the gestation period.

The work of Frisch and Kalecki had limited influence on the further evolution of macroeconomics. This is highly unfortunate, because the early work on fluctuations in the Keynesian tradition is by comparison quite primitive. Several plausible reasons may be given for the neglect of the early econometric cycle models. In the first place, the models had little in common with the static explanation offered by Keynes, as enshrined in the IS–LM model of Hicks. Given the total triumph of Keynesianism, there was little interest in alternative approaches. Secondly, Keynes made an intensive effort to "sell" his ideas; the *General Theory* may be regarded as primarily an effort in persuasion, the conclusion having been already fixed in his mind before he wrote the book. No comparable persuasive effort was made by the econometricians. Frisch wrote only one paper on fluctuations. Tinbergen changed his approach, and pioneered what became the standard style of macroeconometrics of the 1950s and 1960s. Kalecki, the only one to make a sustained effort, remained an outsider unconnected to the mainstream of economic theorizing. Finally, the mathematical difficulty of the mixed difference–differential equations, which might have been regarded positively a few decades later, was an insurmountable barrier to almost all economists at the time.

2.6   *Keynesian macrodynamics*

Two strands of theorizing in the Keynesian tradition began with the work of Harrod and Domar: growth theory and the theory of accelerator-multiplier cycle models. The reason for labeling these models "Keynesian" is that they all built on the ex post identity of saving and investment.

Harrod and Domar set out to correct the static nature of the IS–LM model, which does not take into account either the change in the capital stock resulting from positive net investment or the change in the labor supply resulting from population growth. Their aim was the same as that of Keynes – to explain persistent unemployment – but the explanations they suggested were completely different from Keynes's "pathologies." They discussed two basic reasons for disequilibrium and consequently unemployment: The "warranted" rate of growth (at which saving equals investment) may not correspond to the natural rate of population growth; and a divergence between ex post and ex ante magnitudes can push the economy off the "knife's edge" of equilibrium growth.

Simultaneously with the attempt of Harrod to analyze verbally the behavior of an economy away from the equilibrium growth path, Samuelson (1939) published his mathematical model of cycles, based on a unit lag in the consumption as well as the investment equation. Metzler (1941), following the earlier analysis of Lundberg (1937), constructed a model of the inventory cycle also based on accelerator–multiplier interaction.

The most ambitious attempt at constructing a theory of economic cycles was that of Hicks (1950). Hicks cited Keynes, Frisch, and Harrod as his main sources of inspiration. The book failed to have a significant impact, because it did not contain any striking new ideas and the interest of macroeconomists (including Hicks) shifted to growth theory in the 1960s. Concern with economic fluctuations in macroeconomics disappeared almost completely. When it returned in the form of the New Classical macroeconomics, the break with the earlier tradition was complete.

Starting with Phillips (1961), a small number of economists did continue work on the explanation of economic cycles, using a distinctive approach incorporating Keynesian ideas as well as those of the early econometricians. This is discussed in Section 2.10.

2.7   *Monetarism*[7]

Keynesianism was succeeded by monetarism. Like all paradigmatic revolutions in economics, this one was motivated partly by common sense and partly by ideology. Whereas money is fully integrated into the Keynesian theory, it was believed to be unimportant from an empirical point of view. This opinion was never shared by the Chicago school. The desire to

---

[7] For a more detailed discussion see Cagan (1987).

combat the rising inflation rates of the 1970s was decisive for the decline of Keynesianism and the rise of monetarism. Milton Friedman was the key figure in engineering this paradigmatic revolution.[8]

Monetarism is a complete reversal of Keynesianism in two essential respects. Monetarists denied that the economy has an interesting structure. Consequently, they rejected the IS–LM model at the theoretical level and the large-scale macroeconometric models at the empirical level. Instead, the "St. Louis equation," a simple monocausal effect going from money to output, was postulated. Monetarism rejected the idea of the need or possibility of stabilization policy. Since instability was assumed to be caused by irregular monetary growth, the simple solution was Friedman's proposal of a constant monetary growth rate.

Monetarism involves two propositions: the quantity theory of money, and the idea that output fluctuations are caused by changes in the growth rate of money. The latter is the characteristic innovation of monetarism. In spite of some initial success, the second proposition had to be abandoned on empirical grounds. This rang in the end of monetarism.

2.8   *New classical macroeconomics and real business cycle theory*

Monetarism concentrated on simple empirical hypotheses backed by plausible economic reasoning. The New Classical macroeconomics, which succeeded it, can be understood as a combination of elements taken from monetarism, general equilibrium theory, the rational expectation hypothesis of Muth, as well as pure fantasy. It is the first major economic theory clearly in accord with Friedman's postulate of the irrelevance of the realism of assumptions. This did not prevent the theory from being a huge success, at least for a while. Perhaps the principal reason was that the econometric implementation of the rational expectations hypothesis created considerable technical problems, enough to keep a generation of econometricians busy and happily publishing. Also helpful was the fact that by predicting that monetary policy could have no effect, the theory had a startling implication which fitted well into the rising conservative ideology of the time.

The New Classical macroeconomics must be credited for encouraging empirical testing – which, however, it failed. This led to a second version: real business cycle theory. Here too, the lack of success in econometric testing, as well as the inherent implausibility of the assumptions, have limited the appeal of the theory.

[8] Important references are Friedman (1956) and Friedman and Schwartz (1963).

2.9   *The contemporary mainstream in macroeconomics*

The contemporary mainstream in macroeconomics is fragmented, lacking a central vision and united only in an exaggerated formalism, its emphasis on optimization, and the distance from empirical reality. These remarks apply to various areas of theory such as real business cycle theory, endogenous growth theory, and the asset market approach to open economy macroeconomics. In a different vein, much of the econometric work in macroeconomics has assumed the form of statistical time-series analysis, without significant input from economic theory. This approach has failed to generate a convergence of belief regarding the relevant stylized facts. These remarks apply to such endeavors as testing for Granger causality or for unit roots.

The most concerted efforts at using basic economic theory along with plausible assumptions in order to explain observable stylized facts has been made in the New Keynesian economics, which has largely been a reaction to the New Classical assault on Keynesian assumptions. By focusing exclusively on explaining price–wage rigidities, the New Keynesian macroeconomics has ignored the central concern of both Keynesian and dynamic disequilibrium theory: the explanation of aggregate output fluctuations.

There have been some attempts at moving the New Keynesian macroeconomics beyond static equilibria to a consideration of dynamic disequilibrium adjustment paths. Perhaps the best-known attempt is that of Malinvaud (1980). Other, more recent, approaches are discussed by Colander (1993). These approaches have all remained rudimentary and distant from empirical applications. The consequence is that practical discussion of the major economic problems facing mankind – environmental degradation, population explosion, mass unemployment, and Third World debt – proceed apart from the paradigms of the academic mainstream.

2.10   *The disequilibrium dynamics of cyclical growth and other applications of dynamic disequilibrium modeling*

I conclude the discussion of doctrinal history with the macroeconomic tradition, usually referred to as "continuous time macroeconomics." I will use instead the term "dynamic disequilibrium models of cyclical growth" (DDEMCG), which is more descriptive of its economic content. Because I am myself a part of this tradition, the discussion may lack objectivity; however, this may not be a serious defect, since objectivity is a somewhat nebulous concept and in any case the search for truth is best advanced by the clash of forcefully stated positions. DDEMCG has had a significant and growing impact on the construction of macroeconometric models of an applied nature. It has had a remarkably long and steady evolution over decades during which the mainstream flip-flopped between extreme positions.

The origin of the specific DDEMCG tradition is in the early papers by Phillips (1961) and Bergstrom (1962), but the intellectual origin is the *General Theory* of Keynes, taken in its entirety to include the usually ignored chapters on business cycles. Conventional Keynesian models are dynamizations of the IS–LM model in which output passively equals demand. In DDEMCG, the output decision is modeled directly in relation to anticipated demand and inventory levels, as postulated by Keynes in chapter 5 of the *General Theory.*

Of course, the formalization and extension of ideas contained in the *General Theory* leaves considerable room for judgment. Accordingly, there is variation in detail and emphasis among different contributions to DDEMCG. However, they all contain basically the same dynamic mechanism which is applied in different contexts. I refer to this mechanism as "second-order accelerator" (SOA). The SOA always relates a flow to a stock and assumes that the flow is adjusted continuously. This leads to a second-order differential equation capable of generating cycles. The SOA mechanism can be used to explain how the equipment cycle and the inventory–output cycle are each generated independently within the business sector, rather than requiring multiplier–accelerator interaction as in conventional models.

Interest in the DDEMCG approach has been slowly but steadily growing, and macroeconomic models in this tradition have been estimated for a substantial number of countries. Recent surveys of this work from both substantive and methodological points of view have been provided by Bergstrom (1993a,b), Gandolfo (1993a), and Wymer (1993a,b). The DDEMCG approach deals with national economies, but the general methodology has increasingly been applied to such diverse areas as the markets for financial assets, foreign exchange, and commodities. These developments are surveyed in Wymer (1993b).

3   Aspects of the methodology of the natural sciences[9]

3.1   *Introduction*

Criticism of the methodological procedures of economists has a long tradition and is presently expanding rapidly. Some authors urge that the

---

[9] In Hillinger (1992b) I have discussed some of the topics of this section in greater detail and with references to the literature. It has often been impressed upon me that, despite the burgeoning literature on methodology (which has itself become a specialized field),

methodology of the natural sciences should be embraced more vigorously; others take the opposite view and argue that the pretensions of economics at being scientific do more harm than good and so the aim should be abandoned altogether. This literature is generally abstract and as far removed from the practice of economists as from the concrete practices of the natural sciences.[10]

The methodology expounded in this section evolved in the course of my work on disequilibrium dynamics, specifically cyclical growth. I believe it to be essentially identical with the methodology used in physics. I emphasize certain aspects regarding which economic and econometric practice differs from that of physics. I believe that the power of this methodology has been demonstrated by the stable and replicable results on business cycles obtained at SEMECON, and that this methodology is essential for the long-run success of dynamic disequilibrium modeling.

3.2   *Explanans and explanandum*

One of the most basic aspects of our understanding of the world is that we regard events or phenomena as existing independently of proposed

economists are largely uninformed about the actual practice of the empirical sciences. They also tend to be unaware of the spread of the scientific method to new areas, which is continuously taking place and is the primary cause for optimism regarding the future of economics and other social sciences.

First-rate accounts of scientific advances are legion. I pick out here two recent books, both written by the principal scientists involved. Muller (1989) discusses the phenomenon of mass extinctions of life, which have occurred at intervals of approximately 26 million years. Everything turns on whether seven (!) highly uncertain observations exhibit a genuine periodicity. That in such a situation there is convergence among natural scientists regarding interpretation of the data dramatizes their differences with economists, and explodes the claim that economics and other social sciences are relatively backward because they face greater difficulties with data. The second book is Seligman (1991), which describes the triumph of cognitive psychology over behaviorism. This episode demonstrates the possibility of reaching agreement on factual truth outside of the traditional natural sciences. The book also relates how the dominant school in American psychology was refuted on factual grounds and subsequently disintegrated.

[10] In recent decades, economic methodology has become an active specialty with a strong orientation toward the philosophy of science. In this connection it is important to note that the philosophy of science, like any other field of inquiry, chooses problems and approaches of interest to itself. These happen to be largely of a formal nature. Philosophers of science do not regard it as their job to teach scientists how actually to go about their work.

After completing this paper I became aware of T. Mayer's (1993) *Truth Versus Precision in Economics*. In contrast to most writings on methodology, it contains the methodological reflections of an empiricist. The book nicely complements the present article and deals in much more detail with a number of issues touched upon here.

explanations for them. It is this independence that enables us to entertain different hypotheses to explain given facts. The distinction permeates both ordinary life and science. In the philosophy of science it is reflected in the terminology *explanandum* for that which is to be explained, *explanans* for the explanation. In advanced sciences, the distinction is not a simple one, because a great deal of theory is required to state or verify a "fact." For example, a current problem of cosmology is why less matter is observed than is suggested by physical theory on the basis of other observations. The explanandum in this case is clearly not independent of existing theories. There is, however, enough separation so that alternative explanations and procedures for testing them can be considered. Science, according to the most elementary account given in the philosophy of science, is the systematic application of the *hypothetico-deductive method*. A greatly oversimplified statement of this method is that the scientist is free to invent a hypothesis or proposed explanans, provided he tests the implications against the observed features of the explanandum.

The idea of an explanandum existing independently of the explanans seems to have faded from mathematical economics and econometrics, without this being explicitly noticed and certainly without a debate on the issue. It has been replaced by the idea of statistical testing. The explanans, a mathematical model, is accepted or rejected on the basis of test statistics. The question of whether the data exhibit significant regularities, ascertainable independently of the model, is no longer a major issue.

The origin of the emphasis on statistical testing is simply that researchers (particularly in the Cowles Commission) who established the methodology of econometrics had backgrounds in statistics, not in natural science. The fundamental difference between scientific and statistical hypotheses was overlooked. Scientific applications involve strong substantive hypotheses, although no simple probabilistic interpretation of the error terms is possible. Conversely, typical statistical applications are made in situations for which strong probability assumptions on the error terms are plausible, yet there are no complex hypotheses involving prior theory and knowledge that are being tested. Reflecting their different applications, the discussions of hypothesis testing in statistics and in the philosophy of science are quite different. Econometricians have, unfortunately, opted for the wrong methodology.[11]

---

[11] Probabilistic modeling and statistical inference were introduced into econometrics by Haavelmo (1944). The approach was subsequently elaborated and promoted by a number of researchers (including Haavelmo) at the Cowles Commission, then at the University of Chicago. This approach has come to dominate econometrics so completely that scarcely any econometrician is aware of alternative views. In fact, there is a rich early tradition of nonprobabilistic econometric modeling associated with explicit criticisms

3.3   *Observation, prediction, empirical regularities and explanatory laws*

The concepts of "explanans" and "explanandum" introduced in the previous section are in need of considerable elaboration before a reasonable understanding of the structure of scientific theories and the procedures of scientists can be obtained.

Both explanans and explanandum may belong to different levels of abstraction. The lowest level is that of *observations*. If certain classes of observations reveal characteristic features, these are referred to as *empirical regularities*. In economics it is customary to refer to *stylized facts;* I will use these terms interchangeably. For example, a particular fire is observed to generate heat. This is *explained* as an instance of a general property of combustion. Alternatively, on the basis of the same empirical regularity, we may *predict* that there will be warmth if we light a fire.

An explanans at a higher level is an *explanatory law,* which has as its explanandum a variety of empirical regularities. Perhaps the best-known example in the history of science is Newton's law of universal gravitation. It explains such empirical regularities as Kepler's laws of planetary motion, Galileo's law of falling bodies, and many other phenomena.

The biggest difference between the methodology of the natural sciences and current econometric practices is the virtually complete neglect in the latter of the level of empirical regularities as intermediate between the data and explanatory models. The consequence is that no concerted effort at establishing empirical regularities takes place. Bypassing this intermediate stage, the econometrician attempts to evaluate his explanatory model directly against the data by means of statistical tests. Such tests have played scarcely any role in the evolution of the natural sciences.

A related issue is the meaning of "prediction." In the natural sciences this means prediction of an empirical regularity by a higher-level theory;

regarding the applicability of probabilistic methods. On this early history see Morgan (1990, esp. chap. 8).

A rigorous attack on the probabilistic approach of econometrics was launched in the 1980s by R. E. Kalman. I must confess at the outset that much of his argumentation, couched as it is in the formalism of mathematical systems theory, is not accessible to me. But in important respects Kalman's position is the same as mine; this became particularly clear upon reading Kalman (1985). There he repeats his criticism of probabilistic assumptions and states that theories should explain the data *exactly.* As an example he refers to the fact that Newton's law of universal gravitation explains exactly the elliptical orbit of the planets calculated by Kepler.

My interpretation is that theories explain data not in the sense of observations but rather in the sense of empirical regulation or stylized facts. There can be perfect agreement between the latter and theory.

in this interpretation there is little difference between "explanation" and "prediction." It is natural to use "prediction" when the empirical regularity in question was first deduced from theory and later observed. A famous example is Einstein's prediction that a heavy body, such as the sun, would bend light rays in its vicinity. The econometric interpretation – that models should be tested in relation to their ability to predict data points – is quite different.

3.4   Evaluation of scientific hypotheses

In Section 3.2 I described the hypothetico-deductive method as involving the free invention of hypotheses to be tested. This is a severe oversimplification. Although we cannot describe in detail the mental processes that lead to the invention of a hypothesis, it is clear that these processes operate on our prior knowledge and involve recombinations of elements of that knowledge, a process somewhat resembling the solution of a jigsaw puzzle by trying out different combinations of the pieces. Just as prior knowledge is involved in selecting hypotheses, so too is it involved in rejecting them. Scientists generally do not bother to consider or test hypotheses, of a kind often suggested by outsiders, that are unlikely in terms of the established theories, facts, and beliefs of the discipline.

A scientific hypothesis tends to be accepted if it is plausible given prior beliefs *and* successfully explains the stylized facts. In addition, it is strongly confirmed if it correctly predicts stylized facts that are very improbable given an alternative hypothesis. These three aspects of testing a scientific hypothesis can be explicated in a Bayesian framework (see Hillinger 1992c, chap. 2, sec. 4).

Believing that either prior knowledge alone or empirical testing alone is sufficient for accepting or rejecting a hypothesis are extreme positions. I will refer to the first as *apriorism* and to the second as *falsificationism.*

From the beginning and until quite recently, apriorism was the generally accepted methodological position of economists and was in accordance with their practice. Economic theory, in particular general equilibrium theory, was built on assumptions considered to be self-evident to an informed person. A need for testing the theories was not perceived. In recent decades, falsificationism has replaced apriorism as the principal methodological position of economists.

The turnaround was substantially caused by the confluence of three distinct lines of thought, starting with the penetration into economics of Sir Carl Popper's philosophy of science with its emphasis on falsificationism. Next was the methodology of econometrics as formulated by the Cowles Commission, with its emphasis on statistical inference. It was not seen in this connection that Popper correctly interpreted falsification as a contradiction of theory by some observed stylized facts. Econometric falsificationism, with its focus on statistical tests, is not the same as Popper's falsificationism. By confounding the testing of statistical hypotheses with the testing of scientific theories, econometricians both justified their use of statistics and identified themselves with the most prestigious figure in the contemporary philosophy of science.

The third factor was Friedman's argument that the realism of assumptions is irrelevant. Freidman's position was a direct attack on apriorism, since we judge realism in the light of our prior knowledge. I hold Friedman's argument to be misguided, particularly in economics, because much direct evidence on the validity of basic assumptions can usually be obtained. Stylized facts that refute a specific assumption necessarily refute any theory making that assumption.

From a pragmatic point of view, econometric falsificationism has not been a success. It seems fair to say that there exists no significant economic theory that owes its acceptance to the fact that it has withstood repeated and rigorous testing in the spirit of Popper. Although there has been a substantial amount of econometric activity in macroeconomics and in various applied fields, this is not true of fundamental theory. If one reads textbooks in microeconomics, game theory, international trade theory, and so on, one will scarcely ever encounter the claim that what is being expounded has been empirically tested and found valid.

The needed reconciliation between apriorism and falsificationism in economics may be facilitated by the following interpretation: The acceptance of empirical regularities and explanatory laws within a scientific discipline, at a given moment in time, reflects their past explanatory or predictive successes. A firmly established law has, in the language of Popper, withstood many attempts at falsification. Any new attempt, successful or not, can therefore have only a limited impact. Any reported falsification of a well-established law will be greeted with skepticism as being probably due to experimental or observational errors. On this view, the distinction between apriorism and falsificationism is more pragmatic than fundamental. To be accepted, an economic theory must be based on plausible assumptions *and* must explain some significant stylized facts.

3.5   Example: the scientific method and the explanation of cyclical fluctuations

In order to make the discussion more concrete and to supply specific economic examples, I describe in this section some aspects of an effort at applying the methodology of the natural sciences to the explanation of economic fluctuations. This effort was initiated by myself and continued with my associates at SEMECON. Comprehensive statements of this approach are contained in Hillinger (1992c) and Reiter (1993, 1995). In this economic context I will again use the term "stylized fact" rather than "empirical regularity"; this does not imply any change in emphasis or meaning.

The work originated around 1961 while I was looking for a dissertation topic at the University of Chicago. At that time, the existence of a 40-month inventory cycle in aggregate data was a generally accepted stylized fact for the U.S. economy. At the same time, Metzler's explanatory model for the inventory cycle was well known. I noticed that the stylized facts in this instance were based on casual empiricism rather than systematic investigation. Moreover, there was no attempt at testing Metzler's model as an explanation of the stylized facts. In my dissertation (Hillinger 1963), I attempted both to describe the stylized facts quantitatively and to test Metzler's model relative to them. This was an obvious task if one takes seriously the methodology of the natural sciences.

Later I constructed a model of the interaction of the inventory cycle, the equipment cycle, and secular growth. This model turned out to have the following implications: for deviations from the growth paths, non-durable consumption expenditures exhibit no cycles; equipment investment has the 7–10-year equipment cycle only; and both equipment and inventory cycles appear in aggregate output. These stylized facts were subsequently verified for many countries. They are very hard to explain if the model is not essentially correct.

The work done by Weser (1992) on the aggregation of business cycles turned out to have the unexpected implication that the inventory and equipment cycles would be locked in a particular phase relationship resulting in the characteristic M shape of aggregate fluctuations. This shape had already been noticed by several investigators who could not explain it.

I have offered these examples in order to demonstrate that the confrontation of empirically determined and model-implied stylized facts leads to dramatic confirmations or refutations of alternative theories. Potentially, there is no difference in this regard between the natural sciences and economics.

I conclude this section with some brief remarks on the difference between the SEMECON and conventional econometric methodology for the evaluation of structural models of economic time series, as constructed particularly in macroeconomics. In current econometric practice, the two principal methods for evaluating models are significance tests and out-of-sample forecasts. The probability assumptions underlying econometric tests have already been criticized in Section 3.2. Somewhat milder criticisms are reviewed by Mayer (1993, chap. 10). The idea of testing a structural model by comparing its out-of-sample forecasts with those of a naive model was advanced by Friedman in 1951 and has since been elaborated and applied by numerous investigators. The most detailed elaboration is the SEMTSA methodology advocated by Zellner.[12] Out-of-sample forecast comparison has proven to be an effective evaluative device, casting doubt on the validity of many econometric models.

The conventional methods for validation just described can be contrasted with the SEMECON methodology, which is to establish the stylized facts in the form of the auto-spectra and cross-spectra of the time series being considered. These are then compared with the corresponding spectra implied by the fitted model. The advantages relative to an evaluation by forecasting performance are as follows. First, the spectra contain all of the existing information in both the data and the model. Second, if the process has a large variance but there are many observations, the spectra can be estimated with precision whereas the forecasting performance will necessarily be poor. Third, spectral characteristics such as cyclicity can be intuitively understood and are suggestive of possible explanations (e.g. adjustment lags).[13]

3.6   *Concept formation and the dynamics of scientific theories*

In this section I deal with the evolution of scientific theories and fields. In this context I view science as both an intellectual and a social system. The latter aspect will be developed further in Section 5.[14]

The evolution of scientific fields is a dynamic process guided by both internal and external factors. Internal factors include the existing theories, known facts, and accepted research procedures of the discipline; these determine the type of hypotheses that can be formulated or are deemed worthy of consideration and testing. The external factor is reality itself, which leads to the rejection of particular hypotheses. Even well-established interlocking systems of theories may be thrown into doubt by new evidence.

---

[12] For a description of the SEMTSA approach and references to the literature, see Zellner (1994).

[13] For an up-to-date statement of the SEMECON methodology in this area, see Reiter (1993).

[14] The social system of science is the subject of the sociology of science. This subdiscipline has produced a substantial but almost entirely descriptive literature. More critical accounts, including discussions of immature fields and of the social sciences, can be found in Colander (1991), Ravetz (1971), and Tullock (1966).

The common view of science is that it produces new knowledge, which is reflected in publications. Scientists are rewarded for publishing by career advancement. There is thus a competitive system, analogous to a market economy, that leads to the efficient production of knowledge. This view of science is at best incomplete, and its translation into the practices of the social sciences is problematic. In particular, I shall argue that the drive toward novelty is much less constrained by reality in the social sciences than in the natural sciences, and consequently that the social sciences are more likely to produce trivia than new knowledge.

The most universal assumption regarding science is that it will always generate significant new knowledge, provided only that the scientific field has organized itself properly and has adopted effective research methods. This assumption is a consequence of the explosive growth of knowledge produced by the natural sciences. However, it must be questioned whether this performance can be repeated at any time and in any field.

In forming an opinion on this issue, it is useful first to examine what kind of knowledge has actually been produced by the natural sciences. For this purpose I make a distinction between *vertical* and *horizontal* progress in science. Vertical progress means the discovery of laws at increasing levels of generality. Laws at a lower level, usually those discovered earlier, are shown to be consequences of the more general laws. Horizontal progress means the discovery of new empirical phenomena and of the laws explaining them.

Sustained and impressive vertical progress has, as far as I can see, been limited to theoretical physics and (to a lesser extent) biology. This progress is a consequence of the discovery of previously unknown entities, such as the fundamental forces of physics and elementary particles, and the generation of new observations not previously accessible via the naked senses. Similarly, biology involved the discovery of such new entities as microorganisms and genes. In addition, biology benefited directly from the progress of the physical sciences. Whereas horizontal progress in many areas of science is currently very rapid, it is my impression that vertical progress has largely exhausted itself, particularly in physics. Physicists are still hoping for the "unified theory," which would be the final rung on the ladder.

Examining the social sciences, we see that vertical and horizontal progress generally came early and was not followed by comparable later achievements. Moreover, the progress was never as spectacular or surprising as in the natural sciences. There is a rather obvious reason for this: the social sciences examine phenomena of our direct experience, accessible both through observation and through introspection. In economics, it is hard to imagine finding a more fundamental assumption than utility maximization subject to constraints.[15] Nor can we conceive of the discovery of new entities beyond those already being considered, such as the household, the firm, or the government.

If these points are at least approximately valid then they explain an inherent tendency toward triviality, the manifestations of which are clearly visible in economics and other social sciences. If the most significant ideas of a field are discovered early, and if they are subsequently neglected as being no longer novel or relevant to current research, then novelty will become successively less significant and approach triviality. The existence of large numbers of highly trained and specialized researchers will then simply lead to the rapid exhaustion of novel ideas and to alternating trivial fashions.

In macroeconomics this is illustrated by the fact that its most important problems – inflation, growth, and fluctuations – were identified early and given plausible (if partial) explanations. In contrast are the following hypotheses, all of which played significant roles in the macroeconomics of the past 40 years: that inflation is caused by cost-push/demand-pull, independently of the money supply; that technical progress, like manna flowing from heaven, simply occurs and is not the consequence of investment; that economic fluctuations are solely the result of unanticipated monetary shocks, or of technology shocks. All of these ideas have in common that they sacrificed plausibility in order to achieve novelty.

To reverse the tendencies just described, economics requires a massive shift of emphasis away from novelty and toward the replication of stylized facts and of the conformity of explanatory theories relative to the stylized facts. What this may involve concretely is discussed in the next section in relation to the description and explanation of business cycles.

4   Fundamental issues in dynamic disequilibrium modeling

In this section I deal with basic issues of dynamic disequilibrium theory in the light of the preceding methodological and historical discussion. A central issue is the prospect for dynamic disequilibrium theory to overcome the counterproductive dichotomies that have bedeviled economics in the past and have prevented it from becoming a progressive empirical science. My discussion will focus on the work done at SEMECON because it represents a conscious effort at applying the methodological position outlined earlier and because it is the example I can discuss most

---

[15] Of course, basic concepts of economics such as "utility" are refined and extended in the course of the evolution of economic thought.

competently. Most of my remarks apply directly to other work done in the DDEMCG tradition and substantially apply also to other efforts at dynamic disequilibrium modeling.

4.1   The stylized facts of business cycles

In Section 3.2 I argued that scientific theories are explanations of stylized facts that can be described and verified independently of the various explanatory hypotheses. Accordingly, I begin this section with a discussion of the stylized facts of economic fluctuations.

An extensive literature on business cycles evolved during a period of more than 100 years. This literature began with discussions of economic cycles. A basic contribution was that of Juglar, who was the first to note the recurrent or periodic character of fluctuations. This is the single most important stylized fact regarding fluctuations, and motivated the search for endogenous explanations of business cycles. The subsequent literature contained theory and statistical or historical observations in various proportions. It was for the most part informal and not very systematic. Nevertheless, there was steady progress in agreement on certain basic stylized facts.

A consensus view had evolved by the 1940s and 1950s. There are at least two cycles, a "minor cycle" of 3–4 years' duration, visible mainly in total output and inventory investment, as well as an 8–10-year "major cycle" visible mainly in equipment investment. These, plus possible additional cycles such as a 20-year "building cycle," are superimposed on each other and on other movements such as trends or irregular disturbances. Such a construction is compatible with a highly irregular appearance of observed fluctuations.[16]

The knowledge regarding these stylized facts faded with the declining interest in business cycles beginning in the 1960s. This trend was accentuated by the fact that the stylized facts are incompatible with monetarist or New Classical macroeconomic explanations of business cycles. Also, the findings were not duplicated by time-series methods, a topic to which I now turn.

In the postwar era, various methods and techniques, broadly related to the statistical analysis of time series, entered econometrics on a massive scale. Time-series methods appear to be predestined to establish the stylized facts of dynamical systems independently of a substantive theory.

---

[16] The most detailed and comprehensive statement of the consensus view was given by Matthews (1959). Unfortunately, shortly thereafter, business cycles ceased to be a topic of academic research.

This is, in fact, the role of spectral analysis in the natural sciences. In many applications the empirical spectrum is the explanans, while the relevant theory – which predicts the shape of the spectrum – is the explanandum.

In econometrics, the use of time-series methods has not led to a convergence of belief regarding the relevant stylized facts. On the contrary, the failure to establish stable stylized facts has been a contributing factor to the erosion of belief in the stylized facts that had been established earlier by alternative (and usually less formal) methods.

The use of time series in econometrics began with classical spectral analysis. There was considerable interest in these techniques from the 1950s to the 1970s. The interest was in establishing the stylized facts of economic fluctuations, but the nonparametric methods being used were unsuited to the purpose because they require very long time series, which are difficult to obtain in economics. To obtain large data sets, econometricians turned to financial data, where the observations are closely spaced. But these data tend to be highly irregular and do not display the stylized facts found in series on investment and output. For this and other reasons (discussed more fully in Hillinger and Sebold-Bender 1992), it is not surprising that the traditional stylized facts of business cycles could not be confirmed. The lack of positive results led to a decline of interest in spectral analysis.

The subsequent evolution of time-series techniques in economics was dominated by the work of C. W. Granger and his associates. Interest shifted away from the determination of the stylized facts of economic fluctuations. Key concepts in this connection are *Granger causality, unit roots,* and *co-integration.* Characteristic of these approaches is the stress on statistical testing, rather than on primarily descriptive measures such as the spectrum. The emphasis on statistical testing in econometrics was already criticized in Section 3.2. Other criticisms of these methods can be made. The crucial point is that, in practice, they have not lead to a convergence of belief relative to either stylized facts or explanatory models.

From the beginning of my scientific career in macroeconomics, my aim has been to establish the stylized facts of business cycles and to construct explanatory models for them. To establish the stylized facts I used the greatest variety of evidence and methods that were available or that I was able to construct. This included the use of traditional spectral methods, which I found to yield very weak results and which I therefore abandoned.

In the early 1980s, maximum entropy spectral analysis was brought to my attention by Arnold Zellner. It is a parametric method, designed specifically for the analysis of very short time series and therefore ideally suited to economic applications. It has become the method of choice at SEMECON for establishing the stylized facts of business cycles. The method leads to the full confirmation and also the extension of the traditional stylized facts of business cycles described here.[17]

4.2 Dynamic disequilibrium and equilibrium approaches to the modeling of business cycles

In this section I compare the DDEMCG and rational expectations approaches to the explanation of economic fluctuations. More specifically, I focus on how investment behavior, particularly the characteristic 8–10-year cycles in fixed investment, are modeled by these approaches. I do not attempt a detailed evaluation of either, which would be impossible in a brief space, but rather use them in order to illustrate my methodological position and to derive some general conclusions regarding a suitable methodology for dynamic disequilibrium theory.

The essence of the rational expectations approach is that a sector, or an entire economy, is modeled as being determined by the decisions of a single fully informed and rational agent. The agent solves an intertemporal maximization problem on the assumption that the exogenous variables follow a known stochastic process extending into the indefinite future. The DDEMCG models are in the tradition of Keynesian model building. Behavioral and technological relationships are assumed on the basis of plausibility and simplicity, and the estimated functions can often be interpreted as linear approximations to more complex relationships. A basic distinction is maintained between relationships assumed to hold in equilibrium and adjustment processes out of equilibrium.

A basic assumption regarding the adjustment processes is that they take place in continuous time. Also, neither stock nor flow variables (such as production or investment) are allowed to jump discontinuously. The resulting adjustment processes are represented by second-order differential equations, referred to as second-order accelerator (SOA) mechanisms.

A simple version of SOA for investment in fixed capital, in the absence of trend or depreciation, is

$$\hat{I} = a(K^* - K),$$

$$DI = b(\hat{I} - I),$$

$$DK = I.$$

In this formulation, K is the stock of fixed capital, I net investment, K^* the equilibrium capital stock, and $\hat{I}$ the momentarily desired rate of

[17] For an account of the SEMECON methodology for time-series analysis, see Hillinger and Sebold-Bender (1992).

investment. In the usual flexible-accelerator formulation, actual and desired investment are equal; in the SOA formulation, actual investment adjusts toward the desired level.

In Section 3 I stated that a theory or model should be based on plausible assumptions and should explain the stylized facts. Much of the work done at SEMECON has served to demonstrate that the SOA does explain the stylized facts qualitatively in a variety of contexts, and also quantitatively when fitted to data.[18]

In comparing the plausibility of assumptions employed in the real business cycle and DDEMCG approaches, I will focus on the central and related assumptions of rationality and equilibrium. These are the key assumptions that have, from the beginning, separated mainstream and alternative economics. History demonstrates the difficulty of bridging the conflicting positions on this issue. Nevertheless, I feel that the effort must be made. It would be highly desirable to arrive at a reasoned and convincing position that transcends the tradition of alternative economics and facilitates the acceptance of dynamic disequilibrium theory by the mainstream.

One problem has been that, in the past, mainstream and alternative economics have been more interested in differentiating themselves from each other than in gaining a mutual understanding. One consequence is the tendency of each side to take an extreme position and uphold it like a religious faith. The other is that each side specialized on those problems where its own assumptions are most relevant, while ignoring or downgrading the problems that were the primary concern of the other side. In essence, this means that the mainstream focused on general equilibrium theory and alternative economics on business cycles. It is only in the very recent past that the mainstream has attempted to explain economic fluctuations on the basis of its characteristic optimization assumptions. The attempt took the form of real business cycle theory.

Modern dynamic disequilibrium theory assumes that adjustment speeds are neither infinite (classical case) nor zero (Keynesian case), but instead have an intermediate finite value. The reasons are well known and rather obvious. Nevertheless, I will briefly sketch them for the case of fixed investment.

Consider the lags involved from the occurrence of a major change in demand to the completion of the required adjustment of productive capacity. There are considerable lags before information becomes available to decisionmakers. In large firms, performance reports are typically on a

---

[18] For a discussion of empirical applications of the SOA and further references, see Hillinger and Reiter (1992).

quarterly or annual basis and require time beyond the reporting period to be prepared and submitted to the top management. Further delays occur if the information from many firms is assembled into national statistics. These are typically highly unreliable when they are first reported with about a year's delay. Significant further revisions typically occur over several years. Another delay has to do with the problem of extracting a signal from noisy data. The firm must decide when a change has persisted long enough to be considered permanent rather than transitory. The reaction must then be decided upon. If a new factory is needed, it must be planned and built, and the work force expanded and trained. From the initial planning to routine operation of a new factory, several years will pass. Nor is adjustment any faster in the face of declining demand and necessary retrenchment. This is sufficiently illustrated by the current, protracted world economic crisis.

It should be clear that the existence of adjustment lags is in no sense an indication of irrational behavior. There are costs incurred if the various lags are shortened and other costs if they are lengthened. The optimal lag corresponds to minimal costs, or equivalently to the point at which profits are maximized. This has been recognized in the theoretical literature on adjustment costs, where it is shown that quadratic costs in the deviations of the capital stock from its optimal level and in investment imply that optimal behavior of the firm can be modeled by the conventional flexible accelerator. At SEMECON, the analysis of adjustment costs has been carried considerably further in order to clarify the logic of the SOA adjustment process on which the DDEMCG approach is based.

A basic assumption is that the firm has committed itself to a long-term or equilibrium path for its capital stock along which profits are maximized. Adjustment costs relate to deviations from this path. Let k be the capital stock in deviation form. Investment and the rate of change of investment, also in deviation form, are given by Dk and D^2k. The firm is assumed to minimize a cost function of the form

$$\min_{k(t)} \int_{t_0}^{\infty} [\alpha k^2 + \beta(Dk)^2 + \gamma(D^2k)^2]e^{\rho(t_0-t)} \, dt.$$

The solution to this dynamic optimization problem is the time path (in deviation form) of the firm's net investment and capital stock. A fundamental result is the following: Assume a high value of the discount factor ρ, reflecting strong risk aversion; then the SOA equation approximates the solution path.[19]

[19] For the proof see Hillinger, Reiter, and Weser (1992).

Does the argument just outlined demonstrate that behavior described by the SOA is rational? It depends on what we mean by the term. The SOA cannot be obtained from the currently dominant paradigm of mathematical economics, which requires the maximization of expected profits, discounted by the market interest rate, and where uncertainty is modeled as a known stochastic process extending into the future. This technique of modeling uncertainty has been criticized by several writers, and is not how business decisions are generally made.[20]

If the DDEMCG and real business cycle approaches are compared in order to evaluate the extent to which each is grounded in rational behavior, the aggregation problem must also be considered. The typical real business cycle model assumes that an entire economy can be represented by a single, utility maximizing Robinson Crusoe. Such a theory can be considered seriously only if one accepts the position that the realism of assumptions is irrelevant. I have argued here that this proposition is itself untenable.

In empirical applications, the SOA has also been fitted to aggregate data. There are, however, fundamental aggregation theorems for the SOA that have been proven (Weser 1992). A basic theorem relating to fixed investment is the following: Assume a subset of "coherent" firms that act according to similar but not identical SOA mechanisms, leading to investment cycles of similar but not identical lengths for the firms. The phases of these cycles are initially arbitrary, so that they will substantially cancel out in the aggregate. The remaining "incoherent" firms are ignored. Assume further that the coherent firms have some common input, such as an index of business sentiment. In a suitable nonlinear model embodying these assumptions, it can be shown that the coherent firms will enter a state of *resonance*. This means that the periods of the cycles converge to the average period, the phases converge to the average phase, and the damping of the cycles is reduced so that their amplitudes increase. The result is that a cycle appears in the aggregate investment data, and the movement can be modeled by means of an SOA equation fitted to the aggregate.

As noted in Section 2, concepts evolve with the theories in which they play a role. This clearly applies to the rationality concepts. Dynamic disequilibrium theory has thus far attracted the attention of only a few researchers, and the investigation of the rational underpinnings of dynamic disequilibrium theory is only beginning. Even so, considerable progress has been made, and I hope to have shown that dynamic disequilibrium theory and the assumption of rational behavior need not be strangers.

---

[20] An excellent and detailed exposition of relevant empirical and theoretical issues has been provided by Blatt (1983, book IV).

5 The politics of science and the future of dynamic disequilibrium theory

5.1 Introduction

In this section I make a number of pragmatic observations on the prospects of dynamic disequilibrium theory, both as a fashion and as hard science. In this context I use "fashion" in a nonderogatory sense, meaning more or less the same as "acceptance." No part of economics, or the social sciences generally, has as yet become hard science, but they all contain theories of a greater or lesser degree of empirical relevance and with different degrees of acceptance.

The term "fashion" also reflects the fact that, given the drive toward novelty and the lack of replication, even useful theories have finite life spans. General equilibrium theory – as initiated by Adam Smith and formalized by Walrus, Debreu, and Arrow and Hahn – has been the most enduring fashion in economics, but after more than 200 years it appears to have exhausted itself. Keynesianism, which was a highly successful merging of the mainstream and the alternative, had about a quarter of a century as an academic fashion. If one looks at subsequent macroeconomic fashions – such as monetarism, New Classical economics, or real business cycles – one sees a trend toward fashions that are less comprehensive, less generally accepted, more technique-oriented, and of shorter duration. The reason is that there are now many more economists, with a primarily technical training, who are eager to participate in a new intellectual fashion and by so doing exhaust its formal potential in a shorter time than was formerly the case.

In discussing the prospects for dynamic disequilibrium analysis, I will focus on the explanation of macroeconomic fluctuations, because this is the most central and most highly developed area of dynamic disequilibrium modeling. The general acceptance of dynamic disequilibrium analysis will stand or fall with its success in explaining business cycles.

5.2 The 'story' behind dynamic disequilibrium theory

In order to gain acceptance, it is most important for a scientific theory or movement to have a central and significant message that is plausible and can be communicated effectively. As Colander (1991) pointed out, this is particularly true in economics, because most economists spend most of their time teaching nonspecialized undergraduates. Also, the general and political acceptance of economic theories depends to a large extent on what is communicated in the business sections and editorials of newspapers and business journals.

General equilibrium theory was invented by Adam Smith and sold with the powerful metaphor of the "invisible hand" guiding the selfish actions of individuals to a socially desirable outcome. At the heart of Keynesianism was the message that output adjusts to effective demand and that, in order to avoid unemployment, effective demand must be stabilized by the state. Monetarism had the simple message that output fluctuations are due to monetary disturbances. The New Classical macroeconomics argues that agents anticipate a predictable monetary policy and thereby neutralize the potential impact on the real sector. Real business cycle theory lacks such a simple message, and this accounts for its limited appeal to a wider public.

Is there a simple and convincing message that can be associated with dynamic disequilibrium theory? I believe there is, and that it contains the following elements.

1. The basic conceptualization of the theory: An economy contains *stock* and *flow* variables, the latter being the rates of change of the former. Relative to the usual length of the observation period (i.e., the year or quarter), these variables are *continuous,* because economic activity takes place – and decisions are made – on a daily, hourly, or even shorter basis. By the definition of continuity, the variables do not jump. Dynamic disequilibrium analysis also makes the stronger assumption of *inertia.* This means that the derivatives of the variables cannot become arbitrarily large because of technological constraints, or behavioral and organizational *adjustment costs.* Since even technological constraints generally have some flexibility, it is convenient to postulate adjustment costs as the general explanatory principle and to assume that these increase with deviations from optimal adjustment rates, becoming arbitrarily large for sufficiently large deviations. In this scheme, the persistence of disequilibria is explained by the prohibitive cost of very rapid movements toward equilibrium.

2. The *duration* of business cycles is inversely related to the relevant adjustment speeds. Production can be adjusted relatively rapidly when inventories are too high or low. This causes much short-run variability as well as a typical 3–4-year inventory–output cycle. Equipment investment typically has an 8–10-year cycle. A 20-year cycle has been observed in building. Finally, long cycles of about 50 years have been associated with the diffusion of major innovations.

The basic graphical expository device for dynamic disequilibrium analysis is the *phase diagram.* At an elementary level it can be used without a knowledge of differential equations, and is no more difficult to understand than any of the diagrams used in elementary economics. Figure 1(a) shows a phase diagram for fixed investment. The variables are in deviation form, so that the equilibrium capital stock and the equilibrium investment rate are both zero. At point A in the diagram, the horizontal arrow reflects the identity $DK = I$. The vertical arrow reflects the fact that, given excess capital, a negative net investment rate is desired; the given positive rate can only gradually be moved in this direction. It is clear that, depending on the strength of the vertical arrows at different points, which in turn depend on the nature of the underlying adjustment costs, any kind of movement is possible. This includes a spiral, which would reflect a cyclical movement. An analogous (though somewhat more complex) phase diagram can be given for the inventory–output cycle.

Business forecasters and analysts often predict a rise (fall) in production (investment) if inventories (stocks of fixed capital) are below (above) equilibrium levels. The phase diagrams thus relate directly to what can be read in the business press.[21]

The theoretical phase diagrams can be effectively compared with empirical phase diagrams. Such a diagram for fixed investment in Germany is given in Figure 1(b). This plot strongly suggests that the empirical series on fixed investment follows a cyclical pattern of a kind to be expected on the basis of dynamic disequilibrium theory and the theoretical phase diagram. An even clearer picture of cyclical properties of the data is given by the power spectrum and the cumulative spectrum in Figure 1(c). Finally, the spectra obtained from the data can be compared with the spectra implied by an econometric model estimated from the data; this is shown in Figure 1(d). The relevant SOA equation that was estimated is

$$DK^2 = -0.221DK - 0.526K.$$

The existence of economic disequilibrium is obvious. Dynamic disequilibrium theory has a simple and convincing explanation of why this is so. This explanation can easily be elaborated, but even at a very simple level it provides qualitative and (if need be) quantitative explanations of economic dynamics.

I conclude this section with some remarks on the *nonformal* considerations that play a role in the evaluation of scientific hypotheses. The validation of scientific hypotheses at all levels is essentially a social process. A hypothesis is regarded as verified when independent investigators have convinced themselves of its validity. Ideally, this takes the form of the independent replication of experiments. Where this is not possible – in

---

[21] Kennedy (1992) discussed five macroeconomic relationships that are frequently mentioned by business journalists yet seldom discussed in textbooks. One of these is the influence of inventory levels on subsequent output. He does not mention the effect of capital utilization on expected investment, probably because – in addition to the business press – it is often mentioned in textbooks.

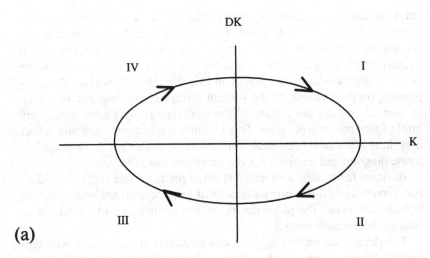

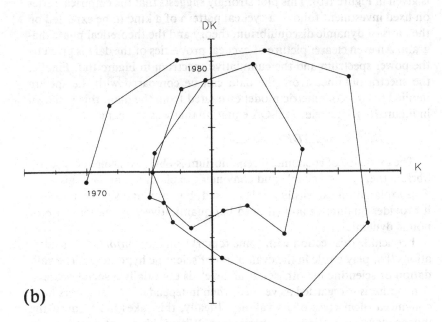

Figure 1. Visual analysis of the equipment cycle for Germany, 1960-89; annual data on fixed investment and capital stock in deviations from trend. (a) Abstract phase diagram. (b) Empirical phase diagram. (c) Data spectrum (maximum entropy). (d) Model spectrum.

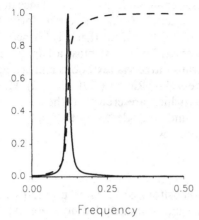

Frequency

| Period | 8.31 | 4.20 |
| Peak Power | 0.67 | 0.03 |

power spectrum
integrated spectrum

(c)

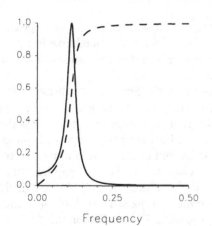

Frequency

| Period | 8.70 |
| Peak Power | 0.30 |

power spectrum
integrated spectrum

(d)

such areas as astronomy, geophysics, or paleontology – the evidence must be independently scrutinized and evaluated.[22] The successful formulation and testing of hypotheses is a craft. This means that it is learned, by example, in close association with practitioners. At most a part of this knowledge can be formalized and transmitted via textbooks and articles. This aspect has been particularly stressed by Ravetz (1971, chap. 3). However, these social and craft aspects, which are crucial to the successful functioning of a science, have been unduly neglected in the evolving literature on the methodology of economics.

6   Conclusion

Macroeconomics has become the repository of research programs that were announced with much fanfare and ultimately led nowhere. All of them – the older business cycles theories, Keynesianism, monetarism, New Classical economics, and real business cycle theory – incorporated some valid ideas but also glaring deficiencies in both content and methodology. I believe that the DDEMCG is the only development in macroeconomics against which such a sweeping criticism cannot reasonably be made. Also, it is not another research program promising empirical success sometime in the future, but can look back on a history of substantial accomplishments in economic theory, econometric methodology, and empirical applications.

Dynamic disequilibrium theory is, of course, much wider in scope than DDEMCG. It is the natural extension of the static maximization paradigm, based on the assumption that agents and organizations have constraints that prevent instantaneous adjustment.

More than any other field of economics, dynamic disequilibrium theory both employs and requires the methodology of the natural sciences. This involves both a great promise and a great challenge. The promise is that dynamic disequilibrium theory could be instrumental in moving economics not only into new substantive areas, but also toward a more effective empirical science methodology. The challenge is that this requires major changes in economists' attitudes and procedures. Required in particular are a much greater effort at determining stylized facts and using them to discriminate between economic theories. The profession must also reorient itself toward a much greater effort at replication, both in publications and in teaching. Finally, the realization of these aims requires appropriate reward structures, particularly for economists at the beginning of their careers.

[22] In contemporary economics "replication" seems to be largely understood as involving the recomputation of an investigator's results on the basis of the same data base. This is a much narrower and almost trivial conception.

REFERENCES

Bergstrom, A. R. (1962), "A Model of Technical Progress, the Production Function and Cyclical Growth," *Economica* 29: 357–70.

(1993a), "The History of Continuous-Time Econometric Models," in Gandolfo (1993b), pp. 13–34.

(1993b), "Survey of Continuous Time Econometrics," Chapter 1 in this volume.

Blatt, J. M. (1983), *Dynamic Economic Systems,* Armonk, NY: M. E. Sharpe.

Cagan, P. (1987), "Monetarism," in Eatwell, Milgate, and Newman (1987), vol. 1, pp. 492–7.

Colander, D. (1991), *Why Aren't Economists as Important as Garbagemen?* Armonk, NY: M. E. Sharpe.

(1992), "New Keynesian Economics in Perspective," *Eastern Economic Journal* 18: 438–48.

(1993), "The Macrofoundations of Micro," *Eastern Economic Journal* 19: 447–57.

Eatwell, J., M. Milgate, and P. Newman (eds.) (1987), *The New Palgrave: A Dictionary of Economics,* London: Macmillan.

Friedman, M. (1956), *Studies in the Quantity Theory of Money.* University of Chicago Press.

Friedman, M., and A. J. Schwartz (1963), *A Monetary History of the United States, 1867–1960.* Princeton, NJ: Princeton University Press.

Frisch, R. (1933), "Propagation Problems and Impulse Problems in Dynamic Economics," in *Economic Essays in Honour of Gustav Cassel.* London: Allen & Unwin. Reprinted in R. A. Gordon and L. K. Klein (eds.) (1965), *Readings in Business Cycles.* Homewood, IL: Irwin.

Gandolfo, G. (1993a), "Continuous-Time Econometrics Has Come of Age," in Gandolfo (1993b), pp. 1–11.

(1993b), *Continuous-Time Econometrics, Theory and Applications.* London: Chapman and Hall.

Haavelmo, T. (1944), "The Probability Approach in Econometrics," *Econometrica* 12 (suppl.): 1–115.

Hicks, J. R. (1950), *A Contribution to the Theory of the Trade Cycle.* Oxford: Clarendon Press.

Hillinger, C. (1963), *A Theory of the Inventory Cycle.* Ph.D. dissertation, Department of Economics, University of Chicago.

(1987), "Keynes and Business Cycles," in G. Gandolfo and F. Marzano (eds.), *Keynesian Theory, Planning Models and Quantitative Economics,* vol. I. Milano: Giuffrè Editore, pp. 77–95.

(1992a), "Paradigm Change and Scientific Method in the Study of Economic Fluctuations," in Hillinger (1992c), pp. 5–46.

(1992b), "The Methodology of Empirical Science," in Hillinger (1992c), pp. 47–60.

(1992c), *Cyclical Growth in Market and Planned Economies.* Oxford: Clarendon Press.

Hillinger, C., and M. Reiter (1992), "The Quantitative and Qualitative Explanation of Macroeconomic Investment and Production Cycles," in Hillinger (1992c), pp. 111–40.

Hillinger, C., M. Reiter, and T. Weser (1992), Micro Foundations of the Second-Order Accelerator and of Cyclical Behaviour," in Hillinger (1992c), pp. 167–80.

Hillinger, C., and M. Sebold-Bender (1992), "The Stylized Facts of Macroeconomic Fluctuations," in Hillinger (1992c), pp. 63–110.

Kalecki, M. (1933), "Outline of a Theory of the Business Cycle," trans. in Kalecki (1971), pp. 1–14.

—— (1935), "A Macrodynamic Theory of Business Cycles," *Econometrica* 3: 327–44.

—— (1954), *Theory of Economic Dynamics*. London: Allen & Unwin.

—— (1971), *Selected Essays on the Dynamics of the Capitalist Economy, 1933–1970,* Cambridge University Press.

Kalman, R. E. (1985), "Identification of Noisy Systems," *Russian Mathematical Surveys* 40: 25–42.

Kennedy, P. (1992), "On Journalists' Use of Macroeconomic Concepts," *Economic Inquiry* 30: 194–201.

Keynes, J. M. (1936), *The General Theory of Employment Interest and Money*. London: MacMillan.

Lundberg, E. (1937), *Studies in the Theory of Economic Expansion*. London: P. S. King: reprinted (1955) by Basil Blackwell, Oxford.

Malinvaud, E. (1980), *Profitability and Unemployment*. Cambridge University Press.

Matthews, R. C. O. (1959), *The Business Cycle*. University of Chicago Press.

Mayer, T. (1993), *Truth versus Precision in Economics*. Brookfield, Elgar.

Metzler, L. A. (1941), "The Nature and Stability of Inventory Cycles," *Review of Economic Statistics* 23: 113–29.

Morgan, M. S. (1990), *The History of Econometric Ideas*. Cambridge University Press.

Muller, R. (1989), *Nemesis: The Death Star*. London: Heinemann.

Petty, W. (1899), *Economic Writings,* 2 vols. (C. Hull, ed.); reprinted (1964) by A. M. Kelly, New York.

Phillips, A. W. (1961), "A Simple Model of Employment, Money and Prices in a Growing Economy," *Economica* 28: 360–70.

Ravetz, J. R. (1971), *Scientific Knowledge and Its Social Problems*. Oxford: Clarendon Press.

Reiter, M. (1993), "Evaluation of Discrete and Continuous Time Dynamic Models by Spectral Methods with an Application to Automobile Demand," Chapter 7 in this volume.

—— (1995), *The Dynamics of Business Cycles: Stylized Facts, Economic Theory, Economic Methodology and Applications*. Heidelberg: Physica.

Roncaglia, A. (1987), "Petty William," in Eatwell et al. (1987), vol. 3, pp. 853–5.

Samuelson, P. A. (1939), "Interaction between the Multiplier Analysis and the Principle of Acceleration," *Review of Economic Statistics* 4: 75–8.

Seligman, M. E. P. (1991), *Learned Optimism*. New York: Knopf.

Smith, A. (1789), *The Nature and Causes of the Wealth of Nations,* 5th ed.; reprinted (1937) by Random House, New York.

Tinbergen, J. (1930), "Ein Schiffsbauzyklus?" *Weltwirtschaftliches Archiv*; reprinted in L. H. Klaasen et al. (eds.) (1959), *Selected Papers by Jan Tinbergen*. Amsterdam: North-Holland, pp. 1–14.

Tullock, G. (1966), *The Organization of Inquiry*. Durham, NC: Duke University Press.

Weser, T. (1992), "The Aggregation Problem for Economic Cycles," in Hillinger (1992c), pp. 181–200.

Wymer, C. R. (1993a), "Continuous-Time Models in Macroeconomics: Specification and Estimation," in Gandolfo (1993b), pp. 35–79.

(1993b), "The Role of Continuous Time Disequilibrium Models in Macroeconomics," Chapter 3 in this volume.

Zellner, A. (1994), "Time Series Analysis, Forecasting and Econometric Modelling, Time Series Analysis (SEMTSA) Approach," *Journal of Forecasting* 13: 215–33.

CHAPTER 3

The role of continuous time disequilibrium models in macroeconomics

Clifford R. Wymer

1 Introduction

This paper discusses an approach to the specification, estimation, and analysis of continuous time models in macroeconomics and in financial and commodity markets. This approach provides the econometric foundations for the development of models that are grounded in economic theory and have a sufficiently rich dynamic structure to provide a satisfactory representation of observed economic behavior. The models are generally relatively small and formulated as disequilibrium systems in continuous time. They are designed to be amenable to mathematical and statistical analysis so that they can be used for the investigation and analysis of macroeconomic behavior, or the behavior of financial and commodity markets, and for policy evaluation. Extensive references to both theoretical and empirical work are given in Wymer (1992).[1] Continuous time models have been used in other areas, for instance in futures or

I am most grateful to Giancarlo Gandolfo for inviting me to the University of Rome, La Sapienza, to continue research in the continuous time field. I much appreciate the interest and comments of Kieran Donaghy and Denis Richard on developments in nonlinear estimation and analysis, and wish to thank them and Giuseppe De Arcangelis for their comments on a draft of this paper. Finally, I wish to record my continuing appreciation to Rex Bergstrom for his interest and discussions over many years.

[1] In some ways the present paper is a companion piece to Wymer (1992), Part I of which was written in 1976 to provide the framework for the econometric work of the U.K. SSRC International Monetary Research Programme at the London School of Economics. That paper, which circulated in mimeograph form, for many years formed the basis for many of the continuous time models with which the author has been associated. Part II of that paper, written in 1992, reviews developments between 1976 and 1992 and contains extensive references to theoretical and empirical work in continuous time econometrics. The present paper is an attempt to define the current position of continuous time models in the econometrics of macroeconomics.

options pricing models in finance such as the asset pricing models of Lo (1988, 1991), but that work is not considered here.

The research on continuous time models in econometrics has developed not just as a method of estimation but as an integrated approach to the specification, estimation, and analysis of economic models involving three aspects: the use of relatively small disequilibrium models based on economic theory and specified as differential equation systems; the derivation of an appropriate discrete model that is stochastically equivalent to the differential equation system, given that economic data are discrete; and the use of full-information maximum likelihood estimators. The aim of this work is to estimate the parameters of the underlying differential equation model as directly as possible, subject to the restrictions inherent not only in the differential model but also in the derivation of the stochastically equivalent discrete system. Although relatively small, theoretically based structural models could be specified as ordinary discrete models and estimated by full-information maximum likelihood techniques, these models have less satisfactory properties than continuous systems; it is the integrated approach to the specification and use of continuous time models that is attractive and provides the benefit of this work.

Throughout this paper it is assumed that the underlying economic system is continuous; the arguments in favor of such a system are overwhelming. Many production processes are continuous or essentially so, as are a number of markets. It is, for example, possible to trade continuously for over five days per week in spot, futures, and options markets for a wide range of commodities and financial assets. While many production processes have more-or-less fixed lags that may be long, especially in primary production and heavy engineering, the products enter markets on a much more continuous basis. More importantly, although individual decisions may be made at regular or irregular intervals, the information on which those decisions are based is likely to be largely continuous and the decisions themselves are likely to concern a broadly continuous path of production, consumption, or transactions. The lags in this process will be much shorter than the observation period of data used for estimation. Moreover, the tertiary sector, which accounts for a substantial and growing proportion of economic activity in many economies, acts very much as a continuous process with very short lags. As macroeconomic behavior is the result of the action and interaction of individual economic agents, aggregation of the microvariables across sectors or markets will produce macrovariables that will tend to be continuous, so that the macroeconomic process can be treated as continuous or as if it were continuous.

It is also assumed throughout that the economic system being studied is dynamic, and only dynamic models will be considered here. The term *ordinary discrete model* will be used to refer to models specified as a set of difference equations that are not derived from a differential equation system, although some of those models may in fact be consistent with a differential equation system.

An important feature of continuous time models is that the estimator uses a discrete model that is satisfied by the observations generated by the differential equation system irrespective of the observation interval of the sample, so that the properties of the parameters of the differential equation system may be derived from the sampling properties of the discrete model. This allows a more satisfactory treatment of distributed lag processes and of the disturbances in the model. In particular, the minimum lag in an economic system is likely to be much smaller than the observation interval, but in continuous time models the lag functions may be specified in a way that allows the length of the lag to be estimated rather than assumed. Thus a continuous time model, unlike ordinary discrete models, can be specified and analyzed independently of the observation interval of the sample to be used for estimation; the forecasting interval is also independent of the observation interval. Moreover, these estimators allow stock–flow models to be handled correctly, since they expressly recognize that although variables such as stocks and prices can be measured instantaneously, other variables such as flows or averages cannot; those variables are observed only as an integral over the observation period. As many behavioral functions in economics involve the interaction between stocks and flows, it is essential that these be treated correctly; this cannot be done in an ordinary discrete model. A simple example using the demand for money was given in Wymer (1992). Reiter (1993), using spectral analysis, showed how misleading results are obtained when a continuous system is mis-specified as an ordinary discrete model.

The approach to continuous time models with which the author has been associated is aimed at specifying an economic system and then estimating that model as directly as possible. This work does not differentiate between the economic system and the data-generating process (as defined for example in Hendry and Richard 1982) other than in the sense that, although the model is formulated as an approximation to the economic system, it must take into account any deficiencies in the sample. The aim, however, is to estimate the parameters of the underlying macroeconomic system. Because some variables in the basic theoretical model may not be observed, or are unobservable, the theory must be extended or modified accordingly. Any modifications of this nature become part of the economic model to be estimated and tested. Although price or quantity expectations are often determinants of some functions of a model, these variables are often unobserved. If observations on such expectations do exist, those variables can be specified as part of the model, perhaps as endogenous variables. Price expectations are sometimes obtained by surveys, and quantity expectations, especially of production in the commodity markets, are provided by specialist firms; for agricultural commodities these data are becoming increasingly reliable through the use of satellites. If observations do not exist, the expectations process may still be specified but the expectations variable is then eliminated by substitution. The resultant model can then be estimated subject to all of the hypotheses and constraints inherent in the basic model, and subject as well to any additional constraints arising from the elimination of unobserved variables.

The models being used are nontâtonnement, so there is no assumption that prices or quantities are in equilibrium at any point in time, let alone at all points in time. Much of the theoretical literature in the past, and even currently, makes assumptions that are essentially those of a Walrasian equilibrium; this includes, for example, much of the rational expectations literature as discussed in Hahn (1983). Such assumptions are far too restrictive to provide a satisfactory representation of an economy. The models developed within the continuous time literature are more general than such Walrasian systems, but their long-run properties are consistent with rational expectations (see e.g. Bergstrom and Wymer 1976, Gandolfo and Padoan 1990, and Bergstrom, Nowman, and Wymer 1992).

Many, and perhaps most, of the models developed and used in the continuous time literature have been disequilibrium models, but this term needs clarification. In this paper (and consistent with most of the literature), a *dynamic disequilibrium* economic model is one that specifies the transition from one long-run equilibrium to another, assuming such equilibria exist, following a change in some exogenous variable or some disturbance. The long-run equilibrium need not be a steady state where all variables grow at some constant rate, but could rather be some form of limit cycle. If the model is nonlinear, it may have a strange attractor leading to aperiodic behavior of deterministic chaos. In this case, the model would exhibit endlessly varying oscillations without an external disturbance or change in exogenous variable, as discussed in Wymer (1995). Of course, if the system is unstable, either generally or under certain conditions, the model may not converge to a new equilibrium; the nature of such instabilities may be derived from the properties of the model. It is emphasized that the use of a "disequilibrium" model does not imply a lack of optimizing behavior by economic agents or that their behavior is irrational. The system as a whole, however, need not be in long-run equilibrium, and the use of these models means that there is no need to make such an assumption; such an equilibrium, if it exists, is a property of the model.

The disequilibrium relationship may be derived from the intertemporal maximization of some profit, cost, or welfare function subject to risk and the costs of adjustment. The economic agents can be assumed to be in equilibrium at all times in the sense that they are on their appropriate supply, demand, or price functions. A linear or log-linear partial adjustment function of the form $Dx(t) = \alpha\{\hat{x}(t) - x(t)\}$, where a variable $x(t)$ adjusts to some desired level $\hat{x}(t)$, can be derived explicitly in this way under simplifying assumptions. In general, though, these derivations become extremely complex, so this function must be considered as an approximation. Investment behavior, fixed capital and financial asset accumulation, and consumer durable behavior can all be formulated within this framework. The overall adjustment process of an economic system, however, requires a much richer specification; this is discussed in Section 3.

Section 2 discusses the role of continuous time models in macroeconomics, and Section 3 details the specification of disequilibrium systems. An outline of the exact and approximate discrete models that are stochastically equivalent (or approximately so) to the differential equation system is given in Section 4, and this is used as a basis for comparison with ordinary discrete models in Section 5. Section 6 discusses the analysis of the dynamic properties of these models and their structural stability, and Section 7 introduces a general framework that allows nonlinear systems to be solved subject to a broad range of constraints.

This paper is essentially a survey and review of some aspects of continuous time modeling, so from that point of view much of the content will be familiar to those working in the area; nevertheless, the discussion of the role of continuous time modeling and some of the techniques available to fulfill that role is new. Thus, those familiar with the field can skip through sections 1, 3, and 4 (at least), while those less familiar with this approach may find more of interest in Sections 1, 2, 5, 6, and 7; Section 5 does, however, depend on Section 4 (and, to a lesser extent, on Section 3). A concise review of the continuous time approach that was written for macroeconomists is Wymer (1992), which also contains a very brief but comprehensive summary of continuous time macroeconomic models, and models of financial and commodity markets, that have been developed along the lines of the approach discussed here.

2   Role of continuous time models

The models considered in this paper all have the characteristic of being relatively small, compact, specified on the basis of economic theory, heavily overidentified, and amenable to mathematical analysis. The reasons for using continuous models are discussed in Bergstrom (1976), Wymer

(1992), and Gandolfo (1981), all of which contain extensive references; these reasons are reviewed in Gandolfo (1992).

Any model is simply a formal representation and approximation designed to capture the essentials of some economic process for the purpose of investigating certain economic behavior and its policy implications. Theoretical models formalize some aspect of economic behavior under a set of assumptions, which are usually chosen so that the model allows an analytical solution. The properties of the model can then be derived and their implications studied. These models are often, by necessity, simplistic (but not simple) and the underlying assumptions very restrictive, so they cannot provide a satisfactory representation of the economic process. Once a theoretical model moves from a static to a dynamic formulation – perhaps because of intertemporal rather than atemporal optimization, the introduction of expectations, or owing to information, decision, or production lags – purely qualitative analysis becomes strictly limited by the difficulty or impossibility of obtaining analytical solutions to the model. It becomes difficult, for example, to obtain useful analytical results once a model involves more than two or three first-order differential equations, or a second-order one, and analytical results rapidly become impossible. Hence much of economic theory, particularly dynamic theory, must necessarily use models that are very small. Simplifications may include assuming away certain feedbacks or assuming some aspects of the economy always to be in equilibrium. While this may be useful for studying some properties of the model, those properties are conditional on the assumptions being made and often these are not realistic. Such models, however, can provide the foundation for a more complete system.

Theoretical models must be validated by appropriate testing if they are to provide a basis for further investigation. Moreover, the properties of even some of the simplest models vary qualitatively depending on the values of the parameters, so it is necessary to obtain estimates of these parameters to allow fuller development of the theory and to provide a guide to the implications of the theory for economic agents.

The emphasis of much of the research in continuous time models is aimed at allowing the study of more realistic models based on economic theory in order to obtain a better understanding of economic behavior, especially dynamic behavior, and to derive the policy implications of this theory. The models are often such that long-run behavior, and to a lesser extent medium-term behavior, can be studied analytically, although this depends of course on the complexity of the model. Economic models are generally too complex to allow short- to medium-term behavior to be studied analytically, but it is possible to derive results which, although numerical, provide information of a similar nature to that which can be obtained from small theoretical models.

The models being considered, whether macroeconomic or of a particular market or sector, are specified to incorporate theory and the institutional structure of the economy in a coherent manner throughout the model. Behavioral functions derived, implicitly or explicitly, by the optimization of some objective function subject to constraints will have a functional form determined by the underlying constrained objective function, and will often be subject to homogeneity, symmetry, and curvature conditions. Institutional and market structures of an economy may also need to be incorporated in the model, perhaps as constraints that are included in the theoretical formulation; in such cases these features will be embodied in the behavioral functions. If the economic theory is not sufficiently well developed to take account of specific market or institutional structures, these features of the economy will need to be superimposed on the more formal theoretical functions so that the more rigorously derived behavioral functions, which are often partial equilibrium functions, are embedded in a wider framework. Thus, the dynamic model may incorporate market rigidities that will exert a major influence in the short run without affecting its long-run properties. The more rigorous the theory from which the functions are derived, the more heavily overidentified will be the model, with parameters often occurring nonlinearly within and across equations. The aim in developing more sophisticated estimators is to allow these functional forms and restrictions on the parameters to be maintained during estimation and analysis of the model, so that the results are consistent with its theoretical formulation.

Continuous time models are ideal for these purposes. They are small enough to be readily understood, and sufficiently compact that there is not a large number of extraneous exogenous variables. They can be as rigorously specified as the theory and data allow, and the estimators allow the constraints on the parameters inherent in the theoretical model to be imposed during estimation, so that the parameters being estimated are those that have been specified in the model. Although most of these models will need to be analyzed numerically, many of these results are more analytical in nature.

For policy purposes – whether for macroeconomic policy by a government or central bank or for decisions of a firm or some other economic agent – a model is required not so much for forecasting purposes but rather to provide a basis for analysis of an economy and the effects of different policies. In institutions such as the International Monetary Fund, the European Economic Commission, and central banks, a major function of an "in-house" model is to focus discussion. Ideally, analytical results would be preferred, but these cannot be obtained except for very small and simple systems. However, the models discussed here provide information that, although numerical, is of direct use in considering the implications of the model for policy; Bruno (1988) emphasizes the usefulness of small, compact models (although not specifically continuous ones) for that purpose. For instance, if the model has a steady state then it may be possible to derive this algebraically, which would allow comparative long-run equilibrium analysis. Dynamic behavior can be investigated using sensitivity analysis to give the partial derivatives of the eigenvalues of a system with respect to its parameters, as shown in Wymer (1992) and discussed in Section 6. A nice feature of these results is that they are compact and can be obtained in a single calculation without the need for simulations or repeated calculations with different parameter values.

Another reason for using these models is for optimal control. Again, the usefulness of optimal control is not that it will be used directly by policy makers, but rather that it helps provide an understanding of the economic system and the extent to which it can be controlled by various policies. A full optimal control solution would provide a baseline against which feedback rules can be evaluated. Given uncertainties in the economy and of some parameter values, a relatively simple feedback rule that provides a satisfactory approximation to the optimal solution may be more useful than full optimal control. Bergstrom (1987) derived the stochastic optimal control solution for linear differential equation systems, and Wymer (1982) provided a nonstochastic optimal control solution using the eigensystem for deterministic models. A useful feature of the latter approach is that it allows the use of sensitivity analysis to give the partial derivatives of the optimal control eigensystem with respect to the parameters of the whole optimal control eigensystem, including the parameters of the objective function. For nonlinear models, a nonstochastic optimal control solution is given in Section 7 that permits nonlinear inequality constraints to be imposed on the control variables. Following LaFrance and Barney (1991), this allows the partial derivative of the optimal value function with respect to the parameters of the economic model and the objective function to be derived as shown in (6.12). Again, these results may be obtained in a single calculation, thus providing information on the effect of changes in parameters in the model without the need for simulation.

A macroeconomic model will usually be estimated with endogenous monetary and fiscal policy feedback equations owing to the endogeneity of these variables. The monetary and fiscal policy equations may then be deleted and replaced by monetary and fiscal control variables derived from the optimization of an intertemporal objective function. The objective function may be defined, for example, as a quadratic form in some target and control variables, but this raises the problem of choosing a relevant set of weights. An alternative is to begin with a more fundamental objective function. For example, one of the problems arising in policy analysis is whether or not some amount of inflation is "bad." This question is difficult to tackle on purely theoretical grounds, because it depends on reactions within the system to changes in inflation in which lags are important. However, the macroeconomic models discussed here are well suited to answer questions of this nature. Rather than defining an objective function in terms of inflation, output, or unemployment, it may be better to maximize a discounted intertemporal welfare function defined in terms of (say) consumption only, so that although this does not target inflation or unemployment directly, the optimal solution for monetary and fiscal policy will reduce inflation, or fluctuations in inflation, but only to the extent that this increases welfare. Of course, this maximization would depend on the form of the welfare function and on the discount rate, but there is considerable literature on these factors, and the number of parameters in the function will be few compared with a quadratic form involving several target and control variables. Inequality constraints on the control variables will almost certainly be necessary, but these may be imposed within the framework outlined in Section 7.

Models incorporating 15 to 25 equations have proved to be a reasonable representation of macroeconomic behavior, including both real and financial sectors. The Knight and Wymer (1978) model of the United Kingdom, a mixed-order system with 21 endogenous variables, includes the main national income aggregates, employment, prices, wages and interest rates, money, bonds, bank advances, and net foreign assets of the private and public sectors. The number of variables can be reduced, however, if the banking system is consolidated with one of the other sectors of the economy, as in the U.K. model of Bergstrom and Wymer (1976). That model has 11 endogenous variables, and is a mixed-order stock–flow model with two second-order equations defining investment and the volume of money. The second-order model of Bergstrom et al. (1992) includes 14 endogenous variables. Similar models are those of Jonson, Moses, and Wymer (1976) for Australia, Gandolfo and Padoan (1990) for Italy, Donaghy (1992) for the United States, and Nieuwenhuis (1995) for the Netherlands. Important feedbacks are likely to be omitted in macromodels with fewer endogenous variables that would seriously affect the dynamic behavior of the system.

The performance of these models has been good, both in commodity and financial models and in macroeconomics. A robust result, holding across many of the macroeconomic models, is that lags are longer than had been accepted previously. The model of the Australian economy of Jonson et al. (1976) predicted high unemployment lasting for over 10 years if the economy were to be deregulated and monetary policy used to control inflation. The policy was not implemented, but similar policies in the United Kingdom under the Conservative government of Mrs. Thatcher and in New Zealand under a Labour government had this result. The policies led to high real interest rates, which increased the cost of investment at a time when the economy was restructuring, thus slowing down the adjustment. The experience of these and other countries (such as German re-unification and the restructuring in Eastern Europe), where many economists argued that adjustment would be rapid, suggests that the adjustment lags were seriously underestimated. In this respect, the models discussed here may be more realistic.

3   Specification

Economic models are often nonlinear.[2] Economic theory often leads to nonlinear functions, and some economic systems may be better represented by a nonlinear model. The use of a nonlinear model may be necessary to represent certain features of an economy or market, as it allows dynamic behavior (including the possibility of limit cycles) that is precluded by a linear system. This is discussed, for example, in Bergstrom (1967), Bailey, Hall, and Phillips (1979), Gandolfo (1981), and Wymer (1979, 1992, 1993a). Nonlinearities may be due to the basic theoretical structure assumed to be underlying the economic system, such as the form of a utility or production function, or due to the institutional or market structure in which the utility or production functions are embedded. Behavioral functions, perhaps derived from utility or profit maximization, are often highly nonlinear and possibly of a logarithmic or transcendental form, while other equations may be linear or simple multiplicative functions of the variables. The institutional or market structure may also be nonlinear. These nonlinearities may have significant implications both in the long run and in the adjustment from one state to another. In a dynamic adjustment model, for example, the rate of adjustment need not be constant but may vary according to the state of the economy or of the market. Such a model could allow for an acceleration in prices and wages or a rise in interest rates as the economy approaches full capacity or full employment and thus incorporate the conditions for a contraction better than a linear model.

A general second-order nonlinear differential equation system may be written as

---

[2] Throughout this paper, a *nonlinear* model means one that is nonlinear in variables. All the models discussed here may be nonlinear in parameters, as even models linear in variables may have coefficients that are nonlinear functions of the parameters of the system.

$$\Phi\{D^2y_1(t), Dy_2(t), Dy_1(t), y_2(t), y_1(t), z(t), \theta\} = v(t), \qquad (3.1)$$

but for the purposes of this paper it is assumed that the system is recursive and can be conveniently but imprecisely written as

$$D^2y_1(t) = \phi_1\{Dy_1(t), y_2(t), y_1(t), z(t), \theta\} + u_1(t),$$
$$Dy_2(t) = \phi_2\{Dy_1(t), y_2(t), y_1(t), z(t), \theta\} + u_2(t), \qquad (3.2)$$

where the $y_i(t)$ are vectors of m_i continuous endogenous variables with $y(t) = [y_1(t)\ y_2(t)]'$, $z(t)$ is a vector of n continuous exogenous variables, and θ is a vector of p parameters; D is the differential operator d/dt. It is assumed that the $u_i(t)$ are vectors of white-noise disturbances, so that the integral $\zeta(t) = \int_0^t u(s)\, ds$ is a homogeneous random process with uncorrelated increments. It can be shown that $\zeta(t)$ is nondifferentiable and hence the process $u(t)$ cannot be rigorously defined, but for the purposes of this section (and as discussed in Wymer 1972) it may be viewed as if it were well defined. A precise definition of the model and the disturbances is given in Section 4. The variables $y(t)$ and $z(t)$ may be stocks or flows; this distinction becomes important for estimation. In this model, the $y_1(t)$ are called second-order variables because this is the highest order in which $y_1(t)$ appears in the model; similarly, the $y_2(t)$ are called first-order variables. Some equations may be identities, in which case the corresponding $u(t)$ are zero. Also, the model may include zero-order equations (i.e., equations defining zero-order variables), which need not be recursive although in many models they are likely to have a causal interpretation.

Ideally, a disequilibrium model of an economic agent or sector would be derived from intertemporal optimization of the utility or profit function (or equivalent objective function) of the sector, subject to the appropriate budget, wealth, or technological constraints and subject also to adjustment costs and uncertainty. Adjustment models[3] of the form

$$Dx(t) = A\{p(t), w(t), \theta\}[\hat{x}(t) - x(t)], \qquad (3.3)$$

where $x(t)$ is a vector of quantities that adjust to their desired level $\hat{x}(t) = f\{p(t), \theta\}$ and $p(t)$ and $w(t)$ are vectors of prices and other costs, have been derived by intertemporal maximization with adjustment costs in the theory of the firm by Eisner and Strotz (1963) for a single variable and more generally by Treadway (1971) for factor demands. The theory of Eisner and Strotz (1963) was generalized to n factors by Lucas (1967) under specific separability conditions on the profit function, but the conditions are stringent; essentially they allow the solution to be diagonalized.

---

[3] For simplicity of notation, disturbances will be omitted from the functions defined in the remainder of this section.

An intertemporal duality approach using flexible functional forms was developed by Cooper and McLaren (1980) and Epstein (1981), and later by Epstein and Denny (1983). However, even under the assumption that the perfectly variable factors always assume their optimal value, so that the intertemporal and atemporal optimization problems are separable as in Eisner and Strotz (1963), the derivation of explicit factor demand functions becomes intractable for more than two semifixed factors of production, and in general only local results can be obtained. These studies assume that prices, or price expectations, are given.

Although the assumption of a tâtonnement process is convenient for theoretical work, there is no reason to suppose that the economic system is a tâtonnement one. Even if this is hypothesized, it is an hypothesis that should be tested. Moreover, the assumption that firms maximize profits or minimize costs, given prices or price expectations, is also a Walrasian concept. It is argued that, even at the disaggregated level, firms operate within a framework of monopolistic competition, so that the formation of quantity expectations may well be as important as price expectations. Once firms are aggregated to the sectoral level, there is even less justification for assuming that the "sectoral" behavioral functions can be derived with given prices; in this case the price determination process becomes an integral part of the system.

If a model is to provide an adequate representation of macroeconomic behavior, it must take into account both price and quantity determination in a nontâtonnement system. The complexity of the intertemporal maximization problem subject to adjustment costs and uncertainty suggests that economic agents, over time, may derive rules that give a sufficiently good (although informal) approximation to the full solution, especially given the degree of uncertainty in expectations and the imprecise nature of their utility function. This is not to argue that firms or individuals do not informally maximize some utility or welfare function, but rather that they can obtain a feasible solution to their intertemporal optimization problem that is an acceptable approximation given the costs of obtaining the information necessary to improve that solution. Furthermore, the lack of a comprehensive theory of monopolistic competition involving adjustment costs, costs of entry (which may be institutional or the result of high initial investment), and uncertainty means that a complete model cannot be derived directly from intertemporal optimization. The economic models considered here are formalizations of the activities of those agents. Although these models are not assumed to be in equilibrium at any point in time, the use of a continuous system allows adjustment to be rapid and does not preclude the system from being at or close to equilibrium; it does enable that hypothesis to be tested.

The approach used in the continuous time models discussed here derives partial equilibrium functions by utility or profit maximization by consumers or firms subject to the usual budget, wealth, or technological constraints, but subject also to short-run constraints on their behavior. These partial equilibrium functions – which may be supply or demand functions for goods, investment functions, functions for desired prices depending on marginal costs or some cost mark-up, or desired holdings of assets – are then embedded in an adjustment framework to give the dynamic model. Some of the partial equilibrium functions will themselves be dynamic, such as the investment functions of Bergstrom (1967), Bergstrom and Wymer (1976), or Hillinger and Reiter (1992), but in other cases the dynamics come from the adjustment function itself.

The specification of these models includes but is not limited to partial adjustment of some variable to the difference between its actual and desired levels:[4]

$$Dx_i(t) = f_i\{\hat{x}_i(t) - x_i(t)\}, \tag{3.4}$$

where $\hat{x}_i(t)$ may refer to the demand or supply of some quantity $x_i(t)$; alternatively, if firms are able to determine prices in the short run, $x_i(t)$ could refer to prices and $\hat{x}_i(t)$ to the marginal cost of production or some mark-up function. Often prices will be determined according to excess demand or supply, so that if the supply of some good is given in the short run, for example, then prices might be determined by

$$Dp_i(t) = h_i\{\hat{q}_i^d(t) - q_i(t)\} \tag{3.5a}$$

or, more generally,

$$Dp_i(t) = h_i\{\hat{q}_i^d(t) - q_i(t), \hat{q}_i^s(t) - q_i(t)\}, \tag{3.5b}$$

where $q_i(t)$ is the actual quantity being traded, $\hat{q}_i^s(t)$ is the desired supply, and $\hat{q}_i^d(t)$ the desired demand; $\hat{q}_i^s(t)$ and $\hat{q}_i^d(t)$ are functions of prices $p_i(t)$ and are derived from profit or utility maximization (or some equivalent) by the producers and consumers of the product. In (3.5b) it is assumed that both supply and demand affect prices but to differing extents or with different lags. These equations may, of course, be of order greater than 1. In the linear case, and where excess demand and supply have similar effects, (3.5b) would collapse to

$$Dp_i(t) = h_i\{\hat{q}_i^d(t) - q_i^s(t)\}. \tag{3.5c}$$

---

[4] Throughout this paper, the discrepancy between the level of a variable and its desired level will be represented as a difference, but this depends on the definition of the variable and on the functional form of the adjustment function. In some cases, especially where some $x(t)$ are defined as natural numbers, a more appropriate representation might be $Dx_i(t) = f_i\{\hat{x}_i(t)/x_i(t)\}$.

Although an equilibrium solution for a first-order model such as this would be $\hat{q}_i^d(t) = \hat{q}_i^s(t) = q_i(t)$ with $Dp_i(t) = 0$ and $Dq_i(t) = 0$, the formulation of the model allows other equilibria where the rate of change of prices and quantities is nonzero. This is shown, for example, in Bergstrom and Wymer (1976).

Another class of disequilibrium relationships, which will just be mentioned here, is defined by the assumption that the actual quantity traded depends on the short side of the market; an early reference is Quandt (1978). Thus $q(t) = \min\{\hat{q}^s(t), \hat{q}^d(t)\}$ where, in its simplest form, prices are assumed to be given. This can be extended to allow price adjustment as in (3.5c), for example. This model is restrictive in that it assumes either that the goods traded are highly perishable or that stocks have no role other than as part of the production process. More generally, and especially at the aggregate level, stocks allow trading to take place off the partial equilibrium supply and demand functions. As shown in equations (3.11), stocks can play a major role in price determination, and prices will change rapidly if stocks are particularly high or low relative to desired holdings.

In a multi-commodity system, the demand and supply functions will, in general, be functions of prices of all commodities, and these functions are subject to all of the homogeneity, symmetry, and curvature conditions inherent in the objective function from which they are derived. These functions will be simplified, however, if the utility or cost functions are separable. It is quite possible that price determination will depend not only on demand and supply for the particular commodity but also on demand and supply for substitutes. Moreover, an excess demand for one commodity will increase its price and thus be reflected in the demand and supply functions of other commodities, and particularly in the demand and supply functions of substitutes. Furthermore, the effect of this excess demand may spill over directly into other markets owing to expectations that prices of substitutes will rise. Thus the price equation (3.5b) or (3.5c) will contain not only the excess demand for commodity i but also the excess demands for other commodities.

In formulating these models, it is necessary to specify the distributed lag function in the adjustment process. There is no reason why the functions should be only first-order. In fact, it is likely that the functions will be of higher order. Thus, if $x(t)$ is assumed to adjust to some desired or expected level $\hat{x}(t)$ with distributed lag $f(s)$, then

$$x(t) = \int_0^\infty f(s)\hat{x}(t-s)\,ds. \tag{3.6}$$

Exponential distributed lag functions provide a useful representation of lag processes in the economy. They have the advantage of being simple, and have the properties of a density function in that $\int_0^\infty f(s)\,ds = 1$, $f(s) >$ 0 for all s, and $\lim_{s\to\infty} f(s) = 0$. These functions are smooth and differentiable to any order, and can be defined to provide realistic "humped" forms with few parameters. These processes may be derived using differential operators, so that the first-order exponential adjustment of $x(t)$ to its desired level $\hat{x}(t)$ given by

$$Dx(t) = \alpha[\hat{x}(t) - x(t)], \quad \alpha > 0, \tag{3.7}$$

may be written as

$$x(t) = \frac{\alpha}{D+\alpha}\hat{x}(t), \tag{3.7a}$$

which is formally equivalent to

$$x(t) = \int_0^\infty \alpha e^{-\alpha s}\hat{x}(t-s)\,ds \quad \text{with } f(s) = \alpha e^{-\alpha s}. \tag{3.7b}$$

This lag process has a mean time lag $\int_0^\infty sf(s)\,ds = 1/\alpha$ or $\int_0^{1/\alpha} f(s)\,ds = 0.63$, so that 63 percent of the adjustment takes place in a time of $1/\alpha$. The distributed lag function corresponding to the second-order process

$$D^2 x(t) = \alpha\beta[\hat{x}(t) - x(t)] - (\alpha+\beta)Dx(t) \quad \text{or}$$
$$x(t) = \frac{\alpha}{D+\alpha}\frac{\beta}{D+\beta}\hat{x}(t), \quad \alpha > \beta > 0, \tag{3.8}$$

is $f(s) = (\alpha\beta/(\alpha-\beta))[e^{-\beta s} - e^{-\alpha s}]$, with a mean time lag of $\int_0^\infty sf(s)\,ds = 1/\alpha + 1/\beta$ and a modal time lag of $\max f(s) = (\log\alpha - \log\beta)/(\alpha-\beta)$. The distributed lag functions for higher order processes can be derived in a similar way. A related class consists of the gamma functions. These distributed lag functions reflect the adjustment costs, gestation or installation lags, uncertainty, and habit persistence faced by economic agents in their intertemporal optimization.

The partial adjustment processes have a distributed lag representation only when a variable is adjusting to its own desired or expected level. Thus, a second-order adjustment process of prices to excess demand as in (3.5), for example, is

$$D^2 p(t) = \gamma\delta[\hat{q}^d(t) - \hat{q}^s(t)] - \gamma Dp(t), \tag{3.9}$$

where the term in $Dp(t)$ has a damping effect on the adjustment to excess demand. This process, which may be written as

$$Dp(t) = \frac{\gamma}{D+\gamma}\delta[\hat{q}^d(t) - \hat{q}^s(t)],$$

involves only a first-order distributed lag process with mean time lag $1/\gamma$. If all variables are in logarithms, δ is the long-run elasticity of the rate of change of prices with respect to excess demand. Estimates of the parameters of the distributed lag, such as α, β, and γ in (3.8) and (3.9), can be used to test the form of the lag function.

A feature of these models is their flexibility in incorporating institutional structures. One example of this is the labor market. In an economy where capital can be considered as fixed in the short run but labor is flexible, and assuming that output is demand determined, the demand-for-labor function may be specified as the inverse of the production function. Assuming second-order log-linear adjustment functions for employment $L(t)$ and wages $w(t)$, these functions may be specified as

$$D^2L(t) = \alpha\beta[\hat{L}^d(t) - L(t)] - (\alpha + \beta)DL(t), \qquad (3.10a)$$

$$D^2w(t) = \gamma\delta[\hat{L}^d(t) - \hat{L}^s(t)] - \gamma Dw(t), \qquad (3.10b)$$

where $\hat{L}^d(t)$ and $\hat{L}^s(t)$ are the demand and supply of labor, and the unemployment rate is $\hat{L}^s(t) - L(t)$. In some countries, and particularly in Europe, rigidities in the labor market mean that the adjustment in (3.10a) is very slow and δ in (3.10b) is small, so that nominal wages are unresponsive to the excess demand for labor. Furthermore, institutional factors such as the various compacts between government, unions, and employers in the United Kingdom during the 1960s and 1970s, or the *scala mobile* in Italy, meant that wages were being maintained in real terms. If wages are index-linked, a more appropriate relationship than (3.10b) is

$$D^2w(t) = \gamma_1[\hat{L}^d(t) - \hat{L}^s(t)] - \gamma_2[Dw(t) - \mu Dp(t)], \qquad (3.10c)$$

where the effect of an excess demand for labor, or perhaps unemployment, is only to modify the level of real wages, and this effect is weak if γ_1 is small. This is unlikely to be the case if, as in some industries under *scala mobile*, μ exceeds unity.

The specific formulation of a model will depend on market structure, production, consumption, and the degree of monopolistic competition existing in the market. In the case of a single commodity – for example, where the commodity is durable and where there is some degree of monopolistic competition in the market – the model may be of the form where production is determined in the short run according to

$$D^2Q(t) = f\{\hat{Q}(t) - Q(t), \hat{V}(t) - V(t), DQ(t)\}, \qquad (3.11a)$$

with consumption given by

$$D^2C(t) = g\{\hat{C}(t) - C(t), DC(t)\}, \qquad (3.11b)$$

prices by

$$D^2p(t) = h\{\hat{Q}(t) - Q(t), \hat{V}(t) - V(t), Dp(t)\}, \qquad (3.11c)$$

and stocks by the discrepancy between output and consumption:

$$DV(t) = Q(t) - C(t), \tag{3.11d}$$

where $\hat{Q}(t)$, $\hat{C}(t)$, and $\hat{V}(t)$ are (respectively) the supply, demand, and inventory functions derived from profit or utility maximization of the producers and consumers, and are functions of prices $p(t)$ as well as of expected prices and adjustment costs. The term $\hat{Q}(t)$ may also be a function of expected consumption, in which case the process determining these expectations would need to be specified. In this model, stocks act as a buffer between supply and demand in that they absorb any discrepancy between production and consumption, but this does not mean that the demand for inventories is eliminated from the model. On the contrary, excess holdings of stocks have been found to be a major, and perhaps crucial, determinant of prices in commodity markets, as shown for example in a prototype model of the world sugar market (Wymer 1975) and in a fully developed model of the world copper market (Richard 1978).

This concept of stocks as a buffer between supply and demand in macroeconomic and commodity markets can be extended to the role of liquid assets, and particularly money balances, in financial markets as shown in Wymer (1973). For its use in macroeconomics see Knight and Wymer (1975), Jonson (1976a,b), and Jonson et al. (1976); this concept is also discussed in Laidler (1984), who provides extensive references.[5]

The demand and supply functions of each sector are assumed to be derived from the optimization of some objective function subject to appropriate constraints. It is assumed that one asset acts as a buffer or residual, so that adjustment functions may be defined for all other goods or assets of a particular sector; this asset then absorbs any discrepancy between supply and demand or receipts and payments of that sector. Thus inventories are the buffer of the goods market, and money balances are the buffer of the private sector. Under uncertainty and in light of transactions and information costs, the private sector is presumed to be willing to allow its actual money balances to change in such a way that its other demands are satisfied subject to their adjustment processes, but this does not preclude the private sector from being concerned about the level of its money balances. These are brought into dynamic equilibrium not by changing money balances directly but rather indirectly, through the effects of excess money balances on the balance of payments, interest rates, and prices. Thus, the excess demand for money balances plays a major

---

[5] Laidler (1984) surveys the literature on money as a buffer stock and contrasts this idea with Keynesian analysis and the neo-Austrian "equilibrium business cycle theory" of Lucas (1975), as well as discussing its implications for the "liquidity preference" versus "loanable funds" controversy and the Brunner and Meltzer (1976) analysis of money supply.

role in determining the adjustment of much of the economic system to changes in exogenous variables or disturbances. Similarly, the differences between desired and actual inventories is a determinant of prices, domestic output, and imports. The inclusion of the budget and wealth constraints in these models is necessary to capture the feedback from output and expenditure decisions to inventories and the rest of the model, and from government expenditure and taxation decisions to the volume of money and the balance of payments.

It is likely that the effect of excess money balances on the economy will be nonlinear in that excess liquidity (i.e., a negative excess demand for money) will cause the rates of adjustment of some nominal variables to increase. The excess demand for money may also play the role of providing information on expected inflation. Thus, in the macroeconomic model of the Australian economy (Jonson et al. 1976), the excess demand for money balances was a determinant of consumption, prices, and wages. Hence wage determination, for example, was specified as

$$D^2 \log w(t)$$
$$= \alpha[\hat{L}^d(t) - \hat{L}^s(t)] - \beta\left[\log \hat{m}(t) - \log \frac{M(t)}{p(t)}\right] - \gamma D \log w(t), \quad (3.12)$$

where $w(t)$ is the wage rate, $p(t)$ the prices level, $M(t)$ the nominal money balances, $\hat{L}^d(t)$ and $\hat{L}^s(t)$ the demand and supply of labor, and $\hat{m}(t)$ the demand for real money balances; it is assumed that real money balances are homogeneous of degree zero in prices. Although money balances entered (3.12) as an additive log-linear term, that could be considered as an approximation to a nonlinear function whereby wages rise faster in times of excess liquidity on the grounds that inflation is expected to increase.

Models of this nature may be extended to the specification of interdependent commodity or asset markets. Let $A(t)$ be a vector of holdings of securities $A_i(t)$, $i = 1, ..., m$, where $A_i(t)$ may be an asset or a liability, and let $r(t)$ be the corresponding vector of interest rates. A second-order adjustment model for asset holdings may be written as

$$D^2 A_i(t) = f_i\{\hat{A}(t) - A(t), DA(t), Dr_i(t)\} \quad \text{for } i = 1, ..., m, \quad (3.13)$$

where $\hat{A}$ is the desired holdings of those securities derived through the optimization of some utility function and f_i is the function defining the adjustment process. Desired holdings of each asset $\hat{A}_i(t)$ will be a function of all interest rates and wealth and subject to all of the homogeneity, symmetry, curvature, and separability conditions inherent in the utility function. Although the process is defined here as a second-order system it may, of course, be of any order. All assets are defined at market value. The term $D_i r(t)$ is included as an argument in f_i to allow for changes in the valuation of an asset $A_i(t)$ following a change in $r_i(t)$; the need for this depends on the nature of the asset. Although f_i is a function of the excess demand for all securities, it is likely that the costs of adjustment and uncertainty will make the effect of some excess demands small relative to others.

At a more general level, therefore, it is necessary to take into account such differences in the nature of the assets as their liquidity and institutional structure. For each sector, desired holdings $\hat{A}_i(t)$ can be considered as being determined subject to some wealth constraint; because holdings need not equal demand yet are subject to the same constraint, each sector may have at least one security that acts as a residual or buffer to satisfy the constraint. Almost by necessity, this security must be very liquid. Holdings of this security act as a shock absorber in that an unexpected change in some asset, which is expected to be short-lived, need not affect the rest of the portfolio. Let this security be $A_1(t)$. The adjustment of these assets may be represented by

$$D^2 A_i(t) = f_i\{\hat{A}_i(t) - A_i(t), \hat{A}_1(t) - A_1(t), DA_i(t), Dr_i(t)\}$$

$$\text{for } i = 2, \ldots, m, \quad (3.14a)$$

and $A_1(t)$ is given by

$$DA_1(t) = DW(t) - \sum_{i=2}^{m} DA_i(t). \quad (3.14b)$$

The additional term $Dr_i(t)$ in (3.14a) is required to allow for changes in the market value of asset $A_i(t)$ following an interest-rate change but where the nominal volume of that asset is unchanged. Thus the system is consistent in that actual holdings satisfy the identity (3.14b) at all times and in equilibrium will equal desired holdings $\hat{A}_i(t)$.

In financial markets at the aggregated level it is likely that some institutions will be able to set interest rates, at least in the short run, yet have little or no control over their holdings of the corresponding asset or liability; an example is bank deposits. Thus, if some institution can set rates $r_i(t)$ on their holdings of an asset or liability $A_i(t)$ but have little or no direct control over these holdings (at least in the short run), then an interest-rate adjustment function may be written as

$$D^2 r_i(t) = h_i\{\hat{A}_i(t) - A_i(t), Dr_i(t)\}, \quad (3.15)$$

where $\hat{A}_i(t)$ is their desired holdings and the volume $A_i(t)$, or expectations of $A_i(t)$, is taken as given.

An exchange and interest model of this nature was presented in Richard (1980) and a related model in Armington and Wolford (1984). The latter, which was used by Wharton Econometric Forecasting Associates for predicting exchange rates, had a forecasting ability superior to any of the nine other models being used at that time in the United States, as shown in Levich (1983). A disequilibrium first-order money demand model for major currencies similar to (3.13) was given in Donaghy and Richard (1992). The money demand functions in these models are rigorously derived from utility maximization and are estimated subject to all of the homogeneity, symmetry, curvature, and regularity conditions inherent in that theory. The latter model is also estimated in both linear and nonlinear form.

These ideas can be extended to a financial sector consisting of several interrelated markets, as in Wymer (1973) in a model of the U.K. banking sector.[6] The structure of financial markets is such that, in effect, one institution absorbs the residual for a particular asset, or is the "market maker" in that asset in the sense that it will supply the financial instrument to other economic agents on demand, but not necessarily at a given price. In fact, these institutions will play this role only if they have a strong influence over the cost or yield of that asset.

Let $A_{ij}(t)$ be the holdings of security i, which may be an asset or a liability, by financial institution j. Assume institution 1 is the market maker in security k and that security l is the most liquid asset (or at least the security that acts as a residual) within the portfolio of this institution; generally this asset will be money balances or something similar. A set of equations defining the actions of this institution may then be written as

$$D^2 A_{i1}(t) = f_{i1}\{\hat{A}_{i1}(t) - A_{i1}(t), \hat{A}_{l1}(t) - A_{l1}(t), DA_{i1}(t), Dr_i(t)\}$$
$$\text{for } i = 1, \ldots, m, \ i \neq k, \ i \neq l, \quad (3.16)$$

with holdings of security k being determined by the actions of other economic agents,

$$A_{k1}(t) = \sum_{j=2}^{m} A_{kj}(t) \quad (3.17)$$

and holdings of the buffer or liquid asset given by

$$DA_{l1}(t) = DW_1(t) - \sum_{\substack{i=1 \\ i \neq l}}^{m} DA_{i1}(t). \quad (3.18)$$

---

[6] In Wymer (1973) the desired asset and liability functions are assumed to be simple linear functions of interest rates and scale variables. At the time that model was developed and estimated (1967/68), nonlinear constraints could not be imposed on the parameters. The first FIML estimator that allowed general nonlinear within- and across-equation restrictions was developed by the author in 1968. Thus the 1973 paper is of interest only for the structure of the model of the financial sector, not for the specification of the desired functions $\hat{A}(t)$; for a thorough derivation of the latter, see Richard (1989) and Donaghy and Richard (1992).

The interest rate on security k is assumed to be determined, at least to a large extent, by this institution, so that

$$D^2 r_k(t) = h_k\{\hat{A}_{k1}(t) - A_{k1}(t), \hat{A}_{l1}(t) - A_{l1}(t), D r_k(t)\}. \tag{3.19}$$

The holdings of other institutions are determined in a similar way, but some interest rates may be determined by the excess holdings of several or all institutions. In the system as a whole, one of the wealth or market identities will be redundant. Thus the market and portfolio constraints are always satisfied and the model is consistent in that, subject to adjustment costs and uncertainty, institutions will hold their desired assets.

The continuous time models are designed to provide estimates of the "deep" parameters of the economic system, that is, parameters which are independent of all other parameters in the system. If that is the case, it is then appropriate to consider the effect on the system of changes in parameters, particularly policy parameters. The correct specification of deep parameters is essential if econometric work is to be able to answer questions about the effects of such policy changes. This requires a structural approach. The coefficients of VARMAX processes (as defined in Section 5) are shallow, so by their very nature those models cannot be used for analyzing problems that involve a change in parameters.

In specifying and estimating a model, it may be found that parameters initially assumed to be fixed will in fact vary over the sample period and so need to be replaced by some functional relationship. This may arise with adjustment parameters, for instance, since they are usually considered as an approximation to some function involving costs and uncertainty. It may also arise with institutional changes or with the introduction of new markets. The model of the Australian economy of Jonson et al. (1976) provides an example of one approach to this question, but another approach is being investigated; both involve the demand for money balances.

In the Australian model it was found that the scaling factor in the demand for real money balances γ in the function $\hat{m}(t) = \gamma e^{-\beta r(t)} Y(t)$ was not constant but increased over time. This was caused by a change in banking regulations and the structure of the financial sector over the sample period, with more substitutes becoming available. Thus γ could not be considered as a deep parameter, but it could be replaced by a function whose parameters could be considered deep. A continuing change in that function would be inconsistent with a steady state, but in the analysis of that model, and particularly steady-state analysis, the function could be assumed fixed by an appropriate choice of those parameter values.

An alternative is to obtain a more appropriate measure of money balances. In many models, the appropriate definition of money balances is some broad measure of monetary or liquid assets rather than money narrowly defined. Various monetary and other highly liquid assets form a continuum, but as the characteristics of these assets vary it is inappropriate to define money balances as a simple sum. Although money balances could be defined as a weighted average (not necessarily with fixed weights) with these relationships being estimated within the model, doing so would require the specification of a financial sector. An alternative approach is based on research conducted by Donaghy and Richard (1992) and by Richard (1993), who is developing a model of multinational money demands along the lines of Barnett (1990) and Barnett, Fisher, and Serletis (1992). Their aim is to produce an economic index of money balances that can then be compared with a continuous Divisia index to see whether the Divisia index provides a suitable approximation to the economic index. If so, then the integral of the Divisia index could be used to provide a monetary aggregate for a group of countries, such as the EEC. The same principle could be applied to domestic money balances or liquid assets. In that case, the integral of the Divisia index could be used in a macroeconomic model instead of money balances as usually defined. The domain of regularity of the functions being used, which are highly nonlinear, could provide the basis for a robust index that would need to be redefined only infrequently.

4   Estimation

It is assumed that the economic system is a causal structure that can be represented by a recursive set of nonlinear, stochastic differential equations of up to order r. To simplify the description, it will be assumed arbitrarily that $r = 3$; the extension to a general mixed-order system is obvious. This model may be written as

$$dD^{r-k}y_k(t) = \phi_k\{D^2y_1(t), Dy_2(t), y_3(t),$$
$$Dy_1(t), y_2(t), y_1(t), D^2z(t), Dz(t), z(t); \theta\} dt$$
$$+ \zeta_k(dt) \quad \text{for } k = 1, ..., r \text{ with } r = 3, \quad (4.1)$$

where the $y_k(t)$ – in this case $y_1(t)$, $y_2(t)$, and $y_3(t)$ – are vectors of m_k endogenous variables and $z(t)$ is a vector of n exogenous variables. Not all levels and derivatives of the exogenous variables need appear in the model. The system is assumed to be such that the differential of the $(r-k)$th derivative of $y_k(t)$ is determined by a function ϕ_k of the $(r-s-i)$th derivatives of the endogenous variables $D^{r-s-i}y_s(t)$ and exogenous variables $D^{r-s}z(t)$ $(i = 0, ..., r-s, s = 1, ..., r)$, where D is the differential operator d/dt defined in the mean-square sense. The variables may be stocks or flows; the distinction is important for estimation. The term θ is a vector of parameters and the $\zeta_k(t)$ are vectors of white-noise innovations. Let $\zeta(t) = [\zeta_1(t) \ \zeta_2(t) \ \zeta_3(t)]'$. Thus it is assumed that

$$E[\zeta(dt)] = 0, \quad E[\zeta(dt)\zeta'(dt)] = |dt|\Omega,$$

and $E[\zeta_i(\Delta_1)\zeta_j'(\Delta_2)] = 0$ for any disjoint sets Δ_1 and Δ_2, where $\zeta(t)$ has $m = m_1 + m_2 + m_3$ elements and Ω is of order m. A rigorous definition of these disturbances and their properties is given in Bergstrom (1983). Some of the equations may be identities, such as the definition of the rate of change of stocks as the difference between production and consumption, in which case the corresponding $\zeta(dt)$ will be identically zero.

In particular, Bergstrom has shown that Gaussian estimators may be obtained under the assumption that the integral of the white-noise innovation process is a Gaussian process, although the innovations themselves are not assumed to have that property. Hence the innovations may be a mixture of Brownian motion and Poisson processes, thus providing a plausible representation of economic behavior in that the innovations may come as discrete jumps at random intervals.

If

$$y^*(t) = [D^2y_1(t) \ Dy_2(t) \ y_3(t) \ Dy_1(t) \ y_2(t) \ y_1(t)]' \quad \text{and}$$

$$z^*(t) = [D^2z(t) \ Dz(t) \ z(t)]',$$

then the mixed-order system (4.1) may be written in the compact first-order form

$$dy^*(t) = \Phi\{y^*(t), z^*(t), \theta\} \, dt + \zeta^*(dt), \tag{4.2}$$

where Φ is a vector of functions such that the first three sets of equations are defined as in (4.1) and the remaining equations are the identities defining the higher-order derivatives

$$dy_4^*(t) = y_1^*(t) \, dt, \quad dy_5^*(t) = y_2^*(t) \, dt, \quad \text{and} \quad dy_6^*(t) = y_4^*(t) \, dt.$$

Therefore, when $r = 3$, $y^*(t)$ contains $m^* = 3m_1 + 2m_2 + m_3$ elements and $z^*(t)$ has $n^* = 3n$ elements; again, not all exogenous variables and their derivatives need appear in the model. The stochastic elements of the vector $\zeta^*(s) = [\zeta_1(s) \ \zeta_2(s) \ \zeta_3(s) \ 0 \ 0 \ 0]'$ have the properties just defined but the corresponding matrix Ω^*, of order m^*, is given by

$$\Omega^* = \begin{bmatrix} \Omega & 0 & \cdots & 0 \\ 0 & 0 & \cdots & 0 \\ & & \cdots & \\ 0 & 0 & \cdots & 0 \end{bmatrix}.$$

Whereas much of the development in the estimation of continuous time models has been made under the assumption that the differential equation system is linear, in empirical work the underlying economic models have usually been nonlinear. It is now possible to obtain estimates of the parameters of the nonlinear model directly by using either an approximate discrete or exact estimator. However, the costs are high and the properties of the exact estimator are not well known and must be inferred heuristically.[7] Because the estimators of linear models are well developed and their asymptotic properties are well known, approximation of the nonlinear model by a Taylor series expansion about some appropriate point (such as the sample mean) or some path (such as the steady state) gives a linearized model that can then be estimated subject to all of the restrictions inherent in the nonlinear model and in the linearization. This provides estimates of the parameters θ of the nonlinear model; these estimates may be used with either the linearized or nonlinear model for hypothesis testing, analysis, and forecasting. However, the approximation error inherent in the linearization means that even if the white-noise innovations or their integrals are Gaussian, this may not be true of the disturbances in the linearized model. These issues are discussed in Wymer (1992, part II).

The general linear rth mixed-order model is defined in Wymer (1975). As an example, consider the linear model corresponding to the mixed third-order model (4.1):

$$dD^{3-k}y_k(t) = [A_{k1}(\theta)D^2y_1(t)+A_{k2}(\theta)Dy_2(t)+A_{k3}(\theta)y_3(t)$$
$$+A_{k4}(\theta)Dy_1(t)+A_{k5}(\theta)y_2(t)+A_{k6}(\theta)y_1(t)]\,dt$$
$$+[B_{k1}(\theta)D^2z(t)+B_{k2}(\theta)Dz(t)+B_{k3}(\theta)z(t)]\,dt$$
$$+\zeta_k(dt), \tag{4.3}$$

where the variables and disturbances are defined as in (4.1). Defining additional variables, this system may be written as the linear first-order model corresponding to (4.2),

$$dy^*(t) = A^*(\theta)y^*(t)\,dt + B^*(\theta)z^*(t)\,dt + \zeta^*(dt), \tag{4.4}$$

where $y^*(t)$, $z^*(t)$, $\zeta^*(t)$, and Ω^* are defined as in (4.2),

$$A^*(\theta) = \begin{bmatrix} A_{11} & A_{12} & A_{13} & A_{14} & A_{15} & A_{16} \\ A_{21} & A_{22} & A_{23} & A_{24} & A_{25} & A_{26} \\ A_{31} & A_{32} & A_{33} & A_{34} & A_{35} & A_{36} \\ I_{m_1} & 0 & 0 & 0 & 0 & 0 \\ 0 & I_{m_2} & 0 & 0 & 0 & 0 \\ 0 & 0 & 0 & I_{m_1} & 0 & 0 \end{bmatrix}, \text{ and } B^*(\theta) = \begin{bmatrix} B_{11} & B_{12} & B_{13} \\ B_{21} & B_{22} & B_{23} \\ B_{31} & B_{32} & B_{33} \\ 0 & 0 & 0 \\ 0 & 0 & 0 \\ 0 & 0 & 0 \end{bmatrix}.$$

---

[7] Although an approximate discrete estimator of the parameters θ of the nonlinear model (4.1) has been available for some time (see Wymer 1979 and Bailey et al. 1979), an exact estimator has only recently been developed (see Wymer 1990). Both estimators are reviewed in Wymer (1992, part II).

The general rth mixed-order model has a similar form except that the order of the identity matrices in A^* varies according to the number of variables of order k, $k = 1, \ldots, r$.

The solution to (4.4) is

$$y^*(t) = e^{\delta A(\theta)} y^*(t - \delta)$$

$$+ \int_{t-\delta}^{t} e^{(t-s)A(\theta)} B^*(\theta) z^*(s)\, ds + \int_{t-\delta}^{t} e^{(t-s)A(\theta)} \zeta^*(ds). \tag{4.5}$$

If the underlying model (4.3) is a first-order instantaneous system then (4.5) can be used to give the exact discrete estimator directly. In higher-order models, $y^*(t)$ contains derivatives of the unobservable endogenous variables $D^k y(t)$, so these variables must be eliminated by successive substitution to give an exact discrete model in terms of observable variables only.

As an illustration, consider a second-order differential equation system in variables (such as stocks and prices) that can be measured instantaneously at a point in time:

$$dDy(t) = A_1(\theta) Dy(t)\, dt + A_2(\theta) y(t)\, dt$$

$$+ B_1(\theta) Dz(t)\, dt + B_2(\theta) z(t)\, dt + \zeta(dt), \tag{4.6}$$

where $y(t)$ is a vector of m endogenous variables, $z(t)$ a vector of n exogenous variables, θ a vector of p parameters, and $\zeta(dt)$ a vector of disturbances defined as in (4.1). Let $E[\zeta(dt)\zeta'(dt)] = |dt|\Omega(\mu)$, where μ is the set of parameters that define Ω. This parameter set would have $m(m+1)/2$ elements if Ω were unrestricted, but would have only m elements if Ω were diagonal. If some equations in (4.6) are identities then the corresponding rows and columns of Ω would be zero and the number of elements in μ reduced accordingly.

The solution to (4.6) may be written as

$$y(t) = F_1(\theta, \delta) y(t - \delta) + F_2(\theta, \delta) y(t - 2\delta) + \Psi(t) + \omega(t), \tag{4.7}$$

where

$$\Psi(t) = \int_{t-\delta}^{t} P_1(t - s)[B_1 Dz(s) + B_2 z(s)]\, ds$$

$$+ \int_{t-2\delta}^{t-\delta} P_2(t - \delta - s)[B_1 Dz(s) + B_2 z(s)]\, ds$$

and

$$\omega(t) = \int_{t-\delta}^{t} P_1(t - s)\zeta(ds) + \int_{t-2\delta}^{t-\delta} P_2(t - \delta - s)\zeta(ds);$$

the F_i and P_i are functions of the elements of the matrix $e^{A(\theta)}$, where

$$A(\theta) = \begin{bmatrix} A_1(\theta) & A_2(\theta) \\ I & 0 \end{bmatrix}.$$

Specifically, as shown in Bergstrom (1983),

$$F_1 = [e^{\delta A}]_{21}[e^{\delta A}]_{11}[e^{\delta A}]_{21}^{-1} - [e^{\delta A}]_{22},$$

$$F_2 = [e^{\delta A}]_{21}[e^{\delta A}]_{12} - [e^{\delta A}]_{21}[e^{\delta A}]_{11}[e^{\delta A}]_{21}^{-1}[e^{\delta A}]_{22},$$

$$P_1(s) = [e^{sA}]_{21}, \quad \text{and}$$

$$P_2(s) = [e^{\delta A}]_{21}[e^{sA}]_{11} - [e^{\delta A}]_{21}[e^{\delta A}]_{11}[e^{\delta A}]_{21}^{-1}[e^{sA}]_{21},$$

where the $[e^{sA}]_{ij}$ are the i, j partitions of order m of the matrix $e^{sA(\theta)}$,

$$E[\omega(t)\omega'(t)] = \delta \int_0^\delta P_1(s)\Omega P_1'(s)\, ds + \delta \int_0^\delta P_2(s)\Omega P_2'(s)\, ds,$$

$$E[\omega(t)\omega'(t-\delta)] = \delta \int_0^\delta P_2(s)\Omega P_1'(s)\, ds,$$

and $E[\omega(t)\omega'(t-k\delta)] = 0$ for all $|k| > 1$.

Assume that the continuous variables are observed every δ time units (so that δ is the length of the observation interval in terms of the basic time units of the system), and let x_τ be the discrete observation of the continuous variable $x(t)$ at time $\tau\delta$, so that $x_\tau = x(\tau\delta)$. Thus, the exact discrete model stochastically equivalent to the continuous model (4.6) is obtained immediately from (4.7). Without any loss of generality, the time unit of the continuous model may be chosen such that the observation interval $\delta = 1$; in this case the exact discrete model becomes

$$y_t = F_1(\theta)y_{t-1} + F_2(\theta)y_{t-2} + \Psi_t + \omega_t \quad \text{for integer } t, \tag{4.8}$$

where Ψ_t and ω_t are defined as in (4.7) but with $\delta = 1$. Because the observations generated by the continuous model (4.6) will satisfy the exact discrete model irrespective of the observation interval, the properties of the estimates of the parameters of the differential system may be obtained from the sampling properties of the discrete model.

If the exogenous variables $z(t)$ in (4.8) are approximated by a quadratic in t, an approximation that is exact if $z(t)$ is a polynomial in t of order 2 or less, then the integral Ψ_t may be approximated by a linear function of z_t, z_{t-1}, and z_{t-2} with coefficients that are explicit functions of θ. Thus, as shown by Bergstrom (1983), given that the conditions on ω_t imply the existence of a set of random vectors ϵ_t such that ω_t can be written as the moving-average process

$$\omega_t = \epsilon_t + G\epsilon_{t-1}$$

(where G is a matrix of order m), the exact discrete model may be represented by the open autoregressive moving average (VARMAX) process

$$y_t = F_1(\theta)y_{t-1} + F_2(\theta)y_{t-2}$$
$$+ E_1(\theta)z_t + E_2(\theta)z_{t-1} + E_3(\theta)z_{t-2} + \epsilon_t + G(\theta, \mu)\epsilon_{t-1}, \qquad (4.9)$$

where $E(\epsilon_t) = 0$, $E(\epsilon_t \epsilon_t') = \Xi(\theta, \mu)$, and $E(\epsilon_s \epsilon_t') = 0$ for all t and s, $s \neq t$. (Here Ξ denotes the error covariance matrix.)

The restrictions inherent in the VARMAX process that is equivalent to a mixed stock–flow model are even more complex. As flows cannot be measured at a point in time but are observed only as the integral over an observation period, the continuous model must be integrated over the observation period to produce a continuous model in observable variables.[8] Briefly, consider the second-order system (4.6) but assume that

$$y(t) = \begin{bmatrix} y^s(t) \\ y^f(t) \end{bmatrix} \quad \text{and} \quad z(t) = \begin{bmatrix} z^s(t) \\ z^f(t) \end{bmatrix},$$

where $y^s(t)$ is a vector of m^s endogenous instantaneous variables, such as stocks and prices, that can be observed at a point in time, $y^f(t)$ is a vector of m^f flow variables observable only as an integral over the observation period, and $z^s(t)$ and $z^f(t)$ are corresponding vectors of n^s and n^f exogenous variables. The model (4.6) may now be written in terms of the observable variables as

$$y^o(t) = \begin{bmatrix} y^s(t) - y^s(t-1) \\ \int_{t-1}^{t} y^f(s)\,ds \end{bmatrix}, \quad z^o(t) = \begin{bmatrix} \frac{1}{2}\{z^s(t) + z^s(t-1)\} \\ \int_{t-1}^{t} z^f(s)\,ds \end{bmatrix}.$$

As shown in Bergstrom (1986), the exact discrete mixed stock–flow model has the VARMAX representation

$$y_t^o = \Gamma_1(\theta)y_{t-1}^o + \Gamma_2(\theta)y_{t-2}^o + E_1(\theta)z_t^o + E_2(\theta)z_{t-1}^o + E_2(\theta)z_{t-2}^o$$
$$+ \epsilon_t + G_1(\theta, \mu)\epsilon_{t-1} + G_2(\theta, \mu)\epsilon_{t-2}, \qquad (4.10)$$

where $E(\epsilon_t) = 0$, $E(\epsilon_t \epsilon_t') = \Xi(\theta, \mu)$, and $E(\epsilon_s \epsilon_t') = 0$, $s \neq t$.

Again, the matrices F_i, E_i, and G_i are functions of the elements of the matrix $e^{A(\theta)}$ and hence of the parameters θ, but these relationships are much more complex than in the instantaneously observable case (4.7). Unlike a second-order stock model, which is stochastically equivalent to a discrete model with a first-order moving-average error process, the exact discrete model corresponding to a second-order mixed stock–flow model has second-order moving-average errors. This also applies to the special case where all variables are flows. In general, an rth-order flow or stock–flow model has an rth-order autoregressive, rth-order moving-average error representation, but the moving-average error process of a model where all variables can be observed instantaneously is of order $r-1$. Note

---

[8] The treatment of variables that are observed only as averages over time, such as implicit price deflators, is analogous to that of flows.

that the order of the moving-average error process in an exact discrete
model equivalent to a mixed-order differential equation system is defined
by the highest-order differential equation.

For estimation purposes, the sample is assumed to contain observa-
tions $y^o(t)$ and $z^o(t)$ for $t = 1, \ldots, T$ and of the initial stock vector $y^s(0)$,
but the other initial state vectors $y^f(0)$ and $Dy(0)$ are unobservable and
must be estimated as part of the parameter set. The estimators of the exact models are developed in detail in Bergstrom (1983, 1985, 1986). Note
that if the disturbances $\zeta(dt)$ are nonstationary then some elements in the
initial state vector must also be estimated, and this leads to a VARMAX
representation where the moving-average error process no longer has fixed
coefficients. It appears, however, that the sequence of these matrices converges rapidly to a limit matrix, so that relatively few matrices need to
be evaluated.

The continuous linear model (4.6) may be approximated by a much simpler discrete model, as shown in Wymer (1972). Again, the discrete approximation to an rth-order flow or stock–flow model will have an rth-order
autoregressive, rth-order moving-average error representation, whereas
the moving-average error process of a model where all variables can be
observed instantaneously is of order $r - 1$. The approximate discrete model where all variables are instantaneously observable has a similar form
to (4.9), but for a mixed stock–flow model the variables in the system
must be integrated over the observation interval to obtain observable variables, and the integral of stock variables $y^s(t)$ must be approximated by
$\frac{1}{2}\{y(t)+y(t-1)\}$. Defining

$$y^a(t) = \begin{bmatrix} \frac{1}{2}\{y^s(t)+y^s(t-1)\} \\ \int_{t-1}^{t} y^f(s)\,ds \end{bmatrix} \quad \text{and} \quad z^a(t) = \begin{bmatrix} \frac{1}{2}\{z^s(t)+z^s(t-1)\} \\ \int_{t-1}^{t} z^f(s)\,ds \end{bmatrix}$$

allows the stock–flow model to be represented as

$$y_t^a = F_1(\theta)y_{t-1}^a + F_2(\theta)y_{t-2}^a + E_1(\theta)z_t^a + E_2(\theta)z_{t-1}^a + E_2(\theta)z_{t-2}^a$$
$$+ \epsilon_t + G_1(\theta, \mu)\epsilon_{t-1} + G_2(\theta, \mu)\epsilon_{t-2}, \tag{4.11}$$

where $E(\epsilon_t) = 0$, $E(\epsilon_t \epsilon_t') = \Xi(\theta, \mu)$, and $E(\epsilon_s \epsilon_t') = 0$, $s \neq t$. Equation (4.11)
is similar in form to (4.10), but the matrices of the approximate discrete
model corresponding to the F_i and E_i of the exact model in (4.9) or (4.10)
are much simpler functions of the parameters θ. Nevertheless, these matrices are still highly nonlinear in the parameters, involving, for example,
elements of $(I - \frac{1}{2}A_1 - \frac{1}{4}A_2)^{-1}$. Specifically,

$$F_1(\theta) = (I - \tfrac{1}{2}A_1 - \tfrac{1}{4}A_2)^{-1}(2 + \tfrac{1}{2}A_2) \quad \text{and}$$

$$F_2(\theta) = (I - \tfrac{1}{2}A_1 - \tfrac{1}{4}A_2)^{-1}(-I - \tfrac{1}{2}A_1 + \tfrac{1}{4}A_2).$$

The moving-average coefficient matrices may be approximated to give an error process that is independent of the parameters of the system, as shown in Wymer (1972). Inverting this process allows the serial correlation inherent in the discrete observable data y_t^a and z_t^a to be removed by a truncated infinite moving-average transformation, thus simplifying the estimation of (4.11).

Exact and approximate discrete estimators of the linear model (4.3) and their asymptotic properties are reviewed in Bergstrom (1990) and Wymer (1992, part II), both of which contain extensive references. Much of the empirical work on continuous time models has used samples of 50 to 300 observations, and for that sample size the estimates provided by the various estimators have been consistent with asymptotic theory. Although the approximate discrete estimators are biased, the bias is of $O(\delta^3)$ so that it decreases rapidly as the observation interval δ decreases; Monte Carlo studies suggest that the bias will be small, and in empirical work the approximate estimator yields parameter estimates that are generally (but not always) close to those of the exact estimator. If all the eigenvalues of the system have negative real parts, then the exact Gaussian estimator of the parameters will converge to the true values at a rate of $O(T^{-1/2})$ as $T \to \infty$. However, Phillips (1991) has shown that if some of the eigenvalues of the system are zero, so that the variables are integrated, then the Gaussian estimator of the exact model is "superefficient" in that the estimator of parameters and their asymptotic standard errors converges at a rate of $O(T^{-1})$ as $T \to \infty$. The theoretical advantage of the exact estimators is reflected in empirical work, where estimates of the asymptotic standard errors of the exact estimators are much smaller than those of the approximate estimator.

Since these models are all estimated using full-information maximum likelihood or Gaussian estimators, the estimates may be used for testing both the overall structure of the continuous model and specific hypotheses, as discussed in Bergstrom (1990). The stochastic equivalence between differential equation systems and a VARMAX process makes a general VARMAX model a useful basis for such a test. Let the unrestricted second-order discrete VARMAX process corresponding to (4.9), (4.10), or (4.11) be

$$y_t = \bar{F}_1(\theta)y_{t-1} + \bar{F}_2(\theta)y_{t-2} + \bar{E}_1(\theta)z_t + \bar{E}_2(\theta)z_{t-1} + \bar{E}_3(\theta)z_{t-2} + \epsilon_t + \bar{G}_1\epsilon_{t-1} + \bar{G}_2\epsilon_{t-2}. \tag{4.12}$$

Although it would be useful to test this VARMAX process against a higher-order one, as Bergstrom (1990) noted, that is likely to be precluded by the size of samples usually available. Still such a test may be feasible in studies of some markets (especially financial ones) where high-frequency data are available, sometimes for a number of years. Such a test would indicate whether the order of the continuous model was consistent with the data. The difficulty which arises is that studies of both financial and commodity markets have shown the importance of stocks – or, more specifically, the excess demand for stocks – in price determination, and stock data are usually observed at a much lower frequency than prices. If such a test is not feasible, however, there are other indicators of whether the order of a particular equation is appropriate. If an equation represents a partial adjustment process then an extremely rapid rate of adjustment, shown by a high adjustment parameter, may indicate that the order of the partial adjustment process is too high; conversely, a very low rate of adjustment may indicate that the actual adjustment process is of higher order. These alternative hypotheses can be tested, but (as noted previously) if testing changes the order r of the continuous system then the order of the whole discrete model will change accordingly. This provides a powerful test of the structure of the continuous model.

Under the assumption that the order of the continuous model, and the corresponding VARMAX process, is correct, the exact or approximate discrete model can be tested against an unrestricted VARMAX process of the same order. This test is described in Bergstrom (1990), and variants of it, often with a partially restricted VARMAX process where the $\bar{F}_i$ and $\bar{E}_i$ are unrestricted but with the $\bar{G}_i$ restricted in some general way, have been used in many of the continuous time studies over the past 25 years.

5   Comparison with ordinary discrete models

Although a linear continuous time model can be written as a VARMAX process, thus providing the link between the estimation of continuous time models, ordinary dynamic discrete models, and time-series analysis, it is here that the distinction between the continuous time approach to econometrics differs from other approaches. In particular, the approach described here, and the research on continuous time estimators, has implications for four areas of econometric research:

(1) the argument that it is possible to derive a model of the economy from a general VARMAX process by deriving a sequence of successively more parsimonious models;

(2) the specification of error correction mechanisms (ECMs) in ordinary discrete models;

(3) the use of "structural" VAR processes; and

(4) the use of a discrete model in investigating aperiodic or dynamic behavior.

5.1   *VARMAX processes*

The exact and approximate models (4.9), (4.10), and (4.11), corresponding to the second-order differential equation system (4.6), may be compared to an unrestricted second-order discrete VARMAX process (4.12).

First, even if the vectors θ and μ are distinct in the continuous model, this is not true of the coefficients of the vector moving-average error process in the stochastically equivalent discrete model. Moreover, even if Ω were a diagonal matrix (so that μ contained only m elements), the error covariance matrix Ξ would still be a full matrix. Thus, simultaneous equation estimators will generally be necessary to estimate the discrete model.

Second, the matrices F_i, E_i, and G or G_i will be functions of the elements of the matrix $e^{A(\theta)}$ in the exact model or of $(I - \frac{1}{2}A_1 - \frac{1}{4}A_2)^{-1}$ in the approximate model. Even if the continuous system (4.6) were linear in parameters and no parameter occurred in more than one equation, the discrete models, whether exact or approximate, would still involve highly nonlinear and cross-equation restrictions, thus requiring the use of full-information techniques. In fact, the coefficients of the differential equation systems being estimated are generally heavily restricted and highly nonlinear functions of the set of parameters θ, with restrictions applying both within and across equations.

In contrast, the elements of $\bar{F}_i$ and $\bar{E}_i$ in an ordinary discrete model are often unrestricted, or the restrictions are of a simple (and often within-equation) nature. An indication of the scale of this difference can be seen from the 24-equation model of the U.K. economy of Knight and Wymer (1978). This model is an economywide nonlinear mixed-order system and so is a special case of (4.1). The model contains five exogenous variables and a constant term. The estimator used in this case is an approximation to (4.11) and transforms the variables in order to eliminate the moving-average process inherent in the data, at least to an approximation. The parameter vector θ has 64 elements and the parameter vector μ defining the matrix Ω has 210 elements; $\Omega(\mu)$ was assumed to be a full matrix apart from the elements corresponding to four equations that were identities. However, since the identities were linearized, the discrete error covariance matrix Ξ is assumed to be unrestricted and thus has 300 elements to be estimated. The unrestricted VARMAX model (4.12) has 1,512 elements in the matrices $\bar{F}_i$ and $\bar{E}_i$ while the error covariance matrix again has 300 elements to be estimated. Differences of a similar scale apply to a number of other economywide models, models of financial and commodity markets, and dynamic demand systems.

If the economic system is, in fact, continuous, then a continuous model will provide not only a consistent but a far more efficient estimator of the parameters of the system, relative to an unrestricted VARMAX process. This allows more powerful tests of the theory inherent in the model. As Bergstrom (1986) has shown, if some variables in the economy are flows and can thus be observed only as integrals over time, then the continuous model cannot be represented by a stochastically equivalent VARMAX process because the coefficients of the error process vary over time. Moreover, as noted in Bergstrom (1990), the exact estimators provide asymptotically unbiased and efficient estimates of the parameters and predictors of postsample data, so that a large gain can be expected in the efficiency of the exact continuous estimates compared with unrestricted VARMAX estimates. The use of a parsimonious VARMAX model as an approximation for prediction purposes would lead to a biased predictor.

Unlike an ordinary discrete model, where a change in the order of an autoregressive process in one equation usually has no effect on other equations, in a continuous model the whole VARMAX process can change when the order of one equation changes. This could arise by changing some lag structure or an expectation. Thus, as mentioned previously, the use of a continuous model provides a powerful test of the structure that is not available in ordinary discrete models.

A comparison of the exact models (4.9) or (4.10), or even the approximate model (4.11), and the unrestricted VARMAX process (4.12) throws serious doubt on the validity and feasibility of the "general-to-specific" methodology which has developed in econometrics during the past 15 years and which postulates that the starting point of econometric analysis should be the unrestricted process (4.12). Such a comparison makes it clear that there is no possibility of deriving the parameters and restrictions inherent in the continuous model (4.6) from the coefficients of (4.12) even in very simple systems, let alone in a model of several equations. If the economy is continuous, or if it can be considered to act approximately as if it were continuous, and if the aim is to study the behavior of the economic system, then it is necessary to proceed from a specific structural model.

Although an unrestricted VARMAX process can be defined and used for testing the overall specification of a linear differential equation system, there is no equivalent general nonlinear VARMAX process and so testing of the overall specification of nonlinear differential equations becomes more difficult. The unrestricted linear VARMAX process could be used to provide a weak test. A general form, with variable coefficients, is

$$y_t = \sum_{i=1}^{k} \bar{F}_i(x_{t-1})y_{t-i} + \sum_{j=1}^{l} \bar{G}_j(x_{t-1})\epsilon_{t-j} + \epsilon_t, \qquad (5.1)$$

where x_t is the set of variables $\{y_t, ..., y_{t-p-1} \ 1 \ \epsilon_t, ..., \epsilon_{t-q-1}\}$ and ϵ_t is a white-noise innovation process. Such a form is suggested by Granger and

Newbold (1986), but in order to make estimation of such a system feasible it would be necessary to restrict the way in which the parameters in the functions of $\tilde{F}_i$ and $\tilde{G}_j$ evolve. A simple form would assume that $\tilde{F}_i$ and $\tilde{G}_j$ are linear in the elements of x_{t-1}, but Priestley (1980) suggested a relationship whereby the parameters become random walks, thus allowing a Kalman filter approach. Such a model could be used to provide a test for the structural model (4.1); there remains, of course, the question of the choice of k, l, p, and q.

The question of whether economic variables are integrated series of some particular order is indicated by the nature of the variable, although a given sample (particularly if short) may lead to another result under test. Interest rates, for example, can be expected to be $I(0)$, except in periods of hyperinflation as in Germany in the 1920s, while output and investment can be expected to be $I(1)$ and the capital stock and other assets approximately $I(2)$. Of course, the degree of integration need not be an integral if the economic system involves some fractional differential process, as in Chambers (1992). These relationships are inherent in a wide range of economic theory and are especially important in the specification of nonlinear models. An indication of whether any assumptions about these series are consistent can be seen from a study of the long-run or steady-state properties of a model.

The importance of the work on co-integration for the continuous time approach is first to determine whether or not the residuals in the model are serially correlated and, if so, to determine what is causing that serial correlation. Again, the aim is to look at this from the point of view of economic theory, to find whether there is a deficiency or mis-specification in the model and to modify it accordingly, rather than to consider it as a statistical problem to be eliminated by using a more sophisticated estimator. The effects on estimation or testing of a model that contains integrated series are largely eliminated if the model is heavily overidentified, like the models considered in this paper. For example, if the interest rate is determined by the excess demand for real money balances, the restriction that the coefficients of nominal money balances and prices be equal will eliminate the problems that arise from these variables being integrated. Restrictions of this nature, which may apply both within and across equations, are derived from the economic theory underlying the model and can be tested either individually or jointly.

For example, it is now common in ordinary discrete models for the variables in an equation to be specified on the basis of equilibrium theory, and to test for nonstationarity: if the sample series is difference-stationary (in that it contains a unit root) then it should be first-differenced; if it is trend-stationary then it should be de-trended. If the sample observations are found to be $I(1)$, the equation is estimated with the variables first-differenced and an error correction term added to satisfy long-run equilibrium, but the restrictions inherent in the theory are not imposed on the first-differenced variables. If the economic system generating the data is continuous, however, it can be seen from (4.9), (4.10), or even from the approximate model (4.11) that differencing discrete observations of the path of the continuous variables will not remove the moving average inherent in those observations. At issue is the link between the current and partial equilibrium values of the variables in the model and how this affects its dynamics.

5.2   *ECM models*

This raises a question about the role of error correction mechanisms (ECMs) in econometrics. Because the continuous models discussed here have a causal structure and often include adjustment according to some excess demand or supply (but not necessarily of the "own" variable, as shown in (3.5c), (3.10b), or (3.11c)), they have an ECM representation. The converse is not true, however. The ECM used in most ordinary discrete modeling does not have a continuous time representation. The approach being used in continuous time work views an excess demand or supply as an economic factor that determines adjustment in the economy and the dynamics of the system. The adjustment process depends on costs, market structures, and the institutional framework, and the economy can be considered to be moving along its optimal path. In other words, the excess is not an "error" to be "corrected." The rationale for the specification is economic, and the difference between the partial equilibrium level of some variable and its current value is not an error in an economic or statistical sense but rather a representation of economic behavior that determines the transition from one equilibrium to another.

In many ordinary discrete models, the ECM is used as a means of satisfying a long-run relationship rather than as a deliberate specification of dynamic economic behavior. If an equation represents adjustment of some variable $x_i(t)$ to its partial equilibrium $\hat{x}_i(t)$ then the distinction may be considered just a matter of semantics, but this is not the case if the adjustment is to some other partial equilibrium function $\hat{x}_j(t)$, such as an excess demand. This use of ECMs appears to have arisen more from atheoretical time-series considerations than from an approach that begins with economic theory. As the ECM models are often just single equations, any mis-specification in the dynamics (such as an omitted feedback) is not relevant and has no repercussions on the behavior of the model; the feedbacks become important once a *system* of equations is being specified.

A problem often arises in ordinary discrete models with the interpretation of these terms. Where some relationship is interpreted as an excess demand, for example, the definition of all the variables in the function must be contemporaneous; it is meaningless to consider an excess demand as the difference between demand at some time t_1 and supply or actual quantity at t_2. Furthermore, if the demand or supply functions involve both stocks (or variables observed at a point) and flows (or averages), this must be explicitly taken into account. For example, if the demand for real money balances in logarithms is $\hat{m} = f(r, Y)$ then the excess demand would be $\hat{m}(t) - [\log M(t) - \log p(t)]$, whereas in the discrete literature this is often specified as $\hat{m}_t - (\log M_{t-1} - \log p_{t-1})$. Furthermore, these functions may appear in the determination of more than one variable and, if so, they must be constrained to be the same. The continuous time approach allows these functions to be specified correctly.

The use of general VARMAX processes in ordinary discrete models must be questioned from another point of view. Consider a structural model that incorporates the behavior of households or firms and assume that the behavior functions depend on real interest rates. If nominal interest rates r and prices p are determined either implicitly or explicitly elsewhere in the model, the coefficients of these variables must be constrained so that the real interest rate $r - D \log p$ is specified consistently throughout the model. If r or $D \log p$ represents expectations, then again the dynamic structure must be constrained; the dynamic structure of the inflation expectations process of a firm or consumer may be expected to be the same as that of the nominal interest rate expectations process, for appropriately defined prices and interest rates.

5.3   Structural VAR processes

The comments on the VARMAX processes have particular relevance to research on "structural" VAR processes (see Sims 1980). This approach is discussed from a discrete time point of view in the papers of Cooley and LeRoy (1985) and Pagan (1987), both of which provide a critique of this methodology and its interpretation. Hence only a brief sketch will be given here.

A general autoregressive process is defined such that

$$x_t = \sum_{i=1}^{q} A_i x_{t-i} + u_i, \tag{5.2}$$

where x_t is a vector of variables and u_t a vector of disturbances such that $E[u_t] = 0$, $E[u_t u_t'] = V$, and $E[u_t u_s'] = 0$ for all t and $s \neq t$. Owing to the interpretation of this process as "structural," the VAR is defined to be stationary, but as Pagan (1987) notes, this is unnecessary for the purpose of estimation. In applications such as Sims (1980) or Blanchard and Quah (1989), a time trend is included in each equation, or deviations about trends are used, or the x_t are defined as first differences. The value of q is chosen, perhaps by a sequence of likelihood ratio tests, and the model estimated either unrestrictedly or to achieve some smoothness criterion. The model is then transformed to provide a process with orthogonal innovations e_t by premultiplying by a matrix K such that $KVK' = I$. Thus, $e_t = Ku_t$ and (5.2) may be written as

$$\sum_{i=0}^{q} B_i x_{t-i} = e_t, \tag{5.3}$$

where $B_0 = K$ and $B_i = -KA_i$ for $i = 1, ..., q$. The process (5.3) is then inverted to give the innovations representation

$$x_t = \sum_{i=0}^{\infty} C_i e_{t-i}. \tag{5.4}$$

In general, the matrix K is not unique and requires at least one assumption to make it "just-identified." This set of identifying assumptions must be such that the elements of K can be determined uniquely from (5.4) given the assumptions and the estimates of the matrices A_i and the covariance matrix V in (5.2). Various identifying assumptions have been made; for example, Sims (1980) assumed K was lower triangular with positive diagonal elements as defined by the Cholesky decomposition, yielding results that depend crucially on the order of variables in x_t, while Blanchard and Quah (1989) assumed that certain innovations have no long-run effect on real output, so that with the first elements of x_t and e_t referring (respectively) to the output and real innovations and their second elements to the monetary variable and nominal innovations, K was chosen such that $\sum_{i=0}^{\infty} [C_i]_{12} = 0$. The coefficients of the C_i provide an impulse response function. However, as pointed out in Cooley and LeRoy (1985), and as emphasized by Pagan (1987), if these impulse functions are to have any meaning then the innovations must be treated as exogenous variables, requiring prior assumption on the causal structure of the economic model.

If the underlying economic system is continuous, the use of structural VAR processes for determining the properties of the system becomes invalid. As shown in (4.9) or (4.10), even if innovations in the continuous model are orthogonal (so that the matrix Ω is diagonal), this will not be true of the covariance matrix of the equivalent discrete model, even in a first-order system, whether or not restrictions are placed on the structural matrices $A_i(\theta)$. The reason for this can be seen from the definition of $\omega(t)$ in (4.7). The problem becomes even more complex in second- or higher-order systems, or in flow or mixed stock–flow models. If impulse functions are required, it is necessary to estimate an appropriately restricted structural model (4.3) and to use that to derive the impulse functions. Questions remain with regard to whether an assumption of orthogonal innovations can be justified economically, and to the interpretation of such innovations.

5.4   *Aperiodic dynamical properties*

An investigation of asymptotic dynamical behavior in a nonlinear model requires a strict distinction between continuous and discrete systems. Although a linear differential system has a discrete VARMAX representation, this does not carry over to nonlinear systems and, in particular, asymptotic dynamic properties of the nonlinear system may not carry over. For example, aperiodic or chaotic behavior can arise in a first-order difference equation, but in a differential model at least three first-order equations are needed. This raises serious questions about the correct framework for economic models. For some well-defined microeconomic behavior it may be possible to define a difference equation model with appropriate integral lags and to use the model properly for an analysis of that behavior. If economic behavior that is essentially continuous is misrepresented by a discrete model that does not take into account the nonintegral nature of the dynamics, the model may exhibit chaotic properties when in fact none exist, resulting in misleading policy prescriptions.

6   Dynamic analysis and structural stability

The nonlinear model (3.1) or (4.1), or the linear or linearized model (4.3), can be used for analysis and forecasting. The theoretical model (3.1) or (4.1) may be used for analysis of the steady state, if it exists, but for other purposes the parameter estimates are required. Although the nonlinear model may be linearized for estimation purposes, all the restrictions inherent in the underlying nonlinear model and in the linearization are imposed during estimation, so that the estimated parameters are those of the nonlinear system. In very small models, or in special cases of nonlinear models, the dynamic behavior can be derived analytically, but for most of the models considered here this will not be possible. Simulation can always be used to investigate the properties of a model, but more sophisticated techniques provide results that are more analytical in nature, although usually dependent on the parameter estimates.

Analysis of the steady-state properties of a model such as (4.1) is discussed, for example, in Wymer (1992), which also provides a simple example. This not only provides information on the dynamics of the system but helps to ensure that the model is economically and mathematically consistent. Even if a steady state does not exist, it may be useful to determine the conditions under which it would exist; this will often require imposing additional restrictions on the system, and the exercise itself may yield insight into the properties of the model. This is discussed, for example, in Knight and Wymer (1978) and Wymer (1979). Macroeconomic theory can indicate which long-run properties the model should exhibit; implausible behavior could indicate a structural defect, or the omission of an important feedback that could affect the predictive performance of the model and its usefulness for policy analysis.

The steady state, if it exists, can be found by considering the deterministic model (4.1) and by assuming that all exogenous variables grow at steady (and consistent) rates. Hence, if

$$z_j(t) = \bar{z}_j e^{\gamma_j t} \quad \text{for all } j, \tag{6.1}$$

then the steady-state solution for the endogenous variables is

$$y_i(t) = \bar{y}_i e^{\rho_i t}, \tag{6.2}$$

where $\rho_i = g_i(\theta, \gamma)$ and $\bar{y}_i = G_i(\theta, \bar{z}, \gamma)$. These functions may then be differentiated with respect to the parameters or the steady state of the exogenous variables to provide comparative steady-state results. The immediate effects of a change in the parameters or the exogenous variables can be seen directly from the model (4.1), while the broad medium-term effects can be traced heuristically, ignoring cyclical behavior.

The stability of the system can also be investigated. For these purposes, it is easiest to consider the model in its first-order form (4.2), with the exogenous variables replaced by their steady state. The model will be asymptotically stable if for some transformation of the variables, say $\tilde{y}(t)$, (4.2) can be written as

$$D\tilde{y}^*(t) = \tilde{A}^*(\theta, \bar{z}^*, \gamma)\tilde{y}^*(t) + h(\tilde{y}^*, \theta, \bar{z}^*, \gamma, t), \tag{6.3}$$

where $\lim_{|\tilde{y}^*| \to 0}[h(\tilde{y}^*, \theta, \bar{z}^*, \gamma, t)/|\tilde{y}^*|]$ is uniformly convergent in t and all eigenvalues have negative real parts. This is discussed, for example, in Wymer (1992), Bergstrom and Wymer (1976), and Gandolfo (1981). A property of many continuous macroeconomic models is that they are satisfied by the logarithmic deviation of the endogenous variables about their steady state.[9] Thus the transformation $\tilde{y}_i^*(t) = \log[y_i^*(t)/\bar{y}_i^* e^{\rho_i t}]$ allows the model to be linearized as in (6.3), with the remainder h being independent

---

[9] In some models, such as Knight and Wymer (1978), certain variables (such as the interest rate) are specified as natural numbers throughout, so that the appropriate transformation is simply the deviation about the steady state rather than the logarithmic deviation.

of t and of lower order of smallness than $|\bar{y}^*|$ as $|\bar{y}^*|$ tends to zero, so that stability is determined by the eigenvalues of $\bar{A}^*$.

The dynamics of the model may also be studied using sensitivity analysis, as discussed in Wymer (1987, 1992). If the eigenvalues of $\bar{A}^*$ are λ_i, some of which may be complex conjugate, then the partial derivatives $\partial\lambda_i/\partial\theta_l$ and $\partial\lambda_i/\partial a_{jk}$ may be found, where a_{jk} are elements of $\bar{A}^*$. These partial derivatives are important for several reasons. First, they give an indication of which parameters or coefficients in the model are critical to its stability; often the number of these parameters is quite small, as shown for example in Knight and Wymer (1978). This has policy implications if those parameters are policy parameters or could otherwise be affected by policy. Second, if $|\partial\lambda_i/\partial\theta_l|$ is large, it may be useful to examine the effects on the dynamics of the model of allowing θ_l to vary within its asymptotic confidence interval; this gives an indication of whether effort should be made to obtain more precise estimates of that parameter. Third, knowledge of these partial derivatives often allows certain parameters and variables, or certain feedbacks, to be associated with particular cyclical behavior within the system, thus giving information on its overall dynamic properties. Sensitivity analysis has been used in a number of studies, such as Bergstrom and Wymer (1976), Knight and Wymer (1978), and Gandolfo and Padoan (1990).

Nonlinearities in these models may lead to much more complex asymptotic behavior. In particular, nonlinear models may have a strange attractor, so that even deterministic solutions can exhibit the appearance of structural change (although no such change has occurred) and have some of the characteristics of stochastic processes. Such aperiodic or chaotic dynamical behavior is not generic to a model: a model may have non-chaotic and stable solutions for one set of parameter values but have chaotic behavior for another, and may oscillate between chaotic and non-chaotic behavior as the parameter values change. Such asymptotic properties can be investigated using a generalization of eigensystem and sensitivity analysis, as discussed in Wymer (1995).

These generalized techniques may be used to examine not only the nature of an attractor of the model for estimated or given parameter values, but also the question of whether the system is structurally stable over some plausible range of parameter values. A model is structurally stable if small changes in parameters do not produce a qualitative change in its dynamic properties, but there may be bifurcation points at which parameter changes do have a qualitative effect. For example, if a nonlinear system has a steady state but the real parts of the eigenvalues of the linearized model about that steady state are not all negative, then the model is not asymptotically stable. Although this suggests that the given parameter set is implausible, it is possible that some other (and perhaps more interesting) attractor exists for values of parameters in the neighborhood of the given parameter set, especially if some real parts of the eigenvalues are close to zero.

Since these more complex properties of nonlinear systems are easier to discuss in phase space, it is useful to make a change in notation. Let the system be the set of autonomous, first-order, nonlinear differential equations,

$$\dot{x} = f\{x(t), \theta\}, \tag{6.4}$$

where $x(t)$ is a vector of n variables, f is a vector function, and θ is a vector of p parameters. It is assumed that this system is coupled in that it is not separable into two independent systems. The system is autonomous and so, given an initial point $x(t_0)$, the system determines a solution path or orbit $x(t) = \phi\{x(t_0), t, \theta\}$ in n-dimensional phase space such that $x(t_0) = \phi\{x(t_0), t_0, \theta\}$; in effect, this is a mapping of the trajectories in time–state space onto phase space, where t is a parameter in phase space. The parameters θ will be omitted where they are fixed. Because a nonautonomous system can be written as a higher-dimensional autonomous system with little loss in generality (but with some change in interpretation), such systems will not be considered explicitly.

An attracting set A in n-dimensional phase space exists if there is an invariant n-dimensional neighborhood U of A such that, for any initial point $x(t_0)$ in this neighborhood and for sufficiently large t, the trajectory $\phi\{x(t_0), t\}$ remains in U and $\phi\{x(t_0), t\} \to A$ as $t \to \infty$. A is an attractor if the attracting set has a dense orbit, that is, an orbit which covers the whole of the attractor; this ensures that the attractor is not the union of two or more smaller attractors. A special case is a fixed point, which is an attractor of a system with a stable steady state in time–state space.

Classical attractors – such as fixed points, limit cycles, and tori – lie on manifolds, which are the analog of surfaces, and so have integer dimension but zero volume in phase space. This dimension can be seen by a suitable mapping of the attractor, so that a fixed point is of dimension 0, while a limit cycle, which can be mapped onto a line, has dimension 1 and is thus a T^1 torus. A T^2 torus has dimension 2 because it can be mapped onto a plane.

A strange attractor, which belongs to a class of attractors that do not lie on manifolds, is defined as an attractor which has a sensitive dependence on the initial conditions $x(t_0)$ in the neighborhood of the attractor, and which is indecomposable in that it does not degenerate into two (or more) distinct attractors. Thus, for an initial point in some neighborhood U of the attractor, the trajectory $\phi\{x(t_0), t\}$ approaches and remains arbitrarily close to the attractor for sufficiently large t, whereas small variations in the initial value of $x(t_0)$ lead to essentially different time paths of the system after some time interval. Although a strange attractor is not, strictly speaking, a surface, it can be visualized as a "surface" consisting of a folded structure having an infinite number of very close layers with a finite volume of phase space between the layers. The attractors are not a closed curve (even of a complicated form) but consist of an aperiodic trajectory. The dimension of a strange attractor is a noninteger or fractal that must be less than the dimension of the phase space but greater than 2. For given parameter values, a dynamical system will exhibit aperiodic or chaotic behavior if it possesses a strange attractor, providing that the trajectory passes through the neighborhood U of the attractor; almost all initial conditions will lead to such a trajectory. Although the system is deterministic and hence a given set of initial conditions leads to uniquely defined trajectories, the sensitivity of the system to those initial conditions means that the behavior of the system is apparently random.

The existence and properties of an attractor of a system may be investigated using a Taylor series expansion, essentially using a generalization of the analysis of a fixed point in phase space. In extending previous work, however, a distinction must be made between conservative and dissipative systems. Dissipative systems always possess attractors, such as fixed points, tori, or strange attractors; conservative or Hamiltonian systems do not, but instead have an infinity of closed orbits such that any initial point will always lie on one of these orbits. The two types of systems can be distinguished using the generalized divergence of f. Consider a set of initial conditions $x(t)$ in a vanishingly small hyperellipsoid V in n-dimensional space. This volume will change as a function of t as $x(t)$ changes, so that

$$\frac{dV}{dt} = \int_V \int \cdots \int \left(\sum_{i=1}^{n} \frac{\partial f_i}{\partial x_i} \right) dx_1 \cdots dx_n. \tag{6.5}$$

The summation term is the generalized divergence of f. Dissipative systems are characterized by contracting volumes, where $dV/dt < 0$, while in conservative Hamiltonian systems, V is constant. If $dV/dt > 0$ then the system is unstable. This term, which is the trace of the Jacobian $J(x, \theta) = \partial f(x, \theta)/\partial x$, is thus equal to the sum of the eigenvalues of the Jacobian. Since all conservative systems are structurally unstable and so do not possess attractors, only dissipative systems will be considered here.

Any trajectory of a dissipative system will approach an attractor as $t \to \infty$. For systems exhibiting chaos in the neighborhood of a strange attractor, the trajectories have a sensitive dependence on the initial conditions, so that the separation of two nearby trajectories increases exponentially with time. This means that there is a stretching of the hyperellipsoid V in one direction which is more than compensated by a contraction in other directions, so that the volume defined by the arbitrary initial conditions decreases with time. The hyperellipsoid cannot always be stretched in the same direction, but must be folded so that it is located in the specified neighborhood of the initial conditions.

Lyapunov exponents provide information on the relative rates of expansion or contraction of this hyperellipsoid in each dimension and hence on the asymptotic properties of a system. Given an initial point $x_0 = \phi(x_0, t_0)$, substituting the solution of the system $\phi(x_0, t)$ into (6.4) and differentiating with respect to x_0 gives the variational (matrix) equation

$$\dot{\Phi}(x_0, t) = J\{\phi(x_0, t)\}\Phi(x_0, t), \tag{6.6}$$

where $\Phi(x_0, t) = \partial\phi(x_0, t)/\partial x_0$ and $\Phi(x_0, t_0) = I$, which is the linearization along the orbit $\phi(x_0, t)$. Thus, if δx_0 is a small perturbation about x_0 then $\delta x(t) = \Phi(x_0, t)\delta x_0$. The Lyapunov exponents are then defined as

$$\lambda_i = \limsup_{t \to \infty} \frac{1}{t} \log|\mu_i| \quad \text{for } i = 1, ..., n,$$

where $\mu_1(t), ..., \mu_n(t)$ are the eigenvalues of $\Phi(x_0, t)$. For simplicity, it will be assumed that the exponents are arranged in descending order such that $\lambda_1 \geq \lambda_2 \geq \cdots \geq \lambda_n$. Corresponding generalized eigenvectors $\eta_1, ..., \eta_n$ of $\Phi(x_0, t)$ can also be defined. Since at least one Lyapunov exponent is positive in chaotic systems, the solutions $\Phi(x_0, t)$ are unbounded as $t \to \infty$ and the matrix is ill-conditioned, so calculation of the Lyapunov exponents is by no means trivial.

Lyapunov exponents are a generalization of the eigenvalues at an equilibrium point. Let x_0 be an equilibrium point such that $J\{\phi(x_0, t)\}$ is time-invariant and (6.6) becomes $\Phi(x_0, t) = e^{J\{\phi(x_0, t)\}t}$. If λ_i^* are the eigenvalues of $J(x^*)$, then $(1/t)\log|\mu_i| = \mathbb{R}(\lambda_i^*)$, so that the Lyapunov exponents of the equilibrium point $\lambda_i = \mathbb{R}(\lambda_i^*)$. Thus, the Lyapunov exponents indicate the rate of expansion or contraction of the hyperellipsoid in the neighborhood of the equilibrium point, or the average rate where $x_0 \neq x^*$, and the subspace within which this occurs is defined by the corresponding eigenvectors.

The Lyapunov exponents λ_i may be used to classify and help determine the form of the attractor. In order for an attractor to exist, the volume of the hyperellipsoid defined by the generalized divergence must contract so that $\sum_{i=1}^{n}\lambda_i < 0$. Haken (1983) has shown that for attractors other than a fixed point, at least one Lyapunov exponent must be zero. Thus, for nonchaotic attractors, for an asymptotically stable equilibrium point $\lambda_i < 0$ for all i, while for an asymptotically stable k-torus, k exponents must be zero and the remainder negative. Hence a limit cycle or T^1 torus has only one zero exponent and the rest negative. A nonchaotic attractor is *nondegenerate* if its dimension equals the number of zero Lyapunov exponents. For chaotic attractors, at least one of the Lyapunov exponents must be positive and at least one zero. In addition, the dimension of a strange attractor must be noninteger; an estimate of this is given by the Lyapunov dimension

$$D^L = k + \frac{\sum_{i=1}^{k} \lambda_i}{|\lambda_{k+1}|},$$

where k is the largest number of eigenvalues such that the sum is positive, that is, k is such that $\sum_{i=1}^{k} \lambda_i > 0$ and $\sum_{i=1}^{k+1} \lambda_i < 0$.

The second question of interest is the structural stability of the solution of the differential system (6.4), that is, whether the asymptotic properties of the system change qualitatively for different values of the parameters. For example, for some parameter values the system may have a stable fixed point whereas for others it may have some form of torus as an attractor or perhaps a strange attractor, and for others still it may be unstable. Such structural stability is of crucial importance when considering the policy implications of a system. A system is structurally stable when small perturbations produce topologically equivalent systems. Heuristically, the system will be structurally stable if there is a one-to-one mapping of the flow of the system for small changes in parameter values; if not, the system is structurally unstable.

In the dynamical system $\dot{x} = f\{x(t), \theta\}$, as the set of parameters θ varies, the phase portrait of the system usually changes gradually so that the system is topologically unchanged, but at some values of θ, or *bifurcation points,* the topology may change, perhaps with a change in the number of fixed points or periodic orbits, or with a change in the nature of the strange attractor; at that point the system becomes structurally unstable. Specifically, a point $\theta = \theta_0$ is a bifurcation point if there exists a θ_1 arbitrarily close to θ_0 such that $f(x, \theta_0)$ and $f(x, \theta_1)$ are topologically different. Such bifurcation points are characterized by a change in the number of eigenvalues of the system with zero real parts at that point, so that the conditions for a bifurcation point can be defined in terms of the Jacobian of $f(x, \theta)$, its eigenvalues, and their partial derivatives. These issues are discussed in Wymer (1995), which also contains more detailed references.

7   Policy analysis

Although the model may be used directly for forecasting or simulation, the properties of the model and their implications can perhaps be better examined by solving the system subject to boundary-point constraints. Optimal control is a special case of this, and has been used in a number of studies. The solution of general deterministic boundary-point problems with linear, or linearized, models using the eigensystem is given in Wymer (1982) and was used by Gandolfo and Petit (1987). A rigorous derivation of stochastic optimal control within the context of linear differential equation systems is given in Bergstrom (1987).

Stochastic optimal control was used by Bergstrom, Nowman, and Wandasiewicz (1994) to derive the feedback equations for optimal monetary and fiscal policy within the linearized second-order model of the United Kingdom given in Bergstrom et al. (1992). The solution shows that monetary policy can be implemented quickly but the lags in its effects are long, whereas fiscal policy can only be implemented more slowly but has more rapid effects. One of the difficulties of optimal control shown by this study is that although a range of plausible weights in the objective function give satisfactory smoothing of the path of the target variables for given initial conditions of the state variables, the initial values of the paths of the control variables are extreme. This suggests that either quite different weights in the objective function are required, or that inequality constraints should be imposed on the control variables. This would almost certainly result in more cyclical paths of the target and control variables, which may decrease the overall rate of convergence of the system to its long-run equilibrium. An alternative possibility, however, is that the nonlinearities in the model are important and that taking these into account explicitly may reduce the extreme initial values of the control variables.

The solution of boundary-point problems in nonlinear differential equation systems is a much more complex problem. Techniques to solve such problems for nonstochastic continuous time models have been implemented by Wymer (1993b) within a general framework. These allow the solution of nonlinear optimal control problems and of "targeting" problems, where some target defined by $F(Dx(t), x(t), z(t))|_T = 0$ is to be achieved at $t = T$ (such as the Maastricht problem), as well as the solution of models involving rational expectations and of differential Nash and Stackelberg games over some interval $(0, T)$.

Let a differential equation model, which may be nonlinear, be defined as the set of first- and zero-order equations

$$Dx_1(t) = g_1\{x(t), z(t), \theta\}, \tag{7.1a}$$

$$g_2\{x(t), z(t), \theta\} = 0, \tag{7.1b}$$

or, more generally,

$$G\{Dx(t), x(t), z(t), \theta\} = 0, \tag{7.2}$$

where x_1 is a vector of first-order endogenous or state or costate variables, x_2 is a vector of m_2 zero-order endogenous variables with $x = [x_1\ x_2]'$,

$z(t)$ is a vector of known exogenous variables or forcing functions, and θ is a vector of parameters. Here $g = [g_1 \ g_2]'$ is the vector of functions defining the system, with the first-order variables defined by g_1 and the zero-order variables by g_2.

The boundary-point problem is that, given the system (7.1) or (7.2), a solution must be found that satisfies a set of functions

$$F_k\{Dx(t), x(t), z(t)\}|_{t=t_k} = 0$$

representing the constraints on the variables at given points $t_k \in (0, T)$ along their path. The F_k will generally (but not necessarily) refer to extreme points only, so that for some given $x_i(0)$ a solution must be found that satisfies a set of functions $F\{Dx(t), x(t), z(t)\}|_{t=T} = 0$. The functions F allow the boundary points to be defined, for example, in terms of ratios of levels of variables or differences between their rates of growth.

The differential equation system (7.1) or (7.2) may be defined to allow endogenous switching between regimes, so that an equation might have two forms, say

$$Dx_i(t) = g_{i1}\{x(t), z(t), \theta\} \quad \text{when some function } h\{x(t), z(t), \theta\} > 0$$

and

$$Dx_i(t) = g_{i2}\{x(t), z(t), \theta\} \quad \text{when } h \le 0,$$

and this may be generalized to allow switching of two or more equations. Moreover, in control problems and especially in optimal control, the control variables may be subject to inequality constraints of the form $a\{x(t), z(t), \theta\} < h\{x(t), z(t), \theta\}$.

Although only first-order systems are treated explicitly, these can be considered as the first-order equivalent of higher-order systems as in (4.1). Of course, these techniques have been implemented in a very general way, so the question of whether a solution exists depends on the particular application and the need for it to be well defined. One class of problems that lies within this framework is that of optimal control.

A general nonlinear optimal control problem may be defined as the maximization of the integral of some point or instantaneous objective function $f\{x(t), u(t), t, \theta\}$ over some interval $(0, T)$, where T may be infinite, subject to constraints imposed by the economic system as in (4.1), and subject to any equality or inequality constraints on the control variables. Formally, the optimal control problem is

$$\text{maximize } Q = \int_{s=0}^{T} f\{x(s), u(s), z(t), \theta\} \, ds + F\{x(T), z(T)\} \tag{7.3}$$

subject to

$$Dx(t) = g\{x(t), u(t), z(t), \theta\}$$

$$\text{for all } t \in \{0, T\} \text{ with } x(0) = x_0 \text{ and } z(t) \text{ given,} \quad (7.3a)$$

$$h\{x(t), u(t), z(t), \theta\} = 0 \quad \text{for all } t \in \{0, T\}, \quad \text{and} \quad (7.3b)$$

$$a\{x(t), u(t), z(t), \theta\} \geq 0 \quad \text{for all } t \in \{0, T\}, \quad (7.3c)$$

where $x(t)$ is a vector of m endogenous or state variables $x(t)$ with given initial state $x(0) = x_0$, $z(t)$ is a vector of n exogenous variables or forcing functions, and $u(t)$ is a vector of control variables. Thus $x(t)$ and $z(t)$ correspond, at least in principle, to $y^*(t)$ and $z^*(t)$ in (4.1), and may also contain derivatives defining a higher-order system as in (4.1). Because the forcing functions are assumed to be known functions of time, or can be approximated by such functions, the vector $z(t)$ may be replaced (without loss of generality) by the scalar t, and the functions f, g, h, and a as well as the parameters θ defined accordingly. The point objective function f may contain a discount factor, so that the intertemporal objective function Q may be defined as the discounted present value of f. Equation (7.3a) is the dynamic model defining the system, with g a vector of nonlinear functions corresponding to Φ in (4.1). Equality constraints on the control variables $u(t)$ are given by (7.3b), and (7.3c) represents any inequality constraints on the $u(t)$. A constraint of the form $a \leq u(t) \leq b$ merely corresponds to defining two inequality constraints of the form (7.3c).

In some economic optimal control problems, the point objective function f and the constraints h and a may be functions of $dx(t)$ but, from a formal point of view, this is omitted since it can be replaced by the corresponding function g. In addition, the economic model (7.3a) may contain zero-order equations but, again from a formal point of view, these may be used to eliminate the corresponding variables from the system. Although these variables may be eliminated formally as assumed in (7.3), (7.3) may be extended to include these variables explicitly; this is shown in the Appendix.

Let the Hamiltonian be

$$H\{x, u, \lambda, \theta\} = f\{x(t), u(t), t, \theta\} + \lambda'(t)g\{x(t), u(t), t, \theta\}, \quad (7.4)$$

which must be maximized subject to any constraints on $u(t)$; $\lambda(t)$ is the vector of Hamiltonian multipliers. The first-order conditions for unconstrained maximization are

$$\frac{\partial H}{\partial \lambda} = \dot{x} = g\{x(t), u(t), t, \theta\}, \quad x(0) = x_0; \quad (7.4a)$$

$$\frac{\partial H}{\partial x} = -\dot{\lambda} = \frac{\partial f}{\partial x} + \left(\frac{\partial g'}{\partial x}\right)\lambda, \quad \lambda(T) = \left.\frac{\partial F}{\partial x}\right|_{t=T}; \quad (7.4b)$$

$$\frac{\partial H}{\partial u} = 0 = \frac{\partial f}{\partial u} + \left(\frac{\partial g'}{\partial u}\right)\lambda. \tag{7.4c}$$

The transversality condition is given by

$$\left(H + \frac{\partial F}{\partial t}\right) + \frac{dx'}{dt}\left(\frac{\partial F}{\partial x} - \lambda\right)\Bigg|_{t=T} = 0. \tag{7.4d}$$

These results also apply when there are equality constraints on the $u(t)$ as in (7.3b) since, from a formal point of view, these may be used to reduce the set of control variables.

When the control variables are subject to inequality constraints such as (7.3c), some of these constraints may be binding over only part of the interval $(0, T)$; moreover, the set of binding constraints may change along the optimal path. Let a *switch point* be the point at which at least one inequality constraint becomes just binding or just nonbinding. Thus the path of at least some variables may not be differentiable at such switch points, in which case the first-order conditions (7.4b) and (7.4c) are no longer valid. This more general problem may be solved by using a dynamic envelope theorem.

The Lagrangian for the constrained case may be defined as

$$\begin{aligned}
L\{x, u, &\lambda, \mu, \nu, t, \theta\} \\
&= f\{x(t), u(t), t, \theta\} + \lambda'(t)g\{x(t), u(t), t, \theta\} \\
&\quad + \mu'(t)h\{x(t), u(t), t, \theta\} + \nu'(t)a\{x(t), u(t), t, \theta\},
\end{aligned} \tag{7.5}$$

where $\mu(t)$ and $\nu(t)$ are the vectors of Lagrangian multipliers corresponding to the equality constraints (7.3b) and inequality constraints (7.3c).

Under the assumptions that the functions f, g, h, and a are twice differentiable, that H is strictly quasiconcave in $u(t)$, that the set of feasible control paths is compact and convex, and that the number of switch points is finite, LaFrance and Barney (1991) showed that a necessary and sufficient set of first-order conditions is:

$$\dot{x} = g(x, u, \theta, t) \quad \text{for fixed } x(0) = x_0; \tag{7.5a}$$

$$\dot{\lambda} = -\left[\frac{\partial f}{\partial x} + \left(\frac{\partial g'}{\partial x}\right)\lambda + \left(\frac{\partial h'}{\partial x}\right)\mu + \left(\frac{\partial a'}{\partial x}\right)\nu\right], \qquad \lambda(T) = \frac{\partial F}{\partial x}\Bigg|_{t=T}; \tag{7.5b}$$

$$\frac{\partial L}{\partial u} = \frac{\partial f}{\partial u} + \left(\frac{\partial g'}{\partial u}\right)\lambda + \left(\frac{\partial h'}{\partial u}\right)\mu + \left(\frac{\partial a'}{\partial u}\right)\nu = 0; \tag{7.5c}$$

$$\frac{\partial L}{\partial \mu} = h(x, u, \theta, t) = 0; \tag{7.5d}$$

$$\frac{\partial L}{\partial \nu} = a(x, u, \theta, t) \geq 0, \quad \nu \geq 0, \quad \nu'a(x, u, \theta, t) = 0. \tag{7.5e}$$

Thus, from (7.5e), v_i is positive if the ith constraint is just binding and zero if it is nonbinding.[10] Under these conditions, the control variables, the state and costate variables, and the Lagrange multipliers all pass through the boundaries of the inequality constraints continuously, and their derivatives with respect to θ are piecewise continuous with at most finite jumps at the switch points.

As an example, consider the solution of the following special case of (7.3):

$$\text{maximize} \int_{s=0}^{T} f\{x(s), u(s), s, \theta\}\, ds \tag{7.6}$$

subject to $Dx(t) = g\{x(t), u(t), z(t), \theta\}$ with $x(0)$ given, and subject to the inequality constraints $a(t) \le u(t) \le b(t)$ where a and b are given functions of time but independent of $x(t)$.

In this case the functions h in (7.3) do not exist, and as $\partial a/\partial x$ and $\partial b/\partial x$ are identically zero the costate equations (7.5b) reduce to those of the unconstrained Hamiltonian (7.4b). However, the first-order conditions $\partial L/\partial u$ in (7.5c), although much simpler than (7.5c), still contain the Lagrangian multipliers v. Specifically, maximizing the Lagrangian incorporating the constraints on $u(t)$,

$$L\{x, u, \lambda, v_1, v_2, z\} = f\{x, u, z\}$$
$$+ \lambda' g\{x, u, z\} + v_1'(u-a) + v_2'(b-u), \tag{7.7}$$

gives

$$\dot{x} = g(x, u, \theta, t) \quad \text{for fixed } x(0) = x_0; \tag{7.7a}$$

$$\dot{\lambda} = -\frac{\partial H}{\partial x}, \qquad \lambda(T) = 0; \tag{7.7b}$$

$$\frac{\partial L}{\partial u} = \frac{\partial H}{\partial u} + v_1 - v_2 = 0; \tag{7.7c}$$

$$u - a \ge 0, \quad b - u \ge 0, \quad v_1 \ge 0, \quad v_2 \ge 0, \quad \text{and}$$
$$v_1'(u-a) + v_2'(b-u) = 0. \tag{7.7d}$$

Thus, from (7.7c) and as shown in Kamien and Schwartz (1981), the solution is such that

---

[10] In the implementation in Wymer (1992), a set of switch functions $s_i(t)$ is defined such that for each inequality constraint a_i, $s_i(t) = 1$ if the constraint is just binding (i.e., if $a_i = 0$) and $s_i(t) = 0$ if $a_i > 0$. Each v_i in (7.5b) and (7.5c) is replaced by $s_i v_i$, and the set of inequality constraints (7.5e) is replaced by the set of equations

$$s_i a_i(x, u, \theta, t) + (1 - s_i)v_i = 0 \quad \text{for all } v_i. \tag{7.5e*}$$

The solution of (7.3) is determined simultaneously with the switch points, which form a finite ordered set $\{s_1(t_1), s_2(t_2), ..., s_k(t_k)\}$ such that $0 < t_1 < \cdots < t_k < T$, where t_l is the point at which at least one $s_i(t)$ changes from 0 to 1 or vice versa.

$$u(t) = a \quad \text{if} \quad \partial H/\partial u < 0,$$
$$a \le u(t) \le b \quad \text{if} \quad \partial H/\partial u = 0, \qquad (7.8)$$
$$u(t) = b \quad \text{if} \quad \partial H/\partial u > 0.$$

In the simplest case, where H is linear in u, the control variables u will take on their extreme values only but may switch between them; often, but not necessarily, there will be only one switch. In this case, the problem becomes one of maximizing

$$\int_{s=0}^{t_1} f(x, u, s) \, ds + \int_{s=t_1}^{T} f(x, u, s) \, ds$$

subject to the constraints given in equations (7.7a) to (7.7b) to yield a set of first-order conditions that must be solved for x, u, and t_1. Given t_1, the control variable $u(t)$ will equal a in one regime and b in the other. The nature of the problem will usually show what the value of u will be at $t = 0$.

Sufficiency conditions can be derived as in Kamien and Schwartz (1981) and Seierstad and Sydsaeter (1977). In the unconstrained case (4.4), if $\{x^*(t), u^*(t)\}$ are the paths satisfying the necessary conditions and if the Hamiltonian is differentiable and concave in (x, u), then $\{x^*(t), u^*(t)\}$ will be optimal provided that $\lambda_i(T) = 0$ if $x_i(t)$ is free, $\lambda_i(T) \ge 0$ if $x_i(T) \ge \bar{x}_i$, and with no conditions on $\lambda_i(T)$ if $x_i(T) = \bar{x}_i$. The same conditions apply to the constrained case if the equality and inequality constraints h and a are differentiable and quasiconcave in (x, u). If the functions f and g are concave in (x, u) then the Hamiltonian is likewise concave in (x, u). In cases where the concavity of f or g is not obvious, the sufficiency condition may be verified by differentiating the relevant functions.

The conditions that the Hamiltonian be concave and that the constraints on the control variables be quasiconcave can be weakened. The latter condition may be replaced by a constraint qualification that ensures some control variable is present in all binding constraints. Let n_h be the number of equality constraints h and n_a the number of inequality constraints a. This constraint qualification is satisfied if

$$\text{rank} \left[\begin{array}{c} \dfrac{\partial h(x, u, \theta, t)}{\partial u} \\[2mm] \dfrac{\partial a_i(x, u, \theta, t)}{\partial u} \end{array} \right]_{\substack{x(t) = x^*(t), u(t) = u^*(t) \\ s_i(t) = 1, i = 1, \ldots, n_a}} = n_h + \sum_{i=1}^{n_a} s_i \quad \text{for all} \quad t \in \{0, T\}.$$

Let $A(t) = \{x : a(x, u, t, \theta) \ge 0 \text{ for some } u\}$. Then $\{x^*(t), u^*(t)\}$ will be optimal if the objective function is a concave function of x on $A(t)$, if each of the a_i is a continuously differentiable function of (x, u), and if the constraint qualification is satisfied.

The sensitivity of the objective function to the parameters of the system may be derived from these results. When Q^* is the optimal value function of (7.3), LaFrance and Barney (1991) showed that under the conditions (7.5), the partial derivative $\partial Q^*/\partial\theta$ is continuous and twice differentiable in θ, and

$$\frac{\partial Q^*}{\partial\theta} = \int_{s=0}^{T} \frac{\partial L(x^*, u^*, \lambda^*, \mu^*, \nu^*, \theta, t)}{\partial\theta}\, dt. \tag{7.9}$$

Thus the partial derivative of Q^* may be obtained easily since the partial derivative of L may be calculated analytically, even for very general systems, and the integral is calculated at the same time as the optimal path.[11] The matrix of second-order partial derivatives $\partial^2 Q^*/\partial\theta\partial\theta'$ may be calculated in a similar way; $\partial^2 Q^*/\partial\theta\partial\theta'$ is symmetric, but this holds only in the integral form and not at a given point in time. These partial derivatives, which may be calculated from (7.9) even for very complex models, provide a useful tool for determining the properties of a model and evaluating its policy implications.

The solution of the optimal control problems (7.4) or (7.5), with the extensions shown in the Appendix, has been implemented by Wymer (1993b) within a more general framework of the solution of boundary-point problems. This program is currently being used for the solution of nonlinear optimal control problems in emissions control (see Donaghy and Mukherjee 1992), traffic planning (Donaghy and Schintler 1994), and the solution of continuous Nash and Stackelberg games. These techniques would also be applicable to such questions as target zones for exchange rates and the Maastricht problem.

Both the linear (or linearized) and nonlinear models may be used for forecasting.[12] An advantage of the continuous time approach here is that models are developed within a theoretical framework and with the aim of having satisfactory long-run properties. This means that, first, the models are likely to provide more satisfactory long-run forecasts since these are constrained by the long-run properties of the model. Second, the emphasis on a theoretical basis for the model means that the model is usually

---

[11] As emphasized by LaFrance and Barney (1991), the Lagrangian must be differentiated prior to substitution of the optimal path of state, costate, and control variables, and the partial derivative then integrated. This is not the same as substituting the optimal solutions into the Lagrangian, differentiating with respect to the parameters, and then integrating.

[12] It should be noted that it is only with a linear (or linearized) model that the asymptotic variance matrix of parameters, and the dynamic forecasting variance matrices, can be calculated analytically. The variance matrix of parameters of the exact nonlinear estimator can only be calculated numerically, and the variance of forecast errors in the nonlinear model must be calculated by Monte Carlo methods.

heavily overidentified and this, together with the asymptotic properties of the estimators, provides efficient forecasts. Third, the use of a continuous time model allows forecasts to be produced at any frequency, independent of the frequency of the data used to estimate the model; this can be seen from (4.7) for the linear case, but the same is true for forecasting using the nonlinear model. The use of linear (or linearized) continuous time models for forecasting is discussed, for example, in Wymer (1992) and in Bergstrom and Wymer (1976), while Bergstrom (1989) gives a rigorous derivation of the optimal forecasting properties of the linear models. The forecasting performance of some of these models is impressive; a brief summary of these models is given in Wymer (1992, part II).

8   Conclusion

The approach to continuous time disequilibrium models discussed here provides a coherent framework for the specification, estimation, and dynamic and policy analysis of economic and particularly macroeconomic models. Although the idea of using continuous models to represent economic behavior is long-standing, it is only during the last 30 years that appropriate estimators have been developed for differential equation systems. Estimation is important. Economic theory is less well developed than in the natural sciences and it is generally not possible to measure or derive parameters from experimental data, so testing of joint hypotheses is required. Although some properties of economic systems can be derived from theory without the need to estimate parameters, much of the more relevant behavior depends crucially on the parameter values. These affect not only transient disequilibrium behavior but also the nature of any equilibrium. Perhaps the most striking example of this is the nature of strange attractors, which can lead to aperiodic or chaotic behavior.

Although Koopmans (1950) first argued for the use of continuous or differential equation models rather than discrete systems in econometrics, it was A. W. Phillips (1959) who first developed a procedure to estimate these systems. His approach was not feasible for overidentified models, especially given the computing resources available at the time, but it stimulated the work of Bergstrom in the early 1960s toward deriving feasible estimators of differential equation systems. It was also A. W. Phillips who emphasized the role of these systems in economic stabilization, using either partial feedback or optimal control. For these purposes, it is essential to take a systemwide view that includes the relevant feedback. It is this thread that has continued through much of the work on continuous systems.

In specifying the differential equation model, it is not necessary to assume that the economic system be in equilibrium, or at least not in a long-run sense. The model is, however, assumed to have a firm theoretical basis, and the constraints implicit in this are maintained throughout estimation and analysis. Exact and approximate Gaussian estimators have been derived for both linear and nonlinear mixed-order stock–flow models. Although these estimators use a sample of discrete observations, the exact estimates are independent of the observation period. The approximate estimates are much faster to calculate than the corresponding exact ones, but they are biased (although the bias is generally small) and have much larger asymptotic standard errors. If the model is nonlinear, it may be estimated directly in that form, but alternatively it may be linearized about some point or path and the linearized model estimated, again subject to all the constraints inherent in the theory and in the linearization. All the estimators are designed to provide estimates of the underlying economic model and are well suited to heavily overidentified systems.

The structure and specification of any particular model and its use will vary according to its purpose. For instance, it may be required for macroeconomic policy, for the investigation or stabilization of some commodity or financial market, or for profit maximization by a firm. Given parameter estimates, the model may be used for hypothesis testing, to investigate its dynamic properties, and for forecasting or simulation. Even if the equilibrium of the model is some attractor other than a steady state or fixed point, it is useful to know how sensitive that attractor is to the parameter values. Computer programs have been developed to implement exact and approximate estimators and the techniques for studying the properties of these models.

The advantages of the estimation and use of continuous time models have, during the past 30 years, become increasingly clear from both a theoretical and empirical point of view. While these techniques are more complex (and for that reason more difficult to use) than standard discrete procedures, an essential difference is that the methodology places much greater emphasis on a satisfactory specification of the economic model. Although this can be time-consuming, it results in better hypothesis testing and more plausible short- and long-run dynamic properties and thus allows superior policy analysis or forecasting of economic behavior.

Appendix

The optimal control problem (7.3) may be extended to allow the systems to include zero-order variables explicitly. Let x_1 be a vector of m_1 first-order endogenous or state variables with given initial state $x_1(0) = x_{10}$, and let x_2 be a vector of m_2 zero-order endogenous variables with $x = [x_1 \ x_2]'$. Let $g = [g_1 \ g_2]'$ be the vector of functions defining the system. The objective function

$$\int_{s=0}^{T} f\{x, \dot{x}_1, u, t, \theta\} \, ds + F\{x(T), T\} \tag{A.1}$$

is to be maximized subject to first-order equations defining $\dot{x}_1$ and zero-order equations defining x_2 as follows:

$$\dot{x}_1 = g_1\{x, u, t, \theta\} \quad \text{for } x_1(0) = x_{10} \text{ given,} \tag{A.1a}$$

$$g_2\{x, \dot{x}_1, u, t, \theta\} = 0, \tag{A.1a$'$}$$

$$h\{x, \dot{x}_1, u, t, \theta\} = 0, \tag{A.1b}$$

$$a\{x, \dot{x}_1, u, t, \theta\} \geq 0. \tag{A.1c}$$

The Lagrangian L may be defined as in (7.5) with $\lambda = [\lambda_1 \, \lambda_2]'$ being the Lagrangian multipliers of the system functions g. The partial derivatives of L with respect to λ will impose the condition that the optimal path satisfies the model (A.1a) and (A.1a$'$), corresponding to (7.5a), and (7.5b) is replaced by the partial derivatives of L with respect to x; that is,

$$\frac{\partial L}{\partial x_1} = -\dot{\lambda}_1 = \frac{\partial f}{\partial x_1} + \left(\frac{\partial g_1'}{\partial x_1}\right)\lambda_1 + \left(\frac{\partial g_2'}{\partial x_1}\right)\lambda_2 + \left(\frac{\partial h'}{\partial x_1}\right)\mu + \left(\frac{\partial a'}{\partial x_1}\right)\nu$$

$$+ \frac{\partial g_1'}{\partial x_1}\left[\frac{\partial f}{\partial \dot{x}_1} + \left(\frac{\partial g_2'}{\partial \dot{x}_1}\right)\lambda_2 + \left(\frac{\partial h'}{\partial \dot{x}_1}\right)\mu + \left(\frac{\partial a'}{\partial \dot{x}_1}\right)\nu\right],$$

$$\lambda(T) = \frac{\partial F}{\partial x}\bigg|_{t=T}; \tag{A.2a}$$

$$\frac{\partial L}{\partial x_2} = 0 = \frac{\partial f}{\partial x_2} + \left(\frac{\partial g_1'}{\partial x_2}\right)\lambda_1 + \left(\frac{\partial g_2'}{\partial x_2}\right)\lambda_2 + \left(\frac{\partial h'}{\partial x_2}\right)\mu + \left(\frac{\partial a'}{\partial x_2}\right)\nu. \tag{A.2b}$$

The solution of (7.3) may also be extended to allow the objective function to depend on both the level u and derivative $\dot{u}$ of a control variable, where $\dot{u}$ is unrestricted. This can be incorporated in the solution (7.5) by defining an additional variable, say $\dot{u} = w$, and corresponding Hamiltonian multiplier κ, introducing κw into the Hamiltonian and replacing $\dot{u}$ by w where it occurs, and then differentiating with respect to w and κ. From a theoretical point of view, the condition $\partial H/\partial w = 0$, or more generally $\partial L/\partial w = 0$, can be solved for κ immediately and the solution differentiated to give $\dot{\kappa}$, which can then be eliminated from the condition $\partial L/\partial u = -\dot{\kappa}$ to give the Euler equation form

$$\frac{\partial L}{\partial u} - \frac{d}{dt}\left(\frac{\partial L}{\partial \dot{u}}\right) = 0. \tag{A.3}$$

The conditions (7.5a)–(7.5e) for a maximum are written as a first-order system, so within the framework considered here all the variables u, w, and κ may be retained and the equations $\partial L/\partial w = 0$ and $\partial L/\partial u = -\dot{\kappa}$ used instead of $\partial L/\partial u = 0$ in (7.5c).

REFERENCES

Armington, P., and C. Wolford (1984), "Exchange Rate Dynamics and Economic Policy," Armington Wolford Associates, Washington, DC.

Bailey, P. W., W. B. Hall, and P. C. B. Phillips (1979), "A Model of Output, Employment, Capital Formation and Inflation," in G. Gandolfo and F. Marzano (eds.) (1987), *Keynesian Theory, Planning Models and Quantitative Economics: Essays in Memory of Vittorio Marrama,* vol. 2. Milano: Giuffré, pp. 703–68.

Barnett, W. (1990), "Developments in Monetary Aggregation Theory," *Journal of Policy Modelling* 12: 205–57.

Barnett, W., D. Fisher, and A. Serletis (1992), "Consumer Theory and the Demand for Money," *Journal of Economic Literature* 30: 2086–2119.

Bergstrom, A. R. (1967), *The Construction and Use of Economic Models.* London: English Universities Press.

(1976), *Statistical Inference in Continuous Time Economic Models.* Amsterdam: North-Holland.

(1983), "Gaussian Estimation of Structural Parameters in Higher Order Continuous-Time Dynamic Models," *Econometrica* 51: 117–52.

(1985), "The Estimation of Parameters in Non-stationary Higher-Order Continuous Time Dynamic Models," *Econometric Theory* 1: 369–85.

(1986), "The Estimation of Open Higher-Order Continuous Time Dynamic Models with Mixed Stock and Flow Data," *Econometric Theory* 2: 350–73.

(1987), "Optimal Control in Wide-Sense Stationary Continuous Time Stochastic Models," *Journal of Economic Dynamics and Control* 11: 425–43.

(1989), "Optimal Forecasting of Discrete Stock and Flow Data Generated by a Higher Order Continuous Time System," *Computers and Mathematics with Applications* 17: 1203–14.

(1990), *Continuous Time Econometric Modeling.* Oxford University Press.

Bergstrom, A. R., K. B. Nowman, and S. Wandasiewicz (1994), "Monetary and Fiscal Policy in a Second Order Continuous Time Macro-Econometric Model of the United Kingdom," *Journal of Economic Dynamics and Control* 18: 731–61.

Bergstrom, A. R., K. B. Nowman, and C. R. Wymer (1992), "Gaussian Estimation of a Second Order Continuous Time Macroeconometric Model of the United Kingdom," *Economic Modelling* 9: 313–51.

Bergstrom, A. R., and C. R. Wymer (1976), "A Model of Disequilibrium Neoclassical Growth and Its Application to the United Kingdom," in A. R. Bergstrom (ed.), *Statistical Inference in Continuous-Time Economic Models.* Amsterdam: North-Holland, pp. 267–328.

Blanchard, O. J., and D. Quah (1989), "The Dynamic Effects of Aggregate Demand and Supply Disturbances," *American Economic Review* 79: 655–73.

Brunner, K., and A. H. Meltzer (1976), "An Aggregative Theory for a Closed Economy," in J. L. Stein (ed.), *Monetary Theory.* Amsterdam: North-Holland.

Bruno, M. (1988), "Econometrics and the Design of Economic Reform," *Econometrica* 56: 275–306.

Chambers, M. J. (1992), "The Estimation of Continuous Time Long-Memory Time Series Models," University of Essex Discussion Paper Series no. 410, Colchester, UK.

Cooper, R. J., and K. R. McLaren (1980), "Atemporal, Temporal and Intertemporal Duality in Consumer Theory," *International Economic Review* 21: 599-609.

Cooley, T. F., and S. F. LeRoy (1985), "Atheoretical Macroeconometrics: A Critique," *Journal of Monetary Economics* 16: 283-308.

Donaghy, K. P. (1992), "A Continuous Time Model of the United States Economy," in G. Gandolfo (ed.), *Continuous Time Econometrics: Theory and Applications.* London: Chapman and Hall, pp. 151-93.

Donaghy, K. P., and J. Mukherjee (1992), "Multilateral Policy Responses to Global Warming: A Differential Game Analysis," presented at Conference of the International Society of Dynamic Games (Grimementz, Switzerland), 14-17 July 1992.

Donaghy, K. P., and D. M. Richard (1992), "Flexible Functional Forms and Generalized Dynamic Adjustment in the Specification of the Demand for Money," in G. Gandolfo (ed.), *Continuous Time Econometrics: Theory and Applications.* London: Chapman and Hall.

Donaghy, K. P., and L. A. Schintler (1994), "Optimal Policies for Reducing Congestion of Major Commuting Arteries in a Growing Urbanized Area," *Journal of Planning Education and Research* 13: 189-98.

Eisner, R. E., and R. H. Strotz (1963), "Determinants of Business Investment," in *Impacts of Monetary Policy* (Commission on Money and Credit). Englewood Cliffs, NJ: Prentice-Hall, pp. 59-236.

Epstein, L. G. (1981), "Duality Theory and Functional Forms for Dynamic Factor Demands," *Review of Economic Studies* 48: 81-95.

Epstein, L. G., and M. Denny (1983), "The Multivariate Flexible Accelerator Model: Its Empirical Restrictions and an Application to U.S. Manufacturing," *Econometrica* 51: 647-74.

Gandolfo, G. (1981), *Quantitative Analysis and Economic Estimation of Continuous-Time Dynamic Models.* Amsterdam: North-Holland.

(1992), "Continuous Time Econometrics Has Come of Age," in G. Gandolfo (ed.), *Continuous Time Econometrics: Theory and Applications.* London: Chapman and Hall, pp. 1-11.

Gandolfo, G., and P. C. Padoan (1990), "The Italian Continuous Time Model: Theory and Empirical Results," *Economic Modelling* 7: 91-132.

Gandolfo, G., and M. L. Petit (1987), "Dynamic Optimization in Continuous Time and Optimal Policy Design in the Italian Economy," *Annales d'Economie et de Statistique* 5/6: 311-33.

Granger, C. W. J., and P. Newbold (1986), *Forecasting Economic Time Series.* London: Academic Press.

Hahn, F. (1983), "Comment" on A. Leijonhufvud, "Keynesianism, Monetarism and Rational Expectations," in R. Frydman and E. S. Phelps (eds.), *Individual Forecasting and Aggregate Outcomes.* Cambridge University Press, pp. 223-30.

Haken, H. (1983), *Advanced Synergetics.* Berlin: Springer-Verlag.

Hendry, D. F., and J.-F. Richard (1982), "On the Formulation of Empirical Models in Dynamic Econometrics," *Journal of Econometrics* 20: 3-33.

Hillinger, C., and M. Reiter (1992), "The Quantitative and Qualitative Explanation of Macroeconomic Investment and Production Cycles," in C. Hillinger (ed.), *Cyclical Growth in Market and Planned Economies*. Oxford: Clarendon Press.

Jonson, P. D. (1976a), "Money and Economic Activity in the Open Economy: The United Kingdom 1880–1970," *Journal of Political Economy* 84: 979–1012.

(1976b), "Money, Prices and Output; an Integrative Essay," *Kredit und Kapital* 4: 499–518.

Jonson, P. D., E. R. Moses, and C. R. Wymer (1976), "A Minimal Model of the Australian Economy," in W. E. Norton (ed.) (1977), *Conference in Applied Economic Research*. Sydney: Reserve Bank of Australia.

Kamien, M. I., and N. L. Schwartz (1981), *Dynamic Optimization*. Amsterdam: North-Holland.

Knight, M. D., and C. R. Wymer (1975), "A Monetary Model of an Open Economy with Particular Reference to the United Kingdom," in M. J. Artis and A. R. Nobay (eds.), *Proceedings of AUTE Conference, 1975*. Cambridge University Press, pp. 153–71.

(1978), "A Macroeconomic Model of the United Kingdom," *IMF Staff Papers* 25: 742–78.

Koopmans, T. C. (1950), "Models Involving a Continuous-Time Variable," in T. C. Koopmans (ed.), *Statistical Inference in Dynamic Economic Models*. New York: Wiley, pp. 384–92.

LaFrance, J. T., and L. D. Barney (1991), "The Envelope Theorem in Dynamic Optimization," *Journal of Economic Dynamics and Control* 16: 355–85.

Laidler, D. (1984), "The Buffer Stock Notion in Monetary Economics," *Conference Papers Supplement to the Economic Journal* 94: 17–84.

Levich, R. M. (1983), "Currency Forecasters Lose Their Way," *Euromoney* (August): 140–7.

Lo, A. W. (1988), "Maximum Likelihood Estimation of Generalized Ito Processes with Discretely Sampled Data," *Econometric Theory* 4: 231–47.

(1991), "Long-Term Memory in Stock Market Prices," *Econometrica* 59: 1279–1313.

Lucas, R. E. (1967), "Optimal Investment and the Flexible Accelerator," *International Economic Review* 8: 78–85.

(1975), "An Equilibrium Model of the Business Cycle," *Journal of Political Economy* 83: 1113–44.

Nieuwenhuis, H. J. (1995), *Continuous Macroeconometric Modelling with an Application to the Dutch Economy*. Den Haag: Labyrinth.

Pagan, A. R. (1987), "Three Econometric Methodologies: A Critical Appraisal," *Journal of Economic Surveys* 1: 3–24; reprinted in C. W. J. Granger (ed.) (1990), *Modelling Economic Series*. Oxford University Press, pp. 97–120.

Phillips, A. W. (1959), "The Estimation of Parameters in Systems of Stochastic Differential Equations," *Biometrika* 46: 67–76.

Phillips, P. C. B. (1991), "Error Correction and Long-Run Equilibrium in Continuous Time," *Econometrica* 59: 967–80.

Priestley, M. B. (1980), "State Dependent Models: A General Approach to Non-Linear Time Series Analysis," *Journal of Time Series Analysis* 1: 47–72.

Quandt, R. E. (1978), "Test of the Equilibrium vs Disequilibrium Hypothesis," *International Economic Review* 19: 435–52.

Reiter, M. (1993), "Evaluation of Discrete and Continuous Time Dynamic Models by Spectral Methods with an Application to Automobile Demand," Chapter 7 in this volume.

Richard, D. (1978), "A Dynamic Model of the World Copper Industry," *IMF Staff Papers* 25: 779–833.

(1980), "A Global Adjustment Model of Exchange and Interest Rates," in D. Bigman and T. Taya (eds.), *The Functioning of Floating Exchange Rates: Theory, Evidence and Policy Implications*. Cambridge, MA: Ballinger, pp. 243–76.

(1993), "National and Multinational Demands for Money and the Construction of Monetary Aggregates," mimeo, IZI, Rome.

Seierstad, A., and K. Sydsaeter (1977), "Sufficient Conditions in Optimal Control Theory," *International Economic Review* 18: 367–91.

Sims, C. A. (1980), "Macroeconomics and Reality," *Econometrica* 48: 1–48.

Treadway, A. B. (1971), "The Rational Multivariate Flexible Accelerator," *Econometrica* 39: 845–55.

Wymer, C. R. (1972), "Econometric Estimation of Stochastic Differential Equation Systems," *Econometrica* 40: 565–77; reprinted in A. R. Bergstrom (ed.) (1976), *Statistical Inference in Continuous Economic Models*. Amsterdam: North-Holland, pp. 81–95.

(1973), "A Continuous Disequilibrium Adjustment Model of the United Kingdom Financial Markets," in A. A. Powell and R. A. Williams (eds.), *Economic Studies of Macro and Monetary Relations*. Amsterdam: North-Holland, pp. 301–34.

(1975), "Estimation of Continuous Time Models with an Application to the World Sugar Market," in W. C. Labys (ed.), *Quantitative Models of Commodity Markets*. Cambridge, MA: Ballinger, pp. 173–91.

(1979), "The Use of Continuous Time Models in Economics," mimeo, International Monetary Fund, Washington, DC.

(1982), "Program Manual: Continest (and supplement)," mimeo, International Monetary Fund, Washington, DC.

(1987), "Sensitivity Analysis of Economic Policy," in G. Gandolfo and F. Marzano (eds.), *Essays in Memory of Vittorio Marrama*. Milano: Giuffré, pp. 953–65.

(1992), "Continuous Time Models in Macro-Economics: Specification and Estimation," part I presented at the SSRC–Ford Foundation Conference on Macroeconomic Policy and Adjustment in Open Economies (Ware, UK), 28 April – 1 May 1976; published with part II in G. Gandolfo (ed.), *Continuous Time Econometrics: Theory and Applications*. London: Chapman and Hall.

(1993a), "Estimation of Non-linear Differential Equation Systems," in P. C. B. Phillips (ed.), *Models, Methods and Applications of Econometrics*. Oxford: Blackwell.

(1993b), "Program Manual: Apredic (and supplement)," mimeo, International Monetary Fund, Washington, DC.

(1995), "Advances in the Estimation and Analysis of Non-linear Differential Equations in Economics," in S. K. Kuipers, L. Schoonbeek, and E. Sterken (eds.), *Methods and Applications of Economic Dynamics*. Amsterdam: North-Holland.

Continuous time models

CHAPTER 4

Nonlinear estimation of a nonlinear continuous time model

Giancarlo Gandolfo, Pier Carlo Padoan,
Giuseppe De Arcangelis, & Clifford R. Wymer

1 Introduction

The advantages of continuous time econometric modeling have been treated in depth elsewhere (see e.g. Gandolfo 1993 and Chapters 1 and 3 in this volume). Hence we will not detail them again, but would like to point out two of them briefly. As we know, econometric methods and models can be used for two main purposes, partly overlapping. One is to test a theory empirically and to discriminate between competing theories; the other is to analyze and simulate different economic policies.

With respect to the first point, consider a dynamic disequilibrium equation of the form

$$Dy = \alpha(x - v), \tag{*}$$

where D denotes the differential operator d/dt and the variables x and v are to be defined; α can represent either a parameter or a sign-preserving function. If we put $x = \hat{y}$ (where $\hat{y}$ denotes the desired or partial equilibrium value of y), $v = y$, and let α be a parameter, then we have a partial adjustment equation in the strict sense. In this case α is an adjustment speed and $1/\alpha$ is the *mean time lag,* that is, the time required for about 63 percent of the discrepancy between $\hat{y}$ and y to be eliminated by the adjustment of y in response to disequilibrium. Many other types of dynamic disequilibrium processes can be modeled through (*) by suitably

We are grateful to the Consiglio Nazionale delle Ricerche and to the University of Rome La Sapienza for generous financial support, and to the Center of Economic Studies (CES) of the University of Munich for offering an ideal environment to Giancarlo Gandolfo in September 1994 for working on the revision of this paper (a preliminary version of which appeared as a CES Working Paper under the title "The Italian Continuous Time Model: Results of the Nonlinear Estimation"). Nonincriminating thanks are also due to two unknown referees, whose comments stimulated a substantial improvement over the version originally submitted.

defining x, y, and α. Of course, higher-order adjustment equations are also possible.

Let us concentrate on the simple partial adjustment equation. The partial adjustment function (and, more generally, all continuously distributed lag adjustment functions) may have very high adjustment speeds and therefore very short mean time lags with respect to the observation period. It may therefore happen that, when the variables are measured in discrete time, the desired value practically coincides with the observed value over the period, so that it is not possible to obtain an estimate of the adjustment speed. With the continuous formulation, however, it is always possible to obtain asymptotically unbiased estimates of the adjustment speed α.

This possibility has important implications, especially when adjustment speeds play a crucial role – for example, in determining which markets clear more rapidly. We know that much theoretical debate is based on different a priori assumptions on the speeds of adjustment of markets and on the relative speeds of adjustment of different variables (e.g., quantities and prices). A neo-Keynesian, for example, will assume that quantities adjust much more rapidly than prices, so that the latter can be taken as constant in short-run dynamics (the fixed-price approach). On the other hand, a new classical macroeconomist will make the opposite assumption that prices adjust much more rapidly than quantities, so that markets clear continuously. These antagonistic assumptions are usually imposed a priori. When there is a debate between competing theories, the respective fundamental antagonistic assumptions should be confronted with the data. However, using standard discrete methods will not enable one to discriminate between speeds of adjustment that occur in a smaller amount of time than the unit period inherent in the data. The issue is so important that the availability of rigorous estimates of the adjustment speeds, independent of the observation interval, should be welcome.

With regard to the second point, suppose that we have a macroeconomic model and that the sample set consists of quarterly observations. In discrete time, after estimating the parameters of the model we can use it to perform policy simulations and forecasts for three-month intervals only. But with the continuous time approach, the estimates of the parameters of the differential equation system can be used to solve it and obtain the *continuous* paths of the endogenous variables. This might be of paramount importance for policy authorities. For example, suppose that – given a discrete time model – a simulation or optimization tells the monetary authorities that they should increase the money supply from 100 today to 102 next period (say, the quarter). But the model does not say just how M is to be brought from 100 to 102 (sudden jump, gradually, etc.) over the quarter. With the continuous time methodology, we obtain the continuous path from 100 to 102.

The Italian continuous time model is a nonlinear dynamic disequilibrium model whose construction was initiated in 1979 (the first version was published in 1980; the current Mark V version is the fifth, published in 1990). All behavioral equations are specified like (*), that is, as dynamic adjustment equations. The method previously available required a linearization for estimation purposes. Although the estimated values of the parameters could be used in the original nonlinear version for simulation and similar exercises, it would be desirable to have nonlinear estimates. This is now possible thanks to Wymer's (1993) ESCONA program. The purpose of this paper is to present these nonlinear estimates and compare the results with the previous linear estimates.

In Section 2 we give a succinct overview of the model, which has been presented at length elsewhere (Gandolfo and Padoan 1990). Section 3 summarizes the empirical results of the linearized model. The nonlinear features of the model are discussed in more depth in Section 4. The results of the nonlinear estimation and their comparison with the linear estimates are examined in Section 5. Section 6 concludes the paper.

2 Overview of the model

Our model is a medium-term disequilibrium model specified and estimated in continuous time as a set of stochastic differential equations that stresses real and financial accumulation in an open and highly integrated economy. (For a detailed treatment see Gandolfo and Padoan 1990; for reference purposes the equations of the model are given in Appendix I of this paper.) The Mark V version includes a detailed specification of the financial sector as well as endogenous determination of the exchange rate.

The model considers stock–flow behavior in an open economy in which both price and quantity adjustments take place. Stocks are introduced with reference to the real sector (where adjustments of fixed capital and inventories to their respective desired levels are present) and to the financial sector, which includes the stock of money, of commercial credit, of net foreign assets, and of international reserves. Real and financial feedbacks are therefore taken into account. Government expenditure and revenues (taxation) are also present, so that the effects of endogenous public deficits are included.

Quantity behavior equations are considered for the traditional macroeconomic variables in real terms (private consumption, net fixed investment, imports and exports of goods and services, inventory changes, net domestic product). Expectations operate through various mechanisms concerning expected real output, the effects of monetary disequilibria on the expected domestic price level, and exchange-rate expectations. A price block is included that determines the domestic price level, the nominal wage rate, and the export price level. Endogenous determination of the latter was considered crucial for an export-led economy such as Italy's, and wage–price spiral effects are explicitly taken into account. The specification of the financial sector was completed by the inclusion of an equation for interest-rate determination. The exchange rate is endogenously determined (see Section 4).

Although the model is a closely interlocked system of simultaneous differential equations, the following causal links may be singled out. Their description also allows a better understanding of the view of the economy that underlies the model itself. Let us start with the real side.

The growth process is both export- and expectations-led. Given foreign demand and prices, real exports grow according to domestic competitiveness and supply constraints. Export growth enhances output growth, which in turn modifies real expectations and consequently real capital formation. Output growth also influences real imports, aggregate public consumption, direct taxes, and the level of private consumption (through the determination of disposable income) which feed back on output. Changes in inventories, whose desired level is linked to expected output, act as a buffer in output determination.

The performance of real aggregates is also deeply influenced by money and by price behavior. The latter depends on cost-push (including exchange-rate effects) and monetary mechanisms as well as on expectations. Prices also enter into the determination of financial variables, whose behavior is closely connected with that of real variables.

A central place in the model is occupied by money and credit. Monetary disequilibria influence consumption demand, the interest rate, and price expectations. The expansion of credit, as determined by the behavior of banks, influences real capital accumulation as well as exports of goods and services. An important role is also played by the rate of interest, for it influences the demand for money (and hence real consumption), credit expansion, and the accumulation of net foreign assets. The rate of interest is determined by both market forces and policy intervention. Policy actions are represented by policy reaction functions for the money supply, the interest rate (in part), and international reserves.

In sum, our model stresses real and financial accumulation in an advanced open economy. Together with expectations, crucial roles are played by aggregate demand and supply on the one hand, and liquidity (i.e. money and credit availability) on the other.

From the formal point of view, the model is specified in logarithmic form for the analytical reasons explained in Gandolfo (1981, sec. 2.2.3), and is a nonlinear dynamic disequilibrium model; all behavioral equations are specified as dynamic adjustment equations.

It should now be stressed that the present paper is not aimed at discussing the economics of the model but rather at presenting the results of nonlinear versus linear estimation. Since our experience shows that readers (especially those unfamiliar with continuous time models) who simply look at the equations of a model may form an incorrect view of its underlying economics, we strongly urge any reader interested in the model as such to read Gandolfo and Padoan (1990) before examining the remainder of the present paper.

3   The linearized model

The log-linear version of the model was obtained by linearizing the nonlinear equations around the sample means. This version was estimated with a sample of quarterly data (running from 1960 to 1984 inclusive) using Wymer's RESIMUL program, which gives FIML estimates of the parameters. The estimated version was then subjected to extensive validation. In addition to the standard procedures (Carter–Nagar system test, standard errors of the parameters, in-sample and out-of-sample dynamic forecasts), we examined the stability properties of the model by computing the eigenvalues of the linear approximation about the steady state and their standard errors. It is interesting to note that the model has both real and complex roots, thus giving rise to cyclical behavior around the steady state, which is stable. Hence the model shows a cyclical growth behavior, which is consistent with the stylized facts of the Italian economy in the period under consideration.

Out-of-sample forecasting of the exchange rate showed that the model was able to outperform the random walk (see Gandolfo, Padoan, and Paladino 1990a,b; Gandolfo, Padoan, and De Arcangelis 1993). Ex ante simulations regarding the liberalization of capital movements were able to predict the Italian lira crisis of September 1992 (for a summary see Gandolfo and Padoan 1991, 1992).

Although we envisage a Mark VI version with many improvements, we feel that the nonlinear estimation of the current version might give useful insights into both the model's structure and the feasibility of the estimation program. Before turning to the estimation results, however, we would like to give a brief overview of the nonlinearities in the model that warrant a nonlinear estimation.

4   Nonlinearities of the model

Because the model was built with a view toward the then-available linear estimation procedure, most of the equations are linear in the logarithms. There are, however, significant nonlinearities in equations (1), (16), (17), (20), and (24) that require a detailed explanation.

In (1), real private consumption C adjusts to its desired level $\hat{C}$, given by the average propensity to consume (which is variable according to several effects) applied to real disposable income $Y - T/P$. The second term in the equation represents the effects of monetary disequilibrium on consumption. Given the logarithmic formulation of the equation, the term $\log(Y - T/P)$ is nonlinear in the logarithms.

Equation (16) is the monetary authorities' reaction function on international reserves, and is quite complicated because of the change in regime (from fixed to floating exchange rates) that occurred in the sample period. This equation has been specified to reflect the regime change, but also contains elements which are independent of the regime in force and which we may call permanent elements in the monetary authorities' behavior. Let us begin with the permanent elements, which are the leaning-against-the-wind policy and the desired reserve ratio. The Italian monetary authorities have generally followed a policy of leaning against the wind (even during the Bretton Woods era) in order to smooth out the path of the exchange rate and/or to prevent excessive fluctuations. This policy implies that international reserves move in the opposite direction to the exchange rate, hence the term $-\delta_7 D \log E$. With regard to the second permanent element, the Bank of Italy has always paid a great deal of attention to the months of financial covering of imports – that is, how long the current flow of imports can be maintained if the existing stock of reserves is used up for this purpose. This implies the existence of a desired ratio (γ_{15}) of R to the value of imports. Thus the term $\delta_8 \log(\hat{R}/R)$ can be interpreted as a partial adjustment equation of R toward $\hat{R}$.

We now come to the elements relating to the exchange-rate regime. During the Bretton Woods era, there was an obligation to maintain the exchange rate within ±1 percent of the official parity E_c. Therefore, when the actual exchange rate tended to exceed the parity, international reserves were used up (and vice versa). Hence we have the term $b\delta_5 \log(E_c/E)$, where b is a variable that takes on the value 1 during the Bretton Woods era and 0 subsequently. During the managed float regime, a constant concern of the monetary authorities has been the competitiveness of domestic goods in foreign markets, which is measured by the ratio $(PXGS/E \cdot PF_f)$. Therefore, assuming a competitiveness target γ_{14} and given $PXGS$ and PF_f, we can define a target exchange rate $\hat{E}$ as the exchange rate that fulfills the competitiveness target: $\hat{E} = PXGS/\gamma_{14}PF_f$. International reserves are used to guide the actual exchange rate toward its target value (we could also see this as a form of the PPP rule), hence the term $(1-b)\delta_6 \log(\hat{E}/E)$. Other terms could have been included, but we preferred not to burden an already overcrowded equation with additional terms. The presence of the multiplicative switching variable b is an important nonlinear feature of the model.

Equations (17), (20), and (24) are definitional equations, linear in the natural values but nonlinear in the logarithms. Equation (17) defines the change in inventories (DV) as a residual in the goods market, (20) defines the change in the public-sector borrowing requirement (DH), and (24) is the balance-of-payments definition. This last equation plays a fundamental role in our model: that of determining the exchange rate.

In order to put this point into proper perspective, we introduce the distinction between models incorporating a specific equation for the exchange rate and models where the exchange rate is implicitly determined by the balance-of-payments equation (i.e., the exchange rate is obtained by solving this equation). From a mathematical point of view the two approaches are equivalent, as can be seen from the following considerations.

Let CA denote the current account, NFA the stock of net foreign assets of the private sector, and R the stock of international reserves. Then the balance-of-payments equation simply states that

$$CA + \Delta NFA + \Delta R = 0. \tag{a}$$

Introduce now the following functional relations:

$$CA = f(F, \ldots), \tag{b}$$

$$\Delta NFA = g(E, \ldots), \tag{c}$$

$$\Delta R = h(E, \ldots), \quad \text{and} \tag{d}$$

$$E = \varphi(\ldots), \tag{e}$$

where E is the exchange rate and the dots indicate all the other explanatory variables, which for the present purposes can be considered as exogenous. Given that system (a)–(e) contains five equations in four unknowns, we can either drop (e) and use (a) to determine the exchange rate, or keep (e) and drop, say, (c) or (d); then (a) can be used to determine the capital movements balance (ΔNFA) or the reserve change (ΔR) residually.

It should be stressed that by using the balance-of-payments definition to determine the exchange rate, one is not necessarily adhering to the traditional or "flow" approach to the exchange rate, as was once incorrectly believed. A few words are in order to clarify this point. In following this approach one is simply using the fact that the exchange rate is determined in the foreign exchange market, which is reflected in the balance-of-payments equation, under the assumption that this market clears instantaneously (as it actually does, if we include the monetary authorities' demand or supply of foreign exchange as an item in this market; in our approach this item is given by (d), which defines the monetary authorities' reaction function). In fact, no theory of exchange-rate determination can be deemed satisfactory if it does not explain how the variables that it considers crucial (whether they are the stocks of assets or the flows of goods or expectations or whatever) actually translate into supply and demand in the foreign exchange market, which – together with supplies and demands coming from other sources – determine the exchange rate. If all these sources – including the monetary authorities through their reaction function (d) on the foreign exchange market – are present in the balance-of-payments equation, then (a) is no longer an identity but becomes a market-clearing condition. Thus it is perfectly legitimate (and consistent with any theory of exchange-rate determination) to use the balance-of-payments equation to calculate the exchange rate once one has specified behavioral equations for *all* the items included in the balance of payments.

A final observation: The balance-of-payments equation (a), which corresponds to equation (24) in the model, is a nonlinear implicit function in the exchange rate, which then turns out to be a nonlinear function of all the other endogenous variables (via the implicit function theorem). Here we have a case in which there is a strong theoretical motive for a variable (the exchange rate) to be nonlinear. Hence the results of Sabani (1993) on the nonlinearity of the exchange rate have a clear theoretical explanation.

5   Results of the nonlinear estimation

The model, after a few manipulations required by the estimation program (see Appendix II), was estimated using Wymer's (1993) ESCONA program for nonlinear estimation. This requires initial parameter values, which have been set equal to the parameter estimates obtained in the linearized version of the model. The data set is of course the same as that used in the estimation of the linearized model (1960-I to 1984-IV) and fully described in Gandolfo and Padoan (1990, apx. 2).

The initial estimation runs of the model have been performed on the mainframe computer (an IBM 3090) of the University of Rome La Sapienza. Owing to the enormous computation time required, the estimation was later transferred to an IBM RISC/6000 Unix workstation. The increase in computation time was only about 20 percent, and thanks to the processor's internal precision, the estimates are much more accurate. Every run usually takes several days of uninterrupted and almost fully dedicated computation before obtaining the first stable parameter estimates.

Table 1. *Estimated adjustment parameters*

Para-meter	Entering equation number	Linear estimates			Nonlinear estimates		
		Point estimate (a)	Asymptotic standard error (b)	(c) = (a)/(b)	Point estimate (a)	Asymptotic standard error (b)	(c) = (a)/(b)
α_1	(1)	1.147	0.214	5.37	2.181	0.227	9.60
α_2	(1)	0.114	0.041	2.77	0.363	0.013	28.67
α_3	(2)	1.003	0.178	5.64	0.109	0.023	4.74
α_4	(2)	0.112	0.014	8.14	0.137	0.043	3.17
α_5	(4)	0.500	0.157	5.90	1.035	0.059	17.43
α_6	(4)	0.329	0.125	2.62	0.094	0.033	2.82
α_7	(4)	0.021	0.010	2.05	0.000[a]		
α_8	(5)	0.869	0.142	6.09	0.917	0.101	9.12
α_9	(5)	0.618	0.219	2.81	−5.941	0.796	7.46
α_{10}	(6)	1.879	0.273	6.88	3.367	0.020	172.04
α_{11}	(6)	0.573	0.058	9.88	0.462	0.002	270.88
α_{12}	(7)	0.493	0.111	4.44	0.105	0.005	22.92
α_{13}	(7)	0.313	0.114	2.75	0.382	0.004	97.65
α_{14}	(7)	0.122	0.058	2.07	0.017	0.003	5.66
α_{15}	(8)	0.340	0.113	3.02	0.359	0.026	13.99
α_{16}	(9)	0.383	0.103	3.71	0.644	0.180	4.29
α_{17}	(10)	0.030	0.007	4.17	-9.73×10^{-6}	1.24×10^{-4}	0.08
α_{18}	(10)	0.073	0.003	25.68	−0.004	0.004	1.20
α_{19}	(10)	0.181	0.007	27.13	0.052	0.005	9.92
α_{20}	(10)	0.049	0.005	13.78	−0.059	0.003	17.38
α_{21}	(10)	0.085	0.004	21.73	−0.008	0.002	4.39
α_{22}	(11)	0.140	0.026	5.35	0.036	0.005	7.37
α_{23}	(11)	−2.904	0.516	5.63	2.425	0.398	6.09
α_{24}	(12)	0.091	0.032	2.84	0.059	0.002	25.09
α_{25}	(12)	−0.182	0.029	6.15	−0.124	0.010	12.07
α_{26}	(13)	4.095	0.938	4.36	4.735	0.020	239.89
α_{27}	(14)	0.155	0.055	2.81	0.076	0.059	1.29
α_{28}	(15)	0.401	0.110	3.61	0.638	0.039	16.42
α_{29}	(15)	−3.410	0.654	5.21	−4.753	0.216	22.00
α'	(2)	0.059	0.004	15.71	0.027	0.005	5.33
η	(3)	0.083	0.025	3.27	0.106	0.004	28.20

[a] Value imposed.

For instance, the last run that gave rise to the estimates reported in this paper took about 160 hours *after* the initialization that produced the Hessian matrix (which itself took about 50 hours).

The estimation results are presented in Tables 1 and 2. For ease of comparison, the estimates obtained through the linearized version (Gandolfo

Table 2. *Other estimated parameters*

Parameter	Entering equation number	Linear estimates			Nonlinear estimates		
		Point estimate (a)	Asymptotic standard error (b)	(c) = (a)/(b)	Point estimate (a)	Asymptotic standard error (b)	(c) = (a)/(b)
β_1	(1)	−1.296	0.299	4.33	2.205	0.009	232.29
β_2	(1)	0.000^a			0.000^a		
β_3	(1),(7),(10)	2.237	0.968	2.31	−0.330	0.641	0.52
β_4	(1),(7),(10)	1.135	0.109	10.43	1.025	0.059	17.50
β_5	(1),(7),(10)	1.480	0.164	9.01	1.245	0.016	77.51
β_6	(4)	0.672	0.140	4.81	0.522	0.021	24.74
β_7	(4)	0.547	0.101	5.41	0.413	0.021	20.13
β_8	(4)	1.166	0.158	7.38	1.497	0.006	251.32
β_9	(5)	0.378	0.082	4.58	0.985	0.163	6.03
β_{10}	(5)	0.500	0.128	5.14	0.465	0.015	30.94
β_{11}	(5)	0.945	0.112	8.49	1.125	0.032	35.55
β_{12}	(7)	0.330	0.047	6.94	0.432	0.045	9.64
β_{13}	(7)	0.501	0.046	10.87	0.510	0.019	26.82
β_{14}	(7)	0.000^a					
β_{15}	(8)	0.480	0.081	5.92	0.133	0.052	2.58
β_{16}	(8)	0.404	0.070	5.79	0.811	0.037	22.20
β_{17}	(9)	0.629	0.041	15.45	0.816	0.031	25.98
β_{18}	(11)	−2.340	0.294	7.96	−5.587	2.104	2.66
β_{19}	(12)	9.026	3.281	2.75	6.171	0.063	93.66
β_{20}	(12)	1.000^a			1.000^a		
β_{21}	(12)	1.000^a			1.000^a		
β_{22}	(14)	1.101	0.048	22.92	1.000^a		
λ_4	(9)	0.019	0.001	16.94	0.012	4.46×10^{-4}	27.97
δ_1	(13)	0.103	0.049	2.08	0.110	0.001	96.64
δ_2	(13)	−0.092	0.080	1.14	−0.081	7.35×10^{-4}	110.60
δ_3	(13)	0.367	0.081	4.51	0.003	0.002	1.79
δ_4	(13)	0.065	0.031	2.02	0.092	7.52×10^{-4}	122.10
δ_5	(16)	−0.390	0.376	1.04	0.000^a		
δ_6	(16)	−0.126	0.200	0.63	0.333	0.042	8.02
δ_7	(16)	0.927	0.188	4.92	1.861	0.028	67.44
δ_8	(16)	0.282	0.038	7.39	0.043	0.004	12.07
γ_1	(1)	0.764	0.005	152.72	0.939	0.439	2.14
γ_2	(1),(7),(10)	0.0006	0.0007	0.83	0.033	0.002	16.79
γ_3	(2)	6.011	0.288	20.84	2.622	0.080	32.77
γ_4	(4)	0.089	0.107	0.82	0.005	5.50×10^{-4}	90.84
γ_5	(4),(6)	1.009	0.061	16.60	1.581	0.050	31.66
γ_6	(5)	0.199	0.197	1.01	9.894	0.240	41.28
γ_7	(7)	1.264	0.226	5.58	1.023	0.485	2.11
γ_8	(8)	1.061	0.022	48.88	1.084	0.113	9.58
γ_9	(9)	0.742	0.017	42.51	0.727	0.026	27.63

Para-meter	Entering equation number	Linear estimates			Nonlinear estimates		
		Point estimate (a)	Asymptotic standard error (b)	(c) = (a)/(b)	Point estimate (a)	Asymptotic standard error (b)	(c) = (a)/(b)
γ_{10}	(11)	0.0095	0.0004	20.67	266.400	11.809	22.56
γ_{11}	(12)	0.00036	0.00007	4.95	omitted		
γ_{12}	(14)	0.134	0.048	2.80	0.173	0.016	10.73
γ_{13}	(15)	0.252	0.007	33.94	0.334	0.009	38.71
γ_{14}	(16)	1.000[a]			0.832	0.153	5.44
γ_{15}	(16)	1.147	0.213	5.37	1.695	0.249	6.81

[a] Value imposed.

and Padoan 1990) are also given in these tables. All parameters are, of course, more or less different. If we adopt $\pm 2\sigma$ intervals around the linear estimates, about 50 percent of the parameters are different; this proportion falls to 42 percent if we adopt the higher confidence interval $\pm 3\sigma$.

At any rate, given that these intervals are only asymptotically meaningful, we feel that in order to extract some economic sense from the numbers it is more important to concentrate on those equations where major differences exist. By "major" differences we mean those that entail the loss of significance of a previously significant parameter and vice versa, or a change in a parameter's sign and hence a qualitatively different economic explanation. We shall also examine minor differences, that is, where the parameter sign does not change but the numerical difference is important from an economic point of view. It should first be noted that the γs are sometimes very different. However, since they usually represent scale parameters, we assume their numerical differences as not relevant in our comparison.

5.1 Major differences

5.1.1 Interest rate
The most important differences pertain to equation (10), the interest-rate determination equation. For the reader's convenience we transcribe the equation here:

$$Di_{TIT} = \alpha_{17}\log(M_d/M) + \alpha_{18}[i_f + \log(FR/E) - i_{TIT}]$$
$$+ \alpha_{19}D\log E + \alpha_{20}Dr + \alpha_{21}Dh.$$

The interest-rate equation is one of the most "crowded" equations in the model, reflecting the hybrid nature of this variable in the Italian economy for the sample period. The first effect is domestic and is represented by the excess demand for money, which may be viewed in either the traditional textbook context or the context of the buffer stock notion discussed in Section 5.1.4. The second term is related to the well-known interest-rate parity condition (IRPC) (see e.g. Gandolfo 1995, sec. 10.7; Gandolfo and Padoan 1990, pp. 100–1). In the Italian economy for the sample period the mobility of capital was far from perfect, so a discrepancy between the two sides of the IRPC gives rise to a limited amount of capital flow – see (12) – and hence to a tendency for the domestic interest rate to move toward closing this discrepancy. The speed of adjustment is measured by α_{18} and depends, inter alia, on the authorities' control on capital movements. The term under consideration thus reflects policy considerations also.

The third term, $a_{19} D \log E$, is the reflection on the interest rate of the monetary authorities' intervention to smooth the behavior of the exchange rate, and must be seen in conjunction with the analogous term in (16). When the authorities follow a policy of leaning against the wind, they use both direct intervention in the foreign exchange market and interest-rate changes to pursue their goal. If, for example, they wish to contrast a devaluation in the exchange rate ($D \log E > 0$), they will both consume international reserves (hence the term $-\delta_5 D \log E$ in (16)) and increase the interest rate to favor capital inflows (or check capital outflows). Similar considerations underlie the fourth term, $\alpha_{20} Dr$. If, in the case under consideration, reserves are being used up at an increasing rate ($Dr > 0$), the increase in the interest rate will tend to be greater, ceteris paribus. If, on the contrary, reserves accumulate at an increasing rate ($Dr > 0$ but with $D \log R$ positive rather than negative), the interest rate can be decreased. Thus α_{20} can be either positive or negative on a priori grounds.

The fifth (and last) term in (10) represents the influence of the rate of change of the public deficit, a proxy for the acceleration of the stock of public debt. In the sample period, what seems to have really mattered in Italy (for institutional reasons) is neither the ratio of public debt to GDP nor the rate of change of public debt but rather the *acceleration* of public debt, whose effect on the rate of interest can be twofold. On the one hand, the higher this acceleration, the higher the interest rate the authorities must offer – ceteris paribus – to convince the public to buy an increasing amount of government bonds ($\alpha_{21} > 0$). On the other hand, when the stock of public debt is accelerating, the authorities try to decrease the interest rate to reduce the burden of interest payments and hence $\alpha_{21} < 0$.

We now come to the empirical results. As can be seen from Table 1, α_{17} (the parameter associated with the excess demand for money) and α_{18} (the parameter associated with the interest-rate differential) are no longer significantly different from zero. Both α_{20} and α_{21}, the parameters associated (respectively) with the rate of change of international reserves and with the rate of change of the public sector's borrowing requirement, now show a negative sign. The only parameter that has remained qualitatively unchanged is α_{19}, which is associated with the rate of change of the exchange rate. Although the change in the sign of α_{20} and α_{21} is consistent with our economic interpretation of the equation, the disappearance of any effect of the excess demand for money, as well as of the interest rate differential, is clearly due to data problems. In fact, the domestic interest rate that should be used in order to be consistent with the theory is the short-term interest rate (i_f is the short-term U.S. interest rate). However, due to data limitations at the time of the linear estimates, the long-term Italian government bond yield was used as a proxy for the domestic interest rate. Hence, what the estimation results really show is that this proxy functions only in a sufficiently small neighborhood (the linear approximation) but not when the exact (nonlinear) structure is used. In future versions of the model we shall certainly use more appropriate data.

5.1.2 *Exports*
Another equation in which a major difference appears is (5), the export function:

$$D \log XGS = \alpha_8 \log(X\hat{G}S/XGS) - \alpha_9 Da, \quad \text{where}$$
$$X\hat{G}S = \gamma_4(PXGS/PF_f \cdot E)^{-\beta_9} YF^{\beta_{10}}(\gamma_3 Y/K)^{-\beta_{11}}.$$

In this equation, real exports of goods and services adjust to their partial equilibrium level as determined by foreign demand for exports and by a supply constraint. Foreign demand, in turn, depends on relative prices and on world income. Given the effect of foreign demand, the partial equilibrium level of exports also reflects the influence of domestic supply, represented by the deviations of the output/capital ratio from its desired value $(1/\gamma_3)$; these can be considered as a proxy for the degree of capacity utilization. In other words, as the utilization of productive capacity increases, the negative impact of a supply constraint will be felt on exports.

The inclusion of the variation of the rate of change of bank advances is due to the observation that, for the sample period, when a credit squeeze occurred the Italian producers tried to increase the expansion of exports. The reason is that by so doing they could circumvent the credit squeeze, which did not hold for export credits. Since $Da = D^2 \log A$ is the acceleration of bank advances, a positive value of Da is consistent with both a restrictive $(D \log A < 0)$ and an expansionary $(D \log A > 0)$ credit scenario; hence α_9 can be either positive or negative on a priori grounds. As Table 1 shows, α_9 has changed sign, becoming significantly negative. This is consistent with the theory and confirms the existence of the effect that Da was meant to capture.

Let us also note a difference that, although minor according to our classification, pertains to the question under consideration and hence is more conveniently examined here than in Section 5.2. This difference pertains to the price elasticity of exports, β_9, which has increased considerably. This shows that elasticity estimates by a linear approximation may be far from the true nonlinear estimates. Given the paramount importance of foreign trade elasticities (consider e.g. the Marshall–Lerner condition) and the fact that actual relative price changes due to exchange-rate swings may be far from "sufficiently small," the possible unreliability of the usual (linear) estimates of these elasticities should be a matter of concern in all policy discussions of exchange-rate management and regimes.

5.1.3   *Monetary authorities' reaction function on international reserves*

A third equation where we find a major difference is (16). As this equation has already been commented on in detail (see Section 4), we can examine the estimation results directly. Table 2 shows that δ_6 (the parameter related to the management of floating exchange rates), which was not significantly different from zero in the linear estimates, is now significantly positive in conformity with our a priori. However, it has not been possible to improve the situation regarding δ_5, which was and remains not significantly different from zero. (In the nonlinear estimates it has actually been constrained to zero, since in earlier stages of estimation it was never significantly different from zero and the constraint improved the efficiency of the estimates.)

Minor differences in this equation concern δ_7 and δ_8, whose numerical values suggest a greater importance of the leaning-against-the-wind policy and a smaller importance of the desired level of international reserves.

5.1.4   *Consumption function*

One major difference is also present in equation (1), the consumption function:

$$D \log C = \alpha_1 \log(\hat{C}/C) + \alpha_2 \log(M/M_d), \quad \text{where}$$

$$\hat{C} = \gamma_1 e^{\beta_1 D \log Y}(P/PMGS_f \cdot E)^{\beta_2}(Y - T/P), \quad \beta_1 \gtrless 0, \quad \beta_2 \gtrless 0.$$

In this equation, real private consumption adjusts to its desired level $\hat{C}$, which is given by the average propensity to consume applied to real disposable income. The propensity to consume, in turn, is a function of other variables. First, it may vary over the trade cycle, either procyclically ($\beta_1 > 0$) or anticyclically ($\beta_1 < 0$); the latter possibility arises if a ratchet effect is operative. Second, in an open economy consumption may vary with the terms of trade. This is known as the Laursen–Metzler effect, which yields an uncertain sign when both domestic and import prices vary at the same time (see Gandolfo and Padoan 1990).

The second term in the equation represents the effect of monetary disequilibrium on consumption. This is an important issue that is related to the role of money as a buffer stock. As shown in Gandolfo and Padoan (1990, p. 96), this role implies that monetary disequilibrium (a discrepancy between actual and desired cash balances) will induce the agents to move toward their long-run target demand for money by changing both their consumption demand (hence the term under consideration) *and* the demand for bonds (hence the monetary disequilibrium term in the interest-rate equation discussed previously). To complete the summary of the role of money in the model, we should note the importance of monetary disequilibrium in the inflationary process. Suppose that we have a price equation of the type

$$D \log P = f(\ldots) + c\pi,$$

where π represents inflationary expectations and the specification of the arguments of f need not concern us here. If we hypothesize that inflationary expectations depend on the excess supply of money, $\pi = n \log(M/M_d)$, we have

$$D \log P = f(\ldots) + \alpha \log(M/M_d), \quad \alpha = cn,$$

which is the formulation used in (7) (to be discussed in Section 5.2).

We now come to the estimates. The difference consists in that, whereas the linear estimate showed a significant anticyclical behavior of the propensity to consume ($\beta_1 < 0$), the nonlinear estimate points to the opposite result of a significant procyclical behavior ($\beta_1 > 0$). Both results are, of course, consistent with the theory of the consumption function, as shown by allowing $\beta_1 \gtrless 0$ in writing the theoretical model.

5.1.5 *Money demand*
Finally, one major difference is also to be found in the ubiquitous demand-for-money function (cf. our previous comments on the role of monetary disequilibrium in the model):

$$M_d = \gamma_2 e^{-\beta_3 i_{T/T}} P^{\beta_4} Y^{\beta_5}, \quad \beta_3 \gtrless 0.$$

Traditional demand-for-money theory requires that the sign of the partial derivative of money demand with respect to the interest rate be negative. Hence, in our specification the interest-rate semielasticity ($-\beta_3$) should be negative. However, since the variable employed to represent the money stock (M2) includes bank deposits whose demand is positively related to the rate of interest on these deposits (a rate that in Italy was closely related to i_{TIT}), the sign of β_3 could be either positive or negative on a priori grounds. In fact, the difference between the linear and nonlinear estimates does show a significant change in the sign of β_3, from positive to negative.

Let us now turn to the minor differences, excluding of course those that have already been examined in conjunction with the major ones.

5.2   Minor differences

These differences mainly concern the price–wage sector, equations (7), (8), and (9). In (7),

$$D \log P = \alpha_{12} \log(\hat{P}/P) + \alpha_{13} Dm + \alpha_{14} \log(M/M_d),$$

$$\hat{P} = \gamma_7 (PMGS_f E)^{\beta_{12}} W^{\beta_{13}} PROD^{\beta_{14}},$$

the domestic price level P adjusts toward a partial equilibrium level $\hat{P}$ that is basically determined by cost-push factors, but the easiness of monetary conditions and expectations also play a crucial role. The determinants of $\hat{P}$ are both domestic and foreign. Import prices capture the effect of an increase in the cost of imported factors of production, as well as a possible foreign competitiveness effect that induces domestic producers to take into account the prices of competing imported goods when they determine the prices of their products. The push from domestic costs is represented both by the level of the nominal wage rate W and, with an inverse relationship, by the level of productivity $PROD$.

The second and third terms in (7) are both related to monetary factors, but have a completely different meaning and should thus be kept distinct. Although the basic determinants of $\hat{P}$ are cost-push factors, the *speed* at which P adjusts to $\hat{P}$ is an increasing function of the easiness of monetary conditions (as represented by Dm), namely $\alpha_{12} = \varphi(Dm)$, $\varphi' > 0$. A suitable approximation then gives the second term under consideration. Finally, the third term represents the effect of inflationary expectations, as already clarified in Section 5.1.4.

Equation (7) must be viewed in conjunction with the wage equation (8), for together they represent the wage–price spiral that was operative in the Italian economy during the sample period:

$$D \log W = \alpha_{16} \log(\hat{W}/W), \quad \hat{W} = \gamma_9 P^{\beta_{17}} e^{\lambda_4 t}.$$

In this equation, the nominal wage rate adjusts to its partial equilibrium level, which is a direct function of the domestic price level. Institutional factors (such as, e.g., a dominant "social pressure" in Hicks's sense) suggest that target nominal wages exceed the level that would be determined by domestic price behavior alone. These factors have been taken into account by introducing a trend among the determinants of $\hat{W}$.

The introduction of a separate equation for export prices,

$$D \log PXGS = \alpha_{15} \log(P X \hat{G} S / PXGS), \quad P X \hat{G} S = \gamma_8 P^{\beta_{15}} (PF_f \cdot E)^{\beta_{16}},$$

is justified by the consideration that exporting firms adjust export prices, taking account not only of the same elements that enter into the determination and adjustment of domestic prices (though with a different weight, hence the parameter β_{15}) but also of the foreign competition barrier. This is represented by the level of foreign competitors' export prices as defined in the export equation, which has an obvious positive effect of the level of $P X \hat{G} S$.

The estimation results concerning (7) and (8) are best examined together. On the one hand, wages show a higher adjustment speed (α_{16} is significantly greater) to the desired level, which in turn is more elastic to domestic prices (β_{17} is significantly greater) and less dependent on exogenous factors (λ_4 is significantly lower). This points to a more dangerous functioning of the price–wage spiral during the sample period with respect to the price/wage ratio. On the other hand, prices show a much lower adjustment speed (α_{12} is significantly much smaller) to the cost-push term, one of whose components is the wage rate. This points to a less dangerous functioning of the price–wage spiral. All in all, the price–wage spiral subsystem remains stable, since the crucial stability condition $\beta_{13}\beta_{17} < 0$ is still fulfilled (see Gandolfo and Padoan 1990, p. 112).

The estimates concerning the partial equilibrium level of export prices show that its elasticity with respect to the domestic price level (β_{15}) is lower, while the elasticity with respect to foreign competitors' prices (β_{16}) is higher.

A final result worth mentioning concerns the investment function:

$$Dk = \alpha_3[\alpha' \log(\hat{K}/K) - k)] + \alpha_4 Da, \quad \hat{K} = \gamma_3 \tilde{Y}.$$

The investment function implicit in this equation is an evolution of the capital stock adjustment principle, which in turn is sufficiently general to accommodate any investment theory. The traditional version of this principle states that actual net fixed investment $I \equiv DK$, is a function of the difference between the desired capital stock $\hat{K}$ and the actual capital stock K. In our opinion, this difference does not give rise directly to net investment, but rather is the determinant of *desired* investment $\hat{I}$. We then assume that the relevant economic agents adjust the actual rate of growth of the capital stock to the desired rate $\hat{k} \equiv \hat{I}/K$ according to the partial adjustment equation $Dk = \alpha_3(\hat{k} - k)$. A second modification that we introduce is that $\hat{K}$ is related not to current output, but rather to expected

Table 3. *Root-mean-square errors for in-sample static forecasts*

Variable	Nonlinear estimates	Linear estimates
C	.018922	.030024
k	.001223	.001603
MGS	.060118	.066917
XGS	.059520	.052224
Y	.027724	.028006
P	.014275	.027197
$PXGS$	.020802	.022233
W	.021175	.032797
i_{TIT}	.007153	.016664
A	.013401	.013023
NFA	.035449	.084420
m	.009573	.013421
T	.046692	.045970
G	.047041	.048399
R	.053497	.156233
V	.026739	.049497
E	.038677	.090363
H	.042999	.043023

output $\tilde{Y}$. This gives rise to the first term in the investment equation (which is very similar to the second-order accelerator developed independently by Hillinger 1992, chap. 8). The second term in the investment function is related to the idea that the speed at which $\hat{k}$ adjusts to k is a function of credit conditions (which in the Italian economy have a great influence also on fixed investment); namely, $\alpha_3 = \psi(Da)$. A suitable approximation then gives the term under consideration.

In the nonlinear estimates, both α_3 and α' are significantly lower, thus reinforcing the results obtained with the linearized version that stocks play the role of "order" variables – in the sense of synergetics (see Gandolfo and Padoan 1990, pp. 92, 110) – in the model. The value of γ_3 has decreased from 6.0 to a more reasonable 2.6.

5.3   Forecasting performance

Let us now consider the in-sample predictive performance of the model. Since our purpose is to compare the goodness of fit of the model with the two sets of parameter estimates, we have computed the in-sample single-period forecasts. (See Gandolfo and Padoan 1984, pp. 10–11, for the continuous time equivalent of the standard discrete time single-period forecasts.)

The results are given in Table 3. It should be remembered that the variables are expressed in logarithms or as percentages; consequently, the root-mean-square (rms) error gives the average error as a proportion of the actual level of the endogenous variable. In most cases the fit is fairly good, and in a few cases very good.

The rms errors obtained using the nonlinear estimates are generally better (and in some cases remarkably better) than those obtained using the linear estimates; in just a few cases, the results are (only slightly) worse. Hence the nonlinear estimation procedure does provide parameter estimates that yield a closer fit of the model to the data.

6   Conclusion

The nonlinear estimation of our nonlinear model has generally confirmed the qualitative robustness of the model. It has also pointed out, however, some interesting differences in the estimates, especially regarding the monetary variables. These differences suggest that a nonlinear estimation of a nonlinear model does provide additional value, since it can more fully extract the information contained in the data and so bring theory and facts closer together. This is also shown in the improvement of the in-sample performance of the model. It is, however, a matter of cost–benefit analysis as to whether this additional value justifies the extraordinarily increased computational time required on the present generation of computers.

Appendix I

Table A.1 lists the equations that constitute the model, and Table A.2 defines the endogenous and exogenous variables used in the equations.

Appendix II

As stated in the text (Section 5) the model had to undergo a few manipulations before being fed to the computer for estimation. These were due to some limitations in the current version of the program, which cannot accept higher-order derivatives of the endogenous variables without specifying them as truly endogenous – that is, without specifying for them the respective behavioral equations or definitions.

Table A.1. *Equations of the model*

Private consumption

$$D \log C = \alpha_1 \log(\hat{C}/C) + \alpha_2 \log(M/M_d), \quad \text{where} \tag{1}$$

$$\hat{C} = \gamma_1 e^{\beta_1 D \log Y}(P/PMGS_f \cdot E)^{\beta_2}(Y - T/P), \quad \beta_1 \gtreqless 0, \ \beta_2 \gtreqless 0;$$

$$M_d = \gamma_2 e^{-\beta_3 i_{TIT}} P^{\beta_4} Y^{\beta_5}, \quad \beta_3 \gtreqless 0. \tag{1.1}$$

Rate of growth in fixed capital stock

$$Dk = \alpha_3[\alpha' \log(\hat{K}/K) - k] + \alpha_4 Da, \quad \text{where} \tag{2}$$

$$\hat{K} = \gamma_3 \tilde{Y}, \quad \gamma_3 = \kappa/u. \tag{2.1}$$

Expected output

$$D \log \tilde{Y} = \eta \log(Y/\tilde{Y}). \tag{3}$$

Imports

$$D \log MGS = \alpha_5 \log(M\hat{G}S/MGS) + \alpha_6 \log(\hat{V}/V) + \alpha_7 PCC, \quad \text{where} \tag{4}$$

$$M\hat{G}S = \gamma_4 P^{\beta_6}(PMGS_f \cdot E)^{-\beta_7} Y^{\beta_8}, \quad \hat{V} = \gamma_5 \tilde{Y}. \tag{4.1}$$

Exports

$$D \log XGS = \alpha_8 \log(X\hat{G}S/XGS) - \alpha_9 Da, \quad \text{where} \tag{5}$$

$$X\hat{G}S = \gamma_6 (PXGS/PF_f \cdot E)^{-\beta_9} YF^{\beta_{10}}(\gamma_3 Y/K)^{-\beta_{11}}. \tag{5.1}$$

Output

$$D \log Y = \alpha_{10} \log(\tilde{Y}/Y) + \alpha_{11} \log(\hat{V}/V). \tag{6}$$

Price of output

$$D \log P = \alpha_{12} \log(\hat{P}/P) + \alpha_{13} Dm + \alpha_{14} \log(M/M_d), \quad \text{where} \tag{7}$$

$$\hat{P} = \gamma_7 (PMGS_f \cdot E)^{\beta_{12}} W^{\beta_{13}} PROD^{-\beta_{14}}. \tag{7.1}$$

Price of exports

$$D \log PXGS = \alpha_{15} \log(PX\hat{G}S/PXGS), \quad \text{where} \tag{8}$$

$$PX\hat{G}S = \gamma_8 P^{\beta_{15}}(PF_f \cdot E)^{\beta_{16}}. \tag{8.1}$$

Money wage rate

$$D \log W = \alpha_{16} \log(\hat{W}/W), \quad \text{where} \tag{9}$$

$$\hat{W} = \gamma_9 P^{\beta_{17}} e^{\lambda_4 t}. \tag{9.1}$$

Interest rate

$$Di_{TIT} = \alpha_{17} \log(M_d/M) + \alpha_{18}[i_f + \log(FR/E) - i_{TIT}] + \alpha_{19} \log E + \alpha_{20} Dr + \alpha_{21} Dh. \tag{10}$$

Bank advances

$$D \log A = \alpha_{22} \log(\hat{A}/A) + \alpha_{23} Dk, \quad \alpha_{23} \gtreqless 0, \quad \text{where} \tag{11}$$

$$\hat{A} = \gamma_{10} e^{\beta_{18} i_{TIT}} M, \quad \beta_{18} \gtreqless 0. \tag{11.1}$$

Net foreign assets

$$D \log NFA = \alpha_{24} \log(N\hat{F}A/NFA) + \alpha_{25} \log(PMGS_f \cdot E \cdot MGS/PXGS \cdot XGS),$$

$$\alpha_{25} < 0, \quad \text{where} \tag{12}$$

$$N\hat{F}A = \gamma_{11} e^{\beta_{19}[i_f + \log(FR/E) - i_T/T]} (PY)^{\beta_{20}} (PF_f \cdot E \cdot YF)^{\beta_{21}}. \tag{12.1}$$

Monetary authorities' reaction function on money supply

$$Dm = \alpha_{26}(\hat{m} - m) + \delta_3 Dh + \delta_4 Dr, \quad \text{where} \tag{13}$$

$$\hat{m} = m^* + \{\delta_1[D \log(PY) - (\rho_P + \rho_Y)] + \delta_2 Di_{T/T}\}, \quad \delta_1 \gtrless 0, \ \delta_2 \gtrless 0. \tag{13.1}$$

Taxes

$$D \log T = \alpha_{27} \log(\hat{T}/T), \quad \text{where} \tag{14}$$

$$\hat{T} = \gamma_{12}(PY)^{\beta_{22}}. \tag{14.1}$$

Public expenditure

$$D \log G = \alpha_{28} \log(\gamma_{13} Y/G) + \alpha_{29} D \log Y, \quad \alpha_{29} \gtrless 0. \tag{15}$$

Monetary authorities' reaction function on international reserves

$$D \log R = b\delta_5 \log(E_c/E) + (1 - b)\delta_6 \log(\hat{E}/E) - \delta_7 D \log E + \delta_8 \log(\hat{R}/R), \quad \text{where} \tag{16}$$

$$\hat{E} = PXGS/\gamma_{14} PF_f, \quad \hat{R} = \gamma_{15} PMGS_f \cdot E \cdot MGS,$$

$$b = \begin{cases} 1 & \text{under fixed exchange rates,} \\ 0 & \text{under floating exchange rates.} \end{cases}$$

Inventories

$$DV = Y + MGS - C - DK - XGS - G. \tag{17}$$

Fixed capital stock

$$D \log K = k. \tag{18}$$

Rate of growth in money supply

$$m = D \log M. \tag{19}$$

Public sector's borrowing requirement

$$DH = PG - T. \tag{20}$$

Rate of growth in international reserves

$$r = D \log R. \tag{21}$$

Rate of growth in bank advances

$$a = D \log A. \tag{22}$$

Rate of growth in H

$$h = D \log H. \tag{23}$$

Balance of payments

$$PXGS \cdot XGS - PMGS_f \cdot E \cdot MGS + (UT_a - UT_p) - DNFA - DR = 0. \tag{24}$$

Table A.2. *Variables of the model*

Endogenous variables

A = nominal stock of bank advances
a = proportional rate of growth of A
C = private consumption expenditure in real terms
E = lira/dollar spot exchange rate
G = public expenditure in real terms
H = public sector borrowing requirement
h = proportional rate of change of H
i_{TIT} = domestic nominal interest rate
K = stock of fixed capital in real terms
k = proportional rate of change of K
M = nominal stock of money (M2)
m = proportional rate of change of M
MGS = imports of goods and services in real terms
NFA = nominal stock of net foreign assets
P = domestic price level
$PXGS$ = export price level
R = nominal stock of international reserves
r = proportional rate of change of R
T = nominal taxes
V = stock of inventories in real terms
W = money wage rate
XGS = exports of goods and services in real terms
Y = real net domestic product and income
$\tilde{Y}$ = expected real net domestic product and income

Exogenous variables

E_c = official lira/dollar parity under fixed exchange rates
FR = forward exchange rate
i_f = foreign nominal interest rate
PF_f = foreign competitors' export price level (in foreign currency)
$PMGS_f$ = import price level (in foreign currency)
$PROD$ = labor productivity
t = time
$UT_a - UT_p$ = net unilateral transfers, in nominal terms
YF = real world income

The model contains a number of second-order derivatives. In particular, Dk and Dm are explicit in (2) and (12), whereas Da, Dr, and Dh must be indirectly derived from the specification of the relative first-order derivatives (i.e., equations (11), (16), and (20)). Whereas no difficulties were encountered for the explicit Dk and Dm, the following strategies have been adopted to circumvent the problem due to the presence of Da, Dr, and Dh.

In estimation, Da has been substituted for a, since the theory about the influence of credit on capital formation (see equation (2)) and on export dynamics (equation (5)) would allow this replacement (see Gandolfo and Padoan 1990).

The solution for the case of the other two variables was more complicated. First, (20) has been divided by H and then differentiated in order to obtain Dh explicitly (note that this causes H to disappear from the model as an endogenous variable). Second, DR has been isolated from (24). Next, both sides of the equation have been divided by R in order to yield r (i.e., $D \log R$) on the left-hand side. Finally, the equation thus obtained has been differentiated to yield Dr. By so doing, the new equation requires $D^2 \log NFA$ (i.e., $DNFA$), which has been obtained by differentiating (11) as well. As a consequence, the value of the intercept term of this last equation, γ_{11}, cannot be estimated since it disappears in the differentiation.

REFERENCES

Gandolfo, G. (1981), *Qualitative Analysis and Econometric Estimation of Continuous Time Dynamic Models*. Amsterdam: North-Holland.

—— (1993), "Continuous Time Econometrics Has Come of Age," in G. Gandolfo (ed.), *Continuous Time Econometrics: Theory and Applications*. London: Chapman and Hall, pp. 1–11.

—— (1995), *International Monetary Theory and Open Economy Macroeconomics* (International Economics, vol. II). Berlin: Springer-Verlag.

Gandolfo, G., and P. C. Padoan (1984), *A Disequilibrium Model of Real and Financial Accumulation in an Open Economy*. Berlin: Springer-Verlag.

—— (1990), "The Italian Continuous Time Model: Theory and Empirical Results," *Economic Modelling* 7: 91–132.

—— (1991), "Liberalizzazione dei movimenti di capitale e disequilibrio macroeconomico. Un'analisi del caso italiano," *Ricerche applicate e modelli per la politica economica*, vol. II. Roma: Banca d'Italia, pp. 535–51.

—— (1992), "The Dynamics of Capital Liberalization: A Macroeconometric Analysis," in M. Baldassarri, M. Di Matteo, and R. Mundell (eds.) (1994), *International Problems of Economic Interdependence*. London: Macmillan, pp. 107–49.

Gandolfo, G., P. C. Padoan, and G. Paladino (1990a), "Structural Models vs Random Walk: The Case of the Lira/$ Exchange Rate," *Eastern Economic Journal* 16: 101–23.

—— (1990b), "Exchange Rate Determination: Single Equation or Economy-Wide Models? A Test Against the Random Walk," *Journal of Banking and Finance* 14: 965–92.

Gandolfo, G., P. C. Padoan, and G. De Arcangelis (1993), "The Theory of Exchange Rate Determination, and Exchange Rate Forecasting," in H. Frisch and A. Wörgötter (eds.), *Open Economy Macroeconomics*. London: Macmillan, pp. 332–52.

Hillinger, C. (ed.) (1992), *Cyclical Growth in Market and Planned Economies*. Oxford University Press.

Sabani, L. (1993), "Testing for Nonlinearity in the Exchange Rate Data Series: An Empirical Investigation of the Lira/Dollar Spot Rate," Chapter 12 in this volume.

Wymer, C. R. (1993), "Estimation of Nonlinear Continuous-Time Models from Discrete Data," in P. C. B. Phillips (ed.), *Models, Methods, and Applications of Econometrics*. Oxford: Blackwell, pp. 91–116.

CHAPTER 5

Endogenous regime switching in a model of accumulation, credit, and monetary policy

D. Delli Gatti, M. Gallegati, & P. C. Padoan

1   Introduction

At present, two polar research strategies are adopted in macroeconomic modeling. On the one hand, theorists prefer small models in order to derive clear-cut analytical results. This goal is reached at a price – namely, the extreme oversimplification necessary to reduce the size of the model to a minimum. On the other hand, econometricians are accustomed to working with much larger models. The obvious drawback is the extreme difficulty in following the interaction among the macrovariables involved.

A way out of this dilemma consists of developing "medium-sized" macromodels. In other words, the size of the model should be increased up to the limit where complexity hinders a clear assessment of the dynamic properties and interactions of the macrovariables. Manageable complexity is the first distinctive feature of the (medium-sized) macrodynamic model described in this paper, a model that is relatively large and yet easy to handle.

The second feature of this model is its specification in continuous time, that is, as a system of nonlinear differential equations. Our model shares this feature with a group of models developed during the 1980s by Gandolfo and Padoan (1980, 1982, 1983a, 1983b, 1984), following a modeling strategy pioneered by Wymer (1972, 1976, 1979).

In our opinion, a medium-sized macrodynamic model specified in continuous time is the best tool for analysis of the interaction between investment activity and the accumulation of debt during the business cycle. The core of the real side of the model is the investment equation, a variant of

We thank the participants in the annual meeting of the Society for Economic Dynamics and Control held in Capri on 20–21 June, 1992, for their insightful comments on a preliminary version of this paper. Financial support from the Italian Ministry for Scientific Research is gratefully acknowledged. Although the authors share responsibility for the whole paper, Domenico Delli Gatti wrote Sections 1 and 3 and the Appendix; Mauro Gallegati wrote Sections 2 and 6, and P. C. Padoan wrote Sections 4 and 5.

151

the stock adjustment mechanism that takes into account the financial determinants of investment expenditure. In fact, it incorporates the assumption that the desired capital/output ratio is a nonlinear increasing function of a simple indicator of financial robustness, namely, the ratio of retained earnings to debt commitments.

The financial view of investment activity is popular among practitioners, but has not been successful in the profession owing to the widely shared Modigliani–Miller irrelevance proposition. Since the mid-1970s, however, the Modigliani–Miller theorem has been convincingly challenged. Because of the presence of asymmetric information on capital markets, changes in the financial structure of the corporate sector must affect investment decisions.

The monetary and financial side of our model is in fact characterized by informational imperfections that generate a financing hierarchy in which retained profits rank first, having a cost advantage over bank loans and the issue of new equities. The flow of internally generated financial resources, therefore, is the most important argument of the investment equation.

As far as the credit market is concerned, we explore the implications of assuming that the rate of interest cannot clear the credit market all the time. As a "quality signal" – a function duly stressed in the literature on credit rationing – the rate of interest cannot efficiently perform its function as an allocating mechanism. Therefore, excess demand for credit (credit rationing) can occur. We allow for persistent disequilibria on the credit market, and focus on the macroeconomic implications of alternative credit regimes (excess demand or excess supply of bank loans). Instead of *assuming* the presence of a particular type of disequilibrium, however, we make the switch from a regime of excess demand to a regime of excess supply (and vice versa) an endogenous one.

In Section 2 we present the equations of the model and discuss their specification and the underlying behavioral assumptions. Section 3 is devoted to the derivation and a brief discussion of the steady-state growth rates of the macrovariables involved. In Section 4 we study the properties of the model by means of numerical simulations. In Section 5 we carry out the stability and sensitivity analysis, and in Section 6 we draw some conclusions. Details on the procedure used to obtain the steady-state growth rates and linear approximations are confined to the Appendix.

2   The model

2.1   *An overview*

For the reader's convenience, we present the equations of the model in Table 1 in deterministic terms. The symbols used to denote the variables

Table 1. *Equations of the model*

Private consumption

$$D \log C = \alpha \log(\hat{C}/C) \tag{1}$$

$$\hat{C} = \gamma_1 \exp(\beta_1 D \log Y)[Y - (T/P)] \tag{1.1}$$

Rate of growth of the capital stock

$$D(D \log K) = \alpha_2[\alpha' \log(\hat{K}/K) - D \log K] + \alpha_3 D \log A \tag{2}$$

$$\hat{K} = \gamma_2 \exp[\beta_2 D \log(\pi PY/iA)]\dot{Y} \tag{2.1}$$

Expected output

$$D \log \dot{Y} = \eta \log(Y/\dot{Y}) \tag{3}$$

Output

$$D \log Y = \alpha_4 \log(\dot{Y}/Y) + \alpha_5 \log(\hat{V}/V) \tag{4}$$

$$\hat{V} = \gamma_3 \dot{Y} \tag{4.1}$$

Price level

$$D \log P = D \log W - D \log Z \tag{5}$$

Money wage

$$D \log W = \alpha_6 \log(\hat{W}/W) \tag{6}$$

$$\hat{W} = \gamma_4 P^{\delta_3} e^{\lambda_1 t} \tag{6.1}$$

Average productivity

$$D \log Z = \log \gamma_5 + \beta_4 D \log K \tag{7}$$

Interest rate

$$Di = \alpha_7 \log(M^d/M) + \alpha_8 D(D \log H) \tag{8}$$

$$M^d = \gamma_6 e^{-\beta_5 i} P^{\beta_6} Y^{\beta_7} \tag{8.1}$$

Public sector's borrowing requirement

$$DH = PG - T + iH \tag{8.2}$$

Credit market

$$D \log A = \alpha_9 \delta D \log A^s + \alpha_{10}(1 - \delta)D \log A^d \tag{9}$$

$$\delta = 0.5 \frac{[(A^d - A^s)^2]^{1/2}}{A^d - A^s} + 0.5 \tag{9.1}$$

$$D \log A^d \equiv DA^d/A^d = EF/A^d = (PI - IF)/A^d = [P(DK) - (\pi PY - iA)]/A^d$$

$$D \log A^d = [P(DK - \pi Y) + iA]/A^d \tag{9.2}$$

$$A^s = \gamma_7 e^{\beta_8 i} M(\pi PY/iA)^{\beta_9} \tag{9.3}$$

$$D \log A^s = \beta_8 Di + D \log M + \beta_9(D \log P + D \log Y - D \log i - D \log A) \tag{9.4}$$

Table 1 *(cont.)*

Monetary authorities' reaction function on money supply

$$D(D \log M) = \alpha_{11}(D \log \hat{M} - D \log M) + \delta_3 D(D \log H) \tag{10}$$

$$D \log \hat{M} = D \log M^* + \delta_i[D \log(PY) - (\mathring{\rho}_P + \mathring{\rho}_Y)] + \delta_2 Di$$
$$\delta_1 \gtreqless 0, \quad \delta_2 \gtreqless 0 \tag{10.1}$$

Taxes

$$D \log T = \alpha_{12} \log(\hat{T}/T) \tag{11}$$

$$\hat{T} = \gamma_8(PY)^{\beta_{10}} \tag{11.1}$$

Public expenditure

$$D \log G \equiv g \tag{12}$$

Inventories

$$DV = Y - C - DK - G \tag{13}$$

Table 2. *List of symbols*

A = nominal stock of bank advances
C = private consumption expenditure in real terms
EF = (need for) external finance (financing gap)
G = public expenditure in real terms
H = public debt
$I \equiv DK$ = net investment
i = rate of interest
IF = internal finance
K = capital stock in real terms
M = nominal stock of money
P = price level
T = taxes in nominal terms
V = stock of inventories in real terms
W = money wage rate
Y = actual output in real terms
Z = per-capita product

---

are listed in Table 2. In order to save on notation, stochastic disturbances are omitted. A hat on a variable (ˆ) denotes the *desired* level of the hatted variable, a knot (°) represents the *expected* value, and a star (*) indicates the *initial* value.

As usual, "log" stands for the natural logarithm; the symbol D is shorthand for the time derivative (d/dt). As a consequence, $D \log x$ represents the *actual* growth rate of the variable x. In the following section we will denote the *steady-state* growth rate by means of the greek letter ρ. Therefore, the dynamic equilibrium is characterized by $D \log x = \rho_x$. All the parameters are assumed to be positive unless otherwise specified.

2.2 *Consumption, investment, and income*

Strictly speaking, the real side of the model consists of equations (1) through (4). In (1) the rate of growth of consumption in real terms is proportional to the difference between (the logarithm of) desired consumption $\hat{C}$ and (the logarithm of) actual consumption C. The parameter α_1 measures the speed of adjustment from C to $\hat{C}$.

According to (1.1), desired consumption is proportional to real disposable income $(Y - T/P)$. The propensity to consume $(\gamma_1 \exp(\beta_1 D \log Y))$ varies with the rate of growth of real income. According to a widely shared view, this propensity is procyclical (i.e. $\beta_1 > 0$). However, if a "ratchet" effect is operative then the propensity to consume may be anticyclical $(\beta_1 < 0)$.

Equation (2) incorporates an investment function that can be thought of as a development of the stock adjustment theory, according to which the change of the level of the actual capital stock (investment) is proportional to the difference between the desired and the actual stock of capital (which will be denoted by $\hat{K}$ and K, respectively). In our framework, which deals with growth rates of the variables involved, the argument can be recast as follows. The change in the growth rate of the actual capital stock is proportional to the difference between the growth rates of the desired and the actual stock of capital:

$$D(D \log K) = \alpha_2 (D \log \hat{K} - D \log K).$$

We assume that the growth rate of the desired capital stock is an increasing function of the gap between the desired and the actual capital stock:

$$D \log \hat{K} = \alpha' \log(\hat{K}/K).$$

Substituting this equation into the previous one, we have

$$D(D \log K) = \alpha_2 [\alpha' \log(\hat{K}/K) - D \log K].$$

The RHS (right-hand side) of this equation is the first term in (2).

In the traditional framework, the desired stock of capital is proportional to (expected) output, so that the (desired) capital/output ratio $\hat{K}/\dot{Y}$ is constant. The second modification that we propose consists of making the desired capital/output ratio endogenous by linking it to the rate of growth of a simple indicator of financial robustness, namely, the ratio of retained earnings πPY to debt commitments iA:

$$FR = \pi PY/iA.$$

Therefore

$$\hat{K}/\hat{Y} = \gamma_2 \exp[\beta_2 D \log(\pi PY/iA)].$$

Re-arranging terms, from the foregoing capital/output equation we may derive (2.1).

Some clarifying remarks are in order with regard to the financial robustness indicator. First of all, for the sake of simplicity, we have assumed that the retention ratio is equal to unity (or, equivalently, that the payout ratio is equal to zero): All the profits are retained within the firm and no dividends are distributed to the shareholders.[1] Therefore, retained earnings coincide with total profits.

In nominal terms, the level of profits is the share of profits in national income (π) multiplied by nominal income PY. By assuming that firms follow a constant mark-up pricing rule, we are entitled to treat as given and constant the share of profits in national income. If we denote the mark-up by μ, the share of profits in national income is equal to $\pi = \mu/(1+\mu)$.

Whereas the ratio of retained earnings to debt commitments is an indicator of financial robustness, the difference between the two aggregates measures the level of *internal finance* in nominal terms.[2] Other things being equal, the higher the stock of debt, the higher will be the volume of interest payment and the lower will be the financial soundness of the non-financial corporate sector and the volume of internally generated funds. Therefore, a higher stock of debt entails a lower desired capital output ratio: The stock of corporate debt negatively affects investment activity through the *debt commitments effect*.

On the other hand, we must take into account the role that the flow of credit plays in stimulating capital accumulation, positively affecting investment through the *credit availability effect*. In order to capture this effect we have assumed that changes in the capital stock growth rate are

[1] As a matter of model consistency, this simplifying assumption should imply that consumer expenditure is linked only to the wage bill: If profits are entirely kept within the firm, there are no dividends and no consumption out of dividends. Equation (1) should be modified accordingly; that is, the desired level of consumer expenditure should be associated to the actual level of disposable labor income. Alternatively, we could assume that firms keep as retained earnings a given and constant proportion of their profits ($0 < \theta < 1$), and modify (2) accordingly. In this case the indicator of financial robustness would be $\theta \pi PY/iA$. From these slight modifications in the specification of the model, however, only negligible changes in the built-in dynamics of the system would follow.

[2] That is, $IF = \pi PY - iA$. From this definition we can derive the following relationship between internal finance and financial robustness: $IF = (FR-1)iA$. The volume of internally generated funds is positive whenever the indicator of financial robustness exceeds unity (and vice versa).

affected also by the rate of change in credit availability: This is why the term $\alpha_3 D \log A$ appears in (2.1).[3]

In (2.1), the desired capital/output ratio depends upon the ratio of retained earnings to interest payments. As a consequence, a positive correlation between investment activity and financial robustness is implicitly assumed in (2). This view of the relationship between capital accumulation and the financial structure of the corporate sector is widely shared among practitioners (bankers and businessmen), but has never been successful in the profession since the 1960s[4] owing to the nearly unanimous acceptance of the Modigliani–Miller irrelevance proposition.[5]

Since the mid-1970s, the basic assumptions of the Modigliani–Miller framework have been convincingly challenged and their main conclusions have been substantially weakened. In particular, if we allow for the presence of asymmetric information on capital markets, changes in the financial structure of the corporate sector must affect investment decisions. This would be true in the presence of equity rationing (Myers and Majluf 1984) even if the credit market were always in equilibrium. In the presence of credit rationing (Stiglitz and Weiss 1981; for a survey, see Jaffee and Stiglitz 1990), the aforementioned dependence of investment decisions on the financial structure and the availability of funds becomes even stronger. The financial view of investment activity can therefore be resurrected and legitimized in light of the burgeoning literature on asymmetric information in capital markets.

Equation (3) incorporates the process of expectation formation. We assume that agents form their expectations according to an adaptive process. The rate of growth of expected output is proportional to the difference between (the logarithm of) expected output $\dot{Y}$ and (the logarithm of) current output Y; η denotes the speed of adjustment from expected to actual output.

The laws of motion of current and expected output in a steady-state dynamic equilibrium are described by

$$Y_t = Y^* \exp(\rho_y t) \quad \text{and} \quad \overset{\circ}{Y}_t = \overset{\circ}{Y}^* \exp(\rho_{y^\circ} t),$$

[3] An increase in the rate of growth of the stock of corporate debt ($D \log A$) will produce the following change in the increase of the growth rate of the capital stock ($D(D \log K)$):

$$-\alpha_2 \alpha' \beta_2 + \alpha_3.$$

The debt commitment prevails if $\alpha_2 \alpha' \beta_2 > \alpha_3$, whereas the credit availability effect prevails if this inequality is reversed.

[4] In the 1950s the so-called Charles River School supported the financial view of investment activity.

[5] The minority view, which maintained that financial variables play a crucial role in investment decisions of the corporate sector, was represented in the profession by Kindleberger and especially Minsky (see e.g. Minsky 1986).

respectively. Substituting these functions into (3) and re-arranging, we obtain

$$\rho_{y^\circ} = \eta[\log(\mathring{Y}^*/Y^*) + (\rho_{y^\circ} - \rho_y)t].$$

We shall assume hereafter as a steady-state condition that $\rho_{y^\circ} = \rho_y$. The previous equation may thus be reduced to

$$\rho_{y^\circ} = \eta[\log(\mathring{Y}^*/Y^*),$$

which implies that

$$\mathring{Y}^* = \exp(\rho_{y^\circ}/\eta)Y^*.$$

According to this expression, at time $t = 0$ the expected output is a constant proportion $(\exp(\rho_{y^\circ}/\eta))$ of current output. The steady-state condition $\rho_{y^\circ} = \rho_y$ assures that proportionality is preserved over time. Note that $\lim_{\eta \to \infty} \exp(\rho_{y^\circ}/\eta) = 1$. In other words, only if the speed of adjustment tends to infinity (i.e., if the adjustment of expected to actual output is instantaneous) will the system be characterized by perfect foresight.

Equation (4) represents the supply decisions of the corporate sector. The rate of growth of current output depends upon the (logarithm of the) ratio of expected to current output and upon the (logarithm of the) ratio of the desired stock $\mathring{V}$ to the actual stock V of inventories.

According to the first term on the RHS of (4), producers' supply decisions aim at matching their expectations concerning future output. While adjusting current output to expected output, firms can run into a shortage of productive capacity, which in turn determines investment expenditure through the accelerator mechanism (see (2)).

The second term on the RHS of (4) can be thought of as a stock adjustment mechanism applied to the inventories of final goods. Producers' supply decisions aim at adjusting current inventories to desired inventories. Changes in output due to this process can be conceived of as the nonfixed component of investment. The desired stock of inventories is in turn proportional to expected output; that is, the ratio γ_3 of desired inventory to expected output is given and constant.

2.3   Prices and wages

We assume that firms follow a simple mark-up pricing rule:

$$P = (1 + \mu)(W/Z),$$

where μ is the mark-up parameter. Equation (5) follows from the pricing rule assuming that the mark-up is given and constant. In this case, of course, the rate of growth of the price level coincides with the rate of growth of unit labor costs, which in turn is defined as the difference between the growth rates of wages and productivity. In our framework, the natural way of dealing with price formation consists of assuming the following adjustment mechanism:

$$D \log P = \alpha \log(\hat{P}/P),$$

where $\hat{P} = \beta W^{\gamma} Z^{-\delta}$. Assuming that $\beta = 1 + \mu$, $\gamma = 1$, and $\delta = 1$, the equation of the desired price level coincides with the mark-up pricing rule just defined. Substituting into the adjustment mechanism the steady-state laws of motion of nominal wages and productivity ($W_t = W^* \exp(\rho_W t)$ and $Z_t = Z^* \exp(\rho_Z t)$) and re-arranging, we have

$$\rho_P = \alpha[\log(\hat{P}^*/P^*) + (\rho_W - \rho_Z - \rho_P)t].$$

The steady state is characterized by $\rho_W - \rho_Z - \rho_P = 0$. Therefore, after simple algebraic manipulation, we end up with the following expression:

$$\hat{P}^* = \exp(\rho_P/\alpha)P^*.$$

At time $t = 0$, the desired price level is a constant proportion $\exp(\rho_P/\alpha)$ of the current price. The steady-state condition $\rho_W - \rho_Z - \rho_P = 0$ assures that proportionality is preserved over time. Because $\lim_{\alpha \to \infty} \exp(\rho_P/\alpha) = 1$ if the speed of adjustment from the desired to the actual price tends to infinity, the two are the same at the beginning of the period.

According to (6), the nominal wage rate adjusts to a desired wage $\hat{W}$, which in turn depends primarily upon the current price level. The term β_3 is the elasticity of the desired wage to the current price. The dependence of the desired wage on the current price captures well-known features of industrial relations and union bargaining processes in Italy. However, institutional and sociopolitical factors (such as a dominant "social pressure" for rising wages) must also be taken into account. This is why an exogenous trend (λ_1) has been added to the target wage equation.

Equation (7) represents the rate of growth of per-capita product as a linear function of the capital stock growth rate; β_4 denotes the sensitivity of the former to the latter. This relation has a Kaldorian flavor, based as it is on the implicit assumption that technical progress is introduced through investment activity. As we shall see, since the steady-state growth rates of the capital stock and of current output coincide, the dynamic equilibrium of the model allows us to interpret (7) as a simple Kaldor–Verdoorn law.

Equations (5) and (6), jointly considered, represent the simplest formalization of a wage–price spiral. An acceleration of capital accumulation boosts productivity (equation (7)), reducing unit labor costs and the inflation rate (see equation (5)). The reduction in the inflation rate, in turn, depresses the rate of growth of wages (equation (6)) and so further reduces inflation.

2.4   *Money and interest*

According to (8), changes in the (representative[6]) interest rate are due, first of all, to money market disequilibria and secondly to changes in the public-debt growth rate. In fact, the first term ($\alpha_7 \log(M^d/M)$) is proportional to the difference between (the logarithm of) the demand for money M^d and (the logarithm of) the supply of money M; the second term ($\alpha_8 D(D \log H)$) is proportional to the change in the rate of growth of public debt. The supply of money is determined by the monetary authorities' reaction function (see (10), to be commented upon later). According to (8.1), the demand for money is a function not only of the rate of interest, but also of the price level and of real income. The price elasticity and output elasticity of the demand for money are constant (and equal to β_6 and β_7, respectively), whereas the interest elasticity is increasing (in absolute value) with the rate of interest.[7]

If we assume that $\beta_6 = \beta_7$, the demand for money becomes a function of the rate of interest and nominal income. Moreover, if we impose the condition $\beta_6 = \beta_7 = 1$ then (8.1) can be rewritten as

$$M^d = \gamma_6 \exp(-\beta_5 i)(PY).$$

This expression is a traditional money demand equation. The demand for money is homogeneous of degree 1 in nominal income. The term $\gamma_6 \exp(-\beta_5 i)$, the ratio of transaction balances to nominal income (usually symbolized by the parameter k in the Cambridge variant of the quantity theory), is the reciprocal of the velocity of circulation with respect to income. Therefore, income velocity is positively correlated to the rate of interest.

The second term in (8) is proportional to a change in the rate of growth of government debt: $D \log H \equiv \rho_H \equiv DH/H$. According to (8.2), the change DH in public debt coincides with the public-sector borrowing requirement, which in turn is defined as the sum of government expenditure on goods and services PG and interest payments iH net of tax revenue T, where all variables are evaluated at current prices.

---

[6] We do not deal formally with the whole structure of interest rates, in order to keep the dimension of the model relatively manageable. Moreover, in empirical analyses concerning Italian capital markets, the rate of interest on government bonds is a reliable proxy for all the other rates and in particular for the rate of interest on bank loans.

[7] In fact, from (8.1) it turns out that the mentioned elasticity is equal to $\epsilon_{Md,i} = -\beta_5 i$.

The steady state is characterized by $Di = D(D \log H) = 0$. This implies, of course, that $M^d = M$. That is, the dynamic equilibrium of the system is inconsistent with the presence of disequilibria in the market for money.

2.5   Credit regimes

Credit availability plays a crucial role in the process of capital accumulation and growth. We allow for structural (persistent) disequilibria on the credit market and focus on the macrodynamic effects of alternative credit regimes (excess demand or excess supply of bank loans). This implies, of course, that the rate of interest cannot be the equilibrating variable on the credit market.

However, instead of merely assuming the presence of a particular type of disequilibrium, we make the switch from a regime of excess demand to a regime of excess supply (and vice versa) an endogenous one by means of an algorithm originally proposed by Wymer (1979) and subsequently applied to Italian data in a different context by Petit (1981). In other words, we are able to explore the macrodynamic consequences of endogenous regime switching.

We assume, for the sake of simplicity, that firms are *equity rationed* (Myers and Majluf 1984). This implies that firms are forced to fill the financing gap by means of bank advances. Therefore, the flow demand for bank loans – that is, the change in the stock demand for bank loans DA^d – coincides with the need for external finance EF, which in turn is defined as nominal investment expenditure I less the flow of internally generated funds IF. Investment expenditure in nominal terms equals the price level multiplied by the change in the capital stock $(P \cdot DK)$, while internal finance is equal to retained profits πPY less debt commitments iA:

$$DA^d = EF = I - IF = P(DK) - (\pi PY - iA) = P(DK - \pi Y) + iA.$$

On the demand side of the credit market, the growth rate of bank advances is the ratio of the flow demand to the stock:

$$D \log A^d \equiv (DA^d/A^d) = [P(DK - \pi Y) + iA]/A^d,$$

which is equation (9.2).

The stock demand for credit is defined as the stock of capital at market value less the integral of internally generated funds:

$$A^d = PK - \int_0^t IF(s)\, ds,$$

where $IF(s) = \pi P(s)Y(s) - iA(s)$. Therefore, in the steady state,

$$A^d = P^*K^* \exp[(\rho_P + \rho_K)t] - \pi \int_0^t P^*Y^* \exp[(\rho_P + \rho_Y)s] \, ds$$

$$+ i^* \int_0^t A^* \exp(\rho_A s) \, ds.$$

By solving the preceding integrals, we derive the following expression:

$$A^d = P^*K^* \exp[(\rho_P + \rho_K)t] - \pi P^*Y^* \{\exp[(\rho_P + \rho_Y)t] - 1\}/(\rho_P + \rho_Y)$$

$$+ i^*A^*[\exp(\rho_A t) - 1]/\rho_A.$$

Since the steady state is characterized by $\rho_K = \rho_Y$ and $\rho_P + \rho_Y = \rho_A$, the foregoing equation may be rewritten as

$$A^d = \exp(\rho_A t)[P^*K^* - (\pi P^*Y^* - i^*A^*)/\rho_A] + (\pi P^*Y^* - i^*A^*)/\rho_A.$$

From the definition of the flow demand for credit we have

$$DA^d = \rho_K P^*K^* \exp[(\rho_P + \rho_K)t] - \pi P^*Y^* \exp[(\rho_P + \rho_Y)t] + i^*A^* \exp(\rho_A t)$$

$$= \exp(\rho_A t)[\rho_K P^*K^* - (\pi P^*Y^* - i^*A^*)].$$

The growth rate of bank advances – that is, the ratio of the flow demand to the stock – is therefore

$$D \log A^d = \frac{\rho_K P^*K^* - (\pi P^*Y^* - i^*A^*)}{P^*K^* - [(\pi P^*Y^* - i^*A^*)/\rho_A] + [(\pi PY - iA)/\rho_A \exp(\rho_A t)]}.$$

With the passing of time, this expression tends to

$$\rho_A^d = \frac{\rho_K P^*K^* - (\pi P^*Y^* - i^*A^*)}{P^*K^* - (\pi P^*Y^* - i^*A^*)/\rho_A}.$$

According to (9.3), the stock of loans supplied by the banking system (A^s) is a function of the stock of money supply (M). In order to simplify the argument, we assume that payments are carried out solely by drawing checks on current accounts, so that the stock of money coincides with bank deposits. By ruling out the presence of currency, we are entitled to assume that high-powered money (HPM) coincides with bank reserves. Therefore, $HPM = rM$, where r is the ratio of bank reserves to deposits. From the very definition of credit ($A = M - HPM$), elementary algebraic manipulations yield

$$r = 1 - (A^s/M).$$

According to (9.3),

$$A^s/M = \gamma_7 \exp(\beta_8 i)(\pi PY/iA)^{\beta_9}.$$

Therefore, (9.3) is implicitly based upon the following behavioral assumption:

$$r = 1 - \gamma_7 \exp(\beta_8 i)(\pi PY/iA)^{\beta_9},$$

which implies that the ratio of bank reserves to deposits is negatively related to the rate of interest and to the indicator of financial health (see Section 2.2).

The presence of an indicator of financial robustness in the equation for the reserves/deposits ratio is based upon the New Keynesian literature on asymmetric information and capital markets. We assume that the banking system links the financial health of corporate clients to their creditworthiness. Such financial indicators as the ratio of retained earnings to debt commitments can be used as screening devices. From (9.3) we quite straightforwardly derive (9.4).

Assuming, for the sake of simplicity, that $\alpha_9 = \alpha_{10} = 1$, at first sight Wymer's algorithm (equation (9)) suggests that the *actual* rate of growth of bank loans is a weighted average of the rates of growth of demand and supply. A quick inspection of (9.1), however, assures us that in disequilibrium the parameter δ can be either zero or unity. If excess demand prevails on the credit market then $\delta = 1$ and so $D \log A = D \log A^s$. Symmetrically, if excess supply prevails then $\delta = 0$ and so $D \log A = D \log A^d$. The switching points are determined endogenously, since both A^d and A^s in (9.1) are endogenous variables.

2.6   Policy equations

Equation (10) is the monetary authorities' reaction function. Let M_{cb} and M_g represent money created (or destroyed) by the central bank and by the government, respectively. The rate of growth of money supply is therefore a weighted average of the rates of growth of the central-bank money stock and the government money stock:

$$D \log M \equiv DM/M = m_{cb} D \log M_{cb} + m_g D \log M_g,$$

where

$$m_{cb} \equiv M_{cb}/M, \quad m_g \equiv M_g/M, \quad D \log M_{cb} \equiv DM_{cb}/M_{cb},$$

$$D \log M_g \equiv DM_g/M_g.$$

The central bank cannot control the stock of money supply created or destroyed by the government. Therefore, given the growth rate of the government money stock, the desired rate of growth of the central-bank money stock ($D \log \hat{M}_{cb}$) is endogenously determined, once the target rate of growth of the money stock ($D \log \hat{M}$) has been established (according to criteria that will be discussed later):

$$D \log \hat{M}_{cb} = (1/m_{cb}) D \log \hat{M} - (m_g/m_{cb}) D \log M_g.$$

The actual rate of growth of the central-bank money stock tends toward the desired rate of growth according to the following adjustment mechanism:

$$D(D \log M_{cb}) = \alpha_{11}(D \log \hat{M}_{cb} - D \log M_{cb}).$$

Multiplying both sides by m_{cb}, substituting the definition of $D \log \hat{M}_{cb}$, adding $m_g D(D \log M_g)$ to both sides, and re-arranging, we end up with

$$D(D \log M) = \alpha_{11}(D \log \hat{M} - D \log M) + m_g D(D \log M_g).$$

Thus $D \log M_g$ is linked to the rate of growth of the public-sector borrowing requirement. For the sake of simplicity we could assume that the ratio of the stock of government money to public debt is constant ($M_g/H = \lambda$), which would imply that

$$D \log M_g = D \log H$$

and hence that $DM_g = \lambda DH$. In other words, a constant proportion λ of the public-sector deficit is monetized. Substituting $D \log M_g = D \log H$ into the previous equation yields (10). In this case, of course, the parameter δ_9 in (10) coincides with m_g.

Equation (10.1) represents the target growth rate of the money supply ($D \log \hat{M}$) as the sum of a permanent component (the steady-state growth rate $D \log M^*$) and two transitory terms. The first term is proportional to the difference $D \log(PY) - (\hat{\rho}_P + \hat{\rho}_Y)$ between the rates of growth of actual and steady-state nominal output. The restriction $\delta_1 > 0$ characterizes a regime of procyclical monetary policy. Symmetrically, the restriction $\delta_1 < 0$ describes a regime of anticyclical monetary policy. The second term is proportional to changes Di in the interest rate. If $\delta_2 < 0$ then monetary authorities are shielding the process of money creation from monetary disequilibria, and the opposite holds true if $\delta_2 > 0$. Both terms are bound to disappear when the system reaches its dynamic steady-state equilibrium.

According to (11), the rate of growth of nominal tax revenue is proportional to the difference between (the logarithm of) desired revenue $\hat{T}$ and (the logarithm of) actual revenue T. Equation (11.1) states that desired revenue is income-elastic, with elasticity of β_{10}. If $\beta_{10} = 1$ then γ_8 would measure the average tax rate.

Equation (12) simply states that the rate of growth of government (autonomous) expenditure g is given and constant.

3   Steady-state growth rates and comparative dynamics

The steady-state growth rates of the endogenous variables are summarized in Table 3. Real magnitudes in the goods market (C, K, $\hat{Y}$, Y, V, T/P) grow

Table 3. *Steady-state growth rates*

Endogenous variable	Growth rate
$C, K, \dot{Y}, Y, V, T/P$	g
P	$\dfrac{\lambda_1 - \log \gamma_5 - \beta_4 g}{-\beta_9 + 1}$
W	$\dfrac{\lambda_1 - \beta_3(\log \gamma_5 + \beta_4 g)}{-\beta_9 + 1}$
Z	$\log \gamma_5 + \beta_4 g$
A, H, T	$\dfrac{\lambda_1 - \log \gamma_5 - (\beta_4 + \beta_3 - 1)g}{-\beta_9 + 1}$
M	$\dfrac{\beta_6(\lambda_1 - \log \gamma_5) - g[\beta_6\beta_4 + \beta_7(\beta_3 - 1)]}{-\beta_9 + 1}$

at the same rate as the exogenous growth rate of government expenditure. As a matter of fact, in a straightforward generalization of the present model G becomes a catch-all variable that includes all forms of autonomous expenditure.

The rate of growth of productivity is a linear function of the growth rate of autonomous expenditure. The rates of growth of the price level and the money wage are linear functions of the rate of growth of productivity. The crucial parameters are the price elasticity and the trend factor in the wage equation.

Nominal magnitudes grow at the same rate as nominal income; this rate is determined by the sum of inflation and the growth rate of output. The rate of growth of nominal income is a linear function of the rate of growth of autonomous expenditure. The parameters involved in this function are those of the wage and productivity equations.

The growth rate of the stock of money is a linear function of the growth rate of autonomous expenditure. The parameters involved in this function are those of the equations for wages, productivity, and money demand. It is worth noting that if $\beta_6 = \beta_7 = 1$ then the growth rate of money, as well as that of credit and public debt, coincides with the growth rate of nominal output.

Along the steady-state growth path, monetary and financial variables have no role to play; they affect neither real variables nor the wage–price interaction. As a matter of fact, just the opposite is true. From the real side of the model we derive the rate of growth of real output (government expenditure provides a real anchor), while the wage–price subsystem

Table 4. *Numerical values of parameters*

α_1	1.0	β_1	−1.0
α_2	1.0	β_2	0.25
α_3	0.25	β_3	0.7
α_4	1.5	β_4	0.2
α_5	0.5	β_5	1.5
α_6	0.4	β_6	1.0
α_7	0.1	β_7	1.0
α_8	0.1	β_8	1.0
α_9	1.0	β_9	1.0
α_{10}	1.0	β_{10}	1.0
α_{11}	2.0	λ_1	0.01
α'	0.1	$\log \gamma_1$	−0.2
δ_1	0.2	$\log \gamma_2$	−0.01
δ_2	0.2	$\log \gamma_3$	0.01
δ_3	0.3	$\log \gamma_4$	−0.3
π	0.5	$\log \gamma_5$	0.3
η	0.1	$\log \gamma_6$	−1.0
		$\log \gamma_7$	−1.0
		$\log \gamma_8$	0.01

yields the steady-state inflation rate. The growth rate of nominal income determines the dynamic path of monetary and financial magnitudes.

4   Calibration and simulation exercises

Most of the parameter estimates adopted to calibrate our model are borrowed from a larger and more complex continuous time macrodynamic model of the Italian economy that was constructed to determine exchange-rate dynamics (Gandolfo and Padoan 1990). The framework devised by Gandolfo and Padoan shares with the present model some basic theoretical and analytical features, although in focusing on the dynamics of the capital stock and corporate debt we have followed a different modeling strategy. Some of the parameters have been inferred from other statistical sources covering the estimation period (1960–1984). Parameter values are reported in Table 4.

The calibrated model has been simulated both in the standard (baseline) version and in a number of variants obtained by changing the value of some key parameters. The simulation exercises were aimed at providing answers to the following questions. What are the effects of an outburst of banks' "euphoria"? What are the consequences of a change in

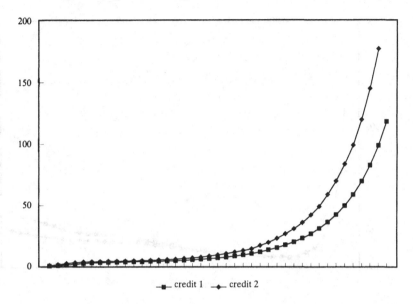

Figure 1. Credit cases 1 and 2.

the way in which firms rank alternative sources of finance in their "financing hierarchy"? To what extent and through which transmission mechanism does monetary policy affect the behavior of the system?

We present four simulation exercises and describe in each case the behavior of three key variables: the flow of profits (πPY), the (logarithm of the) stock of corporate debt actually generated in the credit market ($\log A$), and the growth rate of the capital stock ($D \log K$). The simulation exercises cover 40 quarterly periods, which is equivalent to a 10-year time span.

Case 1: Baseline. The behavior of the actual amount of credit is depicted in Figure 1. We start by assuming that the credit market is characterized by excess demand, so that the effective amount of credit is supply-determined ($A = A^s$). After six periods, a switch in regime from excess demand to excess supply occurs: from $t = 7$ to $t = 38$, credit is demand-determined ($A = A^d$). At $t = 38$, a new credit regime is established in which excess demand prevails and credit is once again supply-determined.

Figures 2 and 3, jointly considered, show that the flow of profits is the mirror image of the rate of capital accumulation, at least from the beginning of the simulation period to $t = 20$. In other words, the correlation of

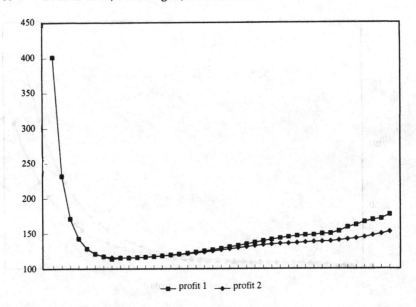

Figure 2. Profit cases 1 and 2.

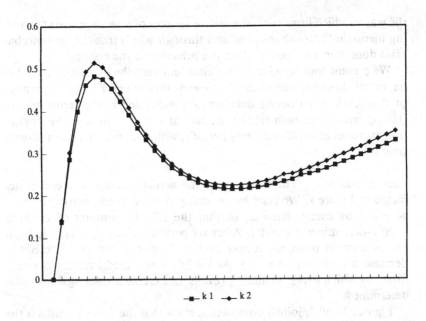

Figure 3. Rate of capital accumulation, cases 1 and 2.

profit and capital accumulation over the business cycle is negative. This result is counterintuitive in a framework which explicitly assumes that capital accumulation is positively linked to the flow of internally generated funds (cf. equation (2)).

This apparently counterintuitive result is due to the law of Kaldor-Verdoorn (see equation (7)), which implies that when the capital stock is growing at an increasing rate (as in Figure 2 from $t = 0$ to $t = 6$), the same must be true of per-capita product. This imparts a deflationary bias to the price level, which in turn has negative repercussions on nominal income and profits. Corporate debt goes up and the same must be true of debt commitments, so that internal finance shrinks. The acceleration of capital accumulation, coupled with the reduction of internal finance, is at the root of excess demand on the credit market.

With the passing of time, the shrinking flow of internally generated funds makes the corporate sector financially fragile, with negative repercussions on the rate of accumulation and the growth rate of per-capita product. An inflationary bias sets in, which is beneficial to profits and reduces the need for external finance. The system enters an excess supply credit regime.

The switch in regime does not interrupt the growth of corporate debt and hence debt commitments. The increasing flow of profits, however, brings about a larger flow of internal finance, which eventually induces a higher rate of capital accumulation (starting from $t = 23$). Excess supply of credit lasts until capital accumulation and the growth of productivity hamper the generation of cash flows, thereby stimulating the need for external finance and pushing the system once again into a regime of excess demand for credit (beginning at $t = 38$).

Case 2: Banks' "euphoria". The elasticity of credit supply to financial robustness (β_9 in (9.3)) – which was equal to unity in the baseline scenario – is now set to 1.5. This increase does not radically reshape the time path of the variables considered (see Figures 1–3 again) but does modify the timing of regime switches. Excess supply of credit sets in earlier (at $t = 3$ versus $t = 7$ in the baseline) as one would expect, but it also ends earlier (at $t = 36$ versus $t = 38$).

This result may be attributed to the credit availability effect. An increase in the propensity to supply credit on the part of banks, other things being equal, pushes up the rate of capital accumulation and hence credit demand with respect to the baseline. Banks' euphoria brings about business euphoria, so that the switching point (from excess supply to excess demand) is anticipated.

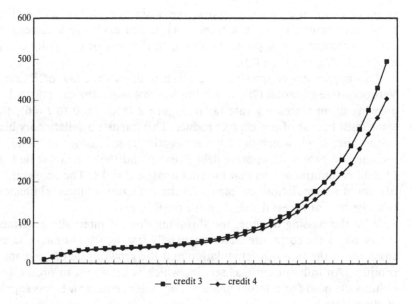

Figure 4. Credit cases 3 and 4.

Case 3: Higher reliance on internal finance.   We simulate the effects of
an increase (decrease) in the relative importance of internal (external)
funds in financing investment expenditure by lowering the value of α_9
(which captures the credit availability effect in (2)) from 0.25 to 0.2 and
increasing the value of β_2 (which links the desired capital output ratio to
the indicator of financial robustness in the same equation) from 0.25 to
0.3 (see Figures 4, 5, and 6).

Contrary to the previous cases, only one regime switch (from excess
demand to excess supply) occurs at $t = 8$ (Figure 4). This result obviously
stems from the higher relative weight attributed to internal finance. It is
worth noting, however, that a lower reliance on credit availability has
negative repercussions on capital accumulation: the rate of growth of the
capital stock, in fact, is lower (albeit only slightly) than in the baseline
scenario (Figure 6).

Case 4: Interest-rate pegging.   In this case we assume that monetary authorities assign a greater weight to interest-rate stabilization. Therefore
we increase the parameter δ_9 by 50 percent in the monetary policy reaction function (equation (10)). Corporate debt (Figure 4) and profits (Figure 5) take on higher values with respect to cases 1 and 2. The system

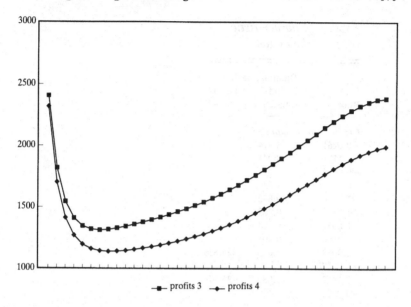

Figure 5. Profit cases 3 and 4.

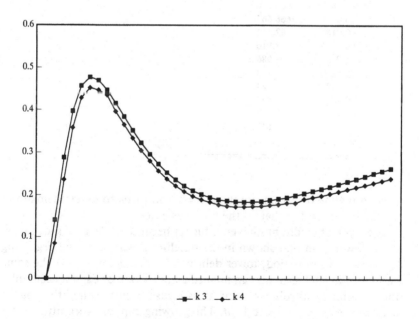

Figure 6. Rate of capital accumulation, cases 3 and 4.

Table 5. *Characteristic roots of the model*

Root	Damping period (quarters)	Period of cycle
Credit = credit supplied		
−0.0261	38.314	
−0.1121	8.921	
−0.2845	3.515	
−0.6150	1.626	
−1.1876	0.842	
−1.3011	0.769	
−1.6031	0.624	
−2.4596	0.401	
−0.00687 ±0.0127i	145.645	429.859
−0.14121 ±0.24567i	7.082	25.576
Credit = credit demanded		
0.0145		
−0.0005	2000.000	
−0.0006	1666.667	
−0.0161	62.112	
−0.0257	38.910	
−0.0715	13.986	
−0.8250	1.212	
−1.6032	0.624	
−2.2078	0.453	
−5.7358	0.174	
−0.1308 ±0.0882i	7.643	71.227

enters a regime of excess supply at $t = 7$ and turns to excess demand at $t = 31$, that is, earlier than in the previous cases.

The stock of credit, moreover, is higher because the level of the interest rate is lower than that shown in the baseline scenario. At the beginning of the simulation period, lower debt commitments imply that the same amount of available credit can finance a higher rate of capital accumulation. The financial robustness of firms is also improved and thus banks increase their propensity to lend. The growing capital expenditure eventually tightens the credit market, and the system enters a regime of excess demand.

Table 6. *Sensitivity analysis with respect to selected parameters: credit = credit supplied*

Root (μ)	-0.0261	-1.6031	-2.4596	-0.00687 $\pm 0.0127i$	-0.14121 $\pm 0.246i$
$\delta\mu/\delta\alpha_4$		-0.9981			
$\delta\mu/\delta\alpha_5$	0.0623	-0.0623			
$\delta\mu/\delta\alpha_6$			-0.1547		-0.4234
$\delta\mu/\delta\alpha$					0.0137
$\delta\mu/\delta\eta$	0.0292				
$\delta\mu/\delta\beta_4$			0.6212	0.0036	
$\delta\mu/\delta\beta_9$				0.0017	0.0148
$\delta\mu/\delta\partial_1$					0.2435

5   Stability and sensitivity analysis

Given the parameter values, we can assess the (local) stability of the model by means of linear approximations around the steady state. Since the model exhibits two regimes – a demand-determined and a supply-determined credit regime – two linear approximations must be computed (see the Appendix for details). The characteristic roots of the model are reported, for the two regimes, in Table 5. The dampening period is the time required for about 63 percent of the initial deviation to be eliminated. The cycle period corresponding to the complex roots is defined in the usual way.

Case 1: Credit is supply-determined. In this case, all the roots are negative in their real part. The model exhibits two pairs of complex roots that bring about a stable cyclical growth movement. Two kinds of cycle are present: a "secular" cycle with a period of more than a century, and a shorter cycle with a period of less than 10 years. Let us now turn to sensitivity analysis, by which we mean the computation of the partial derivatives of the characteristic roots with respect to the parameters of the model.

In Table 6 we report the most relevant results. Several parameters may generate unstable behavior in the model, but the destabilizing influence is not uniform across parameters. By comparing the partial derivative with the value assumed by the parameter, we can detect the bifurcation value.

The first source of instability is the behavior of inventories; an increase in α_5 – the inventory adjustment coefficient in (4) that describes output determination – to 0.419 (80% higher than the estimated value) would make the first root positive. In other words, if firms react too rapidly to a discrepancy between actual and desired inventories then instability emerges.

The second source of instability is an extremely accommodating monetary stance. If monetary authorities increase the relative weight of growth (in nominal terms) in their reaction function for money supply (equation (10)), the second complex root becomes positive in its real part; that is, an unstable policy-induced cycle emerges. For this to happen, δ_1 – the coefficient measuring the reaction of money supply to nominal income – should increase to 0.457 (125% higher than the original value).

This result should be considered jointly with the destabilizing effect of an increase of β_9, the elasticity of the supply of credit to firms' financial position. It is worth noting, however, that this parameter should be increased more than fourfold to push the first root into the unstable region and more than ninefold to make the second root unstable. This possible source of instability is therefore quite unlikely.

Other sources of instability are relevant increases of the following behavioral parameters, which pertain to the nonfinancial corporate sector: α' (equation (2)), η (equation (3)), and β_4 (equation (7)). Both β_4 and α' can eventually generate an unstable cycle.

In sum, a "euphoric" regime could bring about instability and an unstable cyclical growth, a result in line with much of the literature on financial instability. All the agents can be held responsible for such an outcome. It is not with banks, however, that this responsibility lies most. It is rather the euphoric behavior of business firms and monetary authorities that is most likely to push the system toward instability.

Case 2: Credit is demand-determined.   In this case all roots but one are negative and there is one pair of complex roots. Therefore, when credit is demand-determined, the economy follows a dynamic path of cyclical growth movement with a period of almost 18 years. From sensitivity analysis (see Table 7), we conclude that several parameters exert a stabilizing influence on the unstable root: Increases of α_2 and π (see equation (2)), α_6 (equation (6)), β_4 (equation (7)), and β_5 and β_6 (equation (8)) are all stability-enhancing as far as the system's dynamic behavior is concerned.

The strongest effect comes from α_6, the speed of adjustment of nominal wages to their desired value, which should increase to 1.023 (150% higher than the original value) to make the unstable root negative. This is not an implausible value because it implies – given the basic time unit of the model, which is one quarter of a year – a speed of adjustment of less than three months.

Table 7. *Sensitivity analysis with respect to selected parameters: credit = credit demanded*

Root (μ)	0.0145	−1.6032	−5.7358	−0.1308 ±0.0882i
$\delta\mu/\delta\alpha_2$	−0.0019			
$\delta\mu/\delta\alpha_4$		−0.9976		
$\delta\mu/\delta\alpha_6$	−0.0233			
$\delta\mu/\delta\beta_3$				0.1437
$\delta\mu/\delta\beta_4$	−0.0455		3.803	
$\delta\mu/\delta\beta_5$	−0.0028			
$\delta\mu/\delta\beta_6$	−0.0022			
$\delta\mu/\delta\delta_1$				0.0753
$\delta\mu/\delta\pi$	−0.0081			−0.0264

On the other hand, β_4 – the parameter linking the rate of change of productivity to the rate of capital accumulation – should increase to 0.519 (more than 150% higher than the original value) in order to bring the first root into the stable region. Once again this seems to be a reasonable result, yet a further increase in β_4 would bring the tenth (stable) root into the unstable region.

This result is best understood if considered together with the effect of an increase in β_9 on the pair of complex roots. An increase in this parameter to 1.611 (i.e. by about 140%) would generate an unstable cycle. The economic interpretation is as follows. If wage earners succeed in increasing the elasticity of wages to prices (i.e., if they ask for and obtain a higher real wage), and if firms react by boosting productivity through faster accumulation, then the system may eventually become unstable. Another source of instability is an increase in δ_1 (as in case 1), which will generate an unstable cycle.

In sum, if credit is demand-determined then the dynamic behavior of the system is largely dependent on the behavior of firms and their interaction with wage earners. Contrary to the supply-determined case, income distribution effects are crucial. Monetary authorities can exert, once again, a destabilizing role.

6   Conclusions

In this paper we have developed a continuous time macrodynamic model that describes the interactions between firms, banks, households, and policymakers in a more careful and detailed way than usual in models of accumulation and credit.

Owing to the presence of information asymmetries, the credit market is not cleared by a price mechanism (even if the interest rate is flexible), so that a regime of either excess demand or excess supply can occur. The switch in the credit market regime is endogenously determined.

In the steady state, all the real macrovariables grow at the exogenously given growth rate of government expenditure. By assuming a linear relation between the growth of real output to that of average productivity, the Kaldor–Verdoorn law links the real side of the model to the wage–price subsystem, which determines the steady-state growth rate of wages and prices. Finally, in the steady state all monetary and financial macrovariables grow at the growth rate of nominal income.

The properties of the model have been studied through numerical simulations as well as stability and sensitivity analyses. The model has been calibrated using parameter estimates borrowed from a larger and more complicated macromodel of the Italian economy (Gandolfo and Padoan 1990). The analysis of local stability has required two linear approximations around the steady state in order to take into account the disequilibria (excess demand or excess supply) that can emerge in the credit market.

Switches in the credit regime are sensitive to alternative behavioral assumptions, as the sensitivity analysis has shown. The interaction between accumulation, productivity, and income distribution is also important in determining the dynamic performance of the system. Policy-induced instability can emerge if monetary authorities pursue an extremely accommodating policy.

In a regime of supply-determined credit, a high propensity to lend on the part of the banking system may prove destabilizing, but it is firms' "euphoric" behavior that poses the most dangerous threat to a sound performance of the economy. This may occur because of an excessive propensity to invest and/or because of a strong reaction to changes in income distribution. In particular, if wage earners' claims to a higher real wage are countered by firms through an attempt to increase productivity, the system is bound to enter a phase of instability. In a regime of demand-determined credit, on the other hand, a stronger response of per-capita product to the rate of capital accumulation exerts a stabilizing influence on the dynamic path of the system.

In sum, our model seems to provide several interesting insights into the dynamic properties of an advanced economy, where capital and debt accumulation interact. As a relatively large model, it allows us to capture a range of transmission mechanisms and dynamic patterns that cannot be detected in smaller (and perhaps easier-to-handle) macromodels.

Appendix: Derivation of the steady-state growth rates and of the initial conditions

The model in generic form can be represented as follows:

$$f(D \log X_t, X_t, \bar{X}_t, \theta) = 0,$$

where $f(\cdot)$ is a vector of linear or nonlinear differentiable functions, X_t is a vector of n endogenous variables, $\bar{X}_t$ is a vector of exogenous variables, and θ is the vector of parameters. In our framework, there is only one exogenous variable (government expenditure), which is assumed to follow an exogenously given growth path: $G_t = G^* \exp(gt)$.

A *steady state* is a particular solution of the system that has the form $X_{it} = X_i^* \exp(\rho_i t)$ for all $i = 1, 2, ..., n$, where the values of X_i^* (the initial condition, "IC" hereafter) and ρ_i (the steady-state growth rate, "SSGR" hereafter) must be determined. The search for the SSGR is an application of the method of undetermined coefficient (Gandolfo 1981).

In the steady state, $D \log X = \rho_X$. Therefore equations (1)–(13) may be rewritten as follows:

$$\rho_C = \alpha_1 \{ \log \gamma_1 + \beta_1 \rho_Y$$
$$+ \log[Y^* \exp(\rho_Y t) - (T^*/P^*) \exp(\rho_T - \rho_P)t] - \log C^* - \rho_C t \};$$
(A.1)

$$0 = \alpha_2 \alpha' [\log \gamma_2 + \beta_2(\rho_P + \rho_Y - \rho_A) + \log \mathring{Y}^* - \log K^* + (\rho_{\mathring{Y}} - \rho_K)t]$$
$$- \alpha_2 \rho_K + \alpha_3 \rho_A;$$
(A.2)

$$\rho_{\mathring{Y}} = \eta[\log Y^* - \log \mathring{Y}^* + (\rho_{\mathring{Y}} - \rho_Y)t];$$
(A.3)

$$\rho_Y = \alpha_4[\log \mathring{Y}^* - \log Y^* + (\rho_{\mathring{Y}} - \rho_Y)t]$$
$$+ \alpha_5[\log \gamma_3 + \log \mathring{Y}^* - \log V^* + (\rho_{\mathring{Y}} - \rho_V)t];$$
(A.4)

$$\rho_P = \rho_W - \rho_Z;$$
(A.5)

$$\rho_W = \alpha_6[\log \gamma_4 + \beta_3 \log P^* - \log W^* + (\beta_3 \rho_P - \rho_W + \lambda_1)t];$$
(A.6)

$$\rho_Z = \log \gamma_5 + \beta_4 \rho_K;$$
(A.7)

$$0 = \alpha_7[\log \gamma_6 - \beta_5 i^* + \beta_6 \log P^* + \beta_7 \log Y^*$$
$$- \log M^* + (\beta_6 \rho_P + \beta_7 \rho_Y - \rho_M)t];$$
(A.8.1)

$$\rho_H H^* \exp(\rho_H t) = P^* G^* \exp[(\rho_P + g)t]$$
$$- T^* \exp(\rho_T t) + i^* H^* \exp(\rho_H t);$$
(A.8.2)

$$\rho_A = \alpha_9 \delta[\rho_M + \beta_9(\rho_P + \rho_Y - \rho_A)]$$
$$+ \alpha_{10}(1 - \delta) \frac{\rho_K P^* K^* - (\pi P^* Y^* - i^* A^*)}{P^* K^* - (\pi P^* Y^* - i^* A^*)/\rho_A};$$
(A.9)

$$\rho_T = \alpha_{12}\{\log \gamma_8 + \beta_{10}(\log P^* + \log Y^*) - \log T^*$$
$$-[\beta_{10}(\rho_P + \rho_Y) - \rho_T]\}; \qquad \text{(A.11)}$$

$$\rho_V V^* \exp(\rho_V t) = Y^* \exp(\rho_Y t) - C^* \exp(\rho_C t)$$
$$= \rho_K K^* \exp(\rho_K t) - G^* \exp(gt). \qquad \text{(A.13)}$$

The monetary authorities' reaction function (equation (10)) has not been rewritten because it applies only when the actual growth rate is different from the SSGR.

The system of equations (A.1)–(A.13) will be satisfied if the following two sets of conditions are fulfilled.

Set 1:

$$\rho_T - \rho_P = \rho_Y; \qquad \text{(A.14)}$$

$$\rho_P + \rho_Y - \rho_A = 0; \qquad \text{(A.15)}$$

$$\rho_{\dot{Y}} - \rho_K = 0; \qquad \text{(A.16)}$$

$$\rho_{\dot{Y}} - \rho_Y = 0; \qquad \text{(A.17)}$$

$$\rho_{\dot{Y}} - \rho_V = 0; \qquad \text{(A.18)}$$

$$\beta_3 \rho_P - \rho_W + \lambda_1 = 0; \qquad \text{(A.19)}$$

$$\beta_6 \rho_P + \beta_7 \rho_Y - \rho_M = 0; \qquad \text{(A.20)}$$

$$\rho_P + g = \rho_T; \qquad \text{(A.21)}$$

$$\rho_T = \rho_H; \qquad \text{(A.22)}$$

$$\beta_{10}(\rho_P + \rho_Y) - \rho_T = 0; \qquad \text{(A.23)}$$

$$\rho_V = \rho_Y = \rho_C = \rho_K = g. \qquad \text{(A.24)}$$

In the following we assume that $\beta_{10} = 1$, so that (A.23) coincides with (A.14).

Set 2:

$$\log C^* = \log \gamma_1 + \beta_1 \rho_Y + \log[Y^* - (T^*/P^*)] - (\rho_C/\alpha_1); \qquad \text{(A.25)}$$

$$\log K^* = \log \gamma_2 + \log \dot{Y}^* + (\alpha_3 \rho_A - \alpha_2 \rho_K)/(\alpha_2 \alpha'); \qquad \text{(A.26)}$$

$$\log \dot{Y}^* = -(\rho_{\dot{Y}}/\eta) + \log Y^*; \qquad \text{(A.27)}$$

$$\log Y^* = -(\rho_Y/\alpha_4) + [(\alpha_4 + \alpha_5)/\alpha_4] \log \dot{Y}^*$$
$$+ (\alpha_5/\alpha_4)(\log \gamma_3 - \log V^*); \qquad \text{(A.28)}$$

$$\log W^* = -(\rho_W/\alpha_6) + \log \gamma_4 + \beta_3 \log P^*; \qquad \text{(A.29)}$$

$$i^* = (\log \gamma_6 + \beta_6 \log P^* + \beta_7 \log Y^* - \log M^*)/\beta_5; \qquad (A.30)$$

$$\rho_H H^* = P^* G^* - T^* + i^* H^*; \qquad (A.31)$$

$$\rho_A = \alpha_9 \delta \rho_M + \alpha_{10}(1-\delta) \frac{\rho_K P^* K^* - (\pi P^* Y^* - i^* A^*)}{P^* K^* - (\pi P^* Y^* - i^* A^*)/\rho_A}. \qquad (A.32)$$

If $\delta = 1$ (excess demand of credit; credit is supply-determined), then

$$\rho_A = \alpha_9 \rho_M. \qquad (A.32.1)$$

If $\delta = 0$ (excess supply of credit; credit is demand-determined), then:

$$\rho_A = \alpha_{10} \frac{\rho_K P^* K^* - (\pi P^* Y^* - i^* A^*)}{P^* K^* - (\pi P^* Y^* - i^* A^*)/\rho_A}; \qquad (A.32.2)$$

$$\log T^* = -(\rho_T/\alpha_{12}) + \log \gamma_8 + \log P^* + \log Y^*; \qquad (A.33)$$

$$\rho_V V^* = Y^* - C^* - \rho_K K^* + G^*. \qquad (A.34)$$

Set 1 can be solved for the SSGRs of the endogenous variables, while set 2 can be solved for the ICs. Set 1 can be greatly simplified. Conditions (A.16), (A.17), (A.18), and (A.24) may be reduced to

$$\rho_V = \rho_Y = \rho_{\dot{Y}} = \rho_C = \rho_K = g. \qquad (A.35)$$

According to (A.35), the SSGR of each and every *real* variable (expected and actual output, consumption, fixed capital, inventories) is determined by the exogenously given rate of growth of government expenditure.

Substituting g for ρ_K into the Kaldor–Verdoorn law (equation (A.7)), we obtain the SSGR of per-capita product ($\rho_Z = \log \gamma_5 + \beta_4 g$), which in turn can be plugged into the mark-up pricing rule (equation (5)) to yield

$$\rho_P = \rho_W - \log \gamma_5 + \beta_4 g. \qquad (A.36)$$

Equations (A.36) and (A.19) can be solved for the SSGR of the wage and price levels as follows:

$$\rho_P = \frac{\lambda_1 - \log \gamma_5}{1 - \beta_g} - \frac{\beta_4}{1 - \beta_g} \equiv \theta_0 - \theta_1 g;$$

$$\rho_W = \frac{\lambda_1 - \beta_3 \log \gamma_5}{1 - \beta_g} - \frac{\beta_4 \beta_3}{1 - \beta_g} g \equiv \theta_2 - \beta_3 \theta_1 g.$$

In the following, we will assume that the price elasticity of the desired wage is smaller than unity ($\beta_3 < 1$), which implies that the SSGR of per-capita product should be smaller than the exogenously given trend of nominal wages ($\rho_Z < \lambda_1$) in order to have positive SSGRs of prices and wages. It is worth noting that the SSGRs of the wage and price levels are negatively related to the SSGR of output through the Kaldor–Verdoorn law.

For the sake of simplicity we set $\beta_6 = \beta_7 = 1$, so that equations (A.14), (A.15), (A.21), and (A.22) reduce to

$$\rho_A = \rho_H = \rho_T = \rho_M = \rho_P + \rho_Y; \tag{A.37}$$

that is, the SSGR of each nominal magnitude (credit, public debt, money, and tax revenue) is equal to the SSGR of nominal income, which in turn is equal to

$$\rho_{PY} = \rho_P + \rho_Y = \theta_0 + (1 - \theta_1)g. \tag{A.38}$$

The SSGR of nominal income is positively (negatively) related to the SSGR of real income if $\theta_1 < 1$ ($\theta_1 > 1$), that is, if $\beta_3 + \beta_4 < 1$ ($\beta_3 + \beta_4 > 1$).

Taking into account the SSGR computed as solutions of set 1, we can rewrite set 2 as follows:

$$\log\{C^*/[Y^* - (T^*/P^*)]\} = \log \gamma_1 + [\beta_1 - (1/\alpha_1)]g; \tag{A.39}$$

$$\log K^* = \log \gamma_2 + \log \dot{Y}^* + (\alpha_3\theta_0)/(\alpha_2\alpha')$$
$$+ g[\alpha_3(1 - \theta_1) - \alpha_2]/(\alpha_2\alpha') \tag{A.40}$$

$$\log \dot{Y}^* = -(g/\eta) + \log Y^*; \tag{A.41}$$

$$\log Y^* = -(g/\alpha_4) + [(\alpha_4 + \alpha_5)/\alpha_4] \log \dot{Y}^*$$
$$+ (\alpha_5/\alpha_4)(\log \gamma_3 - \log V^*); \tag{A.42}$$

$$\log W^* = -(\theta_2 - \theta_1\beta_3 g)/\alpha_6 + \log \gamma_4 + \beta_3 \log P^*. \tag{A.43}$$

The mark-up pricing rule implies that

$$\log P^* = \log W^* - \log Z^* - \log(1 - \pi), \tag{A.44}$$

since $1 + \mu = (1 - \pi)^{-1}$.

If $\delta = 1$ then $\rho_A = \alpha_9\rho_M$. From set 1 we know that $\rho_A = \rho_M$, so we will assume $\alpha_9 = 1$. (Of course, symmetry requires $\alpha_{10} = 1$.) This means that the ratio of money to credit remains unchanged through time, whatever its value at the beginning of the period:

$$H^* = (P^*G^* - T^*)/[\theta_0 + (1 - \theta_1)g - i^*]; \tag{A.45}$$

$$\log T^* = -[\theta_0 + (1 - \theta_1)g]/\alpha_{12} + \log \gamma_9 + \log P^* + \log Y^*; \tag{A.46}$$

$$Y^* = g(V^* + K^*) + C^* + G^*. \tag{A.47}$$

Substituting (A.41) into (A.40) and (A.42) and re-arranging, we obtain

$$\log K^*/Y^* = \log \gamma_2 + (\alpha_3\theta_0)/(\alpha_2\alpha')$$
$$+ g[\alpha_3(1 - \theta_1) - \alpha_2]/[(\alpha_2\alpha') - (1/\alpha') - (1/\eta)], \tag{A.40'}$$

$$\log V^*/Y^* = \log \gamma_3 - g[(\eta + \alpha_4 + \alpha_5)/\eta\alpha_5]. \tag{A.42'}$$

Given Z^*, the subsystem (A.43)–(A.44) can be solved for $\log W^*$ and $\log P^*$ as follows:

$$\log W^* = \{\log \gamma_4 - (\theta_2/\alpha_6) - \beta_3[\log Z^* + \log(1-\pi)]\}/(1-\beta_3)$$
$$+ [\beta_3\theta_1/\alpha_6(1-\beta_3)]g,$$
$$\equiv \theta_3 + [\beta_3\theta_1/\alpha_6(1-\beta_3)]g, \tag{A.43'}$$

$$\log P^* = \theta_4 + [\beta_3\theta_1/\alpha_6(1-\beta_3)]g, \tag{A.44'}$$

where $\theta_4 = \theta_3 - \log Z^* + \log(1-\pi)$.

From (A.43') and (A.44') we have

$$W^* = \exp\{\theta_3 + [\beta_3\theta_1/\alpha_6(1-\beta_3)]g\}, \tag{A.43''}$$

$$P^* = \exp\{\theta_4 + [\beta_3\theta_1/\alpha_6(1-\beta_3)]g\}. \tag{A.44''}$$

From (A.47) we derive the average tax rate as

$$T^*/P^*Y^* = \gamma_3 \exp\{-[\theta_0 + (1-\theta_1)g]/\alpha_{12}\}.$$

Equation (A.39) therefore becomes:

$$\log C^*/Y^* = \log(1 - T^*/P^*Y^*)$$
$$+ \log \gamma_1 + [\beta_1 - (1/\alpha_1)]g; \tag{A.39'}$$

$$C^*/Y^* = \gamma_1(1 - \gamma_3 \exp\{-[\theta_0 + (1-\theta_1)g]/\alpha_{12}\})$$
$$\times \exp\{[\beta_1 - (1/\alpha_1)]g\}. \tag{A.39''}$$

Taking the levels, equations (A.40') and (A.42') become

$$K^*/Y^* = \gamma_2 \exp\{(\alpha_3\theta_0)/(\alpha_2\alpha')$$
$$+ g[\alpha_3(1-\theta_1) - \alpha_2]/[(\alpha_2\alpha') - (1/\alpha') - (1/\eta)]\}; \tag{A.40''}$$

$$V^*/Y^* = \gamma_3 \exp[-g(\eta + \alpha_4 + \alpha_5)/\eta\alpha_5]. \tag{A.42''}$$

Equation (A.47) can be rewritten as

$$Y^* = G^*/\{1 - g[(V^*/Y^*) + (K^*/Y^*)] + (C^*/Y^*)\}. \tag{A.49}$$

Substituting (A.39''), (A.40''), and (A.42'') into (A.49), we can compute the IC of real income (Y^*), given the IC of government expenditure and its growth rate (i.e., G^* and g). Of course, once we obtain Y^*, by substitution into (A.39''), (A.40''), and (A.42'') we obtain the ICs of consumption C^*, capital stock K^*, and inventories V^*, respectively.

The IC of expected income is easily derived from equation (A.41):

$$\mathring{Y}^* = Y^* \exp(-g/\eta). \tag{A.41'}$$

The IC of the tax revenue in nominal terms (T^*) can be derived from (A.47'), having established the ICs of real income and the price level.

Taking the levels of (A.30), we can write the IC of the money stock as a function of the steady-state interest rate, given the ICs of real income and the price level:

$$M^* = \gamma_6 \, P^* Y^* \exp(-\beta_5 i^*). \tag{A.30'}$$

According to (A.45) and (A.46), the ICs of credit and government debt (A^* and H^*, respectively) also are functions of the interest rate.

In Section 2 we assumed that money created to finance government expenditure ("govenment money," for short) is a constant proportion of the money stock. Moreover, we assumed that a constant proportion of the deficit is monetized, which implies that the ratio of government money to public debt is constant. Jointly considered, the two assumptions imply that

$$H^*/M^* = m_g/\lambda. \tag{A.50}$$

Substituting (A.46) and (A.30') into (A.50), we have

$$(P^* G^* - T^*) \exp(\beta_5 i^*)/\gamma_6 \, P^* Y^* [\theta_0 + (1 - \theta_1)g - i] = m_g/\lambda,$$

which can be solved for i^*. Of course, by substitution into (A.30'), (A.45), and (A.46) we can compute the ICs of (respectively) money, credit, and public debt.

REFERENCES

Gandolfo, G. (1981), *Qualitative Analysis and Econometric Estimation of Continuous Time Dynamic Models.* Amsterdam: North-Holland.

Gandolfo, G., and P. C. Padoan (1980), "A Macrodynamic General Disequilibrium Model for the Determination of the Equilibrium Exchange Rate," in J. Gutenbaum and M. Niezgodka (eds.), *Applications of System Theory to Economics, Management and Technology.* Warsaw: Polish Scientific Publishers.

(1982), "Policy Simulations with a Continuous Time Macrodynamic Model of the Italian Economy: A Preliminary Analysis," *Journal of Economic Dynamics and Control* 4: 205–24.

(1983a), "Cyclical Growth in a Non-linear Macrodynamic Model of the Italian Economy," in R. M. Goodwin, M. Kruger, and A. Vercelli (eds.), *Non-Linear Models of Fluctuating Growth.* Berlin: Springer-Verlag.

(1983b), "Inflation and Economic Policy in an Open Economy: Some Simulations with a Dynamic Macroeconometric Model," in T. Basar and L. F. Pau (eds.), *Dynamic Modelling and Control of National Economies.* Oxford: Pergamon.

(1984), *A Disequilibrium Model of Real and Financial Accumulation in an Open Economy.* Berlin: Springer-Verlag.

(1990), "The Italian Continuous Time Model: Theory and Empirical Results," *Economic Modelling* 7: 91–132.

Jaffee, D., and J. Stiglitz (1990), "Credit Rationing," in B. Frieman and F. Hahn (eds.), *Handbook of Monetary Economics*. Amsterdam: North-Holland, Chapter 16.

Minsky, H. P. (1986), *Stabilizing an Unstable Economy*. New Haven, CT: Yale University Press.

Myers, S., and E. Majluf (1984), "Corporate Financing and Investment Decisions When Firms Have Information that Investors Do Not Have," *Journal of Financial Economics* 13: 187-221.

Petit, M. L. (1981), "Modelli di squilibrio e metodi di stima: un'applicazione al mercato delle esportazioni italiane," *Note Economiche* 2: 62-81.

Stiglitz, J., and A. Weiss (1981), "Credit Rationing in Markets with Imperfect Information," *American Economic Review* 71: 393-410.

Wymer, C. R. (1972), "Econometric Estimation of Stochastic Differential Equation Systems," *Econometrica* 40: 565-77.

(1976), "Continuous Time Models in Macroeconomics: Specification and Estimation," presented at the SSRC-Ford Foundation Conference on Macroeconomic Policy and Adjustment in Open Economies (Ware, UK), 28 April - 1 May.

(1979), "The Use of Continuous Time Models in Economics," mimeo, International Monetary Fund, Washington, DC.

CHAPTER 6

A note on continuous time dynamic disequilibrium macroeconometric modeling of the United Kingdom

K. B. Nowman

1   Introduction

Bergstrom, Nowman, and Wymer (1992; hereafter "BNW") developed the first continuous time dynamic disequilibrium macroeconometric model of the United Kingdom economy to be formulated as a complete system of second-order differential equations. The major aim of their study was to test the feasibility of new exact Gaussian estimation econometric methods developed by Bergstrom (1983, 1985, 1986) for second-order continuous time dynamic models with mixed stock and flow data and associated new forecasting methods by Bergstrom (1989) (see also Bergstrom 1990; Nowman 1991, 1992, 1993; Gandolfo 1981, 1993). The model has more recently been applied to monetary and fiscal policy analysis by Bergstrom, Nowman, and Wandasiewicz (1994).

The model used in the BNW study was estimated over the period 1974 to 1984 inclusive using quarterly United Kingdom data. In this note we re-estimate the model on more recent data for the period 1974 to 1989 inclusive, and apply the forecasting algorithm of Bergstrom (1989) for the period 1990 to 1991 to see if the model can capture the U.K. recession that started in 1990. We also use the monetary aggregate M0, which currently is officially monitored by HM Treasury.

The plan of this note is as follows. In Section 2 we give a very brief overview of the model. Section 3 discusses the empirical results, and Section 4 offers some conclusions.

I would like to thank Professor G. Gandolfo, the editors of this proceedings volume, and two anonymous referees for helpful comments and suggestions. Special thanks go to Rex Bergstrom for his constant help and support in my research on continuous time modeling. I would also like to thank Professors P. C. Padoan, P. Zadrozny, and C. R. Wymer for helpful comments on an earlier version of this paper.

185

2   Overview of the model

The model of the United Kingdom (which is presented in Table 1 for reference purposes) is thoroughly discussed in BNW and is essentially based on the smaller first-order model of Bergstrom and Wymer (1976). Like that prototype model, it synthesizes real and monetary phenomena and cycles and growth in an integrated system, makes intensive use of economic theory to obtain a parsimonious parameterization, and is designed in such a way as to permit a rigorous mathematical analysis of its steady state and its asymptotic stability properties. The structure of the model will be briefly outlined here.

The model comprises a system of 14 second-order differential equations with 63 structural parameters, including 27 long-run propensities or elasticities, 33 speed-of-adjustment parameters, and 3 trend parameters representing the rate of technical progress, the rate of growth of the labor supply (the nonaccelerating inflation level of employment), and the target rate of growth of the money supply. The first equation of the model is the consumption adjustment equation. The acceleration of the logarithm of private consumption is assumed to depend both on the deviation of the current proportional growth rate of consumption from the expected long-run growth rate of income and on the ratio of the partial equilibrium level of consumption to its current level. The assumption of long-run rational expectations is incorporated by assuming that the expected long-run growth rate of income is equal to the steady-state growth rate of real income obtained from the steady-state solution of the complete model (see BNW).

Most of the other equations of the model have a similar general form, with the acceleration of the logarithm (or, in some cases, the natural value) of the variable depending on the deviation of its current rate of change from the steady-state rate of change, as well as on the ratio of the partial equilibrium level to the current level of the variable. Equations (2) to (6) of the model are concerned with the production sector of the economy and include adjustment equations for capital, employment, output, prices, and wages. They are closely related through the parameters of a production function with constant elasticity of substitution. Equation (7), the interest-rate adjustment equation, reflects the dynamic behavior of the market for long-dated bonds. Equations (8) to (12) represent the adjustment of the balance-of-payments items, including imports, exports, international transfers, international flows of profit, interest and dividends, and international capital flows. Finally, equations (13) and (14) are the adjustment equations for (respectively) the money supply and the exchange rate.

Table 1. *Equations of the model*

Real private consumption

$$D^2 \log C = \gamma_1(\lambda_1 + \lambda_2 - D \log C)$$

$$+ \gamma_2 \log\left[\frac{\beta_1 e^{-\{\beta_2(r - D \log p) + \beta_3 D \log p\}}(Q+P)}{T_1 C}\right] \tag{1}$$

Employment

$$D^2 \log L = \gamma_3(\lambda_2 - D \log L)$$

$$+ \gamma_4 \log\left[\frac{\beta_4 e^{-\lambda_1 t}(Q^{-\beta_6} - \beta_5 K^{-\beta_6})^{-1/\beta_6}}{L}\right] \tag{2}$$

Amount of fixed capital

$$D^2 \log K = \gamma_5(\lambda_1 + \lambda_2 - D \log K)$$

$$+ \gamma_6 \log\left[\frac{\beta_5(Q/K)^{1+\beta_6}}{r - \beta_7 D \log p + \beta_8}\right] \tag{3}$$

Real net output

$$D^2 \log Q = \gamma_7(\lambda_1 + \lambda_2 - D \log Q)$$

$$+ \gamma_8 \log\left[\frac{\{1 - \beta_9(qp/p_i)^{\beta_{10}}\}(C + G_C + DK + E_n + E_o)}{Q}\right] \tag{4}$$

Price level

$$D^2 \log p = \gamma_9[D \log(w/p) - \lambda_1]$$

$$+ \gamma_{10} \log\left[\frac{\beta_{11}\beta_4 T_2 we^{-\lambda_1 t}\{1 - \beta_5(Q/K)^{\beta_6}\}^{-(1+\beta_6)/\beta_6}}{p}\right] \tag{5}$$

Wage rate

$$D^2 \log w = \gamma_{11}[\lambda_1 - D \log(w/p)] + \gamma_{12} D \log(p_i/qp)$$

$$+ \gamma_{13} \log\left[\frac{\beta_4 e^{-\lambda_1 t}(Q^{-\beta_6} - \beta_5 K^{-\beta_6})^{-1/\beta_6}}{\beta_{12} e^{\lambda_2 t}}\right] \tag{6}$$

Interest rate

$$D^2 r = -\gamma_{14} Dr + \gamma_{15}[\beta_{13} + r_f - \beta_{14} D \log q + \beta_{15}\{p(Q+P)/M\} - r] \tag{7}$$

Volume of imports

$$D^2 \log I = \gamma_{16}[\lambda_1 + \lambda_2 - D \log(p_i I/qp)]$$

$$+ \gamma_{17} \log\left[\frac{\beta_9(qp/p_i)^{\beta_{10}}(C + G_C + DK + E_n + E_o)}{(p_i/qp)I}\right] \tag{8}$$

Real non-oil exports

$$D^2 \log E_n = \gamma_{18}(\lambda_1 + \lambda_2 - D \log E_n)$$

$$+ \gamma_{19} \log\left[\frac{\beta_{16} Y_f^{\beta_{17}}(p_f/qp)^{\beta_{18}}}{E_n}\right] \tag{9}$$

Table 1 *(cont.)*

Real current transfers abroad

$$D^2F = -\gamma_{20}DF + \gamma_{21}[\beta_{19}(Q+P)-F] \tag{10}$$

Real profits, interest, and dividends from abroad

$$D^2P = -\gamma_{22}DP + \gamma_{23}[\{\beta_{20}+\beta_{21}(r_f - D\log p_f)\}K_a - P] \tag{11}$$

Cumulative net real investment abroad

$$D^2K_a = -\gamma_{24}DK_a$$
$$+ \gamma_{25}[\{\beta_{22}+\beta_{23}(r_f - r) - \beta_{24}D\log q - \beta_{25}d_x\}(Q+P) - K_a] \tag{12}$$

Money supply

$$D^2\log M = \gamma_{26}(\lambda_3 - D\log M) + \gamma_{27}\log\left[\frac{\beta_{26}e^{\lambda_3 t}}{M}\right]$$
$$+ \gamma_{28}D\log\left[\frac{E_n + E_o + P - F}{(p_i/qp)I}\right] + \gamma_{29}\log\left[\frac{E_n + E_o + P - F - DK_a}{(p_i/qp)I}\right] \tag{13}$$

Exchange rate

$$D^2\log q = \gamma_{30}D\log(p_f/qp) + \gamma_{31}\log\left[\frac{\beta_{27}p_f}{qp}\right]$$
$$+ \gamma_{32}D\log\left[\frac{E_n + E_o + P - F}{(p_i/qp)I}\right] + \gamma_{33}\log\left[\frac{E_n + E_o + P - F - DK_a}{(p_i/qp)I}\right] \tag{14}$$

Endogenous variables
C = real private consumption
E_n = real non-oil exports
F = real current transfers abroad
I = volume of imports
K = amount of fixed capital
K_a = cumulative net real investment abroad (excluding change in official reserves)
L = employment
M = M0 money supply
P = real profits, interest, and dividends from abroad
p = price level
Q = real net output
q = exchange rate (price of sterling in foreign currency)
r = interest rate
w = wage rate

Exogenous variables
d_x = dummy variable for exchange controls ($d_x = 1$ for 1974-79, $d_x = 0$ for 1980 onward)
E_o = real oil exports
G_c = real government consumption
p_f = price level in leading foreign industrial countries
p_i = price of imports (in foreign currency)
r_f = foreign interest rate

T_1 = total taxation policy variable $((Q+P)/T_1$ is real private disposable income)
T_2 = indirect taxation policy variable $(Q/T_2$ is real output at factor cost)
Y_f = real income of leading foreign industrial countries
  t = time

3   Empirical results

In this section we discuss the empirical results with reference to the previous results of BNW, which contains a detailed discussion of the estimation methodology and data set. The exact Gaussian estimates of the structural parameters are given in Table 2. We now discuss the main changes to the earlier estimates. The trend parameters imply a rate of technical progress of about 1.8 percent per annum ($\lambda_1 = 0.0044$) and a rate of growth of the labor supply (the nonaccelerating inflation level of employment) of about 2.8 percent per annum ($\lambda_2 = 0.0071$). These have both increased in value. The estimate of the long-run target rate of growth of the M0 money supply of 4 percent per annum ($\lambda_3 = 0.0100$) is now very plausible compared to the previous long-run target rate of zero growth. Indeed, the current monitoring range of M0 by the U.K. Treasury is 1 to 4 percent per annum.

The main long-run parameters imply, in particular, that the private propensity to consume β_1 (when the real interest rate and the inflation rate are zero) is 0.95, the elasticity of substitution between labor and capital is 0.77 ($\beta_6 = 0.2966$), the propensity to import β_9 (when the real exchange rate is at its base level) is 0.1972, the price elasticity of demand for imports is 0.67 ($\beta_{10} = 0.3333$), and the price elasticity of demand for exports β_{18} is 0.52. These are all consistent with the earlier study. Of particular interest are the estimates of the parameters β_2 and β_3, which imply a rather weak negative effect of the real interest rate on consumption but a strong negative effect of inflation on consumption (as was found in the earlier study).

Turning now to parameters of the speeds of adjustment, the new estimates imply that consumption (γ_1), output (γ_7), exports (γ_{18}), transfers (γ_{20}), and profits, interest, and dividends from abroad (γ_{22}) all have high speeds of adjustment and should therefore be modeled as first-order equations. These results confirm the earlier estimates of these parameters.

The interpretation of the estimates of the speed-of-adjustment parameters is illuminated by the implied continuous time-lag distributions derived by BNW using convolution integrals through which the current values of the variables depend on the past values of variables on which they are causally dependent. The mean and modal time lags (see BNW

Table 2. *Exact Gaussian estimates for U.K. model,*
1974Q1–1989Q4

Parameter	Estimate	Standard error	Parameter	Estimate	Standard error
β_1	0.9500	0.0253	γ_1	3.9990	0.5214
β_2	0.2015	0.8716	γ_2	0.5882	0.7294
β_3	3.4971	0.7159	γ_3	2.7977	0.0842
β_4	0.1693	0.0135	γ_4	0.0768	0.0105
β_5	0.2426	0.0698	γ_5	0.1218	0.0246
β_6	0.2966	0.0170	γ_6	0.0009	0.0001
β_7	0.1535	0.0754	γ_7	3.9503	0.2343
β_8	0.0070	0.0037	γ_8	0.2388	0.7579
β_9	0.1972	0.0280	γ_9	0.2227	0.0579
β_{10}	−0.3333	0.2083	γ_{10}	0.0023	0.0202
β_{11}	1.0000	2.4580	γ_{11}	3.9590	0.1874
β_{12}	23.2551	0.6437	γ_{12}	0.7216	0.4317
β_{13}	−0.0721	0.0252	γ_{13}	0.1200	0.0834
β_{14}	0.1448	0.1745	γ_{14}	0.4489	0.2120
β_{15}	0.0073	0.0062	γ_{15}	0.0324	0.0054
β_{16}	19.0000	0.6399	γ_{16}	1.4137	0.0173
β_{17}	0.5378	0.4060	γ_{17}	0.2155	0.0027
β_{18}	0.5161	0.3434	γ_{18}	3.9968	0.0483
β_{19}	0.0056	0.0022	γ_{19}	0.4437	0.0054
β_{20}	0.0100	0.0084	γ_{20}	3.9995	0.0445
β_{21}	0.2520	0.6022	γ_{21}	1.0167	0.0124
β_{22}	−0.1185	0.7957	γ_{22}	3.9997	0.0481
β_{23}	57.0548	0.6388	γ_{23}	2.0944	0.0255
β_{24}	0.1577	0.6776	γ_{24}	0.1839	0.0022
β_{25}	0.0007	0.1861	γ_{25}	0.0040	0.00005
β_{26}	14.5787	0.6789	γ_{26}	0.4537	0.0055
β_{27}	0.9263	0.2526	γ_{27}	0.0216	0.0003
			γ_{28}	0.1301	0.0016
λ_1	0.0044	0.00005	γ_{29}	0.0856	0.0010
λ_2	0.0071	0.00009	γ_{30}	3.3950	0.0414
λ_3	0.0100	0.0001	γ_{31}	0.1826	0.0022
			γ_{32}	0.0024	0.00003
			γ_{33}	0.0008	0.00001

for precise formulas) are presented in Table 3. The long mean time lag of 135 quarters for investment is longer than the earlier estimate, and suggests that the total stock of capital should be disaggregated into total residential, private nonresidential, and public nonresidential investment.

The steady-state solution of the model and levels of the steady-state growth paths were derived by BNW under certain assumptions concerning

Table 3. *Estimated time-lag parameters*

Variable	Mean time lag (quarters)	Standard error	Modal time lag (quarters)	Standard error
$\log C$	6.7987	8.2109	0.8732	0.2922
$\log L$	36.4284	5.0517	1.6790	0.0564
$\log K$	135.3333	17.0046	25.1727	3.3639
$\log Q$	16.5423	52.3740	1.0838	0.7497
r	13.8549	6.6483	5.1391	0.9766
$\log I$	6.5601	0.1151	1.8430	0.0113
$\log E_n$	9.0079	0.1546	0.9356	0.0065
F	3.9338	0.0648	0.7570	0.0046
P	1.9097	0.0326	0.6146	0.0037
K_a	45.9750	0.7924	13.7833	0.0840

Table 4. *Derived steady-state growth rates*

Variable	Instantaneous growth rate (percent per annum)
$C, K, Q, I, E_n, F, P, K_a$	2.56
L	0.80
p	1.44
w	3.20
r	0.00
M	4.00
q	0.00

the behavior of the exogenous variables that we also use here. Following the reasons given in BNW, we adjusted two parameters of the model for the purpose of computing the steady-state paths: λ_2 and β_{18}, which were changed to 0.002 and 1.0, respectively. We also adjusted β_{26} from the estimated value of 14.58 to 9.77. These adjustments yield a steady-state level in 1991Q4 that is equal to the actual 1991Q4 value. The money supply will then continue to grow at 4 percent per annum, which is realistic given the official monitoring range of HM Treasury. The derived steady-state growth rates of the endogenous variables are shown in Table 4. All the main real aggregates grow at the instantaneous rate of 2.56 percent per annum, the price level at 1.44 percent per annum, and the nominal wage rate at 3.2 percent per annum. These values are comparable to the

Table 5. *Derived steady-state levels*

Variable	Steady-state–level parameter	Steady-state level in last quarter of 1991	Actual level in last quarter of 1991
C	61.2653	97.1239	69.1235
L	23.2551	26.8569	25.6640
K	720.6377	1142.4269	1089.0000
Q	86.1543	136.5804	95.4884
p	1.0601	1.3738	1.4215
w	2.9739	5.2903	3.7849
r	0.0090	0.0090	0.0230
I	13.9213	22.0694	33.9840
E_n	29.4903	46.7510	23.9365
F	0.4710	0.7467	0.1871
P	0.0791	0.1254	0.0788
K_a	6.4987	10.3024	−7.1755
M	9.7707	20.0730	20.0730
q	0.3837	0.3837	1.0650

earlier results. The levels of the steady-state growth paths are shown in Table 5. In addition to the level parameters, this table shows the steady-state and actual levels of the variables in the final quarter of 1991.

A notable implication of the numbers in Table 5 is that, over the sample period, the change in the structure of the production parameters compared to the earlier estimates has resulted in a much higher steady-state level of output in the final quarter of 1991 owing to various technological changes in the U.K. economy in the mid- to late 1980s. The actual path will continue to move toward the steady-state path but over a much longer period. Another notable implication of these numbers (together with the data and assumptions about foreign prices used in BNW) is that the steady-state real exchange rate is about 65 percent below the actual real exchange rate in the final quarter in 1991. This is mainly due to the assumption used in BNW that oil exports are zero in the steady state. Another factor contributing to the implied long-run fall in the real exchange rate is that the increase in import demands resulting from the increase in real income in the steady state exerts downward pressure on the exchange rate. This fall in the exchange rate tends both to increase exports and decrease imports to the extent necessary to eliminate the deficit in the balance of payments arising from the factors mentioned.

The stability of the steady state is given by the eigenvalues of the matrix C in equation (79) of BNW; these eigenvalues for the linear (in logarithms)

Table 6. *Eigenvalues for linear approximation about the steady state*

Real part	Standard error	Imaginary part	Standard error
−3.9089	0.6191		
−3.7761	0.3411		
−3.7332	0.0489		
−3.6334	0.4143		
−3.3865	0.0594		
−2.7700	0.0848		
−1.2412	0.0202		
−0.6261	0.0142		
−0.4391	0.0758		
−0.2768	0.0897		
−0.2547	0.1285		
−0.1649	0.0000		
−0.1262	0.0891		
−0.1147	0.0012		
−0.0534	0.0000		
−0.0277	0.0281		
−0.0073	0.0114		
−0.0025	0.0098		
−3.9124	0.4596	±0.0246	0.2057
−0.2612	0.0318	±0.0887	0.1366
−0.0250	0.0069	±0.0773	0.0212
−0.0248	0.0202	±0.0183	0.0246
0.0060	0.0213	±0.0297	0.0364

approximation about the steady state are shown in Table 6. All but two of these eigenvalues have negative real parts. The positive real part is included in the complex pair $0.0060 \pm 0.0297i$. The real parts of these eigenvalues are so small that we cannot reject the hypothesis that the steady state is asymptotically stable. It should be noted that the positive real part of the complex root is much smaller than obtained in the BNW study, which had in addition a very small positive real root.

The forecasting algorithm of Bergstrom (1989) for obtaining optimal dynamic postsample forecasts is now used for the period 1990–1991. A full description of the method is contained in Bergstrom (1989). We compare the forecasts of the continuous time model with some discrete time models. The first discrete time model is a second-order autoregressive model in both the endogenous and exogenous variables, and will be denoted ARX. We produce dynamic forecasts not only from the ARX model but also from a "naive" model, in which all variables are assumed to change

Table 7. *Summary forecast statistic,
root-mean-square error*

Variable	Model		
	Continuous time	ARX	Naive
$\log C$	0.0822	0.0619	0.0570
$\log L$	0.0176	0.0398	0.0515
$\log K$	0.0026	0.0048	0.0107
$\log Q$	0.0914	0.0412	0.0756
$\log p$	0.0870	0.0374	0.0199
$\log w$	0.1875	0.0231	0.0096
$\log I$	0.1313	0.0289	0.0238
$\log E_n$	0.0366	0.0458	0.1985
$\log M$	0.0202	0.0101	0.0346
$\log q$	0.1172	0.0257	0.2164
r	0.0062	0.0039	0.0024
F	0.4283	0.4675	0.9821
P	0.3977	1.0445	0.4980
K_a	11.6320	8.7760	3.0057

at the same rate as they did during the last year of the sample period. We report the root-mean-square error (RMSE) as a forecasting accuracy measure in Table 7.

As can be seen, the results imply in particular that the continuous time model performs well with regard to forecasts for labor, capital, exports, transfers, and finally profits, interest, and dividends from abroad. The comparatively large errors in the forecasts for output, consumption, wages, and prices are most likely due to our use of a single deterministic time trend for technical progress and labor supply; a better approach would be to use stochastic trends. Similar conclusions are drawn from the earlier results.

4   Conclusions

In this note we have re-estimated the Bergstrom et al. (1992) model of the United Kingdom using more recent data. The results of these studies indicate that the next stage of research is to develop the exact Gaussian estimation method for mixed first- and second-order systems with mixed stock and flow data and to incorporate stochastic trends. The methods could then be applied to a modified mixed-order version of the model used in this note, allowing some equations with fast speeds of adjustment (e.g. consumption and output) to be modeled as first-order equations and the incorporation of stochastic trends. The investment equation should also be disaggregated. It is hoped that the results of such a study will be completed in the next few years by the author and Professor Bergstrom.

REFERENCES

Bergstrom, A. R. (1983), "Gaussian Estimation of Structural Parameters in Higher Order Continuous Time Dynamic Models," *Econometrica* 51: 1117-52.
(1985), "The Estimation of Parameters in Nonstationary Higher Order Continuous Time Dynamic Models," *Econometric Theory* 1: 369-85.
(1986), "The Estimation of Open Higher Order Continuous Time Dynamic Models with Mixed Stock and Flow Data," *Econometric Theory* 2: 350-73.
(1989), "Optimal Forecasting of Discrete Stock and Flow Data Generated by a Higher Order Continuous Time System," *Computers and Mathematics with Applications* 17: 1203-14.
(1990), *Continuous Time Econometric Modelling*. Oxford University Press.
Bergstrom, A. R., K. B. Nowman, and S. Wandasiewicz (1994), "Monetary and Fiscal Policy in a Second Order Continuous Time Macroeconometric Model of the United Kingdom," *Journal of Economic Dynamics and Control* 18: 731-61.
Bergstrom, A. R., K. B. Nowman, and C. R. Wymer (1992), "Gaussian Estimation of a Second Order Continuous Time Macroeconometric Model of the United Kingdom," *Economic Modelling* 9: 313-52.
Bergstrom, A. R., and C. R. Wymer (1976), "A Model of Disequilibrium Neoclassical Growth and Its Application to the United Kingdom," in A. R. Bergstrom (ed.), *Statistical Inference in Continuous Time Economic Models*. Amsterdam: North-Holland, pp. 267-328.
Gandolfo, G. (1981), *Qualitative Analysis and Econometric Estimation of Continuous Time Dynamic Models*. Amsterdam: North-Holland.
(ed.) (1993), *Continuous Time Econometrics: Theory and Applications*. London: Chapman and Hall.
Nowman, K. B. (1991), "Open Higher Order Continuous Time Dynamic Model with Mixed Stock and Flow Data and Derivatives of Exogenous Variables," *Econometric Theory* 7: 404-8.
(1992), "Computer Program for Estimation of Continuous Time Dynamic Models with Mixed Stock and Flow Data," *Economic and Financial Computing* 2: 25-38.
(1993), "Finite Sample Properties of the Gaussian Estimation of an Open Higher Order Continuous Time Dynamic Model with Mixed Stock and Flow Data," in G. Gandolfo (ed.), *Continuous Time Econometrics: Theory and Applications*. London: Chapman and Hall, pp. 93-116.

CHAPTER 7

Evaluation of discrete and continuous time dynamic models by spectral methods with an application to automobile demand

Michael Reiter

1   Introduction

The aim of this paper is to present a powerful method for evaluating dynamic economic models. It rests on the methodological tenet that the principal desideratum of a dynamic model is not to pass some formal statistical tests, but rather to explain the stylized facts that can be uncovered from the data. This methodological position is dominant in the natural sciences, and has been advocated in economics since the 1960s by Hillinger and associates and is now a firm constituent of the work at SEMECON, Munich (Hillinger 1992). Since the method of this paper does not rely on statistical tests, it can be used to evaluate estimated as well as calibrated models.[1]

In order to see whether a model is able to explain the observed stylized facts, it is necessary to investigate thoroughly the dynamic properties of the data as well as of the explanatory model. A thorough dynamic analysis of estimated econometric models is seldom performed in econometric applications. A pioneering contribution in this field was made by Adelman and Adelman (1959), who investigated the Klein–Goldberger model. Important contributions to the analysis of the long-run properties of dynamic models came from the advocates of continuous time econometrics (see e.g. Bergstrom and Wymer 1976, Gandolfo 1981). We have strong a priori conceptions (e.g. stability) concerning the long-run properties of models, although it is hard to extract information from available economic time series, which are typically short. The situation is completely different with the *cyclical* aspects of dynamic models, to which this paper

I wish to thank G. Gandolfo, C. Hillinger, B. Nowman, U. Woitek, and two anonymous referees for helpful comments on previous drafts of this manuscript.
[1] Calibrated models may need some additional stochastics to fit the data; cf. Watson (1993).

is devoted. We have very few a priori beliefs about those, but are able to extract them from the data.

To identify stylized facts concerning cyclical dynamics, it is appropriate to perform the analysis in the frequency domain – that is, by use of spectral methods. The spectrum is a complete characterization of linear processes, and it can be applied to certain types of nonlinear models by use of some appropriate linearization. Therefore, I propose to compare the multivariate spectra of the economic model with spectral estimates obtained from the data by time-series methods. The univariate and bivariate spectral parameters such as coherence and phase shift (see Section 6.1) give information about the model and the data that is easily interpretable and highly useful in business cycle analysis.

The idea of comparing the model dynamics with the dynamics of the data as identified by time-series methods is, of course, not new. It was advocated, for example, by Howrey (1980), but it did not receive the attention it deserves. One reason for this is certainly that comparison of the dynamics of the data and of the model does not easily lead to a formal statistical test, which many econometricians seem to regard as the only legitimate means of model evaluation. In contrast, I think that the role of informal judgment should be strengthened relative to formal testing. The main argument for this is that formal statistical methods test whether the econometric model is true in a literal sense (including all stochastic assumptions). Yet economic models today are not true in such a strong sense, and probably never will be. If they are not, then refutation depends on the power of the test, which in turn is largely a matter of the sample size (this and other arguments are brought forward in more detail in Reiter 1995). However, even if a model can be formally rejected, it may still be highly useful if it explains the basic features of the dynamics of the data. This can be uncovered by the dynamic analysis suggested in this paper.

Because calibrated models cannot be subjected to statistical testing in the standard way, it is common practice to analyze whether their dynamic properties fit the sylized facts. Unfortunately, most of the literature in this field confines itself to a very rudimentary analysis, such as citing some covariances. A methodology for the thorough dynamic analysis of calibrated models was developed by Watson (1993), who also provided a fine example of the power of spectral methods in model evaluation. Contrary to the present paper, Watson did not treat the trend problem and did not consider multivariate spectra.

Besides the stress on formal statistical testing, there are two further reasons why spectral methods are not frequently used in economics: First, classical spectral methods are nonparametric and can be applied satisfactorily only to relatively long data series, which are typically not available in economics. This problem can be overcome by the use of parametric spectral estimation methods such as the AR (autoregressive) spectrum. (Burg 1967 provided a strong foundation for the use of AR spectra in terms of the maximum entropy formalism; an economic application was given by Sebold-Bender 1990.) The second problem is that the time series under consideration have a trend as well as a cyclical component. In order to perform spectral analysis it is necessary to eliminate the trend component, which is a difficult task that can lead to distorted results (early references are Chan, Hayya, and Ord 1977 and Nelson and Kang 1981). The existence of exogenous variables has the same effect as a trend, rendering the model unstationary unless the exogenous variables are themselves assumed to follow stationary processes. A main contribution of this paper is to provide techniques for removing the trend of a model and the effects of exogenous variables in a way that is consistent with the model to be tested. I start with the Beveridge–Nelson decomposition and generalize it to handle models with arbitrary roots and exogenous variables. This paper considers a very comprehensive class of linear models, treating continuous as well as discrete time models – both in the state-space formulation, which allows unobservable variables. The analysis of nonlinear models cannot be general; this paper is confined to demonstrating the procedure with two simple models.

The plan of the paper is as follows. Section 2 briefly discusses some problems related to the detrending of economic time series, and then provides suitable stable transformations for a comprehensive class of linear discrete time models. The analysis is carried over to continuous time models in Section 3 and to nonlinear models in Section 4. The rest of the paper serves to illustrate the proposed methodology: Section 5 presents a model for the purchases of durable goods, and Section 6 contains the empirical results for German automobile data.

2   A detrending procedure for discrete time dynamic systems

2.1   *Detrending economic time series*

To apply spectral analysis, it is necessary to find appropriate stationary transformations of the data as well as of the original model. Data detrending procedures can be classified according to whether they are based on explicit assumptions about the nature of the trend generating process, or use a pragmatic methodology that is expected to yield an at least approximately stationary series for a wide class of models. I will call these methods model-based and model-independent, respectively. Applying a Hodrick–Prescott filter is a typical example of the latter, whereas taking

nth differences is of the first type, if one explicitly assumes that the series is integrated of order n. Differencing can also be used in a model-independent way, if no special assumptions about the series are made.

It is now well-known that the detrending of time series is extremely problematic, since the choice of the wrong detrending procedure (for example, fitting deterministic trend functions to integrated time series) leads to severe distortions of the cyclical structure. Dickey–Fuller tests are widely used to determine the nature of the trend generating process, but the short economic time series contain insufficient information to decide the issue, so that standard tests have little power (see e.g. Phillips, Kwiatkowsky, and Schmidt 1991).

In the present context of evaluating models of cyclical growth, we can avoid these problems and apply a detrending procedure that is strictly consistent with the model under investigation. In other words, the data can be subjected to the same transformation as is applied to the model to make it stationary. This model-based detrending procedure has the further advantage that it can distinguish between endogenous dynamics and the impact of exogenous variables, whereas a purely statistical detrending procedure eliminates only the long-run component of a time series.

The central part of the proposed evaluation procedure is therefore the comparison of the spectrum of the model with an estimate of the spectrum of the data, where the data series was made stationary in the same way as the model. In addition, I think it is informative to consider the estimated spectrum of the data detrended by a model-independent method. If the results for the two data series diverge significantly, this calls for a closer investigation. Perhaps the discrepancy is due to the inadequency of the model-independent detrending, but it may also be due to the impact of exogenous variables, or to a deficient treatment of the trend component in the economic model.

Model-based detrending methods play a double role in our case, yielding a transformation that renders the model, as well as the data, stationary. The rest of this section is concerned with developing reasonable detrending procedures for several classes of linear models. Nonstationarity in a linear model may arise from the endogenous dynamics (e.g. unit roots) or from the impact of exogenous variables, or from both. Sections 2.3–2.6 treat these cases separately; the general model is first presented in Section 2.2.

2.2   *Discrete time models*

I assume that the model is in state-space form:

$$x_{t+1} = Ax_t + Bz_t + u_{t+1}, \tag{1a}$$

$$y_t = Zx_t + v_t, \tag{1b}$$

where x_t is a vector of unobserved state variables that evolves according to the transition equation (1a). The vector of observations y_t, also called the *output process,* is linked to the state variables by the observation equation (1b). The random vectors u_t and v_t are serially and mutually uncorrelated; more precisely,

$$E(u_t u_t') = Q, \quad E(v_t v_t') = R \quad \forall t,$$

$$E(u_t u_s') = 0, \quad E(v_t v_s') = 0 \quad \forall s \neq t,$$

$$E(u_t v_r') = 0 \quad \forall t, r.$$

Equations (1a) and (1b) imply that the observations follow a vector ARMAX process. Conversely, for every ARMAX process, a state-space model can be specified that implies the same output process. Higher-order AR terms can be brought into first-order form by including lagged variables in the state vector. The handling of MA (moving-average) terms of arbitrary order is treated, for example, in Hannan and Deistler (1988, sec. 1.2). The matrix A may have eigenvalues greater than or equal to unity, so that co-integrated systems are a special case. This shows that vector ARMAX models and state-space models are equivalent in the sense that they imply the same output processes. The advantage of the state-space representation is that its simple standardized form allows the use of the Kalman filter (see Section 2.3).

2.3 *Detrending co-integrated models*

In this section it is assumed that all variables are integrated of order at most 1.[2]

A suitable stationary transformation of the variables must be found. For any model there are, of course, several different stable transformations. For example, the vector of first differences of the variables is stable, so one can compare the spectrum of the differenced data to the theoretical spectrum of the differences of the variables as implied by the model. This solution has the advantage of simplicity. I think, however, that it is more appropriate to use the decomposition suggested by Beveridge and Nelson (1981), abbreviated hereafter as the "BN decomposition." It is explained in what follows, and convenient ways of computation are given for the type of processes that are of interest to us. The BN decomposition has the following advantages when compared to taking first differences.

    (1)   It is necessary to identify the structure of the detrended data by time-series methods. Even if the original model has a finite autoregressive representation, first differences do not if there are

---

[2] See note 3 for higher-order integrated models.

co-integration relationships (Engle and Granger 1987, p. 259). In that case, the cyclical component in the BN decomposition has a simpler structure, as we shall demonstrate.

(2)   Taking differences will amplify the noise in the series. Assume, for example, that the model (3) exactly describes the path of the actual variables but that the data contain a white-noise measurement error. Taking differences introduces an MA component, which has a greater variance than the original measurement error. The BN decomposition avoids this pitfall.

(3)   Taking differences renders models with real unit roots stationary. In the context of economic models, however, eigenvalues of the system matrix with absolute value greater than unity, or cyclical unstable roots, might occur. This case can be handled by a generalization of the BN decomposition introduced in Section 2.4.

The literature has criticized the BN decomposition on several grounds. For example, the trend estimate at time t uses information only up to time t (cf. equation (2)), unlike smoothed estimates. I do not deny that it is possible to find better decompositions for many purposes. In our context, the BN decomposition can be very easily used and generalized to cover all important cases. Because we are ultimately interested in a comparison of the dynamics of the model and the data, the choice of the decomposition is less important than the fact that model and data are detrended in exactly the same way.

The BN decomposition is defined for vector stochastic process ξ_t where all variables are integrated of order 1, so that the first differences are stationary; this allows the Wold representation

$$\Delta \xi_t = d + b(L)\epsilon_t$$

with a drift vector d. The BN decomposition splits ξ_t additively into a permanent and a transitory component,

$$\xi_t = \bar{\xi}_t + \tilde{\xi}_t,$$

where $\bar{\xi}_t$ is defined as the original variable plus the limit of the sum of future expected changes, corrected for the drift term:

$$\bar{\xi}_t = \xi_t + \lim_{k \to \infty} \sum_{i=1}^{k} [E_t(\xi_{t+i} - \xi_{t+i-1}) - d]. \tag{2}$$

The operator E_t denotes the linear projection of a variable on the set of past values of ξ up to ξ_t. In case $d = 0$, $\bar{\xi}_t$ is simply the limit of the expectation of ξ_k for $k \to \infty$.

An attractive feature of the BN decomposition is that it can be easily computed and interpreted if the series at hand has an AR representation.

Take the special case of the state-space model (1), without exogenous variables and with all state variables observable. The variables follow the transition equation

$$x_t = Ax_{t-1} + u_t \tag{3}$$

with white-noise error u_t. Assume that A can be diagonalized, so that the vector x_t can be expressed as a linear combination of the eigenvectors of A. It is well-known from linear system theory that the components belonging to eigenvalues with absolute value smaller than unity will asymptotically approach zero in expectation. The components belonging to unit eigenvalues are expected to stay constant. The permanent component of x_t is therefore the sum of the components belonging to unit eigenvalues. The stationary component $\bar{x}_t$ is the sum of the components belonging to the stable eigenvalues.

A formal exposition is as follows: Let the co-integration rank be $m < n$, so that there exists a co-integration matrix C with rank m such that Cx_t is a stationary process. Assuming that A can be diagonalized,[3] we have $GAG^{-1} = \Lambda$ with diagonal Λ. From the transformation

$$Gx_t = \Lambda Gx_{t-1} + Gu_t$$

we see that a version of the co-integration matrix is the submatrix consisting of the rows of G belonging to diagonal entries of Λ smaller than unity. The columns of G^{-1} are the eigenvectors of A. The components of x_t belonging to the m-dimensional stable subspace are the fluctuating components of the series. More precisely, express x_t by

$$x_t = \sum_{i=1}^{n} \alpha_{it} g_i, \tag{4}$$

where g_i are the eigenvectors of A. If the roots are distinct (if not, see note 12), such a representation exists because the eigenvectors span the n-dimensional space. Assume that the eigenvalues are ordered so that the first m are smaller than unity. The cyclical component, also called the "detrended series," can then be expressed as

$$\bar{x}_t = \sum_{i=1}^{m} \alpha_{it} g_i. \tag{5}$$

This series contains the stable components of x_t; the components belonging to the unstable roots are filtered out.

---

[3] This assumption is not essential and is made solely for simplicity of exposition. If it is violated, as is the case for variables integrated of order 2, the following operations can be performed with generalized eigenspaces. The concept of a generalized eigenspace is explained in Hirsch and Smale (1974, p. 110).

The cyclical component $\tilde{x}_t$ is a linear transformation of the original data, so we can rewrite equations (4) and (5) as

$$\tilde{x}_t = Mx_t, \tag{6}$$

where

$$M = G^{-1}EG, \quad E = \begin{bmatrix} I_m & 0 \\ 0 & 0 \end{bmatrix}.$$

Here, I_m denotes the m-dimensional identity matrix and the zero matrices are appropriately sized. Accordingly, the stationary component $\bar{x}_t$ can be obtained by

$$\bar{x}_t = \bar{M}x_t, \quad \bar{M} = I - M.$$

If the model is correct, the detrended data follow the stationary process

$$\tilde{x}_t = (AM)\tilde{x}_{t-1} + Mu_t \tag{7}$$

because $AM = MA$ and $M^2 = M$, as can be easily verified. Formula (7) shows that if the original data follow an autoregressive scheme then so do the detrended data $\tilde{x}_t$, contrary to the vector of first differences. The system matrix AM has the same eigenvalues as A, except that unit eigenvalues are replaced by zeros.

We turn now to the general state-space model (1) with unobserved variables (we continue to ignore exogenous variables). In order to handle this case we must introduce the Kalman filter, which is a recursive algorithm for computing best linear estimates of the unobserved state variables. When all variables are Gaussian, the estimates are conditional expectations.

We need the following definitions: Y_t is the stacked vector of observations up to time t: $[y_1', \ldots, y_t']'$; $x_{n|m}$ and $y_{n|m}$ are the conditional expectations of x_n and y_n with respect to Y_m; $P_{n|m}$ is the conditional covariance matrix relating to $x_{n|m}$; and F_t is the innovation covariance matrix. The Kalman filter consists of the prediction equations

$$x_{t|t-1} = Ax_{t-1|t-1}, \tag{8a}$$

$$y_{t|t-1} = Zx_{t|t-1}, \tag{8b}$$

$$P_{t|t-1} = AP_{t-1|t-1}A' + Q, \tag{8c}$$

$$F_t = ZP_{t|t-1}Z' + R \tag{8d}$$

and the updating equations

$$x_{t|t} = x_{t|t-1} + K_t(y_t - Zx_{t|t-1}), \tag{9a}$$

$$P_{t|t} = P_{t|t-1} - K_tF_tK_t', \tag{9b}$$

where the Kalman gain K_t is defined as

$$K_t = P_{t|t-1} Z' F_t^{-1}. \tag{10}$$

We can now use the Kalman filter estimates to obtain forecasts of the output variables. Since the optimal forecast of x_s based on Y_t is given by $A^{s-t} x_{t|t}$, it is obvious that $\bar{y}_t = Z\bar{M}x_{t|t}$, so

$$\bar{y}_t = ZMx_{t|t} + (y_t - Zx_{t|t}). \tag{11}$$

This equation defines a stationary transformation of the model. Given estimates of M, we can obtain a detrended data series and compare the estimated spectrum of the data to the theoretical spectrum of (11) as implied by the model. A formula for the theoretical spectrum of (11) is derived in Appendix A.

2.4 A generalization of the Beveridge–Nelson decomposition

The BN decomposition is designed to detrend models with unit roots. Estimated structural economic models sometimes have roots (more precisely, eigenvalues of the system matrix) with absolute value greater than unity, or unstable cyclical roots. Furthermore, it might happen that roots are smaller than but very close to unity. In this case the model has a spectral density, but most of the spectral mass is in the low-frequency range. I therefore propose to eliminate the impact of those roots that are not significantly different from unity.[4] The interpretation of the BN decomposition given in Section 2.3 suggests an obvious generalization of the BN decomposition that can handle these cases. Start with the diagonalized transition equation

$$Gx_t = \Lambda Gx_{t-1} + Gu_t,$$

and assume

$$\Lambda = \begin{bmatrix} a_1 & & & & & \\ & \ddots & & & 0 & \\ & & a_m & & & \\ & & & b_1 & & \\ & 0 & & & \ddots & \\ & & & & & b_{n-m} \end{bmatrix}.$$

---

[4] One of the referees pointed out that Aoki (1989) has developed a transformation that is very similar to the one proposed here. It is also based on the idea of filtering out the components related to unstable eigenvalues of the system matrix. Aoki's decomposition is more elegant from a theoretical point of view, but less simple.

The a_i represent stable eigenvalues; the b_j denote unstable eigenvalues – that is, those with absolute value greater than or equal to unity, or perhaps eigenvalues that are smaller than unity but not significantly so. We can now define a detrended series by (6) and proceed as in Section 2.3.

2.5   *Detrending models with exogenous variables*

Consider the state transition equation (1a),

$$x_{t+1} = Ax_t + Bz_t + u_{t+1},$$

and assume that the matrix A has all eigenvalues inside the unit circle. The nonstationarity arises because of the vector of exogenous variables z_t. If these variables follow a trend, they also imply a trend for the state vector x_t. A familiar example are neoclassical growth models, where the trend is induced by the exogenous growth of the labor force and by technical progress, which are related to the exogenous variable time (see Section 4).

Using the lag operator L, we can write

$$x_{t+1} = (I - AL)^{-1}(Bz_t + u_{t+1}).$$

From this we see that

$$\tilde{x}_t = x_t - (I - AL)^{-1}Bz_{t-1} = (I - AL)^{-1}u_t \tag{12}$$

is a stationary series. It is obtained by subtracting from x_t the cumulated impact of the exogenous variables, thereby eliminating the trend. Given estimates of A, B, and the error covariance matrix R, the spectral density of $\tilde{x}_t$ can be computed.

It remains to find a stationary transformation of the data. First, let us assume that all state variables are observable. It would be desirable to transform the data in the manner given by (12). This expression cannot be directly calculated, however, because the infinite past of z_t is not known (except for constants or time trends). We must therefore refer to the difference equation

$$\tilde{x}_{t+1} = A\tilde{x}_t + u_{t+1}, \tag{13}$$

which can be easily inferred from (1a). If we take the estimated system parameters as the true values then the error term on the right-hand side of (13) can be replaced by its estimated value $\hat{u}_t$, so that

$$\tilde{x}_{t+1} = A\tilde{x}_t + \hat{u}_{t+1}. \tag{14}$$

The problem is therefore reduced to finding the starting values $\tilde{x}_1$. If the given time series is sufficiently long, then our choice of the initial state has only a small influence on most of the data points and therefore on the estimated spectral density of the series. However, in case of the short series typical of economic data, the choice of x_1 may be of some importance. Our options at this point may be summarized as follows.

(1) Extrapolate the exogenous variables backwards and construct starting values by (12). Because the extrapolation is arbitrary, this method may generate very unreasonable results and so is not considered further.

(2) Obtain initial values by model-independent detrending. This procedure seems reasonable, but is possible only when all state variables are observed.

(3) Compute the variance of x_1 under the assumption of stationarity and draw a realization from a random-number generator. This technique is consistent with the model, but has the disadvantage of introducing a further stochastic element in the computation of the detrended series. Also, it does not yield a uniquely determined detrended series.

(4) If we are not interested in a uniquely determined detrended series but rather in the spectral density or some parametric representation of the series (e.g., an AR representation), then procedure (3) can be repeated sufficiently often in order to compute the expected value of this representation.

(5) Initialize x with its unconditional expectation – that is, a vector of zeros. This method can be considered as an approximation to procedure (4) because it yields the same results for a linear transformation of the data, such as the periodogram. In cases where (2) cannot be applied, I would recommend this procedure, also because of its simplicity; it will be used in Section 6.

The generalization to the case where the state vector is only partially observed is straightforward. Given estimates $x_{t|t}$, we can define $\hat{u}_{t|t}$ and $\hat{v}_{t|t}$ by

$$\hat{u}_{t|t} = x_{t|t} - Ax_{t-1|t-1} - Bz_{t-1},$$

$$\hat{v}_{t|t} = y_t - Zx_{t|t}.$$

Now define the detrended series $\bar{x}_t$ by

$$\bar{x}_t = A\bar{x}_{t-1} + \hat{u}_{t|t},$$

where an initial vector $\bar{x}_1$ was found via one of the foregoing procedures; the detrended data series is then obtained by

$$\bar{y}_t = Z\bar{x}_t + \hat{v}_{t|t}.$$

This eliminates the cumulated impact of the exogenous variables on x_t and on y_t. The empirical spectrum of the detrended series $\tilde{y}_t$ can be compared to the theoretical spectrum of the model without exogenous variables, which is given by

$$F_y(\omega) = Z(I - Ae^{-i\omega})^{-1}Q\overline{(I - Ae^{-i\omega})^{-1}}Z' + R,$$

where the bar denotes the complex conjugate transpose.

The procedure proposed here can be interpreted in the following way: Equation (14) defines a transformation of the estimated errors, and we investigate afterward whether this transformation exhibits the same dynamic behavior (measured by the spectrum) as one would expect under the assumptions on the error term as stated by the model. If the model states that the u_t are white noise, the whole procedure can be seen as a test of whether the $\hat{u}_t$ really are white noise. For a formal test, it would probably be better to perform a white-noise test directly on the u_t. Our aim is not to provide a formal test but instead to gather interesting information about the performance of the model, information that can be easily interpreted and used to improve the model. It is therefore useful to consider the transformation (6).

2.6   *Detrending co-integrated models with exogenous variables*

The procedures of Sections 2.4 and 2.5 can be combined in an obvious way to detrend a model with both sources of nonstationarity, that is, a model of the form (1) where the system matrix has some unit roots. First eliminate the impact of the exogenous variables by the transformation (12), then eliminate the unit roots by the transformation (6). The theoretical spectrum of the detrended series is again given by formula (32) in Appendix A.

3   Continuous time models

This section describes briefly how the methods developed in Section 2 carry over to continuous time models. This paper does not treat the estimation problem. It is assumed that estimates by the methods of Bergstrom (1983, 1985, 1986), Harvey and Stock (1985), or Zadrozny (1988) can be obtained.

The general linear continuous time dynamic model can be written in state-space form as[5]

---

[5] The model can be further generalized to handle mixed frequency data (cf. Zadrozny 1988).

$$d\alpha(t) = [A\alpha(t) + Bz(t)]\,dt + \zeta(dt), \tag{15a}$$

$$y_\tau^s = Z^s\alpha(t_\tau) + \xi_\tau^s, \tag{15b}$$

$$y_\tau^f = Z^f \int_0^\delta \alpha(t_{\tau-1} + s)\,ds + \xi_\tau^f. \tag{15c}$$

The state transition equation (15a) is a system of first-order stochastic differential equations[6] in the state vector $\alpha(t)$. The vector $z(t)$ is exogenous, and $\zeta(dt)$ is a continuous time white-noise error with covariance matrix Σ. The model contains two measurement equations, (15b) for stock data y_τ^s such as capital, which can be measured at a point in time, and (15c) for flow data y_τ^f such as consumption, which are measured as an integral over the observation period. Each equation allows for measurement errors, ξ_τ^s and ξ_τ^f respectively.

Continuous time models are typically handled by finding a discrete analog to the continuous system. An exact method uses an exact discrete analog – that is, a system of stochastic difference equations defining the same process as the stochastic differential equations imply for a set of discrete points $\alpha(t_1), \alpha(t_2), \dots$. For example, (15a) implies in the special case $z(t) = 0$ that

$$\alpha(t) = e^A \alpha(t-1) + \epsilon_t,$$

$$E(\epsilon_t) = 0,$$

$$E(\epsilon_t \epsilon_t') = \Omega = \int_0^1 e^{rA} \Sigma e^{rA'}\,dr,$$

$$E(\epsilon_s \epsilon_t') = 0, \quad s \neq t$$

(cf. Bergstrom 1984, pp. 1167ff). One can see that the discrete values $\alpha(0), \alpha(1), \dots$ obey a first-order vector autoregressive model with system matrix $e^A := \sum_{i=0}^\infty (A^i/i!)$ and covariance matrix Ω.

The treatment of the state-space model (15) is complicated by the presence of the flow variables y_τ^f. To apply the detrending procedures of the previous section, and to compute spectra for these models, it is necessary to find an exact discrete analog of the general model (15) that is of the form (1). Methods for this have been provided in the literature, and for completeness are summarized in Appendix B.

4 Nonlinear models

Spectral analysis is primarily a tool for investigating time series generated by linear models. Because most models of cyclical growth are nonlinear,

---

[6] These can be interpreted as Ito differential equations (cf. Oksendal 1989) or in the sense of Bergstrom (1984).

the method of this paper can gain wider application only if it can be used in connection with some common types of nonlinear models. This involves some linearization of the model, which implies that we can consider only nonlinear models that fulfill the following conditions.

(1)   The model must possess a path about which it is reasonable to linearize. This will typically be a steady-state path.

(2)   The dynamics of the model near the steady-state path must be well approximated by a linear model. This condition is typically fulfilled if the model is asymptotically stable; it is not fulfilled when the model is locally unstable and the dynamics is characterized by a limit cycle.

Most of the empirical models used today satisfy these requirements.

As in the case of linear models, we must find a stable transformation of the model as well as of the data. I will illustrate the procedure with two simple discrete time models. Again, we need to distinguish whether the instability is caused by the endogenous dynamics or by exogenous variables. For the latter case, consider a version of the neoclassical growth model with a Cobb–Douglas production function:

$$K_{t+1} = se^{\mu t}K_t^{\alpha}L_t^{1-a} + (1-\delta)K_t + u_t.$$

Capital K grows by the fraction s of gross output, subject to the error term u_t, and is written off with the factor δ. Labor supply L is assumed to be exogenous. Productivity grows at the exogenous rate μ. To achieve stationarity, the effect of the exogenous variables (here, of L_t and t) must be cancelled by equating them to a constant[7] but – unlike with linear models – not necessarily to zero. In the previous equation it is convenient to set $t = 0$ and $L = 1$, yielding

$$K_{t+1} = sK_t^{\alpha} + (1-\delta)K_t + u_t. \tag{16}$$

Ignoring the error term, the model allows the constant steady-state path $K_t = (s/d)^{1/(1-\alpha)}$. Linearizing about the steady state yields

$$K_{t+1} \approx \left(\frac{s}{\delta}\right)^{1/(1-\alpha)} + [1-(1-\alpha)\delta]\left(K_t - \left(\frac{s}{\delta}\right)^{1/(1-\alpha)}\right) + u_t. \tag{17}$$

Next we must find a data series $\tilde{K}_t$ that is detrended consistently with the model. This can be done in complete analogy to the linear case: Initialize $\tilde{K}_0$ by the steady-state value and use (16), replacing u_t by the estimated errors $\hat{u}_t$. The result is

---

[7]   To avoid misunderstandings, this relates to time as an *exogenous variable*. As an index for other variables, time retains its normal role, of course.

$$\tilde{K}_{t+1} = s\tilde{K}_t^\alpha + (1-\delta)\tilde{K}_t + \hat{u}_t. \tag{18}$$

Alternatively, one can generate the detrended data series by using the linearized model (17). This has the advantage that the linearization error does not impair the comparison of model and data.

The foregoing model can be handled so easily because it is stationary once the impact of the exogenous variables is eliminated. The situation is more complicated if the nonstationarity results from endogenous dynamic forces, when it becomes necessary to find stable combinations of the variables. Consider the following model, where the productivity parameter Θ_t is an endogenous variable (for simplicity, the exogenous variable L_t has already been removed):

$$K_{t+1} = (s\Theta_t K_t^\alpha + (1-\delta)K_t)e^{u_{1t}}, \tag{19a}$$

$$\Theta_{t+1} = \beta\Theta_t e^{u_{2t}}, \quad \beta > 1. \tag{19b}$$

Ignoring shocks, this model allows a steady state where Θ_t and K_t grow with the constant rates $\ln\beta$ and $\ln\beta/(1-\alpha)$, respectively. This suggests that the variable $\xi_t = K_t^{1-\alpha}\Theta_t^{-1}$ is stationary, which can be considered as the nonlinear generalization of a cointegration relationship. Using equations (19), it is easy to check that

$$\xi_{t+1} = \beta^{-1}[s\xi_t^{\alpha/(1-\alpha)} + (1-\delta)\xi_t^{1/(1-\alpha)}]^{1-\alpha}e^{(1-\alpha)u_{1t}-u_{2t}} \tag{20}$$

and that the stationary value is $\xi = s/\delta$. It is now possible to linearize (20) about the stationary value, probably after taking logarithms. Notice that the dimension of the stationary system (20) is lower than that of (19). This is analogous to the linear case, where the matrix M in equation (6) is not of full rank, projecting the state vector into a lower-dimensional subspace. The method described here can be generalized to models of higher dimension if it is possible to find stationary transformations of the variables.

With respect to continuous time models, the linearization about the steady state is well documented in the literature for a widely employed class of models (Gandolfo 1981); I shall not supply the details here. Detrended data series can be obtained using the ideas set out in this section.

We have shown that the treatment of nonlinear models can be based on the same ideas already employed with linear models.

(1) Eliminate the impact of exogenous variables by equating them to a constant.
(2) Find stable combinations of the variables. Find a differential equation system in the stable variables. Linearize about the steady-state values.
(3) Obtain detrended data by using the stationarized model, replacing the theoretical error terms by its estimated values. Initialize using the steady-state value.

5   A model for the consumption of durables

5.1   *The continuous time model*

The methods developed in the preceding sections will now be illustrated with a small model explaining the purchases of consumer durables and some related variables. First I develop the basic continuous time model. Section 5.2 will derive a simple discrete analogue, and both versions will be estimated and compared.

Attention will focus on the consumption equation, which is thought to be structural. The other variables are modeled in an ad hoc, time-series fashion. These variables include disposable income and the real interest rate, which are important variables for explaining durable consumption, as well as fixed investment, which is a main driving force of the business cycle and helps to model the other variables satisfactorily. A basic assumption is that consumers draw utility not from the purchases of durable goods C but rather from the services rendered by the available stock of goods S. It is therefore natural to specify a *desired level of stocks* of durable goods S^*. The desired stock of durables depends on current disposable income and on the real interest rate R. A look at our data suggests that the desired ratio of stocks to income has changed over the sample period; this may be due, for example, to the rise in income or to changes in relative prices. To account for these changes in a simple way, I specify the ratio of desired stocks to income as a second-order polynomial in t. The resulting expression for S^* must be linearized in variables:

$$S^* = (v_0 + v_1 t + v_2 t^2)Y + v_r R$$
$$\approx (v_0 + v_1 \bar{t} + v_2 \overline{t^2})Y + \bar{Y}(v_1 t + v_2 t^2) - \bar{Y}(v_1 \bar{t} + v_2 \overline{t^2}) + v_r R, \tag{21}$$

where $\bar{x}$ denotes the sample average of any variable x. Stocks adjust to their desired levels by the following second-order adjustment process:[8]

$$C^* = a_s(S^* - S) + \delta S + DS^*, \tag{22a}$$

$$DC = a_d(C^* - C). \tag{22b}$$

Desired purchases C^* partly fill the gap between desired and actual stocks, and account for the depreciation of stocks and also for the change in desired stocks. Actual purchases adjust to their desired value with a time lag, reflecting the assumption that changes in the rate of purchase of

---

[8] A very similar model was estimated by Bergstrom and Chambers (1990). They derive their equation from an intertemporal linear quadratic maximization calculus.

durable goods are costly. Combining the equations in (22) and representing DS^*, for simplicity, by $v_0 DY$, we have the consumption equation

$$DC = a_d[a_s(S^* - S) + \delta S + v_0 DY - C].\tag{23}$$

Stocks of durable goods evolve according to the familiar equation

$$DS = C - \delta S,\tag{24}$$

where a constant rate of depreciation δ is assumed. The rest of the model is in the VAR style:

$$D^2 I = \beta_{10} + \beta_{11} I + \beta_{12} DI + \beta_{13} Y + \beta_{14} DY,\tag{25a}$$

$$D^2 Y = \beta_{20} + \beta_{21} I + \beta_{22} DI + \beta_{23} Y + \beta_{24} DY + \beta_{25} C,\tag{25b}$$

$$DR = \beta_{30} + \beta_{31} DI + \beta_{32} DY + \beta_{33} C + \beta_{34} R.\tag{25c}$$

For estimation, equations (23) and (25) were supplemented by error terms. Equation (24) was used in deterministic form. This should increase the stability of the estimates, since data on the value of the stocks of automobiles are not available for Germany.

5.2 The simple discrete analog

We now formulate a simple discrete analog to the model of Section 5.1, with the differential operator replaced by the forward difference operator. There is some choice in the timing of variables, but it must be guaranteed that all endogenous variables in an equation are lagged. The investment equation now reads

$$\Delta^2 I_t = \beta_{10} + \beta_{11} I_t + \beta_{12} \Delta I_t + \beta_{13} Y_t + \beta_{14} \Delta Y_t,$$

where Δ is the forward differencing operator. This yields, after shifting the right-hand side back in time,

$$I_t = \beta_{10} + (2 + \beta_{12}) I_{t-1} + (\beta_{11} - \beta_{12} - 1) I_{t-2} + \beta_{14} Y_{t-1} + (\beta_{13} - \beta_{14}) Y_{t-2}.$$

Analogously, for Y and R we have

$$Y_t = \beta_{20} + \beta_{22} I_{t-1} + (\beta_{21} - \beta_{22}) I_{t-2}$$
$$+ (2 + \beta_{24}) Y_{t-1} + (\beta_{23} - \beta_{24} - 1) Y_{t-2} + \beta_{25} C_{t-1},$$

$$R_t = \beta_{30} + \beta_{31}(I_{t-1} - I_{t-2}) + \beta_{32}(Y_{t-1} - Y_{t-2})$$
$$+ \beta_{33} C_{t-1} + (1 + \beta_{34}) R_{t-1}.$$

The S_t term is the beginning-of-period stock of durables, which evolves according to

$$S_t = (1 - \delta) S_{t-1} + C_{t-1}.\tag{26}$$

Finally, for the purchases of consumer durables we have

$$S_t^* = (v_0 + v_1\bar{t} + v_2\overline{t^2})Y_t + \bar{Y}(v_1 t + v_2 t^2)$$
$$- \bar{Y}(v_1\bar{t} + v_2\overline{t^2}) + v_r R, \tag{27}$$

$$\Delta C_t = a_d[a_s(S_t^* - S_t) + \delta S_t + v_0\Delta Y_{t-1} - C_t],$$

which was transformed to

$$C_t = C_{t-1} + a_d[a_s(S_{t-1}^* - S_t) + \delta S_t + v_0(Y_{t-1} - Y_{t-2}) - C_{t-1}]. \tag{28}$$

Inserting (27) and (28) into (29) yields an equation with lagged endogenous variables.

6   Empirical results

6.1   Discrete time model

In Sections 6.1 and 6.2 we apply the models of Section 5 to annual German data of automobile demand, 1960–89,[9] and investigate them by the methods developed previously. Toward this end, Figures 1–5 present autospectra of both series and the three most important two-dimensional spectral parameters: the coherence, the phase spectrum, and the gain. A thorough interpretation of these parameters can be found, for example, in Koopmans (1974). Briefly, the *coherence* (which is also known as "squared coherency") at frequency λ is a number between zero and unity that indicates the strength of the relationship between both series at this frequency. The *phase spectrum* gives the expected value of the phase shift of one series relative to the other. Finally, the *gain* describes how the amplitude of a series is changed by the transmission to the other series.

As a first step in the analysis, I try to extract the most salient features of the data process using spectral estimates obtained from data that are detrended by a model-independent technique. I have argued in Section 2.1 that this is a useful supplement to the model-dependent methods.

Figure 1 shows the spectra for the Hodrick–Prescott filtered series (cf. Prescott 1986; the smoothness parameter has been set to 100). The spectra are obtained from an estimated third-order bivariate autoregressive model (this holds also for Figures 3 and 5). Both series exhibit a sharp peak at a frequency corresponding to a cycle of about 7.5 years. The coherence at this frequency is very high, about 0.9, and the phase spectrum shows that income lags at this frequency by about 1 year (a positive value of the gain spectrum means a lag of the first series, disposable income). The gain is about 5.

[9] The data are reported in Appendix C.

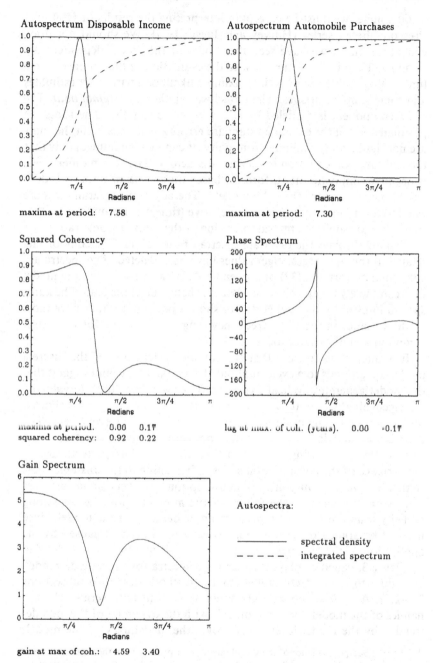

Figure 1. Multichannel spectral analysis: Germany 1960–89, data detrended by HP(100); disposable income and automobile purchases.

Of course, we must be careful in interpreting the results of Hodrick-Prescott filtered series (Harvey and Jaeger 1991). We should not draw conclusions until we have seen the results of the model-dependent detrending. Therefore, we turn now to the evaluation of the simple discrete time analog. Table 1 reports the maximum likelihood parameter estimates and some simple statistics. The model was applied to *original data*. The trend component is modeled by two roots close to unity. The roots are less than 0.9, but the estimated standard errors are large, so that the roots are not significantly different from unity. It can be seen immediately that the consumption equation is very unsatisfactory. The R^2 (in differences) is negative, implying that a forecast based on a random walk with drift would perform better than the model.[10] The adjustment parameters are estimated very low, and v_0 is even negative (time was normalized so that v_0 is approximately the midsample value of the stock/income ratio).

Figure 2 displays the bivariate spectra of the model. The components related to the two largest eigenvalues have been deleted. The spectra are computed by formula (32) of Appendix A. It can be seen that the model fails completely to reproduce the dynamic behavior of the data. The autospectra implied by the model do not show a peak, but rather have most of the variance in the short-frequency range. This is true for both consumption and disposable income.

It is interesting to note that the complex eigenvalue of the discrete model corresponds to a cycle of about 11.5 years. This would suggest that the model generates cyclical dynamics. However, the absolute value of the eigenvalue is only 0.69. This means that, in the absence of shocks, the amplitude of the cycle would reduce by 31 percent every year. The cycle is so much damped that it does not show up in the spectrum. The gain is very high, owing to the fact that the model interprets almost all the variance of the consumption series as belonging to the unstable root, so that the cyclical component of consumption has a very small variance.

It is unclear whether the failure of the model to produce the strong cyclicity found in Figure 1 represents an inadequacy of the model, since it could be argued that the strong cyclicity is an artefact caused by the application of the Hodrick-Prescott filter. This question can be decided by Figure 3, which displays the estimated spectra for the data detrended according to the discrete model (by the methods described in Sections 2.3–2.6). A cycle of about eight years appears in both series. The dynamics of the model does not coincide with the dynamics of the data detrended by the model itself. This proves the inadequacy of the model,

---

[10] The very bad performance of the model might be surprising. I ran the numerical maximization procedure with different starting values, but could not find better parameter values. Perhaps the numerical procedure did not reach the global maximum.

Table 1. *Results for the discrete time model*

Equation for	Parameters							R^2	Korr.
	a_s	a_d	δ	v_0	v_1	v_2	v_r		
C	0.010[a]	0.129 (0.082)	0.150[b]	-0.009 (0.145)	0.050 (0.007)	-0.002 (0.001)	47.656 (49.385)	-0.065	0.330
	β_{10}	β_{11}	β_{12}	β_{13}	β_{14}				
I	46.726 (18.842)	-0.266 (0.085)	-0.771 (0.154)	-0.012 (0.012)	0.096 (0.138)			0.472	0.041
	β_{20}	β_{21}	β_{22}	β_{23}	β_{24}	β_{25}			
Y	125.360 (32.109)	-0.150 (0.116)	-0.337 (0.235)	-0.180 (0.056)	-1.285 (0.179)	2.702 (0.871)		0.229	-0.014
	β_{30}	β_{31}	β_{32}	β_{33}	β_{34}				
R	2.398 (0.679)	-0.010 (0.016)	-0.002 (0.012)	0.016 (0.016)	-0.773 (0.173)			0.277	0.208
Eigenvalues									
Real part	0.899 (0.179)	0.873 (0.246)	0.834 (0.090)	0.590 (0.117)	0.201 (0.274)	-0.078 (0.332)			
Imaginary part	0.000	0.000	0.000	±0.358 (0.139)	0.000	0.000			

Notes: Standard errors are given in parentheses. R^2 refers to the changes in the variables, where $R^2 = 1 - (\text{Var(prediction error)}/\text{Var(differences of data)})$. "Korr." denotes the first-order serial correlation of the prediction error.
[a] Estimated at boundary of parameter space.
[b] Preset value.

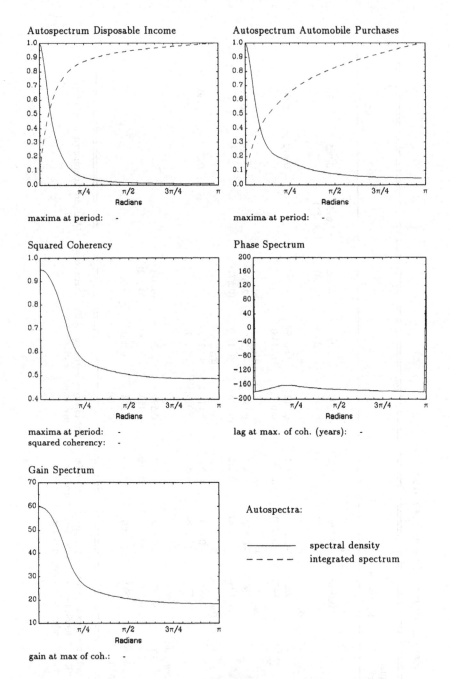

Figure 2. Multichannel spectral analysis: Germany 1960–89, discrete time model; disposable income and automobile purchases.

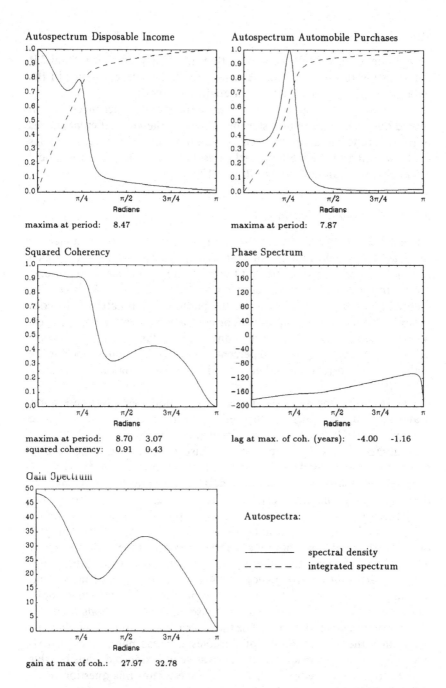

Figure 3. Multichannel spectral analysis: Germany 1960–89, data detrended by discrete time model; disposable income and automobile purchases.

219

even if one is not yet fully convinced that the eight-year cycle is "real." It is interesting to observe that the strong eight-year cycle remains in the data even if detrended by a very unsatisfactory model.

This example was rather extreme, since the model under investigation turned out to be very poorly specified. We saw the very different shapes of the theoretical and the empirical spectra in such a case. More examples of the working of the method, and cases where the failure of the model is less obvious, can be found in Reiter (1995).

6.2   *Continuous time model*

Table 2 presents the results for the continuous time model, estimated by the exact Gaussian estimator of Harvey and Stock (1985)[11] and applied to original data. It is obvious that the continuous time model represents a huge improvement over the simple discrete analog. The R^2 is considerably higher for all variables, and the parameter estimates of the consumption equation are reasonable. The complex eigenvalues imply a cycle with a period of 8.4 years, which is only slightly damped (in the absence of shocks, it reduces by only 10 percent a year). A disturbing aspect is the high negative correlation of the error in the consumption and income equations.

The results of the dynamic analysis of the model are given in Figures 4 and 5. Figure 4 shows the theoretical spectrum of the model, where the component belonging to the eigenvalue with real part −0.064 has been filtered out. This component was also removed from the data to obtain the model-based detrended series (cf. Sections 2.3–2.6). Figure 5 shows the estimated spectrum of the data. We see that the model mimics the dynamics of the data very well. For both series, the spectra of the model as well as of the data exhibit sharp peaks at a period of about 8.5–9 years. The cycle in the data seems to be somewhat longer than predicted by the model, but not much. The coherence at the cycle frequency is very high, showing that the 9-year cycles in both series are strongly interrelated. At this frequency, the gain and the phase of model and data approximately coincide. The model reproduces the interesting empirical finding that the cycle in the purchases of durable goods *leads* by about a year relative to income. The theoretical explanation is that income determines the desired *stocks* of durables whereas purchases approximate the change in stocks, and the derivative of a sinusoid leads relative to the series itself (Reiter 1995, chap. 6, investigates this question more closely). At frequencies with low coherence, the predictions of the model

---

[11] For details, see Reiter (1995).

Table 2. Results for the continuous time model

Equation for	Parameters							σ	R^2	Korr.
C	a_s 2.189 (0.396)	a_d 0.327 (0.040)	δ 0.150[a]	v_0 0.143 (0.003)	v_1 0.004 (0.000)	$v_2\times1000$ -0.129 (0.013)	v_r -1.072 (0.680)	2.316 (0.311)	0.596	-0.390
I	β_{10} 31.550 (41.508)	β_{11} -0.401 (0.194)	β_{12} -1.634 (0.258)	β_{13} -0.015 (0.025)	β_{14} 1.809 (0.044)			20.308 (3.676)	0.502	0.023
Y	β_{20} 3058.746 (765.633)	β_{21} -6.667 (2.680)	β_{22} -10.000[b]	β_{23} -3.887 (1.135)	β_{24} -10.000[b]	β_{25} 53.494 (17.332)		279.232 (36.162)	0.274	-0.254
R	β_{30} 5.336 (2.605)	β_{31} -0.095 (0.036)	β_{32} 0.022 (0.007)	β_{33} 0.047 (0.040)	β_{34} -1.973 (0.806)			2.149 (0.605)	0.433	0.029
Eigenvalues										
Real part	-0.064 (0.042)	-0.098 (0.052)	-0.586 (0.189)	-2.414 (1.109)	-4.436 (1.267)	-6.387 (0.719)				
Imaginary part	0.000	±0.748 (0.070)	0.000	0.000	0.000	0.000				

Notes: Standard errors are given in parentheses. The column headed by σ presents the standard deviation of the continuous time error process for each equation. R^2 refers to the changes in the variables, where $R^2 = 1 - (\text{Var}(\text{prediction error})/\text{Var}(\text{differences of data}))$. "Korr." denotes the first-order serial correlation of the prediction error.
[a] Preset value.
[b] Estimated at boundary of parameter space.

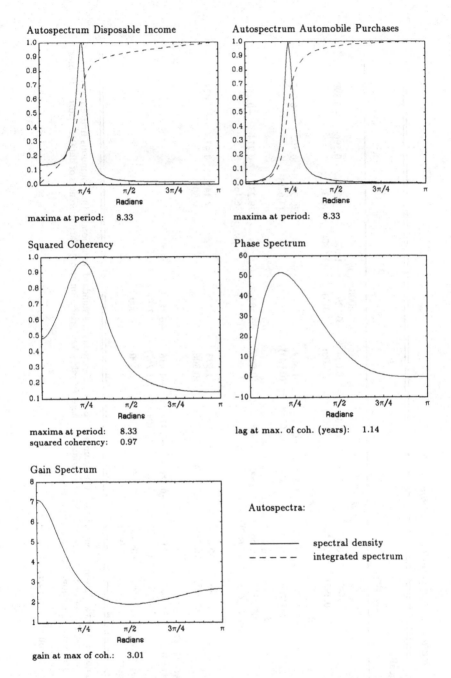

Figure 4. Multichannel spectral analysis: Germany 1960–89, continuous time model; disposable income and automobile purchases.

222

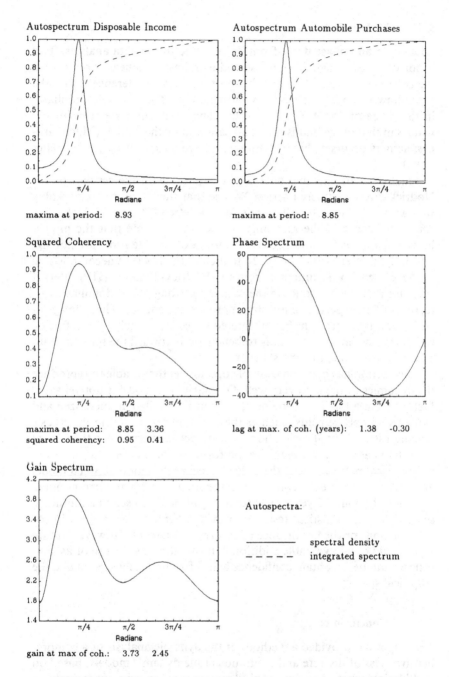

Figure 5. Multichannel spectral analysis: Germany 1960–89, data detrended by continuous time model; disposable income and automobile purchases.

223

about gain and phase differ from those found in the data analysis. This is not very disturbing, since phase and gain have significance only when the coherence is high. Perhaps the most important difference is that the data show some coherence between income and automobile purchases in the range of about 3.5-year cycles. This might indicate relevant dynamics in that range that is not at all captured by the model. (Much business activity occurs within the aforementioned frequency range; cf. Reiter 1995.)

Finally, let us examine once again Figure 1 with the results for the Hodrick–Prescott filtered series. We see that they conform remarkably well with the results for the model-based detrended series, which gives some confidence in the reliability of the results. Note that the model-based trend is of the unit-root type (more exactly, the roots are not significantly different from unity). In that case, the BN type decomposition we have used is very different from the Hodrick–Prescott (HP) filter. It confirms that the dynamics in the data is so strong that it dominates distortions of the spectra caused by improper detrending. That the cycles are somewhat shorter in the HP filtered series is probably an artefact of the filter: The fitted trend tends to bend closely toward the series at both ends of the sample, thereby shortening cycles.

This section has given an example of a model that is able to reproduce the dynamics of the data very well. Of course, the model is not yet satisfactory from a theoretical point of view. It is heavily parameterized and contains ad hoc elements, such as the exogenous variation in the stock/income ratio. A final evaluation of a model must consider theoretical plausibility as well as the empirical performance on a given sample. From an empirical point of view, the only significant deviation between model and data seems to be the coherence in the frequency range corresponding to cycles of about 3.5 years. The term "significant" is used in an intuitive sense, since no statistical tests are provided here. I have argued in the introduction for the importance of informal judgment. However, future work could obtain valuable additional information by the use of asymptotic techniques to obtain confidence bands for the model spectra and the empirical spectra.

7   Conclusions

This paper has provided a method for the dynamic analysis of a comprehensive class of discrete and continuous time dynamic models, based on multivariate spectral analysis. This dynamic analysis can serve to evaluate the merits of a model by its ability to explain the stylized facts regarding the cyclical structure of the time series. To uncover this structure, it is necessary to remove nonstationarities arising from the endogenous dynamics or from exogenous variables. The method developed here achieves stationarity of the data not by relying on arbitrary statistical assumptions, but rather by utilizing the trend mechanism of the structural economic model under investigation.

An illustrative example has compared two variants of a simple continuous time model: the exact discrete analog and a crude discrete approximation to the model. The exact discrete analog is able to reproduce the main characteristics of the multivariate spectrum of the data, whereas the failure of the crude approximation is drastically visible. The example has also demonstrated that economic data contain enough cyclical structure for the application of spectral methods to be highly informative.

Appendix A: Spectrum of detrended state-space model

The prediction and updating equations (8)–(10) of the Kalman filter in Section 2.2 can be combined to yield

$$P_{t+1|t} = A[P_{t|t-1} - P_{t|t-1}Z'(ZP_{t|t-1}Z'+R)^{-1}ZP_{t|t-1}]A' + Q. \tag{29}$$

In the following we denote by P the stationary solution to (29), that is, the solution of the algebraic Riccati equation

$$P = A[P - PZ'(ZPZ'+R)^{-1}ZP]A' + Q.$$

To obtain the spectrum of the detrended variable in (11), note from (8) and (9) that

$$Mx_{t|t} = AMx_{t-1|t-1} + MK(y_t - Zx_{t|t-1}).$$

This defines a transition equation in the variable Mx_t with an error covariance $MKFK'M'$, where $F = (ZPZ'+R)^{-1}$ and $K = PZ'F^{-1}$. We first treat the case $R = 0$. The variance of the prediction error is then ZPZ', the detrended data are given by $\bar{y}_t = ZMx_{t|t}$, and the spectral density of $\bar{y}_t$ is

$$F_{\bar{y}} = Z(I - Ae^{-i\omega})^{-1}MPZ'(ZPZ')^{-1}ZP\overline{(I - Ae^{-i\omega})^{-1}MZ'}. \tag{30}$$

To derive the analogous result for the case $R \neq 0$, it is convenient to write the model in an equivalent way with an augmented state space, treating the observation errors as state variables:

$$\begin{bmatrix} x_t \\ v_t \end{bmatrix} = A^* \begin{bmatrix} x_{t-1} \\ v_{t-1} \end{bmatrix} + \begin{bmatrix} u_t \\ v_t \end{bmatrix},$$

$$y_t = Z^* \begin{bmatrix} x_t \\ v_t \end{bmatrix}, \tag{31}$$

with

$$A^* = \begin{bmatrix} A & 0 \\ 0 & 0 \end{bmatrix}, \qquad Z^* = [\, Z \ I \,].$$

For the augmented state space, the analogs to the matrices M, P, and K are

$$M^* = \begin{bmatrix} M & 0 \\ 0 & I \end{bmatrix}, \qquad P^* = \begin{bmatrix} P & 0 \\ 0 & R \end{bmatrix}, \qquad K^* = \begin{bmatrix} PZ \\ R \end{bmatrix} (ZPZ' + R)^{-1}.$$

Applying (30) to the enlarged state space (31) yields, after a little algebra, the following formula for the spectral density of (11):

$$F_{\bar{y}} = [Z(I - Ae^{-i\omega})^{-1}MPZ' + R](ZPZ' + R)^{-1}$$
$$\times [ZP\overline{(I - Ae^{-i\omega})^{-1}MZ'} + R']. \tag{32}$$

This computation supposes that the algebraic Riccati equation has a unique solution. This is not very restrictive. Sufficient conditions are that the system be detectable and stabilizable. For more information, see Harvey (1989, p. 119).

Appendix B: Exact discrete analog of the continuous time state-space model

This appendix briefly describes how to transform the continuous time state-space model (15) into a discrete time state-space model (1). The material is based on Harvey and Stock (1985, 1988), Zadrozny (1988), and Reiter (1995). Since the impact of exogenous variables is filtered out by detrending, they do not affect the spectrum and can be omitted for notational simplicity.

In order to cope with the difficulties of a mixed sample, I will use the device of constructing an enlarged state space and apply the standard Kalman filter to it (Harvey and Stock 1988). Define the new discrete time state vector β_τ as

$$\beta_\tau = \begin{bmatrix} \alpha(t_\tau) \\ \alpha_\tau^{f*} \end{bmatrix}, \qquad \alpha_\tau^{f*} = Z^f \int_0^\delta \alpha(t_{\tau-1} + s)\, ds. \tag{33}$$

The variable α_τ^{f*} was chosen such that

$$y_\tau^f = \alpha_\tau^{f*} + \xi_\tau^f.$$

Next we must find a transition equation for α_τ^{f*}. To simplify the following formulas, I use the notation $\int_a^b \zeta(c + dr)$ as equivalent to $\int_{c+a}^{c+b} \zeta(dr)$. It follows from (15a) that

$$\alpha(t_{\tau-1} + s) = e^{As}\alpha(t_{\tau-1}) + \int_0^s e^{A(s-r)}R\zeta(t_{\tau-1} + dr)$$

and therefore

$$\alpha(t_\tau) = e^{A\delta}\alpha(t_{\tau-1}) + \int_0^\delta e^{A(\delta-r)}R\zeta(t_{\tau-1}+dr).$$

Using (33) we obtain

$$\alpha_\tau^{f*} = Z^f\left[\int_0^\delta e^{As}\alpha(t_{\tau-1})\,ds + \int_0^\delta \int_0^s e^{A(s-r)}R\zeta(t_{\tau-1}+dr)\,ds\right].$$

We therefore have the following exact discrete analog to (15a)–(15c):

$$\beta_{\tau+1} = T\beta_\tau + \epsilon_{\tau+1}, \tag{34a}$$

$$y_\tau = Z\beta_\tau + \xi_\tau, \tag{34b}$$

$$T = \begin{bmatrix} e^{A\delta} & 0 \\ Z^f W(A,\delta) & 0 \end{bmatrix}, \quad W(A,\delta) = \int_0^\delta e^{As}\,ds, \tag{34c}$$

$$\epsilon_\tau = \begin{bmatrix} \int_0^\delta e^{A(\delta-s)}R\zeta(t_{\tau-1}+ds) \\ Z^f \int_0^\delta \int_0^s e^{A(s-r)}R\zeta(t_{\tau-1}+dr)\,ds \end{bmatrix}, \tag{34d}$$

$$A = \begin{bmatrix} Z^s & 0 \\ 0 & I \end{bmatrix}, \quad \xi_\tau = \begin{bmatrix} \xi_\tau^s \\ \xi_\tau^f \end{bmatrix}. \tag{34e}$$

These equations constitute a discrete time system of the form (1), so that the methodology of Section 2 can be applied.

It remains only to give formulas for the matrix $W(A,\delta)$ and the error covariance Σ_ϵ. The following formulas suppose that the system matrix A can be diagonalized so that[12]

$$A = G\Lambda G^{-1}$$

with Λ diagonal, containing the eigenvalues of A. The columns of G are the eigenvectors of A.

Now the matrix $W(A,\delta)$ is given by

$$W(A,\delta) = GW(\Lambda,\delta)G^{-1}.$$

Here $W(\Lambda,\delta)$ is a diagonal matrix. Its diagonal elements are given by

$$\{W(\Lambda,\delta)\}_{ii} = w(\lambda_i,\delta),$$

$$w(x,\delta) = \begin{cases} (1/x)(e^{\delta x}-1) & \text{if } x \neq 0, \\ \delta & \text{if } x = 0, \end{cases}$$

where $\lambda_i = \Lambda_{ii}$ is the ith eigenvalue of A.

The covariance matrix of ϵ_t in (34) is

$$\Sigma_\epsilon := E(\epsilon_t\epsilon_t') = \begin{bmatrix} GQ\bar{G} & Z^f GQ^f\bar{G} \\ \bar{G}QGZ^{f\prime} & GQ^{ff}\bar{G} \end{bmatrix},$$

---

[12] Formulas for the case where A cannot be diagonalized can be found in Zadrozny (1988).

where

$$Q_{ij} = \Gamma_{ij} w(\lambda_i + \bar{\lambda}_j, \delta);$$

$$(Q^{ff})_{ij} = \begin{cases} \dfrac{\Gamma_{ij}}{\lambda_i + \bar{\lambda}_j} \left[w(\lambda_i; \delta) w(\bar{\lambda}_j; \delta) \right. \\ \qquad \left. - \dfrac{w(\lambda_i; \delta) - \delta}{\lambda_i} - \dfrac{w(\bar{\lambda}_j; \delta) - \delta}{\bar{\lambda}_j} \right], & \lambda_i + \bar{\lambda}_j \neq 0, \\[2ex] \dfrac{2\Gamma_{ij}}{\lambda_i^2} \left[\dfrac{\sinh(\lambda_i \delta)}{\lambda_i} - \delta \right], & \lambda_i + \bar{\lambda}_j = 0; \end{cases}$$

$$(Q^f)_{ij} = \begin{cases} \dfrac{\Gamma_{ij}}{\lambda_i + \bar{\lambda}_j} e^{\lambda_i \delta} [w(\bar{\lambda}_j; \delta) - w(-\lambda_i; \delta)], & \lambda_i + \bar{\lambda}_j \neq 0, \\[2ex] \dfrac{\Gamma_{ij}(w(\lambda_i; \delta) - \delta)}{\lambda_i}, & \lambda_i + \bar{\lambda}_j = 0; \end{cases}$$

and $\Gamma = G^{-1} R \Sigma R' \bar{G}^{-1}$. The bar denotes the complex conjugate transpose.

Appendix C: Data

The following table reports the data used in the empirical part of this paper; these are annual German data from 1960 to 1989. I denotes net fixed investment, Y is private personal disposable income deflated by the GNP deflator, and C is consumer purchases of new cars. All series are in millions of 1980 deutsche marks. R denotes the real interest rate in percent, computed as nominal interest rate of newly issued bonds ("Emissionsrendite festverzinslicher Wertpapiere") minus expected inflation rate

I	134.270	141.650	144.050	141.290	159.810	164.800	161.770	139.070
	142.630	160.960	179.270	189.410	190.120	181.780	145.270	125.180
	130.190	135.300	143.580	159.560	162.060	139.710	117.660	121.630
	118.820	113.950	119.500	121.180	132.160	149.740		
Y	518.406	528.065	545.721	556.516	595.762	637.183	651.131	655.615
	696.403	724.152	757.450	766.273	804.012	816.325	819.624	844.144
	879.222	891.114	926.805	959.864	962.490	964.962	952.320	975.682
	998.565	1007.802	1044.564	1070.846	1123.227	1139.766		
C	7.400	8.790	10.050	10.550	11.490	13.910	14.370	13.090
	14.520	19.210	23.160	24.680	24.580	23.350	18.940	24.490
	29.480	34.720	35.620	35.080	31.320	30.220	29.510	33.460
	32.910	33.470	42.650	45.420	44.680	45.550		
R	2.577	1.687	2.587	2.575	2.739	3.178	4.674	4.764
	3.375	2.744	2.366	2.071	3.392	3.108	4.416	3.545
	3.994	1.977	1.933	3.641	3.944	6.467	4.472	4.617
	4.890	3.819	2.827	3.530	3.415	3.971		

$\hat{P}_t = E_t \sum_{i=0}^{3} \hat{P}_{t+i}/4$, where $\hat{P}_t$ is the growth rate of the GNP deflator and E_t denotes the expectation with information up to time t. The expectation is based on an AR(3) representation of $\hat{P}$. The nominal interest-rate series is from Deutsche Bundesbank. All other series are from Statistisches Bundesamt.

REFERENCES

Adelman, I., and F. L. Adelman (1959), "The Dynamic Properties of the Klein-Goldberger Model," *Econometrica* 28: 596–625.

Aoki, M. (1989), "A Two-Step State Space Time Series Modeling Method," *Computers and Mathematics with Applications* 17: 1165–76.

Bergstrom, A. (1983), "Gaussian Estimation of the Structural Parameters in Higher Order Continuous Time Dynamic Models," *Econometrica* 51: 117–52.

(1984), "Continuous Time Stochastic Models and Issues of Aggregation over Time," in Z. Griliches and M. Intriligator (eds.), *Handbook of Econometrics*, Amsterdam: North-Holland.

(1985), "The Estimation of Parameters in Nonstationary Higher Order Continuous Time Dynamic Models," *Econometric Theory* 1: 369–85.

(1986), "The Estimation of Open Higher Order Continuous Time Dynamic Models with Mixed Stock and Flow Data," *Econometric Theory* 2: 350–73.

Bergstrom, A., and M. Chambers (1990), "Gaussian Estimation of a Continuous Time Model of Demand for Consumer Durable Goods with Applications to Demand in the United Kingdom, 1973–84," in A. Bergstrom (ed.), *Continuous Time Econometric Modelling*. Oxford University Press.

Bergstrom, A., and C. Wymer (1976), "A Model of Disequilibrium Neoclassical Growth and Its Applications to the United Kingdom," in A. Bergstrom (ed.), *Statistical Inference in Continuous Time Economic Models*. Amsterdam: North-Holland.

Beveridge, S., and C. R. Nelson (1981), "A New Approach to Decomposition of Economic Time Series into Permanent and Transitory Components with Particular Attention to Measurement of the 'Business Cycle'," *Journal of Monetary Economics* 7: 151–74.

Burg, J. (1967), "Maximum Entropy Spectral Analysis," in D. Childers (ed.), *Modern Spectrum Analysis*. Piscataway, NJ: IEEE Press.

Chan, K., J. Hayya, and J. Ord (1977), "A Note on Trend Removal Methods: The Case of Polynomial Regression versus Variate Differencing," *Econometrica* 45: 737–44.

Engle, R. F., and C. Granger (1987), "Co-integration and Error Correction: Representation, Estimation, and Testing," *Econometrica* 55: 251–76.

Gandolfo, G. (1981), *Qualitative Analysis and Econometric Estimation of Continuous Time Dynamic Models*. Amsterdam: North-Holland.

Hannan, E., and M. Deistler (1988), *The Statistical Theory of Linear Systems*. New York: Wiley.

Harvey, A. (1989), *Forecasting, Structural Time Series Models and the Kalman Filter*. Cambridge University Press.

Harvey, A., and A. Jaeger (1991), "Detrending, Stylized Facts and the Business Cycle," Discussion Paper no. EM91/230, London School of Economics.

Harvey, A. C., and J. H. Stock (1985), "The Estimation of Higher-Order Continuous Time Autoregressive Models," *Econometric Theory* 1: 97–117.

    (1988), "Continuous Time Autoregressive Models with Common Stochastic Trends," *Journal of Economic Dynamics and Control* 12: 365–84.

Hillinger, C. (ed.) (1992), *Cyclical Growth in Market and Planned Economies.* Oxford: Clarendon Press.

Hirsch, M., and S. Smale (1974), *Differential Equations, Dynamical Systems, and Linear Algebra.* San Diego: Academic Press.

Howrey, E. P. (1980), "The Role of Time Series Analysis in Econometric Model Evaluation," in J. Kmenta and J. B. Ramsey (eds.), *Evaluation of Econometric Models.* New York: Academic Press.

Koopmans, L. (1974), *The Spectral Analysis of Time Series.* New York: Academic Press.

Nelson, C., and H. Kang (1981), "Spurious Periodicity in Inappropriately Detrended Time Series," *Econometrica* 49: 741–51.

Oksendal, B. (1989), *Stochastic Differential Equations,* 2nd ed. Berlin: Springer-Verlag.

Phillips, P., D. Kwiatkowsky, and P. Schmidt (1991), "Testing the Null Hypothesis of Stationarity against the Alternative of a Unit Root: How Sure Are We That Economic Time Series Have a Unit Root?," Discussion Paper no. 979, Cowles Foundation.

Prescott, E. C. (1986), "Theory Ahead of Business-Cycle Measurement," *Carnegie-Rochester Conference Series on Public Policy,* no. 25, Amsterdam: North-Holland.

Reiter, M. (1995), *The Dynamics of Business Cycles: Stylized Facts, Economic Theory, Econometric Methodology and Applications.* Heidelberg: Physica.

Sebold-Bender, M. (1990), "Stilisierte Fakten Makroökonomischer Schwankungen," Ph.D. thesis, University of Munich.

Watson, M. M. (1993), "Measures of Fit for Calibrated Models," *Journal of Political Economy* 101: 1011–41.

Zadrozny, P. (1988), "Gaussian Likelihood of Continuous-Time ARMAX Models When Data Are Stocks and Flows at Different Frequencies," *Econometric Theory* 4: 109–24.

CHAPTER 8

A continuous time method for modeling optimal investment subject to adjustment costs and gestation lags

Peter A. Zadrozny

1   Introduction

This paper derives a method for formulating, solving, estimating, fore-casting, and simulating with a continuous time linear quadratic optimal control model of firms' decisions on production inputs and output, where investment in capital inputs is subject to convex internal adjustment costs and to a gestation lag. Convex internal adjustment costs arise when, for a given technology and for given levels of inputs, firms face a diminishing marginal returns trade-off between producing output and investing in capital inputs. That is, in addition to purchasing costs, there are internal resource costs of building or putting capital into place. Gestation lags are defined as the time required to build or to put capital into place for productive use.

Following Lucas (1981b) and Lucas and Prescott (1971), in this model the optimal control problem of a representative firm in an industry is specified as a social planning problem whose solution represents a competitive rational expectations equilibrium in the industry. A single type of productive capital is specified, although several types of capital could be specified, each with its own gestation lag. The gestation lag is allowed to be any nonnegative number. In particular, it is not restricted to being a multiple of a discrete sampling interval. Thus, flexibility is gained for studying how capital fixity arises from adjustment costs and gestation lags. However, allowing the gestation lag to assume any nonnegative value necessitates a continuous time analysis, which is substantially more complicated than a discrete time analysis.

There is an extensive literature in which firms' production and investment decisions are treated as explicit solutions of optimal control problems

231

involving (convex, internal) adjustment costs. Examples include theoretical continuous time studies by Eisner and Strotz (1963), Lucas (1967a,b, 1981a,b), and Gould (1968), as well as theoretical and empirical (mostly) discrete time studies by Sargent (1978), Hansen and Sargent (1980, 1981), Berndt, Fuss, and Waverman (1980), and Zadrozny (1980). Only linear quadratic structures or linear quadratic approximations of non-linear quadratic structures are treated in this literature, because solutions of non-linear quadratic optimal control problems generally cannot be characterized analytically.

Earlier interest in gestation lags as propagators of business cycles (e.g. Frisch 1933 and Kalecki 1935) waned with the ascendance of Keynesian analysis (see Hillinger 1992, pp. 18–22, for a brief review). Examples of rekindled interest in gestation lags are heuristic studies (i.e., without explicit dynamic optimization) by Jorgenson (1963, 1966), employing theoretical discussions in continuous time and empirical applications in discrete time. Lucas's (1981a) theoretical continuous time study seems to be the only previous study that treats both adjustment costs and gestation lags in terms of an explicit optimal control problem. Lucas considered a general notion of gestation lags that includes the present time-to-build notion as a special case. However, he did not explicitly solve the optimal control problem, as is done here. In discrete time, Kydland and Prescott (1982) turned attention away from adjustment costs and toward time-to-build gestation lags. They argued that such gestation lags, but not adjustment costs, help explain cyclical fluctuations in the United States. Other recent studies of gestation lags as propagators of business cycles are Brody (1992) and Tarjan (1992).

This paper contributes in several ways. First, the present continuous time analysis offers an approach for unifying the largely disparate theoretical and empirical literature on adjustment costs and gestation lags as sources of capital fixity. Second, illustrative numerical solutions of the model show that the present approach is econometrically tractable. Third, step-response simulations of the solved model show that the present approach can offer useful insights about how adjustment costs and gestation lags interact to produce similar as well as different aspects of capital fixity.

The discussion will proceed as follows. Section 2 specifies the model and restates it in a state-space form in order to facilitate solving its optimal control problem. Section 3 derives first-order conditions of the optimal control problem and describes a numerical strategy for solving them. Section 4 shows how to transform continuous time equations of the solved model into econometrically useful discrete time equations. Section 5 reports and interprets step-response simulations of the solved model. Section 6 contains concluding remarks.

2   Specification of the model

Consider an industry that is adequately described by behavior of a representative firm. Accordingly, except for differences in scale, firm- and industry-level variables are identical. The analysis starts at some moment in time, t_0. At this moment and at every subsequent moment, $t \geq t_0$, the representative firm maximizes expected present value of profits,

$$V(t, h) = \lim_{h \to \infty} E_t \int_{\tau=t}^{h} e^{-\delta(\tau-t)} \pi(\tau) \, d\tau, \tag{2.1}$$

with respect to a class of constant linear feedback decision rules, for an infinite planning horizon, where maximization is subject to laws of motion to be specified, E_t denotes expectations conditioned on the firm's information at t, $\delta > 0$ is a constant real discount factor, and $\pi(\tau)$ denotes real profits. Throughout, a real value is a nominal (current-dollar) value divided by some aggregate price index. The firm's optimal control problem – in particular, the class of its feedback decision rules – is precisely stated at the end of this section.

To obtain a solution to this problem that represents a competitive rational expectations equilibrium in the industry output market, as in Lucas (1981b) and Lucas and Prescott (1971) sales revenues in $\pi(t)$ are set to the area under the industry output demand curve. Therefore: $\pi(t) = r_q(t) - c_q(t) - c_n(t)$ with $r_q(t) = \int_{x=0}^{q(t)} p_q[x, \xi_q(t)] \, dx$, where $p_q[\cdot]$ is the inverse demand curve for the industry's output, $q(t)$ is the instantaneous rate of production of output, $\xi_q(t)$ determines the demand curve's position, $c_q(t)$ is production costs, and $c_n(t)$ is direct investment costs. If $r_q(t) = p_q[q(t), \xi_q(t)] q(t)$ then the solution would represent the monopoly equilibrium.

To obtain estimation equations that are linear in variables, $r_q(t), c_q(t)$, and $c_n(t)$ are specified to be linear quadratic in variables. This assumption makes computation of the optimization problem's solution tractable and allows linear time-series estimation, simulation, and forecasting methods to be used.

Assume that the inverse demand curve for output is

$$p_q[q(t), \xi_q(t)] = -\eta q(t) + \xi_q(t), \tag{2.2}$$

where $\eta > 0$ is a constant demand slope parameter and $\xi_q(t)$ is an unobservable disturbance generated by the stationary continuous time AR(1) process

$$D\xi_q(t) = -a_q \xi_q(t) + \epsilon_q(t), \tag{2.3}$$

where D is the mean-squared time derivative, and where a_q is a constant parameter, and $\epsilon_q(t)$ is an unobservable Gaussian white-noise disturbance with constant positive intensity σ_q^2. Equation (2.2) implies that $r_q(t) = -\frac{1}{2}\eta q(t)^2 + q(t)\xi_q(t)$.

These assumptions on $\epsilon_q(t)$ imply that it has Gaussian increments, zero mean, autocovariance function $\sigma_q^2 \Delta(s-\tau)$ (where $\Delta(\cdot)$ is the Dirac delta generalized function with unit mass at zero and $s \geq \tau$ are points in time), and is independent of $\xi_q(s)$ for $t \geq s$. Strictly speaking, $\epsilon_q(t)$ and hence process (2.3) are not well-defined; however, there is a well-defined (mean-squared) stochastic integral equation corresponding to process (2.3) that gives it a rigorous foundation (see e.g. Astrom 1970, pp. 13–90, or Priestley 1981, pp. 150–83).

Assume that $\xi_q(t)$ and the other exogenous processes to be introduced in what follows are stationary and mean-adjusted. Stationarity is the natural assumption for statistical inference. Although most economic data are nonstationary, they can usually be put into stationary form by differencing. Harvey and Stock (1989) describe a way of doing this in estimation of linear continuous time models. The necessary and sufficient condition for process (2.3) to be stationary, $a_q > 0$, is assumed to hold. Stationarity, mean adjustment, and the white-noise properties of $\epsilon_q(t)$ imply that $E\xi_q(t) = 0$, where E denotes unconditional expectation.

To begin specification of $c_q(t)$, assume that the firm uses inputs (k, l, m) to produce outputs (q, n), where k is capital stock, l is labor stock, m is materials usage rate, q is output-good production rate, and n is gross investment rate in k (t is occasionally dropped in order to save notation). Assume that the firm's production technology has the separable form $f \cdot g(k, l, m) = h(q, n)$, where f is an input-neutral technology index. Following Kydland and Prescott's (1982) treatment of the utility function, assume that $g(\cdot)$ and $h(\cdot)$ are constant elasticity functions

$$g(k, l, m) = (\alpha_1 k^\beta + \alpha_2 l^\beta + \alpha_3 m^\beta)^{1/\beta} \quad \text{and}$$
$$h(q, n) = (\gamma_1 q^\rho + \gamma_2 n^\rho)^{1/\rho}, \tag{2.4}$$

where $\alpha_1 > 0$, $\alpha_2 > 0$, $\alpha_3 > 0$, $\alpha_1 + \alpha_2 + \alpha_3 = 1$, $\beta < 1$, $\gamma_1 > 0$, $\gamma_2 > 0$, $\gamma_1 + \gamma_2 = 1$, and $\rho > 1$. Production technology (2.4) will be approximated by a linear quadratic dual variable cost function. CES $= (\beta - 1)^{-1} < 0$ is the constant elasticity of substitution between inputs, and CET $= (\rho - 1)^{-1} > 0$ is the constant elasticity of transformation between outputs.

In principle, assume that $f(t)$ is the sum of a possibly nonstationary mean function $\mu_f(t)$ and a stationary disturbance $\xi_f(t)$. Usually, the mean function of the technology index is assumed to be a polynomial or an exponential function. Assume that any data to be used in estimation are first put into a stationary mean-adjusted form. When this is done properly, $\mu_f(t)$ and its effects on endogenous variables are removed. Therefore, assume that $\mu_f(t) = 0$, so that $f(t) = \xi_f(t)$ and $\mu_f(t)$ can be ignored.

In equations (2.5), $\xi_f(t)$ is specified to be generated by a continuous time AR(1) process.

Convex internal adjustment costs arise when, for given values of technology index f and inputs k, l, m, the production technology implies that transformation curves between outputs q and n are concave to the origin. Such adjustment costs are called convex because the implied dual variable cost function is convex in (q, n). Hall's (1973) analysis shows that separability of technology into $g(\cdot)$ and $h(\cdot)$ is a necessary condition for output transformation curves to be concave. In this CET case, $\rho > 1$, the necessary and sufficient condition for transformation curves to be concave, is assumed; the transformation curves become more curved (i.e., the degree of adjustment costs increases) as ρ increases. Similarly, $\beta < 1$, the necessary and sufficient condition for input isoquants to be convex to the origin, is assumed; the isoquants become more curved as $\beta \to -\infty$.

Let $c_q = p_l l + p_m m$, where p_l is the real hiring price of labor and p_m is the real purchase price of materials, and let $c_n = p_n n$, where p_n is the real purchase price of investment goods. Because l and m are variable (not subject to adjustment costs or a gestation lag) and k is fixed (subject to adjustment costs and a gestation lag), c_q and c_n are, respectively, variable and fixed production costs. More specifically, let c_q denote the dual variable cost function: For given $z = (z_1, \ldots, z_6)^T = (q, n, k, p_l, p_m, \xi_f)^T$ (superscript T denotes transposition), $c_q(z) = \min_{\{l, m\}}\{p_l l + p_m m\}$, where minimization is subject to technology (2.4).

The constant term in π does not affect optimal decisions in the approximate linear quadratic optimal control problem; moreover, linear terms in π contribute to the optimal decision rule only an additive constant term, which is removed by mean adjustment of data. Therefore, without loss of generality, constant and linear terms in π are ignored and $c_q(z)$ is approximated by $c_q(z) = \frac{1}{2}z^T \nabla^2 c_q(z_0)z$, where $\nabla^2 c_q(z_0)$ denotes the Hessian matrix of second partial derivatives of $c_q(z)$ evaluated at $z = z_0$. Hessian $\nabla^2 c_q(z_0)$ is evaluated in equations (B.1) of Appendix B for $z_0 = (1, 1, 1, \alpha_2, \alpha_3, 1)^T$, a normalization that results in the simplest expression for $\nabla^2 c_q(z_0)$. So far, then, $\pi = -\frac{1}{2}\eta q^2 + q\xi_q - \frac{1}{2}z^T \nabla^2 c_q z - p_n n$.

Evidently, $\nabla^2 c_q$ is symmetric (henceforth, for simplicity, $\nabla^2 c_q(z_0)$ is written as $\nabla^2 c_q$). Ideally, $\frac{1}{2}z^T \nabla^2 c_q z$ would have the following inherited properties for all values of z: (i) linear homogeneity in (q, n, k); (ii) convexity in (q, n, k); (iii) strict convexity in (q, n), (n, k), and (q, k); (iv) linear homogeneity in (p_l, p_m); and, (v) strict concavity in p_l and p_m. In fact, homogeneity restrictions (i) and (iv) hold for $z = z_0$ and curvature restrictions (ii), (iii), and (v) hold for all z.

Although it is tempting to specify $\nabla^2 c_q$ as a general matrix with desired curvature properties, $\nabla^2 c_q$ has instead been derived from the CES-

CET technology in order to keep the number of parameters to a minimum. The CES–CET underpinning facilitates analysis of the roles of basic economic components. For example, c_{11} equals the $(1,1)$ element of $\nabla^2 c_q = \partial^2 c_q / \partial q^2 =$ the slope of the marginal cost of output curve $= \gamma_1 \gamma_2(\rho - 1) + \alpha_1(1 - \beta)\gamma_1^2/(1 - \alpha_1)$. As expected, this equation states that c_{11} increases with the degree of adjustment costs ($\partial c_{11}/\partial \rho > 0$) and equals infinity when the only input is fixed ($\alpha_1 \to 1$ implies $c_{11} \to +\infty$). It would be difficult to obtain such insights with a general $\nabla^2 c_q$ that is not grounded in a well-understood economic structure.

Assume that p_n, p_l, p_m, and ξ_f are exogenous to the industry and are generated by stationary continuous time AR(1) processes as follows:

$$Dp_n(t) = -a_n p_n(t) + \epsilon_n(t),$$

$$Dp_l(t) = -a_l p_l(t) + \epsilon_l(t),$$

$$Dp_m(t) = -a_m p_m(t) + \epsilon_m(t),$$

$$D\xi_f(t) = -a_f \xi_f(t) + \epsilon_f(t),$$

(2.5)

where a_n, a_l, a_m, and $a_f > 0$ are constant parameters and $\epsilon_n(t)$, $\epsilon_l(t)$, $\epsilon_m(t)$, and $\epsilon_f(t)$ are unobservable Gaussian white-noise disturbances with constant intensities σ_n^2, σ_l^2, σ_m^2, and $\sigma_f^2 > 0$. As in process (2.3), $a's > 0$ makes the processes stationary. Stationarity, mean adjustment, and white-noise properties of disturbances imply that $Ep_n(t) = Ep_l(t) = Ep_m(t) = E\xi_f(t) = 0$. Also, assume that $\xi_q(t)$, $p_n(t)$, $p_l(t)$, $p_m(t)$, and $\xi_f(t)$ are mutually independent, so that $\epsilon_q(t)$, $\epsilon_n(t)$, $\epsilon_l(t)$, $\epsilon_m(t)$, and $\epsilon_f(t)$ are mutually independent.

Assume that the capital law of motion is

$$Dk(t) = -a_k k(t) + n(t - \lambda) + \epsilon_k(t),$$

(2.6)

where $a_k > 0$ is a constant depreciation factor, $\lambda > 0$ is the gestation lag, and $\epsilon_k(t)$ is an unobservable Gaussian white-noise disturbance, independent of previously stated disturbances, with constant positive intensity σ_k^2. As before, $a_k > 0$ renders the law of motion (2.6) stationary.

Equation (2.6) states that capital is built in a single investment stage of duration λ. Within limits, the present approach can handle other, multistage specifications of gestation lags. For example,

$$Dk(t) = -a_k k(t) + (1/\lambda) \int_{\tau=0}^{\lambda} n(t - \tau) \, d\tau$$

specifies that capital is built in a continuum of investment stages with durations from 0 to λ. This law of motion is a continuous time variant of Kydland and Prescott's (1982) discrete time multi-stage gestation lag.

The model's components have now been specified. Next, in order to simplify the optimal control problem, q is eliminated by maximizing π with respect to q. Because q is not a control variable in any law of motion, conditional on n being at its optimal value, the optimal value of q is given by maximizing π with respect to q. The first-order condition $\partial \pi / \partial q = 0$ yields

$$q = -(c_{11} + \eta)^{-1}(c_{12}n + c_{13}k + c_{14}p_l + c_{15}p_m + c_{16}\xi_f - \xi_q), \qquad (2.7)$$

where $(c_{11}, \ldots, c_{16})$ is the first row of $\nabla^2 c_q$.

Similarly, elimination of l and m from the optimal control problem is justified in the construction of $c_q(z)$ because l and m are not control variables in any law of motion. Optimal values of l and m conditional on q and n being at their optimal values, recovered with Shepard's lemma (Diewert 1971, p. 495), are

$$l = \partial c_q / \partial p_l = c_{41}q + c_{42}n + c_{43}k + c_{44}p_l + c_{45}p_m + c_{46}\xi_f, \qquad (2.8)$$

$$m = \partial c_q / \partial p_m = c_{51}q + c_{52}n + c_{53}k + c_{54}p_l + c_{55}p_m + c_{56}\xi_f, \qquad (2.9)$$

where $(c_{41}, \ldots, c_{46})$ and $(c_{51}, \ldots, c_{56})$ are the fourth and fifth rows of $\nabla^2 c_q$.

Of course, optimality of decision rules (2.8) and (2.9) also rests on $c_q = \frac{1}{2}z^T \nabla^2 c_q z$ being a good approximation of technology (2.4). It is straightforward to derive analogous rules for l and m with the exact cost function implied by technology (2.4). However, such rules are nonlinear in variables, a significant complication for estimation, simulation, or forecasting. Whether exact or approximate rules are used to account for decisions on l and m, the approximate linear quadratic optimal control problem remains unchanged.

To solve the problem, put it in a general state-space form. Define the control vector $u = (n)$ and the state vector $x = (k, p_n, p_l, p_m, \xi_f, \xi_q)^T$. Then, eliminate q with decision rule (2.7) and write $\pi = -\frac{1}{2}\eta q^2 + q\xi_q - \frac{1}{2}z^T \nabla^2 c_q z - p_n n$ as $\pi = u^T R u + 2u^T S x + x^T Q x$. Then, partition x as $x = (x_1^T, x_2^T)^T$, where $x_1 = (k)$ is endogenous and $x_2 = (p_n, p_l, p_m, \xi_f, \xi_q)^T$ is exogenous, and write

$$\pi = u^T R u + 2u^T S_1 x_1 + 2u^T S_2 x_2 + x_1^T Q_{11} x_1 + 2x_1^T Q_{12} x_2 + x_2^T Q_{22} x_2. \qquad (2.10)$$

Without loss of generality, let R and Q (and hence Q_{11} and Q_{22}) be symmetric.

Section 3 shows that the solution of the optimal control problem that gives optimal investment decisions is independent of Q_{22}. Also, decision rules (2.7)–(2.9) show that optimal decisions on q, l, and m are independent of Q_{22}. As a result, Q_{22} is not constructed. The values of R, S_1, S_2, Q_{11}, and Q_{12} are given in equations (B.4) in Appendix B.

Corresponding to the general representation of the profit function by equation (2.10), the laws of motion (2.3), (2.5), and (2.6) are assembled into state equation $Dx(t) = Fx(t) + Gu(t-\lambda) + H\epsilon(t)$; that is,

$$\begin{bmatrix} Dx_1(t) \\ Dx_2(t) \end{bmatrix} = \begin{bmatrix} F_{11} & F_{12} \\ 0 & F_{22} \end{bmatrix} \begin{bmatrix} x_1(t) \\ x_2(t) \end{bmatrix} + \begin{bmatrix} G_1 \\ 0 \end{bmatrix} u(t-\lambda) + \begin{bmatrix} H_1 \\ H_2 \end{bmatrix} \epsilon(t), \qquad (2.11)$$

where $F_{11} = [-a_k]$, $F_{12} = 0$, $F_{22} = \text{diag}[-a_n, -a_l, -a_m, -a_f, -a_q]$, $G_1 = [1]$, $H = [H_1^T, H_2^T]^T = I_6$ (the 6×6 identity matrix), and $\epsilon(t) = (\epsilon_k(t), \epsilon_n(t),$ $\epsilon_l(t), \epsilon_m(t), \epsilon_f(t), \epsilon_q(t))^T$, with intensity matrix $\Sigma_\epsilon = \text{diag}[\sigma_k^2, \sigma_n^2, \sigma_l^2, \sigma_m^2,$ $\sigma_f^2, \sigma_q^2]$.

In the standard $\lambda = 0$ linear quadratic optimal control problem, under the assumption that disturbances are Gaussian and the state vector is fully observed, the optimal controller has the linear form $u(t) = Kx(t)$. The solution of the $\lambda > 0$ control problem proposed here has the same form. Roughly speaking, the representative firm is assumed to maximize expected present value (2.1) with respect to K such that $u(t) = Kx(t)$ and $x(t)$ follows state equation (2.11). Actually, as discussed in Section 3, K is a function of a matrix P, so that the maximization is with respect to P.

3   Solution of the optimal control problem

This section uses definitions and rules of matrix differentiation that are discussed in Appendix A. The reader should review Appendix A before proceeding. In this section we first review the standard solution of the $\lambda > 0$ linear quadratic optimal control problem in which $u(t)$ feeds back on $x(t)$ and on a convolution of $u(\tau)$ for $t - \lambda \le \tau < t$. We then proceed to derive a more tractable formulation and solution of the $\lambda > 0$ problem, one in which $u(t)$ feeds back only on $x(t)$.

3.1   Standard solution of the $\lambda > 0$ problem

For simplicity, $\delta = 0$ and $S = 0$ are assumed in the review of the standard solution of the $\lambda > 0$ problem (in any case, $\delta = 0$ and $S = 0$ can always be achieved by transforming $u(t)$ and $x(t)$). When $\delta = 0$ and $S = 0$, the $\lambda > 0$ problem is restated as the $\lambda = 0$ problem by transforming the control vector to $\hat{u}(\tau) = u(\tau - \lambda)$. The implied $\lambda = 0$ problem is to maximize $V(t, \infty) = E_t \int_{\tau=t+\lambda}^{\infty} [\hat{u}(\tau)^T R\hat{u}(\tau) + x(\tau)^T Qx(\tau)] d\tau$ with respect to $\{\hat{u}(\tau)\}_{\tau=t+\lambda}^{\infty}$, subject to $Dx(\tau) = Fx(\tau) + G\hat{u}(\tau) + H\epsilon(\tau)$, for $\tau \ge t \ge t_0$. Because $\{x(\tau)\}_{\tau=t}^{t+\lambda}$ is predetermined with respect to $\{u(\tau)\}_{\tau=t}^{\infty}$, the part $\int_{\tau=t}^{t+\lambda} x(\tau)^T Qx(\tau) d\tau$ of the objective function is considered irrelevant for the purpose of determining the optimal controller, and is therefore ignored.

The standard theory for the $\lambda = 0$ problem (Kawkernaak and Sivan 1972, pp. 201-53) then yields the certainty-equivalent optimal controller

$\hat{u}(t+\lambda) = P^{\dagger}E_{t+\lambda}x(t+\lambda)$ for $t \geq t_0$, where $P^{\dagger} = -R^{-1}G^{\mathrm{T}}W^{\dagger}$, $W^{\dagger}$ is the negative semidefinite ($W^{\dagger} \leq 0$) solution of the continuous time algebraic Riccati equation $P^{\dagger\mathrm{T}}RP^{\dagger} + Q + \Phi^{\dagger\mathrm{T}}W^{\dagger} + W^{\dagger}\Phi^{\dagger} = 0$, and $\Phi^{\dagger}$ is the closed-loop matrix defined by $\Phi^{\dagger} = F + GP^{\dagger}$. In particular, the linear quadratic structure, additivity, Gaussianity, and whiteness of disturbances causes the controller to be certainty-equivalent (see e.g. Astrom 1970, pp. 256–7).

To transform $\hat{u}(t+\lambda) = P^{\dagger}E_{t+\lambda}x(t+\lambda)$ to a controller for $u(t)$ in variables dated t or earlier, take E_t of $\hat{u}(t+\lambda) = P^{\dagger}E_{t+\lambda}x(t+\lambda)$, use the law of iterated expectations to replace $E_t[E_{t+\lambda}x(t+\lambda)]$ with $E_t x(t+\lambda)$, and replace $\hat{u}(t+\lambda)$ with $u(t)$ to obtain the predictive optimal controller $u(t) = P^{\dagger}E_t x(t+\lambda)$.

Consider any predictive controller $u(t) = PE_t x(t+\lambda)$, that is, where P is any element of $\mathbb{R}^{m \times n}$. To write $E_t x(t+\lambda)$ explicitly in variables dated t or earlier, integrate equation (2.11) over $[t, t+\lambda]$ to obtain

$$x(t+\lambda) = e^{F\lambda}x(t) + \int_{\tau=0}^{\lambda} e^{F(\lambda-\tau)}[Gu(t-\lambda+\tau) + H\epsilon(t+\tau)]\,d\tau. \qquad (3.1)$$

Gaussianity and whiteness of disturbances imply that

$$E_t x(t+\lambda) = e^{F\lambda}x(t) + \int_{\tau=0}^{\lambda} e^{F(\lambda-\tau)}Gu(t-\lambda+\tau)\,d\tau. \qquad (3.2)$$

Next, combine the predictive controller and (3.2) to obtain a controller in variables dated t or earlier:

$$u(t) = Pe^{F\lambda}x(t) + \int_{\tau=0}^{\lambda} Pe^{F(\lambda-\tau)}Gu(t-\lambda+\tau)\,d\tau. \qquad (3.3)$$

If $P = P^{\dagger}$ then (3.3) is the standard optimal controller in the $\lambda > 0$ problem (see e.g. Mee 1973).

Every time controller (3.3) is applied, the convolution in u,

$$\int_{\tau=0}^{\lambda} Pe^{F(\lambda-\tau)}Gu(t-\lambda+\tau)\,d\tau,$$

must be computed, a tedious task that can only be done numerically (see e.g. Lee and Chang 1987 and the references therein). Moreover, the convolution in u creates serious complications for analysis in discrete time such as estimation, forecasting, or simulation. As a first step toward obtaining a convolution-free, pure-state feedback controller, (3.3) will be restated in a different (but mathematically equivalent) form.

3.2   *Derivation of a pure-state feedback controller*

Write $u(t) = PE_t x(t+\lambda)$ as

$$u(t-\lambda) = Px(t) - P[x(t) - E_{t-\lambda}x(t)]. \qquad (3.4)$$

Equations (3.1) and (3.2) imply that the state prediction error is

$$x(t) - E_{t-\lambda}x(t) = \int_{\tau=0}^{\lambda} e^{F(\lambda-\tau)} H\epsilon(t-\lambda+\tau)\,d\tau. \tag{3.5}$$

Combine (2.11), (3.4), and (3.5) to obtain the closed-loop state equation

$$Dx(t) = \Phi x(t) + H\epsilon(t) + \psi_1(t),$$

$$\psi_1(t) = -\int_{\tau=0}^{\lambda} GPe^{F(\lambda-\tau)} H\epsilon(t-\lambda+\tau)\,d\tau, \tag{3.6}$$

where, as before, $\Phi = F + GP$. Then, integrate (3.6) over $[t, t+\lambda]$ to obtain

$$x(t+\lambda) = e^{\Phi\lambda}x(t) + \int_{s=0}^{\lambda} e^{\Phi(\lambda-s)} H\epsilon(t+s)\,ds$$

$$+ \int_{s=0}^{\lambda} e^{\Phi(\lambda-s)}\psi_1(t+s)\,ds. \tag{3.7}$$

Changing variables of integration in the second double integral and re-using τ and s as the variables of integration allows (3.7) to be written as

$$x(t+\lambda) = e^{\Phi\lambda}x(t) - \int_{\tau=0}^{\lambda}\left[\int_{s=0}^{\tau} e^{\Phi(\lambda-s)} GPe^{F(\lambda+s-\tau)}\,ds\right] H\epsilon(t-\lambda+\tau)\,d\tau$$

$$+ \int_{\tau=0}^{\lambda}\left[e^{\Phi(\lambda-\tau)} - \int_{s=\tau}^{\lambda} e^{\Phi(\lambda-s)} GPe^{F(s-\tau)}\,ds\right] H\epsilon(t+\tau)\,d\tau. \tag{3.8}$$

Because the first and second sets of integrals in (3.8) involve (respectively) predetermined past disturbances and undetermined future disturbances, (3.8) implies

$$E_t x(t+\lambda) = e^{\Phi\lambda}x(t) - \int_{\tau=0}^{\lambda}\left[\int_{s=0}^{\tau} e^{\Phi(\lambda-s)} GPe^{F(\lambda+s-\tau)}\,ds\right] H\epsilon(t-\lambda+\tau)\,d\tau. \tag{3.9}$$

In particular, Gaussianity and whiteness of future disturbances imply that the conditional expectation of the second set of integrals is zero. Then, combine $u(t) = PE_t x(t+\lambda)$ with (3.9) to obtain

$$u(t) = Kx(t) + \psi_2(t),$$

$$K = Pe^{(F+GP)\lambda}, \tag{3.10}$$

$$\psi_2(t) = -\int_{\tau=0}^{\lambda}\left[\int_{s=0}^{\tau} Pe^{\Phi(\lambda-s)} GPe^{F(\lambda+s-\tau)}\,ds\right] H\epsilon(t-\lambda+\tau)\,d\tau.$$

The gain in restating controller (3.3) as (3.10) is that the convolution in u is replaced with the more tractable disturbance $\psi_2(t)$. If $\psi(t) = (\psi_1(t)^{\mathrm{T}}, \psi_2(t)^{\mathrm{T}})^{\mathrm{T}}$ is deleted, then (3.6) and (3.10) reduce to

$$Dx(t) = \Phi x(t) + H\epsilon(t) \tag{3.11}$$

and

$$u(t) = Kx(t) \tag{3.12}$$

so that $\Phi = F + GP$ and $K = Pe^{\Phi\lambda}$.

We now propose the following pure-state feedback controller: Maximize objective (2.1) with respect to P, subject to $u(t) = Kx(t)$, where $K = Pe^{\Phi\lambda}$, and to state equation (3.11). The resulting optimized predictive control, closed-loop, and feedback control matrices are denoted by P^*, $\Phi^* = F + GP^*$, and $K^* = P^*e^{\Phi^*\lambda}$, respectively.

Equations (3.11) and (3.12) are mathematically equivalent to equations (2.11) and (3.3) if and only if $\epsilon(t) = 0$ almost everywhere for all t. In this nonstochastic case, each pair of state controller equations yields the same value of $V(t, \infty)$ for a given value of P. Moreover, P yields a larger value of $V(t, \infty)$ at P^* than at $P^\dagger$, because P^* takes into account the effect of P on $\{x(\tau)\}_{\tau=t}^{t+\lambda}$ in $V(t, \infty)$ but $P^\dagger$ does not. Accordingly, P^* depends on λ but $P^\dagger$ does not. The latter property helps in econometric analysis because it makes the estimation objective function (e.g., the Gaussian likelihood function) more sensitive to λ and thereby reduces the estimated standard error of λ.

In the stochastic case, deleting ψ in order to obtain (3.11) and (3.12) can be justified by the following argument, which hinges on the more limited role of continuous time structural disturbances – when compared with discrete time residuals – in econometric analysis of the model. Structural disturbances represent the firm's uncertainty about x. Residuals not only incorporate the firm's uncertainty about x, but also account for an econometrician's inevitable specification error, which manifests itself as "secondary" serial correlations laid over "primary" serial correlations of structural disturbances $H\epsilon + \psi_1$ and ψ_2. It can be shown that primary serial correlations of $H\epsilon + \psi_1$ and ψ_2 are nonzero up to order $\text{int}(\lambda/\Delta)$, where $\text{int}(\cdot)$ denotes the integral part of a number and Δ denotes a constant sampling interval.

Although Hansen and Sargent (1980, 1981) emphasized the theoretical advantages of deriving residual serial correlations from structural disturbances, in practice not all such correlations can be derived from theoretically motivated structural disturbances. To obtain an adequately fitting model, a significant part of the residual serial correlations usually must be determined empirically. Accordingly, one might as well merge the primary and secondary layers of residual serial correlations into a single empirically determined layer. By defining x appropriately, any serial correlations of residuals in the class of discrete time samples of continuous time rational spectral processes can be accounted for by (3.11).

In sum, (3.11) and (3.12) are appropriate for an econometric analysis of investment subject to adjustment costs and a gestation lag, because they capture the essential optimizing behavior of the representative firm in the model and because (3.11) can account for any residual serial correlations encountered in practice.

3.3   *Restrictions on parameters*

The following three restrictions on parameters are borrowed from the standard $\lambda = 0$ problem. The investment model satisfies these assumptions.

3.3.1   *Stabilizability*

To account for discounting, define $\tilde{\Phi} = \Phi - (\delta/2)I$ or, equivalently, $\tilde{\Phi} = \tilde{F} + GP$, where $\tilde{F} = F - (\delta/2)I$. Assume that the pair of matrices $(\tilde{F}, G)$ is stabilizable. Following Kwakernaak and Sivan (1972, pp. 53–65), because the pair of matrices $(\tilde{F}, G)$ is in controllability canonical form, stabilizability means that (a) the controllability matrix $[G_1, \tilde{F}_{11}G_1, ..., (\tilde{F}_{11})^{\rho-1}G_1]$ has full (row) rank ρ, where ρ is the dimension of x_1; and (b) $\tilde{F}_{22}$ is stable. A square matrix is (continuous time) stable when the real parts of all of its eigenvalues are negative. Condition (a) implies that x_1 can be moved from any initial value to any target value in a finite amount of time. Condition (b) states that x_2 is expected to grow at less than the exponential rate $\delta/2$, and so permits exogenous variables to be nonstationary within this bound.

3.3.2   *Concavity*

Assume that $\pi(t)$, as defined by (2.10), is both (a) concave in the endogenous variables $u(t)$ and $x_1(t)$ and (b) strictly concave in $u(t)$. Here assumption (a) implies $\begin{bmatrix} R & S \\ S^T & Q \end{bmatrix}$ is negative semidefinite ($\begin{bmatrix} R & S \\ S^T & Q \end{bmatrix} \leq 0$) and assumption (b) implies R is negative definite ($R < 0$).

3.3.3   *Detectability*

Define $\hat{Q} = Q - S^T R^{-1} S$. Concavity as just described implies that $\hat{Q}$ is negative semidefinite. Because $\hat{Q}$ is symmetric negative semidefinite, it has the (non-unique) factorization $\hat{Q} = -J^T J$. Assume that the pair of matrices $(\tilde{F}, J)$ is detectable; this assumption is equivalent to the pair of matrices $(\tilde{F}^T, J^T)$ being stabilizable (Kwakernaak and Sivan 1972, pp. 79–81). Here, as in most economic models, detectability is implied by $\hat{Q}_{11} < 0$.

Stabilizability ensures that there is a P for which $\lim_{h \to \infty} V(t, h)$ is finite, and hence that the infinite-horizon problem is well-formulated. Concavity ensures that the second-order condition of the optimal control problem holds. Detectability strengthens concavity and thereby helps to ensure that $\tilde{\Phi} = \tilde{F} + GP$, but not necessarily $\Phi = F + GP$, is stable for $P = P^\dagger$ or P^*.

3.4 First-order conditions for P^*

Because P^*, like $P^\dagger$, is certainty-equivalent, its first-order conditions are more easily derived with nonstochastic state controller equations. Accordingly, with ϵ suppressed, (3.11) and (3.12) imply that $V(t,h) = x(t)^{\mathrm{T}} W(t,h) x(t)$, where $W(t,h)$ is given by

$$W(t,h) = \int_{\tau=t}^{h} e^{\tilde{\Phi}^{\mathrm{T}}(\tau-t)}[K^{\mathrm{T}}RK + K^{\mathrm{T}}S + S^{\mathrm{T}}K + Q]e^{\tilde{\Phi}(\tau-t)}\,d\tau. \tag{3.13}$$

Premultiply (3.13) by $\tilde{\Phi}^{\mathrm{T}}$, postmultiply (3.13) by $\tilde{\Phi}$, add the products together, and integrate the sum by parts. Assuming $\tilde{\Phi}$ is stable, the limit as $h \to \infty$ of the resulting equation is

$$e^{\Phi^{\mathrm{T}}\lambda}P^{\mathrm{T}}RPe^{\Phi\lambda} + e^{\Phi^{\mathrm{T}}\lambda}P^{\mathrm{T}}S + S^{\mathrm{T}}Pe^{\Phi\lambda} + Q + \tilde{\Phi}^{\mathrm{T}}W + W\tilde{\Phi} = 0, \tag{3.14}$$

where $W = \lim_{s \to \infty} W(0,s) = \lim_{h \to \infty} W(t,h)$. Symmetry of W, which is evident from (3.13), is used in (3.14).

In general, W exists and equations (3.13) and (3.14) are equivalent only if $\tilde{\Phi}$ is stable. It is well-known that when $\lambda = 0$ and restrictions 3.3.1–3 hold, $\tilde{\Phi}^\dagger = \tilde{F} + GP^\dagger$ is stable. The standard proof of this result (Kwakernaak and Sivan 1972, pp. 237–43) continues to apply when the state and controller equations are (3.11) and (3.12) and $\lambda > 0$ (apply the standard proof in terms of K and ignore the dependence of K on P). Therefore, under restrictions 3.3.1–3, predictive control matrices P are restricted to values that imply stable values of $\tilde{\Phi}$ and hence treat (3.13) and (3.14) as equivalent.

Let d denote a differential of a scalar or matrix function of P with respect to an infinitesimal variation in P. For $\lambda \geq 0$, the immediate first-order condition for maximizing $V(t,\infty)$ with respect to P is $dV(t,\infty) = 0$. Because $x(t)$ is predetermined and can assume any value, $dV(t,\infty) = x(t)^{\mathrm{T}} dW x(t)$, so that $dV(t,\infty) = 0$ implies $dW = 0$. To see what $dW = 0$ implies, execute the following steps: differentiate (3.14) with respect to P using differentiation rules (A.1) and (A.3) of Appendix A; impose $dW = 0$; take the trace of the last result; use $\operatorname{tr}(AB) = \operatorname{tr}(BA)$ to write the last result as $\operatorname{tr}(dP^{\mathrm{T}}B) = 0$; and use rule (A.2) to reduce $\operatorname{tr}(dP^{\mathrm{T}}B) = 0$ to $B = 0$. Therefore,

$$\lambda G^{\mathrm{T}} \int_{s=0}^{1} e^{\Phi^{\mathrm{T}}\lambda s}P^{\mathrm{T}}[RPe^{\Phi\lambda} + S]e^{\Phi^{\mathrm{T}}\lambda(1-s)}\,ds + [RPe^{\Phi\lambda} + S]e^{\Phi^{\mathrm{T}}\lambda} + G^{\mathrm{T}}W = 0. \tag{3.15}$$

A generally reliable, accurate, and quick method for computing the matrix exponential $e^{\Phi\lambda}$ and the integral in (3.15) is as follows. First, compute

$e^{\Phi\lambda}$ using the method of Padé approximation with scaling and squaring (Ward 1977, 1985). Let Ψ be the block upper triangular matrix defined by $\Psi = \begin{bmatrix} A & B \\ 0 & C \end{bmatrix}$, where $A = \Phi\lambda$, $B = [K^{\mathrm{T}}R + S^{\mathrm{T}}]P$, and $C = \Phi\lambda$. Then, compute e^{Ψ} using the method of Padé approximation with scaling and squaring. Let e^{Ψ} be written as $\begin{bmatrix} X & Y \\ 0 & Z \end{bmatrix}$. Then Van Loan's (1978) analysis implies that

$$Y^{\mathrm{T}} = \int_{s=0}^{1} e^{\Phi^{\mathrm{T}}\lambda s} P^{\mathrm{T}} [RPe^{\Phi\lambda} + S] e^{\Phi^{\mathrm{T}}\lambda(1-s)} \, ds, \qquad (3.16)$$

the integral in (3.15).

Equations (3.14) and (3.15) are a computationally useful form of the first-order condition $dW = 0$. As expected, when $\lambda = 0$, (3.14) and (3.15) reduce to the first-order condition of the $\lambda = 0$ problem. In particular, if $\lambda = 0$ then (3.15) reduces to $P = -R^{-1}[S + G^{\mathrm{T}}W]$. After eliminating P from (3.14) with this result, (3.14) becomes the continuous time algebraic Riccati equation. If $\lambda > 0$ then (3.15) cannot be first explicitly solved for P, so that (3.14) and (3.15) must be solved simultaneously for P and W.

Second-order conditions for P^* are discussed in Appendix C.

3.5   Numerical solution of the first-order conditions for P^*

Because $F_{21} = 0$ and $G_2 = 0$, (3.14) can be simplified considerably. Let P and K be conformably partitioned with $x = (x_1^{\mathrm{T}}, x_2^{\mathrm{T}})^{\mathrm{T}}$ as $P = [P_1, P_2]$ and $K = [K_1, K_2] = [P_1, P_2]e^{\Phi\lambda}$. Similarly, let Φ, $\tilde{\Phi}$, and W be partitioned into quadrants Φ_{ij}, $\tilde{\Phi}_{ij}$, and W_{ij} for $(i, j) = (1, 1)$, $(1, 2)$, $(2, 1)$, and $(2, 2)$. Then $G_2 = 0$ implies $G^{\mathrm{T}}W = [G_1^{\mathrm{T}}W_{11}, G_1^{\mathrm{T}}W_{12}]$ in (3.15), so that only the parts W_{11} and W_{12} of W are relevant for determining P^*. Also, $F_{21} = 0$ and $G_2 = 0$ imply that W_{11}^* and W_{12}^* are determined by respective parts of (3.14) as follows:

$$K_1^{\mathrm{T}}RK_1 + K_1^{\mathrm{T}}S_1 + S_1^{\mathrm{T}}K_1 + Q_{11} + \tilde{\Phi}_{11}^{\mathrm{T}}W_{11} + W_{11}\tilde{\Phi}_{11} = 0, \qquad (3.17)$$

$$K_1^{\mathrm{T}}RK_2 + K_1^{\mathrm{T}}S_2 + S_1^{\mathrm{T}}K_2 + Q_{12} + \tilde{\Phi}_{11}^{\mathrm{T}}W_{12} + W_{11}\tilde{\Phi}_{12} + W_{12}\tilde{\Phi}_{22} = 0. \qquad (3.18)$$

The simplification involves replacing (3.14) with (3.17) and (3.18), and ignoring W_{22} and the part of (3.14) by which it is determined. Thus, the number of equations to be solved in the nonlinear system is reduced by the number of nonredundant elements of W_{22}. For example, in the present model, (3.14) involves 21 distinct equations, whereas (3.17) and (3.18) involve only 7 distinct equations, a 67-percent reduction. If $\lambda = 0$ then (3.15) partitions similarly, so that (3.17) and (3.18) can be solved sequentially for W_{11}^* and W_{12}^* as in the analogous discrete time problem (Hansen and Sargent 1981, pp. 136–9). However, if $\lambda > 0$ then the presence of exponentials involving Φ prevents (3.15) from being decomposed into equations for P_1^* and P_2^*, so that (3.15), (3.17), and (3.18) must be solved simultaneously for P^*, W_{11}^*, and W_{12}^*. In the present model, (3.15), (3.17), and (3.18) comprise 12 distinct equations to be solved for the 12 nonredundant elements of P, W_{11}, and W_{12}.

Equations (3.15), (3.17), and (3.18) may be solved for P, W_{11}, and W_{12} as follows. First, compute the $\lambda = 0$ solution with a Schur decomposition method (Laub 1979, Arnold and Laub 1983). Then use the $\lambda = 0$ solution as a starting point to compute the desired $\lambda = \lambda^*$ solution with a trust-region method (Moré, Garbow, and Hillstrom 1980, Moré et al. 1984, Dennis and Schnabel 1983).

If λ^* is too large for the $\lambda = 0$ solution to be a good starting point for the $\lambda = \lambda^*$ solution, then the $\lambda = \lambda^*$ solution can be computed in N steps. The trust-region method can be applied to the $\lambda = \lambda_j$ problem for $j = 1, \dots, N$, taking as a starting point the $\lambda = \lambda_{j-1}$ solution, where $0 = \lambda_0 < \lambda_1 < \cdots < \lambda_j < \cdots < \lambda_N = \lambda^*$ is a uniform grid on $[0, \lambda^*]$ (i.e., $\lambda_j - \lambda_{j-1} = 1/N$).

The multi-step trust-region (MSTR) method was applied to solve (3.15), (3.17), and (3.18) for various values of parameters. When λ was too large and N and γ were too small (γ denotes the convergence criterion), the MSTR method often converged to inadmissible solutions – that is, solutions at which either Φ was not stable or W was not negative semidefinite. However, for $\lambda \leq 1$, $N \geq 5$, and $\gamma \geq 0.01$, the MSTR method always converged to an admissible solution. Therefore, for appropriate values of λ, N, and γ, the MSTR method is a reliable and speedy method for computing P^*. Each application was executed in FORTRAN within 20 seconds on a personal computer operating at 50-MHz clock speed.

4 Estimating, forecasting, or simulating with the model

4.1 *Discrete time state-space representation*

To estimate, forecast, or simulate with the model, its equations must be converted to discrete time form. In the present state-space approach, this involves integrating continuous time state equation (3.11) to discrete time form and specifying a discrete-time observation equation that incorporates controller (3.12).

As before, suppose that t_0 is the instant at which the decisionmaker in the model initiates an optimal policy, let Δ be a constant sampling interval, and let $t = t_0 + \Delta j$ ($j = 1, \dots, N$) be instants at which variables of the

Table 1. *Classification of variables*

Number	Variable	Observed	State variable
1	q	Yes	No
2	n	Yes	No
3	k	No	Yes
4	l	Yes	No
5	m	No	No
6	p_q	Yes	No
7	p_n	Yes	Yes
8	p_l	Yes	Yes
9	p_m	No	Yes
10	ξ_f	No	Yes
11	ξ_q	No	Yes

model are observed. The value of a variable at $t_0 + \Delta j$ is denoted by its symbol with a subscript j; for example, $x_j = x(t_0 + \Delta j)$.

Integrate continuous time state equation (3.11) over sampling intervals $[t_0, t_0 + \Delta j]$ for $j = 1, \ldots, N$ in order to obtain the discrete time closed-loop state equation

$$x_j = \bar{\Phi} x_{j-1} + \zeta_j, \tag{4.1}$$

where $\bar{\Phi} = e^{\Phi \Delta}$ and $\zeta_j = \int_{\tau=0}^{\Delta} e^{\Phi(\Delta - \tau)} H \epsilon(t_0 + \Delta(j-1) + \tau) \, d\tau$. Disturbance ζ_j inherits Gaussianity and whiteness from ϵ; in particular, $\zeta_j \sim \text{NIID}(0, \Sigma_\zeta)$, where

$$\Sigma_\zeta = \int_{s=0}^{\Delta} e^{\Phi(\Delta - s)} H \Sigma_\epsilon H^T e^{\Phi^T(\Delta - s)} \, ds \tag{4.2}$$

(see e.g. Zadrozny 1988a). Like the integral in (3.15), Σ_ζ can be computed by Van Loan's method: Let $e^{\Psi \Delta} = \begin{bmatrix} X & Y \\ 0 & Z \end{bmatrix}$, where $\Psi = \begin{bmatrix} A & B \\ 0 & C \end{bmatrix}$, $A = -\Phi$, $B = H \Sigma_\epsilon H^T$, and $C = \Phi^T$; then $\Sigma_\zeta = \bar{\Phi} Y$.

To obtain an observation equation, the variables in the model must be classified according to whether they are observed. It is also convenient to recall which variables are state variables. Table 1 provides these classifications.

Let $y = (p_q, q, l, n, p_n, p_l)^T$ be the vector of observed variables, and recall that $x = (k, p_n, p_l, p_m, \xi_f, \xi_q)^T$ and $\epsilon = (\epsilon_k, \epsilon_n, \epsilon_l, \epsilon_m, \epsilon_f, \epsilon_q)^T$. Then the observation equation is

$$y_j = M x_j + v_j \quad \text{for } j = 1, \ldots, N, \tag{4.3}$$

where v_j is an optional vector of discrete time observation errors distributed as $v_j \sim \text{NIID}(0, \Sigma_v)$; in particular, v_j is distributed independently of all values of ϵ.

To compute M, first solve output inverse demand curve (2.2), optimal output rule (2.7), and optimal labor input rule (2.8) for p_q, q, and l in terms of n, k, p_l, p_m, ξ_q, and ξ_f. Then, use optimal investment rule $n = Kx$ to eliminate n. The coefficients of the resulting three equations, which express p_q, q, and l in terms of x, are the first three rows of M. The fourth row of M is $K = (K_1, K_2)$, where $K_1 = (K_{1,1})$ and $K_2 = (K_{2,1}, ..., K_{2,5})$. The remaining (fifth and sixth) rows of M consist of zeros and ones that select p_n and p_l out of x. M is given in detail in equations (B.3) of Appendix B.

Discrete time state equation (4.1) and observation equation (4.3) comprise a discrete time state-space representation that is useful for estimation, forecasting, or simulation.

Suppose that any identities have been previously removed, so that a sample of observations, $Y_N = \{y_j\}_{j=1}^{N}$, has a nonsingular (empirical frequency) distribution. Then, to estimate the model (e.g., by maximum likelihood), the model and sampling scheme must impart a nonsingular (theoretical probability) distribution to Y_N. Because H is nonsingular, the state equation transmits the nonsingular distribution of ϵ to x. In turn, because M is generally nonsingular, the observation equation transmits the nonsingular distribution of x to y. The transfer-function representation $y(t) = M(D - \Phi)^{-1} H \epsilon(t)$ states exactly how the model transmits variations from ϵ to y. Possible observation errors v_j add further stochastic variation to y. In sum, y is a full-rank process if either $M(D + \Phi)^{-1} H \epsilon(t)$, v_j, or some "combination" of these terms is a full-rank process.

Table 1 attributes all variations in y to ϵ, making it unnecessary to introduce observation errors in order to have a nonsingular distribution of y. By contrast, in a multivariate model, G. D. Hansen and Sargent (1988) specified only a single structural (technology) disturbance, thereby necessitating the addition of observation errors (of course, this was their intention). Table 1 classifies materials as unobserved. For U.S. manufacturing industries, depending on the sampling frequency, materials may or may not be observed. If materials are indeed observed then their observations should be used in estimation, and another structural disturbance or observation error must be introduced.

4.2   *Maximum likelihood estimation*

First, we must clarify the following relationships among the underlying time unit, the measure of the sampling interval (Δ), and the measure of the gestation lag (λ).

The (actual) sampling interval, the measure of the sampling interval, and the underlying time unit are related as follows:

"sampling interval" = $\Delta \times$ "underlying time unit."

Therefore, for a given value of Δ, the underlying time unit may be defined in terms of the sampling interval or vice versa. For example, a sampling interval of one quarter measured by $\Delta = 0.25$ implies an underlying time unit of one year.

The measure of the gestation lag, λ, is the only structural parameter whose value depends on time and has been defined implicitly in terms of the underlying time unit. In terms of the sampling interval, the gestation lag is λ/Δ. For example, if (as before) the underlying time unit is one year, $\Delta = 0.25$, and the sampling interval is one quarter, then a gestation lag of $\lambda = 0.75$ years is equivalent to a gestation lag of three quarters.

Of course, two measures of time are unneeded, so that either Δ or λ can and should be normalized. If the sampling interval is constant over a sample then it seems simplest to set $\Delta = 1$, so that the sampling interval equals the underlying time unit. However, Appendix C and Section 3.5 explain that, to compute P^* reliably and accurately, λ must be neither too small nor too large. Accordingly, it might be best to normalize λ (to $\lambda = 1$, for example) and thereby reparameterize the gestation lag from λ to Δ.

To estimate the model by maximum likelihood, the Gaussian likelihood function can be computed by applying the Kalman filter to equations (4.1) and (4.3) (see e.g. Zadrozny 1988a; see also Bergstrom 1983, 1986). For simplicity, here all elements of y are treated as stocks at the same frequency. In practice, y is more likely to be a mixture of stocks and flows at different frequencies. Sampling intervals may also vary over a sample. Equations (4.1) to (4.3) are readily extended to account for all of these sampling complications (Zadrozny 1988a, Bergstrom 1986).

4.3   Forecasting and simulation

Consider using a specified or estimated model to forecast y beyond a sample Y_N. For $j = 1, 2, ..., J$, let $x_{N+j|N}$ and $y_{N+j|N}$ denote expectations of x_{N+j} and y_{N+j} conditional on Y_N. Using the model, run the Kalman filter over Y_N to obtain $x_{N+1|N}$. Then, for $j = 1, 2, ..., J$, $y_{N+j|N} = Mx_{N+j|N}$, where $x_{N+j|N}$ is generated recursively with $x_{N+j+1|N} = \bar{\Phi} x_{N+j|N}$, starting with $x_{N+1|N}$.

Nonstochastic impulse–response simulations, like those reported in Section 5, are computed as follows. The simulations concern y_j for $j = 1, 2, ..., J$. First, set $x_0 = 0$. For each $i = 1, ..., 6$, consider the simulation in which element i of ϵ experiences a "standard" impulse of σ_i/γ over an interval of length γ, where σ_i is the square root of element (i, i) of ϵ's intensity matrix, Σ_ϵ, and $0 < \gamma \le \Delta$. In particular, $\epsilon_i(\tau) = \sigma_i/\gamma$ for $0 \le \tau \le \gamma$, $\epsilon_i(\tau) = 0$ for $\tau > \gamma$, and $\epsilon_\nu(\tau) = 0$ for $\nu \ne i$ and $\tau \ge 0$. Then $y_j = Mx_j$, where x_j is generated recursively with $x_j = \bar{\Phi}x_{j-1}$ for $j = 2, 3, ..., J$, starting with $x_1 = \bar{H}e_i$ where $\bar{H} = (1/\gamma)\int_{s=0}^{\gamma} e^{\Phi(\Delta - s)}ds$ and e_i is the 6×1 vector with σ_i in position i and zeros elsewhere.

Like Σ_ζ, $\bar{H}$ can be computed by Van Loan's method: Let $e^{\Psi\Delta} = \begin{bmatrix} X & Y \\ 0 & Z \end{bmatrix}$, where $\Psi = \begin{bmatrix} A & B \\ 0 & C \end{bmatrix}$, $A = \Phi$, $B = I_6$, and $C = 0$; then $\bar{H} = (1/\gamma)Y$. In general, Φ may be singular; if Φ is nonsingular, then $\bar{H}$ may be computed more directly as $\bar{H} = e^{\Phi\Delta}(\gamma\Phi)^{-1}(I - e^{-\Phi\gamma})$. In the limit as $\gamma \to 0$, $\epsilon_i(\tau)$ is a Dirac delta generalized function with mass σ_i centered at zero and $\bar{H} = e^{\Phi\Delta}$. Simulations reported in Section 5 are based on $\sigma_i = 1$ for $i = 1, ..., 6$ and $\gamma = \Delta$; any other value of γ in the interval $0 < \gamma < \Delta$ (including the limit as $\gamma \to 0$) yields qualitatively the same results. Of course, the model can also be simulated stochastically, by iterating equation (4.1) with pseudo-random values of ζ_j drawn from the distribution NIID$(0, \Sigma_\zeta)$.

5   Illustrative step-response simulations

Step responses illustrate short-run and long-run responses of the representative firm in the model. Many possible responses could be shown, but space constraints limit the discussion to the four sets of responses in Figure 1. Each row of Figure 1 depicts responses of price, output, labor, and capital to a permanent outward shift in demand for output by one unit, that is, responses of p_q, q, l, and k to a unit step in ζ_q. The responses were computed as responses to impulses in ϵ_q according to Section 4.3, but are equivalent to responses to steps in ξ_q because ξ_q follows a random walk. Before ξ_q is shocked by the impulse in ϵ_q, the firm is assumed to be in an initial long-run equilibrium represented by the origin, so that graphed responses denote deviations from the initial equilibrium. Recall that adjustment costs increase with ρ and decrease with CET $= (\rho - 1)^{-1}$. The rows of Figure 1 depict, respectively, responses for the following four combinations of adjustment costs and gestation lag: (1) relatively low adjustment costs ($\rho = 2$ or CET $= 1$) and no gestation lag ($\lambda = 0$); relatively high adjustment costs ($\rho = 6$ or CET $= 0.2$) and no gestation lag; relatively low adjustment costs ($\rho = 2$) and a unit gestation lag ($\lambda = 1$); and relatively high adjustment costs ($\rho = 6$) and a unit gestation lag.

Remaining structural parameters are set to the following values: $\Delta = 1$ equates the time unit and sampling interval, presumed to be a quarter. A continuous discount rate of $\delta = 0.0074$ implies an identical quarterly discount rate. A slope of -1 of the demand curve for output is set by $\eta = 1$.

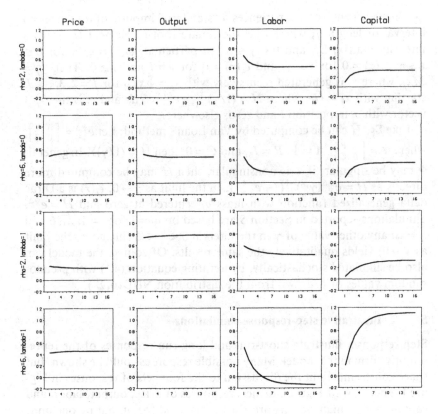

Figure 1. Responses of variables to a unit step in ξ_q.

Production inputs and outputs are weighted equally by $\alpha_1 = \alpha_2 = \alpha_3 = 0.333$ and $\gamma_1 = \gamma_2 = 0.5$. Input substitutability of CES = 1.111 is set by $\beta = 0.1$. A continuous capital depreciation rate of $a_k = 0.0181$ (inferred from average capital depreciation rates in U.S. SIC manufacturing industries 28, 30, and 32 as reported by Jorgenson and Stephenson 1967) implies a quarterly capital depreciation rate of about 0.0178. All exogenous processes are random walks, so that $a_q = a_n = a_l = a_m = a_f = 0$. Because ϵ_q experiences a unit impulse, in effect $\sigma_6^2 = 1$, where σ_6^2 denotes element $(6, 6)$ of Σ_ϵ. The rest of Σ_ϵ is irrelevant for these simulations.

In terms of conventional economic theory, responses of p_q and q are determined by intersections of the demand curve for output and a sequence of short-run marginal cost (SRMC) of output curves. Under assumed restrictions on parameters, the dual variable cost function derived in Section 2 implies $\partial^2 c / \partial^2 q = c_{11} = \gamma_1 \gamma_2 (\rho - 1) + \alpha_1 (1 - \beta) \gamma_1^2 / (1 - \alpha_1) > 0$ and

Table 2. *Transition time in quarters*
between long-run equilibria

Row in Figure 1	Adjustment costs	Gestation lag	Transitional quarters
1	Low	0	11
2	High	0	13
3	Low	1	16
4	High	1	16

$\partial^2 c/\partial q \partial k = c_{13} = -\alpha_1(1-\beta)\gamma_1/(1-\alpha_1) < 0$. The SRMC curve therefore has a positive slope, which increases as adjustment costs increase; the SRMC curve shifts to the right as k increases. The SRMC curve does not depend on the gestation lag.

Immediately after the shock to demand for output, p_q and q increase along the SRMC curve, positioned by the amount of k at the instant of the shock. The rise in p_q and q stimulates the firm to accumulate k. As k is accumulated, the SRMC curve shifts to the right, causing p_q to fall and q to rise. Because higher adjustment costs result in a steeper SRMC curve, p_q is higher and q is lower in rows 2 and 4 in Figure 1 than in rows 1 and 3. In all rows, $p_q + q = 1$ because the demand curve for output has risen by one unit and its slope is -1. The only conflict with this supply-and-demand explanation is the steady increase in p_q and steady decrease in q in rows 2 and 4, that is, when adjustment costs are relatively high. It is unclear why these responses occur.

Perhaps because the SRMC curve is independent of gestation lag λ, the patterns of responses of p_q and q appear to be independent of λ. Although the *patterns* of the p_q and q responses are independent of λ, an increase in λ does *stretch out* those responses. That is, an increase in λ results in an increase in the transition time from the initial long-run equilibrium (LRE) to the final LRE. Because k is the only factor subject to adjustment costs and gestation lags, transition time from the initial LRE to the final LRE is a measure of capital fixity. However, the final LRE is reached only when all variables have converged, not just when k has converged. Table 2 summarizes the transition times in the figures.

Consider now the responses of l and k in terms of scale effects in production. The permanent increase in demand for output is expected to stimulate an increase in demand for all production inputs. Adjustment costs discourage and gestation lags prevent k from increasing quickly. Therefore, k rises slowly and steadily to its final LRE value and, in the

Table 3. *Long-run equilibrium changes in labor and capital*

Row in Figure 1	Adjustment costs	Gestation lag	Δl	Δk	$\Delta l - \Delta k$
1	Low	0	0.426	0.344	0.082
2	High	0	0.176	0.346	−0.170
3	Low	1	0.433	0.326	0.107
4	High	1	−0.136	1.112	−1.248

short run, the unexpected increase in demand for output is met mostly by increasing freely variable l (and m) inputs. As k accumulates, l declines from its initially high values. These features are qualitatively identical in all rows in Figure 1, and are quantitatively very similar in rows 1 through 3.

Conventional economic theory predicts that, with constant linear homogeneous production technology and constant input prices, a permanent increase in output demand should stimulate proportional LRE increases in all production inputs. Let subscripts 0 and 1 denote (respectively) initial and final LRE values, and let Δ denote absolute changes in values from LRE_0 to LRE_1. In other words, conventional economic theory predicts that $\Delta(l/k) = 0$. The normalization $z = z_0$, imposed in Section 2, sets $l_0 = k_0 = 1$, which implies that $\Delta(l/k) = \Delta l - \Delta k$. In contrast to the conventional result, Table 3 reports that $\Delta(l/k) > 0$ when adjustment costs are low and $\Delta(l/k) < 0$ when adjustment costs are high, regardless of whether a gestation lag is present.

In sum, the simulations show that the present modeling approach is computationally feasible and that it can reveal unknown, complex, and interesting responses of representative optimizing firms arising from interactions of adjustment costs and gestation lags. Therefore, the simulations show the present modeling approach to be a useful tool for studying dynamic firm behavior.

6   Concluding remarks

This paper proposes a continuous time method for modeling analysis of investment in capital inputs subject to adjustment costs and to a gestation lag. The method may be called the "P^*-short" method because it sets the predictive control matrix $P = P^*$ and "shortens" state and controller equations (3.6) and (3.10) by dropping the disturbance vector ψ. Implicitly, the paper also proposes related "P^*-long," "$P^\dagger$-short," and "$P^\dagger$-long" methods, where "$P^\dagger$" means $P = P^\dagger$ (the standard predictive control matrix) and "long" means using state controller equations (3.6) and (3.10) with ψ retained. As noted in Section 3.2, sensitivity to gestation lag λ gives P^* certain modeling advantages over $P^\dagger$, at the cost of significantly more difficult computations. The discrete time state-space representation in Section 4 can be extended to incorporate ψ exactly, also at the cost of significantly more difficult computations. Experience will determine which of the four methods offers the best mix of adequate specification and computational tractability.

The paper illustrates in detail a general method with the particular gestation lag of equation (2.6). As noted in Section 2, within limits the method applies to other specifications of gestation lags. Ignoring disturbances, a capital law of motion is expressed in transfer-function form as $k(t) = \Gamma(D)n(t)$, where $\Gamma(D)$ is a function of the mean-squared time derivative D. For example, (2.6) implies $\Gamma(D) = (D + a_k)^{-1}e^{-D\lambda}$. Any continuous $\Gamma(D)$, such as the frequently considered gamma "distributed lags," can be arbitrarily well-approximated by a rational function of the form $A(D)/B(D)$, where $A(D)$ and $B(D)$ are finite polynomials in D such that degree$[B(D)] >$ degree$[A(D)]$. Any such approximate ARMA-type capital transfer function can be restated in state-space form (see e.g. Zadrozny 1988a) and handled by any of the four related methods.

Appendix A: Matrix differentiation and vectorization rules

Let $A(\theta)$ be a real, differentiable, $m \times n$ matrix function of the real $p \times 1$ vector $\theta = (\theta_1, ..., \theta_p)^T$, where m, n, and p are any positive integers and T denotes transposition (the text definitions of k, m, n, p, and q are overridden in this appendix). In particular, θ can be the vectorization of a matrix with a total of p elements. Let the $m \times n$ matrices $\partial_k A = \{\partial A_{ij}/\partial \theta_k\}$ ($k = 1, ..., p$) collect first-order derivatives of $A(\theta)$ in partial derivative form, where A_{ij} is the (i, j) element of A. Let $dA_{ij} = \sum_{k=1}^{p}(\partial A_{ij}/\partial \theta_k)\,d\theta_k$, where $d\theta_k$ is an infinitesimal variation in θ_k. Then the $m \times n$ matrix $dA = \{dA_{ij}\}$ is the differential form of first-order derivatives of $A(\theta)$.

Let $A(\theta)$ and $B(\theta)$ be real, differentiable, $m \times n$ and $n \times q$ matrix functions of the real $p \times 1$ vector θ, where m, n, p, and q are any positive integers. Componentwise application of the usual scalar product rule of differentiation yields

$$d(AB) = dA \cdot B + A \cdot dB \tag{A.1}$$

(Magnus and Neudecker 1988, p. 148).

Consider tr$(dA \cdot B)$, where A and B continue to be $m \times n$ and $n \times m$ and where dA assumes all possible values in $\mathbb{R}^{m \times n}$. Here A may be a differentiable function of a vector θ, so that dA is induced by $d\theta$. Then

$\operatorname{tr}(dA \cdot B) = 0$ for all dA in $\mathbb{R}^{m \times n}$ implies that $B = 0$.   (A.2)

To prove (A.2) let $dA = 0$, except that $dA_{ik} \neq 0$ for some i and k. Then $\operatorname{tr}(dA \cdot B) = \sum_{j=1}^{m} \sum_{\nu=1}^{n} dA_{j\nu} \cdot B_{\nu j} = 0$ implies $B_{ki} = 0$. Repeat this argument for all i and k to obtain $B = 0$.

Let A be a real $m \times m$ matrix. The matrix exponential e^A is defined by $e^A = I + A + (1/2!)A^2 + \cdots + (1/k!)A^k + \cdots$. Then, restating in terms of differentials the argument given by Graham (1981, pp. 109-10) yields

$$d[e^A] = \int_{\tau=0}^{1} e^{A(1-\tau)} dA\, e^{A\tau}\, d\tau.   \tag{A.3}$$

Of course, A may be a differentiable function of θ, so that dA is induced by $d\theta$.

Appendix B: Statement of $\nabla^2 c_q(z_0)$, R, S, Q, and M

Because $\nabla^2 c_q(z_0)$ is symmetric, it suffices to state its upper triangular part. Let c_{ij} denote the (i, j) element of $\nabla^2 c_q(z_0)$. Then, for

$$z_0 = (1, 1, 1, \alpha_2, \alpha_3, 1)^{\mathrm{T}},$$

we have the following.

Equations (B.1):

$$c_{11} = \gamma_1 \gamma_2 (\rho - 1) + \alpha_1 (1 - \beta) \gamma_1^2 / (1 - \alpha_1),$$

$$c_{12} = -\gamma_1 \gamma_2 (\rho - 1) + \alpha_1 (1 - \beta) \gamma_1 \gamma_2 / (1 - \alpha_1),$$

$$c_{13} = -\alpha_1 (1 - \beta) \gamma_1 / (1 - \alpha_1),$$

$$c_{14} = \gamma_1 / (1 - \alpha_1),$$

$$c_{15} = \gamma_1 / (1 - \alpha_1),$$

$$c_{16} = -\gamma_1 + \alpha_1 (1 - \beta) \gamma_1 / (1 - \alpha_1),$$

$$c_{22} = \gamma_1 \gamma_2 (\rho - 1) + \alpha_1 (1 - \beta) \gamma_2^2 / (1 - \alpha_1),$$

$$c_{23} = -\alpha_1 (1 - \beta) \gamma_2 / (1 - \alpha_1),$$

$$c_{24} = \gamma_2 / (1 - \alpha_1),$$

$$c_{25} = \gamma_2 / (1 - \alpha_1),$$

$$c_{26} = -\gamma_2 + \alpha_1 (1 - \beta) \gamma_2 / (1 - \alpha_1),$$

$$c_{33} = \alpha_1 (1 + \alpha_1 \alpha_2 \alpha_3 \beta)(1 - \beta) / (1 - \alpha_1),$$

$$c_{34} = -\alpha_1 / (1 - \alpha_1),$$

$$c_{35} = -\alpha_1/(1-\alpha_1),$$

$$c_{36} = -\alpha_1(1-\beta)/(1-\alpha_1),$$

$$c_{44} = -\alpha_3/(1-\alpha_1)\alpha_2(1-\beta),$$

$$c_{45} = 1/(1-\alpha_1)(1-\beta),$$

$$c_{46} = 1/(1-\alpha_1),$$

$$c_{55} = -\alpha_2/(1-\alpha_1)\alpha_3(1-\beta),$$

$$c_{56} = 1/(1-\alpha_1),$$

$$c_{66} = -2 + \alpha_1(1-\beta)/(1-\alpha_1).$$

The c_{66} term has also been given (for completeness), although it does not affect any optimal decisions.

Next, we give the coefficient matrices R, S_1, S_2, Q_{11}, and Q_{12} appearing in (2.10). Matrices R, S_1, and Q_{11} are scalars, and S_2 and Q_{12} are 1×5 matrices; that is, $S_2 = (S_{2,1}, ..., S_{2,5})$ and $Q_{12} = (Q_{12,1}, ..., Q_{12,5})$. For simplicity, to eliminate the common factor $\frac{1}{2}$ in the coefficients, π is rescaled by multiplying it by 2; this is possible because optimal decisions are invariant to the scale of π. Setting $c_0 = (\eta + c_{11})^{-1}$ then yields the following.

Equations (B.2):

$$R = c_0(c_{12})^2 - c_{22};$$

$$S_1 = c_0 c_{12} c_{13} - c_{23},$$

$$S_{2,1} = -1,$$

$$S_{2,2} = c_0 c_{12} c_{14} - c_{24},$$

$$S_{2,3} = c_0 c_{12} c_{15} - c_{25},$$

$$S_{2,4} = c_0 c_{12} c_{16} - c_{26},$$

$$S_{2,5} = -c_0 c_{12};$$

$$Q_{11} = c_0(c_{13})^2 - c_{33},$$

$$Q_{12,1} = 0,$$

$$Q_{12,2} = c_0 c_{13} c_{14} - c_{34},$$

$$Q_{12,3} = c_0 c_{13} c_{15} - c_{35},$$

$$Q_{12,4} = c_0 c_{13} c_{16} - c_{36},$$

$$Q_{12,5} = 0.$$

Finally, we give the 6×6 coefficient matrix M of observation equation (4.2). Recall that K is a 1×6 vector partitioned as $K = (K_1, K_2)$, where $K_1 = (K_{1,1})$ and $K_2 = (K_{2,1}, ..., K_{2,5})$, and let M_{ij} denote the (i, j) element of M. Then, with $c_0 = (\eta + c_{11})^{-1}$ again and $c_1 = \eta/(c_{11} + \eta)$, we have the following.

Equations (B.3):

$$M_{11} = c_1(c_{12}K_{1,1} + c_{13}),$$

$$M_{12} = c_1 c_{12} K_{2,1},$$

$$M_{13} = c_1(c_{12}K_{2,2} + c_{14}),$$

$$M_{14} = c_1(c_{12}K_{2,3} + c_{15}),$$

$$M_{15} = c_1(c_{12}K_{2,4} + c_{16}),$$

$$M_{16} = c_1(c_{12}K_{2,5} - 1) + 1,$$

$$M_{21} = -c_0(c_{12}K_{1,1} + c_{13}),$$

$$M_{22} = -c_0 c_{12} K_{2,1},$$

$$M_{23} = -c_0(c_{12}K_{2,2} + c_{14}),$$

$$M_{24} = -c_0(c_{12}K_{2,3} + c_{15}),$$

$$M_{25} = -c_0(c_{12}K_{2,4} + c_{16}),$$

$$M_{26} = -c_0(c_{12}K_{2,5} - 1),$$

$$M_{31} = -c_0 c_{41}(c_{12}K_{1,1} + c_{13}) + c_{42}K_{1,1} + c_{43},$$

$$M_{32} = (-c_0 c_{41} c_{12} + c_{42})K_{2,1},$$

$$M_{33} = -c_0 c_{41}(c_{12}K_{2,2} + c_{14}) + c_{42}K_{2,2} + c_{44},$$

$$M_{34} = -c_0 c_{41}(c_{12}K_{2,3} + c_{15}) + c_{42}K_{2,3} + c_{45},$$

$$M_{35} = -c_0 c_{41}(c_{12}K_{2,4} + c_{16}) + c_{42}K_{2,4} + c_{46},$$

$$M_{36} = -c_0 c_{41}(c_{12}K_{2,5} - 1) + c_{42}K_{2,5};$$

$$(M_{41}, ..., M_{46}) = (K_{1,1}, K_{2,1}, K_{2,2}, K_{2,3}, K_{2,4}, K_{2,5}),$$

$$(M_{51}, ..., M_{56}) = (0, 1, 0, 0, 0, 0),$$

$$(M_{61}, ..., M_{66}) = (0, 0, 1, 0, 0, 0).$$

Appendix C: Second-order conditions for P^*

In general, (3.14) and (3.15) yield multiple solutions. Let $(P^{\ddagger}, W^{\ddagger})$ denote a solution of (3.14) and (3.15), and let (P^*, W^*) denote the solution that maximizes $V(t, \infty)$. In order for $(P^{\ddagger}, W^{\ddagger}) = (P^*, W^*)$, it must satisfy two additional conditions. First, concavity and detectability assumptions 3.3.2 and 3.3.3 and the form of (3.13) imply that $W^{\ddagger} \leq 0$ (negative semidefinite), which may be called the "transversality" condition because it corresponds to the transversality condition in the calculus of variations. Second, $(P^{\ddagger}, W^{\ddagger})$ must satisfy the second-order condition $d^2 W_{\lambda}^{\ddagger} \leq 0$, where $d^2 W_{\lambda}^{\ddagger}$ denotes the second-order differential of W with respect to P at $(P^{\ddagger}, W^{\ddagger})$ for $\lambda > 0$. If $d^2 W_{\lambda}^{\ddagger} < 0$ (negative definite) then $(P^{\ddagger}, W^{\ddagger})$ achieves a unique local maximum of $V(t, \infty)$. If multiple solutions $(P^{\ddagger}, W^{\ddagger})$ achieve local maxima of $V(t, \infty)$, then the one yielding the greatest value of $V(t, \infty)$ is designated (P^*, W^*).

Let $d^2 W_0^{\dagger}$ denote the second-order differential of W with respect to P at $(P^{\ddagger}, W^{\ddagger}) = (P^{\dagger}, W^{\dagger})$, that is, for $\lambda = 0$. An envelope-theorem argument (cf. Zadrozny 1988b) shows that the equation which characterizes $d^2 W_0^{\dagger}$ reduces to

$$\tilde{\Phi}^{\mathrm{T}} d^2 W_0^{\dagger} + d^2 W_0^{\dagger} \tilde{\Phi} + dP^{\mathrm{T}} R dP = 0, \tag{C.1}$$

where dP denotes any nonzero infinitesimal variation in P. Because $\tilde{\Phi}$ must be stable in order for W and $d^2 W$ to be finite for $h = \infty$, (C.1) is equivalent to

$$d^2 W_0^{\dagger} = \int_{\tau=0}^{\infty} e^{\tilde{\Phi}^{\mathrm{T}} \tau} dP^{\mathrm{T}} R dP e^{\tilde{\Phi} \tau} d\tau. \tag{C.2}$$

Because $R < 0$ by assumption and because a matrix exponential always has full rank, $d^2 W_0^{\dagger} \leq 0$ for any nonzero infinitesimal variation dP and $d^2 W_0^{\dagger} < 0$ for any nonsingular infinitesimal variation dP. That is, $dP = \eta X$ such that $\eta \downarrow 0$ and X is any nonsingular matrix in $\mathbb{R}^{m \times n}$.

Analogous equations for $d^2 W_{\lambda}^{\ddagger}$ are difficult to derive and are even more difficult to use for checking $d^2 W_{\lambda}^{\ddagger} \leq 0$. Continuity of $d^2 W_{\lambda}^{\ddagger}$ with respect to λ is assumed to imply $d^2 W_{\lambda}^{\ddagger} \leq 0$. In particular, because $d^2 W_0^{\dagger} \leq 0$, λ sufficiently close to zero is assumed to imply $d^2 W_{\lambda}^{\ddagger} \leq 0$. As explained in Section 4, λ can be normalized to any positive value. Therefore, $d^2 W_{\lambda}^{\ddagger} \leq 0$ is assumed to hold at an admissible solution $(P^{\ddagger}, W^{\ddagger})$, computed with sufficiently many steps N of the MSTR method. (A solution is *admissible* if $\tilde{\Phi}^{\ddagger} = \tilde{F} + GP^{\ddagger}$ is stable and $W^{\ddagger} \leq 0$; the MSTR method is described in Section 3.5.) Intuitively, because $(P^{\ddagger}, W^{\ddagger})$ is the end of a sequence of solutions, if the sequence index from $\lambda = 0$ to the desired $\lambda = \lambda^*$ is sufficiently fine, then all solutions in the sequence are expected to inherit $d^2 W_{\lambda}^{\ddagger} \leq 0$ from $d^2 W_0^{\dagger} \leq 0$. (A sequence index is *sufficiently fine* if, within the chosen convergence criterion, an increase in N results in no change in the last solution $(P^{\ddagger}, W^{\ddagger})$ in the sequence.) Note also that if λ is too close to zero, it will have no detectable effect on $(P^{\ddagger}, W^{\ddagger})$. In practice, $\lambda \cong 1$ appears to be sufficiently small to ensure $d^2 W_{\lambda}^{\ddagger} \leq 0$ yet is sufficiently large to have a detectable effect on $(P^{\ddagger}, W^{\ddagger})$.

REFERENCES

Arnold, W. F., and A. J. Laub (1983), "A Software Package for the Solution of Generalized Algebraic Riccati Equations," *Proceedings of the 22nd IEEE Conference on Decision and Control.* Piscataway, NJ: Institute of Electrical and Electronics Engineers, pp. 415–17.

Astrom, K. J. (1970), *Introduction to Stochastic Control Theory.* Boston: Academic Press.

Bergstrom, A. R. (1983), "Gaussian Estimation of Structural Parameters in Higher Order Continuous Time Dynamic Models," *Econometrica* 51: 117–52.

(1986), "The Estimation of Open Higher Order Continuous Time Dynamic Models with Mixed Stock and Flow Data," *Econometric Theory* 2: 350–73.

Berndt, E. R., M. A. Fuss, and L. Waverman (1980), "Dynamic Adjustment Models of Industrial Energy Demand: Empirical Analysis for U.S. Manufacturing, 1947–1974," Report no. EA-1613, Electric Power Research Institute, Palo Alto, CA.

Brody, A. (1992), "Gestation Lags and the Explanation of Investment Cycles in Socialist Economics," in Hillinger (1992), pp. 149–55.

Dennis, J. E., and R. B. Schnabel (1983), *Numerical Methods for Unconstrained Optimization and Nonlinear Equations.* Englewood Cliffs, NJ: Prentice-Hall.

Diewert, W. E. (1971), "An Application of the Shepard Duality Theorem: A Generalized Leontief Production Function," *Journal of Political Economy* 79: 481–507.

Eisner, R., and R. Strotz (1963), "Determinants of Business Investment," in *Impacts of Monetary Policy* (Commission on Money and Credit). Englewood Cliffs, NJ: Prentice-Hall.

Frisch, R. (1933), "Propagation Problems and Impulse Problems in Dynamic Economics," reprinted in R. A. Gordon and L. R. Klein (eds.) (1965), *Readings in Business Cycles.* Homewood, IL: Irwin.

Gould, J. P. (1968), "Adjustment Costs in the Theory of Investment of the Firm," *Review of Economic Studies* 35: 47–55.

Graham, A. (1981), *Kronecker Products and Matrix Calculus: With Applications.* Chichester, UK: Ellis Horwood.

Hall, R. E. (1973), "The Specification of Technology with Several Kinds of Output," *Journal of Political Economy* 81: 878–92.

Hansen, G. D., and T. J. Sargent (1988), "Straight Time and Overtime in Equilibrium," *Journal of Monetary Economics* 21: 281–308.

Hansen, L. P., and T. J. Sargent (1980), "Formulating and Estimating Dynamic Linear Rational Expectations Models," *Journal of Economic Dynamics and Control* 2: 7–46.

(1981), "Linear Rational Expectations Models for Dynamically Interrelated Variables," in Lucas and Sargent (1981), pp. 127–56.

Harvey, A. C., and J. H. Stock (1989), "Estimating Integrated Higher-Order Continuous-Time Autoregressions with an Application to Money-Income Causality," *Journal of Econometrics* 42: 319–36.

Hillinger, C. (ed.) (1992), *Cyclical Growth in Market and Planned Economies.* Oxford: Clarendon Press.

Jorgenson, D. W. (1963), "Capital Theory and Investment Behavior," *American Economic Review* 53: 247–59.

(1966), "Rational Distributed Lags," *Econometrica* 32: 135-49.

Jorgenson, D. W., and J. Stephenson (1967), "The Time Structure of Investment Behavior in United States Manufacturing, 1947-1960," *Review of Economics and Statistics* 49: 16-27.

Kalecki, M. (1935), "A Macrodynamic Theory of Business Cycles," *Econometrica* 3: 327-44.

Kwakernaak, H., and R. S. Sivan (1972), *Linear Optimal Control Systems*. New York: Wiley.

Kydland, F. E., and E. C. Prescott (1982), "Time to Build and Aggregate Fluctuations," *Econometrica* 50: 1345-70.

Laub, A. J. (1979), "A Schur Method for Solving Algebraic Riccati Equations," *IEEE Transactions on Automatic Control* 24: 913-21.

Lee, T. T., and Y. F. Chang (1987), "Analysis of Time-Varying Delay Systems via General Orthogonal Polynomials," *International Journal of Control* 45: 169-81.

Lucas, R. E., Jr. (1967a), "Optimal Investment Behavior and the Flexible Accelerator," *International Economic Review* 8: 78-85.

(1967b), "Adjustment Costs and the Theory of Supply," *Journal of Political Economy* 75: 321-34.

(1981a), "Distributed Lags and Optimal Investment Policy," in Lucas and Sargent (1981), pp. 39-53.

(1981b), "Optimal Investment with Rational Expectations," in Lucas and Sargent (1981), pp. 55-66.

Lucas, R. E., Jr., and E. C. Prescott (1971), "Investment Under Uncertainty," *Econometrica* 39: 659-81.

Lucas, R. E., Jr., and T. J. Sargent (eds.) (1981), *Rational Expectations and Econometric Practice,* vol. 1. Minneapolis: University of Minnesota Press.

Magnus, J. R., and H. Neudecker (1988), *Matrix Differential Calculus with Applications in Statistics and Econometrics.* New York: Wiley.

Mee, D. H. (1973), "An Extension of Predictor Control for Systems with Time Delays," *International Journal of Control* 18: 1151-68.

Moré, J. J., B. S. Garbow, and K. E. Hillstrom (1980), "User Guide for MINPACK-1," Report no. ANL-80-74, Argonne National Laboratory, Argonne, IL.

Moré, J. J., D. C. Sorensen, B. S. Garbow, and K. E. Hillstrom (1984), "The MINPACK Project," in W. R. Cowell (ed.), *Sources and Development of Mathematical Software.* Englewood Cliffs, NJ: Prentice-Hall, pp. 88-111.

Priestley, M. B. (1981), *Spectral Analysis and Time Series,* vol. 1. Boston: Academic Press.

Sargent, T. J. (1978), "Estimation of Dynamic Labor Demand Schedules under Rational Expectations," *Journal of Political Economy* 86: 1009-44.

Tarjan, T. G. (1992), "Macroeconomic Fluctuations Based on Gestation Lags: A Formal Analysis," in Hillinger (1992), pp. 157-63.

Van Loan, C. F. (1978), "Computing Integrals Involving the Matrix Exponential," *IEEE Transactions on Automatic Control* 23: 395-404.

Ward, R. C. (1977), "Numerical Computation of the Matrix Exponential with Accuracy Estimate," *SIAM Journal on Numerical Analysis* 14: 600-10.

(1985), PADEXP, FORTRAN source code (personal communication), Martin Marietta Energy Systems, Oak Ridge, TN.

Zadrozny, P. A. (1980), "Estimation of Linear-Quadratic Adjustment Cost Models Under Rational Expectations: A Theory with an Application to the

260   **Peter A. Zadrozny**

Demand for Inventories and Labor," Ph.D. dissertation, Department of Economics, University of Chicago.

(1988a), "Gaussian Likelihood of Continuous-Time ARMAX Models When Data Are Stocks and Flows at Different Frequencies," *Econometric Theory* 4: 109–24.

(1988b), "Analytic Derivatives for Estimation of Discrete-Time Linear-Quadratic Dynamic Optimization Models," *Econometrica* 56: 467–72.

Business cycles and growth

CHAPTER 9

Monopolistic price setting, subjective demand, and the business cycle

Alfred Maussner

1   Introduction

There is a long tradition of attempts that assign a central role to agents' expectations of future market conditions in explaining recurrent fluctuations in aggregate employment and output. Pigou (1927) identified errors of optimism and pessimism as triggers of upswings and downswings. Keynes (1936) blamed entrepreneurs' volatile expectations as the source of fluctuations in investment spending that transmit into aggregate demand variability via the multiplier principle.

The rational expectations hypothesis, which emerged in the seventies, downplays the role of expectations as an endogenous cause of business cycles. The confusion between nominal and real shocks, coupled with a signal extraction problem, accounts only for the persistence of nominal demand shocks in the business cycle model of Lucas (1975). The real business cycle theory, originating in the papers by Kydland and Prescott (1982) and Long and Plosser (1983), denies any independent influence of expectations on business activity at all.

The concept of sunspot equilibria in Azariadis (1981), Cass and Shell (1983), and Azariadis and Guesnerie (1986) tries to give a choice-theoretic underpinning to Pigou's and Keynes's ideas within the framework of rational expectations. It is well known that nonlinear rational expectation models may have a multiplicity of equilibria with periodic orbits among them. For example, a deterministic two-period cycle may be considered as the limiting case of an equilibrium with self-fulfilling expectations: The probability $\pi_{a,b}$ of a switch from state a to state b and vice versa is 1, and agents correctly foresee the price p_a (p_b) if state a (b) prevails. Yet, as Azariadis and Guesnerie (1986) show, by continuity there is a neighborhood

I would like to thank Charles van Maarewijk and the conference participants for helpful comments and suggestions.

$N(\bar{\Pi})$ of the transition matrix $\bar{\Pi} = \left(\begin{smallmatrix} 1 & 0 \\ 0 & 1 \end{smallmatrix}\right)$ that contains matrices with non-zero off-diagonal elements. If agents condition their price expectations upon an arbitrary matrix $\Pi \in N(\bar{\Pi})$, they will find the price p_a (p_b) whenever state a (b) is randomly selected. Any two-stage Markov process with transition matrix $\Pi \in N(\bar{\Pi})$ implies a different stationary two-stage stochastic equilibrium with self-fulfilling expectations. Thus, equilibrium allocations are determined by agents' beliefs in any observable stochastic variable (e.g., sunspot activity) that by itself does not influence preferences or production possibilities.

In this paper I shall advocate yet another mechanism by which expectations may account for economic fluctuations. It is based upon the very fact that price and quantity signals reveal private information that other agents cannot know in advance. The rational expectations hypothesis excludes the possibility of misinterpreting price and quantity signals by crediting agents with the capability to compute market-clearing prices up to an unsystematic error term. Misinterpretations of price and quantity signals, I believe, are closer in spirit to Pigou's errors of optimism and pessimism than are sunspot equilibria.

But why may those errors persist? – I think for two reasons. First, the process of acquiring information is not costless. Simple rules of thumb, requiring less information than sophisticated estimation techniques, may do better in terms of costs and benefits of forecasts. As Naish (1993) has shown and as can be demonstrated also in my model, the loss of profits incurred by firms with simple forecasting rules as compared to firms with rational expectations may be quite small. This is the consequence of the envelope theorem and due to the same reasoning as applied in the menu-costs literature (see e.g. Akerlof and Yellen 1985) to rationalize price rigidities.

Second, forecast errors, even if permanent, may not be sufficiently revealing to agents as to suggest an alternate method of forecast. In models with aperiodic time paths, a firm's sales statistics closely resemble a stochastic process. The firm may therefore attribute its forecast errors to highly irregular, unforeseeable events instead of to an inappropriate forecasting rule.

I shall give an example of a model where the interaction between quantity signals and actions taken by agents in response to perceived signals might create endogenous fluctuations in prices and income. Toward this end I consider a general equilibrium model with monopolistically competitive firms. Each firm knows the fixed true price elasticity of its individual demand but not the forthcoming level of demand, which depends upon aggregate income and the price level. These two variables, in turn, depend upon the pricing policy of all firms and upon consumers' choices. Thus, they are revealed to firms only after markets have closed, and firms must form expectations with respect to the shift parameter of their individual demand function. Firms forecast this parameter adaptively.

In the case of decreasing returns to scale, firms finally discover the true value of the shift parameter. In the case of increasing returns to scale, permanent cycles and irregular time paths may arise depending upon the speed of adjustment of expectations. As in Benhabib and Miyao (1981), the speed of adjustment plays the role of a bifurcation parameter. The unique stationary equilibrium loses stability, and a stable two-period cycle emerges, when the speed of adjustment exceeds a critical level. Further increases in the speed of adjustment generate cycles of all orders as well as irregular time paths.

The remainder of this paper consists of three sections: Section 2 describes the model, Section 3 presents the model's dynamic properties, and Section 4 offers concluding remarks. An appendix covers the proof of the paper's proposition.

2 The model

Consider an economy with J firms. Each firm produces one good, using labor services as the single factor of production. A representative household supplies a given amount of labor $\bar{N}$ irrespective of the real wage. The nominal wage W is constant. Firms are never rationed on the labor market. The household consumes the J goods and holds money balances. Its demand for goods and money is limited by its initial stock of money $\bar{M}$, labor, and dividend income. Incorporating the specification of the household's utility function in Section 2.1 yields a variant of the prototype New Keynesian model (see e.g. Ball and Romer 1989, Blanchard and Kiyotaki 1987, Rotemberg 1987, Startz 1989, and Weitzman 1985).

2.1 *Demand*

Let the function

$$U := C^{\theta}\left[\frac{M}{P}\right]^{(1-\theta)}, \quad C := J^{1/(1-\epsilon)}\left\{\sum_{j=1}^{J} C_j^{(\epsilon-1)/\epsilon}\right\}^{\epsilon/(\epsilon-1)}, \quad \epsilon > 1, \quad \theta \in (0,1) \tag{1}$$

describe the utility of the household. Utility is a linear homogeneous function of the household's real money balances M/P and of the consumption index C, which is itself a CES (constant elasticity of substitution) function of the quantities of the J goods consumed C_j.[1]

---

[1] Putting real money balances into the utility function is just one approach of introducing money into the model. A cash-in-advance constraint or an overlapping generations structure leads to almost identical demand functions. The cash-in-advance model, maximizing

The household's budget constraint is

$$\sum_{j=1}^{J} P_j C_j + M \le PY + \bar{M}, \tag{2}$$

where Y is aggregate real income, PY aggregate nominal income, $\bar{M}$ the given stock of money, and P_j the price of good $j = 1, 2, ..., J$. The household chooses a consumption bundle $(C_1, C_2, ..., C_J)$ that maximizes (1) subject to (2). The solution to this decision problem gives the demand for good j:

$$C_j = \left(\frac{P_j}{P}\right)^{-\epsilon} \theta \frac{PY + M}{JP}, \tag{3}$$

where P is the price level,

$$P := \left\{\frac{1}{J} \sum_{j=1}^{J} P_j^{1-\epsilon}\right\}^{1/(1-\epsilon)}, \tag{4}$$

and aggregate nominal income PY satisfies

$$PY = \sum_{j=1}^{J} P_j Y_j. \tag{5}$$

2.2   Supply

Production Y_j of firm $j = 1, 2, ..., J$ is a function of labor input N_j. The elasticity of production with respect to labor input α is constant. For convenience, I assume the following form for this function:

$$Y_j = f(N_j) := \frac{1}{\alpha} N_j^{\alpha}, \quad \alpha > 0. \tag{6}$$

When firm j must set its price P_j it neither knows the price level P nor aggregate income Y. These two variables, together with the given stock of money $M = \bar{M}$, compose the shift parameter z of firm j's demand curve:

$$z := P^{\epsilon} \left[\frac{PY + M}{JP}\right]. \tag{7}$$

The firm correctly believes that z is independent of its price decision. I denote the firm's expectation of z by z_j. Hence, expected demand of firm j is:

C subject to $M \ge PC$, produces $C_j = (P_j/P)^{-\epsilon}(M/JP)$ instead of (3). The overlapping generations model, maximizing $C_1^{\theta} C_2^{1-\theta}$ subject to $PC_1 \le PY - M$ and $PC_2 \le M$, yields $C_j = (P_j/P)^{-\epsilon}(\theta Y + M/P)/J$. Hence, none of my results is changed by considering either one of these two alternatives.

$$C_j^e = P_j^{-\epsilon} z_j. \tag{8}$$

The firm's price P_j solves the profit maximizing problem

maximize $\quad P_j Y_j - W N_j$

subject to $\quad Y_j \le \dfrac{1}{\alpha} N_j^\alpha$ and $Y_j \le P_j^{-\epsilon} z_j$

and is thus a function of z_j and of the model's parameters – that is, of W, α, and ϵ:

$$P_j(z_j) := \delta z_j^\eta, \quad \delta := \left[\frac{\epsilon}{\epsilon - 1} W \right]^{\alpha/[\alpha + \epsilon(1-\alpha)]} \alpha^\eta, \quad \eta := \frac{1-\alpha}{\alpha + \epsilon(1-\alpha)}. \tag{9}$$

The firm's price satisfies the property

$$P_j = \mu \frac{W}{f'(N_j)}, \quad \mu := \frac{\epsilon}{\epsilon - 1} > 1, \tag{10}$$

where $\mu - 1$ is the mark-up on marginal costs $W/f'(N_j)$.

The condition sufficient for a profit maximum is satisfied in the case of $\alpha < 1$. If $\alpha > 1$ (i.e., with increasing returns to scale) then the elasticity of substitution between two consumer goods ϵ must satisfy

$$\epsilon < \frac{\alpha}{\alpha - 1} \tag{11}$$

for a profit maximum to exist.

At the set price, firm j produces according to forthcoming demand. There are two arguments to justify this assumption. (1) The firm incurs fixed costs whenever it adjusts its price intraperiodically. Under this assumption, there exists a period of length $h > 0$ within which no firm adjusts its price.[2] (2) Alternatively, assume $h > 0$ is the time needed to gather information on sales at given prices. In fact, announcing the selling price and watching sales at that price is the sole means of discovering whether demand expectations have been correct.

2.3 Temporary equilibria

Suppose firms share the same technique of production and hold identical expectations. Then all firms set the same price and the price level coincides

---

[2] Let $h > 0$ denote units of time between two successive time periods t and $t + h$. Suppose that there are costs $c > 0$ if the firm adjusts its price within the given time period. Let $\Delta G(P_j, P_0)$ be the reduction of profits per time unit incurred by keeping one's price fixed at P_j, where P_0 is profit maximizing. Assume that $\Delta G(P_j, P_0)$ is constant. The firm will keep the price P_j if $K = c - h\Delta G(P_j, P_0) > 0$. Since $\lim_{h \to 0}(K/h) = \infty$, there does exist a $h > 0$ such that P_j is fixed between t and $t + h$ for all $\Delta G(P_j, P_0) < \infty$.

with the price of firm j, which is now representative for the $J-1$ other firms, $P = P_j$. Aggregate production is J times the production of firm j, $Y = JY_j$. Thus, equation (3) uniquely determines demand and production of firm j:

$$Y_j(z_j) := \frac{\theta}{1-\theta} \frac{M}{JP_j(z_j)} \tag{12}$$

given z_j, the firm's expectations of z.

2.4   *Expectations and the sequence of temporary equilibria*

Given its sales, firm j is able to deduce the actual shift parameter z. According to equation (8), z is a function of z_j:

$$z(z_j) := [P_j(z_j)]^\epsilon Y_j(z_j). \tag{13}$$

With adaptive expectations, firm j estimates the shift parameter in period $t+1$ according to the formula

$$z_j(t+1) = z_j(t) + \psi[z(z_j(t)) - z_j(t)], \quad \psi \in (0,1). \tag{14}$$

The parameter ψ governs the proportion of the forecasting error $z - z_j$ considered in the estimation of next period's shift parameter $z_j(t+1)$. I do not consider the polar cases $\psi = 0$ and $\psi = 1$. With $\psi = 0$, expectations are stationary; that is, $z_j(t) = z_j(0)$ for all t. In case $\psi = 1$, the current shift parameter is expected to prevail for the next period: $z(t) = z_j(t+1)$.

The stationary equilibrium of the learning process described by equation (14) is the perfect foresight value of z. This value z_j^* solves

$$z_j^* = [P_j(z_j^*)]^{\epsilon-1}\left[\frac{\theta}{1-\theta}\frac{M}{J}\right] \tag{15}$$

and is found to be given as

$$z_j^* = \alpha^{(\epsilon-1)(1-\alpha)}\left[\frac{\epsilon}{\epsilon-1}W\right]^{\alpha(\epsilon-1)}\left[\frac{\theta}{1-\theta}\frac{M}{J}\right]^{\alpha+\epsilon(1-\alpha)}. \tag{16}$$

3   **Dynamic properties of the model**

3.1   *Returns to scale and stability*

Equations (9), (12), (13), and (14) imply the following nonlinear difference equation in the expected shift parameter of firm j's demand curve z_j:

$$z_j(t+1) = \Phi[z_j(t)] := (1-\psi)z_j(t) + \psi\gamma[z_j(t)]^{(\epsilon-1)\eta},$$

$$\gamma := \frac{\theta}{1-\theta}\frac{M}{J}\delta^{\epsilon-1}. \tag{17}$$

The following proposition, proved in the Appendix, summarizes the properties of this equation.

Proposition.   (a) *In case of decreasing returns to scale, $\alpha < 1$, the unique fixed point of equation* (17) *is globally stable in the interval* $(0, \infty)$, *irrespective of* $\psi \in (0, 1)$.

   (b) *In case of increasing returns to scale, $\alpha > 1$, and for*

$$\epsilon \in \left(\frac{\alpha - 0.5}{\alpha - 1} ; \frac{\alpha}{\alpha - 1} \right),$$

the following statements obtain.

   (b1)   *There exists a $\Delta > 0$ such that, for all $\psi \in (\psi_0, \psi_0 + \Delta)$ with $\psi_0 :=$ $2[\alpha + \epsilon(1 - \alpha)]$, there is a stable two-period cycle.*

   (b2)   *For all $\psi \in [\psi_0 + \Delta, 1)$ there is an interval $I(\psi) := [\alpha(\psi), b(\psi)]$ such that no path starting in I ever leaves I. Either almost all paths starting in I converge to a uniquely determined cycle with period $n > 2$, or observed dynamic patterns depend upon the initial point chosen.*

The elasticity of production with respect to labor input is decisive for the dynamics of the system. If $\alpha < 1$ then the elasticity of firm j's price with respect to the expected shift parameter of its demand curve, η, is less than unity. Suppose firm j expects z to rise 1 percent; it will then increase its price by $\eta < 1$ percent. Because aggregate demand has a price elasticity of unity, the price increase lowers aggregate demand, also by η percent. Accordingly, firm j's actual sales decrease by η percent. The firm attributes the reduction of demand to its higher price and to the actual change of the shift parameter z. From equation (8) and equation (13), it concludes that $\epsilon\eta$ is the price effect and $(\epsilon - 1)\eta$ the actual shift of z. The estimation error is thus $[1 - (\epsilon - 1)\eta] < 1$. With an estimation error of less than 1 percent, the firm expects next period's z to increase by less than 1 percent. Hence, expected and actual demand converge. This stability result does not depend upon the speed of adjustment of expectations ψ. Yet, convergence is the faster the closer is ψ to unity.

   Suppose instead that $\alpha > 1$. The elasticity of price with respect to z_j is now negative and, in absolute terms, not bounded from above. Its absolute value increases as ϵ approaches $\alpha/(\alpha - 1)$. Upon this fact rests the potential instability of the learning process: Consider again a 1-percent increase of z_j. The firm lowers its price proportional to its expected decrease of marginal costs. Sales increase by η percent. Firm j attributes $-\epsilon\eta$ percent of the observed increase of sales to its lower price, and concludes that z has shifted downward by $(\epsilon - 1)\eta < -1$ percent. Instead of a

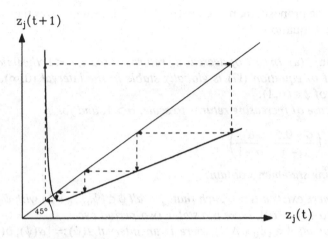

Figure 1.

further increase, the firm expects next period's z to decrease. If the speed of adjustment of expectations is small, $\psi < \psi_0$, the expected decrease of demand is small. The firm will raise its price and will conclude from its sales that z has increased, although z was expected to fall. Yet, this unexpected increase is less than unity. Thus, cyclically expected and actual demand converge.

The stationary equilibrium loses stability if expectations adjust quickly, $\psi > \psi_0$. The initial expectation is cyclically amplified: Estimating z to rise by 1 percent, the firm is subsequently convinced that z will fall by more than 1 percent but in fact observes z to have soared by more than it was expected to plunge. However, this process cannot go on forever. Sufficiently high values of z_j imply that observed z is quite small. In that case the linear part of equation (17), $(1 - \psi)z_j$, determines the forecast of z and demand expectations become gradually more and more pessimistic. If expected demand z_j is small, the high prices convince firms that actual z is large. The nonlinear part of (17), $\psi \gamma z_j^{(\epsilon - 1)\eta}$, dominates the forecast and hence demand expectations, quite suddenly, become optimistic. Figure 1 illustrates this cycle.

The actual dynamic behavior of the model depends upon the existence of a (weakly) stable cycle.[3] If such a cycle exists, it attracts almost all initial points. Thus, despite their possible existence, it is practically impossible to observe irregular time paths. If, instead, no such cycle exists, then

---

[3] A k-period cycle $(x_1, x_2, \ldots, x_k)$ of the difference equation $x_{t+1} = f(x_t)$ is *weakly stable* if $|f'(x_1)f'(x_2)\cdots f'(x_k)| \leq 1$, where $f'(x_t)$ is the derivative of f evaluated at x_t.

all kinds of dynamic patterns – periodic or aperiodic – will arise. In that case, the observed path depends upon the initial point chosen.

Numerical calculations show that, at least for certain values of α and ϵ (e.g. $\alpha = 1.1$, $\epsilon = 10.0$), the family of maps defined by (17) and $\psi \in [\psi_0, \psi_1]$ with $\psi_1 = 0.45$ is "full" as defined by Grandmont (1986, p. 242).[4] In the Appendix, I demonstrate that every map of this family has the properties required by Theorem 9 of Grandmont (1986). The theorem implies the existence of a ψ_∞ such that, for all $\psi \in [\psi_0, \psi_\infty]$, the dynamics of the model is governed by a stable cycle. There is an uncountable set of values of ψ in $(\psi_\infty, \psi_1]$ for which (17) has no stable cycle.

3.2   Bifurcation of cycles and speed of adjustment

This point is further illustrated by Figure 2, which highlights the role of the speed of adjustment of expectations in creating cycles. It is a typical bifurcation diagram for nonlinear difference equations of first order. The abscissa depicts ψ in the interval $I = [0.19, 0.45]$. With a step size of $0.26/200$, I increased ψ and iterated equation (17) for each of these values 400 times. The ordinate depicts the last 100 points from each of the 200 simulations. Hence, Figure 2 shows the points that a time path will approach, or at most 100 points of an irregular time path. I chose W and M/J to yield $z_j^* = 0.5$. As can be seen, the unique fixed point is stable for $\psi < \psi_0 = 0.2$. At $\psi = 0.2$, a stable two-period cycle bifurcates from the now unstable fixed point. Increasing ψ still further leads to the well-known period doubling. However, as the diagram reveals, there is no monotone relationship between ψ and the periodicity of cycles. Suddenly, short-period cycles follow long-period cycles, thus creating the "windows" in Figure 2.

3.3   Sensitive dependence on initial conditions

The bifurcation diagram suggests that there are values of the speed of adjustment of expectations where no (weakly) stable cycle exists. These values can be detected with the aid of another numerical tool. Figure 3 shows calculations of the Lyapunov exponents λ for $\alpha = 1.1$, $\epsilon = 10.0$,

---

[4] Let $\Phi_\psi(z_j)$ denote the map defined by equation (17) for $\alpha > 1$ and $z_{j\psi}^{min}$ its minimizer. The family of maps $\Phi_\psi(z_j)$, $\psi \in [\psi_0, \psi_1]$, is said to be *full* if (a) $\Phi_{\psi_0}^2(z_{j\psi_0}^{min}) < z_{j\psi_0}^{min}$, (b) $\Phi_{\psi_1}^2(z_{j\psi_1}^{min}) > z_{j\psi_1}^{min}$, and (c) $\Phi_{\psi_1}^3(z_{j\psi_1}^{min}) < z_{j\psi_1}^{min}$, where $\Phi_\psi^i(z_j)$ $(i = 2, 3)$ denotes the second and third iterate of $\Phi_\psi(z_j)$, respectively. Figure 1 has been drawn for $\alpha = 1.1$, $\epsilon = 10.0$, and $\psi = 0.45$. It demonstrates that (b) and (c) are fulfilled. Because the two-period cycles occurring for ψ_0 (see Figure 2) consist of points on the negatively sloped left half of the graph of Φ, it should be intuitively clear that (a) holds at ψ_0 for $\alpha = 1.1$ and $\epsilon = 10.0$.

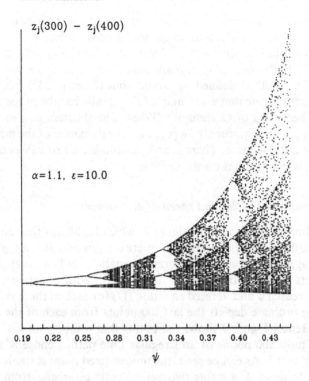

$z_j(300) - z_j(400)$

$\alpha=1.1, \ \varepsilon=10.0$

0.19   0.22   0.25   0.28   0.31   0.34   0.37   0.40   0.43

ψ

Figure 2.

and $\psi \in [0.19, 0.45]$.[5] Positive values of λ imply that the time path of the expected shift parameter of the demand function depends upon the initially expected value. As can be seen, there exist three subintervals for ψ with positive Lyapunov exponents.

3.4   *Costs of adaptive expectations*

One can get an idea of the costs of adaptive expectations by comparing the profit of firms holding such expectations to the profit of firms holding rational expectations (Naish 1993). Consider a firm i knowing the true structure of the model. It sets its price, taking into account the prices of the remaining $J-1$ firms that forecast their shift parameter adaptively. Firm i's profit must be higher than the profits of its competitors. Yet,

---

[5] Formally, the Lyapunov exponent of $x_{t+1} = f(x_t)$ is defined as

$$\lambda = \lim_{n \to \infty} (1/n) \log_2 |f'(x_1) f'(x_2) \cdots f'(x_n)|$$

(see e.g. Lorenz 1993, p. 215). Figure 3 is based on numerical calculations with $n = 500$ and a step size of 0.004 for $\psi \in [0.186, 0.45]$.

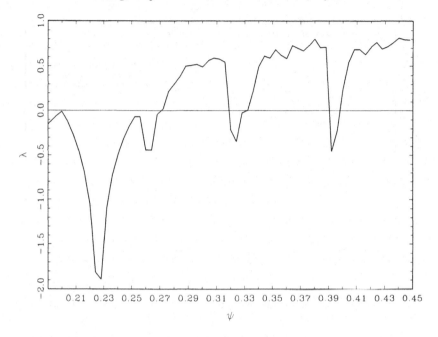

Figure 3.

from the envelope theorem, we know that the magnitude of the difference between i's profit and the profit of any other firm is of second order. Applying the reasoning used in Maussner (1992) to compute the costs of fixed prices to this model, I computed the loss of profits incurred to the $J-1$ firms that forecast adaptively.

Figures 4(a) and 4(b) give examples of the behavior of adaptive and rational expectations. Figure 4(a) shows the case of decreasing returns to scale, $\alpha < 1$. The rational forecast of firm i stays close to the adaptive forecast of other firms, which converges toward the perfect foresight equilibrium $z^* = 0.5$ after about 32 periods. A firm switching from adaptive to rational forecasts could increase its profit per period on average by about 0.002 percent of its revenue. This figure does not change much with other values of $\alpha < 1$, ϵ, or ψ.

Figure 4(b) depicts the case of increasing returns to scale. Here ψ has been selected to give rise to a stable two-period cycle around the stationary equilibrium $z^* = 0.5$. Adaptive and rational expectations now move in opposite directions. The distance between both forecasts increases with the elasticity η of firm j's price ($j \neq i$) with respect to the shift parameter of its demand function, z_j. Profits lost owing to adaptive forecasting are still small, but about 13 times greater than in the case of decreasing

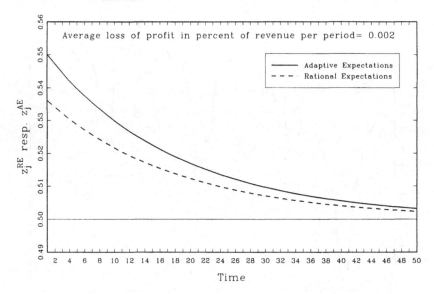

Figure 4. (a) Simulation parameters: $\alpha = 0.70$; $\epsilon = 10.00$; $\psi = 0.201$.

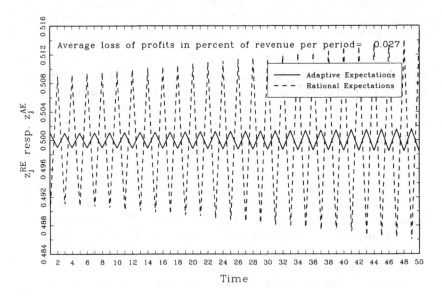

Figure 4. (b) Simulation parameters: $\alpha = 1.10$; $\epsilon = 10.00$; $\psi = 0.201$.

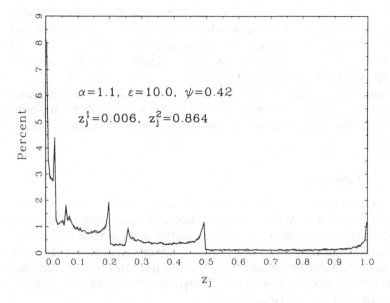

Figure 5.

returns. Moreover, these losses depend critically upon ϵ and ψ; they easily exceed 1 percent of revenue if ψ is increased toward unity.

3.5   Statistical regularity of aperiodic time paths

Despite its nonconvergence, there is a reason why firms might stick with their simple forecasting rule. Time paths with long periods, as well as irregular paths, disguise systematic forecast errors. In fact, aperiodic time paths may even be thought of as realizations of a stochastic process. In that case, the map Φ defined in equation (17) is called *ergodic*. I am not able to offer a rigorous proof of the ergodicity of this map for certain values of the speed of adjustment of expectations. Numerical experiments, however, give a hint that there might be values of ψ for which (17) is ergodic.

Consider Figure 5. It shows two histograms computed from two time paths with 50,000 observations each. The time paths start at z_j^1 and z_j^2, respectively. I normalized the values obtained from iterating the starting values 50,000 times to fall into the interval $[0, 1]$. This interval was divided into 400 subintervals of equal length. I counted the $z_j(t)$, $t = 0, 1$, ..., 50,000, falling within each subinterval. These numbers, in percent, can be read off from the ordinate. The thick line portrays the histogram obtained from the starting value 0.006. It is almost the same as the histogram obtained from the starting value 0.864, shown by the thin line. Virtually the same picture emerges with other starting points $z_j(0)$. Thus, arbitrary time paths, despite being quite different as to their actual time profile, yield almost the same histogram.

Under these circumstances, the actual sales statistic of a firm closely resembles a stochastic process. Forecast errors may well be attributed to highly irregular or unforeseeable events, but not to a false forecasting rule.

4   Conclusion

I considered a model of the business cycle with basically Keynesian ingredients: a fixed money wage, adaptive demand expectations of monopolistically competitive firms, increasing returns, and intraperiodically fixed prices of produced goods. These four assumptions give rise to endogenous cycles. Hence the model differs sharply not only from the real business cycle models, but also from the New Keynesian models that assume firms know their objective demand curve.

Endogenous fluctuations emerge from the interplay between price and quantity signals observed by firms, the interpretations firms give to these signals, and firms' pricing policy in response to their beliefs. Typical properties of the fluctuations are procyclical demand expectations with a one-year period lead, procyclical real wages, procyclical labor productivity, and countercyclical price movements. All these are well in line with the stylized facts of postwar business cycles (cf. Backus and Kehoe 1992, Brandner and Neusser 1992).

The sawtooth pattern of time paths generated by nonlinear difference equations of first order clearly does not resemble the actual pattern of business cycles. In a sense, the model presented here is an approximation of a more realistic setting that would give rise to a less erratic dynamic pattern.[6] Invernizzi and Medio (1991) showed that discrete lag models may be thought of as the limiting case of an economy where reaction lags

[6] Enlarging the state space is, of course, another way to smooth the model's cycles. A referee pointed out that exit and entry of firms might accomplish this. Imagine a certain fraction of firms exiting if their actual profits fall short of expected profits and consider a two-period cycle, where period 1 is the boom and period 2 the slump. Because expected profits increase with z_j whereas realized profits decrease, firms exit at the end of period 1. The level of demand, $\theta M/JP(1-\theta)$, therefore increases in period 2, and the observed z is higher than it would otherwise be. This cycle may lose its stability. However, as numerical examples show, this effect depends critically on the timing and the size of the fraction of exiting firms. With a time lag between changed profits and exit, the cycle is amplified. If the fraction is large, the cycle is reversed.

(forecast intervals in my model) are gamma distributed over an indefinitely large set of agents. Furthermore, there is an equivalence between my model and the model of a representative agent reacting to inputs with a continuous, multiple exponential lag of order n. In the latter model, irregular time paths may emerge for n sufficiently large. Those paths behave more smoothly than those of first-order nonlinear difference equations.

Undoubtedly, the most controversial assumption of the model are adaptive expectations. This is used to make a more general point. The perfect foresight or rational expectations approach to business cycles neglects the role that markets play in gathering and transmitting privately held information. The paper gives an example to show that learning within a market environment might be a source of coordination failure.

Appendix

Consider the map $\Phi: (0, \infty) \to (0, \infty)$ defined by

$$\Phi(z_j) = (1 - \psi)z_j + \psi\gamma(z_j)^{(\epsilon - 1)\eta},$$

$$\eta = \frac{1 - \alpha}{\alpha + \epsilon(1 - \alpha)}, \quad \gamma = \left[\frac{\epsilon}{\epsilon - 1}W\right]^{\alpha(\epsilon - 1)/[\alpha + \epsilon(1 - \alpha)]}\left[\frac{\theta}{1 - \theta}\frac{M}{J}\right]^{\alpha(\epsilon - 1)\eta}, \tag{A1}$$

and observe that

$$\begin{aligned}\alpha \in (0, 1) \wedge \epsilon \in (1, \infty) &\Rightarrow \eta \in (0, 1), \\ \alpha \in (1, \infty) \wedge \epsilon \in (1, (\alpha/(\alpha - 1)) &\Rightarrow \eta \in (-\infty, 0).\end{aligned} \tag{A2}$$

The first derivative of Φ is given by

$$\Phi' = 1 + \psi\left[(\epsilon - 1)\eta\frac{z}{z_j} - 1\right], \quad \frac{z}{z_j} := \gamma(z_j)^{[(\epsilon - 1)\eta - 1]}. \tag{A3}$$

At the stationary equilibrium, $z/z_j^* = 1$. Hence

$$\begin{aligned}\alpha \in (0, 1) &\Rightarrow \Phi'(z_j^*) \in (0, 1) \quad \forall\psi \in (0, 1), \\ \alpha \in (1, \infty) &\Rightarrow \Phi'(z_j^*) \in (-1, 0) \quad \forall\psi \in (0, \psi_0), \\ \alpha \in (1, \infty) &\Rightarrow \Phi'(z_j^*) \in (-\infty, -1)\forall\psi \in (\psi_0, 1),\end{aligned} \tag{A4}$$

where $\psi_0 := 2[\alpha - \epsilon(\alpha - 1)]$ and $\alpha < 1$ implies the local stability of z_j^*. Formula (A3) implies that Φ' declines and approaches $(1 - \psi) < 1$ as z_j approaches ∞. The graph of Φ is therefore as shown in Figure A1, and all z_j starting in $(0, \infty)$ converge to z_j^*. This proves part (a) of the proposition.

In case $\alpha > 1$, there is a "flip" bifurcation in the sense of Theorem 3.5 of Lorenz (1993) at $\psi = \psi_0 = 2[\alpha - \epsilon(\alpha - 1)]$. According to that theorem, there exists a $\Delta > 0$ such that, for all $\psi \in (\psi_0, \psi_0 + \Delta)$, stable two-period cycles exist if at (z_j^*, ψ_0)

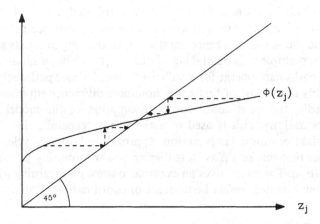

Figure A1.

$$A := \left(\frac{\partial \Phi}{\partial \psi}\frac{\partial^2 \Phi}{\partial(z_j)^2} + 2\frac{\partial^2 \Phi}{\partial z_j \partial \psi}\right) = \frac{-2}{\alpha - \epsilon(\alpha - 1)} < 0 \quad \text{and}$$

$$B := -2\left(\frac{\partial^3 \Phi}{\partial(z_j)^3}\right) - 3\left(\frac{\partial^2 \Phi}{\partial(z_j)^2}\right) \tag{A5}$$

$$= \frac{4\psi_0}{(z_j^*)^2}\frac{(\epsilon - 1)(\alpha - 1)}{[\alpha - \epsilon(\alpha - 1)]^3}\{2[\alpha - \epsilon(\alpha - 1)] - 1\} < 0.$$

It is easily checked that, under the parameter restriction

$$\epsilon \in \left(\frac{\alpha - 0.5}{\alpha - 1}, \frac{\alpha}{\alpha - 1}\right),$$

both terms are indeed negative, thus proving part (b1) of the proposition.

Let $\psi \in [\psi_0 + \Delta, 1)$; then $\Phi'(z_j^*) < -1$. At the left of z_j^*, the absolute value of Φ' does increase, and the graph of Φ approaches the ordinate. At the right of z_j^*, the graph of Φ approaches the linear curve $(1 - \psi)z_j$. Hence, $\Phi(z_j)$ has exactly one minimum. Let a denote this minimal value of z_j. Define $\bar{z}_j$ implicitly by $a = \Phi(\bar{z}_j)$. Since $\Phi(z_j)$ declines monotonically for z_j ranging from a to $\bar{z}_j$, it follows that $b = \Phi(a) \geq \Phi(z_j)$ for all $z_j \in [a, \bar{z}_j]$. Furthermore, $\Phi(z_j) < z_j$ for all $z_j \in [\bar{z}_j, b]$. Therefore, the graph of Φ has the shape depicted in Figure A2. No time path starting in $[a, b]$ can ever leave this interval.

The linear change of coordinates

$$y = b - z_j, \quad z_j \in [a, b], \tag{A6}$$

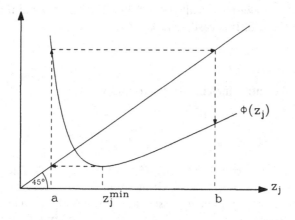

Figure A2.

is a homeomorphism. In the new coordinates, the dynamics of the model is governed by

$$g(y) := b - \Phi(b - y), \tag{A7}$$

where g and Φ are topological conjugates (cf. e.g. Devaney 1987, pp. 44–8). The map $g(y)$ has a maximum at $\bar{y} = b - \bar{z}_j$, is strictly increasing in the range $[0, \bar{y}]$, and is strictly decreasing in the range $[\bar{y}, b - a]$. Furthermore, $g(y)$ is differentiable to arbitrary order. We therefore have the following conditions.

(S1) $g(y)$ is C^1-unimodal as defined in Grandmont (1986, p. 231).

(S2) $g(y)$ is three times continuously differentiable.

(S3) The Schwarzian derivative of $g(y)$,

$$Sg(y) := \frac{g'''(y)}{g'(y)} - \frac{3}{2}\left[\frac{g''(y)}{g'(y)}\right]^2 = \frac{\Phi'''(z_j)}{\Phi'(z_j)} - \frac{3}{2}\frac{[\Phi''(z_j)]^2}{[\Phi'(z_j)]^2},$$

equals the Schwarzian derivative of Φ,

$$S\Phi(z_j) = \frac{\psi(\epsilon - 1)\eta[(\epsilon - 1)\eta - 1]\dfrac{z}{(z_j)^3}}{\left[(1 - \psi) + \psi(\epsilon - 1)\eta\dfrac{z}{z_j}\right]^2}$$

$$\times \left\{(1 - \psi)[(\epsilon - 1)\eta - 2] - \frac{1}{2}\psi(\epsilon - 1)\eta[(\epsilon - 1)\eta + 1]\frac{z}{z_j}\right\},$$

and hence is negative for all $y \neq \bar{y}$ if $[(\epsilon - 1)\eta - 2] < 0$ and if also $[(\epsilon - 1)\eta + 1] < 0$. It is easily checked that

$$\epsilon \in \left(\frac{\alpha - 0.5}{\alpha - 1}, \frac{\alpha}{\alpha - 1} \right)$$

is necessary and sufficient for this to apply.

(S4″) $g(y) > y$ for all $y \in [0, \bar{y}]$.

(S5) $g''(\bar{y}) = -\Phi''(\bar{z}_j) = -\psi(\epsilon - 1)\eta[(\epsilon - 1)\eta - 1]\dfrac{z}{\bar{z}_j} < 0$.

Therefore, $g(y)$ satisfies conditions (S1)–(S4″) of Theorem 2 and conditions (S1)–(S5) of Proposition 4 of Grandmont (1986). According to Grandmont's Theorem 2, $g(y)$ does possess at most one stable cycle, and according to his Proposition 2 the Lebesgue measure of points not attracted by this cycle is zero. This proves part (b2) of my proposition.

REFERENCES

Akerlof, G. A., and J. L. Yellen (1985), "A Near-Rational Model of the Business Cycle, with Wage and Price Inertia," *Quarterly Journal of Economics* 100: 823–38.

Azariadis, C. (1981), "Self-Fulfilling Prophecies," *Journal of Economic Theory* 25: 380–96.

Azariadis, C., and R. Guesnerie (1986), "Sunspots and Cycles," *Review of Economic Studies* 53: 725–37.

Backus, D. K., and P. J. Kehoe (1992), "International Evidence on the Historical Properties of Business Cycles," *American Economic Review* 82: 864–88.

Ball, L., and D. Romer (1989), "Are Prices too Sticky?" *Quarterly Journal of Economics* 104: 507–24.

Benhabib, J., and T. Miyao (1981), "Some New Results on the Dynamics of the Generalized Tobin Model," *International Economic Review* 22: 589–96.

Blanchard, O. J., and N. Kiyotaki (1987), "Monopolistic Competition and the Effects of Aggregate Demand," *American Economic Review* 77: 647–66.

Brandner, P., and K. Neusser (1992), "Business Cycles in Open Economies: Stylized Facts for Austria and Germany," *Weltwirtschaftliches Archiv* 128: 67–87.

Cass, D., and K. Shell (1983), "Do Sunspots Matter?" *Journal of Political Economy* 91: 193–227.

Devaney, R. L. (1987), *An Introduction to Chaotic Dynamical Systems*. Redwood City, CA: Addison-Wesley.

Grandmont, J.-M. (1986), "Periodic and Aperiodic Behavior in Discrete, One-Dimensional, Dynamical Systems," in W. Hildebrand and A. Mas-Colell (eds.), *Contributions to Mathematical Economics*. New York: North-Holland, pp. 225–46.

Invernizzi, S., and A. Medio (1991), "On Lags and Chaos in Economic Dynamic Models," *Journal of Mathematical Economics* 20: 521–50.

Keynes, J. M. (1936), *The General Theory of Employment, Interest and Money.* New York: Harcourt Brace.

Kydland, F. E., and E. C. Prescott (1982), "Time to Build and Aggregate Fluctuations," *Econometrica* 50: 1345–70.

Long, J. B., and C. I. Plosser (1983), "Real Business Cycles," *Journal of Political Economy* 91: 39–69.

Lorenz, H.-W. (1993), *Nonlinear Dynamical Economics and Chaotic Motion,* 2nd ed. Berlin: Springer-Verlag.

Lucas, R. E., "An Equilibrium Model of the Business Cycle," *Journal of Political Economy* 83: 1113–44.

Maussner, A. (1992), *Monopolistische Preisbildung und Nachfrageerwartungen in Makroökonomischen Modellen.* Tübingen: Mohr.

Naish, H. F. (1993), "The Near Optimality of Adaptive Expectations," *Journal of Economic Behavior and Organization* 20: 3–22.

Pigou, A. C. (1927), *Industrial Fluctuations.* London: Macmillan.

Rotemberg, J. J. (1987), "The New Keynesian Microfoundations," *NBER Macroeconomics Annual* 2: 69–104.

Startz, R. (1989), "Monopolistic Competition as a Foundation for Keynesian Macroeconomic Models," *Quarterly Journal of Economics* 104: 737–52.

Weitzman, M. L. (1985), "The Simple Macroeconomics of Profit Sharing," *American Economic Review* 75: 937–53.

CHAPTER 10

The G7 countries: a multivariate description of the business cycle stylized facts

Ulrich Woitek

1 Introduction

The aim of business cycle theory is to explain the fluctuations of economic series around a time trend. This aim requires information on the structure of these fluctuations. Therefore, it is necessary first to describe the stylized facts independently of the explanatory model in order to find answers to the following important questions (see Hillinger 1992a,b).

(1) Are the observed fluctuations irregular or do they show cyclical structure – that is, do they exhibit maxima and minima at regular time intervals?

(2) If the fluctuations show a cyclical structure, how many superimposed cycles can be identified?

(3) What can be said about the length of these cycles?

(4) How important are they? That is, how large a part of the variance of the fluctuations can be explained by the variance of a particular cycle, and how strong is the influence of noise?

(5) What can be said about lead–lag relationships between cycles in different series?

There are a number of stylized facts concerning these questions, which have been identified beginning with the nineteenth-century work of Juglar. An overview of the literature on stylized facts of business cycles may be found in Hillinger (1992a).

The most precise answer to these questions is provided by spectral analysis. In recent years maximum entropy (ME) spectral estimation, a method developed by Burg (1975), has been successfully applied at SEM-ECON to the description of the stylized facts regarding macroeconomic

I am indebted to Claude Hillinger, Michael Reiter, Giuseppe De Arcangelis, Peter Zadrozny, and two anonymous referees for helpful comments and various suggestions.

fluctuations. Hillinger and Sebold-Bender (1992) contains an extensive description of the methods used to estimate a univariate ME spectrum and an application to 15 OECD countries.

Univariate spectral analysis can answer only the first four questions. For the last question – the lead–lag relationships between cycles in different series – a multivariate extension is needed. In Section 2 I briefly describe multivariate ME spectral estimation, and discuss some of the problems connected with the application to economic series. In Section 3, a univariate and multivariate spectral analysis of the GDP and its components for the G7 countries is given.

2   Methodology

A method for describing the cyclical characteristics of a time series is to transform it from the time domain to the frequency domain and then to compute the spectral density function, which provides the measures needed to find answers to the questions of Section 1. In the following, a brief overview of the spectral measures used in this paper is given. For a detailed description, see for example Brockwell and Davis (1991, pp. 434–43), Koopmans (1974, pp. 119–64), and Priestley (1981, vol. II).

2.1   Univariate and multivariate spectral measures

The spectral density matrix $\mathbf{F}(\omega)$ of a n-dimensional stochastic process is the Fourier transform of the covariance function of the process:

$$\mathbf{F}(\omega) = \frac{1}{2\pi} \sum_{\tau=-\infty}^{+\infty} \mathbf{\Gamma}(\tau)e^{-i\omega\tau}, \quad -\pi \le \omega \le \pi, \tag{1}$$

with

$$\mathbf{\Gamma}(\tau) = \begin{pmatrix} \gamma_{11}(\tau) & \cdots & \gamma_{1n}(\tau) \\ \vdots & \ddots & \vdots \\ \gamma_{n1}(\tau) & \cdots & \gamma_{nn}(\tau) \end{pmatrix}, \quad \mathbf{F}(\omega) = \begin{pmatrix} f_{11}(\omega) & \cdots & f_{1n}(\omega) \\ \vdots & \ddots & \vdots \\ f_{n1}(\omega) & \cdots & f_{nn}(\omega) \end{pmatrix}.$$

Because $\mathbf{F}(\omega)$ is an even function, it is sufficient to examine it in the interval $[0, \pi]$. The diagonal elements $f_{11}(\omega), \ldots, f_{nn}(\omega)$ are the real-valued *autospectra* or *power spectra* of the n individual series:

$$f_{jj}(\omega) = \frac{1}{2\pi}\left(\gamma_{jj}(0) + 2\sum_{\tau=-\infty}^{+\infty} \gamma_{jj}(\tau)\cos(\omega\tau)\right), \quad j = 1, \ldots, n. \tag{2}$$

The area under the power spectrum equals the process variance $\gamma_{jj}(0)$:

$$\gamma_{jj}(0) = \int_{-\pi}^{\pi} f_{jj}(\omega)\, d\omega. \tag{3}$$

In this paper, the normalized power spectrum is used; that is, the power spectrum $f_{jj}(\omega)$ is divided by the process variance $\gamma_{jj}(0)$:

$$\tilde{f}_{jj} = \frac{f_{jj}(\omega)}{\gamma_{jj}(0)}. \tag{4}$$

Hence, the area under the normalized power spectrum equals unity. Now assume that the autospectrum $f_{jj}(\omega)$ has a peak at the frequency ω^*. Then the expression

$$\frac{2}{\gamma_{jj}(0)} \int_{\omega^*-0.1\omega^*}^{\omega^*+0.1\omega^*} f_{jj}(\omega)\, d\omega \tag{5}$$

can be interpreted as the part of the variance $\gamma_{jj}(0)$ that is explained by the variance of oscillations with frequencies within the range of ± 10 percent around the peak frequency ω^*. In the following, this expression is called the *peak power* of a cycle with frequency ω^*.

One measure for judging the spread of a peak (i.e., the damping of a cycle) is the *bandwidth*, the range in which the peak halves: The sharper the peak at a frequency ω^*, the smaller the bandwidth (see Priestley 1981, pp. 513–17). The bandwidth has the disadvantage that it cannot be computed if the respective cycle is too strongly damped or if two peaks are too close. Therefore, it is more informative to look at the moduli of the corresponding complex roots of the characteristic polynomial of the autoregressive (AR) model used to estimate the univariate spectrum, as explained in what follows.

Another important measure is the *signal-to-noise ratio*. It measures the influence of noise on a series j, and is defined as the ratio of the variance of the signal to the variance of the noise (see Koopmans 1974, pp. 146–7):

$$\text{SNR} = \frac{\int_{-\omega}^{\omega} f_{jj}(\omega)\, d\omega - \sigma_{uj}^2}{\sigma_{uj}^2}. \tag{6}$$

The elements $f_{jk}(\omega)$, $j \neq k$, are called *cross-spectra*. In general, they are not real-valued, since the cross-covariances $\gamma_{jk}(\tau)$, $j \neq k$, are not symmetric. Therefore, $f_{jk}(\omega)$ can be written as

$$f_{jk}(\omega) = \frac{1}{2\pi} \sum_{\tau=-\infty}^{+\infty} \gamma_{jk}(\tau)e^{-i\omega\tau} = c_{jk}(\omega) - iq_{jk}(\omega),$$
$$j = 1, ..., n, \ \ k = 1, ..., n, \ \ j \neq k, \tag{7}$$

where $c_{jk}(\omega)$ is the *cospectrum* and $q_{jk}(\omega)$ is the *quadrature spectrum*. From these spectra of two series j and k it is possible to compute measures for the lead–lag relationships between them. These measures are the phase spectrum, the gain spectrum, and the squared coherency.

The *squared coherency* can be interpreted in the same way as the correlation coefficient in a regression model. It measures the degree of linear relationship between a cycle of frequency ω in the series j and a cycle of the same frequency in the series k. If it equals 1 at a frequency ω then there is an exact linear relationship between the cycles with frequency ω in the two series; if it equals 0 then there is no relationship between the two cycles. The squared coherency is defined as

$$\kappa_{jk}^2(\omega) = \frac{|f_{jk}(\omega)|^2}{f_{jj}(\omega)f_{kk}(\omega)}. \tag{8}$$

The multiplicative change of the amplitude of a cycle, if transformed from series j to series k, is measured by the *gain spectrum*, which is defined as

$$g_{jk}(\omega) = \frac{|f_{jk}(\omega)|}{f_{jj}(\omega)}. \tag{9}$$

The *phase spectrum*

$$\phi_{jk}(\omega) = \arctan \frac{-q_{jk}(\omega)}{c_{jk}(\omega)} \tag{10}$$

measures the phase lead of the series j over the series k at a frequency ω. If the squared coherency $\kappa_{jk}(\omega)^2$ equals 1 then there is a fixed linear relationship between the two series at the frequency ω. If it is less than 1 then the phase and the gain must be interpreted as expected values. Therefore, it is sensible to examine lead–lag relationships of cycles only where the squared coherency reaches values near unity.

2.2   Detrending

For the application of spectral analysis it is necessary to have a stationary series. However, since most economic time series are nonstationary, the trend component must be removed from the original data before estimating the spectrum. Beginning with the influential work of Chan, Hayya, and Ord (1977) and Nelson and Kang (1981), there is a body of literature concerning detrending procedures and their possibly distorting effects on the structure of the residuals. Incorrect detrending may cause spurious cyclicity, or destroy existing cyclical structure.

A recently developed and widely used detrending procedure is the Hodrick–Prescott (HP) filter (Hodrick and Prescott 1980). This filter is defined by

$$\min_{\bar{y}_t} \left(\sum_{t=1}^{N} (y_t - \bar{y}_t)^2 + \mu \sum_{t=2}^{N-1} \{(\bar{y}_{t+1} - \bar{y}_t) - (\bar{y}_t - \bar{y}_{t-1})\}^2 \right), \tag{11}$$

where the y_t are the original data and the $\bar{y}_t$ are chosen to minimize the expression. The parameter μ determines the relative weight between the first term, which measures the goodness of fit, and the second term, which is a measure for the variation of the trend. For annual data, this parameter is usually set to 100.

Since it is well known that the HP filter can generate cycles in the residuals if applied to a difference stationary (DS) series, it cannot be used without examining the type of nonstationarity present. In cases where the nonstationarity is due to a unit root, it is appropriate to use a difference filter. But if a difference filter is applied to a series for which the nonstationarity is not due to a unit root, the cyclical structure of the residuals is seriously distorted.[1] This effect can be seen in Figure 1, which plots the power transfer functions (PTFs) of the respective filters.

The PTF measures the multiplicative change of the input spectrum if transformed to the spectrum of the output series of the filter, and is defined as the squared absolute value of the Fourier transform of the filter. The PTF of the HP(100) filter if applied to a series that is integrated of order 0 (I(0)) shows that components with very low frequencies are removed, while components with frequencies greater than about 0.4 are left unchanged. Applying a difference filter to a I(0) series leads to the result that the influence of components with frequencies less than 1/6 is reduced, while the influence of components with frequencies greater than 1/6 is enlarged. In the case where an I(1) series is detrended using the HP(100) filter, the PTF shows a peak at the frequency 0.07. The output spectrum at this frequency has a value that is about three times higher than the value of the input spectrum of the series.

In the bivariate case, HP-detrended random walks might show high correlations between spurious cycles. Harvey and Jaeger (1991) showed this by computing the asymptotic distribution of the sample cross-correlations of two independent stationary series, which is given by

$$\rho_{jk}(\tau) \sim AN\left(0, N^{-1} \sum_{h=-\infty}^{\infty} \rho_{jj}(h)\rho_{kk}(h)\right). \tag{12}$$

The spectra of the two HP(100)-filtered random walks can be computed by

$$f_i(\omega) = \frac{8(1-\cos(\omega))^3}{[1/\mu + 4(1-\cos(\omega))^2]^2} \frac{\sigma_i^2}{2\pi}, \quad i = j, k. \tag{13}$$

Taking the inverse Fourier transform of the spectra gives the autocovariances and the autocorrelations of the two series:

---

[1] For more on the effects of filters see Canova (1991), Cogley and Nason (1992), Harvey and Jaeger (1991), and King and Rebelo (1993).

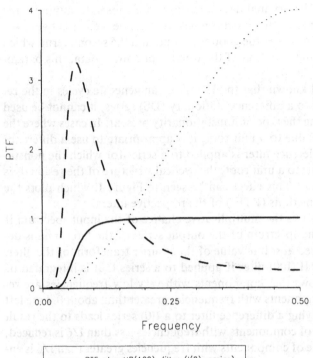

Figure 1. Power transfer function (PTF) of the HP(100) filter and the difference filter.

$$\gamma_{ii}(\tau) = \frac{\sigma_i^2}{2\pi} \int_{-\pi}^{\pi} \frac{\cos(\omega\tau)8(1-\cos(\omega))^3}{[1/\mu + 4(1-\cos(\omega))^2]^2} \, d\omega,$$

$$\rho_{ii}(\tau) = \frac{\gamma_{ii}(\tau)}{\gamma_{ii}(0)}, \quad \tau = 1, ..., i = j,k.$$

(14)

Harvey and Jaeger (1991) set $\sigma_i^2 = 1$ and use the first 100 autocorrelations to approximate the infinite sum in (12). Doing this for our special problem (annual data, i.e. $\mu = 100$, for sample size $N = 30$), one obtains for the cross-correlations a standard deviation of 0.26. Assuming a normal distribution implies a probability of about 34 percent of cross-correlations exceeding 0.25 in absolute value.

These considerations show that the distorting effect of the HP(100) filter and the difference filter on an I(1) and an I(0) series (respectively) is not negligible in either the univariate or the multivariate case. This is a disturbing result, and motivates use of the Dickey–Fuller test (Dickey 1976, Fuller 1976) to judge whether a series requires differencing or whether it is I(0).

The well-known result of applying unit-root tests is that, for a great number of economic time series, the DS hypothesis cannot be rejected (see e.g. Nelson and Plosser 1982) and so a difference filter must be applied to make the series stationary. In this paper, an augmented Dickey–Fuller test is used. A linear time trend superimposed by an AR(p) model is fitted to the data using ordinary least squares (OLS):[2]

$$y_t = \mu + \beta t + \sum_{j=1}^{p} \alpha_j y_{t-j} + u_t,$$

which can be re-arranged as

$$y_t = \mu + \beta t + \rho_1 y_{t-1} + \sum_{j=2}^{p} \rho_j (y_{t-j+1} - y_{t-j}) + u_t \qquad (15)$$

with

$$\rho_j = \sum_{k=j}^{p} \alpha_k, \quad j = 1, ..., p.$$

It is now possible to test for a unit root – that is, $\rho_1 = \sum_{j=1}^{p} \alpha_j = 1$ – using the test statistic $\hat{\tau}_s = (\hat{\rho}_1 - 1)/\hat{\sigma}_{\hat{\rho}_1}$. If $\hat{\tau}_s$ exceeds the critical values given, for example, in Fuller (1976, p. 373, table 8.5.2), the null hypothesis of a unit root can be rejected; otherwise, we would need to use a difference filter in order to render the series stationary.

Unfortunately, unit-root tests have well-known drawbacks, especially with the very short time series we must deal with. It has been shown (see Rudebusch 1992, 1993) that one cannot be sure, on the basis of these tests, whether the nonstationarity of the GDP and its components is in fact of DS type. Therefore, the following procedure seems reasonable: After presenting the outcome of the augmented Dickey–Fuller test, I examine the cyclical structure of both the HP- and the difference-filtered series to compare the resulting characteristics and so distinguish the stylized facts that can be looked upon as robust from those that are probably due to the chosen detrending procedure.

2.3   Spectral estimation

To estimate the spectral density matrix, the theoretical covariance function $\Gamma(\tau)$ is inferred from the estimated covariance function $\hat{\Gamma}(\tau)$, which

---

[2] The problem is not whether the series in fact contains a linear trend, since the TS (trend stationary) as well as the DS model allow for it, but whether the *residuals* of this trend are DS or not (see Dickey, Bell, and Miller 1986, p. 14).

is known only for $|\tau| \leq N-1$. Classical spectral analysis solves this problem by assuming that the covariances are zero outside the observation period. This method has well-known defects (see e.g. the discussion in Koopmans 1974, pp. 294–336): The unsmoothed empirical spectrum (the periodogram) is an asymptotically unbiased but inconsistent estimate for the true spectral density matrix. A consistent estimate can be found by smoothing it using spectral windows, but this method has the disadvantage that it reduces resolution, that is, the ability to distinguish between peaks in the spectra. This problem becomes very serious with the short macroeconomic time series typically encountered in econometrics. In order to use the information that spectral analysis can provide for describing business cycle stylized facts, a method based on more reasonable assumptions must be found. This was accomplished by Burg (1975), using the maximum entropy principle (or "first principle of data reduction") developed by Shannon and Jaynes.[3]

The maximum entropy principle can be stated as follows (Ables 1974, p. 383): *The result of any transformation imposed on the experimental data shall incorporate and be consistent with all relevant data and be maximally noncommittal with regard to unavailable data.* In light of this principle, we choose – from the spectra which are compatible with the sample autocovariances – that spectrum which is least informative concerning out-of-sample autocovariances. Burg (1975, pp. 68–77) shows that the estimate takes the form:

$$\mathbf{F}(\omega)_A = \mathbf{A}(\omega)_p^{-1} \Sigma_p^f \mathbf{A}(\omega^{-1})_p^T,$$

$$\mathbf{A}(\omega)_p = \mathbf{I}_n + \mathbf{A}_{p,1} e^{-i\omega} + \mathbf{A}_{p,2} e^{-i2\omega} + \cdots + \mathbf{A}_{p,p} e^{-i\omega p}, \tag{16}$$

where $\mathbf{A}(\omega)_p$ is the Fourier transform of a multivariate forward prediction filter of order p, and Σ_p^f is the prediction error variance–covariance matrix of the filter. Since the process is stationary, the polynomial given by the determinant of the filter has all of its roots outside the unit circle. The parameter matrices $\mathbf{A}_{p,j}$, $j = 1, \ldots, p$, are determined by an equation system that is formally identical to the Yule–Walker equations of a VAR(p) process:

$$\begin{bmatrix} \Gamma(0) & \Gamma(-1) & \cdots & \Gamma(-p) \\ \Gamma(1) & \Gamma(0) & \cdots & \Gamma(-p+1) \\ \vdots & \vdots & \ddots & \vdots \\ \Gamma(p) & \Gamma(p-1) & \cdots & \Gamma(0) \end{bmatrix} \begin{bmatrix} \mathbf{I}_n \\ \mathbf{A}_{p,1}^T \\ \vdots \\ \mathbf{A}_{p,p}^T \end{bmatrix} = \begin{bmatrix} \Sigma_p^f \\ \mathbf{0} \\ \vdots \\ \mathbf{0} \end{bmatrix}. \tag{17}$$

To obtain the ME spectrum, we therefore estimate an AR or VAR (vector autoregressive) model and compute the respective spectra. The

---

[3] See the review in Jaynes (1985).

estimation algorithms in this paper are based on the fact that, in the frequency domain, the direction of time is not important. Therefore, estimating the parameters by minimizing both the forward and the backward prediction errors leads to a unique parameterization of the spectrum. Algorithms using this property proved to be superior to the OLS algorithm in terms of resolution of the resulting spectra (see Swingler 1979). In the univariate case, I use the Burg algorithm (Burg 1975) or, if the estimates do not fulfill the stationarity condition, the Fougere algorithm (Fougere 1985). In the multivariate case, the Vieira–Morf algorithm is applied (Morf et al. 1978).[4]

A problem that might arise in multivariate ME spectral estimation is the so-called feed-across effect, where peaks that should be present only in one of the series' autospectra occur also in the autospectra of the other series. As shown by Marple and Nuttal (1983), the feed-across effect is unavoidable. They proposed restricting the use of multivariate spectra to estimating lead–lag relationships between the series. To describe the cyclical characteristics of single series, examining the univariate spectral estimate is preferable to analyzing the result of the autospectra derived from a multivariate estimate.

2.4   *Model selection*

In Section 2.3 it was assumed that the order p of the filter is known. In practice, p must be estimated. In this paper, the Bayesian autoregressive criterion (BAC) developed by Heintel (1994) is applied. This criterion is based on the framework of Bayesian time-series analysis. In this framework it is possible to use prior information about the order of the process, which can be very easily modeled since it results in a discrete distribution.

From a theoretical point of view, the BAC is preferable to the widely used information criteria because the latter determine the order by minimizing the sum of the estimated error variance and a more or less arbitrary penalty term, and prior information can be taken into account in a way that is replicable. A simulation study currently under way at SEM-ECON shows that the BAC is preferable also from a more practical view. It results in more robust order estimates (i.e., results that are not dependent on the characteristics of the data-generating process) than the other model selection criteria, even in the noninformative case where we do not have prior information about the order. The criterion is based on the continuous version of Bayes's theorem (see e.g. Judge et al. 1988, pp. 117–20):

---

[4] For a more detailed explanation of the univariate algorithms and their application in macroeconometrics, see Hillinger and Sebold-Bender (1992). A description of the Vieira-Morf algorithm and a comparison with other estimators can be found in Marple (1987, pp. 404–5, 409–16).

$$f(\theta\,|\,\mathbf{y}) \propto L(\theta\,|\,\mathbf{y})f(\theta),$$

where θ is the parameter vector to be estimated, $\mathbf{y}$ is the vector of observations, $f(\theta)$ is the prior distribution of the parameter vector θ, $L(\theta\,|\,\mathbf{y})$ is the likelihood function (i.e., the sample information on θ), and $f(\theta\,|\,\mathbf{y})$ is the resulting posterior distribution of θ.

In the case of the G7 countries, we assume as prior information that the order is equally distributed in the range $0, ..., h$, where h is the highest possible order; the magnitude of h must be determined in advance. The resulting posterior distribution is

$$f(p\,|\,\mathbf{y}) \propto \frac{f(p)\Gamma^*(a_1^{(p)}/2)}{(2\pi)^{a_1^{(p)}/2}|\mathbf{F}^{(p)}|^{1/2}(b_1^{(p)}/2)^{a_1^{(p)}/2}}, \quad p = 0, ..., h, \tag{18}$$

where

$$f(p) = 1/(h+1),$$

$$a_1^{(p)} = N - p - 1,$$

$$\mathbf{F}^{(p)} = \mathbf{X}^{(p)^T}\mathbf{X}^{(p)},$$

$$b_1^{(p)} = \mathbf{y}^T(\mathbf{I} - \mathbf{X}^{(p)}(\mathbf{F}^{(p)})^{-1}\mathbf{X}^{(p)^T})\mathbf{y}.$$

Here $\Gamma^*(\cdot)$ denotes the gamma function, $\mathbf{y} = (y_1, y_2, ..., y_N)^T$ is the vector of observations, and $\mathbf{X}^{(p)}$ is the $N \times (p+1)$ matrix consisting of N rows with the value 1 and the p lagged observations per time t, $t = 1, ..., N$.[5] The BAC estimate of the order p is the mode of the posterior distribution $f(p\,|\,\mathbf{y})$.

Because a multivariate extension of the BAC is not yet available, we need to make a reasonable choice from the large number of widely used information criteria to estimate the order of a VAR process.[6] I decided to use the multivariate CAT (criterion for autoregressive transfer functions), because the autospectra computed from VAR models for which the order is determined by CAT exhibit characteristics that are similar to the respective univariate spectra. The multivariate CAT is given by:

$$\text{CAT}(k) = \text{tr}\left\{\frac{n}{N}\sum_{j=1}^{k}(\Sigma_u^j)^{-1} - (\Sigma_u^k)^{-1}\right\}, \tag{19}$$

$$\Sigma_u^j = \frac{N}{N-nj-1}\sum_{t=j+1}^{N}\mathbf{u}_t^T\mathbf{u}_t, \quad j = 1, 2, ..., h, \tag{20}$$

where the $\mathbf{u}_t$ are the residuals of the estimated VAR(j) model, n is the dimension of the VAR model, and h is again the highest possible order. The order is chosen for which the criterion reaches a minimum.

---

[5] The starting values $y_{-p+1}, ..., y_0$ are the first p observations.

[6] See Lütkepohl (1985; 1991, pp. 135-9) for an overview and comparison of multivariate information criteria.

Table 1. *Results of the augmented Dickey–Fuller test*

Country	GDP	GFCF	II	RD
Germany	−2.230	−2.983	−3.409	−2.085
United Kingdom	−3.292	−2.755	−5.630	−3.324
France	−2.110	−2.401	−2.717	−2.029
Italy	−3.243	−3.877	−3.869	−1.946
United States	−3.165	−5.521	−5.100	−2.188
Canada	−3.176	−3.143	−2.887	−2.018
Japan	−2.286	−2.715	−2.420	−2.945

3　Results

3.1　*Estimation of the GDP/GFCF/II/RD spectra*

This section describes how the methodology is used to obtain a description of the cyclical characteristics of the G7 GDP (gross domestic product) and its components, at constant prices: GFCF (gross fixed capital formation); II (inventory investment); and RD (residual demand), which sums private consumption, governmental consumption, and the exports minus the imports. The breakdown was chosen in order to focus on the investment series, which are traditionally looked upon as being mainly responsible for the cyclical structure of the GDP. The observation period is 1960–91, with annual data.[7]

First, an augmented Dickey–Fuller test (see equation (15)) with the AR order fixed at 2 is applied to obtain an impression of the long-run characteristics of the series. The results of this test are displayed in Table 1. Comparing the outcome with the critical values given in table 8.5.2 of Fuller (1976, p. 373), we see that only for the U.S. and Italian GFCF and the U.K., U.S., and Italian II can the hypothesis of a unit root be rejected at the 5 percent significance level.

Because the type of nonstationarity cannot be reliably determined, given the small number of observations ($N = 30$), results for both the HP filter and the difference filter are displayed.[8] This procedure makes it

---

[7] Data source: "OECD Economic Outlook," *Statistics on Microcomputer Diskettes* 54 (December 1993). The observation period for (West) Germany is 1960–1989.

[8] A similar comparison of detrending procedures with respect to their influence on stylized facts can be found e.g. in Baxter (1991) for U.S. data and in Correia, Neves, and Rebelo (1992) for U.S. and U.K. data. Because the series turn out to be not always stationary after taking first differences, I decided to detrend them after differencing with a linear time trend. Allowing for higher orders of the difference filter would have caused the filtered series to be too short. The data transformation did not use logarithms to overcome

possible to analyze the robustness of the stylized facts with respect to the detrending method.

In the next step, the univariate and multivariate spectra for the GDP, GFCF, II, and RD series are estimated using the algorithms mentioned in Section 2.3. In both the univariate and the multivariate case, the order is estimated with highest possible order h fixed at 6. The multivariate spectra are estimated for the GFCF/II/RD systems. The spectral density matrix for the complete GDP/GFCF/II/RD system can be obtained by using the following relationships:

$$\underbrace{F_{(IV)}(\omega)}_{\text{GDP/GFCF/II/RD}} = Z \underbrace{F_{(III)}(\omega)}_{\text{GFCF/II/RD}} Z^T, \text{ with}$$

$$Z = \begin{bmatrix} 1 & 1 & 1 \\ 1 & 0 & 0 \\ 0 & 1 & 0 \\ 0 & 0 & 1 \end{bmatrix}. \tag{21}$$

3.2   *Results of the spectral estimation*

The univariate results concerning the first four questions asked in Section 1 are given in Tables 2 and 3. To make the interpretation of the outcome easier, Figure 2 contains a summary of cycle lengths, the importance of the cycles, and the regularity of the fluctuations, which is measured by the signal-to-noise ratio (SNR). The importance of the cycles is represented by the peak power (PP) only, because the modulus contains essentially the same information.[9] Because simply using the mean when looking for stylized facts might be misleading in some cases, an error-bar type plot is used to give a visual impression of the variation of the results.

As a typical example of the univariate spectra of the G7 GDPs and their components, Figure 3 displays the GDP, GFCF, II, and RD spectra of Germany for the HP-filtered series.[10] We see that there is a long cycle in the GDP with a length of about 8 years and a PP of 0.17. The long cycle can also be found in GFCF with a PP of 0.53. The cycle in II is clearly

---

the problem of heteroscedasticity because, for estimation of the multivariate spectra, the bookkeeping identity GDP = GFCF + II + RD is needed; this identity does not hold for logarithms.

[9] The higher the modulus, the higher the PP. The bandwidth (BW) is not plotted because of the problems described in Section 2.1. As additional information, both BW and the moduli can be found in Tables 2 and 3.

[10] The spectral densities are normalized (divided by their maximum value) to fit into the same box as the integrated spectrum. In this way it is possible to put information on both the spectral shape and the importance of the cycles into a single graph.

Table 2. *HP-filtered series, univariate spectra*

	Period	PP	BW	Moduli	SNR	AR order
Canada						
GDP	10.319	0.581	1.013	0.971	15.128	6
	4.414	0.075	1.169	0.856		
GFCF	7.656	0.641	0.911	0.953	20.487	4
II	9.863	0.179	3.107	0.909	6.616	6
	4.486	0.244	0.170	0.914		
RD	8.460	0.301	1.342	0.872	10.241	3
France						
GDP	9.027	0.131	—	0.667	9.743	2
GFCF	9.062	0.358	3.084	0.896	18.965	3
II	—	—	—	—	—	0
RD	—	—	—	—	—	0
Germany						
GDP	7.705	0.169	13.676	0.714	9.672	2
GFCF	8.373	0.534	1.448	0.938	24.193	4
II	4.699	0.171	6.107	0.583	4.747	2
RD	6.810	0.134	—	0.600	6.261	2
Italy						
GDP	8.611	0.413	1.735	0.931	9.648	5
	3.413	0.078	—	0.748		
GFCF	7.521	0.302	2.858	0.862	14.661	4
II	6.790	0.071	2.842	0.842	7.028	5
	3.180	0.329	0.473	0.870		
RD	10.535	0.557	1.528	0.959	18.001	5
Japan						
GDP	10.700	0.340	3.390	0.916	13.816	4
	3.182	0.054	1.114	0.778		
GFCF	9.577	0.528	1.656	0.947	30.317	5
	2.983	0.021	0.621	0.830		
II	—	—	—	—	—	0
RD	10.447	0.614	1.106	0.970	15.702	5
	3.163	0.051	0.893	0.784		
United Kingdom						
GDP	10.734	0.325	2.867	0.928	14.766	6
	5.166	0.104	—	0.833		
GFCF	12.345	0.220	4.774	0.912	13.852	6
	5.029	0.171	1.194	0.884		
II	4.583	0.289	2.158	0.747	6.404	2
RD	7.976	0.335	3.007	0.872	15.286	3
United States						
GDP	6.523	0.205	5.842	0.733	8.484	2
GFCF	7.561	0.330	1.878	0.911	12.250	6
	5.027	0.185	—	0.832		
II	7.591	0.094	—	0.832	7.263	6
	4.151	0.276	0.254	0.902		
RD	9.153	0.488	1.930	0.932	23.332	3

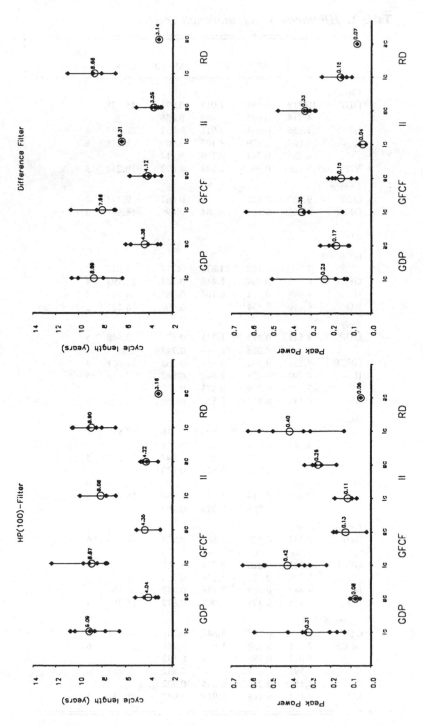

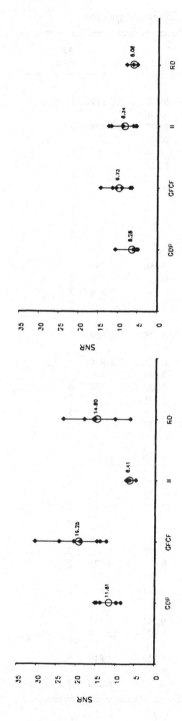

Figure 2. Univariate results.

Table 3. *Difference-filtered series, univariate spectra*

	Period	PP	BW	Moduli	SNR	AR order
Canada						
GDP	10.589	0.493	1.135	0.970	10.579	6
	4.088	0.108	0.733	0.880		
GFCF	8.430	0.626	0.538	0.977	14.406	6
	4.042	0.073	1.061	0.845		
II	—	—	—	—	—	0
RD	8.041	0.097	22.112	0.688	5.132	3
France						
GDP	—	—	—	—	—	0
GFCF	—	—	—	—	—	0
II	2.903	0.306	—	0.611	6.118	2
RD	—	—	—	—	—	0
Germany						
GDP	5.990	0.115	—	0.486	4.765	2
GFCF	6.960	0.142	—	0.628	6.800	2
II	3.511	0.282	1.751	0.668	5.370	2
RD	—	—	—	—	—	0
Italy						
GDP	7.865	0.177	2.486	0.836	5.669	5
	3.240	0.252	0.655	0.887		
GFCF	6.824	0.310	1.601	0.903	8.938	6
	3.514	0.179	0.516	0.889		
II	6.290	0.025	—	0.838	12.466	6
	3.216	0.335	0.385	0.895		
RD	10.977	0.245	2.993	0.928	7.828	5
	3.144	0.071	—	0.759		
Japan						
GDP	10.040	0.120	10.529	0.796	5.921	4
	2.996	0.191	0.673	0.811	—	
GFCF	10.669	0.336	3.138	0.922	11.376	4
	2.936	0.099	0.522	0.838		
II	3.027	0.277	1.894	0.593	5.524	2
RD	—	—	—	—	—	0
United Kingdom						
GDP	6.248	0.134	—	0.575	5.578	2
GFCF	5.643	0.194	5.516	0.682	6.371	2
II	5.080	0.320	1.028	0.888	8.756	4
RD	6.824	0.123	—	0.597	5.114	3
United States						
GDP	5.574	0.209	3.432	0.741	5.155	3
GFCF	6.924	0.311	1.250	0.927	10.466	6
	4.441	0.213	—	0.863		
II	6.337	0.058	—	0.854	11.816	6
	3.785	0.466	0.148	0.937		
RD	8.780	0.147	12.636	0.749	6.250	3

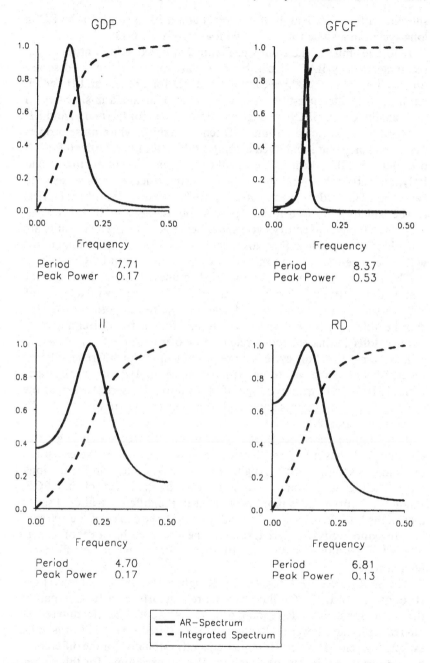

Figure 3. Germany, univariate spectra (HP-filtered series).

shorter, with a cycle length of 4–5 years and a PP of 0.17. In the RD, a long cycle can also be found, but with a PP of only 0.13.

Before examining the results in Figure 2, we take a look at the order recommended by BAC. It can be seen that, for the HP-filtered series, order 0 is estimated in three cases (II and RD for France, and II for Japan); for the difference-filtered series, it is recommended in six cases (II for Canada; GDP, GFCF, and RD for France; RD for Germany; and RD for Japan). In particular, II and RD tend to exhibit white-noise properties, a tendency that is enlarged if using a difference filter. Order 0 for RD does not mean that the noninvestment components do not fluctuate regularly, but rather that – taken together – their cyclical structures seem to cancel out. That order 0 is estimated for the Japanese II (HP-filtered series) can be explained by "just-in-time" production. In this case, there is no reason why a typical inventory cycle should emerge. The French results are something of an outlier: For most of the series, order 0 is recommended; with difference-filtered data this holds even for GDP and GFCF.

The first part of Figure 2 and the third column of Tables 2 and 3 show that, in the GDPs and the component series, a long cycle with a length of 8–9 years and a short cycle of 3–4 years can be found both for the HP- and the difference-filtered series. The results for the two detrending procedures differ in that the long cycle is more often seen in the HP-filtered series whereas the short cycle is more prominent in the difference-filtered series. This outcome was to be expected, since the HP filter exaggerates cycles in the low-frequency range (if applied to a DS series) whereas the short cycle amplifies cycles in the high-frequency range (if applied to a TS series; see Section 2.2).

Judging the importance of the cycles using PP, we see that in general the long cycle has a higher PP than the short cycle, with the exception of II; in this series, the PP is higher for the short cycle than for the long cycle. The highest PP on average is achieved by the long cycle in GFCF. Again, the short cycle is more prominent in the difference-filtered series than in the HP-filtered series. Especially for RD, the choice of the detrending procedure leads to different results: The long cycle has a PP of 40 percent in the HP-filtered series but a PP of only 20 percent in the difference-filtered series.

The SNR of the HP-filtered series is highest for GFCF and lowest for II; in other words, GFCF fluctuates more regularly than II. Comparing the results for the two detrending procedures, we see that the difference-filtered series have lower SNRs than the HP-filtered series. This was to be expected, given that order 0 is more frequently estimated for the difference-filtered series. Again, the outcome for II is an exception; for this series, the SNR is higher after differencing. As in the case of PP, the chosen detrending procedure has the strongest impact on RD: After taking differences, the SNR is about 7 on average but about 15 for the HP-filtered series. For the other series, the difference is not so clear.

Figure 4 and Tables 4 and 5 contain the multivariate results. In the third column of Tables 4 and 5, the cycle length at the maxima of the GDP autospectrum is displayed, which is taken as a reference series. The following columns contain the maximum squared coherency (MSC), the phase shift (phase lead of component series over GDP), and the gain at the maxima of the GDP autospectrum; the last column lists the order recommended by the multivariate CAT criterion. In Figure 4 the coherency, the (absolute) phase shift, and the gain are plotted.

As expected, the peaks in the GDP autospectra differ from the corresponding univariate spectra. However, in most cases the differences are very small; that is, cycles found in the autospectra are very often present also in the univariate spectra. In the case of the difference-filtered French GDP/GFCF/II/RD system, where BAC estimated order 0 for the GDP, GFCF, and RD, I nevertheless used order 2 as recommended by the multivariate CAT criterion. Still, the univariate results should be kept in mind.

An interpretation of phase shift and gain is possible only if the coherency is reasonably high at the respective frequency (see Section 2.1). We see that this is certainly the case for GDP/GFCF, especially at the long cycle (average coherency of 0.93 for the HP-filtered series, 0.89 for the difference-filtered series). The coherency of GDP/II also reaches high values at both cycle lengths. After differencing, the average coherency between GDP and II at the short cycle is higher than for the long cycle.

It is striking that the results for GDP/GFCF are very close to their mean if compared with GDP/II and GDP/RD. Particularly for GDP/RD, the variation is remarkably high; moreover, the average coherencies are clearly smaller than for GDP/GFCF and GDP/II. Therefore, it is hardly possible to find any regularities for the lead–lag relationships of GDP and RD. Of course, the coherency cannot be used for causal interpretation, but this result suggests seeking a causal relationship between the cyclical structure in the GDP and the investment series rather than between the GDP and RD.

The phase shift between GDP and the long cycle of GFCF and between GDP and the short cycle in II is smaller than one year on average; together with the high coherencies, this is another indication that the respective cyclical structure in the GDP might be due to the investment series. The average (absolute) phase shift between the long cycle in GDP and II is about a year; Tables 4 and 5 show that the long cycle in II lags behind the long cycle in GDP.

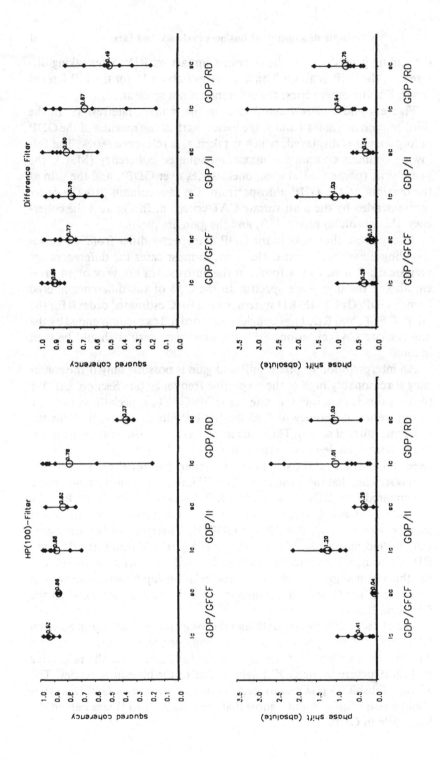

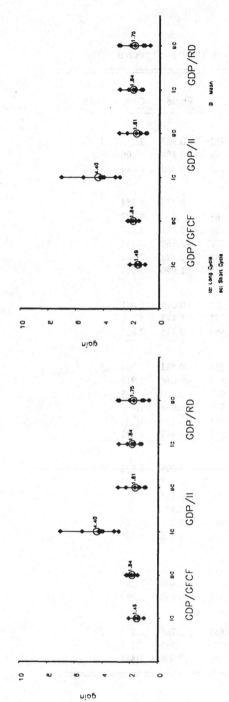

Figure 4. Multivariate results.

Table 4. *HP-filtered series, multivariate spectra*

	Period	MSC	Phase	Gain	VAR order
Canada					
GDP/GFCF	8.264	0.952	−0.967	2.003	3
GDP/II	8.264	0.964	0.884	5.406	
GDP/RD	8.264	0.979	0.510	1.784	
France					
GDP/GFCF	10.309	0.977	0.370	1.254	3
	3.597	0.863	0.003	1.727	
GDP/II	10.309	0.976	1.367	3.727	
	3.597	0.799	−0.269	1.165	
GDP/RD	10.309	0.889	−2.292	2.382	
	3.597	0.315	1.096	0.961	
Germany					
GDP/GFCF	7.407	0.907	−0.075	1.451	2
GDP/II	7.407	0.777	1.145	3.146	
GDP/RD	7.407	0.584	−0.715	2.025	
Italy					
GDP/GFCF	8.696	0.954	−0.523	1.954	3
	3.717	0.853	−0.038	1.911	
GDP/II	8.696	0.697	2.070	7.075	
	3.717	0.959	0.068	1.440	
GDP/RD	8.696	0.945	0.209	1.734	
	3.717	0.352	−1.613	3.011	
Japan					
GDP/GFCF	9.804	0.943	0.099	1.020	2
	3.344	0.877	0.085	1.362	
GDP/II	9.804	0.897	0.758	9.027	
	3.344	0.738	−0.537	2.319	
GDP/RD	9.804	0.181	−2.615	1.715	
	3.344	0.436	0.378	1.701	
United Kingdom					
GDP/GFCF	7.874	0.939	−0.163	2.239	2
GDP/II	7.874	0.928	0.904	5.587	
GDP/RD	7.874	0.933	−0.150	2.017	
United States					
GDP/GFCF	8.621	0.861	0.706	2.327	2
GDP/II	8.621	0.920	1.296	7.221	
GDP/RD	8.621	0.955	−0.606	1.431	

Table 5. *Difference-filtered series, multivariate spectra*

	Period	MSC	Phase	Gain	VAR order
Canada					
GDP/GFCF	7.407	0.851	−0.959	1.609	3
	4.219	0.796	0.049	1.876	
GDP/II	7.407	0.904	0.795	4.091	
	4.219	0.676	0.571	2.875	
GDP/RD	7.407	0.900	0.575	1.712	
	4.219	0.812	−0.307	1.728	
France					
GDP/GFCF	7.463	0.818	0.074	1.353	2
	2.907	0.845	0.055	1.653	
GDP/II	7.463	0.667	0.815	2.830	
	2.907	0.903	−0.180	0.863	
GDP/RD	7.463	0.363	−0.853	1.278	
	2.907	0.674	1.169	1.157	
Germany					
GDP/GFCF	8.264	0.872	−0.022	1.411	3
	3.367	0.734	0.127	2.256	
GDP/II	8.264	0.742	1.400	3.151	
	3.367	0.576	0.177	0.951	
GDP/RD	8.264	0.614	−0.830	1.853	
	3.367	0.190	−0.634	0.645	
Italy					
GDP/GFCF	7.519	0.941	−0.402	1.400	3
	3.413	0.853	−0.069	2.022	
GDP/II	7.519	0.543	1.963	4.265	
	3.413	0.977	0.073	1.352	
GDP/RD	7.519	0.847	0.296	2.195	
	3.413	0.413	−1.536	2.907	
Japan					
GDP/GFCF	11.765	0.907	0.223	0.970	2
	3.226	0.887	0.082	1.420	
GDP/II	11.765	0.662	0.413	7.022	
	3.226	0.754	−0.470	2.291	
GDP/RD	11.765	0.154	−3.226	1.156	
	3.226	0.497	0.371	2.033	
United Kingdom					
GDP/GFCF	8.065	0.850	−0.226	2.059	2
	3.311	0.340	−0.211	1.428	
GDP/II	8.065	0.862	1.093	3.966	
	3.311	0.847	−0.148	1.301	
GDP/RD	8.065	0.853	−0.257	1.855	
	3.311	0.322	0.555	1.026	

Table 5 *(continued)*

	Period	MSC	Phase	Gain	VAR order
United States					
GDP/GFCF	5.747	0.984	0.096	1.658	3
	3.236	0.963	−0.131	2.200	
GDP/II	5.747	0.953	0.702	5.460	
	3.236	0.874	−0.070	1.631	
GDP/RD	5.747	0.955	−0.524	2.824	
	3.236	0.525	0.684	2.788	

The gain shows that the amplitude of the long and the short cycle in GDP is about as high as the amplitude of the respective cycles in the investment series, with the exception of GDP/II. For the long cycle we see that the amplitude of the GDP cycle is 4 to 6 times higher than the long II cycle.

4   Conclusion

Our analysis has confirmed that traditional univariate business cycle stylized facts apply to the G7 GDPs and their components. To these results were added multivariate stylized facts concerning lead–lag relationships between the series. The comparison of the results for the HP- and difference-filtered series made it possible to avoid the danger of interpreting spurious cyclical structure. It has been shown that spectral analysis is a powerful tool for the description of cyclical characteristics of macroeconomic time series.

In the G7 GDPs, a long cycle with a length of 8–9 years and a short cycle with a length of 3–4 years can be found; the long cycle has the determining influence on the cyclical structure of the GDP. Both cycles can also be seen in the component series, where the long cycle is most prominent in GFCF (Juglar cycle) and the short cycle in II (Kitchin cycle), which are well-known stylized facts (see Zarnowitz 1985, p. 530).

Looking at the multivariate results, we see that there is a strong relationship between the cycles in the investment components and the GDP. The phase shift between the cycles in GDP and the investment series is less than a year; in other words, the investment series are procyclical. This is also a well-established stylized fact (see e.g. Fiorito and Kollintzas 1992 and Backus and Kehoe 1992), but there is an exception: the long cycle in II. For this series, the long cycle lags behind the respective GDP cycle with a phase shift of about a year.[11]

The amplitudes of the GDP cycles are 1 to 2 times higher than the amplitudes in the component series, again with the exception of the long cycle in II, for which the amplitude of the GDP is 4 to 6 times higher.

In general, the stylized facts for the GDP and the investment series are robust with respect to the detrending procedure, which is not the case for RD. The cyclical structure in this series is very sensitive regarding the assumption of the nonstationarity type. It was therefore not possible to identify reliably stylized facts for this component. This result does not mean that there is no cyclical structure in the noninvestment series.[12] However, taken together, the effects of its components cancel each other out.

In sum: There exists a striking set of stylized facts, largely those of traditional business cycle theory. They are robust across different countries and are to a large extent independent to the choice of the detrending methods. The ability to replicate these stylized facts should be an acid test for explanatory macroeconomic models.[13]

REFERENCES

Ables, J. G. (1974), "Maximum Entropy Spectral Analysis," *Astronomy and Astrophysics Supplement Series* 15: 383-93; reprinted in D. G. Childers (ed.), *Modern Spectrum Analysis.* New York: IEEE Press, pp. 23-33.

Backus, D. K., and P. J. Kehoe (1992), "International Evidence on the Historical Properties of Business Cycles," *American Economic Review* 82: 864-88.

Baxter, M. (1991), "Business Cycles, Stylized Facts, and the Exchange Rate Regime: Evidence from the United States," *Journal of International Money and Finance* 10: 71-88.

Blackburn, K., and M. O. Ravn (1992), "Business Cycles in the United Kingdom: Facts and Fictions," *Economica* 59: 383-401.

Brockwell, P. J., and R. A. Davis (1991), *Time Series: Theory and Methods,* 2nd ed. Berlin: Springer-Verlag.

Burg, J. P. (1975), "Maximum Entropy Spectral Analysis," Ph.D. dissertation, Stanford University, CA.

Canova, F. (1991), "Detrending and Business Cycle Facts," Working Paper no. 91/58, Department of Economics, European University Institute, Florence.

---

[11] For the U.S. and U.K. economies, different results were obtained by Kydland and Prescott (1990) and by Blackburn and Ravn (1992), who analyzed quarterly macroeconomic data in the time domain. They found that the cross-correlations between GDP and inventories peak at lag 0, i.e., that the series is procyclical (Kydland and Prescott 1990, p. 12, table 3; Blackburn and Ravn 1992, p. 389, table 2). From our analysis it can be seen that this is true only for the short cycle, if it is present.

[12] See e.g. the results of Backus and Kehoe (1992), who found cyclical structure in the noninvestment components with the exception of governmental consumption.

[13] A methodology for testing against stylized facts is elaborated in Reiter (1993).

Chan, K. H., J. C. Hayya, and J. K. Ord (1977), "A Note on Trend Removal Methods: The Case of Polynomial Regression versus Variate Differencing," *Econometrica* 45: 737–44.

Cogley, T., and J. M. Nason (1992), "Effects of the Hodrick–Prescott Filter on Trend and Difference Stationary Time Series: Implications for Business Cycle Research," Discussion Paper no. 92-23, Department of Economics, University of British Columbia, Vancouver.

Correia, I., J. A. L. Neves, and S. Rebelo (1992), "Business Cycles from 1850 to 1950: New Facts about Old Data," *European Economic Review* 36: 459–67.

Dickey, D. A. (1976), "Estimation and Hypothesis Testing in Nonstationary Time Series," Ph.D. dissertation, Iowa State University, Ames.

Dickey, D. A., W. R. Bell, and R. B. Miller (1986), "Unit Roots in Time Series Models: Tests and Implications," *American Statistician* 40: 12–26.

Fiorito, R., and T. Kollintzas (1992), "Stylized Facts of Business Cycles in the G7 from a Real Business Cycles Perspective," Discussion Paper no. 681, Center for Economic Policy Research, London.

Fougere, P. F. (1985), "A Review of the Problem of Spontaneous Line Splitting in Maximum Entropy Power Spectral Analysis," in C. R. Smith and W. Grandy (eds.), *Maximum-Entropy and Bayesian Methods in Inverse Problems*. Dordrecht: Reidel, pp. 303–14.

Fuller, W. A. (1976), *Introduction to Statistical Time Series*. New York: Wiley.

Harvey, A. C., and A. Jaeger (1991), "Detrending, Stylized Facts and the Business Cycle," Discussion Paper no. EM/91/230, London School of Economics.

Heintel, M. (1994), "A Bayesian Way to Identify the Order of Autoregressive Processes," Münchner Wirtschaftswissenschaftliche Beiträge 94-03, Department of Economics, University of Munich.

Hillinger, C. (1992a), "The Methodology of Empirical Science," in C. Hillinger (ed.), *Cyclical Growth in Market and Planned Economies*. London: Oxford University Press.

(1992b), "Paradigm Change and Scientific Method in the Study of Economic Fluctuations," in C. Hillinger (ed.), *Cyclical Growth in Market and Planned Economies*. London: Oxford University Press.

Hillinger, C., and M. Sebold-Bender (1992), "The Stylized Facts of Macroeconomic Fluctuations," in C. Hillinger (ed.), *Cyclical Growth in Market and Planned Economies*. London: Oxford University Press.

Hodrick, R., and E. Prescott (1980), "Postwar U.S. Business Cycles: An Empirical Investigation," Discussion Paper no. 451, Carnegie-Mellon University, Pittsburgh.

Jaynes, E. (1985), "Where Do We Go from Here?" in C. R. Smith and W. Grandy (eds.), *Maximum-Entropy and Bayesian Methods in Inverse Problems*. Dordrecht: Reidel, pp. 21–58.

Judge, G. G., R. C. Hill, W. E. Griffiths, H. Lütkepohl, and L. Tsuong-Chao (1988), *Introduction to the Theory and Practice of Econometrics*, 2nd ed. New York: Wiley.

King, R. G., and S. T. Rebelo (1993), "Low Frequency Filtering and Real Business Cycles," *Journal of Economic Dynamics and Control* 17: 207–31.

Koopmans, L. H. (1974), *The Spectral Analysis of Time Series*. New York: Academic Press.

Kydland, F. E., and E. C. Prescott (1990), "Business Cycles: Real Facts and a Monetary Myth," *Federal Reserve Bank of Minneapolis Quarterly Review* 14: 3-18.

Lütkepohl, H. (1985), "Comparison of Criteria for Estimating the Order of a Vector Autoregressive Process," *Journal of Time Series Analysis* 6: 35-52.

(1991), *Introduction to Multiple Time Series Analysis.* Berlin: Springer-Verlag.

Marple, S. L. (1987), *Digital Spectral Analysis with Applications.* Englewood Cliffs, NJ: Prentice-Hall.

Marple, S. L., and A. H. Nuttal (1983), "Experimental Comparison of Three Multichannel Linear Prediction Spectral Estimators," *IEEE Proceedings* 130: 218-29.

Morf, M., A. Vieira, D. T. Lee, and T. Kailath (1978), "Recursive Multichannel Maximum Entropy Spectral Estimation," *IEEE Transactions on Geoscience Electronics* 16: 85-94.

Nelson, C. R., and H. Kang (1981), "Spurious Periodicity in Inappropriately Detrended Time Series," *Econometrica* 49: 741-51.

Nelson, C. R., and C. I. Plosser (1982), "Trends and Random Walks in Macroeconomic Time Series," *Journal of Monetary Economics* 10: 139-62.

Priestley, M. (1981), *Spectral Analysis and Time Series.* London: Academic Press.

Reiter, M. (1993), "Evaluation of Discrete and Continuous Time Dynamic Models by Spectral Methods with an Application to Automobile Demand," Chapter 7 in this volume.

Rudebusch, G. D. (1992), "Trends and Random Walks in Macroeconomic Time Series: A Re-examination," *International Economic Review* 33: 616-80.

(1993), "The Uncertain Unit Root in Real GDP," *American Economic Review* 83: 264-72.

Swingler, D. (1979), "A Comparison between Burg's Maximum Entropy Method and a Nonrecursive Technique for the Spectral Analysis of Deterministic Signals," *Journal of Geophysical Research* 84: 679-85.

Zarnowitz, V. (1985), "Recent Work on Business Cycles in Historical Perspective: A Review of Theories and Evidence," *Journal of Economic Literature* 23: 523-80.

PART IV

Testing for nonlinearity

CHAPTER 11

Comparisons of the available tests for nonlinearity and chaos

William A. Barnett, A. Ronald Gallant,
Melvin J. Hinich, Mark Jensen, & Jochen Jungeilges

1   Introduction

In recent years there has been growing interest in testing for nonlinearity and chaos in economic data, but much disagreement and controversy has arisen about the available results. For example, Barnett and Chen (1986, 1988a,b) published a case in which successful detection of chaos was claimed with economic data. That published claim generated considerable controversy, as in Ramsey, Sayers, and Rothman (1990), who raised similar questions regarding virtually all of the other published tests of chaos. In short, there seems to be little agreement about the existence of nonlinearity or chaos in economic data; some economists continue to insist that linearity remains a good assumption for all economic time series, despite the fact that economic theory provides virtually no support for such an assumption. This paper outlines the beginnings of a large-scale research project designed to explore the reasons for these empirical difficulties. This ongoing project includes comparisons with real monetary aggregate data and a controlled competition based upon the use of simulated data. Our objectives are to explore the powers of the various competing tests against various alternatives, the nature of the null hypotheses of the tests, and the robustness of the tests with respect to the method of data aggregation, sample size, and testing method. As a result of the scale of this project, the results necessarily must appear in a series of papers. This paper is the first in the series and outlines the methods of generating the data, the methods of aggregation compared, and the various tests included in the comparisons and in the competition.

This research is receiving support from the National Science Foundation in the United States (Barnett, Gallant) and the German Science Foundation in Germany (Jungeilges). Mark Jensen was funded as a research assistant under Barnett's NSF grant while he was a graduate student at Washington University.

313

In earlier papers of more limited scope, Barnett and Hinich (1992, 1993) argued that the controversies stem primarily from two sources: the high noise level that exists in most aggregated economic data, and the relatively low sample sizes that are available with economic data. The algorithms currently available to detect chaos, such as the Liapunov exponent test and the Grassberger–Procaccia dimension computation, were devised primarily for use with experimental data. Since physicists can often generate very large samples of high-quality data from laboratory experimentation, physicists find these algorithms to be directly applicable to their research. Unfortunately, economists have found the successful use of these algorithms with economic data to be difficult. As a possible solution to the problem, Barnett and Hinich proposed the use of sophisticated advances in index number theory to generate low-noise data, and they then proposed the use of a bispectral method for nonlinearity testing.

In a sense, the controversies regarding the existence of chaos in economic data seem surprising. The tests used in this paper, as well as the conventional deterministic tests used by Barnett and Chen, do not test for the existence of chaos produced from within the structure of the economy. In fact, the tests have no way of determining the source of the chaos because they have no way of knowing the boundaries of the economic system. Hence any of these tests could find chaos even in an economic system that is entirely linear and stable if that system is subject to chaotic shocks from the surrounding environment. If these shocks from the surrounding "weather" system are important in explaining economic fluctuations, low-dimensional chaos could be found in economic data despite the fact that the chaos actually originates in the nonlinear dynamics of weather formation.

In order to isolate the source of the chaos within the structure of the economy, we would need a parametric structural model of the economy; we would then need to test the hypothesis that the parameters lie within the subset of the parameter space that supports chaos. However, mathematicians currently do not have the ability to solve for the boundary of that set when the number of parameters exceeds three. So for plausible structural economic models we do not have the ability to locate the boundaries of the set that define the null hypothesis of chaos within the economic structure, and hence we do not have the ability to test for chaos within such a structure.

Because the available tests are not structural and hence have no ability to identify the source of detected chaos, the alternative hypothesis of the available nonparametric, nonstructural tests is that no natural deterministic explanation exists for the observed economic fluctuations anywhere in the universe. In other words, the alternative hypothesis is that the economic fluctuations are produced by supernatural shocks. Considering the extreme implausibility and unscientific nature of the alternative hypothesis, one would think that findings of chaos in such a nonparametric test would produce little controversy, while any claims to the contrary would be subjected to careful examination. Yet, the opposite seems to be the case.

The controversies that have arisen regarding the nonparametric tests for economic chaos seem to be far out of proportion to the nature of the very weak null hypothesis in those tests. As a result, it would appear that the controversies must be produced by the nature of the tests themselves, rather than by the nature of the hypothesis. In particular, there may be very little robustness with such tests. That the likelihood function has been found to be extremely irregular under chaos (see e.g. Geweke 1989 and El-Gamal 1991) might suggest that results that are consistent across variations in sample size, test method, and aggregation method may be difficult to find. That possibility is the subject of this paper.

We are using the currently most reputable tests for nonlinearity or chaos, we are varying the sample size, and we are using four competing index numbers to measure the same variable. By these means we investigate the robustness of the inference to variations in sample size, variation in the inference method, and variation in the statistical index number used to generate the aggregated data. So far, we are finding limited robustness across these three dimensions. It appears that each of the tests has its own relative advantages under certain circumstances or against certain alternatives, and that none of the tests uniformly dominates the others.

To pursue these matters further, we have decided to produce simulated data from known models and to send the data to experts in running each of the tests. The experts were not told of the source of the data, so the controlled experiments run in this manner may be viewed as a competition between tests. This competition is ongoing and incomplete at the present time. The generating models are known at present only to William Barnett and Mark Jensen, who are not advocates of any one of the competing tests. The other co-authors and participants in the experiments are not yet aware of the generating models, since they are continuing to run their tests with the simulated data sent to them via electronic mail by Barnett and Jensen.

Although Barnett and Hinich's (1992, 1993) results tended to support Barnett and Chen's (1986) findings of chaos, or at least of nonlinearity, our current results suggest that there are enough nearly arbitrary degrees of freedom available to economic researchers to permit them to find whatever they may wish to find. However, once this project is finished in all of its objectives, we believe that it will become possible to choose among tests based upon their relative powers against various alternatives, and to target tests based upon objectives. If there are many objectives then many tests may have to be run, but each used for a particular purpose rather than each treated as a competitor of the others.

2   Data aggregation

A possible reason for the apparent success of the research in Barnett and Chen (1988a) is the unusually high quality of the data. Instead of using data produced from governmental accounting identities, Barnett and Chen (1988a) used Barnett's (1980, 1987) Divisia monetary aggregates, which are produced from careful application of the principles of economic index number and aggregation theory. Hence, although the sample size was not comparable to that available from physics experiments, the data used in Barnett and Chen (1988a) were of higher quality than those available from usual governmental sources. In particular, Barnett's Divisia monetary aggregates are produced from the Törnqvist discrete time approximation to the continuous time Divisia line integral. In continuous time, the Divisia index is known to track the unknown exact aggregate without error (see Hulten 1973). Diewert (1976) has proven that in discrete time the Törnqvist index is within Diewert's "superlative" class, defined to consist of index numbers producing a second-order approximation to the exact theoretical aggregate of economic aggregation theory. Hence the Divisia monetary aggregates, being second-order approximations, have third-order remainder terms. In contrast, the highest-quality data typically available from governmental sources is based upon Laspeyres or Paasche indexes, which produce only first-order approximations. The Federal Reserve System's simple-sum monetary aggregates are not even first-order approximations to the economic variable, and hence have first-order remainder terms. In brief, the noise in the Divisia monetary aggregates is very low relative to that in most economic data.

Two sets of data were used in Barnett and Chen (1988a): the Federal Reserve's official simple-sum monetary aggregates, and Barnett's Divisia monetary aggregates. In the current paper, we also use a recent addition to this list of competitors: the Rotemberg, Driscoll, and Poterba (1991) CE ("currency equivalence") index. As in Barnett and Hinich (1992, 1993), we use monthly data on the monetary aggregates. But we also use updated data, including the most recent observations, as a means of iterating on sample size to explore robustness to sample size variations.

In considering our results on robustness with respect to the aggregation method, we must examine the issue of stock versus flow. If each of our three methods of aggregation were a measure of the flow of monetary services from the same component assets, then indeed we would have a robustness issue. But if one method of aggregation (such as Divisia) measures the flow of services while another (such as CE) measures the economic capital stock, then we might argue that Divisia and CE methods of aggregation produce different variables and are therefore not comparable. Although it is clear from the available published theory that Divisia monetary aggregates measure the service flow, there is a difference of opinion regarding CE. Hence we shall present some theory that is intended to clarify the stock-versus-flow issue regarding CE aggregation of monetary assets.

2.1   The economic stock of money

Barnett (1987, p. 160, sec. 12; 1990) defined the economic stock of money to be the discounted present value of expenditure on the services of monetary assets. Barnett (1978, p. 148, eq. 2; 1980, eq. 3.3; 1981, p. 196, eq. 7.3) derived that discounted present value in the form displayed here as equation (2.2). Also see Barnett, Hinich, and Yue (1991, sec. 3) for the same result, but with less discussion.

During period s, let p_s^* denote the true cost-of-living index, M_{is} the nominal balances of monetary asset i, and r_{is} the nominal expected holding-period yield on monetary asset i; define $m_{is} = M_{is}/p_s^*$ to be real balances of monetary asset i. The current period is defined to be period t, so that $s \geq t$. Define R_t to be the benchmark rate of return, which is the maximum expected available rate of return in the economy. In principle, the benchmark rate is the rate of return on a pure investment asset, producing no services other than its monetary yield. Define the discount rate for period s to be

$$\rho_s = \begin{cases} 1 & \text{for } s = t, \\ \prod_{u=t}^{s-1}(1+R_u) & \text{for } s > t. \end{cases} \tag{2.1}$$

Allowing the planning horizon T to approach infinity in the second term of Barnett (1978, p. 148, eq. 2; 1980, eq. 3.3; 1981, p. 196, eq. 7.3) yields the following definition for the economic stock of money.

Definition 1.   Under risk neutrality, the economic stock of money (ESM) during period t is

$$V_t = \sum_{s=t}^{\infty} \sum_{i=1}^{n} \left[\frac{p_s^*}{\rho_s} - \frac{p_s^*(1+r_{is})}{\rho_{s+1}} \right] m_{is}. \tag{2.2}$$

The concept of economic stock used to produce Definition 1 is the user cost–evaluated expenditure on the services of the n component monetary assets. It should be observed that the procedure used in Barnett (1978, p. 148, eq. 2; 1980, eq. 3.3; 1981, p. 196, eq. 7.3) to acquire that discounted present value was simply back substitution and algebraic manipulation of the sequence of flow-of-funds identities, collapsing that sequence into a single Fisherine discounted wealth constraint. Hence our conclusion is produced entirely from accounting identities.

If we now substitute (2.1) and $m_{is} = M_{is}/p_s^*$ into (2.2), we acquire the following result:

$$V_t = \sum_{s=t}^{\infty} \sum_{i=1}^{n} \left[\frac{R_s - r_{is}}{\prod_{u=t}^{s}(1+R_u)} \right] M_{is}. \tag{2.3}$$

Our problem is to determine the conditions under which (2.3) reduces to the CE index, which is defined as follows.

Definition 2. The CE index is

$$V_t = \sum_{i=1}^{n} \frac{R_t - r_{it}}{R_t} M_{it}. \tag{2.4}$$

We seek to find conditions under which (2.4) will equal (2.3). Toward that end, suppose that expectations are stationary in the sense that $r_{is} = r_{it}$ and $R_{is} = R_{it}$ for all $s \geq t$, and consider the static portfolio $(M_{1s}, M_{2s}, ..., M_{ns}) = (M_{1t}, M_{2t}, ..., M_{nt})$ for all $s \geq t$. Equation (2.3) reduces to

$$V_t = \sum_{i=1}^{n} \sum_{s=t}^{\infty} \left[\frac{R_t - r_{it}}{(1+R_t)^{s-t+1}} \right] M_{it}. \tag{2.5}$$

However, observe that

$$\sum_{s=t}^{\infty} \frac{R_t - r_{it}}{(1+R_t)^{s-t+1}} = \frac{R_t - r_{it}}{R_t}, \tag{2.6}$$

since the left-hand side of (2.6) is a convergent geometric series (minus the first term in the series). The series is convergent under the assumption that rates of return are less than 100 percent. Substituting (2.6) into (2.5) yields the following result.

Theorem 1. *Under stationary expectations, the CE index is equal to the economic money stock.*

2.2   Implications for simple-sum aggregation

Theorem 1 is especially interesting as a means of illustrating the source of confusion that has existed in recent years regarding the role of official simple-sum monetary aggregates. In particular, it is sometimes argued that the simple-sum monetary aggregates measure the stock of money, while the Divisia monetary aggregates measure the service flow. Hence, use of the simple-sum aggregates is sometimes defended on the grounds that the stock measures are needed for some applications of monetary data. For example, monetary wealth is relevant to modeling the real balance effect, which is intended to explain the monetary transmission mechanism through a wealth effect.

However, it is evident both from the CE index and from the more general money stock formula in Definition 1 that the simple-sum aggregates do not measure the economic stock of money. In this section we consider the reasons why the accounting stock does not equal the economic stock.

It is perhaps worth observing that at one time the use of simple-sum aggregates as measures of the money stock may have been justified. The reason is that, up until recent decades, the only assets that were viewed as candidates for inclusion in monetary assets were those yielding zero own rates of return.[1] Consideration of broad monetary assets has been a relatively recent phenomenon within the central banks of the world, and has largely resulted from the expanded role of financial intermediation along with the increased nominal yield on money substitutes in the inflationary environment of recent decades. Inspection of the CE index reveals immediately that simple-sum aggregation is correct when $r_{it} = 0$ for all i.[2]

Although this observation may provide a comforting explanation for the historical use of simple-sum monetary aggregation by central banks, we still are left with a paradox. In order to acquire the services of the nominal portfolio $(M_{1t}, M_{2t}, ..., M_{nt})$, we must pay $\sum_{i=1}^{n} M_{it}$, although under stationary expectations the economic value of the money stock is given by (2.4). How can that be?

The answer is acquired by discounting to present value the portfolio's investment yield as well as expenditure on the service flow. In particular, under the stationary expectations assumption we can easily discount to present value the expected investment yield flows, $r_{is}M_{is} = r_{it}M_{it}$ for $s \geq t$, to obtain the following capitalized value:

$$V_t^* = \sum_{s=t}^{\infty} \sum_{i=1}^{n} \left[\frac{r_{it}M_{it}}{(1+R_t)^{s-t+1}} \right]. \tag{2.7}$$

Again we have a convergent geometric series in the summation over s at any given i, so that

---

[1] Some economists believe that demand deposits have always yielded a positive implicit rate of return. If so, then the simple-sum aggregates have never measured the economic stock of money.

[2] Actually, the same is true for the Divisia index of monetary services when own rates are all zero, although the demonstration is less self-evident than with the CE index.

$$V_t^* = \sum_{i=1}^{n} \frac{r_{it}}{R_t} M_{it}. \tag{2.8}$$

Adding (2.8) to (2.4), we have

$$V_t + V_t^* = \sum_{i=1}^{n} M_{it}. \tag{2.9}$$

The conclusion is clear. The simple-sum monetary aggregates measure the stock of money only if the investment (interest) yield of the monetary components is treated as a monetary service. Yet it is difficult to identify a single macroeconomic school of thought that has ever viewed the interest yield on monetary assets to be a monetary service. In fact, that possibility was carefully considered and then rejected unequivocally in Pesek and Saving (1967).

2.3   The economic stock of money and the Divisia monetary aggregate

Expenditure on the monetary service flow was evaluated in Definition 1 by summing the user cost–evaluated expenditures over individual monetary assets. We now shall ask whether there exists a connection between that monetary stock aggregate and the aggregation-theoretic aggregator function $M(\mathbf{m}_t)$, which measures the service flow. Barnett has long advocated the use of the Divisia monetary aggregate, since that index number tracks the aggregator function $M(\mathbf{m}_t)$ in discrete time to within a third-order remainder term, regardless of the form of the unknown aggregator function M. In continuous time the tracking is exact, with no remainder term at all, regardless of the form of the unknown aggregator function; see Diewert (1976).

2.3.1   The Divisia index

Under risk neutrality, the decision of each of the agents modeled in this section can be solved in two stages. In the first stage, expenditure is budgeted to aggregates. In the second stage, the budgeted expenditure on each aggregate is allocated over its components. For details of the two-stage budgeting solutions, see Barnett (1987). Only the contemporaneous second-stage decision is relevant to our purposes. For each of our economic agents, the contemporaneous second-stage decision is to maximize the current-period service flow produced from the components of the aggregate, subject to the budgeted constraint on current-period expenditure on those components. The service flow objective function is the agent's separable aggregator function over the components. Since that second-stage decision has the same form for firms and consumers (aside from a change in notation for variables and functions), we present the second-stage decision only for one economic agent, the consumer.

In the perfect certainty case, Barnett (1978, 1980) proved that the nominal user cost of the services of m_{it} is π_{it}, where

$$\pi_{it} = p^* \frac{R_t - r_{it}}{1 + R_t}. \tag{2.10}$$

The corresponding real user cost is π_{it}/p^*. In the risk neutral case, the user cost formulas are the same as in the perfect certainty case, but with the interest rates replaced by their expected value. The second-stage decision is as follows.

Problem 1. Choose $m_t \geq 0$ to maximize $M(m_t)$ subject to $m_t' \pi_t = E_t$, where E_t is total expenditure budgeted to m_t in the first stage.

It can be shown that the solution value of the exact monetary aggregate $M(m_t)$ can be tracked without error (see e.g. Barnett 1980) by the Divisia index:

$$d \log M_t = \sum_{i=1}^{k_1} s_{it} \, d \log m_{it}, \tag{2.11}$$

where the flawless tracking ability of the index in the risk neutral case holds regardless of the form of the unknown aggregator function M.

2.3.2 The dual

By Fisher's factor reversal test, we know that there must exist a user cost price aggregate $\Pi(\pi_t)$ dual to the exact service quantity aggregate $M(m_t)$ such that $M(m_t)\Pi(\pi_t) = m_t' \pi_t$. Hence expenditure on aggregate monetary services $M(m_t)$ must equal the sum of the user cost–evaluated expenditures on the components m_t. As a result, we can derive monetary wealth by discounting to present value either the expenditure flow $m_s' \pi_s$ for $s \geq t$ or the exactly equal aggregate expenditure flow $M(m_s)\Pi(\pi_s)$ for $s \geq t$. In fact if the user costs are themselves already computed as discounted present values, we need only sum the expenditure flow to obtain

$$V_t = \sum_{s=t}^{\infty} \Pi(\pi_s)M(m_s). \tag{2.12}$$

It is clear from (2.3) that the discounted user costs π_s in (2.12) must be

$$\pi_{is} = \frac{R_s - r_{is}}{\prod_{u=t}^{s}(1 + R_u)},$$

as has been explicitly derived by Barnett (1978, p. 148; 1980, eq. 3.4; 1981, p. 196, eq. 7.4).

If we impose the stationarity assumption used to acquire the CE index in Definition 2, we find that

$$V_t = M(\mathbf{m}_t) \sum_{s=t}^{\infty} \Pi(\pi_s),$$

where

$$\pi_{is} = \frac{R_t - r_{it}}{(1+R_t)^{s-t+1}}.$$

Hence we see that, under the assumption of implicit stationary expectations, the CE index is proportional to the monetary service flow $M(\mathbf{m}_t)$, which is measured by the Divisia monetary index. But the proportionality factor $\sum_{s=t}^{\infty} \Pi(\pi_s)$ need not be a constant over time when actual ex post data on the interest rates is used. In any case, it is clear from (2.12) that the economic stock of money equals the discounted present value of expenditure on the aggregate service flow $M(\mathbf{m}_s)$, $s \geq t$, regardless of whether or not expectations are stationary. The Divisia index tracks that aggregate flow $M(\mathbf{m}_s)$, $s \geq t$, very accurately (to within a third-order remainder term in the changes).

2.3.3   The CE index as a measure of service flow

Strong separability in currency produces an interesting special case of the Divisia index. In particular, that special case produces the CE or "currency equivalence" index advocated by Rotemberg (1991) and Rotemberg et al. (1991). In this section, we prove that the CE index is a fully nested special case of the Divisia index.

As demonstrated in Section 2.3.1, derivation of the Divisia monetary index requires the assumption of blockwise weak separability of monetary assets from other goods and assets in the utility function, so that an exact monetary aggregate will exist. In addition to that fundamental existence condition, we also need perfect certainty (or risk neutrality) with respect to contemporaneous current-period prices and interest rates, but not necessarily with respect to future prices and interest rates. Although for convenience we have assumed linear homogeneity of the monetary asset category utility function M, that assumption is not required. If M is not linearly homogeneous then M is not the monetary asset aggregator function; rather, the distance function is, and the Divisia index then tracks the distance function. See Barnett (1987, sec. 7 and 8).

As we now show, the derivation of the CE index requires the category utility function M to be linearly homogeneous and also to be strongly separable in currency. Both assumptions are empirically implausible, but the CE index does produce a potentially useful special case under certain circumstances. In particular, the CE index is completely linear and hence can be aggregated over economic agents more easily than the Divisia index. The CE index can also be used to measure the stock of money, rather than the flow of monetary services, as shown in Section 2.1 and first proven by Barnett et al. (1991).

Under the foregoing assumptions of linear homogeneity and strong separability, the monetary asset category utility function over m_t can be written $M(\mathbf{m}_t) = \phi m_{1t} + h(m_{2t}, ..., m_{k_1 t})$, where ϕ is an unknown constant parameter and h is the aggregator function over noncurrency monetary assets. Setting $\phi = 1$ is a harmless positive linear transformation of the category utility function M, and hence we shall follow Rotemberg et al. (1991) by normalizing ϕ at 1 so that $M(\mathbf{m}_t) = m_{1t} + h(m_{2t}, ..., m_{k_1 t})$. Observe that the marginal utility $\partial M/\partial m_{jt}$ is independent of currency holding m_{1t}, and that $\partial M/\partial m_{1t} = 1$ independently of the holding of other assets $m_{2t}, ..., m_{k_1 t}$. These implications of the CE assumptions are empirically most unappealing, but the implied form of $M(\mathbf{m}_t)$ as a simple sum of m_{1t} and of the exact aggregate over other monetary assets, $h(m_{2t}, ..., m_{k_1 t})$, clearly produces the currency equivalent interpretation. In particular, the exact aggregate over other monetary assets is required by the assumed form of M to be a perfect substitute for currency, so that $M(\mathbf{m}_t)$ is the sum of currency and a perfect substitute for currency.

We now further explore the implications of the condition $\partial M/\partial m_{1t} = 1$. In particular, we multiply through by $m_{1t}/M(\mathbf{m}_t)$ to obtain

$$\frac{\partial \log M_t}{\partial \log m_{1t}} = \frac{m_{1t}}{M_t}. \tag{2.13}$$

We now see what happens to the Divisia monetary index under the CE restriction (2.13). From the Divisia index formula (2.11), we know that

$$\frac{\partial \log M_t}{\partial \log m_{1t}} = s_{1t}. \tag{2.14}$$

From (2.13) and (2.14) we have that $M_t = m_{1t}/s_{1t} = (\mathbf{m}_t' \boldsymbol{\pi}_t/m_{1t}\pi_{1t})m_{1t}$, so that

$$M_t = \sum_{i=1}^{k_1} \frac{R_t - r_{it}}{R_t} m_{it}, \tag{2.15}$$

which is the CE index.

Clearly, the CE index is acquired as a special case by imposing two very strong and entirely unnecessary assumptions upon the Divisia index. Furthermore, the CE index possesses a very undesirable property, which to my knowledge is not possessed by any reputable index number: It is not locally linearly homogeneous. Hence, even if all components are growing at exactly the same rate, the CE index need not be growing at that rate. In fact, the growth rate of the index could even have a different sign from the sign of the growth rate of all of the components.

This can be seen by taking the total differential of (2.15) and dividing through by (2.15):

$$d \log M_t = \sum_{i=1}^{k_1} s_{it} \, d \log m_{it} + \sum_{i=1}^{k_1} s_{it} \, d \log \pi_{it}. \tag{2.16}$$

The problem is evident by comparing (2.16) with the Divisia index (2.11). In the Divisia index, if $d \log m_{it} = \lambda$ for all i then $d \log M_t = \lambda$, because $\sum_{i=1}^{k_1} s_{it} = 1$. Hence the Divisia index supplies the right answer in the one case in which everyone would agree on the right answer. In contrast, the CE index will yield the wrong answer in that case, unless the second term of (2.16) is exactly equal to zero, where the second term is the Divisia user cost aggregate for monetary services. It is small consolation that (2.16) would exactly track linearly homogeneous $M(\mathbf{m}_t) = m_{1t} + h(m_{2t}, ..., m_{k_1 t})$, if that were exactly the utility function over $\mathbf{m}_t$ and if the Euler equations were exactly satisfied by the data.

Nevertheless, the CE index, unlike the Divisia index, is linear in the levels of the component monetary assets. Hence aggregation over economic agents is simple.[3] In addition, Barnett et al. (1991) showed that the CE index is the discounted present value of expenditure on the services of the Divisia aggregate under stationary expectations. That result permits the CE index to be interpreted as the stock aggregate implied by the Divisia flow aggregate, under stationary expectations. In fact, that interpretation provides a resolution of the troublesome issue raised by the nonhomogeneity of (2.16), since (2.16) can be written as

$$d \log Q_t = d \log[M(\mathbf{m}_t)\Pi(\pi_t)],$$

where Q_t is the CE index, $M(\mathbf{m}_t)$ the Divisia quantity index, and $\Pi(\pi_t)$ the Divisia user cost index. The result is Barnett's (1991) interpretation as user-cost–evaluated expenditure on the services of $\mathbf{m}_t$. Under stationary expectations, the same result is acquired after discounting the future stream of such expenditures over an infinite horizon to produce a stock aggregate.

If the CE aggregate is thereby interpreted as $M(\mathbf{m}_t)\Pi(\pi_t)$, we should not expect that aggregate to have the same properties that we require for an index measuring $M(\mathbf{m}_t)$, and hence (2.16) should not bother us. Fur-

---

[3] With the Divisia index, formal aggregation usually requires subaggregation over similar demographic groups followed by Divisia aggregation over the groups. See Barnett (1987, sec. 9) and Barnett and Serletis (1990). Hence data are required for asset holdings by those demographic groups, unless Gorman's or Muellbauer's assumptions for the existence of a representative economic agent are satisfied (see Barnett 1981, apx. B1.2).

thermore, the ease of aggregation over consumers should not surprise us, since the index is in expenditure units rather than quantity-demanded units.

2.3.4   *Conclusions about the CE index theory*

With given monetary asset components, we have considered whether Divisia and CE aggregation should be viewed as alternative methods of measuring the same economic variable. If we were to accept the view of Rotemberg et al. (1991), both methods of aggregation would produce measures of the service flow generated by the components. Hence different results produced from chaos tests with those two series would create a robustness issue. However, we have seen that the CE index can be viewed as a measure of the service flow only under assumptions that create a strictly nested special case of the Divisia aggregate. Under that interpretation, the Divisia, CE, and simple-sum aggregate over a fixed set of monetary asset components are measures of the same economic variable. But in theory, the simple-sum index is nested within the CE, which in turn is nested within the Divisia index. Hence inconsistencies between chaos inferences can be resolved by the observation that the Divisia data are of higher quality than the other two, and hence should produce the preferred inference.

As we have seen, our preferred interpretation of the CE index is as a stock index that discounts to present value the Divisia service flow under stationary expectations. Under that interpretation, the CE and Divisia index measure different economic variables.

Rotemberg et al. (1991) proposed fitting a centered moving average to CE aggregate data as a means of smoothing the aggregate's growth rates. However, averaging the data in that manner damages its connection with the underlying economic theory. Moreover, the value of a moving average centered about the current period does not, in principle, exist during the current period. Hence the averaged CE index does not exist during the current period and is defined only in the past. For these reasons, we consider the CE index without the averaging transformation to be more interesting than the data transformed by a centered moving average. Nevertheless, we shall report results both with and without the centered averaging advocated by Rotemberg et al. (1991).

3   Test methods and capabilities

In addition to varying the sample size, comparing three index aggregation methods, and using simulated as well as real data, we use various inference methods to test for nonlinearity or chaos. These methods include the Hinich bispectrum test, the BDS test, the Liapunov exponent estimator of Nychka et al. (1992), White's test for nonlinearity, and the more recent Kaplan approach.

The tests used in Barnett and Chen (1988a) are those commonly used in the experimental physics literature. With noise-free data, the connection between those tests and chaos is well understood (see e.g. Brock and Dechert 1988 for proofs of the relevant theorems). However, the appropriate way to use those tests with noisy data is not entirely clear, since the sampling distributions of the test statistics are not known. This ambiguity is one source of the controversies that have arisen in economics regarding testing for chaos.

In the current paper, we outline the testing methods introduced so far into this comparison project. The Hinich bispectral test is a test in the frequency domain of flatness of the bispectrum. The sampling properties of the test statistic are known, and the approach is based upon conventional time-series inference methodology. White's test is a time-domain test for nonlinearity of a stochastic process. The BDS test is a test for whiteness that can be used to test for residual nonlinear structure after any linear structure has been removed through prior prewhitening. The NEGM test (Nychka et al. 1992) is a nonparametric test for positivity of the maximum Liapunov exponent. All of these tests are explicitly derived for use with noisy data. The most recently introduced test included in this project is the Kaplan test, the details of which will appear in later papers produced from this project as the implementation of this approach becomes more clearly defined.

4   Available conventional tests

By using conventional stochastic process methods to test for complex nonlinear dynamics, we are mainly limited to tests for nonlinearity, which is necessary but not sufficient for chaos. There are two important tests currently in use for testing for nonlinearity: the BDS test (Brock, Dechert, and Scheinkman 1986) and the Hinich bispectrum test.

The BDS test provides an important advance in testing for stochastic dependence and is hence a significant new contribution to the field of statistics. But the BDS test does not currently provide a direct test for either nonlinearity or chaos, since the sampling distribution of the test statistic is not known - either in finite samples or asymptotically - under a null hypothesis of nonlinearity, linearity, chaos, or the lack of chaos. The asymptotic distribution is known under the null of independence. Hence the hypotheses of nonlinearity and chaos are nested within the alternative hypothesis, which includes both nonwhite linear and nonwhite nonlinear processes.

In conventional statistical methodology, one tests a hypothesis by equating it with the null or with the total alternative hypothesis – not by using the power of the test to try to discriminate between subsets of the alternative hypothesis. Under the latter nonstandard approach, virtually every known hypothesis would be a "test for nonlinearity or chaos," since every statistical test contains nonlinearity and chaos as subsets somewhere within either the null or the alternative hypothesis. Nevertheless, it is possible to use BDS to test independence against any null hypothesis, if all other alternative hypotheses have been removed by prefiltering. For example, if all linear possibilities have been removed by fitting the best possible linear model, the BDS test can be used to test the residuals for remaining nonlinear dependence. Likewise, if all nonchaotic possibilities have been removed by fitting the best possible nonchaotic model, the BDS test can be used to test the residuals for remaining chaotic dependence.

Filtering out all possible nonchaotic possibilities with certainty seems to be beyond the state of the art. Hence it is not clear how the BDS test can be used to produce a convincing inference regarding chaos. Filtering out all possible linear possibilities with certainty is difficult at best, but prefiltering by ARIMA (autoregressive integrated moving average) fit is often viewed as a reputable means of prewhitening; hence we use BDS to test for remaining nonlinear dependence in the residuals of an ARIMA process fitted by the Box–Jenkins approach. There have been a number of other recent attempts to apply the BDS test to nonlinearity testing of filtered data. For an interesting example see Scheinkman and LeBaron (1989). We describe the BDS test in Section 6.

The Hinich bispectrum approach provides a direct test for nonlinearity as well as a direct test for Gaussianity, since Hinich's approach produces a test statistic having known asymptotic sampling distribution under the null of linearity, as well as another test statistic having known asymptotic sampling distribution under the null of Gaussianity. In Section 5 we describe the Hinich bispectrum approach, which is related to that of Subba Rao and Gabr (1980).

Although the BDS and Hinich tests appear to be among the best available tests for nonlinearity in noisy data, we believe that there is currently only one credible candidate for a test for chaos in noisy data. That is the NEGM test, which is described in Section 7. A connection exists between the NEGM test for chaos and White's test for nonlinearity, since both use neural nets; White's test is described in Section 8. Our intent is to include the Kaplan test in these comparisons as well, although the null of that test depends upon the way in which the test surrogate data series are produced. Until we have made those decisions, it will be unclear whether we shall incorporate the Kaplan test among those for nonlinearity or for chaos.

5   The Hinich bispectral approach

5.1   *Definitions and background*

If $\{x(t)\}$ is a zero-mean third-order stationary time series, then the mean $\mu_x = E[x(t)] = 0$, the covariance $c_{xx}(m) = E[x(t+m)x(t)]$, and the general third-order moments $c_{xxx}(s, r) = E[x(t+r)x(t+s)x(t)]$ are independent of t. If $c_{xx}(m) = 0$ for all nonzero m then the series is white noise. Priestly (1981) and Hinich and Patterson (1985) stressed that, although a series may be white noise, $x(n)$ and $x(m)$ may be stochastically dependent unless $\{x(t)\}$ is multivariate Gaussian. Only under multivariate Gaussianity are lack of correlation (whiteness) and stochastic independence the same. If the distribution of $\{x(n_1), ..., x(n_N)\}$ is multivariate normal for all $n_1, ..., n_N$, then the series is defined to be Gaussian, where N is the sample size.[4] Hinich and Patterson (1985, p. 70) fault Box and Jenkins (1970, p. 8 vs. p. 46) and Jenkins and Watts (1968, p. 149 vs. p. 157) for blurring the definitions of whiteness and independence.

We define a pure white-noise series as one in which $x(n_1), ..., x(n_N)$ are independent random variables for all values of $n_1, ..., n_N$. All pure white-noise series are white. All white-noise series are not pure white noise, unless in addition they are Gaussian.

In addition to stationarity, whiteness, and pure whiteness, another often-assumed property of a time series is linearity. Many researchers implicitly assume that the errors of their models are Gaussian, and test for pure white noise by using the covariance function $c_{xx}(m)$, but ignore the information regarding possible nonlinear relationships found in the third-order moments $c_{xxx}(s, r)$. This suggests the need to test for both nonlinearity and Gaussianity, in addition to testing in the usual manners for whiteness.

5.2   *The test method*

Hinich (1982) argued that the bispectrum in the frequency domain is easier to interpret than the multiplicity of third-order moments $\{c_{xxx}(r, s): s \leq r, r = 0, 1, 2, ...\}$ in the time domain. For frequencies f_1 and f_2 in the principal domain

---

[4] In accordance with time series conventions, we equate Gaussianity of the time series with multivariate Gaussianity.

$$\Omega = \{(f_1, f_2): 0 < f_1 < \tfrac{1}{2}, f_2 < f_1, 2f_1 + f_2 < 1\},$$

the bispectrum $B_{xxx}(f_1, f_2)$ is defined by

$$B_{xxx}(f_1, f_2) = \sum_{r=-\infty}^{\infty} \sum_{s=-\infty}^{\infty} c_{xxx}(r, s) \exp[-i2\pi(f_1 r + f_2 s)]. \qquad (5.1)$$

The bispectrum is the double Fourier transformation of the third-order moments function.[5]

The statistical tests based on the sample bispectrum that we briefly discuss in this section were applied with success to the study of acoustic signals and noise by Brockett, Hinich, and Wilson (1987) and to stock prices and exchange rates by Hinich and Patterson (1985, 1989) and Brocket, Hinich, and Patterson (1988).

The skewness function $\Gamma(f_1, f_2)$ is defined in terms of the bispectrum as follows:

$$\Gamma^2(f_1, f_2) = |B_{xxx}(f_1, f_2)|^2 / S_{xx}(f_1) S_{xx}(f_2) S_{xx}(f_1 + f_2), \qquad (5.2)$$

where $S_{xx}(f)$ is the (ordinary power) spectrum of $x(t)$ at frequency f. Since the bispectrum is complex-valued, the absolute value (vertical) lines in (5.2) designate modulus. Brillinger (1965) proved that the skewness function $\Gamma(f_1, f_2)$ is constant over all frequencies $(f_1, f_2) \in \Omega$ if $\{x(t)\}$ is linear, and zero over all frequencies if $\{x(t)\}$ is Gaussian. Linearity and Gaussianity can be tested using a sample estimator of the skewness function $\Gamma(f_1, f_2)$. We now outline the procedure used to obtain the bispectrum.

5.3   Computation of the test statistics

Let $f_k = k/N$ for each integer k. For the sample $\{x(0), x(1), \dots, x(N-1)\}$, define $F_{xxx}(f_j, f_k)$ to be an estimate of the bispectrum of $\{x(t)\}$ at the frequency pair (f_j, f_k) such that

$$F_{xxx}(f_j, f_k) = X(f_j) X(f_k) X^*(f_j + f_k)/N, \qquad (5.3)$$

---

[5] The bispectrum is the third-order polyspectrum, while the ordinary power spectrum is the second-order polyspectrum. Strictly speaking, the polyspectrum of order k is the Fourier transform of the cumulant function (not the moment function) of order k.

Cumulants are defined to be the coefficients of the terms in the power series expansion of the *logarithm* of the characteristic function of a distribution, whereas the moments are the coefficients of the terms in the power series expansion of the *level* of the characteristic function of the distribution. Unlike the moments, the cumulants have the merit of being semi-invariants. However, for a stationary time series with zero mean, the second- and third-order cumulant functions are identical to the second- and third-order moment functions. Only at the fourth and higher orders do the cumulant functions differ from the moment functions. Because we use only the second and third orders (under the assumption of stationarity and zero mean), we need draw no distinction betweem moments and cumulants.

where

$$X(f_j) = \sum_{t=0}^{N-1} x(t) \exp(-i2\pi f_j t).$$

The asterisk in (5.3) designates complex conjugate.

The function $F_{xxx}(f_j, f_k)$ must be smoothed to form a consistent estimator. Let $\langle B_{xxx}(f_m, f_n) \rangle$ denote a smooth estimate of $B_{xxx}(f_m, f_n)$, which is obtained by averaging over values of $F_{xxx}(f_j, f_k)$ at adjacent frequency pairs such that

$$\langle B_{xxx}(f_m, f_n) \rangle = M^{-2} \sum_{j=(m-1)M}^{mM-1} \sum_{k=(n-1)m}^{nM-1} F_{xxx}(f_j, f_k). \qquad (5.4)$$

This estimator, $\langle B_{xxx}(f_m, f_n) \rangle$, is the average of the $F_{xxx}(f_j, f_k)$ over a square on M^2 points. It is a consistent and asymptotically complex normal estimator of the bispectrum $B_{xxx}(f_1, f_2)$ if the sequence (f_m, f_n) converges to (f_1, f_2) (see Hinich 1982).

As discussed earlier, the estimated skewness function $\Gamma(f_m, f_n)$ will not be significantly different from a constant at any frequency pair in Ω under the null hypothesis of linearity. If the null hypothesis is Gaussianity as well as linearity, then that constant is zero. The skewness function can be used to motivate construction of the normalized test statistic $2|\delta(f_m, f_n)|^2$, where

$$\delta(f_m, f_n) = \frac{\langle B_{xxx}(f_m, f_n) \rangle}{[(N/M^2)\langle S_{xx}(f_m) \rangle \langle S_{xx}(f_n) \rangle \langle S_{xx}(f_m + f_n) \rangle]^{1/2}}. \qquad (5.5)$$

In this formula, $\langle S_{xx}(\cdot) \rangle$ is defined to be a consistent and asymptotically normal estimator of the power spectrum $S_{xx}(\cdot)$, and f_m is defined by $f_m = (2m-1)M/2N$ for each integer m. Hinich (1982) has shown that $2[\delta(f_m, f_n)]^2$ is approximately distributed as an independent noncentral chi-squared variate with two degrees of freedom at frequency pair (f_m, f_n).

The larger is M, the less is the finite sample variance and the larger is the sample bias. Because of this trade-off, there is no unique M that is appropriate to use for performing nonlinearity and Gaussianity tests based upon the estimated statistics given by (5.5). If M is large then the bandwidth is large, the variance is reduced, and the resolution of the tests is small, since there are too few terms for the linearity test. If M is small then there is a large number of terms to sort for the linearity tests, the variance may be too large, and the chi-square approximation used for the linearity test may not be good. Hinich (1982) suggested that M should be selected to be approximately the square root of the number N of observations.

Let P denote the number of frequency pairs in the principal domain Ω, and let

$$D = \{(m, n): (f_m, f_n) \in \Omega\},$$

so that P is the cardinal number of the set D. Hinich (1982) showed that the P values of $2|\delta(f_m, f_n)|^2$ for $(m, n) \in D$ are approximately distributed as independent, noncentral chi-square variates with noncentrality parameter $\lambda(f_m, f_n)$, where

$$\lambda(f_m, f_n) = (2M^2/N)|B_{xxx}(f_m, f_n)|^2/S_{xx}(f_m)S_{xx}(f_n)S_{xx}(f_m + f_n)$$
$$= (2M^2/N)\Gamma^2(f_m, f_n). \tag{5.6}$$

Define the test statistic

$$\text{CHISUM} = 2 \sum_{(m, n) \in D} \sum |\delta(f_m, f_n)|^2. \tag{5.7}$$

The distribution of CHISUM is approximately a noncentral chi square with $2P$ degrees of freedom and a noncentrality parameter that is the sum of the $\lambda(f_m, f_n)$ over all $(m, n) \in D$.

Under the null hypothesis that $\{x(t)\}$ is Gaussian, and thus that the skewness function $\Gamma(f_m, f_n)$ is identically zero over all $(m, n) \in D$, CHISUM is approximately a central chi-square $2P$ variate. Equation (5.7) gives us an asymptotic chi-square test of the Gaussianity hypothesis. If the time series is linear but not necessarily Gaussian then the skewness function is constant, which implies from (5.6) that the noncentrality parameters are constant. The Hinich linearity test uses the empirical distribution function of $\{2|\delta(f_m, f_n)|\}$ in the principal domain to test the null hypothesis that the $\lambda(f_m, f_n)$ are all the same. A robust single test statistic for this dispersion is the 80th quantile of these statistics.

For details of the test, see Hinich (1982), Hinich and Patterson (1985, 1989), and Ashley, Patterson, and Hinich (1986). In particular, the final transformed test statistics are distributed as standard normal random variates under the respective null hypotheses. When the null is Gaussianity, the resulting test statistic is denoted by H. When the null is linearity, the test statistic is denoted by Z. In both cases, the distribution of the standard normal is used to produce a one-sided test in which the null is rejected if the test statistic is large.

Ashley et al. (1986, p. 174) presented an equivalence theorem proving that the Hinich bispectral linearity test statistic is invariant to linear filtering of the data. This important result proves that the linearity test can be applied either to the raw series or to the residuals of a linear model fitted to the data. Hence there is no need to choose among possible linear methods of detrending or prefiltering the data. An additional important implication of the theorem is that if $x(t)$ is found to be nonlinear then the residuals of a linear model of the form $y(t) = f(x(t))$ will also be nonlinear, since the nonlinearity in $x(t)$ will pass through any linear filter f.

Ashley et al. (1986) also reported tables on the power of the Hinich linearity test for detecting violations of the linearity and Gaussianity hypotheses for a number of sample sizes and M values. The tables indicate substantial power for both tests, even when N is as small as 256, if the value of M used is between 12 and 17. For this sample size, the power of the test falls off as M increases above 17.

6   The BDS test

6.1   General features of the test

The details of the BDS test (Brock et al. 1986) are well known. The test uses the correlation function (integral) as the test statistic. This choice is in contrast to the Grassberger–Procaccia test, which uses the correlation dimension. The correlation function is needed in deriving the correlation dimension, but the two are not the same. The correlation dimension's value has a direct connection with the Hausdorff dimension of the attractor, and hence the correlation dimension, in principle, has a direct connection with chaos. In particular, low fractional Hausdorff dimension is the result sought by those looking for useful chaos.

While correlation dimension is therefore potentially very useful in testing for chaos, the sampling properties of the correlation dimension are unknown. If the only source of stochasticity is noise in the data, and if that noise is slight, then it is possible to filter the noise out of the data and use the correlation dimension test deterministically. However, if the economic structure that generated the data contains a stochastic disturbance within its equations, the correlation dimension is stochastic and its derived distribution is important in producing a reliable inference.

The BDS test uses the correlation function as the test statistic. The asymptotic distribution of the correlation function is known under the null hypothesis of pure whiteness (independent and identically distributed observations). As a result, the BDS test can be used to produce a formal statistical test of whiteness against general dependence. However, the sampling distribution of the BDS test statistic is not known under the nulls of chaos, nonlinearity, or linearity. We are left with an uncomfortable choice between (a) the correlation dimension, which produces a direct test for chaos, but only when no stochastic shocks exist within the model, and (b) the correlation function, which possesses known sampling properties when such shocks do exist, but only under a different null hypothesis (i.e., whiteness).

Nevertheless, the BDS test can be used to produce a form of indirect evidence about nonlinearity. In particular, an ARIMA process can be fitted to the data in an attempt to remove linear structure. The BDS test then can be used to determine whether there is evidence of remaining dependence in the data. If all linear dependence has already been removed, then any remaining dependence should be nonlinear. In principle, there are some difficulties with this approach. The Box–Jenkins estimate of the ARIMA process may not succeed in removing all forms of linear dependency. In addition, the sampling distribution of the BDS test statistic is affected in largely unknown ways by the nonzero variances of the coefficient estimators in the ARIMA process. Despite such necessary qualifications about pretesting, we are including the BDS test in our comparisons and competition.

In particular, we use the Box–Jenkins approach to fit an ARIMA(i, j, k) model to the data, where i is the order of the AR(i) autoregressive part, k is the order of the MA(k) moving-average part, and j is the number of times that the data are differenced before fitting the moving average.

Formally, the equation of an ARMA(i, k) process x_t is:

$$x_t = \sum_{n=1}^{i} a_n x_{t-n} + \sum_{n=1}^{k} b_n u_{t-n},$$

where u_t is a zero-mean white-noise process. The AR(i) autoregressive part is $\sum_{n=1}^{i} a_n x_{t-n}$, while the MA$(k)$ moving-average part is $\sum_{n=1}^{k} b_n u_{t-n}$. As mentioned previously, an ARIMA(i, j, k) process becomes an ARMA(i, k) process if differenced j times.

The BDS test statistic is a transformation of the correlation function. That transformed test statistic asymptotically becomes a standard normal Z statistic, under the null of whiteness. The null of whiteness is rejected if the test statistic is large. By convention, with a Z statistic "large" means larger than 2 or perhaps 3. Strictly speaking, the definition of "large" should depend upon sample size.

The correlation function has two arguments (variables) and one free parameter. The arguments are the embedding dimension m and the metric bound ϵ, which is the maximum difference between pairs of observations counted in computing the correlation function. In the case of the Grassberger–Procaccia test, ϵ and m are not free, since the limit of those two variables is taken in defining the correlation dimension. In particular, in defining the correlation dimension, the limit is taken as ϵ goes to zero and as m goes to infinity. But the BDS test uses the correlation function, rather than the correlation dimension, and the values of those two variables is finite and arbitrary in the definition of the correlation function.

In addition to the two variables, there is a free parameter in the correlation function. That parameter is the time delay used in embedding the univariate observations into a multivariate phase space. In this case, a finite choice for that parameter must be made in both the Grassberger–Procaccia and the BDS test. In the BDS test, the convention is to set the time delay equal to unity so that m successive observations are stacked, without skipping any intervening observations, in producing the embedded phase-space vectors. There is much controversy regarding the best choice of the time delay for the Grassberger–Procaccia test; various competing selection methods have been proposed, including one based upon information theory. In the case of the BDS test, the argument for the use of the unitary time delay rests upon the prewhitening by ARIMA fit of the data used with the BDS test.

The need to choose the values of ϵ and m can be a complication in using the BDS test. In our comparisons, we adopt the approach used by advocates of the test: we set ϵ equal to the standard deviation of the data.[6] At our chosen setting for ϵ, we are currently producing the BDS test statistic for all embedding dimensions from 2 to 8, in the hope that the same inference will be produced at each dimension.

Hsieh and LeBaron (1988) found that type I error is large with the BDS test when the sample size is not adequately large, since the nonzero standard error of the ARIMA coefficient estimators biases the BDS test. By their criterion, our sample size is barely adequate. Hence, to avoid rejecting a true null hypothesis, we should refrain from rejecting the null unless the test statistic is very large: Instead of rejecting when the test statistic exceeds the conventional critical values of 2 or 3, perhaps we should resist rejecting unless the test statistic exceeds 4. In addition, Brock, Hsieh, and LeBaron (1991) found that the asymptotic properties of the BDS test deteriorate when the embedding dimension increases to more than 3 at sample sizes comparable to ours.

6.2   Details of the test statistic

The preceding discussion assumes knowledge of the correlation function (integral) and correlation dimension formulas. For convenient reference, the formulas are supplied in this section.

Suppose we have a time series of observations on a scalar random variable m_t. We first embed them into a multivariate phase space as follows.

---

[6] Through Monte Carlo studies, Hsieh and LeBaron (1988) found that the power and size of the test is maximized when ϵ is selected to be between 0.5 and 1.5 times our choice, which is thus in the center of that region. We further investigated variations of the setting throughout that range. Our inferences were not changed at either the upper or lower bound of the region. Lower settings for ϵ, including the square of the standard deviation, produced results evidencing domination of the test by noise in the data. In particular, the test statistic became a strong function of embedding dimension and varied between very positive and very negative values as m was increased at fixed ϵ.

Select an embedding dimension n, and then stack the resulting n values of m_t into an n-dimensional vector, with successive elements of the vector being separated by τ periods. If the first observation in the n-history is m_t, then we can designate the resulting n-history at t by $\mathbf{m}(n,\tau)_t$, where we define

$$\mathbf{m}(n,\tau)_t = (m_t, m_{t+\tau}, m_{t+2\tau}, \ldots, m_{t+(n-1)\tau})$$

at each t. For notational simplicity, in what follows the τ will usually be omitted in $\mathbf{m}(n,\tau)_t$; the existence of the argument τ should be understood.

We first define the Grassberger–Procaccia method of measuring dimension. The dimension measure resulting from that method is called the correlation dimension, since the procedure uses the correlation function $C_n(\epsilon)$ defined by

$$C_n^*(\epsilon) = \frac{\#\{(i,j): \|\mathbf{m}(n)_i - \mathbf{m}(n)_j\| < \epsilon,\, 1 \le i \le N_n,\, 1 \le j \le N_n,\, i \ne j\}}{N_n^2 - N_n}, \quad (6.1)$$

where $N_n = N - (n-1)\tau$ is the number of n-histories that can be produced from a sample of size N with time lag τ, and $\#A$ denotes the cardinality of (number of distinct points in) the set A. The correlation function measures the correlation of points along the time series. (In practice, there is no need to divide by $N_n^2 - N_n$.)

The Grassberger–Procaccia correlation dimension in phase space is defined to be

$$D(n) = \lim_{\epsilon \to 0}(\log_2 C_n^*(\epsilon)/\log_2 \epsilon). \quad (6.2)$$

If we take the limit as the embedding dimension goes to infinity and then apply the Takens embedding theorem, we get the correlation dimension of the attractor set in state space,

$$D = \lim_{n \to \infty} D(n). \quad (6.3)$$

As discussed before, the BDS test is based upon the correlation function $C_n^*(\epsilon)$, which has n, τ, and ϵ as unspecified parameters. The Grassberger–Procaccia test is based upon D, in which only ϵ remains free and unspecified. However, the sampling distribution of D is unknown for stochastic data.

7   The Liapunov exponent test

7.1   *General features of the test*

When there are stochastic shocks within the structure of a system, measures of dimension are sensitive to the amount of noise in the system. An

alternative method of testing for chaos is to compute the dominant Liapunov exponent. Testing for a positive value of that exponent for a bounded
system is equivalent to testing for the sensitivity-to-initial-conditions property of chaos. Hence, testing for positivity of that exponent produces a
direct test for chaos.

Algorithms for estimating the Liapunov exponent fall into two classes:
the Jacobian method (see e.g. Ellner et al. 1991) and the direct method.
In the past, such computations were applied deterministically. In physics
experiments with very large sample sizes and no stochastic shocks internal
to the system, noise in the data can be filtered out (see e.g. Smith 1992)
and the Liapunov exponent computed by one of the two approaches. Recently an estimator became available that is applicable to more modest
sample sizes and to systems containing internal stochastic shocks. The
estimator is presented and explored with simulated and biological data
by Nychka, Ellner, Gallant, and McCaffrey (1992; hereafter NEGM). The
approach proceeds as follows.

Assume that the data $\{x_t\}$ are real-valued and are generated by a nonlinear autoregressive model of the form

$$x_t = f(x_{t-L}, x_{t-2L}, ..., x_{t-dL}) + e_t \tag{7.1}$$

for $1 \le t \le N$, where L is the time-delay parameter and d is the length of
the autoregression. Here f is a smooth unknown function, and $\{e_t\}$ is a
sequence of independent random variables with zero mean and unknown
constant variance. According to Takens's theorem (Eckmann and Ruelle
1985) for dynamical systems, the nonlinear autoregression (7.1) can represent any deterministic chaotic system on an attractor with finite dimension. NEGM fitted f nonparametrically using either a spline or a neural
net. They then computed the Liaponuv exponent from the fitted function, f, using the Jacobian approach.

Based upon the findings of NEGM, we use the neural net approach.
As in their study, we use the feed-forward single hidden-layer networks
with a single output. The neural net approach to nonlinear regression has
a selection parameter q, which equals the number of units in the hidden
layer of the neural net. Hence, in addition to the coefficients of the neural
net, there are three parameters that must be selected in the NEGM approach: q, L, and d. The approach uses a Bayesian information criterion
(BIC) to select these parameters. We use the neural net fit and the BIC
criterion in the same manner used by NEGM. In particular, the value of
the triple (q, L, d) is determined to minimize BIC, while the coefficients
of the neural net are selected to minimize least squares conditional upon
(q, L, d). For more details regarding the neural net fit, see McCaffrey et al.
(1992). For proof of the consistency of the nonparametric function estimator by neural net, see Gallant and White (1981).

In principle, it should be possible to produce a standard error for the Liapunov exponent point estimate, perhaps by bootstrapping. But when noise is large, the properties of such a bootstrapped standard error are not known, and there has not yet been any published research on the computation of a standard error for the NEGM Liapunov exponent estimate.

7.2   Point estimation

In this section we provide a more technical discussion of the NEGM approach to estimation of the maximum Liapunov exponent λ. We begin by producing a state-space representation of (7.1) as follows. Define the vectors

$$X_t = \begin{pmatrix} x_t \\ x_{t-L} \\ \vdots \\ x_{t-dL+L} \end{pmatrix}, \quad F(X_{t-L}) = \begin{pmatrix} f(x_{t-L}, \ldots, x_{t-dL}) \\ x_{t-L} \\ \vdots \\ x_{t-dL+L} \end{pmatrix}, \quad E_t = \begin{pmatrix} e_t \\ 0 \\ \vdots \\ 0 \end{pmatrix}.$$

The state-space representation is

$$X_t = F(X_{t-L}) + E_t. \tag{7.2}$$

Data analyses based on Takens's theorem include the widely used method of "attractor reconstruction in time-delay coordinates" (Schuster 1988). Thus, the nonlinear autoregressive model in (7.1) is a generalization of attractor reconstruction to allow for random perturbations. Most methods of attractor reconstruction are data-intensive, because they rely on the availability of a large number of nearly identical data segments that are separated in time to generate various numerical approximations to the local behavior of the system. The method of McCaffrey et al. (1992) is more efficient in its use of data, because it uses nonparametric statistical methods to approximate f directly.

Ruelle (1989) provided a definition of chaos that extends to noisy dynamic systems such as the nonlinear autoregressive model: A system is chaotic if it exhibits sensitive dependence to initial conditions for all initial conditions. A quantitative measure of the rate at which similar trajectories diverge is the dominant Liapunov exponent, λ. A bounded system with positive λ is one operational definition of chaotic behavior. See NEGM for a discussion of Liapunov exponents that is specific to the nonlinear autoregressive model.

NEGM use a Jacobian-based method to estimate λ through the intermediate step of estimating the individual Jacobian matrices,

$$J_t = \frac{\partial F(X_t)}{\partial X'}.$$

After examining several nonparametric methods, McCaffrey et al. (1992) recommended using either thin plate splines or neural nets to estimate J_t. Here we use neural nets and follow the protocol described in NEGM. Briefly, the method is as follows.

The neural net with q units in the hidden layer is

$$f(X_{t-L}, \theta) = \beta_0 + \sum_{j=1}^{q} \beta_j \psi\left(\gamma_{0j} + \sum_{i=1}^{d} \gamma_{ij} x_{t-Li}\right),$$

where

$$\psi(u) = \frac{u(1 + |u/2|)}{2 + |u| + u^2/2}$$

and where the parameter vector

$$\theta = (\beta_0, \beta_1, ..., \beta_q, \gamma_{01}, \gamma_{11}, \gamma_{21}, ..., \gamma_{d1}, ..., \gamma_{0q}, \gamma_{1q}, \gamma_{2q}, ..., \gamma_{dq})$$

is fit to data by nonlinear least squares. That is, one computes the estimate $\hat{\theta}$ to minimize the sum of squares

$$S(\theta) = \sum_{t=1}^{N} [x_t - f(X_{t-1}, \theta)]^2,$$

and uses

$$\hat{F}(X_t) = \begin{pmatrix} f(X_t, ..., x_{t-dL+L}, \hat{\theta}) \\ x_{t-L} \\ \vdots \\ x_{t-dL+L} \end{pmatrix}$$

to approximate $F(X_t)$.

The surface of $S(\theta)$ is replete with local minima. In view of this, NEGM suggested that one randomly select on the order of 1,000 starting values for θ and iterate each to a local minimum using the nonlinear optimizer NPSOL (Gill et al. 1986) with a lax termination criterion. The 20 best of these are then used as starting values with a stringent termination criterion. The value of $\hat{\theta}$ that corresponds to the smallest $S(\theta)$ of these 20 is selected as the estimate.

Because appropriate values of d, L, and q are unknown, they must be estimated. NEGM recommended selecting that value of the triple (d, L, q) that minimizes the BIC criterion (Schwarz 1978) jointly in (d, L, q, θ), where

$$\text{BIC} = S(\hat{\theta}) + p \log(N);$$

here $p = 1 + q(d+1)$ is the number of elements in θ. As shown by Gallant and White (1992), we can use $\hat{J}_t = \partial \hat{F}(X_t)/\partial X'$ as a nonparametric estimator of J_t when (d, L, q) are selected to minimize BIC. The estimate of the dominant Liapunov exponent is then

$$\hat{\lambda} = \frac{1}{2N} \log|\nu_1(N)|,$$

where $\nu_1(N)$ denotes the largest eigenvalue of the matrix $\hat{T}_N'\hat{T}_N$ and where $\hat{T}_N = \hat{J}_N\hat{J}_{N-1}, ..., \hat{J}_1$.

7.3 Precision

Although the standard error of the estimate $\hat{\lambda}$ is not known, NEGM (1992, p. 422) displayed plots that are informative about precision. One plot illustrates the sensitivity of the estimate of λ to variations in the initial conditions used in estimating the coefficients θ of the neural net and to variations in (L, d). The other plot illustrates the sensitivity of the estimate of λ to variations in (L, d), and also indicates the precision of the point estimate of (L, d). The first plot is an indication of the sensitivity of $\hat{\lambda}$ to variations in θ about the least squares estimate at various settings of (L, d), and the second plot is an indication of the sensitivity of $\hat{\lambda}$ to variations in (L, d) about the BIC estimator of (L, d, q) and of the sensitivity of the BIC level itself to those variations.

In our experiments and comparisons, the procedure for producing the first plot is the following. For each setting of (L, d), where $L = 1, 2, ..., 5$ and $d = 1, 2, ..., 6$, the value of q that minimizes BIC conditional upon (L, d) is found. Let $\hat{q}(L, d)$ be that value. The estimation of θ proceeds by first narrowing down the estimates of that vector to 20 possibilities, through a nested optimization procedure. The one among the 20 that minimized least squares is then selected as the optimum estimate. In the resulting figure, box plots are displayed indicating the range of values of the estimated dominant Liapunov exponent at each setting of (L, d), with q set at $\hat{q}(L, d)$. The range within the box is acquired at each such setting of $(L, d, \hat{q})$ by varying θ over the 20 possibilities for θ attained through the nested iteration. A bar within each box indicates the median of the estimates among the 20 possibilities. The scatter with a box illustrates the numerical stability of recovering a similar estimate of λ when only the starting values of θ are varied. Moving between boxes indicates the sensitivity of the estimate of λ to variations in (L, d).

The procedure for producing the second plot is as follows. At each of the settings of $(L, d, \hat{q}(L, d))$ used in the plot, the value of the BIC criterion and of the Liapunov exponent are computed; the value of BIC is then plotted against λ for each case. Each resulting point in that space appears as a circle in the plot. Within the circle is the setting of L that produced the point. The value of d is not indicated on the plot. Since d as well as L are being varied, the circle that contains a given L is not unique.

The point in the plot that produces the lowest value of BIC among all of the points defines the optimum point estimate of λ, and the circle about that point contains the value of L that produced $\hat{\lambda}$.

8   White's test

Jochen Jungeilges has offered to enter White's neural net test into the competition. The basic idea of White's test involves modeling the elements of the generating process as being generated by an augmented single hidden-layer feed-forward network. Recent simulation studies have produced evidence demonstrating that the test has power against a variety of nonlinear processes. All results using White's test in this competition are obtained using an implementation programmed and applied by Jochen Jungeilges. In the balance of this section we provide a sketch of the neural network test.

Prior to running the neural network test, each time series was plotted and checked for noteworthy observations. The use of graphical techniques, recommended as one of the early steps in an analysis focusing on the linear or nonlinear character of a series, was suppressed, since the task was to arrive at a conclusion only by applying a sole specific testing technology.

The test procedure applied is essentially due to White's (1989a,b) proposed neural network test. Efforts to study the operational characteristics of this test for nonlinearity were undertaken by Lee, White, and Granger (1993) and Jungeilges (1993). These studies demonstrated that the test has appropriate size as well as power against various types of nonlinearity. The version of the test used in the current investigation is equivalent to the version called NEURAL1 by Lee et al. (1993). Details of the algorithm used are given in Jungeilges (1993).

The rationale for White's test can be summarized as follows: Under the hypothesis of linearity in the mean, the theoretical residuals obtained by applying a linear filter to the process (i.e., the affine part of the network) should not be correlated with any measurable function of the history of the process under scrutiny. When carrying out White's test, one correlates the residuals from an affine network with the output generated by the hidden-layer phantom units of a single hidden-layer feed-forward network. White chose an exponential cumulative density function as the measurable test function. The vector of connection strengths associated with the signals arriving at each of the hidden-layer phantom units is chosen at random and independently of the process at hand. This amounts to randomly choosing the direction in which the test looks for nonlinearity. This strategy appears to be a viable way out of the dilemma generated by the fact that the connection strength parameters can be identified only under the alternative of nonlinearity in the means (see e.g. White 1989a and Kuang and White 1991).

In White (1989b) it is pointed out that, under certain assumptions, the parameters of the network need not be estimated. White argued that a procedure involving regression and the extraction of principal components leads to an equivalent test procedure, and showed that the test statistic of the network test is asymptotically equivalent to a function of the multiple correlation between the residuals from the affine network and a low-dimensional representation of the hidden-layer output. See White (1989b), Lee et al. (1993), and Jungeilges (1993). The current investigations utilize the following specification of the test: There are ten hidden units in the phantom layer, and the two largest principal components (after dropping the largest component) are extracted.

The dimension of the affine network (i.e., the order of the AR process) is chosen by a conventional selection criterion. For each series, we choose the order that minimized the Schwarzian Bayesian information criterion (SBIC). This criterion provides asymptotically unbiased order estimates. Alternatives such as Akaike's AIC are known to overestimate the order. In the light of results presented by Theiler and Eubank (1993), it may be preferable to have parsimonious order-selection criteria when testing for nonlinearity. Moreover, Jungeilges (1993) demonstrated that choosing the dimension of the affine part of the network via the SBIC criterion may improve the power of White's test against nonlinear chaotic data-generating processes relative to the power of versions of the test that incorporate alternative selection criteria. The SBIC criterion suggested an AR(1) process for each time series.

9   Kaplan's test

All of the tests described so far are well known among econometricians. Considering the evidence of nonrobustness across sample sizes and tests that we are finding in these comparisons, it may be interesting to look at a newer and less well-known approach. Following the suggestion of researchers at the Santa Fe institute, we decided to introduce into these experiments a test being developed by Daniel Kaplan at the Center for Nonlinear Dynamics (Department of Physiology, McGill University). For details on the method that he advocates, see Kaplan (1993a,b).

10   The data

Two sources of data are being used in these comparisons. One source is simulated data. Since the competition based upon that simulated data is still under way, we cannot reveal the details of those Monte Carlo data.

However, our other comparisons are based upon the use of monetary aggregate data, the sources for which are described next.

The data used in Barnett and Chen (1988a) and Barnett and Hinich (1992, 1993) included Barnett's Divisia monetary aggregates, which provide second-order approximations to the exact monetary aggregates of economic theory, as well as the Federal Reserve's official simple-sum monetary aggregates, which have no known approximation properties relative to the exact theoretical monetary aggregates. The data were used at two levels of monetary aggregation: M1 and M2. We are including both of those data sources, in their monthly growth-rate form, among the data included in the current comparisons. The monthly sample is from February 1969 through February 1985. To investigate robustness with respect to sample size, we are repeating our tests with updated data acquired from the Federal Reserve Bank of St. Louis for the months from January 1960 through December 1990. The backwards extrapolation to the months of the early 1960s probably augments the sample with noisier data than the more recent data, since data from the early 1960s were of lower quality. There are 377 observations in the updated data.

We also are including data with the CE index proposed by Rotemberg et al. (1991). The extended data are used at four levels of monetary aggregation: M1, M2, M3, and M4, where M4 is the broadest of the four aggregates (called "L" by the Federal Reserve).

Because of the sample-size problems that exist in using the testing algorithms produced within the literature on chaos, Barnett and Chen used weekly data. However, some degree of interpolation exists in virtually all governmental sources of weekly data, because not all component variables used in computing the aggregates are available on a weekly basis. For this reason, Barnett and Chen's results were criticized by Ramsey et al. (1988). On the other hand, monthly monetary data are of very high quality and make *no* use of interpolated or splined variables in the generation of the data. In the current comparisons, we are using the monthly data with no splining or interpolation.

As a further check on the conclusions in Barnett and Chen (1988a), we preprocess the data by logarithmic first differencing to acquire growth rates.

11   Conclusions

As a result of the scale of this project, we expect the results to appear in a series of papers rather than in any one publication. Many of the results acquired so far are scheduled to appear in Barnett, Gallant, and Hinich (1995) and Barnett et al. (1995a,b).

REFERENCES

Ashley, R., D. M. Patterson, and M. Hinich (1986), "A Diagnostic Test for Non-linear Serial Dependence in Time Series Fitting Errors," *Journal of Time Series Analysis* 7: 165–78.

Barnett, W. A. (1978), "The User Cost of Money," *Economics Letters* 1: 145–9.
  (1980), "Economic Monetary Aggregates: An Application of Index Number and Aggregation Theory," *Journal of Econometrics* 14: 11–48.
  (1981), *Consumer Demand and Labor Supply: Goods, Monetary Assets, and Time*. Amsterdam: North-Holland.
  (1987), "The Microeconomic Theory of Monetary Aggregation," in W. A. Barnett and K. Singleton (eds.), *New Approaches to Monetary Economics* (Proceedings of the Second International Symposium in Economic Theory and Econometrics). Cambridge University Press, pp. 115–68.
  (1990), "Developments in Monetary Aggregation Theory," *Journal of Policy Modeling* 12: 205–57.

Barnett, W. A., and P. Chen (1986), "Economic Theory as a Generator of Measurable Attractors," *Mondes en Developpement* 14; reprinted in I. Prigogine and M. Sanglier (eds.) (1988), *Laws of Nature and Human Conduct: Specificities and Unifying Themes*. Brussels: G.O.R.D.E.S., pp. 209–24.
  (1988a), "The Aggregation-Theoretic Monetary Aggregates Are Chaotic and Have Strange Attractors: An Econometric Application of Mathematical Chaos," in W. A. Barnett, E. Berndt, and H. White (eds.), *Dynamic Econometric Modeling* (Proceedings of the Third International Symposium in Economic Theory and Econometrics). Cambridge University Press, pp. 199–246.
  (1988b), "Deterministic Chaos and Fractal Attractors as Tools for Nonparametric Dynamical Econometric Inference," *Mathematical Computer Modeling* 10: 275–96.

Barnett, W. A., A. R. Gallant, and M. J. Hinich (1995), "A Comparison of Nonparametric Tests for Chaos," in W. A. Barnett, A. Kirman, and M. Salmon (eds.), *Nonlinear Dynamics and Economics* (Proceedings of the Tenth International Symposium in Economic Theory and Econometrics). Cambridge University Press (forthcoming).

Barnett, W. A., A. R. Gallant, M. J. Hinich, J. A. Jungeilges, D. T. Kaplan, and M. J. Jensen (1995a), "Robustness of Nonlinearity and Chaos Tests to Measurement Error, Inference Method, and Sample Size," *Journal of Economic Behavior and Organization* 27: 301–20.
  (1995b), "A Single-Blind Controlled Competition between Tests for Nonlinearity and Chaos," *Journal of Econometrics* (forthcoming).

Barnett, W. A., and M. J. Hinich (1992), "Empirical Chaotic Dynamics in Economics," *Annals of Operations Research* 37: 1–15.
  (1993), "Has Chaos Been Discovered with Economic Data," in P. Chen and R. Day (eds.), *Evolutionary Dynamics and Nonlinear Economics*. Oxford University Press.

Barnett, W. A., M. J. Hinich, and P. Yue (1991), "Monitoring Monetary Aggregates under Risk Aversion," in M. T. Belongia (ed.), *Monetary Policy on the 75th Anniversary of the Federal Reserve System* (Proceedings of the Fourteenth Annual Economic Policy Conference of the Federal Reserve Bank of St. Louis). Boston: Kluwer.

Barnett, W. A., and A. Serletis (1990), "A Dispersion-Dependency Diagnostic Test for Aggregation Error: With Applications to Monetary Economics and Income Distribution," *Journal of Econometrics* 43: 5–34.

Box, G. E. P., and G. M. Jenkins (1970), *Time Series Analysis – Forecasting and Control*. San Francisco: Holden-Day.

Brillinger, D. R. (1965). "An Introduction to Polyspectrum," *Annals of Mathematical Statistics* 36: 1351–74.

Brock, W. A., and W. D. Dechert (1988), "Theorems on Distinguishing Deterministic from Random Systems," in W. A. Barnett, E. Berndt, and H. White (eds.), *Dynamic Econometric Modeling* (Proceedings of the Third International Symposium in Economic Theory and Econometrics). Cambridge University Press, pp. 247–68.

Brock, W. A., W. D. Dechert, and J. Scheinkman (1986), "A Test for Independence Based on the Correlation Dimension," *Econometric Reviews* (forthcoming).

Brock, W. A., D. A. Hsieh, and B. LeBaron (1991), *Nonlinear Dynamics, Chaos, and Instability: Statistical Theory and Economic Evidence*. Cambridge, MA: MIT Press.

Brockett, P. L., M. J. Hinich, and G. R. Wilson (1987), "Nonlinear and Non-Gaussian Ocean Noise," *Journal of the Acoustical Society of America* 82: 1386–94.

Brockett, P. L., M. J. Hinich, and D. Patterson (1988), "Bispectral-Based Test for the Detection of Gaussianity and Linearity in Time Series," *Journal of the American Statistical Association* 83: 657–64.

Diewert, W. E. (1987), "Exact and Superlative Index Numbers," *Journal of Econometrics* 4: 115–45.

Eckmann, J.-P., and D. Ruelle (1985), "Ergodic Theory of Chaos and Strange Attractors," *Reviews of Modern Physics* 57: 617–56.

El-Gamal, M. (1991), "Non-parametric Estimation of Deterministically Chaotic Systems," *Economic Theory* 1: 147–67.

Ellner, S. A., R. Gallant, D. McCaffrey, and D. Nychka (1991), "Convergence Rates and Data Requirements for Jacobian-Based Estimates of Liapunov Exponents from Data," *Physics Letters A* 153: 357–63.

Gallant, A. R., and H. White (1981), "There Exists a Neural Network That Does Not Make Avoidable Mistakes," in *Proceedings of the Second IEEE International Conference on Neural Networks* (San Diego, 24–27 July). San Diego: SOS Printing, pp. I.657–64.

   (1982), "On Learning the Derivatives of an Unknown Mapping with Multilayer Feedforward Networks," *Neural Networks* 5: 129–38.

Geweke, J. (1989), "Inference and Forecasting for Chaotic Nonlinear Time Series," Discussion Paper no. 89–06, Institute of Statistics and Decision Sciences, Duke University, Durham, NC.

Gill, P. E., W. Murray, M. A. Saunders, and M. H. Wright (1986), "Users Guide for NPSOL (version 4.0): A Fortran Package for Nonlinear Programming," Technical Report no. 86-2, Systems Optimization Laboratory, Stanford University.

Hinich, M. J. (1982), "Testing for Gaussianity and Linearity of a Stationary Time Series," *Journal of Time Series Analysis* 3: 169–76.

Hinich, M. J., and D. Patterson (1985), "Identification of the Coefficients in a Non-Linear Time Series of the Quadratic Type," *Journal of Econometrics* 30: 269–88; reprinted in W. Barnett and R. Gallant (eds.) (1989), *New*

Approaches to Modelling, Specification Selection, and Econometric Inference (Proceedings of the First International Symposium in Economic Theory and Econometrics). Cambridge University Press.

(1989), "Evidence of Nonlinearity in the Trade-by-Trade Stock Market Return Generating Process," in W. Barnett, J. Geweke, and K. Shell (eds.), *Economic Complexity: Chaos, Sunspots, Bubbles, and Nonlinearity* (Proceedings of the Fourth International Symposium in Economic Theory and Econometrics). Cambridge University Press, pp. 383–409.

Hsieh, D., and B. LeBaron (1988), "Finite Sample Properties of the BDS Statistic," mimeo, University of Chicago and University of Wisconsin – Madison.

Hulten, C. R. (1973), "Divisia Index Numbers," *Econometrica* 63: 1017–26.

Jenkins, G., and D. Watts (1968), *Spectral Analysis and Its Applications.* San Francisco: Holden-Day.

Jungeilges, J. A. (1993), "Operational Characteristics of White's Test for Neglected Nonlinearities," working paper, Department of Economics, Washington University in St. Louis, MO.

Kaplan, Daniel T. (1993a), "Analysis of Determinism in the Washington University Time Series," private correspondence, Centre for Nonlinear Dynamics, Department of Physiology, McGill University, Montreal, Quebec.

(1993b), "Exceptional Events as Evidence for Determinism," *Physica D* (forthcoming).

Kuang, C., and H. White (1991), "Artificial Neural Networks: An Econometric Perspective," working paper, Department of Economics and Institute for Neural Computation, University of California at San Diego.

Lee, T. H., H. White, and C. Granger (1993), "Testing for Neglected Nonlinearities in Time Series Models," *Journal of Econometrics* 56: 269–90.

McCaffrey, D. F., S. Ellner, A. R. Gallant, and D. W. Nychka (1992), "Estimating the Lyapunov Exponent of a Chaotic System with Nonparametric Regression," *Journal of the American Statistical Association* 87: 682–95.

Nychka, D., S. Ellner, R. Gallant, and D. McCaffrey (1992), "Finding Chaos in Noisy Systems," *Journal of the Royal Statistical Society B* 54: 399–426.

Pesek, B. P., and T. R. Saving (1967), *Money, Wealth, and Economic Theory.* New York: Macmillan.

Priestley, M. (1981), *Spectral Analysis and Time Series,* vol. 2. New York: Academic Press.

Ramsey, J. B., C. L. Sayers, and P. Rothman (1990), "The Statistical Properties of Dimension Calculations Using Small Data Sets: Some Economic Applications," *International Economic Review* 31: 991–1020.

Rotemberg, J. J. (1991), "Commentary: Monetary Aggregates and Their Uses," in M. T. Belongia (ed.), *Monetary Policy on the 75th Anniversary of the Federal Reserve System* (Proceedings of the Fourteenth Annual Economic Policy Conference of the Federal Reserve Bank of St. Louis). Boston: Kluwer.

Rotemberg, J., J. Driscoll, and J. Poterba (1991), "Money, Output, and Prices: Evidence from a New Monetary Aggregate," Working Paper no. 3326-91-EFA, Sloan School of Management, Massachusetts Institute of Technology, Cambridge.

Ruelle, D. (1989). *Chaotic Evolution and Strange Attractors.* Cambridge University Press.

Scheinkman, J., and B. LeBaron (1989), "Nonlinear Dynamics and GNP Data," in W. Barnett, J. Geweke, and K. Shell (eds.), *Economic Complexity: Chaos, Sunspots, Bubbles, and Nonlinearity* (Proceedings of the Fourth Interna-

346   W. A. Barnett, A. R. Gallant, M. J. Hinich, M. Jensen, & J. Jungeilges

tional Symposium in Economic Theory and Econometrics). Cambridge University Press, pp. 213–27.

Schuster, H. G. (1988), *Deterministic Chaos: An Introduction,* 2nd ed. Weinheim: VCH.

Schwarz, G. (1978), "Estimating the Dimension of a Model," *Annals of Statistics* 6: 461–4.

Smith, R. L. (1992), "Estimating Dimension in Noisy Chaotic Time Series," *Journal of the Royal Statistical Society B* 54: 329–51.

Subba Rao, T., and M. Gabr (1980), "A Test for Linearity of Stationary Time Series," *Journal of Time Series Analysis* 1: 145–58.

Theiler, J., and S. Eubank (1993), "Don't Bleach Chaotic Data," working paper, Center for Nonlinear Studies and Theoretical Division, Los Alamos National Laboratory, NM.

White, H. (1989a), "Some Asymptotic Results for Learning in Single Hidden-Layer Feedforward Network Models," *Journal of the American Statistical Association* 84: 1003–13.

    (1989b), "An Additional Hidden Unit Test for Neglected Nonlinearity in Multilayer Feedforward Networks," in *Proceedings of the International Joint Conference on Neural Networks* (Washington, DC). New York: IEEE Press, pp. II.451–5.

CHAPTER 12

Testing for nonlinearity in the exchange-rate data series: an empirical investigation of the lira/dollar spot rate

Laura Sabani

1   Introduction: testing for nonlinear structure

In the last ten years there has been a growing interest in the study and application of statistical and mathematical methods to detect nonlinearities in asset price and macro data series. The interest is motivated by the realization that an (apparently) totally "random" behavior can be generated by nonlinear *deterministic* systems (chaos).[1] In this paper we apply some of these procedures to test for nonlinearities in the lira/dollar exchange-rate data series.

There are two primary goals of this analysis. The first is to show that the Meese and Rogoff (1983) result does not imply that exchange rates really evolve as random walks, but rather that the random walk is the best *linear* approximation to the nonlinear structure underlying exchange-rate dynamics. The second is to attempt to discriminate between nonlinearities arising through persistence in variance and through persistence in conditional means.

With respect to the first point, there exists plenty of evidence suggesting that exchange rates only apparently behave as random walks. The results can be categorized into two groups: those using tests for nonlinear structure derived from the theory of stochastic nonlinear time series

Financial assistance from the Ministry of the University and of Scientific and Technological Research Ateneo 1990 rif. 05-15-01-006, is gratefully acknowledged. I am greatly indebted to Giancarlo Gandolfo for inspiring this research and to Blake Le Baron for providing the computer program to calculate the BDS statistic. I also wish to thank Alberto Bagnai, who provided the computer algorithms to estimate the ARCH model, and William Barnett for suggesting useful references. It goes without saying that I am responsible for possible deficiencies that might remain.

[1]   For an analysis of much of the mathematical theory dealing with deterministic chaos, see e.g. Barnett and Chen (1988).

analysis (see e.g. Diebold 1988; Diebold and Nerlove 1989; Hsieh 1988, 1989); and those using tests derived from the mathematics of chaos, based on Liapunov exponents and the correlation dimension (see e.g. Hsieh 1989).

These analyses show that the changes in the spot exchange rate (weekly or daily data) are linearly uncorrelated and nonlinearly dependent, where the rejection of the null hypothesis of identical and independent distribution – whose acceptance is fundamental to support the random-walk hypothesis – can be attributed to changing conditional means and/or conditional variances.

Whether the nonlinearities arise through persistence in conditional means (additive dependence) or in conditional variances (multiplicative dependence) is a very important question to sort out. In fact, only in the case of additive dependence can the nonlinearities be exploited to generate improved point predictions, whereas in the case of multiplicative dependence the correct identification of the nonlinear structure can only help to construct superior prediction intervals.

The empirical studies that try to identify which type of nonlinearity is effectively operating in exchange rate data use different methods and often arrive at different conclusions. More precisely, these analyses are unanimous in identifying the presence of multiplicative dependence in all the major dollar spot rates, whereas only a few studies find evidence of additive dependence and even then only for some particular spot rate.

Diebold and Nason (1990) addressed this issue by directly estimating nonparametrically the nonlinear conditional means functions of the ten major dollar spot rates. Their results did not support the presence of additive dependence. Hsieh (1989) attempted to identify the types of nonlinearities by applying to five dollar spot rates a new test designed to discover additive dependence. His results supported the finding that multiplicative dependence accounts for the major part of nonlinearities in the data (Hsieh's study did not consider the lira/dollar exchange rate). By contrast, Diebold and Pauly (1988) found evidence of additive dependence for the yen/dollar, the sterling/dollar, and the mark/dollar exchange rates. They obtained this result by fitting an ARCH-M and a GARCH-M model to the data. Bagnai and Sabani (1992) found evidence of additive dependence by fitting a SGARCH-M model to five lira forward exchange rates (including the lira/dollar forward exchange rate).

In the following two sections we give a brief introduction to the nonlinear stochastic systems used in econometric studies and to the nonlinearity tests that we will implement. Finally, in the last section we present our empirical results.

2   Nonlinear stochastic systems

Let us take a time-series model in state-space form:

$$y_t = Z\alpha_t + d_t + \epsilon_t, \quad \alpha_t = T\alpha_{t-1} + c_t + R\eta_t, \tag{1}$$

where Z, T, and R are (respectively) $N \times m$, $m \times p$, and $m \times p$ matrices, d and c are $N \times 1$ and $m \times 1$ vectors, and ϵ_t and η_t are $N \times 1$ and $p \times 1$ serially uncorrelated disturbances with mean zero and covariance matrices H and Q.

The model is said to be *nonlinear* when either the system matrices depend on past observations or the measurement and the transition equations are functionally nonlinear – that is, when observations in the measurement equation are no longer a linear function of the state vector α_t, or the state vector itself is no longer a linear function of α_{t-1} (Harvey 1989).

The first type of nonlinearity identifies, together with the hypothesis of conditionally Gaussian disturbances, the most important class of nonlinear models: conditionally Gaussian models. Some well-known examples of models belonging to this class are the bilinear model (Granger and Andersen 1978), the threshold autoregressive model (Tong and Lim 1980), the ARCH(p) model (Engle 1982), and the ARCH(p)-M model (Engle, Lilien, and Robins 1987).

Times series generated by these systems all exhibit little or no serial correlation, and yet they are not stochastically independent of past observations. In the first two models, nonlinearities arise through persistence in conditional means; in the ARCH model, nonlinearities are responsible only for persistence in conditional variances; and in the ARCH-M model, nonlinearities are responsible both for persistence in conditional means and conditional variances.

3   Test description

In this section we describe five of the main tests used in the literature.

3.1   *Box–Pierce Q-statistics*

McLeod and Li (1983) showed that the Box–Pierce Q-statistics applied to the squared residuals of an ARMA model (or to the squared raw data) can be used to test for nonlinear dependence. Let $Q_{yy}(k)$ be the statistics for the first k autocorrelations of $\{y_t^2\}$. Under the null hypothesis of absence of serial correlation, it is possible to show that $Q_{yy}(k)$ follows asymptotically a $\chi^2(k)$ distribution (the same as the Box–Pierce statistics).

Finding no serial correlation in raw data and yet important serial correlation in squared data indicates that the sample contains nonlinearity.

3.2   Engle's test for ARCH

Engle (1982) showed that it is possible to test for an ARCH(p) process by regressing the squared residuals of a fitted linear model on an intercept and p own lags. The statistic TR^2, where T is the number of observations and R^2 is the coefficient of multiple correlation obtained from the regression, is distributed as a $\chi^2(p)$ under the null hypothesis of no ARCH(p). The Engle test is clearly related to the Box–Pierce statistic on squared data, since the latter uses the autocorrelation coefficients of $\{y_t^2\}$ while the former uses their partial autocorrelation coefficients.

3.3   BDS test

The BDS statistic was developed by Brock, Dechert, and Scheinkman (1987) to test the null hypothesis of a random independently and identically distributed system. The test makes use of the idea of "correlation integral" introduced by Grassberger and Procaccia (1983) as a method of measuring the fractal dimension of deterministic data. In essence, the correlation integral is a measure of the frequency with which temporal patterns are repeated in the data. Given a time series $\{y_t\}$, the correlation integral $C(\epsilon)$ is defined as

$$C(\epsilon) = \lim_{T \to \infty} \frac{2}{T(T-1)} \sum_{i<j} I_\epsilon(y_i, y_j),$$

where $I_\epsilon(y_i, y_j)$ is an indicator function that equals unity if $\|y_i, y_j\| < \epsilon$ and zero otherwise ($\|\cdot\|$ is the sup-norm).

The correlation integral $C(\epsilon)$ is used to distinguish between chaotic deterministic systems and stochastic systems. Alternatively, Brock et al. (1987) utilized $C(\epsilon)$ to propose a statistic that tests the null of IID (independent and identically distributed) systems and has power against both deterministic chaos and nonlinear stochastic systems. Theorems and proofs regarding the BDS test can be found in Brock et al. (1987, 1990); here, we give only a brief exposition of the ideas underlying the test.

Let $\{y_t\}$ be a sequence of observations that are IID. Consider the m-histories

$$y_t^m = (y_t, y_{t-1}, \ldots, y_{t+m-1}),$$

where m is called the *embedding dimension*. Compute the correlation integral

$$C_m(\epsilon, T) = \frac{2}{T_m(T_m - 1)} \sum_{i<j} I_m(y_i^m, y_j^m),$$

where $T_m = T - m + 1$.

Brock et al. (1987) show that under the null that $\{y_t\}$ is IID,

$$\lim_{T \to \infty} C_m(\epsilon, T) = C_1(\epsilon)^m$$

and

$$\lim_{T \to \infty} \text{Prob}\{|C_m(\epsilon, T) - C_1(\epsilon)^m| < k\} = 1 \quad \text{for all } k \text{ arbitrarily small.}$$

The BDS statistic is defined by

$$\text{BDS}(m, \epsilon) = \frac{\sqrt{T}\{C_m(\epsilon, T) - C_1(\epsilon)^m\}}{\sigma_m(\epsilon, T)},$$

where the denominator $\sigma_m(\epsilon, T)$ is the estimated standard deviation of the numerator $\sqrt{T}\{C_m(\epsilon, T) - C_1(\epsilon)^m\}$. Under the null hypothesis, $\text{BDS}(m, \epsilon)$ has a standard normal limiting distribution.

Once a series has been purged of its linear patterns, large values of the BDS statistic are indications of nonlinear structure.

3.4   Tsay's test

Tsay (1986) proposed a new test for nonlinearity based on the analysis of the correlation of nonlinear terms such as $(y_{t-1}y_{t-2})$ with the residuals of fitted linear models. The test consists of the following steps:

(1) regress y_t on an intercept and M own lags and save the residual vector e_t;
(2) regress the m-dimensional vector $z_t = (y_{t-1}^2, y_{t-1}y_{t-2}, ..., y_{t-M}^2)$, where $m = (M/2)(M+1)$, on $(1, y_{t-1}, ..., y_{t-M})$ and save the residual vectors x_t^i;
(3) regress the vector e_t on the residual vectors x_t^i, $t = M+1, ..., T$, and let $\hat{F}$ be the F ratio of the mean square of regression to the mean square of errors.

Under the null hypothesis that y_t is a linearly filtered series from IID noise, the statistic $\hat{F}$ follows approximately an $F(m, T - M - m - 1)$ distribution.

The Tsay test can be run for any number of cross-terms. In this paper we will compute the Tsay statistic for $M = 2$, $M = 4$, and $M = 6$. Simulations have shown that Tsay's test has good power against bilinear and nonlinear moving-average models, but has low power against ARCH processes (Hsieh 1989, Tsay 1986).

3.5   *Hsieh's test*

Hsieh (1988) proposed a test specifically designed to detect additive dependence. Let e_t be a vector of residuals of a linearly filtered series y_t, and consider such terms as $(e_{t-j}e_{t-i})$, $(y_{t-j}e_{t-i})$, and $(y_{t-j}y_{t-i})$. Multiplicative dependence implies that e_t is not correlated with these terms, whereas additive dependence implies that e_t is correlated with at least some of these terms. The test is implemented as follows.

Step 1:   Define

$$\rho_{eee}(i,j) = E\left(\frac{e_t e_{t-j} e_{t-i}}{\sigma_e^3}\right)$$

and estimate $\rho_{eee}(i,j)$ by the statistic

$$r_{eee}(i,j) = \frac{(1/T)\sum e_t e_{t-j} e_{t-i}}{[(1/T)\sum e_t^2]^{1.5}}.$$

Step 2:   Hsieh (1989) then showed that, under the null of $\rho_{eee}(i,j) = 0$ and other auxiliary assumptions (which can be found in central limit theorems for martingale differences), $r_{eee}(i,j)$ is asymptotically normally distributed with mean zero and variance consistently estimated by

$$W_{ij} = \frac{(1/T)\sum e_t^2 e_{t-j}^2 e_{t-i}^2}{[(1/T)\sum e_t^2]^3};$$

therefore,

$$H = \frac{\sqrt{T}\, r_{eee}(i,j)}{\sqrt{W_{ij}}} \sim N(0,1).$$

Simulations performed by Hsieh (1989) show that this test rejects the null hypothesis of zero third-order moments at approximately the nominal size of 1% for the AR1, MA1, and ARCH models (which have no additive nonlinearity), and rejects the null at about the 99% level for the threshold autoregression model (which does have additive nonlinearity). The rejection rate for a hybrid model like ARCH-M is 64% (the power of the test against ARCH-M increases with the number of observations; the percentage reported here is from a sample of about 2,000 observations).

The Tsay test and the Hsieh test are very similar. However, it is worthwhile to note that even though the Tsay test has low power against ARCH, it still maintains some power because of the hypothesis of IID disturbances. By contrast, the Hsieh test corrects for possible heteroskedasticity and is therefore able to distinguish between additive and multiplicative dependence.

Table 1. *Summary statistics, weekly nominal
lira/dollar exchange-rate changes*

Sample mean	0.001606
Standard deviation	0.013931
Variance	0.000194
Standard deviation of mean	0.000544
T statistic for mean $= 0$	2.977325 (0.002907)
Skewness	0.274899 (0.004162)
Kurtosis	10.578760 (0.000000)
Minimum value	−0.080467
Maximum value	0.108922

Note: Significance levels in parentheses.

4   Data and empirical results

4.1   *Empirical findings on raw and linearly filtered data series*

We analyze the weekly lira/dollar spot exchange rates from the first week
of July 1973 to the third week of December 1985. The sample consists of
656 observations, and all data are interbank closing spot prices (bid side,
Wednesday).[2]

All the tests are implemented on the rates of change of the data series,
calculated by taking the logarithmic differences between successive observations. Our primary concern is to detect nonlinear departure from
white-noise behavior. Table 1 provides summary statistics of the rates-of-
change series.

It is evident from the kurtosis value that the distribution exhibits consistent leptokurtosis (10.5787 versus a zero value for a normal distribution). This finding is consistent with the presence of ARCH effects; in
fact, ARCH processes are characterized by fat-tailed unconditional densities and normal conditional distributions (Diebold 1988).

Table 2 provides the Box–Pierce statistics $Q_y(k)$, $Q_{yc}(k)$, and $Q_{yy}(k)$.
$Q_y(k)$ and $Q_{yc}(k)$ are applied to the raw data, and the difference between
the two arises because the second is adjusted for heteroskedasticity according to Diebold (1988).[3] The $Q_{yy}(k)$ statistic is applied to squared data.

---

[2] Following Diebold (1988), Wednesday was chosen because very few holidays occur on
that day; when they did, we used the observation for the following Thursday.

[3] Diebold showed how the presence of ARCH renders the usual Bartlett standard error
bands overly conservative relative to the main 5% test size, and developed an ARCH-
corrected standard error estimate. This leads to the construction of ARCH-adjusted Box–
Pierce Q-statistics.

354   **Laura Sabani**

Table 2. *Box–Pierce statistics, weekly nominal lira/dollar exchange-rate changes (raw and squared data)*

$Q_y(10)$	13.22914	$Q_{yc}(10)$	5.34229	$Q_{yy}(10)$	115.5899
	(0.21114)		(0.86717)		(0.00000)
$Q_y(20)$	22.04764	$Q_{yc}(20)$	16.84315	$Q_{yy}(20)$	118.0133
	(0.33793)		(0.66313)		(0.00000)
$Q_y(30)$	28.56896	$Q_{yc}(30)$	24.44552	$Q_{yy}(30)$	119.3043
	(0.54031)		(0.75150)		(0.00000)
$Q_y(40)$	34.98652	$Q_{yc}(40)$	31.90524	$Q_{yy}(40)$	120.5487
	(0.69511)		(0.81554)		(0.00000)
$Q_y(50)$	39.19358	$Q_{yc}(50)$	37.07883	$Q_{yy}(50)$	123.0349
	(0.86478)		(0.91240)		(0.00000)
$Q_y(60)$	45.42324	$Q_{yc}(60)$	44.69143	$Q_{yy}(60)$	125.3095
	(0.91844)		(0.92997)		(0.00000)
$Q_y(70)$	58.44095	$Q_{yc}(70)$	50.99776	$Q_{yy}(70)$	193.6212
	(0.83630)		(0.95747)		(0.00000)
$Q_y(80)$	69.45188	$Q_{yc}(80)$	59.81027	$Q_{yy}(80)$	209.2990
	(0.79398)		(0.95548)		(0.00000)
$Q_y(90)$	71.70185	$Q_{yc}(90)$	62.98685	$Q_{yy}(90)$	212.0054
	(0.92197)		(0.98640)		(0.00000)
$Q_y(100)$	73.92589	$Q_{yc}(100)$	65.67162	$Q_{yy}(100)$	214.6829
	(0.97646)		(0.99683)		(0.00000)

Notes: Significance levels in parentheses. $Q_{yc}(k)$ statistics are adjusted for heteroskedasticity.

The Box–Pierce statistics applied to the raw data show no serial correlation, but the $Q_{yy}(k)$ are highly significant for every k. This result corroborates the inference that the data contain nonlinearities. In Table 3 we report the results of Engle's test for ARCH(p), for raw variables as well as for AR(2) and AR(3) residuals. We test for ARCH effects of order $p = 1, 4, 6, 9$. The existence of strong ARCH effects is clear (all the statistics are highly significant). However, this test is of little use for determining the appropriate order of the ARCH process, since it tests the null hypothesis that $\alpha_0, \alpha_1, ..., \alpha_p$ are jointly zero.

Table 4 reports the BDS values, which indicate substantial nonlinear dependence in the data. Following Hsieh (1989) and Hsieh and Le Baron (1988), we report the BDS results for values of the embedding dimension from 2 to 6, and choose values of ϵ between 0.5 and 2 times the standard deviation divided by the spread of the data (σ/s). When the number of observations exceeds 600, we use the standard normal tables to assess

Table 3. *Engle's test, weekly nominal lira/dollar exchange-rate changes*

	Raw data	AR(2) residuals	AR(3) residuals
ARCH(1)	45.19200 (0.00000)	45.46390 (0.00000)	46.23400 (0.00000)
ARCH(4)	49.15700 (0.00000)	49.3953 (0.00000)	49.90870 (0.00000)
ARCH(6)	49.30840 (0.00000)	49.46120 (0.00000)	49.87120 (0.00000)
ARCH(9)	97.91420 (0.00000)	99.21464 (0.00000)	98.69407 (0.00000)

Note: Significance levels in parentheses.

Table 4. *BDS statistics (raw data)*

$\epsilon s/\sigma$	m	BDS
0.5	2	10.647
0.5	3	14.985
0.5	4	20.506
0.5	5	29.242
0.5	6	44.819
1.0	2	7.584
1.0	3	10.795
1.0	4	13.209
1.0	5	15.024
1.0	6	17.390
1.5	2	6.158
1.5	3	8.277
1.5	4	9.882
1.5	5	10.620
1.5	6	11.204
2.0	2	6.673
2.0	3	7.891
2.0	4	8.679
2.0	5	8.837
2.0	6	8.894

Note: All BDS values are significant at the 1% level.

Table 5. *Tsay's test, weekly nominal
lira/dollar exchange-rate changes*

$M = 2$, $F(3,649)$	2.667086
	(0.0468782)
$M = 3$, $F(6,647)$	1.397396
	(0.2131561)
$M = 4$, $F(10,645)$	0.9281840
	(0.5064418)

Note: Significance levels in parentheses.

Table 6. *Hsieh's test, weekly nominal
lira/dollar exchange-rate changes*

$H(1,1)$	0.00290	$H(2,2)$	−0.28671
	(0.99768)		(0.77433)
$H(1,2)$	0.23482	$H(2,3)$	0.02418
	(0.81434)		(0.98070)
$H(1,3)$	0.00392	$H(3,3)$	0.05498
	(0.99687)		(0.95616)

Note: Significance levels in parentheses.

significance, since the small-sample properties become important only for sample sizes less than 500 (Hsieh and Le Baron 1988).

The results of the Tsay test are reported in Table 5. It is interesting that the test is able to detect nonlinearities only for $M = 2$ (5% significance level); for $M = 3$ and $M = 4$, the null hypothesis of no nonlinearities is accepted.

This first set of results allows us to say that the weekly lira/dollar exchange-rate changes are not independent of past changes, and that the dependence is not linear. The presence of multiplicative dependence (ARCH effects) is confirmed, whereas the results of Tsay's test, which has low power against ARCH, support the hypothesis that additive dependence – if any – accounts for only a small part of the nonlinearities in the data.

In order to check this hypothesis we ran the Hsieh test. Table 6 reports the results obtained by applying the test to the residuals from an AR(3) autoregression model. None of the coefficients computed are significant at the 10% level. The results do not change when varying the identification procedure (AR(2) or AR(4)) or when using the raw data (these findings are not reported in the table).

Table 7. *Maximum likelihood estimation results for heteroskedasticity coefficients*

Parameter	Estimate
α_0	0.0000426
	(2.4762)
α_1	0.35202
	(3.6240)
LL = 1930.71289	

Notes: T statistics in parentheses. LL = maximum value of Log-likelihood function.

4.2   *Empirical findings on standardized data series*

In this section we will concentrate on estimating conditional heteroskedasticity using Engle's (1982) ARCH model in order to obtain a standardized data series. We will then apply the nonlinearity tests on this data series in order to ascertain the presence of residual nonlinearity once ARCH effects[4] are allowed for.

We estimated a simple ARCH(9) model specified as follows:

$$y_t = \epsilon_t,$$

$$h_t = \alpha_0 + \alpha_1(0.5\epsilon_{t-1}^2 + 0.45\epsilon_{t-2}^2 + \cdots + 0.1\epsilon_{t-9}^2),$$

$$\epsilon_t|_{(\epsilon_{t-1}, ..., \epsilon_{t-9})} \sim N(0, h_t),$$

where y_t is the logarithmic grow rate of the exchange rate and h_t is the conditional variance.

We constrained the squared innovations coefficients to be linearly declining. This accommodates the basic intuition of the ARCH model, which is that "high" volatility today must be followed by "high" volatility tomorrow and vice versa (Engle 1982, Diebold 1988). Following Engle (1982), we performed a maximum likelihood estimation with the method of scoring, which involves an iterative sequence of least squares regressions on the transformed variable.

The estimates of the linearly constrained model are given in Table 7. After estimation, we performed diagnostic tests on the standardized data series $z_t = y_t/\sqrt{\hat{h}_t}$, where $\hat{h}_t$ is the estimated variance. Table 8 reports the

---

[4] See Barnett and Hinich (1992) for a critical discussion of the methodology used here to detect residual nonlinearity.

Table 8. *Box–Pierce statistics, weekly nominal lira/dollar exchange-rate changes (standardized data)*

$Q_z(10)$	20.20950 (0.02733)	$Q_{zz}(10)$	3.26761 (0.97440)
$Q_z(20)$	29.73853 (0.07420)	$Q_{zz}(20)$	5.12578 (0.99966)
$Q_z(30)$	37.33097 (0.16769)	$Q_{zz}(30)$	6.98801 (0.99999)
$Q_z(40)$	43.87940 (0.31047)	$Q_{zz}(40)$	8.82660 (1.00000)
$Q_z(50)$	47.05173 (0.59242)	$Q_{zz}(50)$	12.37934 (1.00000)
$Q_z(60)$	56.93863 (0.58830)	$Q_{zz}(60)$	26.45850 (0.99994)
$Q_z(70)$	66.1631 (0.60786)	$Q_{zz}(70)$	73.71384 (0.68837)
$Q_z(80)$	69.72767 (0.78709)	$Q_{zz}(80)$	65.58074 (0.87760)
$Q_z(90)$	73.20888 (0.90122)	$Q_{zz}(90)$	66.28553 (0.97136)
$Q_z(100)$	77.88709 (0.95036)	$Q_{zz}(100)$	71.56510 (0.98583)

Note: Significance levels in parentheses.

$Q_z(k)$ and the $Q_{zz}(k)$ statistics. As expected, the squared standardized data are uncorrelated. The $Q_z(k)$ detect little serial correlation (only $Q_z(10)$ is significant at the 5% level).

These two tests support the hypothesis that an ARCH(9) process fits our data. Nonetheless, we then added the Tsay test and the BDS test. It is clear from Table 9 that the Tsay test still finds evidence of nonlinear dependence at $M = 2$. With respect to the BDS test, the results reported in Table 10 clearly show that allowing for conditional heteroskedasticity lowers all the BDS values. However, we still find evidence of nonlinearity since the null hypothesis of an IID system can be rejected at the 1% level for each value of the embedding dimension when ϵ ranges from 0.5 to 1.5 times σ/s.

These results lead us to conjecture that nonlinearities may be present in conditional means other than conditional variances. Although this inference contrasts with the results of Hsieh's test, it must be recalled that

Table 9. *Tsay's test, weekly nominal*
lira/dollar exchange-rate changes
(standardized data)

$M = 2$, $F(3,640)$	2.720179
	(0.04368)
$M = 3$, $F(6,636)$	1.48360
	(0.18020)
$M = 4$, $F(10,631)$	1.106398
	(0.35460)

Note: Significance levels in parentheses.

Table 10. *BDS statistics*
(standardized data)

$\epsilon s/\sigma$	m	BDS
0.5	2	5.887
0.5	3	8.178
0.5	4	11.327
0.5	5	16.542
0.5	6	25.793
1.0	2	4.624
1.0	3	5.799
1.0	4	6.416
1.0	5	6.704
1.0	6	7.222
1.5	2	2.755
1.5	3	3.887
1.5	4	4.287
1.5	5	4.033
1.5	6	3.699
2.0	2	1.639
2.0	3	2.293
2.0	4	2.372
2.0	5	1.979
2.0	6	1.534

Note: All BDS values for ϵ ranging
from 0.5 to 1.5 times σ/s are significant at the 1% level.

this test has low power against such hybrid models as ARCH-M and GARCH-M. Therefore, it is probable that an ARCH-M or a GARCH-M model may fit the data series sufficiently well.

5   Conclusion

The nonlinearity tests that we have applied to the lira/dollar exchange-rate data series find evidence of nonlinearity. This evidence points to the presence of the stronger form of nonlinearity (additive dependence) as well as the weaker form (multiplicative dependence). This implies that by enlarging the class of models used to describe exchange-rate behavior to include nonlinear models, it would be possible to generate improved point predictions. The precise identification of the functional form of nonlinearity in the data is the concern of our ongoing research.[5]

REFERENCES

Bagnai, A., and L. Sabani (1992), "Mercato dei cambi a termine e premio per il rischio: una applicazione del modello SGARCH-M," *Quaderni di Econometria e Statistica* 14: 15–25.

Barnett, W. A., and P. Chen (1988), "The Aggregation-Theoretic Monetary Aggregates Are Chaotic and Have Strange Attractors: An Econometric Application of Mathematical Chaos," in W. Barnett, E. Berndt, and H. White (eds.), *Dynamic Econometric Modeling* (Proceedings of the Third International Symposium in Economic Theory and Econometrics). Cambridge University Press, pp. 199–245.

Barnett, W. A., and M. J. Hinich (1992), "Empirical Chaotic Dynamics in Economics," *Annals of Operation Research* 37: 1–15.

Brock, D., W. D. Dechert, and J. Scheinkman (1987), "A Test for Independence Based on the Correlation Dimension," unpublished manuscript, Department of Economics, University of Wisconsin, Madison.

Brock, D., W. D. Dechert, J. Scheinkman, and B. Le Baron (1990), "A Test for Independence Based on the Correlation Dimension," unpublished manuscript, Graduate School of Business, University of Chicago.

Diebold, F. X. (1988), *Empirical Modelling of Exchange Rate Dynamics.* Springer-Verlag, New York.

Diebold, F. X., and J. Nason (1990), "Nonparametric Exchange Rate Predictions," *Journal of International Economics* 28: 315–32.

Diebold, F. X., and M. Nerlove (1989), "The Dynamics of Exchange Rate Volatility: A Multivariate Latent Factor ARCH Model," *Journal of Applied Econometrics* 4: 1–22.

Diebold, F. X., and P. Pauly (1988), "Endogenous Risk in a Rational Expectations Portfolio Balance Model of DM/$ Rate," *European Economic Review* 32: 27–54.

[5] In Gandolfo, Padoan, and Sabani (1991), the lira/dollar exchange rate was estimated using a general nonlinear disequilibrium macrodynamic model of the Italian economy. The model produced forecasts that outperformed those of the benchmark random walk.

Engle, R. (1982), "Autoregressive Conditional Heteroskedasticity with Estimates of the Variance of U.K. Inflation," *Econometrica* 50: 987–1007.

Engle, R., D. M. Lilien, and R. P. Robins (1987), "Estimating Time Varying Risk Premium in the Term Structure: the ARCH-M Model," *Econometrica* 55: 391–407.

Gandolfo, G., P. C. Padoan, and L. Sabani (1991), "Exchange Rates: Linear or Not Linear?" Working Paper no. 6, Centro Interdipartimentale di Economia Internazionale, Roma.

Granger, C. W. J., and A. P. Andersen (1978), *Introduction to Bilinear Models*. Göttingen: Vandehoeck & Ruprecht.

Grassberger, P., and I. Procaccia (1983), "Measuring the Strangeness of Strange Attractors," *Physica D* 9: 189.

Harvey, A. C. (1989), *Forecasting Structural Time Series Models and the Kalman Filter*. Cambridge University Press.

Hsieh, D. A. (1988), "The Statistical Properties of Daily Foreign Exchange Rates: 1974–83," *Journal for International Economics* 24: 129–45.

(1989), "Testing for Nonlinear Dependence in Foreign Exchange Rates: 1973–83," *Journal of Business* 2: 339–68.

Hsieh, D. A., and B. Le Baron (1988), "Small Sample Properties of the BDS Statistic," Graduate School of Business, University of Chicago.

McLeod, A., and W. Li (1983), "Diagnostic Checking of ARMA Time Series Models Using Squared Residuals Autocorrelations," *Journal of Time Series Analysis* 4: 269–73.

Meese, R. A., and K. Rogoff (1983), "Empirical Exchange Rate Models of the Seventies: Do They Fit the Sample?" *Journal of International Economics* 14: 3–24.

Tong, H., and K. Lim (1980), "Threshold Autoregression, Limit Cycles and Cyclical Data," *Journal of the Royal Statistical Society B* 42: 245–92.

Tsay, R. (1986), "Nonlinearity Tests for Time Series," *Biometrika* 73: 461–66.

PART V

Rationing and disequilibrium dynamics

CHAPTER 13

Dynamic stochastic choice modeling of disequilibrium in an economy

B. Dejon, F. Graef, H.-J. Meier, & J. Novotný

1   Introduction

The goal of this paper is to present a flexible formal framework for the dynamics of stochastic choice processes, together with an application to disequilibrium modeling of a production and exchange economy. Our conceptual starting point is random-utility maximization by economic agents. However, we stress that – after proper modification of the deterministic part of the utility functions of the economic agents – random-utility maximization may be cast as an arbitrage problem with respect to the properly modified utility functions (see Sections 2.3.3 and 2.3.4). The random-utility maximization paradigm will be put to work first in a static context (Section 2) and then in a dynamic one (Section 3). In each case, random-utility maximization is effected by having the economic agents behave as arbitrageurs of the properly modified utility values of the available choice alternatives.

Within a production and exchange economy, the choice alternatives of the economic agents typically consist of tuples of price–quantity pairs to be chosen at the markets for labor and for capital services, as well as at the markets for consumption and for capital goods. This, by the way, means that we model economic agents not as price takers but rather as price and quantity setters. (The technical device that permits us to do so consists of introducing a rationing penalty incurred by an economic agent for any price level at which he or she is being rationed. Typically, demanders find themselves rationed at the lower price levels of a market,

We should like to express our sincere thanks to Professor M. Neumann (University of Erlangen-Nürnberg) for his continued interest in our work over the past years, and we gratefully acknowledge assistance by Dr. G. Leha (University of Passau) at early attempts to formalize our heuristic arguments concerning "nonlinear" Markov chains.

while the upper price levels are the ones at which suppliers are generically rationed.)

The mathematical background of the dynamics of stochastic choice processes consists of what we propose to call *nonlinear* Markov chains (Section 3.3), a subject somewhat neglected in probability theory even though there exist early contributions by eminent workers in the field (see Section 3.4(iii)). Working with nonlinear Markov chains enables us to keep the state spaces of our Markov chains – one chain per population of agents dealt with – relatively small: They contain only the action sets of respective populations. This may be contrasted to a second approach, originating in interacting particle physics, which adopts the (generically extremely large) set of all possible combinations of macroconfigurations (see Section 2.4) of the various populations as the state space of some "linear"[1] (as we would say) Markov chain. As a consequence, however, one must pass on to mean-value equations in order to achieve manageable orders of differential equation systems (see Section 3.4(iii)). Another argument in favor of modeling dynamic stochastic choice processes as nonlinear Markov chains is that such chains provide an apparently novel theoretical basis for panel data analysis and for Monte Carlo simulations of dynamic stochastic choice processes.

2   Static stochastic choice modeling: a brief overview

2.1   *Populations, action sets, and flow states*

A stochastic choice system consists, to start with, of finitely many agents grouped by behaviorally nearly homogeneous populations, such as producers, private households, investors, and so on. In the sequel, the set of all these populations will be designated by N.

To each population n in N there is associated a nonnegative number, P^n, the *size* of the population (P^n may change with time and, for technical reasons, need not be an integer). In addition, for each population n there is a finite set, A^n, of *actions* among which every agent of population n is supposed to make a choice (which may well be revised as time goes on). Let $\pi^n(a, t)$ in $[0, 1]$ designate the probability that an agent of population n practices action a at time t. The product

$$P^n(a, t) := P^n(t)\pi^n(a, t) \tag{1}$$

will be called the *occupation number* of action a, and the tuple

$$\mathbf{P}(t) := (P^n(a, t))_{n \in N, a \in A^n}$$

---

[1] "Linear" Markov chains (time homogeneous or inhomogeneous) are the ones commonly treated in the textbook literature.

of all occupation numbers is called the *distribution* or *flow state,* at time t, of the stochastic choice process. The designation "flow state" is self-explanatory in an application like transportation analysis, where occupation numbers $P^n(a, t)$ typically denote numbers of trips on "route" a. In pure economics, the flow is of a more indirect nature: For example, households make choices from sets of alternative consumption plans (including prices, since households are being modeled as price and quantity setters) and thereby cause a flow of values (if one thinks, e.g., in terms of a circular-flow representation of an economy).

2.2 Stocks and stock and flow states

In a number of stochastic choice models, and especially in economies, stocks of certain storable goods play a sizable role. Therefore, to the previously introduced constitutive elements of a stochastic choice model we add a vector of *stocks,*

$$\mathbf{B}(t) := (B_g(t))_{g \in GS},$$

where GS denotes the set of all relevant storable goods. These stocks are related to flows by a system of first-order differential equations:

$$\mathbf{B}'(t) = \Psi(\mathbf{B}(t), \mathbf{P}(t)). \tag{2}$$

More explicitly,

$$B_g'(t) = G_g(\mathbf{P}(t)) - \rho_g B_g(t), \quad g \in GS,$$

is the equation of stock balances of the model, where ρ_g designates the depreciation rate of good g and $G_g(\mathbf{P}(t))$ is an expression that is typically (piecewise) linear in the occupation numbers $P^n(a, t)$. The pair $(\mathbf{B}(t), \mathbf{P}(t))$ will be called the *stock and flow state,* at time t, of the dynamic stochastic choice system.

Let $(\mathbf{B}(\leq t), \mathbf{P}(\leq t))$ designate the stock and flow history, up to and including time t, of the system. In later utility functions we shall, in general, not make use of the full information contained in $(\mathbf{B}(\leq t), \mathbf{P}(\leq t))$, but only of some aggregate information about $(\mathbf{B}(\leq t), \mathbf{P}(\leq t))$ that we shall designate by $\mathbf{F}_t$. For the time being, there is no need to spell out in any more detail how $\mathbf{F}_t$ is obtained from $(\mathbf{B}(\leq t), \mathbf{P}(\leq t))$.

2.3 Random utility and desired flow states

2.3.1 Basic notions and assumptions
Many authors in the field start from the assumption that all agents i in all populations n of a stochastic choice system exhibit utility maximizing

behavior, guided by some more-or-less conscious (individual) *utility vector* $u_i^n(\cdot; F_t, \Xi): A^n \to \Re$ that depends parametrically on aggregate information F_t as well as on some unobserved set of parameters Ξ. Part of the unobserved parameters may derive from the personal history of agent i. The individual utility vectors are supposed to form a random sample from some random (utility) vector $u^n(\cdot; F_t)$.

We imagine that the agents of the various populations, or at least many of them, nearly continually re-evaluate their actions and form beliefs about which of the available actions appear to be optimal under prevailing conditions. The result of this process is modeled by desired distributions or *desired flow states*, $\tilde{P}(F_t) := (\tilde{P}^n(a; F_t))_{n \in N, a \in A^n}$, with

$$\tilde{P}^n(a; F_t) := P^n(t) \, \mathrm{pr}\{u^n(a; F_t) \geq u^n(a'; F_t) \, \forall a' \in A^n\}. \tag{3}$$

Here $\mathrm{pr}\{\cdots\}$ denotes the probability of event $\{\cdots\}$.

The number $\tilde{P}^n(a; F_t)$ may be interpreted as (an approximation to) the number of votes that may be obtained by action a from the agents of population n if each agent i votes for an action that i considers optimal under the prevailing conditions. In Section 3, when formulating dynamic laws of behavior, we go somewhat further and interpret $\tilde{P}^n(a; F_t)$ as (an approximation to) the number of agents in population n that *plan* to perform action a (somewhere in the not-too-distant future).

With regard to the random-utility vector $u^n(\cdot; F_t)$, most authors make the following assumption.

Additive random-utility assumption. For each population n and each action a in A^n,

$$u^n(a; F_t) = u^n(a; F_t) + \epsilon^n(a), \tag{4}$$

where $u^n(\cdot; F_t)$ is a deterministic vector and the randomness of u^n is absorbed in the random vector ϵ^n.

In this context, $u^n(\cdot; F_t)$ is typically called the *mean* or *systematic* or *deterministic utility* vector of population n, while $\epsilon^n(\cdot)$ is said to be the *random utility* part.

2.3.2   *Special case: multinomial logit*
For a particular class of random-utility vectors, the desired distributions $\tilde{P}^n(\cdot; F_t)$ may be calculated explicitly. Under the additive random-utility assumption just stated, let us make in addition the following.

IIDG assumption. For each population n, the random variables $\epsilon^n(a)$ for a in A^n are independent and identically Gumbel distributed, with dispersion parameter $\lambda^n > 0$.[2]

---

[2] That is, their common distribution function is $F(x) = \exp[-\exp(-x/\lambda^n)]$.

Then we obtain the following celebrated formula.

Multinomial logit formula.

$$\tilde{P}^n(a; \mathbf{F}_t) = C^n \exp[u^n(a; \mathbf{F}_t)/\lambda^n],^3 \tag{5}$$

where C^n is a normalizing factor,

$$C^n = \frac{P^n(t)}{\Sigma_a \exp[u^n(a; \mathbf{F}_t)/\lambda^n]}.$$

2.3.3   An equivalent arbitrage problem: logit arbitrage
Subsequent developments will be strongly motivated by the fact that the multinomial logit formula may be obtained as the solution of the following problem.

Logit arbitrage problem.   For each population n, determine the distribution $(\tilde{P}^n(a))_{a \in A^n}$ (of votes) that satisfies:

(a)   the *balance equation*

$$P^n(t) = \Sigma_{a \in A^n} \tilde{P}^n(a);$$

as well as

(b)   the following *arbitrage condition*: The *logitized mean utility* of action a,

$$\hat{u}^n(a; \mathbf{F}_t) := u^n(a; \mathbf{F}_t) - \lambda^n \ln \tilde{P}^n(a), \tag{6}$$

should be the same for all $a \in A^n$; that is, there should be some real $\tilde{V}^n$ (say) such that

$$u^n(a; \mathbf{F}_t) - \lambda^n \ln \tilde{P}^n(a) = \tilde{V}^n \quad \forall a \in A^n. \tag{7}$$

Equivalently (with $\gamma^n := 1/\lambda^n$), the problem may be stated as follows: For each population n, determine $\tilde{W}^n = \gamma^n \tilde{V}^n$ such that

$$\gamma^n u^n(a; \mathbf{F}_t) - \ln \tilde{P}^n(a) = \tilde{W}^n \quad \forall a \in A^n. \tag{8}$$

Solving (7) for $\tilde{P}^n(a)$, one obtains the multinomial logit formula (5) with $C^n = \exp(-\tilde{V}^n/\lambda^n)$. Hence C^n (and thereby $\tilde{V}^n$) are readily calculated by inserting the expression just obtained for $\tilde{P}^n(a)$ into the balance equation given in (a).

Terminology. $\tilde{V}^n$ is called the *arbitrage value* (or *equilibrated value*) of the logitized mean utility vector $(\hat{u}^n(a; \mathbf{F}_t))_{a \in A^n}$.

The arbitrage condition (6) is frequently expressed by the requirement that no arbitrage opportunities persist. We should emphasize here that

---

[3] See e.g. McFadden (1978) or Anderson, de Palma, and Thisse (1992).

our intention is not to insinuate that economic agents, when allocating their votes to the various actions available, would think in terms of arbitrage. On the contrary, we want to stress that the economic agents being modeled as solvers of a logit arbitrage problem may in reality be (and typically are) simply random-utility maximizers.

2.3.4   Nonlogit arbitrage

In the arbitrage condition (7), replacing the function $\tilde{P}^n(a) \mapsto \lambda^n \ln \tilde{P}^n(a)$ with some other monotonic increasing function $h^n(\tilde{P}^n(a))$ of $\tilde{P}^n(a)$ results in what may be called a *nonlogit arbitrage problem*. More flexibly, one may even work with functions $h_a^n(\cdot)$ that depend on the various actions $a \in A^n$. In Section 3, which concerns the dynamics of stochastic choice processes, we shall deal with expressions of the type

$$h_a^n(\tilde{P}^n(a)) := \alpha \ln(\tilde{P}^n(a)/\hat{P}^n(a)) \tag{9}$$

(cf. (20)), with the denominator (here, $\hat{P}^n(a)$ for $a \in A^n$) a given a priori distribution of population n across its action set and where $\hat{P}^n(a) > 0$ for all a. This yields the following.

Arbitrage problem with prior information.   For population n, determine the distribution $(\tilde{P}^n(a))_{a \in A^n}$ that satisfies

(a)   the *balance equation*

$$P^n(t) = \Sigma_{a \in A^n} \tilde{P}^n(a),$$

as well as

(b)   the *prior information arbitrage condition*:

$$u^n(a; \mathbf{F}_t) - \lambda^n \ln(\tilde{P}^n(a)/\hat{P}^n(a)) = \tilde{V}^n \quad \forall a \in A^n, \tag{10}$$

for some properly chosen constant $\tilde{V}^n$.

Because

$$u^n(a; \mathbf{F}_t) - \lambda^n \ln(\tilde{P}^n(a)/\hat{P}^n(a)) = u^n(a; \mathbf{F}_t) + \lambda^n \ln \hat{P}^n(a) - \lambda^n \ln \tilde{P}^n(a),$$

the prior information arbitrage problem with respect to the mean utility vector $(u^n(a; \mathbf{F}_t))_{a \in A^n}$ may be viewed as a logit arbitrage problem with respect to the modified mean utility vector $(u^n(a; \mathbf{F}_t) + \lambda^n \ln \hat{P}^n(a))_{a \in A^n}$. Therefore, when we model (in Section 3) the movers of the various populations of economic agents as solvers of prior information arbitrage problems, we imagine those movers to be random-utility maximizers.

Finally, let us draw attention to the following: For positive values, the larger is λ^n, the closer is the solution $(\tilde{P}^n(a))_{a \in A^n}$ of the previous prior information arbitrage problem to the a priori distribution $(\hat{P}^n(a))_{a \in A^n}$. For small values of λ^n, the distribution $(\tilde{P}^n(a))_{a \in A^n}$ will be heavily concentrated at the actions a for which the mean utility $u^n(a; F_t)$ is maximal.

2.4   *Equilibrium*

Definition.   Consider some stochastic choice model

$$(N, (A^n)_{n \in N}, (u^n(\cdot, \cdot))_{n \in N}),$$

frequently together with some vector **B** of stocks, and in any case together with a set $\mathfrak{F}$ that comprises all possible information vectors **F** (see Section 2.2). The couple $(\mathbf{P}, \mathbf{F})$ of a flow state **P** and an information vector **F** is said to constitute a *stochastic flow equilibrium* if

$$\tilde{\mathbf{P}}(\mathbf{F}) = \mathbf{P}; \tag{11}$$

$(\mathbf{B}, \mathbf{P}, \mathbf{F})$ is called a *stochastic stock and flow equilibrium* if

$$\tilde{\mathbf{P}}(\mathbf{F}) = \mathbf{P} \quad \text{and} \quad \Psi(\mathbf{B}, \mathbf{P}) = 0 \qquad \text{(cf. (2)).} \tag{12}$$

Note: For a stochastic choice system that is evolving in time, a stochastic (stock and) flow equilibrium is said to *prevail* at time t if $(\mathbf{P}(t), \mathbf{F}_t)$ is a stochastic flow equilibrium or (respectively) if $(\mathbf{B}(t), \mathbf{P}(t), \mathbf{F}_t)$ is a stochastic stock and flow equilibrium, where $0 \le t \le +\infty$. The simplest and frequently considered special case is the one where $\mathbf{F}_t = \mathbf{P}(t)$ or $\mathbf{F}_t = (\mathbf{B}(t), \mathbf{P}(t))$, respectively. (This is the case where, at any time t, economic agents form their utility judgments on the basis of information only about the current state of the system.) In this case, by the way, one may simply speak of $\mathbf{P}(t)$ as a stochastic flow equilibrium, or (respectively) of $(\mathbf{B}(t), \mathbf{P}(t))$ as a stochastic stock and flow equilibrium, prevailing at t.

Microlevel aspects

A *microconfiguration* of a system $(n, A^n)_{n \in N}$ of populations n, with sizes P^n that are integers and with respective choice sets A^n, is a family of maps

$$\text{cfg} = (\text{cfg}^n : n \to A^n)_{n \in N}$$

assigning to each economic agent i of any population n some particular action $a \in A^n$.

The *macroconfiguration* pertaining to some given microconfiguration cfg is

$$\text{CFG}(\text{cfg}) := (Z^n(a))_{n \in N, a \in A^n},$$

where $Z^n(a) :=$ number of $i \in n$ with $\text{cfg}^n(i) = a$. In other words, CFG(cfg) is a listing, for each action available to a population, of the number of agents practicing that action; cfg is said to be a *realization* of CFG(cfg).

We call a microconfiguration cfg a *microequilibrium* if each agent i of any population n considers the current action $cfg^n(i)$ to be optimal by his or her current individual utility vector, $\mathbf{u}_i^n(\cdot; \mathbf{F}_t, \Xi)$. A macroconfiguration is called a *macroequilibrium* if at least one of its realizations constitutes a microequilibrium.

The notion of a macroequilibrium is the proper analog, on this level of analysis, to the preceding notion of a stochastic flow equilibrium. More precisely, this is so whenever the parameter sets $\mathbf{F}_t$ and Ξ, entering the individual utility vectors $\mathbf{u}_i^n(\cdot; \mathbf{F}_t, \Xi)$, depend only on macroconfigurations (present or past) and not on any microconfigurational information. In that situation, let CFG be some macroequilibrium and cfg any realization of CFG. Then CFG is obtainable as the result of a voting process, where each agent $i \in n$ gives his or her vote to an action $a \in A^n$ that is optimal under $\mathbf{u}_i^n(\cdot; \mathbf{F}_t, \Xi)$. (If cfg_0 is a realization of CFG that constitutes a microequilibrium, then each agent $i \in n$ in the microconfiguration cfg may, e.g., vote for the action $cfg_0(i)$.)

2.5   *Notes and references*

(i) A review of early work on random utility, starting from its beginnings in the field of psychology (see Thurstone 1927), may be found in Luce and Suppes (1965). In the seventies and eighties, the random-utility approach found widespread applications in the realms of urban and regional economics; see for example Ben-Akiva and Lerman (1989), to mention but one of the numerous contributions in this field. An application of random utility in the context of product differentiation is Anderson et al. (1992).

(ii) The logit arbitrage problem, for any one population n, constitutes a (first-order) necessary and sufficient optimality condition of the maximum problem

$$\max\{\textstyle\sum_{a\in A^n}[u^n(a; \mathbf{F}_t)\tilde{P}^n(a) - \lambda^n \tilde{P}^n(a)\ln\tilde{P}^n(a)]\,|$$
$$\tilde{P}^n(a) \geq 0 \text{ and } \textstyle\sum_{a\in A^n}\tilde{P}^n(a) = P^n(t)\},$$

and, after some minor re-arrangement of terms, also of the following maximum problem:

$$\max\{\textstyle\sum_{a\in A^n}[-\tilde{P}^n(a)\ln\tilde{P}^n(a)]\,|\,\tilde{P}^n(a) \geq 0, \sum_{a\in A^n}\tilde{P}^n(a) = P^n(t),$$
$$\text{and } \textstyle\sum_{a\in A^n}u^n(a; \mathbf{F}_t)\tilde{P}^n(a) = \hat{u}^n\},$$

where $\hat{u}^n$ designates some given average utility to be achieved by population n when maximizing the *entropy*, $-\sum_{a\in A^n}\tilde{P}^n(a)\ln\tilde{P}^n(a)$, of its desired distribution $(\tilde{P}^n(a))_{a\in A^n}$. In the first of these two maximum problems, the dispersion parameter λ^n is given, with average utility $\hat{u}^n$ resulting from it; $\hat{u}^n$, by the way, turns out to relate negatively to λ^n. In the second maximum problem, λ^n comes out as a reciprocal Lagrange multiplier of the last equality constraint. The entropy maximization aspect has found broad and fruitful coverage in the work of A. G. Wilson and others; see for example Wilson et al. (1981).

(iii) Nonlogit arbitrage may well be considered as an endeavor complementary to the work on broadening the IIDG assumption–based random-utility approach by, for example, probit or dogit analysis. In this context, the open question is whether there exist general functional relationships between nonlogit arbitrage and nonlogit random utility.

(iv) In the field of game theory, Harsanyi (1973) introduced "disturbed" games and defined a notion of equilibrium that bears a strong resemblance to our notion of stochastic flow equilibrium, in particular if $\mathbf{F}_t = \mathbf{P}(t)$.

(v) In game theory, the treatment of the existence question for flow equilibria (i.e., of equilibria in mixed strategies) is standard, by way of continuity and convexity arguments; see for example Aubin (1993). Müller (1990) has extended this technique to an existence proof for stock and flow equilibria.

3   Dynamic stochastic choice modeling: a framework

3.1   *Basic concepts*

With respect to flow states, we distinguish two sources of change: internal migration and external processes.

3.1.1   *Internal migration and internal balance equations*

When (in interpretative terms) agents change their decisions, switching from one action a to another b, we say they *migrate* from a to b. The rate of migration (number of agents migrating per unit of time) from a to b will be designated by M_{ab}.[4]

The *mover pool* of action a is defined as

$$M_a := \sum_b M_{ab},$$

and

$$\mu_a := M_a / P(a, t)$$

is what we call the *mobility* (of the agents) at a. The *conditional migration rates,* or *conditional transition probabilities,* are

$$R_{ab} := M_{ab}/M_a. \tag{13}$$

---

[4] As to the case $a = b$, in some applications M_{aa} will always equal 0, in others not. In this section on dynamics, as long as there is no risk of confusion, we suppress the superscript n and write e.g. $P(b, t)$ instead of $P^n(b, t)$, or M_{ab} instead of M_{ab}^n.

They form a stochastic matrix:

$$\sum_b R_{ab} = 1 \quad \forall a \quad \text{(and } R_{ab} \geq 0\text{)}.$$

The *internal balance equations* read

$$\begin{aligned} P'(b, t) &= \sum_a M_{ab} - M_b \\ &= \sum_a R_{ab} M_a - M_b \\ &= \sum_a R_{ab} \mu_a P(a, t) - \mu_b P(b, t), \end{aligned} \tag{14}$$

where $P'(b, t)$ denotes the part of the time rate of change of $P(b, t)$ that is attributable to internal migration.

A migration pattern $(^0M_{ab})$ is said to be *balanced* if

$$\sum_a {}^0M_{ab} - {}^0M_b = 0 \quad \forall b$$

or, equivalently, if

$$\sum_a {}^0R_{ab}{}^0M_a - {}^0M_b = 0 \quad \forall b.$$

The latter equality states that the mover pool vector (^0M_a) is a left eigenvector, to the eigenvalue 1, of the conditional transition probabilities matrix $(^0R_{ab})$.

A *rank-1 migration pattern* is one where, for each population, the rows of the matrix (R_{ab}) are identical; that is, for each row a, $R_{ab} = r_b$ for all b.

Standard rank-1 conditional migration pattern.

$$R_{ab}(t) = r_b(t) := P(b, t) / \sum_c P(c, t). \tag{15}$$

Standard mover-pool pattern.

$$M_a(t) := \mu P(a, t)$$

where μ denotes the mobility of the population.

When combined, the standard rank-1 conditional migration pattern and the standard mover-pool pattern yield the following.

Standard rank-1 balanced migration pattern.

$$^0M_{ab}(t) = \underbrace{\mu P(a, t)}_{^0M_a(t)} \underbrace{P(b, t) / \sum_c P(c, t)}_{^0R_{ab}(t) = {}^0r_b(t)}. \tag{16}$$

A migration pattern $(^0M_{ab})$ is said to exhibit *detailed balance* if the matrix $(^0M_{ab})$ is symmetric, that is, if $^0M_{ab} = {}^0M_{ba}$ for all a, b, or (equivalently) if net migration $^0M_{ab} - {}^0M_{ba}$ vanishes for all a, b.

Observation: Obviously, if there is detailed balancedness then there is balancedness as well. Moreover, in the rank-1 case, detailed balance is the only way of achieving balancedness, because the latter implies that $^0M_a = {}^0r_a \sum_c {}^0M_c$ for all a, whence $^0M_{ab} = {}^0M_{ba}$ for all a, b.

Note: We do not want to restrict ourselves to the rank-1 case, as we do not want to be restricted to detailed balance as the only form of balancedness. One reason is that we do not want to preclude intransitivities of the following kind:

$$^0M_{ab} > {}^0M_{ba} \quad \text{and} \quad {}^0M_{bc} > {}^0M_{cb}, \quad \text{yet} \quad {}^0M_{ac} < {}^0M_{ca},^5$$

which says that positive net migration from a to b, combined with positive net migration from b to c, does not necessarily imply positive net migration from a to c.

Another reason for not restricting ourselves to the rank-1 case is an empirical one: In spatial migration processes (where action sets consist, e.g., of geographical regions), the mover pools from two different regions – a and b, say – are known generically not to spread in identical ways across the various destination regions. (According to empirical evidence, neighboring regions are preferred to distant ones.)

3.1.2 *External processes and full dynamic balance equations*
External processes are processes that change sizes of populations. If $\dot{P}(t)$ denotes the time rate of change of the size of some population under consideration, one may posit that the impact of $\dot{P}(t)$ on the various occupation numbers $P(b, t)$ of the population is proportional to their values:

$$\dot{P}(b, t) = \dot{P}(t)\pi(b, t), \tag{17}$$

where $\pi(b, t)$ denotes the probability of action b (cf. (1)).

Other impact rules for $\dot{P}(t)$ may reasonably be devised, depending on the particular application at hand. In this paper, however, we do not want to study external processes in any more detail. Suffice it to say that the (total) time rate of change, $d_t P(b, t)$, of any occupation number is obtained by superposition of its internal and its external time rates of changes:

$$d_t P(b, t) = P'(b, t) + \dot{P}(b, t).$$

More explicitly, we have the following full dynamic balance equation:

$$d_t P(b, t) = \sum_a R_{ab}\mu_a P(a, t) - \mu_b P(b, t) + \dot{P}(t)\pi(b, t). \tag{18}$$

---

[5] Goodchild and Smith (1980) analyze such intransitivities in spatial migration.

Finally, we observe that external processes may be either exogenous or endogenous. For example, if the size of the population of private households changes because of some autonomously varying net birth rate (equal to $\dot{P}^n(t)$ where n stands for "private households"), then that change is an exogenous external process. On the other hand, market entry of entrepreneurs may be modeled by an endogenous external process. Toward this end, let n_0 designate the population of all potential entrepreneurs (i.e., active and inactive ones), and let their action set $A^{n_0} := \{$inactivity, activity$\}$. Further, let n_1 designate the population of active entrepreneurs. Then the size $P^{n_1}(t)$ of population n_1 (i.e., the number of active entrepreneurs) is equal to the occupation number $P^{n_0}(\text{activity}, t)$, and

$$d_t P^{n_0}(\text{activity}, t) = \dot{P}^{n_1}(t).$$

The external process that changes the size of population n_1 is part of an endogenous stochastic choice process on the level of population n_0.

3.2   *Disequilibrium migration patterns*

Disequilibrium migration patterns are obtained as modifications of balanced migration patterns. The modifications are such that they are nil if and only if the prevailing flow state is a flow equilibrium. Thus, any stock and flow equilibrium will be a steady state provided that, for the prevailing stock and flow equilibrium, $\mathbf{F}_t$ does not change with time and that there are no ongoing exogenous processes that would change any parameters of the model.

3.2.1   *Conditional migration rates*

We obtain the conditional migration rates R_{ab} (cf. (13)) as solutions of an arbitrage problem for movers. Toward this end, we associate with each action a (of each population) some *disutility* $D_a(t)$ of lingering at a such that[6]

$$D_a(t) > 0 \Leftrightarrow \tilde{P}(a; \mathbf{F}_t) < P(a, t) \quad \text{and}$$
$$D_a(t) = 0 \Leftrightarrow \tilde{P}(a; \mathbf{F}_t) = P(a, t) \quad \text{and thence}$$
$$D_a(t) < 0 \Leftrightarrow \tilde{P}(a; \mathbf{F}_t) > P(a, t).$$

Thus, $(\mathbf{P}(t), \mathbf{F}_t)$ is a flow equilibrium if and only if $D_a(t) = 0$ for all a.

For any one action a of the population under consideration, the agents in the still unknown mover pool M_a behave as solvers of the following problem.

---

[6] A frequent choice made in our simulation work is $D_a(t) := -\alpha \ln(\tilde{P}(a, \mathbf{F}(t))/P(a, t))$ (for $\alpha > 0$ as with (20)).

Movers' arbitrage problem. Find (R_{ab}) or, equivalently, find $(M_{ab}) = (R_{ab}M_a)$ such that the following balance equation (19) and arbitrage condition (20) hold:

$$\Sigma_b M_{ab} = M_a, \tag{19}$$

$$D_b + \alpha \ln(M_{ab}/^0M_{ab}) = \tilde{D}_a \quad \forall b \quad \text{(for appropriate } \tilde{D}_a), \tag{20}$$

where $\alpha > 0$ is an empirical weighting factor.

The utility expression on the left-hand side of (20) is of the prior information type, introduced in the context of formula (10).

Solving (20) for M_{ab}, one obtains

$$M_{ab} = {}^0M_{ab} \exp(-\beta D_b) \exp(\beta \tilde{D}_a) \quad \text{with } \beta := 1/\alpha. \tag{21}$$

Inserting M_{ab} into the balance equation yields

$$\exp(\beta \tilde{D}_a) = \frac{M_a}{\Sigma_b {}^0M_{ab} \exp(-\beta D_b)}, \tag{22}$$

whence

$$M_{ab} = M_a \frac{{}^0M_{ab} \exp(-\beta D_b)}{\Sigma_c {}^0M_{ac} \exp(-\beta D_c)} \tag{23}$$

or

$$R_{ab} = \frac{{}^0R_{ab} \exp(-\beta D_b)}{\Sigma_c {}^0R_{ac} \exp(-\beta D_c)}. \tag{24}$$

3.2.2 The mover pool
The still unknown mover pool M_a, or rather $M_a/^0M_a$, will be obtained as follows.

Inverse demand equation for moving.

$$f(M_a/^0M_a) = \tilde{D}_a - D_a, \tag{25}$$

where the *inverse demand function* $f(\cdot)$ typically is monotonic decreasing (though not necessarily strictly) and $f(1) = 0.$[7]

From (22) and (25) one obtains:

$$\frac{M_a}{\Sigma_b {}^0M_{ab} \exp(-\beta D_b)} = \exp(\beta D_a) \exp\left(\beta f\left(\frac{M_a}{^0M_a}\right)\right)$$

or

---

[7] Unlike more common inverse demand functions, $f(\cdot)$ may take negative values (viz., for $x > 1$). This may be necessary because the "prices" in (25) are differences of disutilities that may very well turn out to be negative.

$$\frac{M_a}{^0M_a}\exp\left(-\beta f\left(\frac{M_a}{^0M_a}\right)\right) = \frac{\Sigma_b\,^0R_{ab}\exp(-\beta D_b)}{\exp(-\beta D_a)},$$

or, finally,

$$\frac{\mu_a}{^0\mu_a} = \frac{M_a}{^0M_a} = \Phi\left[\frac{\exp(-\beta D_a)}{\Sigma_b\,^0R_{ab}\exp(-\beta D_b)}\right], \tag{26}$$

where $x = \Phi(y)$ is the solution of $x\exp(-\beta f(x)) = 1/y$.[8]

3.2.3   Final formulas
Let us introduce first what one may call the *attraction*, $V(a, t)$, of action a at time t:

$$V(a, t) := \exp(-\beta D_a).[9] \tag{27}$$

The quantity

$$\bar{V}_a(t) := \Sigma_c\,^0R_{ac}V(c, t) \tag{28}$$

is a weighted average of the various attractions, $V(c, t)$. The weights $^0R_{ac}$ ($c \in A^n$) vary – in non–rank-1 cases (cf. Section 3.1.1) – with the action a from which the movers considered are departing. Therefore, $\bar{V}_a(t)$ will be called the *mean attraction as perceived from a*. In the same vein,

$$V_a^{\text{rel}}(b, t) := V(b, t)/\bar{V}_a(t) \tag{29}$$

is called the *relative* attraction of b as perceived from a.

The formulas for the out-of-equilibrium mobilities and conditional migration rates may now be cast in the following form:

$$\mu_a = \Phi(V_a^{\text{rel}}(a, t))\,^0\mu_a \quad \text{(cf. (26))} \tag{30}$$

$$R_{ab} = V_a^{\text{rel}}(b, t)\,^0R_{ab} \quad \text{(cf. (24))} \tag{31}$$

Because of the conspicuous role of relative attractions in these formulas, we speak of *attraction-regulated* migration laws.

As to the mobility modifier, $\Phi(\cdot)$, it is helpful to note that $\Phi(y) > 0$ for $y > 0$ and that $\Phi(\cdot)$ is strictly monotonic decreasing[10] with $\Phi(1) = 1$. In other words, the disequilibrium mobility μ_a (of agents) at any one action a is lower, the higher is the relative attraction of that action.

---

[8] Existence of this solution is guaranteed if, e.g., the inverse demand function $f(\cdot)$ is (not necessarily strictly) monotonic decreasing. In case of differentiability of $f(\cdot)$, this is a consequence of the derivative of $x\exp(-\beta f(x))$ being everywhere larger than 0.

[9] With $D_a(t) := -\alpha \ln(\tilde{P}(a; F_t)/P(a, t))$ (see note 6), the attraction is

$$V(a, t) = \tilde{P}(a; F_t)/P(a, t).$$

[10] Because the derivative of the function $x \mapsto x\exp(-\beta f(x))$ is everywhere larger than 0, its inverse function ($\Psi(\cdot)$, say) has positive derivative, too; therefore, the derivative of $\Phi(y) := \Psi(1/y)$ is negative.

3.2.4 *Particular cases*

(a) *Standard rank-1 case:* "Rank-1" implies that the *mean* attraction $\bar{V}_a(t)$ is independent of a:

$$\bar{V}_a(t) = \bar{V}(t).$$

Inserting *standard* attraction $V(a, t) := \tilde{P}(a; \mathbf{F}_t)/P(a, t)$ (see note 9), one obtains

$$\bar{V}(t) = \Sigma_c \frac{P(c, t)}{\Sigma_b P(b, t)} \frac{\tilde{P}(c; \mathbf{F}_t)}{P(c, t)} = 1,$$

and therefore

$$V^{\text{rel}}(b, t) = V(b, t) = \tilde{P}(b; \mathbf{F}_t)/P(b, t).$$

(b) *Perfectly elastic mover pools:* $f(M_a/{}^0M_a) \equiv 0$. In this case, $\Phi(y) = 1/y$ by (26). Thus, in the standard rank-1 case with the balanced migration pattern

$${}^0M_{ab}(t) = {}^0\mu P(a, t)P(b, t)/\Sigma_c P(c, t) \qquad \text{(cf. (16))}$$

and with $V^{\text{rel}}(b, t) = V(b, t)$ as in case (a), one obtains

$$M_{ab}(t) = {}^0\mu[P(a, t)/V(a, t)][V(b, t)P(b, t)/\Sigma_c P(c, t)]$$
$$= {}^0\mu[P(a, t)^2/\tilde{P}(a; \mathbf{F}_t)][\tilde{P}(b; \mathbf{F}_t)/\Sigma_c P(c, t)]. \qquad (32)$$

Note that, in this case of perfectly elastic mover pools, the inverse demand equation for moving (equation (25)) reduces to $\tilde{D}_a = D_a$, with the consequence that the movers' arbitrage problem (equations (19) and (20)) is no longer a genuine arbitrage problem. Equation (20) may immediately be solved for M_{ab}:

$$M_{ab} = {}^0M_{ab} \exp[(D_a - D_b)/\alpha] = {}^0M_{ab}V(b, t)/V(a, t) \qquad \text{(cf. (27))}.$$

With the standard rank-1 balanced migration pattern ($^0M_{ab}$) of (16) and the standard attraction as given in note 9, one again obtains (32).

(c) *Perfectly inelastic mover pools:* The inverse demand function f is set-valued:

$$f\left(\frac{M_a}{{}^0M_a}\right) := \begin{cases} \Re & \text{for } M_a/{}^0M_a = 1, \\ \varnothing & \text{otherwise.} \end{cases}$$

Equivalently, the demand function for moving is identically equal to unity:

$$M_a/{}^0M_a = 1 \quad \text{for all "prices."}$$

In this case, for movers from any action a,

$$\Phi(y) = 1 \quad \forall y. \tag{33}$$

Thus, in the standard rank-1 case with the balanced migration pattern

$$^0M_{ab}(t) = {}^0\mu P(a, t)P(b, t)/\sum_c P(c, t) \qquad \text{(cf. (16))}$$

and with $V^{\text{rel}}(b, t)$ as in case (a), one obtains

$$M_{ab}(t) = {}^0\mu P(a, t)V(b, t)P(b, t)/\sum_c P(c, t)$$
$$= {}^0\mu P(a, t)\tilde{P}(b; \mathbf{F}_t)/\sum_c P(c, t).$$

Note that here the internal balance equations (14) take a particularly simple form:

$$P'(b, t) = {}^0\mu[\tilde{P}(b; \mathbf{F}_t) - P(b, t)].$$

(d) *Explicitly obtainable mobility modifiers:*

$$f(x) := -\tau \ln x, \quad 0 < \tau < \infty,$$

is a strictly monotonic decreasing inverse demand function, with $f(1) = 0$. The corresponding mobility modifier Φ is easily seen to be

$$\Phi(y; \tau) = (1/y)^{1/(1+\beta\tau)},$$

where y may be replaced by respective relative attractions. Note that

   (i) as $\tau \to 0$, $\Phi(y; \tau) \to 1/y$ (perfectly elastic mover-pool case); and
   (ii) as $\tau \to \infty$, $\Phi(y; \tau) \to 1$ (perfectly inelastic mover-pool case).

3.3   *Underlying "nonlinear" Markov chains*

We shall point out, for each population, a *continuous time Markov chain* X_T defined on any time interval T for which the differential equations of stock and flow dynamics (equations (2) and (18)) possess a solution for given initial values of $\mathbf{P}(\cdot)$ and $\mathbf{B}(\cdot)$. The *state space* of the chain will be formed by the action sets A of the respective populations, and the one-dimensional probability distribution of the chain at time $t \in T$ will be

$$\text{pr}\{X_t = a\} = P(a, t)/P(t) \quad \forall a \in A \qquad \text{(cf. note 4)}.$$

In order to specify the proclaimed Markov chain more closely, we shall establish its matrices of *transition probabilities,*

$$\mathbf{T}(s, t) = (\pi_{ab}(s, t))_{a, b \in A} \quad \text{for } s, t \in T \text{ with } s \leq t,$$

where $\pi_{ab}(s, t) := \text{pr}\{X_t = b \mid X_s = a\}$ denotes a conditional probability (as is common in this context).

The term $\pi_{ab}(s, t)$ may be interpreted as follows. If $\langle a, s \rangle$ denotes the subpopulation of the population under consideration that practices action

a at time s, then a fraction $\pi_{ab}(s, t)$ of subpopulation $\langle a, s \rangle$ will be practicing action b at time t:

$$P^{\langle a, s \rangle}(b, t) = P^{\langle a, s \rangle}(t) \pi_{ab}(s, t),$$

where $P^{\langle a, s \rangle}(t)$ denotes the size of subpopulation $\langle a, s \rangle$ at time t,[11] and $P^{\langle a, s \rangle}(b, t)$ the number of agents from subpopulation $\langle a, s \rangle$ that practice action b at time t.

With respect to the time rate of change of $P^{\langle a, s \rangle}(b, t)$, in interpretative terms we make the following assumptions.

(1) At time t, the agents in the fraction $P^{\langle a, s \rangle}(b, t)$ of subpopulation $\langle a, s \rangle$ exhibit the same mobility μ_b and the same conditional migration rates R_{bc} as do all the other agents that practice action b at time t. This assumption appears to be legitimate insofar as the information vectors $\mathbf{F}_t$ comprise only aggregate data. Individual data are absorbed by the random-utility parts $\epsilon^n(\cdot)$ of the random-utility vectors $\mathbf{u}^n(\cdot; \mathbf{F}_t)$ (see Section 2.3.1).

(2) The impact of an external time rate of change $\dot{P}(t)$ of the population under consideration on *any* of its subpopulations is proportional to the size of that subpopulation.[12]

Expressing this in formal terms, one obtains the following.

Forward Kolmogorov equations. For $P^{\langle a, s \rangle}(b, t)$ with $a, b \in A$:

$$d_t P^{\langle a, s \rangle}(b, t) = \frac{\dot{P}(t) P^{\langle a, s \rangle}(b, t)}{P(t)}$$
$$- \mu_b(t) P^{\langle a, s \rangle}(b, t) + \sum_c \mu_c(t) P^{\langle a, s \rangle}(c, t) R_{cb}(t),$$

where the initial conditions are

$$P^{\langle a, s \rangle}(b, s) = \begin{cases} P^{\langle a, s \rangle}(s) & \text{for } b = a, \\ 0 & \text{otherwise.} \end{cases}$$

Note: In the differential equations (18) of flow dynamics, the mobilities $\mu_c(t)$ and the conditional migration rates $R_{cb}(t)$ are *indirect* functions of time t, for they depend *directly* only upon the relative attractions $V_a^{\text{rel}}(a, t)$ as well as on $^0\mu_a$ and on $^0R_{ab}$ (cf. (30) and (31)), which in turn depend on time (albeit in an indirect manner). After solving equations (2) and (18) of stock and flow dynamics, one may express – in principle at least – all relative attractions as functions of time and insert these into the expressions for the various coefficients μ_c and R_{cb}. After treating the

[11] Like sizes of entire populations, sizes of subpopulations may also change with time.
[12] Compare with the impact rule specified as (17).

underlying balanced migration patterns $^0M_{ab}$ (i.e., $^0\mu_a$ and $^0R_{ab}$) in a similar fashion, one finally obtains the $\mu_c(t)$ and the $R_{cb}(t)$ as direct functions of time. These are the functions that are meant to be used in the preceding forward Kolmogorov equations. In the same vein, the functions $\dot{P}(t)$ and $P(t)$, obtained by solving equations (18) and (2), are meant to be given as direct functions of time. Our point is that the forward Kolmogorov equations are thereby *linear* differential equations, with the consequence that one may establish the validity of the following.

Chapman–Kolmogorov equations.

$$\mathbf{T}(s, t)\mathbf{T}(t, z) = \mathbf{T}(s, z) \quad \forall s \le t \le z \text{ (in } \mathbf{T}).$$

As a consequence of the semigroup property of the transition probability matrices, one concludes that one is actually dealing with a *Markov chain*, as announced previously. There is indeed such a Markov chain for each of the populations. These Markov chains are coupled by way of the utility vectors $u^n(\cdot; \mathbf{F}_t)$, $n \in N$, or (more specifically) by way of the information vectors $\mathbf{F}_t$ that serve as common transmitters of information to all agents in the system.

Terminology.   The forward Kolmogorov equations for the $P^{\langle a, s\rangle}(\cdot, t)$ (all a) are nonlinear at the outset, and become linear only after the treatment outlined in the foregoing Note. Thus we are induced to speak of *"nonlinear" Markov chains,* as opposed to the standard linear (time homogeneous or inhomogeneous) Markov chains.

Remarks: (a) If one works with the plausible (albeit special) impact rule for external processes expounded as (17), the forward Kolmogorov equations for the transition probability matrices $\mathbf{T}(s, t)$ take the following simple form in which no external processes are discernible:

$$\partial_t \mathbf{T}(s, t) = \mathbf{T}(s, t)\mathbf{H}(t),$$

where

$$\mathbf{H}(t) := (\mu_a(t)(R_{ab}(t) - \delta_{ab}))_{a, b \in A},$$

$$\delta_{ab} := \begin{cases} 1 & \text{for } b = a, \\ 0 & \text{otherwise,} \end{cases} \quad \text{(the Kronecker symbol)}$$

is the *infinitesimal generator* of the semigroup $\mathbf{T}(\cdot, \cdot)$. (Note that the forward Kolmogorov equations were obtained by differentiating $\pi_{ab}(s, t) := P^{\langle a, s\rangle}(b, t)/P^{\langle a, s\rangle}(t)$ with respect to t.)

(b) The modeling of dynamic stochastic choice processes as coupled nonlinear Markov chains yields a novel theoretical basis for the analysis of panel data, the longitudinal data sets of which appear to lend themselves to an interpretation as samples from the path spaces of the respective Markov chains. (More precisely, the longitudinal data set pertaining to any one of the observed individual agents would be interpreted as a sampled path of the respective Markov chain, sampled at some finite number of points in time.) Finally, nonlinear Markov chains appear to provide a firm theoretical basis for Monte Carlo simulations of dynamic stochastic choice processes.

3.4   Notes and references

(i) The movers' arbitrage problem, together with the inverse demand equation for moving, may be cast as a "network equilibrium" problem; see Dejon (1983). For a discussion of networks in economics, see Nagurney (1993). The formalism used there to describe and analyze network equilibria is that of variational inequalities, whereas the largely equivalent formalism used in Dejon (1983) is that of subdifferential calculus (or complementarity theory) as propounded, for example, in Rockafellar (1984).

(ii) The question of global existence of solutions to the differential equations of stock and flow dynamics was analyzed by Schefczik (1989), with positive results under rather weak conditions. Schefczik (1989) also studied the question of asymptotic stability, and formulated some sufficient conditions.

(iii) Nonlinear Markov chains appear to have aroused comparatively weak interest hitherto, although there are early contributions by such eminent workers in the field as McKean (1966) who in turn referred to Kac (1958). The interacting particle theoretical mainstream of interest in mathematics, as portrayed for example by Ligget (1985), was stimulated by findings in interacting particle physics and inspired by the seminal work of R. L. Dobrushin and F. Sptizer (circa 1970). The theory deals with interacting particle systems by way of linear Markov processes but pays the tribute of working with the extremely large state space of *all* macroconfigurations of the system. In order to achieve manageable orders of differential equation systems, one passes to (deterministic!) mean-value equations. In the realm of sociology this technique was propounded by de Palma and Lefèvre (1983) as well as by Weidlich and Haag (1983).

(iv) Monte Carlo simulations of dynamic stochastic choice processes on the level of an urban economy were reported by Wegener (1985).

4   A production and exchange economy

In this section we sketch one of many conceptually possible ways to model the evolution of a disequilibrium economy as a dynamic stochastic choice process. The populations, action sets, and utility functions proposed are by no means mandatory. With the aim of providing but a basic feasibility study, we try to keep our choices as simple as possible. We observe that the monetary sector could also be modeled along the same lines as expounded for the real sector.

4.1   Typical populations

In modeling a production and exchange economy, we propose to distinguish the following constituents:

consumers (i.e., private households in their roles as consumers), specified by income class and possibly also by age and/or training;

workers (i.e., private households in their roles as workers, offering labor services at the labor market), possibly specified by age and/or training;

producers, typically specified by sector and possibly also by production technology employed (e.g., low vs. high capital intensity);

investors, who buy buildings and equipment at the capital goods markets; and

lessors, who lease buildings and equipment to producers.

In a spatial economy, these constituent populations would have to be specified by their location as well. The government will enter the picture in a very rudimentary fashion, as a mere collector of taxes that are subsequently spent at the commodity markets.

4.2   Typical action sets

For each market g, we introduce a finite grid of admissible prices,

$$\mathbf{PC}_g := \{p_{g,1} < \cdots < p_{g,l}\},$$

as well as finite grids of admissible quantities,

$$\mathbf{Q}_g^n := \{0 = q_{g,0} < q_{g,1}^n < \cdots < q_{g,k}^n\},$$

that in general are specific for each population n. The finitely many price levels in $\mathbf{PC}_g$ are suitable for all populations. The finitely many quantity levels in $\mathbf{Q}_g^n$, however, may vary with population n, with a tendency toward small quantities for consumers, for instance, and toward large quantities for producers.

The agents of any population n choose, at each of their activity markets g, some price level $p_g \in \mathbf{PC}_g$ as well as some quantity level $q_g \in \mathbf{Q}_g^n$.

Such a choice by an agent of population n means that the agent wants to sell or to buy (respectively) q_g physical units, per unit of time, of good g at price p_g. (The choice of $q_{g,0} = 0$ physical units of good g may be interpreted as temporary inactivity at market g; the price level p_g is then irrelevant.) Thus, if G^n designates the set of all activity markets of population n, then the actions of that population are formalized as tuples of *price-quantity pairs* $(p_g, q_g^n)_{g \in G^n}$.

4.3   *Typical information vectors*

Information vectors, $\mathbf{F}_t$, typically consist of aggregate market data as follows.

$D_g^n(p_g)$: Intended purchases by demander population n at price level p_g of market g,

$$D_g^n(p_g) := \sum_a^* P^n(a, t) q_g(a). \tag{34}$$

The summation $\sum_a^*$ extends over those actions $a \in A^n$ the price components of which, at market g, equal p_g; $q_g(a)$ denotes the quantity component of action a at market g.

$D_g(p_g) := \sum_n D_g^n(p_g)$: Total intended purchases at price level p_g of market g.

On the supply side we distinguish sales from stock (SS) and sales from current production (SC).

$SC_g^n(p_g)$: Intended sales from current production by supplier population n at price level p_g of market g, computed analogously to $D_g^n(p_g)$ (formula (34)).

$SS_g^n(p_g)$: Intended sales from stock by population n at price level p_g of market g,

$$SS_g^n(p_g) := \sigma_g^n B_g^n(t) SC_g^n(p_g) / \sum_{p_g} SC_g^n(p_g).$$

For a first approach, σ_g^n will depend in a rather simplistic way on $B_g^n(t)$ (the stock of commodity g held by population n) so as to keep $B_g^n(t)$ above some minimal level of stock.[13]

$S_g^n(p_g) := SS_g^n(p_g) + SC_g^n(p_g)$: Total intended sales by population n at price level p_g of market g.[14]

$S_g(p_g) := \sum_n S_g^n(p_g)$: Total intended sales at price level p_g of market g.

[13] A more sophisticated approach would implement some inventory optimization scheme.

[14] Increasing σ_g^n leads to an increase in total intended sales and thereby, in general, to an increase in actual sales as well.

The single most important aggregate (albeit price-level specific) market data we work with is *relative demand* (or *degree of rationing*) at any price level p_g of market g:

$$r_g(p_g) := D_g(p_g)/S_g(p_g),$$

with $r_g(p_g) := +\infty$ for $S_g(p_g) = 0$ and $D_g(p_g) > 0$. (The case of $S_g(p_g) = D_g(p_g) = 0$ is practically irrelevant, at least when the dispersion parameters $\lambda^n > 0$; cf. the multinomial logit formula (5).)

Rationing: Actual sales at price level p_g equal intended sales at that price level if intended purchases are at least that high. Otherwise, suppliers are rationed at price level p_g, and actual sales amount to intended purchases only. Analogously, if demanders are rationed at price level p_g, actual purchases amount only to sales intended at that price level.[15]

4.4   Mean utility vectors and soft rationing

4.4.1   Soft-rationing penalty terms

Our approach of modeling the economic agents' reactions to being rationed at certain price levels of one or more markets is based on *penalty terms* introduced into the expressions for the agents' mean utility vectors:

$$u^n(a; \mathbf{F}_t) := u_0^n(a; \mathbf{F}_t) - z^n(\mathbf{r}(a)), \qquad (\text{cf. (4)}) \qquad (35)$$

where

   $u_0^n(a; \mathbf{F}_t)$ designates the intrinsic utility of action $a \in A^n$ ("intrinsic" in the sense of "valid irrespective of any rationing that may be incurred") and

   $z^n(\mathbf{r}(a))$ is a rationing penalty depending on the vector $\mathbf{r}(a) = [r_g(p_g(a))]_{g \in G^n}$ of relative demands at the price levels $p_g(a)$ of action a, at the various activity markets $g \in G^n$ of population n.

More explicitly, we posit $z^n(\mathbf{r}(a))$ as a *sum* of penalties incurred at the various activity markets:

$$z^n(\mathbf{r}(a)) := \sum_{g \in G^n} z_g^n[r_g(p_g(a))] := \sum_{g \in G^n} \zeta_g^n[r_g(p_g(a))]q_g(a), \qquad (36)$$

where $\zeta_g^n[r_g(p_g(a))]$ represents the *unit cost* of being rationed at price level $p_g(a)$ of market g. The $z_g^n[r_g(p_g(a))]$ are to be expressed in terms of *utils* of population n in order to allow for subtraction of $z^n(\mathbf{r}(a))$ from intrinsic utility (cf. (35)).

---

[15] So far we work with *proportional* rationing; each population is rationed proportionally to its engagement on the various price levels.

On the demand side, rationing penalties may be interpreted as search costs, and on the supply side as storage costs. Notice that $\zeta_g^n(r_g)$ typically is strictly monotonic increasing: as

(i) $r_g > 1$ increases, and population n is on the demand side; or as
(ii) $r_g < 1$ decreases, and population n is on the supply side.

More briefly, $\zeta_g^n(r_g)$ increases as rationing increases.[16]

Note: If an economic agent changes his or her current action by moving, at some market g, from price level $p_{g,\sigma}$ to (say) the next preferable one (i.e., to $p_{g,\sigma+1}$ if the agent is a supplier, or to $p_{g,\sigma-1}$ in the case of a demander), then intrinsic utility is being increased. However, this increase may be offset by an even stronger increase of the rationing penalty incurred, depending on the prevailing market situation (i.e., on the current stock and flow state $(\mathbf{B}(t), \mathbf{P}(t))$). Such offsetting effects prevent, at all markets, suppliers and demanders from drifting too far apart on the price axis. (Without rationing penalties, suppliers would keep moving to the upper price levels and demanders to the lower ones.) Briefly speaking, owing to the introduction of rationing penalties, one is able to model economic agents as both price and quantity setters.

Introducing rationing penalties is technically equivalent to what happens in optimization theory when inequality constraints are replaced by penalties for violating such constraints. These penalty functions are sometimes called *soft* constraints, as opposed to hard constraints in the form of inequalities that must be obeyed strictly. In the same vein, rationing that is induced by penalties may be termed *soft rationing*.

4.4.2   *Examples of mean utility functions in production and consumption*

Producers: We consider a highly aggregated economy with a single compound good g, a single market for labor services ls, and a single market for capital services cs. We assume that there is a single population pr of producers of the compound good g who have static expectations that offering the compound good g at price level p_g will, on average, lead to proceeds $\hat{r}_g(p_g)p_g q_g$ (with $\hat{r}_g(p_g) = r_g(p_g)$ for $r_g(p_g) < 1$ and with $\hat{r}_g(p_g) = 1$ for $r_g(p_g) \geq 1$).

On the assumption that producers' decisions are guided by expected undistributed profits after taxes, the intrinsic utility function of producers is

---

[16] So far, we frequently have $\zeta_g^n(\cdot)$ increase exponentially. More and deeper investigations into the proper analytic form of rationing penalties will surely be required.

$$u_0^{pr}(p_{ls}, q_{ls}, p_{cs}, q_{cs}, p_g, q_g)$$
$$:= [\hat{r}_g(p_g)p_g q_g(1-\tau_i) - p_{ls}q_{ls} - p_{cs}q_{cs}](1-\tau_d)(1-dp),$$

where τ_i denotes the rate of indirect taxes, τ_d the rate of direct taxes, and dp the quota of distributed profits.

We remark that, according to the strict meaning of intrinsic utility (cf. Section 4.4.1), the factor $\hat{r}_g(p_g)$ in the preceding expression for u_0^{pr} would need to be replaced by the constant 1 in order not to account for any rationing effects within u_0^{pr}. In return, the difference

$$[1 - \hat{r}_g(p_g)]p_g q_g(1-\tau_i)(1-\tau_d)(1-dp)$$

would be included as part of the rationing penalty at price level p_g. Rationing at the input markets (i.e., at the labor market and at the market for capital services) is separately accounted for by additional penalty terms (cf. 36)).

Workers: For simplicity's sake, we assume that there is a single population wk of workers, and that $\mathbf{Q}_{ls}^{wk} = \{0 = q_{ls,0} < q_{ls,1}^{wk}\}$ with $q_{ls,1}^{wk} = 60$ hours per week, say. A private household that chooses $q_{ls,0}$ thereby chooses voluntary unemployment. In a first stage, private households make a choice between activity at the labor market and inactivity (voluntary unemployment). In a second stage, those who have opted for activity make, in addition, a choice of one of the wage levels $p_{ls} \in \mathbf{PC}_{ls}$.

Evidently, the intrinsic utility $u_0^{wk}(p_{ls})$ attributed by (activity-seeking) workers to the wage level p_{ls} should relate positively to p_{ls}. For the time being, we work with $u_0^{wk}(p_{ls}) := \ln p_{ls}$. More and deeper investigations into the proper analytic form of $u_0^{wk}(p_{ls})$ are surely required.

Consumers: We distinguish consumers by income classes, where income consists of wage income and distributed profits. Let an income class be denoted by its average income y. The consumers in income class y make a choice of the quantity $q_g \in \mathbf{Q}_g^y$ as well as of the price $p_g \in \mathbf{PC}_g$ at which they want to shop at the market g of the compound good. In a first approach, we adopt the following intrinsic utility function of economic agents in income class y:

$$u_0^y(p_g, q_g) := \beta^y u_0(q_g) + (1-\beta^y)\acute{u}_0(y, p_g, q_g),$$

where $u_0(q_g)$ denotes a standard utility of consumption and $\acute{u}_0(y, p_g, q_g)$ the utility derived from increasing wealth (in case $p_g q_g < y$) or from lowering wealth (in case $p_g q_g > y$); $0 < \beta^y < 1$ is an empirical parameter reflecting the degree of consumption preference of private households in income class y.

Lessors and investors: Under formal aspects, lessors and investors are treated much like workers and consumers, respectively: Lessors and workers are both (potentially) active at respective factor markets, while investors and consumers both act as demanders at commodity markets.

On the assumption that lessors always offer all of their stocks of capital goods at the market for capital services, the only choice to be made is that of the rent (or leasing price) p_{cs}. Analogously to the intrinsic utility function of workers, the intrinsic utility $u_0^{les}(p_{cs})$ attributed by lessors to the leasing price p_{cs} should relate positively to it. For the time being, we work with $u_0^{les}(p_{cs}) := \ln p_{cs}$.

Investors, analogously to consumers, are split up into several populations, inv-pcs, according to the price level p_{cs} at which they currently offer their capital services. The actions of investors consist of choosing a quantity $q_g \in \mathbf{Q}_g^{\text{inv-pcs}}$ and a price level $p_g \in \mathbf{PC}_g$ at the market g of the compound good. We assume that investors value these actions by the present value of expected future returns, net of purchasing cost (in turn corrected by investment subsidies) as well as of adjustment costs incurred during installation of newly bought physical capital:

$$u_0^{\text{inv-pcs}}(p_g, q_g) := \left[\frac{ra}{i+d} - (1-s)p_g - c_{\text{adj}}(q_g) \right] q_g.$$

Here ra denotes average rent achieved at the market for capital services: $ra := p_{cs}\hat{r}_{cs}(p_{cs})$, where $\hat{r}_{cs}(p_{cs})$ equals 1 if relative demand at rent level p_{cs} is larger than or equal to 1 and where $\hat{r}_{cs}(p_{cs}) = r_{cs}(p_{cs})$ otherwise. Furthermore, i denotes the interest rate, d the depreciation rate, s the rate of investment subsidies, and c_{adj} unit adjustment costs.[17]

4.4.3 Effects of soft rationing in connection with a corporate tax-rate change

We start with a standard marginal analysis of the price-taking producer (firm), but with one special feature: We do not differentiate the intrinsic utility function $u_0^{pr}(\cdot)$ of producers but rather the mean utility function $u^{pr}(\cdot) := u_0^{pr}(\cdot) - z^{pr}(\cdot)$. Working with input functions $q_g \mapsto q_{ls}(q_g)$ and $q_g \mapsto q_{cs}(q_g)$ that describe the input price vector–dependent expansion path of the firm, one obtains:

$$\frac{du_0^{pr}(p_{ls}, q_{ls}(q_g), p_{cs}, q_{cs}(q_g), p_g, q_g)}{dq_g} - \frac{dz^{pr}(\mathbf{r}(a))}{dq_g} = 0$$

if and only if

---

[17] Unit adjustment costs are assumed to be strictly increasing with q_g.

$$p_g(1-\tau_i) - p_{ls}\frac{\partial q_{ls}}{\partial q_g} - p_{cs}\frac{\partial q_{cs}}{\partial q_g}$$

$$= \frac{\zeta_g^{pr}(r_g(p_g)) + \zeta_{ls}^{pr}(r_{ls}(p_{ls}))\dfrac{\partial q_{ls}}{\partial q_g} + \zeta_{cs}^{pr}(r_{cs}(p_{cs}))\dfrac{\partial q_{cs}}{\partial q_g}}{(1-\tau_d)(1-dp)}. \quad (37)$$

Given standard decreasing returns to scale of the production function, the solution q_g of the preceding equation *decreases* as the value of the right-hand side *increases*. The latter occurs if, for example, the direct income-tax rate of producers (i.e., the corporate tax τ_d) is raised and producers are simultaneously rationed in at least one of their activity markets g, ls, or cs. (Generically, at the output market g, producers are rationed at the upper price levels; at the input markets, they are rationed at the lower price levels.[18])

Near flow equilibrium, the actual distribution of producers concentrates, at every price level, near the respective optimal quantity level (i.e., in terms of mean utility). Therefore, after a corporate tax rise – with ensuing decreases of optimal output quantities, at price levels with rationing of producers – it appears natural at rationed price levels to expect the actual distributions of producers to shift downward to lower levels of output.

A case in proof, dealing with the previously exhibited highly aggregated model economy, is presented in Figures 1–4. At time $t = 0$, a corporate tax rise from 25 percent to 30 percent has just taken place, with an ensuing reduction of after-tax profits. As suggested by (37), output of the composite good goes down (Figure 1). On the simplistic assumption that government spends its total tax revenues with the same consumption preference as households do, nominal consumption and average price paid at the output market both increase (Figure 2). Because of reduced output there is also reduced input of labor services, which – in combination with a rising price index – leads to reduced real wages (Figure 3). The interplay of these various entities leads to a rise in after-tax real profits (Figure 4) that is, at least in this example, not strong enough by far to offset the initial lowering of after-tax profits triggered by the rise of the corporate tax rate.

4.5   Notes and references

(i) Soft rationing combined with dynamic stochastic choice modeling of the behavior of economic agents may be viewed as a way of operational-

---

[18] Only those (typically few) producers whose intended output price is low and intended input prices are high are generically not rationed.

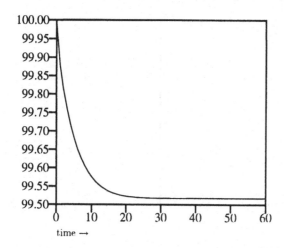

Figure 1. Real output of the composite good.

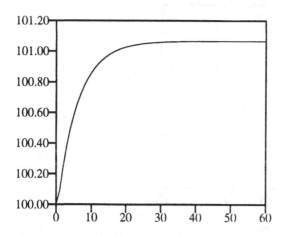

Figure 2. Price index.

izing Clower's (1965) "dual decision hypothesis." An analog of Clower–Benassy-type effective demand (cf. Benassy 1982), albeit in an environment of price and quantity dispersion, may be seen in our desired distributions $\tilde{P}(F_t)$.

(ii) Concerning the question of tax incidence (see e.g. Recktenwald 1966), the foregoing attempt at an analysis based on soft-rationing effects appears to provide arguments in favor of the entrepreneurs' capability, even in a competitive economy, to pass on part of the burden of a corporate tax rise to private households and government.

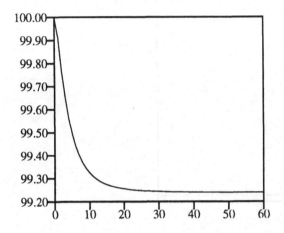

Figure 3. Real wages.

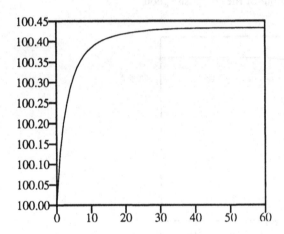

Figure 4. After-tax real profits.

(iii) The smaller the dispersion parameter λ^n in the logit arbitrage problem (cf. (6)) for some population n, the more pronouncedly $\tilde{P}^n(a)$ will concentrate at actions a with maximal values $u^n(a; F_t)$ of mean utility. Necessarily, the same holds for $\hat{P}^n(a)$ if $(\hat{P}, F_t)$ designates some flow equilibrium. In Dejon, Güldner, and Wenzel (1989) it was shown, under rather weak conditions, that in the case of a market economy a flow equilibrium $(\hat{P}, F_t)$ – and a stock and flow equilibrium $(\hat{P}, \hat{B}, F_t)$, as well – concentrates at each market g near a single (equilibrium) price level $\hat{p}_g$ as λ^n tends to zero for all populations n.

REFERENCES

Anderson, S. P., A. de Palma, and J.-F. Thisse (1992), *Discrete Choice Theory of Product Differentiation.* Cambridge, MA: MIT Press.

Aubin, J.-P. (1993), *Optima and Equilibria. An Introduction to Nonlinear Analysis.* Berlin: Springer-Verlag.

Ben-Akiva, M., and St. R. Lerman (1989), *Discrete Choice Analysis. Theory and Application to Travel Demand.* Cambridge, MA: MIT Press.

Benassy, J.-P. (1982), *The Economics of Market Disequilibrium.* New York: Academic Press.

Clower, R. (1965), "The Keynesian Counterrevolution: A Theoretical Appraisal," in F. H. Hahn and F. P. R. Brechling (eds.), *The Theory of Interest Rates* (proceedings of a conference held by the International Economic Association). London: Macmillan.

Dejon, B. (1983), "Attraction-Regulated Dynamic Models of Migration of the Multiplicative Type," in D. A. Griffith and A. C. Lea (eds.), *Evolving Geographical Structures.* The Hague: Martinus Nijhoff, pp. 12–23.

Dejon, B., B. Güldner, and G. Wenzel (1989), "Direct Equilibria of Economies and Their Perfect Homogeneity Limits," in Å. E. Andersson, D. F. Batten, B. Johansson, and P. Nijkamp (eds.), *Advances in Spatial Theory and Dynamics.* Amsterdam: Elsevier, pp. 81–105.

de Palma, A., and C. Lefèvre (1983), "Individual Decision-making in Dynamic Collective Systems," *Journal of Mathematical Sociology* 9: 103–24.

Goodchild, M., and T. Smith (1980), "Intransitivity, the Spatial Interaction Model and U.S. Migration Streams," *Environment and Planning A* 12: 1131–44.

Harsanyi, J. C. (1973), "Games with Randomly Disturbed Payoffs: A New Rationale for Mixed Strategy Equilibrium Points," *International Journal of Game Theory* 2: 1–23.

Kac, M. (1958), *Probability and Related Topics in the Physical Sciences.* New York: Interscience.

Ligget, T. M. (1985), *Interacting Particle Systems.* New York: Springer-Verlag.

Luce, R., and P. Suppes (1965), "Preference, Utility and Subjective Probability," in R. Luce, R. Bush, and E. Galanter (eds.), *Handbook of Mathematical Psychology,* vol. 3. New York: Wiley.

McFadden, D. (1978), "Modelling the Choice of Residential Location," in A. Karlqvist, L. Lundqvist, F. Snickars, and J. W. Weibull (eds.), *Spatial Interaction Theory and Residential Location.* Amsterdam: North-Holland, pp. 75–96.

McKean, H. P., Jr. (1966), "A Class of Markov Processes Associated with Nonlinear Parabolic Equations," *Proceedings of the National Academy of Sciences* 56: 1907–11.

Müller, G. (1990), "Modellierung einer monetären Ökonomie als attraktivitätsgesteuertes Spiel," Ph.D. dissertation, University of Erlangen–Nürnberg.

Nagurney, A. (1993), *Network Economics: A Variational Inequality Approach.* Dordrecht: Kluwer.

Rockafellar, R. T. (1984), *Network Flows and Monotropic Optimization.* New York: Wiley.

Recktenwald, H.-C. (1966), *Steuerüberwälzungslehre.* Berlin: Duncker & Humboldt.

Schefczik, P. (1989), "Untersuchungen zur Existenz und Stabilität stationärer Punkte in einem dynamischen Alternativenwahlmodell," Ph.D. dissertation, University of Erlangen–Nürnberg.

Thurstone, L. (1927), "A Law of Comparative Judgement," *Psychological Review* 34: 273–86.

Wegener, M. (1985), "The Dortmund Housing Market Model: A Monte Carlo Simulation of a Regional Housing Market," in K. Stahl (ed.), *Microeconomic Models of Housing Markets*. Berlin: Springer-Verlag, pp. 144–91.

Weidlich, W., and G. Haag (1983), *Concepts and Models of a Quantitative Sociology*. Berlin: Springer-Verlag.

Wilson, A. G., J. D. Coelho, S. M. Macgill, and H. C. W. L. Williams (1981), *Optimization in Locational and Transport Analysis*. New York: Wiley.

CHAPTER 14

Nonlinear models of employment adjustment

Werner Smolny

Workers who walk out of the factory gate
on a Friday afternoon will typically return
through the same gate on a Monday morning,
if not before.

Stephen J. Nickell

1 Introduction

In many theoretical factor demand models, employment is still treated as the flexible factor while analyzing the inflexibility of the demand for capital. On the other hand, the quasifixity of labor and the efficiency of long-run worker–employer relationships have long been recognized by economic theory.[1] In addition, it is argued that the slow adjustment of employment was one reason for the persistence of high unemployment in Germany in the eighties. This paper deals with the dynamic adjustment of employment within the context of a rationing model. It builds on previous work on dynamic factor demand and extends this work by introducing additional constraints on the employment adjustment.[2] In the model, it is assumed that wages and prices do not adjust instantaneously to clear the market at every moment of time. Labor supply can differ from labor demand, and the dynamics of matching (i.e., employment determination) is the key issue of the study.

There are different themes connected to the dynamics of employment adjustment that appear under several headlines in the literature.[3] First, the detailed studies of Becker and Oi derive the efficiency of long-term worker–employer relationships on the basis of investments in firm-specific

I am indebted to an anonymous referee for helpful comments on an earlier draft.
[1] See Becker (1962) and Oi (1962).
[2] See Smolny (1993b).
[3] For an overview, see Nickell (1986).

human capital.[4] Fixed employment costs arise from investments of firms in hiring and training activities, which implies that labor cannot be treated as a flexible factor of production. Similar arguments for the quasifixity of the employment relation were derived within the theory of implicit "full employment" contracts on the basis of reputation losses for firms in case of frequent dismissals.[5] A third argument is based on legal or explicit contractual clauses on periods of notice for employees. All three arguments are in favor of a cautious hiring policy to avoid hiring and/or firing costs, and all favor "natural" fluctuation (i.e., quits and retirement) as a tool for achieving downward adjustments of the labor force.

Another strand of the literature on employment dynamics analyzes interrelated factor demand functions and macroeconomic consequences of the quasifixity of the employment decision.[6] Usually, any constraints on the adjustment of one factor lead to an overshooting of the demand for a more flexible factor, at least if substitution is possible. This caused serious problems for the first models of dynamic factor demand, which were based on the assumptions of a quasifixed capital demand and flexible labor. These models imply an overshooting of employment and an anti-cyclical behavior of labor productivity, which contrasts sharply with the observed slow adjustment of employment and the procyclical development of labor productivity. These shortcomings were removed with the introduction of a "putty-clay" technology, adjustment costs for labor, and other flexible factor inputs such as working time and the utilization of labor and capital.

A third theme of adjustment models of labor demand is related to the shape of the adjustment cost function. This issue had been discussed in detail within the context of distributed lag models of investment behavior.[7] More recently, it has also been introduced into the discussion of labor demand models. Most traditional models of dynamic factor demand rely on approximating the adjustment cost function by a linear quadratic polynomial in net or gross adjustment. This assumption – together with some further restrictive simplifications such as absence of uncertainty, static expectations, and linear homogeneity of the model – allows one to derive a simple partial adjustment model for the demand of the quasifixed factor. However, the aforementioned causes for the slow adjustment of employment (e.g., partial irreversibility and fixed costs of screening and training) fit badly into the quadratic cost approach. This argument is important, because fixed costs of adjustment imply a quite different behavior of labor demand at the firm level: convex adjustment costs imply a slow ad-

4 See Becker (1962) and Oi (1962).
5 See Okun (1981).
6 See Nadiri and Rosen (1969), Pindyck and Rotemberg (1983), and Palm and Pfann (1990).
7 See Rothschild (1971) and Nickell (1978).

justment with respect to equilibrium values; fixed costs lead to a "lumpy" adjustment.[8] On the other hand, the aggregate consequences of both models have some similarities. Suppose there is a shock in the target level of employment; with fixed adjustment costs, some firms adjust completely while others stay with the previous employment level. The aggregate outcome in both models is a partial adjustment of employment. However, for large shocks, the adjustment in the fixed-cost model is faster, since the hazard increases with the distance between actual and target employment levels. A related issue is the symmetry of adjustment costs and the adjustment of employment. Hiring is quite different from firing; one may think, for example, of linear adjustment costs for hiring and of fixed or linear costs for firing.[9]

Finally, there is the literature about the Beveridge curve and the matching function.[10] These models introduce some interesting aspects into the discussion of dynamic employment adjustment. The first is that employment dynamics cannot be understood solely in terms of labor demand; labor supply and unemployment are also important. A second is the idea that matching takes time. For instance, it can be argued that it takes less time to find one worker when looking for two than to find 50 workers when looking for 100. In this case, the adjustment hazard decreases with the size of the desired adjustment. This is just the opposite of the case for the fixed-cost model. Third, the matching function literature is concerned with gross flows that are usually much larger than net employment changes.

The dynamic model of employment adjustment derived here is mostly related to the matching function literature. In the basic model, the idea of a delayed adjustment is introduced (Section 2). This allows for a simple derivation of decision rules. Interdependent factor demand is taken into account by assuming larger delays for the capital adjustment and a putty-clay technology. In Section 3, the matching function is augmented by linear constraints on the adjustment speed. The estimation results (Section 4) reveal that even this extended model is too simple an approximation of the observed adjustment processes for employment. Final estimates of a nonlinear error correction model give some rough idea about the adjustment process found in the data.

2 The basic model

This section is based on a model that is presented in more detail in Smolny (1993b), so the discussion here will be short. The macroeconomic structure

---

[8] See Hamermesh (1989, 1990a,b, 1993) and Caballero and Engel (1992a,b).

[9] See Bentolila and Bertola (1990), Bertola and Caballero (1990), Bertola (1991), Pfann (1993), and Pfann and Palm (1993).

[10] See Blanchard and Diamond (1989, 1992), Pissarides (1992), and Franz and Smolny (1993).

of the model relies on the concept of micromarkets. The aggregate goods and labor market can be divided into a number of micromarkets, with homogeneous labor and output in each micromarket but with limited mobility between micromarkets. This allows for a straightforward introduction of structural imbalances between supply and demand at the aggregate level, while preserving homogeneity at the microeconomic level. A micromarket is defined by a single firm operating in it. Each firm is engaged on one market for its output, one labor market, and one market for capital goods. Aggregate wages and prices are assumed to adjust sluggishly with respect to demand; at the micro level, they are treated as being exogenous.

In the basic model, it is assumed that adjustment costs depend solely on the delay between the decision to change a factor input and the completion of adjustment. It is further assumed that adjustment costs are negligible if firms take account of a factor-specific adjustment delay τ_j, and prohibitive if firms try to adjust faster. This results in constant adjustment delays for labor and capital. Adjustment delays are probably smaller for labor than for capital, and the production technology is approximated by a putty-clay production function. Finally, it is assumed that output can be adjusted rather quickly with respect to demand changes in the presence of sufficient capacity and labor. These assumptions allow us to reduce the dynamic decision problem of the firm to three static problems, which can be solved sequentially.

1. Short-run adjustment of output YT_i, with predetermined employment LT_i, capital stock K_i, and the capital/labor ratio. Output is given by the minimum of goods supply YS_i and demand YD_i:

$$YT_i = \min(YS_i, YD_i) \tag{1}$$

   The index i refers to micromarkets. Output supply is given by a short-run limitational production function:

$$YS_i = \min[\pi_{l,i} \cdot LT_i, \pi_{k,i} \cdot K_i] = \min(Y_{LT_i}, YC_i), \tag{2}$$

   where Y_{LT_i} denotes an employment constraint; YC_i, capacities; $\pi_{l,i}$, the technical productivity of labor; and $\pi_{k,i}$, the technical productivity of capital. The factor productivities are predetermined by the capital/labor ratio and the production function.

2. Medium-run adjustment of employment with uncertain output, predetermined capital stock, and the capital/labor ratio. Employment is determined by the minimum of labor supply LS_i and demand LD_i:

$$LT_i = \min(LD_i, LS_i). \tag{3}$$

3. Long-run adjustment of the capital stock and the capital/labor ratio, with uncertain output and employment.

Neglecting overtime work and inventory adjustment, the optimal output of the firm is given by (1) and (2). The employment decision for time t must be made at time $t - \tau_L$, that is, τ_L periods before demand realization and thus under uncertainty of goods demand. Labor supply for time t is known in advance and assumed to be exogenous for the firm. The capital stock at time t and the capital/labor ratio must be chosen *before* the employment decision, so capacities and labor productivity are also fixed. Assuming risk neutrality, optimal employment is derived from:

$$\max_{\rightarrow LT_i} p_i \cdot {}_{t-\tau_L} E(YT_i) - w_i \cdot LT_i - c_i \cdot K_i + \lambda_{LS_i} \cdot (LS_i - LT_i), \qquad (4)$$

where p_i is the output price, w_i are wages, and c_i are the user costs of capital. The term ${}_{t-\tau_L} E(YT_i)$ is the expected value of output in t, with expectations formed at $t - \tau_L$. For the determination of employment, three cases can be distinguished.

Case 1: No constraints. If the firm is constrained neither by the available labor supply nor by the existing capital stock, the first-order condition is given by

$$p_i \cdot \text{prob}(YD_i > Y_{LT_i}) \cdot \pi_{l,i} \overset{!}{=} w_i. \qquad (5)$$

$$\underbrace{\hphantom{p_i \cdot \text{prob}(YD_i > Y_{LT_i}) \cdot \pi_{l,i}}}_{\text{expected marginal returns}} \quad \underbrace{\hphantom{w_i}}_{\text{marginal costs}}$$

The firm chooses employment so as to equalize expected marginal returns and marginal wage costs. Marginal returns are given by the price, multiplied by the probability of the supply-constrained regime on the goods market, and labor productivity. In the optimum, the probability of the supply-constrained regime is equal to the full-employment labor share sl_i^*. Optimal employment is determined from

$$LT_i^* = L_i^* = \frac{F_{YD_i}^{-1}(1 - sl_i^*)}{\pi_{l,i}} \quad \text{with} \quad sl_i^* = \frac{w_i}{p_i \cdot \pi_{l,i}}, \qquad (6)$$

where $F_{YD_i}^{-1}$ denotes the inverse of the cumulative distribution function of demand YD_i. Optimal employment is determined by the productivity of labor, the share of labor costs in nominal full-employment output, and the parameters of the distribution function of goods demand. The partial derivative of L_i^* with respect to the real wage is negative. The effect of a higher productivity of labor on optimal employment is ambiguous: There is an employment-increasing effect on profitability sl_i^*, but there is also a decreasing effect because less labor is needed to produce a given output. The effect of a higher expected demand on employment is positive, while increased uncertainty (i.e., a higher variance of demand) may increase or decrease employment, depending on the value of sl_i^* and depending on the particular form of the distribution function of demand. For example, if the distribution function is symmetric around the expected value, the critical value of sl_i^* is 0.5. If $sl_i^* > 0.5$ then optimal employment will decrease with higher uncertainty, and vice versa. However, this property cannot be generalized for skewed distributions.

Case 2: Capacity constraint. If the firm is constrained by the existing capital stock, no more workers will be demanded than can be employed with the (predetermined) capital stock. Optimal employment is determined according to

$$LT_i^* = L_{YC_i} = \frac{YC_i}{\pi_{l,i}} = \pi_{k,i} \cdot \frac{K_i}{\pi_{l,i}}. \tag{7}$$

Employment is given by the available number of working places. This implies that the employment constraint is also binding for goods supply YS_i.

Case 3: Labor supply constraint. In the case of insufficient labor supply, the firm has not enough applicants to fill all vacancies. Employment cannot exceed this constraint, so optimal employment is equal to the labor supply:

$$LT_i^* = LS_i. \tag{8}$$

The three cases can be summarized by a minimum condition for optimal employment:

$$LT_i^* = \min(L_i^*, L_{YC_i}, LS_i). \tag{9}$$

In the model, the utilization of labor varies procyclically, with higher utilization in the presence of positive (unexpected) demand shocks and hence a *procyclically* varying measured productivity of labor. This property is in accordance with observed stylized facts and stands in contrast to conventional models of dynamic factor input adjustment, which allow for immediate adjustment of employment and short-run substitution of capital and labor and hence imply an *anticyclical* movement of the productivity of labor. On the other hand, optimal labor hoarding will decrease with lessened uncertainty of demand, and less labor hoarding will be observed in the presence of labor supply or capacity constraints.

The investment decision must be made τ_K periods before demand realization with uncertainty about labor supply and goods demand. It fixes capacities as well as the capital/labor ratio. The results are presented in detail in Smolny (1993b), where it is shown that the optimal capacities depend on profitability and the possible constraints on the goods and labor market. The optimal factor productivities are determined by real factor costs, weighted by the utilization of the factors and the shadow price of the labor supply constraint.

The aggregation procedure of micromarkets in different regimes rests on a derivation put forward by Lambert (1988). For lognormally distributed micromarkets, a very simple analytical expression for aggregate employment LT can be derived. If the weighted probabilities of the regimes are approximated by a logistic curve, it can be shown to yield the following CES-type function for aggregate employment:

$$LT = \{LD^{-\rho_m} + LS^{-\rho_m}\}^{-1/\rho_m}. \tag{10}$$

Variables without the index i refer to aggregate values, and ρ_m serves as a mismatch parameter with

$$\frac{\partial LT}{\partial \rho_m} > 0, \quad \lim_{\rho_m \to \infty} LT = \min(LD, LS).$$

Aggregate employment can be determined from aggregate supply and demand and the mismatch parameter ρ_m, depending on the variance of the logarithmic difference of both variables on the micro level. Labor demand, in turn, is given by the minimum of the capacity constraint and demand-determined employment. For this case, the CES property can be applied as well. The distribution of the minimum of two lognormally distributed variables can again be closely approximated by a lognormal distribution, and aggregate employment can be determined from[11]

$$LT = \{LS^{-\rho_m} + [L^{*-\rho_f} + L_{YC}^{-\rho_f}]^{\rho_m/\rho_f}\}^{-1/\rho_m}. \tag{11}$$

This example shows that the aggregation procedure, which was originally designed to capture the case of micromarkets in disequilibrium situations, can also be applied to those kind of firm's (or household's) behavior, which can be expressed by minimum conditions. Two CES functions can be stated, one for the labor market and one for the labor demand of the firm; these functions can be nested to determine aggregate employment in terms of labor supply, capacity employment, and demand-determined employment.

The complete model of the firm consists of five behavioral relations. Output is given by the minimum of goods supply and demand, and supply is in turn determined by employment. Employment depends on expected demand, the labor supply, and capacities. Optimal capacities depend on

[11] See Smolny (1993a).

profitability and possible constraints on the goods and labor market; the optimal factor productivities are determined by real factor costs, weighted by the utilization of the factors and the shadow price of the labor supply constraint. The estimation is carried out in two steps. The first step consists of the determination of the technical productivities of labor and capital. Observed productivities deviate from the technical ones by the respective degree of utilization of the factor in question. This implies the following relations between actual productivities, factor costs, the shadow price of the labor supply constraint, and the utilization of the factors:

$$\frac{YT}{LT} = \pi_l \cdot DUL, \tag{12}$$

$$\frac{YT}{K} = \pi_k \cdot DUC. \tag{13}$$

By using indicators for the degrees of utilization of labor DUL and capital DUC, the productivity equations can be expressed completely in terms of observable variables and can thus be estimated. For the utilization of capital, an indicator is given by the business survey series on capacity utilization q for industry (published by the ifo institute, Munich). The indicator for utilization of labor within the firm is based on the correlation of the utilizations of labor and capital: The most important source of underutilization are unexpected demand shocks, with employment adjusting faster to those shocks; this is captured by a dynamic specification of q.

The significance of this indicator provides also a test of the assumptions made in the derivation of the model. Significant underutilization of labor stresses the role of a delayed adjustment of employment, as well as of a delayed adjustment of the capital/labor ratio. With an immediate adjustment of employment and a putty-clay technology, the productivity of labor should not be cyclical at all. An immediate adjustment of employment together with short-run substitution possibilities between labor and capital would imply an anticyclical productivity of labor. A procyclical productivity of labor within the firm can occur only in the case of a slow adjustment of employment and the capital/labor ratio. The underutilization of labor and capital is also an indicator of price rigidities. In a model with perfectly flexible prices, firms can always lower prices in case of a negative demand shock. This should increase utilization, so if firms instead prefer underutilization of labor and capital then there is some form of price rigidity. The estimated degree of utilization of labor is based on the estimation of productivity equations, which are presented in Smolny (1993b). This estimate is given by[12]

---

[12] The estimation is based on quarterly data of the private sector of the West German economy. The data sample is 1960Q1–1989Q4.

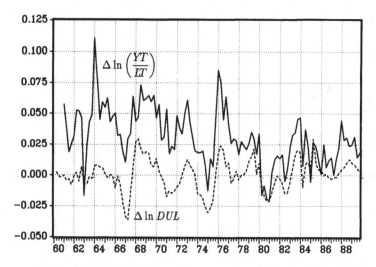

Figure 1. Annual changes in labor productivity and utilization.

$$\ln DUL_t = 0.44 \cdot (\ln q_t - 0.408 \cdot \ln q_{t-1}) - \text{const.}, \qquad (14)$$
$$\qquad\quad (0.06) \qquad\quad (0.10)$$

where standard errors are reported in parentheses. The constant stands for the observed maximum of the variable. Very significant coefficients were found for the utilization indicator. The short-run correlation between labor productivity and utilization can be seen in Figure 1. The estimated coefficients imply an average utilization of labor of about 97 percent. This corresponds to an average amount of labor hoarding of about 600,000 workers; in recession periods, labor hoarding exceeds 1,000,000 workers. The implied amount of labor hoarding can be seen from Figure 2.[13] The term LT denotes actual employment and L_{YT} the number of workers necessary to produce output:

$$L_{YT} = YT/\pi_t. \qquad (15)$$

Here, π_t is again taken from the estimation of the productivity equations. This result accentuates the importance of labor hoarding and the dynamic adjustment of employment. It also gives a hint for understanding business cycle asymmetries: The reaction of output with respect to demand is bounded upward by supply, but has no similar bound in case of negative demand shocks.

The optimal productivities are necessary ingredients for the calculation of capacity employment. Capacities are calculated from capital productivity and the stock of capital, and capacity employment is given by:

[13] The data depicted in the figures are seasonally adjusted by constant seasonal factors.

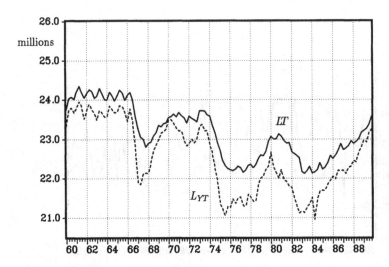

Figure 2. Labor hoarding.

$$L_{YC} = YC/\pi_l = \pi_k \cdot K/\pi_l. \tag{16}$$

For the determination of excess demand, it is assumed that domestic demand can always be realized by switching to the foreign markets in case of supply constraints on the domestic market. This gives an instruction for the calculation of demand: The excess demand for domestic products is given by those imports that are caused by supply constraints on the domestic market *plus* that part of exports not carried out owing to the supply constraints of domestic firms. Trade equations are estimated with the most important determinants of exports and imports included, and containing also an indicator for supply constraints on the domestic market. This yields an estimate for the excess demand. The estimation results are again taken from Smolny (1993b). Aggregate demand is calculated according to

$$YD = YT + \text{excess demand}, \tag{17}$$

and demand-determined employment follows from

$$L_{YD} = YD/\pi_l. \tag{18}$$

Labor supply is given by employment plus the number of unemployed:

$$\overline{LS} = LT + U. \tag{19}$$

These series are an important outcome of our approach; they are depicted in Figures 3 and 4, together with actual employment LT. The labor supply was treated as an exogenous variable for the derivation of the basic model, but the endogeneity of the labor supply will be taken into account

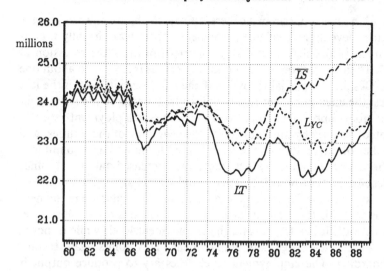

Figure 3. Employment series I: LT, L_{YC}, $\overline{LS}$.

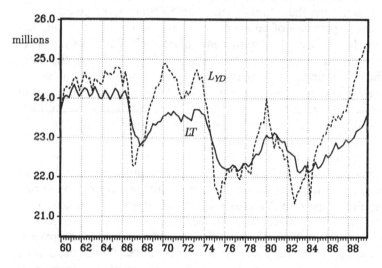

Figure 4. Employment series II: LT, L_{YD}.

for the derivation of the dynamic adjustment of employment in what follows. From Figure 3, it can be seen that the labor supply is an endogenous variable on the aggregate level also. It decreased during recessions and increased during boom periods. Factors accounting for this are the dependence of international factor mobility on the employment situation in the FRG and the inverse relation between the unemployment rate and the participation rates of German workers.[14] From the figure one can also see the distinct development of unemployment. There was virtually no unemployment in the sixties until 1973, apart from the short recession in 1966–67. Then the number of unemployed persons increased to about one million. Despite the partial recovery of the employment level in the late seventies, the unemployment rate remained high owing to the sharply increasing labor supply. The mild decrease in the unemployment rate was terminated abruptly by the recession at the beginning of the eighties, and the number of unemployed persons increased to more than two million. Since then, it has remained rather stable and decreased only slowly since 1986, despite the enormous increase in employment since 1983.

The most striking characteristic of demand-determined employment L_{YD} in Figure 4 is the high variance over the business cycle. During recession periods, it lies far beyond the employment level, while in boom periods it increases faster than employment. This points again toward labor hoarding. The employment level necessary to produce output is always less than or equal to L_{YD}, and $L_{YD} < LT$ implies labor hoarding. On the other hand, during boom periods, demand-determined employment increases faster than employment. These distinct developments again indicate the importance of adjustment constraints for employment. Referring solely to Figure 4, employment adjusts only slowly with respect to demand during the upswing and during the downswing. On the other hand, the development of capacity employment is smoother than actual employment. The recessions of 1966–67 and 1974 are less pronounced in L_{YC} than in employment. In addition, L_{YC} lags behind employment, indicating the slower adjustment of capacities with respect to demand.

Taken together, these figures draw a rather detailed picture of the economic situation in the FRG. Until 1966, an equilibrium situation obtained. The labor supply was slightly below capacity employment, the demand for goods approximately equaled capacities, and the unemployment rate stayed at about 1 percent. Employment and the degrees of utilization of labor and capital remained fairly stable. This picture changed sharply with the recession in 1966. Demand-determined employment decreased, and the unemployment figures increased to above 500,000 people, despite the remigration of many guest workers. Capacities adjusted downward, and gross investment in the first quarter of 1967 was nearly 20 percent below the corresponding level of the preceding year. However, the recession was short-lived and demand increased again until 1970, brought about mainly by higher exports caused by the undervaluation of the deutsche

---

[14] The endogeneity of the aggregate labor supply is not analyzed in this work. Some determinants of the labor supply in the FRG are analyzed by Franz and Smolny (1990) and Smolny (1992).

mark and high growth rates of the world economy. The labor supply and capacities adjusted only slowly, and in 1970 the shortages of capital and labor supply were the main factors restraining a higher growth rate of the economy. The subsequent slowdown of demand in 1971 had hardly any consequences for employment and investment, and the economy boomed until the first oil-price shock hit the German economy. High inflation rates at the beginning of the seventies – caused by an enormous wage push in 1970 and increases in monetary growth in the course of the breakdown of the Bretton Woods exchange-rate system – induced the Deutsche Bundesbank to switch to a restrictive policy, and short-run interest rates exceeded 14 percent. These high interest rates reduced investment and consumption demand, and exports declined in consequence of the slowdown of world demand. In 1975, the unemployment figure exceeded one million and the utilization of labor and capital decreased to very low levels. The partial recovery since then was terminated with the second oil-price shock. Again, high inflation rates induced a restrictive monetary policy.[15] Between 1979 and 1981, the money supply remained below the minimum of the target set by the Deutsche Bundesbank, and interest rates were high. As a result, investment and consumption decreased in real terms. Furthermore, the fiscal authorities changed to a restrictive course and in 1983 the unemployment figure exceeded two million. Since then, the economy has switched to a path of sustained growth. Figures 3 and 4 indicate that one factor inhibiting employment growth is probably the adjustment constraints of employment; that is, the persistence of unemployment in the eighties can partly be attributed to the dynamics of employment adjustment. Only at the end of the eighties did the slow adjustment of capacities become the dominant constraint for employment.

The figures give also a hint for understanding the asymmetric behavior of employment during the business cycle. In case of positive demand shocks, there is an upper bound on the target level of employment given by capacities and the labor supply. No similar bound prevents the reduction of employment in case of negative demand shocks.

3   Dynamic employment adjustment

Employment cannot exceed the labor supply. However, the labor supply consists of those already employed in the firm as well as job applicants. It therefore seems sensible to allow for a dependence of the current labor supply on the past employment level. A similar dependence on past employment can be stated for the demand for labor. Investments in firm-

---

[15] Another reason for the restrictive monetary policy was a deficit in the trade balance and a devaluation of the deutsche mark.

specific human capital, implicit full-employment contracts, and reputation losses give rise to costs of dismissing workers and so tend to restrict the downward adjustment of employment to normal fluctuations (i.e., quits and retirement). In addition, the limited capacity for training entrants may prevent a too-rapid growth of employment. One way to introduce these aspects into the employment decision is to assume a constraint on the adjustment *speed* of employment. For labor demand, this can be formalized as

$$LD_{t,i} = \min\{(1+\delta_i^c)\cdot LT_{t-1,i}, \max[LD_{t,i}^*, (1-\delta_i^s)\cdot LT_{t-1,i}]\}, \qquad (20)$$

where t is the time index and $LD_{t,i}^*$ is the target level of labor demand to which the firm wants to adjust. The parameter δ_i^c is determined by the capacity for training entrants, and the minimum condition in (20) restricts the maximum amount of adjustment of employment within one period to δ_i^c percent of the past employment level. The maximum condition implies a limit on the downward adjustment, and δ_i^s is the maximum rate of downward adjustment of employment.[16] If the costs of dismissing are prohibitive then δ_i^s can be identified with the rate of normal separations. A similar model can be applied to the supply of labor:

$$LS_{t,i} = \min[(1+\delta_i^a)\cdot LT_{t-1,i}, \overline{LS}_{t,i}]. \qquad (21)$$

Equation (21) reflects a constraint on the absolute level of labor supply $\overline{LS}$, as well as on the maximum rate of applications. It implies that the labor supply increases if the firm increases employment, but only until it reaches an exogenous level constraint $\overline{LS}_{t,i}$. It seems important to allow for both kinds of constraints. In the short run and during recessions, the number of applications within a time period restricts employment growth, whereas it is plausible that a low overall *level* of labor supply prevents higher employment in the long run and during boom periods.

Now there are four restrictions causing employment to differ from the target level of labor demand $LD_{t,i}^*$: First, the level of employment is retricted by the exogenous level constraint on labor supply $\overline{LS}_{t,i}$; second, the decrease in employment cannot exceed maximum (optimal) separations; third, employment increases must be carried out with limited training capacities; and finally, the number of job applicants with a time period can be binding. The last two restrictions can be combined. Defining $\delta_i^h = \min(\delta_i^a, \delta_i^c)$, optimal employment is determined by

$$LT_{t,i} = \min\{\overline{LS}_{t,i}, (1+\delta_i^h)\cdot LT_{t-1,i}, \max[LD_{t,i}^*, (1-\delta_i^s)\cdot LT_{t-1,i}]\}. \qquad (22)$$

---

[16] δ_i^s can also be interpreted as the optimal rate of downward adjustment. A dependence of δ_i^s on the expected persistence of low labor demand, for instance, is plausible.

An interesting property of this kind of adjustment constraints is the simple way of allowing for different restrictions on upward and downward adjustments of employment. For $\delta_i^s < \delta_i^h$, for instance, the downward adjustment is more impeded than the upward adjustment; as a special case, $\delta_i^h = \infty$ ($\delta_i^s = 1$) implies an unconstrained upward (downward) adjustment.

However, in the dynamic model here, the optimal target level of employment differs from those derived in the static context. Again, $LD_{t,i}^*$ depends on the number of workers that can be employed with the capital stock, L_{YC_i}. However, it may be profitable to employ more workers than L_{YC_i}. For example, if the firm is installing capacities at time t_1, it can start earlier with employment adjustment in light of the difficulties in finding applicants. The additional wage costs incurred by an earlier hiring may be more than compensated by the earlier use of the new machine. The expected demand for goods is also a determinant for $LD_{t,i}^*$, but once again the strong minimum condition (9) need not hold. In the face of an expected temporary demand shock, for instance, the employment level may adjust only partially. Employment depends not only on current constraints on adjustment, but also on expected employment changes and expected future constraints on employment adjustment.

This model of employment adjustment has in some respects features that are just the opposite of those of the fixed-costs model mentioned previously. In the model here, firms adjust completely if the desired adjustment is *within* some small range given by the δ parameters. In the fixed-cost model, firms adjust only if the desired adjustment is *outside* some range determined by the extent of those costs. Both models imply a partial adjustment of aggregate employment with respect to shocks, but with increasing hazards in the fixed-cost model and decreasing hazards in the model here.

The aggregation procedure of micromarkets in disequilibrium situations can also be applied to capture these extensions of the model. Equation (22) contains a maximum condition, but it can be shown (in a procedure analogous to those applied for the aggregation of the minimum condition) that the aggregate maximum of two lognormally distributed variables can be approximated as well by a CES function.[17] The only modification is given by a change in the sign of the mismatch parameter. It should be noted that the δ parameters need not be equal for all firms; the only requirement is the close approximation of the distribution of all variables by a lognormal distribution.

[17] See Smolny (1993a).

4   Estimation results

In the empirical application of the model, three mechanisms for the dynamic adjustment of labor demand and supply with respect to equilibrium values are tested. The first corresponds to the aggregate version of (22) and implies a lower and upper bound on the adjustment speed of actual employment with respect to its target level. Alternatively, a more standard specification of the dynamic adjustment of employment is tested, one that relies on convex adjustment costs instead of adjustment constraints. The adjustment path implied by convex adjustment costs is approximated by a partial adjustment mechanism for labor demand. Actual employment is again determined by supply and demand, and the target level of employment is determined by the available number of working places and expected demand for goods. This combination of minimum conditions and a partial adjustment mechanism seems to be another promising basis for the specification of dynamic adjustment processes for employment. Compared with a standard partial adjustment mechanism for employment, it has the advantage that the restriction $LT \le \overline{LS}$ is implied; compared with a sole specification in terms of constraints, it has the advantage of fewer nonlinearities and that fewer coefficients must be estimated. Finally, the dynamic adjustment of employment is estimated by a linear and a nonlinear error correction model. This procedure is not derived within the context of the theoretical model, but it can give indications of nonlinearities and asymmetries of the observed employment adjustment.

In Table 1, estimation results of the CES employment equations are reported.[18] The first rows depict the results from a static CES employment function. The fitted values of this equation will be used later for the estimation of the error correction model. Otherwise, these results should be seen only as a reference point for the tabulation of the dynamic employment functions displayed thereunder. In the next version displayed, the dynamic adjustment of employment is specified solely in terms of minimum and maximum conditions. The estimated coefficient for the constraint on the speed of the upward adjustment δ^h is about 0.006, which implies that the firms (on average) cannot increase their labor force by more than 0.6 percent per quarter. This coefficient is rather low, but stable in the different specifications tested. The result seems to be plausible; it can be seen from Figures 3 and 4 that the maximum observed employment

---

[18] Of course, demand-determined employment L_{YD} is an endogenous variable from an econometric point of view. However, results changed only negligibly if an instrumental variable technique was applied, which may be due to a slow adjustment of demand with respect to employment. We therefore proceeded with NLS estimates.

Table 1. *Employment dynamics: CES specification*

(1) *Static CES function*

$$LT_t = \{LS_t^{-\rho} + LD_t^{-\rho}\}^{-1/\rho}$$
$$LD_t = \{L_{YD_t}^{-\rho} + L_{YC_t}^{-\rho}\}^{-1/\rho}$$

$$1/\rho = 0.0127$$
$$(0.002)$$

SEE: 0.0143   DW: 0.538

(2) *CES adjustment*

$$LT_t = \{LS_t^{-\rho} + LD_t^{-\rho}\}^{-1/\rho}$$
$$LS_t = \{\overline{LS}_t^{-\rho} + [(1 + 0.0062) \cdot LT_{t-1}]^{-\rho}\}^{-1/\rho}$$
$$(0.001)$$
$$LD_t = \{LD_t^{*\rho'} + [(1 - 0.0101) \cdot LT_{t-1}]^{\rho'}\}^{1/\rho'}$$
$$(0.003)$$
$$LD_t^* = \{L_{YD_t}^{-\rho} + L_{YC_t}^{-\rho}\}^{-1/\rho}$$

$$1/\rho = 0.0080 \qquad 1/\rho' = 0.0194$$
$$(0.001) \qquad\qquad (0.005)$$

SEE: 0.0045   BP(8): 82.2

(3) *Partial adjustment*

$$LT_t = \{LS_t^{-\rho} + LD_t^{-\rho}\}^{-1/\rho}$$
$$LS_t = \overline{LS}_t$$
$$LD_t = 0.204 \cdot LD_t^* + (1 - 0.204) \cdot LT_{t-1}$$
$$(0.023) \qquad\qquad (*)$$
$$LD_t^* = \{L_{YD_t}^{-\rho} + L_{YC_t}^{-\rho}\}^{-1/\rho}$$

$$1/\rho = 0.0057$$
$$(0.001)$$

SEE: 0.0043   BP(8): 85.9

Notes: DW: Durbin–Watson statistic. BP(8): Box–Pierce Q-statistic, eight lags. Data sample: 1960Q1–1989Q4. The estimation sample is shortened to allow for lags. Standard errors in parentheses. The estimation is carried out in logs. All equations include seasonal dummies but no constant.

increases are about in this dimension.[19] The estimated coefficient δ^s implies that the downward adjustment is slightly less impeded. The maximum downward adjustment is estimated to be about 1 percent per quarter. However, the difference between these coefficients is not significant. In the last rows, the results obtained from a partial adjustment specification of

[19] It should be noted that seasonal dummies were included in the estimated equation. The data for the figures are also seasonal-adjusted with constant seasonal factors. It should be noted that the observed seasonal changes are larger than the estimated coefficients.

labor demand are depicted.[20] The results achieved with this combination of minimum conditions and the usual partial adjustment mechanism are encouraging. Only two coefficients are estimated, and the standard error of the equation is below 0.5 percent. The estimated dynamic adjustment is similar to those obtained from the pure CES specification, and the adjustment coefficient λ is about 0.2.

From these versions of the employment function, the following conclusions can be drawn. First, the dynamic adjustment of employment is very pronounced. Allowing for a dynamic adjustment yielded a remarkably better explanation of actual employment as compared with a static equation. The estimated adjustment is rather slow: The partial adjustment model yielded an estimate of 20 percent adjustment of labor demand per quarter,[21] while the CES approach yielded a maximum adjustment per quarter not above 1 percent of the previous employment level. This is in accordance with the model and can explain the considerable amount of labor hoarding during recession periods. The results indicate that it is difficult to discriminate between these approaches, despite their different implications. Recall that the CES specification of employment dynamics implies a slower adjustment in case of large deviations of actual employment from the target level; that is, the adjustment hazard is decreasing in the desired adjustment. In addition, both employment equations are plagued by enormous serial correlation. We therefore attempted to extract some further information about employment dynamics by estimating a more general error correction model.

The results from the error correction specification of employment adjustment are displayed in Table 2. The target level of employment LT^* is taken from the fitted values of the static CES employment function in Table 1, and is depicted together with actual employment in Figure 5. We have shown that the target level derived from this equation is always below its arguments (i.e., demand-determined employment, capacity employment, and the labor supply). The bad fit of this equation is therefore not surprising.[22] In addition, one can see an asymmetry of the differences between actual employment and the target level: In case of negative demand shocks, the target level of employment falls far below actual

---

[20] A similar combination of the CES function and the partial adjustment mechanism was used by Sneessens and Drèze (1986). See also the papers in Drèze and Bean (1990), especially Entorf et al. (1990).

[21] It should be noted that the adjustment of employment is lower in case of labor supply constraints.

[22] One may even question the stationarity of the residuals of this equation. The t-statistic of an augmented Dickey–Fuller test is 2.76. However, the residuals are significant in the dynamic error correction model (see the following discussion).

Table 2. *Employment dynamics: error correction specification (dependent variable:* $\Delta \ln LT_t$)

Explanatory variables	Version			
	(1)	(2)	(3)	(4)
$\Delta \ln LT_t^*$	0.194 (0.03)	0.182 (0.02)	0.015 (0.04)	0.060 (0.03)
$\ln LT_{t-1} - \ln LT_{t-1}^*$	−0.143 (0.03)	−0.090 (0.03)		
$\ln LT_{t-2} - \ln LT_t^*$			−0.179 (0.05)	−0.150 (0.04)
$(\ln LT_{t-2} - \ln LT_t^*)^2$			0.527 (0.62)	1.473 (0.69)
$(\ln LT_{t-2} - \ln LT_t^*)^3$			28.36 (26.3)	25.79 (27.6)
$(\ln LT_{t-2} - \ln LT_t^*)^4$			−432.2 (282.0)	−468.7 (267.0)
$\Delta \ln LT_{t-1}$	0.320 (0.07)	0.384 (0.08)	0.154 (0.09)	0.256 (0.10)
$\Delta \ln LT_{t-2}$	−0.118 (0.06)		−0.158 (0.06)	
$\Delta \ln LT_{t-3}$	−0.177 (0.05)		−0.163 (0.05)	
$\Delta \ln LT_{t-4}$	0.600 (0.06)		0.611 (0.06)	
$\Delta \ln LT_{t-5}$	−0.492 (0.06)		−0.493 (0.06)	
AR(4)		0.788 (0.06)		0.800 (0.06)
SEE	0.00288	0.00311	0.00286	0.00301
serial correlation: χ^2	9.95 [0.27]	13.1 [0.11]	12.8 [0.12]	9.1 [0.33]
Wald χ^2			4.7 [0.20]	9.6 [0.02]

Notes: The constant and the seasonal dummies are not reported. Standard errors in parentheses. AR(4): coefficient of autocorrelation, eight lags. The test for autocorrelation is the Breusch/Godfrey-Lagrange multiplier test with eight lags. The coefficient restriction of the Wald test concerns the exclusion of the three nonlinear error correction terms. The significance levels are reported in brackets.

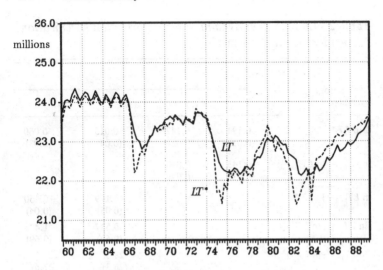

Figure 5. Employment series III: *LT, LT**.

employment; in case of a positive demand shock, insufficient capacities prevent a quick increase of the target level. One can also see that the actual employment is below the target level in the second half of the eighties, which points toward the importance of adjustment constraints for explaining the persistence of unemployment during this period.

In the first two versions displayed in Table 2, a linear error correction model is estimated. In version (1), employment changes are explained by changes in the target level of employment, the lagged residuals of the static CES equation, and additional lags of the endogenous variable. The short-term impact of a change in the target level is about 0.2, the error correction coefficient is about −0.15, and a rather strong effect is found for the first lagged endogenous variable. In addition, the seasonal lags account for fourth-order autocorrelation. The adjustment speed is similar to the foregoing dynamic CES equations, but the error correction model accounts also for the positive autocorrelation of employment changes. This lends further support to the argument that adjustment takes time – that is, an intended change of employment takes more than one period. The large seasonal changes of employment correspond to the large gross flows emphasized in the matching function literature, as compared with the rather low net annual changes of employment. In version (2), the seasonal autocorrelation is captured by an AR(4) process for the residuals instead of for the lagged endogenous variables, which nonetheless yields about the same results.

Versions (3) and (4) in Table 2 test for additional nonlinearities in the adjustment process of employment. More specifically, the adjustment coefficient is approximated by a higher-order polynomial of the difference between the target level of employment and lagged employment. This should give some information on whether adjustment hazards are asymmetric and/or increasing or decreasing in the size of the desired adjustment. Taking the comparable importance of the actual change in the target, the lagged equilibrium error, and the lagged change of the endogenous variable, we tested for nonlinearity in the coefficient of $(\ln LT_{t-2} - \ln LT_t^*)$. The nonlinearity was also specified in terms of $(\ln LT_{t-1} - \ln LT_t^*)$ and $(\ln LT_{t-1} - \ln LT_{t-1}^*)$, versions that yielded the same qualitative results (not reported). In the displayed versions, up to fourth-order polynomial terms of this difference were used as regressors; higher-order polynomials of this difference did not contribute significantly to the explanation. The versions correspond to the linear error correction models (1) and (2): In version (3), seasonal autocorrelation is specified in terms of the endogenous variable; in version (4), an autoregressive model for the residuals is employed. Both versions include as special cases the corresponding linear error correction models, thereby enabling a test for the significance of these terms.

In version (4), the nonlinearity contributes significantly to the explanation of employment changes. The implied adjustment coefficient λ, defined as

$$\lambda = \frac{\partial(\Delta \ln LT_t)}{\partial(\ln LT_{t-2} - \ln LT_t^*)},$$

is displayed in Figure 6. A histogram of the frequency of the observations is given in Figure 7. It can be seen that the absolute value of the adjustment coefficient has a relative maximum for small negative differences between lagged employment and the target level. The estimated adjustment is fastest if the target level is slightly higher than lagged employment, that is, for small increases in employment. The adjustment coefficient is lower (in absolute value) for larger increases in employment and has a relative minimum for medium-size downward adjustments of the labor force. For large decreases in employment (i.e. recessions), the estimated coefficients imply an increase in the adjustment speed. However, it should be noted that this estimation result is based on only two observations within this range and hence should be viewed with caution. Version (3) reveals substantially the same conclusions for the adjustment coefficient. The significance of the nonlinearity of the adjustment is lower, which may be partly due to multicollinearity of lagged employment changes and the nonlinear error correction terms.

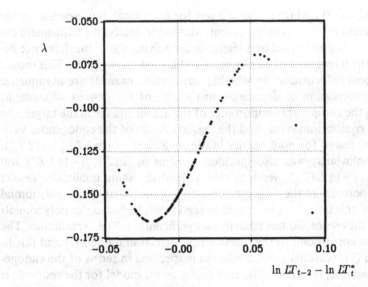

Figure 6. Adjustment coefficient.

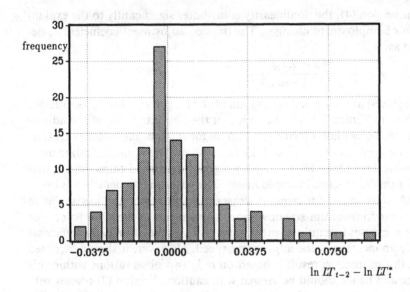

Figure 7. Residual histogram.

What can be learned from these estimation results? First, less than 20 percent of a desired change in employment is carried out within the first quarter. This accounts for the considerable amount of labor hoarding during recession periods, and also accentuates the importance of supply constraints on the goods market in case of demand increases. Second, the observed adjustment appears to be more complicated than a simple partial adjustment scheme. The estimated adjustment is asymmetric as well as decreasing in the size of the desired change of employment. This result is in accordance with matching function models, and stands in contrast to the model with fixed costs of adjustment. One interpretation of this result is that adjustment takes time, and a larger adjustment takes a longer time. Only in deep recession does the adjustment speed seem to increase. Third, there is considerable seasonal variation of employment changes. This corresponds to the observed large gross employment flows, and stands in contrast to the estimated slow seasonal adjusted changes of aggregate employment. One interpretation is that a different mechanism drives the adjustment of employment in those parts of the economy with strong seasonal changes in labor demand.

5   Conclusion

The main objectives of this paper are the investigation of the dynamic adjustment of employment and the analysis of the resulting inefficiencies. An excess supply on the goods market that is not immediately removed by price or quantity adjustments implies underutilization of labor, and excess supply on the labor market is unemployment. The slow adjustment of quantities increases the persistence of these disequilibria, and is seen as an important component for an explanation of the business cycle. A dynamic model of the firm is derived and supplemented by an aggregation procedure for firms in disequilibrium situations. At any moment of time, different firms face different constraints on the goods and labor market. The aggregate transacted quantity can be approximated by an explicit functional relation that depends on aggregate supply, aggregate demand, and a mismatch parameter. The aggregation procedure allows an easy transformation of the firm-specific variables into aggregate quantities, and the model can be tested by using merely aggregate data.

The results of the estimation of the model generally confirm the assumptions used in its derivation. Significant underutilizations of labor were found, which indicates a slow adjustment of employment and the production technology; they indicate also a downward rigidity of prices. For employment, it takes more than two quarters before half of the adjustment is carried out. The adjustment appears to be asymmetric, and the adjustment speed appears to decrease with the size of the desired adjustment. One outcome of the approach is the different measures of disequilibrium on the goods and labor markets. A measure of the short-run excess supply or demand on the goods market is provided by the utilization of labor. On the labor market, Keynesian labor demand and capacity employment can be determined, in addition to the labor supply. The employment series reveal the importance of demand for the medium-run determination of employment. Demand is the driving force for employment changes.

In the short and medium run, employment growth can be limited by adjustment constraints for employment. These aspects provide a partial explanation for the persistence of high unemployment in Germany in the eighties. At the beginning of the eighties, the demand breakdown in the course of the second oil-price shock reduced employment. After the recovery of demand in 1984, employment growth was impeded mainly by adjustment constraints for employment. Only at the end of the eighties did the slow adjustment of capacities constrain employment.

REFERENCES

Becker, G. S. (1962), "Investment in Human Capital: A Theoretical Analysis," *Journal of Political Economy* 70: 9–49.

Bentolila, S., and G. Bertola (1990), "Firing Costs and Labour Demand: How Bad Is Eurosclerosis?" *Review of Economic Studies* 57: 381–402.

Bertola, G. (1991), "Labor Turnover and Average Labor Demand," Working Paper no. 3866, National Bureau of Economic Research, Cambridge, MA.

Bertola, G., and J. Caballero (1990), "Kinked Adjustment Costs and Aggregate Dynamics," *NBER Macroeconomics Annual,* pp. 237–95.

Blanchard, O. J., and P. Diamond (1989), "The Beveridge Curve," *Brookings Papers on Economic Activity* 1: 1–76.

(1992), "The Flow Approach to Labor Markets," *American Economic Association, Papers and Proceedings* 82: 354–9.

Caballero, R. J., and E. M. R. A. Engel (1992a), "Beyond the Partial-Adjustment Model," *American Economic Association, Papers and Proceedings* 82: 360–4.

(1992b), "Microeconomic Adjustment Hazards and Aggregate Dynamics," Working Paper no. 4090, National Bureau of Economic Research, Cambridge, MA.

Drèze, J. H., and C. Bean (1990), *Europe's Unemployment Problem.* Cambridge, MA: MIT Press.

Entorf, H., W. Franz, H. König, and W. Smolny (1990), "The Development of German Employment and Unemployment: Estimation and Simulation of a Disequilibrium Macro Model," in J. H. Drèze and C. Bean (eds.), *Europe's Unemployment Problem.* Cambridge, MA: MIT Press, pp. 239–87.

Franz, W., and W. Smolny (1990), "Internationale Migration und wirtschaftliche Entwicklung: Eine theoretische und empirische Analyse mit Hilfe eines

Mengenrationierungsmodells," in B. Felderer (ed.), *Bevölkerung und Wirtschaft.* Berlin: Duncker & Humboldt, pp. 195–209.

(1993), "The Measurement and Interpretation of Vacancy Data and the Dynamics of the Beveridge-Curve – The German Case," Diskussionspapier no. 3, Center for International Labor Economics, Universität Konstanz.

Hamermesh, D. S. (1989), "Labor Demand and the Structure of Adjustment Costs," *American Economic Review* 79: 647–89.

(1990a), "Aggregate Employment Dynamics and Lumpy Adjustment Costs," *Journal of Monetary Economics* (suppl.) 33: 93–130 (Carnegie–Rochester Conference Series on Public Policy).

(1990b), "A General Model of Dynamic Labor Demand," Working Paper no. 3356, National Bureau of Economic Research, Cambridge, MA.

(1993), "Spatial and Temporal Aggregation in the Dynamics of Labor Demand," in J. C. van Ours, G. A. Pfann, and G. Ridder (eds.), *Labor Demand and Equilibrium Wage Formation.* Amsterdam: Elsevier, pp. 91–108.

Lambert, J.-P. (1988), *Disequilibrium Macroeconomic Models – Theory and Estimation of Rationing Models Using Business Survey Data.* Cambridge University Press.

Nadiri, M. I., and S. Rosen (1969), "Interrelated Factor Demand Functions," *American Economic Review* 59: 457–71.

Nickell, S. J. (1978), *The Investment Decision of Firms.* Cambridge University Press.

(1986), "Dynamic Models of Labour Demand," in O. Ashenfelter and R. Layard (eds.), *Handbook of Labor Economics,* vol. I. Amsterdam: Elsevier, pp. 473–522.

Oi, W. Y. (1962), "Labor as a Quasi-fixed Factor," *Journal of Political Economy* 70: 555–88.

Okun, A. M. (1981), *Prices and Quantities: A Macroeconomic Analysis.* Oxford: Basil Blackwell.

Palm, F. C., and G. A. Pfann (1990), "Interrelated Demand Rational Expectations Models for Two Types of Labour," *Oxford Bulletin of Economics and Statistics* 52: 45–68.

Pfann, G. A. (1993), "The Thin Edge of the Wedge: Non-linearity in Stochastic Labor Market Dynamics," in J. C. van Ours, G. A. Pfann, and G. Ridder (eds.), *Labor Demand and Equilibrium Wage Formation.* Amsterdam: Elsevier, pp. 23–48.

Pfann, G. A., and F. C. Palm (1993), "Asymmetric Adjustment Costs in Nonlinear Labour Demand Models for the Netherlands and U.K. Manufacturing Sectors," *Review of Economic Studies* 60: 397–412.

Pindyck, R. S., and J. I. Rotemberg (1983), "Dynamic Factor Demands under Rational Expectations," *Scandinavian Journal of Economics* 85: 223–38.

Pissarides, C. (1992), "Search Theory at Twenty-one," Discussion Paper no. 90, Center for Economic Performance.

Rothschild, M. (1971), "On the Costs of Adjustment," *Quarterly Journal of Economics* 85: 605–22.

Smolny, W. (1992), "Macroeconomic Consequences of International Labour Migration," in H.-J. Vosgerau (ed.), *European Integration in the World Economy.* Berlin: Springer-Verlag, pp. 376–408.

420   **Werner Smolny**

(1993a), "Die Aggregation von Mikromärkten in Ungleichgewichtssituationen," in B. Gahlen, H. Hesse, and H.-J. Ramser (eds.), *Makroökonomik unvollständiger Märkte*. Tübingen: Mohr, pp. 137–67.

(1993b), *Dynamic Factor Demand in a Rationing Context: Theory and Estimation of a Macroeconomic Disequilibrium Model for the Federal Republic of Germany*. Heidelberg: Physica.

Sneessens, H. R., and J. H. Drèze (1986), "A Discussion of Belgian Unemployment, Combining Traditional Concepts and Disequilibrium Econometrics," *Economica* 53: S89–S119.

CHAPTER 15

A simulation study of disequilibrium price dynamics

Claus Weddepohl

1   Introduction

It it known that a discrete time tâtonnement process in an exchange economy need not converge to an equilibrium price vector, but can instead generate erratic dynamics with cyclical or chaotic paths (Bela and Majumdar
1992, Day and Pianigiani 1991, Saari 1985, Weddepohl 1995). That equilibrium prices are quickly obtained cannot be taken for granted, and disequilibrium might persist too long to postpone trade. The purpose of the
present paper is to study price adjustment in a disequilibrium model:
trade occurs at disequilibrium prices before the prices are adjusted. To
make such an exercise possible, a consistent adjustment model must be
formulated that takes disequilibrium phenomena into account, with a
Walrasian equilibrium as a fixed point of the process, so that a path indeed converges to an equilibrium if it converges at all.

In simulations of a discrete tâtonnement process in exchange economies with two and three goods (Weddepohl 1994, 1995), it appeared
that, because of overshooting, prices may jump up and down again and
again and the system may "explode." By restricting the rate of change
of prices, not only the volatility is diminished but also the amplitude:
the nonconverging paths remain within a neighborhood of the equilibrium price. The same technique is applied here in simulations in a three-
goods economy (the smallest number for disequilibrium adjustment with
numéraire to differ from tâtonnement). This gives rise to similar results.

In Section 2 the basic model is introduced. Section 3 contains a discussion on adjustment models and the model of this paper is presented. There
is trade in one market at a time: markets open consecutively and transactions are carried out at disequilibrium prices, which requires rationing.

The author thanks Cars Hommes for valuable conversation and for help with the construction of the figures.

New prices are set for the next period as a function of the level of excess demand. Since there is trade in each market separately, the sequence of trades can lead to deficits or surpluses of value. This requires some monetary asset. In Section 4 the different parts of the simulation processes are introduced, and a number of ways in which agents optimize in order to obtain excess demands is defined. In Section 5 the simulation model is summarized and some remarks on stability are made. The results of a series of simulations are given in Section 6.

2   The exchange economy

A standard exchange economy $E = \{\{u^h\}, \{X^h\}, \{w^h\}\}$ is studied with c consumers ($h = 1, 2, ..., c$) and n commodities ($i = 1, 2, ..., n$). The consumption set of consumer h is $X^h = \mathbb{R}^n_+$, with u^h and w^h denoting (respectively) the consumer's utility function and resource vector. Maximizing utility under consumer h's budget constraint $B^h(p) = \{x \in X^h : px \le pw^h\}$, given a price $p \in \mathbb{R}^n$, yields the demand function

$$x^h(p) = \arg\max\{u^h(x) \mid x \in B^h(p)\}. \tag{2.1}$$

A Walrasian equilibrium consists of an allocation x^{h*} for each h and a price vector p^* such that $x^{h*} = x^h(p^*)$ and

$$\sum_h x^{h*} = \sum_h w^h. \tag{2.2}$$

The excess demand functions are defined by

$$z^h(p) = x^h(p) - w^h, \tag{2.3}$$

with aggregate excess demand $z(p) = \sum_h z^h(p)$. Equation (2.2) is equivalent to $z(p^*) = 0$. In the sequel we shall frequently write $u^h(z^h)$ instead of $u^h(z^h + w^h) = u^h(x^h)$ and shall use the budget constraint $B^h(p) = \{z \mid z + w^h \in X^h \text{ and } pz \le 0\}$. Under the assumptions that, for all h, (i) u^h is strictly monotonous, strictly quasiconcave, and continuous, and (ii) $w^h > 0$, it is well-known that Walras's law holds (for all p: $pz(p) = 0$) and that a Walrasian equilibrium exists ($\{p^*, z^{h*}, h = 1, 2, ..., c\}$ such that $z(p^*) = 0$). It is further assumed that:

> the economy is stationary: the utilities and the resources are the same in each period; and
>
> consumers maximize utility over a single period only and have no intertemporal preferences; that is, they do not want to transfer income from one period to the next.

This means that utility depends only on a single commodity bundle and not on future consumptions, and implies that money is not included in the utility function (although money will be introduced as a medium of exchange). In a sequence of equilibria the same price $p(t) = p^*$ will obtain again and again, and the same trades z^{h*} are established in each period t.

3   Price adjustment models

3.1   Traditional models

The problem is how a Walrasian equilibrium can be established, that is, how the equilibrium price vector is to be realized. In the literature, different processes have been proposed that are unconvincing for different reasons. (Only discrete time processes are considered here, although continuous time versions also have been studied in the literature.)

A tâtonnement process starts with an initial price $p(0)$. In each stage $s = 1, 2, \ldots$, prices are adjusted on the basis of excess demand:

$$p(s+1) = \varphi(z(p(s))), \tag{3.1.1}$$

with φ such that $p_i(s+1) \gtrless p_i(s)$ if $z_i(p(s)) \gtrless 0$. Formula (3.1.1) is a difference equation whose equilibrium is a fixed point; that is, $p^* = \varphi(z(p^*))$. The standard interpretation is that an auctioneer proposes a price vector, agents express their individual excess demands, and the auctioneer adjusts the prices using (3.1.1) after computing aggregate excess demand $z(p(s))$. During the process there is no trade; transactions are carried out only after an equilibrium price has been found. Stages s remain within a single period t. Hence a price p^* established in period 1 could remain constant over time in our stationary economy. In an alternative interpretation, stages s coincide with periods t. In each period there is trade at the going price, but next period's price follows from "notional" excesses defined by (2.3). What trade is realized at disequilibrium prices is left open and is irrelevant for the adjustment. If at some t an equilibrium price is established, it will remain constant. Note, however, that in this interpretation demand is determined by maximizing u^h with respect to $B^h(p)$, as in (2.1), so the agents do not take into account the rationing they experienced. That is, there are no spillover effects, and the value of individual excess demand remains zero.

A nontâtonnement process results in a final allocation within a single period (Hahn and Negishi 1962). The initial allocation $x^h(0) = w^h$ and an initial price $p(0)$ are given. If $z(p(t)) \neq 0$ then some trade is carried out at $p(t)$, with zero net value for each h, leading to a new allocation. The excess generates a new price, as in the tâtonnement process. In the next stage, given the new allocation, trade is at the new price:

$$p(s+1) = \varphi(z(p(s), x(s-1))), \tag{3.1.2}$$

$$x_i^h(s) = x_i^h(s-1) + \bar{z}_i^h(s), \tag{3.1.3}$$

with $\sum_h \bar{z}_i^h(s) = 0$ and $\sum_i p_i(s) \bar{z}_i^h(s) = 0$, and where some rule on trade $\bar{z}_i^h(s)$ is needed. This continues until no excess remains, as no trade is desired at the final price. The final allocation is not a Walrasian but rather a Pareto efficient allocation. The final price is not an equilibrium price, so it need not constitute a better start for the next period. (In any case, I have been unable to find any studies that examine this question.) If p^* is the initial price then no adjustment is necessary: p^* is a fixed point of (3.1.2), that is, $p^* = \varphi(z(p^*, w))$, while $x_i^{h*} = w_i^h + z_i^{h*}$. The process I have in mind is not a nontâtonnement process in the sense just described because there will be trade in each commodity within a period only once.

A third method is to consider a sequence of fixed-price equilibria. Given p, a fixed-price equilibrium consists of a set of trades and a rationing scheme $\{z^h, \underline{\sigma}^h, \bar{\sigma}^h\}$ (the rationing scheme consists of supply constraints $\underline{\sigma}_i^h \le 0$ and demand constraints $\bar{\sigma}_i^h \ge 0$) such that

(i) $z^h(p; \underline{\sigma}^h, \bar{\sigma}^h) = \arg\max\{u(z) \mid z \in B^h(p), \underline{\sigma}_i^h \le z_i \le \bar{\sigma}_i^h\}$ (constrained excess demand);
(ii) $\sum_h z^h(p; \underline{\sigma}^h, \bar{\sigma}^h) = 0$;
(iii) for each i, no constraint is binding on two sides; and
(iv) constraints $\underline{\sigma}^h, \bar{\sigma}^h$ satisfy some condition (to be specified).

In a fixed-price equilibrium, prices are given but now an equilibrium set of constraints is to be determined. Condition (i) replaces (2.1): utility is maximized with respect to trades that satisfy not only the budget constraint but also the quantity restrictions. Condition (iii) excludes simultaneous demand and supply rationing of the same good. By (iv), a rationing system must be specified – for example, uniform rationing (identical for all h) as in Drèze (1975), or proportional rationing as in Benassy (1975). The fixed-price equilibrium at p^* coincides with the Walrasian equilibrium, and there are no binding constraints. A price adjustment process runs as follows: Given $p(t)$, a fixed-price equilibrium with an equilibrium rationing scheme is determined. Then $p(t+1)$ is set on the basis of binding constraints: If a supply (demand) constraint for good i is binding, its price is decreased (increased). Such a process might converge to an equilibrium price p^* (Veendorp 1975, Laroque 1981). In this case, spillovers are taken into account.

A drawback of all three processes is simultaneity: All markets are "visited" simultaneously by all agents; likewise, transactions are carried out and prices are adjusted simultaneously. For both computational and conceptual reasons I have decided to model each step in a simpler manner.[1]

3.2   *Consecutive markets*

Before we can study disequilibrium dynamics and perform simulations, we must describe the functioning of the markets. Rather than assuming that all trade is carried out simultaneously, I believe it is more realistic to assume that agents visit the markets consecutively – though it is not quite clear what "more realistic" means with respect to an exchange economy, since this is a pedagogical construct designed in order to achieve insight into exchange processes as such. In the real world with producers and dealers, a consumer tends to buy one commodity at a time and does not make purchases conditional on the trade possibility on markets visited later. If consumer h cannot satisfy his or her demand then h buys less, which might affect purchases at the market visited next. But if h has traded at market s then h will not undo this trade in response to rationing in market $s+1$.

I study models where, in each period, markets are open in a given order (the order of the goods index i). Each period is divided into n subperiods, where n denotes the number of commodities. Market i is open in subperiod (t, i) of period t,[2] which yields the sequence of markets $..., (t, 1)$, $(t, 2), ..., (t, n), (t+1, 1), (t+1, 2), ..., (t+1, n), ...$. At the beginning of each period, all prices are given. If market (t, i) does not clear, the given price vector is not an equilibrium; the ith price will be adjusted and $p_i(t+1)$ will be next period's price of good i.

The main question is: How is the excess demand $z_i^h(t)$ of each agent in subperiod (t, i) determined? There are still (at least the following) two ways to do this (the index h is suppressed).

Single-period optimization: During period t, an agent maximizes the utility $u(z(t))$ of the consumption bundle of period t, realized sequentially

---

[1] When I started this research on disequilibrium price adjustment, my first idea was to simulate sequences of fixed-price equilibria. But then I realized that determining a fixed-price equilibrium is at least as complex as determining the Walrasian equilibrium price. To find the constraints, a process similar to tâtonnement has to be designed. It is not clear why it should be assumed, on the one hand, that an equilibrium price cannot be found immediately, but that the more complex (simultaneous) equilibrium rationing scheme can be.

[2] A possibly more satisfactory construction would be to assume that all markets are open in every subperiod, but that each consumer visits each market only once. Each market is then visited by a subset of the consumers; these subsets could be made representative for the economy. In this case all prices are revised in each subperiod.

by trade in $(t, 1), (t, 2), ..., (t, n)$. In stage (t, i) the agent plans trades for $(t, i), (t, i+1), ..., (t, n)$, given realized trades $\bar{z}_1(t), \bar{z}_2(t), ..., \bar{z}_{i-1}(t)$. Thus the agent makes the plan

$$z_i(t, i), z_{i+1}(t, i), ..., z_n(t, i),$$

and his or her (excess) demand is $z_i(t) = z_i(t, i)$. If this trade is realized then the plan made in $(t, i+1)$ will coincide with the old plan of (t, i) for $j > i$, but if a constraint holds in (t, i) then the new plan will differ: $z_{i+1}(t, i+1) \neq z_{i+1}(t, i)$.

Gliding optimization: In each stage (t, i), the agent maximizes utility for a full demand vector and makes a plan for the n subperiods (t, i), $(t, i+1), ..., (t, n), (t+1, 1), ..., (t+1, i-1)$ consisting of

$$(z_i(t, i), z_{i+1}(t, i), ..., z_n(t, i), z_1(t, i), ..., z_{i-1}(t, i)),$$

without taking into account what happened before. Hence, in stage (t, i) the agent makes a plan for the next n subperiods and comes to the market with $z_i(t) = z_i(t, i)$.

Both models will be explored in what follows, because we cannot choose on a priori grounds. The question of which is the true model becomes important if the results are different. This will appear not to be the case, but to arrive at this conclusion we first had to perform the experiment.

3.3   *Money and credit*

Since there is trade in only one good in each subperiod, the budget constraint changes after each trade. It cannot be assumed that all payments are cleared at the end of a period, because (out of equilibrium) an agent's trade in the period need not have zero net value. We need to determine in each step how much can still be spent. Credit or money, as a medium of exchange, must be introduced. Let $m_i^h(t)$ denote h's monetary position at the end of subperiod (t, i), after the trade $\bar{z}_i^h$ has been realized. Given $m_{i-1}^h(t)$ and $\bar{z}_i^h(t)$, we have

$$m_i^h(t) = m_{i-1}^h(t) - p_i(t)\bar{z}_i^h(t); \tag{3.3.1}$$

here $m^h(t) \equiv m_n^h(t) = m_0^h(t+1)$ is the position at the end of period t. The term $m_i^h(t)$ can most easily be interpreted as the position of h's bank account, which means that all sales are paid for by transfers to the seller's account; however, it can also be seen as cash plus bank accounts plus claims on other consumers minus debts to other consumers. A priori the position can be negative, but restrictions will be introduced and $m_i^h(t)$

may appear in the budget restriction. In some versions of the model $m_i^h(t)$ can be interpreted as cash, which cannot become negative.

Given the trades $\bar{z}_i^h(t)$, $s_i^h(t)$ is h's trade surplus of period t at the end of subperiod (t, i):

$$s_i^h(t) = -[p_1(t)\bar{z}_1^h(t) + p_2(t)\bar{z}_2^h(t) + \cdots + p_i(t)\bar{z}_i^h(t)], \quad i = 1, 2, \ldots, n.$$

$$(3.3.2)$$

Here $s_i^h(t) > 0 \, (< 0)$ means that h has sold (bought) more than he bought (sold). Obviously, for all (t, i), $\sum_h s_i^h(t) = 0$. The net surplus of period t is $s^h(t) \equiv s_n^h(t)$ (with $s^h(0) \equiv 0$). The minimum value that h's surplus took on during t is

$$\sigma^h(t) = \min_i s_i^h(t).$$

$$(3.3.3)$$

In an equilibrium $\{p^*, z^*\}$ all markets clear and hence $\bar{z} = z^*$, giving the trade surpluses

$$s_i^{h*} = -\sum_{j=1}^{i} p_j^* z_j^{h*}, \quad i = 1, 2, \ldots, n,$$

$$(3.3.4)$$

where $\sigma^{h*} \leq s_n^{h*} = s^{h*} = 0$ is the minimum surplus in the equilibrium sequence. If the system is in equilibrium from t onward, each consumer's surplus will repeatedly follow the same pattern s_i^{h*}. If an agent h is a buyer in an initial sequence of subperiods and a seller later, then h's surplus will first be negative and then increase to zero. Out of equilibrium, the period's surplus $s^h(t)$ can be positive or negative. By (3.3.1) and (3.3.2),

$$m_i^h(t) = m^h(t-1) + s_i^h h(t).$$

$$(3.3.5)$$

The minimum position in period t is

$$\mu^h(t) = m^h(t-1) + \sigma^h(t).$$

$$(3.3.6)$$

If $m^h(t-1) \geq -\sigma^h(t)$, then $m_i^h(t)$ remains nonnegative during t and $\mu^h(t) \geq 0$. Stipulating $m^{h*} \geq -\sigma^{h*}$ ensures that h does not have to borrow in equilibrium. Let $M = \sum_h m^h(0)$ be the total initial amount of money (sum of all bank accounts or cash); then, for all (t, i),

$$\sum_h m_i^h(t) = M.$$

$$(3.3.7)$$

Suppose agents are not permitted (or do not want) to have a debt and do not want to hold more money than is strictly necessary. The equilibrium must then satisfy the extra condition that no agent's money holdings ever become negative; hence the initial money holdings must equal $-\sigma^{h*}$. This requires that there be a positive amount of money (which can now be called "cash") in the economy and so defines a "cash-in-advance equilibrium" (cf. Clower 1967).

Definition. A cash-in-advance equilibrium in economy E, given total cash M, is an allocation $\{x^{h*}\}$, a price p^*, and initial cash holdings $\{m^{h*}\}$ such that $\{x^{h*}, p^*\}$ is a Walrasian equilibrium and furthermore (i) $m^{h*} = -\sigma^{h*}$ and (ii) $\sum m^{h*} = M$.

Let $\{z^{h*}, p^\circ\}$ be a Walrasian equilibrium, with an equilibrium price p°. Given M, there exist $p^* = \theta p^\circ$ and $\{m^{h*}\}$ such that $M = \sum m^{h*}$ and $m^{h*} = -\sigma^{h*}$. This implies that the total stock of money serves as the numéraire. At p^*, h's demand for cash and supply are denoted (respectively) by $-\sigma^{h*}$ and m^{h*}, with excess demand being $-\mu^{h*} = (\sigma^{h*} + m^{h*})$. The consumer's budget restriction then becomes

$$p^* z^h \le (\sigma^{h*} + m^{h*}); \tag{3.3.8}$$

hence the system is in equilibrium only if the term within parentheses is zero and thus $\mu^{h*} = 0$.

The next section introduces adjustment processes (i) in models with numéraire $p_n = 1$ and no stock of money ($M = 0$), and (ii) in models that have a case-in-advance equilibrium for given M and where M is the numéraire. In processes focusing on cash-in-advance equilibrium, the excess demand for money (out of equilibrium) is approximated by the minimum money holdings of the previous period, giving – instead of (3.3.8) –

$$p(t) z^h(t) \le \mu^h(t-1). \tag{3.3.9}$$

4   Components of the simulation models

For simulations, the difference equations $p_i(t+1) = \varphi_i(p(t), m^1(t-1), \ldots, m^c(t-1))$ and $m^h(t) = \psi^h(p(t), m^1(t-1), \ldots, m^c(t-1))$ must be constructed that generate paths for $p(t)$ and $m^h(t)$ and that have p^* (and m^* in the case of a cash-in-advance equilibrium) as fixed points. The components that together constitute the difference equations are:

(a)   demand schemes for $z_i^h(t)$ as functions of $p(t)$ and $m^h(t-1)$ and also, in the case of single-period optimization, of $\bar{z}_1^h(t), \ldots, \bar{z}_{i-1}^h(t)$;

(b)   rules that determine trades $\bar{z}_i^h(t)$ from demands $(z_i^1(t), z_i^2(t), \ldots, z_i^c(t))$; and

(c)   a price adjustment rule where excess supply $\sum_h z_i^h(t)$ determines $p_i(t+1)$.

Because (b) in particular is complex, we cannot hope to find a closed-form expression for the difference equations φ_i and ψ^h. These will remain implicit in the computer programs.

In Sections 4.1 and 4.2, the problems (c) and (b) are studied. The rules will be the same for all simulation models. Sections 4.4 and 4.5 deal with problem (a) by introducing the models for single-period and gliding optimization, respectively.

4.1   Price adjustment

The standard method of adjusting prices as a function of aggregate excess demand $z_i(t)$ is

$$p_i(t+1) = p_i(t) + \lambda z_i(t), \tag{4.1.1}$$

where the constant λ represents the velocity of adjustment. For the sake of simplicity a single λ will be applied, but for each good a different λ_i could be specified. Since in the real world price changes are usually in percentages, I prefer a proportional adjustment rule such as

$$p_i(t+1) = (1 + \lambda z_i(t)) p_i(t), \tag{4.1.2}$$

which has the advantage that it is homogeneous of degree 1 in prices. For

$$D_i = \sum_h \max\{z_i^h(t), 0\} \quad \text{and} \quad S_i = -\sum_h \min\{z_i^h(t), 0\}, \tag{4.1.3}$$

we can define an alternative rule, based on the ratio of excess demand and excess supply, as follows:

$$p_i(t+1) = \{1 + \lambda[(D_i/S_i) - 1]\} p_i(t), \tag{4.1.4}$$

which also is homogeneous of degree 1 in prices. Equations (4.1.1), (4.1.2), and (4.1.4) are special cases of (3.1.1). It seems, however, that the choice of the adjustment rule does not make much difference for the dynamic behavior.

The system may become very volatile. It can be proved that the path in the tâtonnement process can be kept in a neighborhood of the equilibrium price if in each step a price cannot increase by more than a given percentage, say 30 percent. This could be rationalized by assuming that the agents who adjust prices are "cautious" (cf. Weddepohl 1994, 1995). This is assumed in the present study. With r_+ the maximum rate of increase and r_- the maximum rate of decrease, the bounded adjustment is achieved by replacing (4.1.2) with

$$p_i(t+1) = \min\{1 + r_+, \max\{1 - r_-, 1 + \lambda z_i(t)\}\} p_i(t). \tag{4.1.5}$$

4.2   Rationing and trade

Given $z_i^h(t)$, the trade $\bar{z}_i^h$ must be determined such that the market clears: $\sum_h \bar{z}_i^h(t) = 0$, which requires rationing. Though a host of alternative rules exist, for sake of simplicity we will apply the proportional rationing rule: on the long side of the market, each agent's trade is a fraction of his or her excess demand. With S_i and D_i defined by (4.1.3), we obtain the following.

(1)   If $D_i \geq S_i$ then

$$\bar{z}_i^h(t) = \begin{cases} (S_i/D_i)z_i^h(t) & \text{for } z_i^h(t) > 0, \\ z_i^h(t) & \text{for } z_i^h(t) \leq 0; \end{cases} \qquad (4.2.1)$$

(2)   if $D_i < S_i$ then

$$\bar{z}_i^h(t) = \begin{cases} z_i^h(t) & \text{for } z_i^h(t) \geq 0, \\ (D_i/S_i)z_i^h(t) & \text{for } z_i^h(t) < 0. \end{cases} \qquad (4.2.2)$$

4.3   Single-period processes

In this section the consumer superscript h is suppressed. In subperiod (t, i) the agent has realized the trades $\bar{z}_1(t), \bar{z}_2(t), ..., \bar{z}_{i-1}(t)$ and so maximizes

$$u(\bar{x}_1(t), \bar{x}_2(t), ..., \bar{x}_{i-1}(t), x_i(t, i), ..., x_n(t, i)) \qquad (4.3.1)$$

under one of the budget constraints (to be specified). The optimum values at (t, i), $z_j(t, i)$ for $j \geq i$, differ from $z_j(t, i-1)$ obtained at $(t, i-1)$ (spill-over effects), if the realized trade $\bar{z}_{i-1}(t)$ was different from $z_{i-1}(t) = z_{i-1}(t, i-1)$, for two reasons: (i) the utilities of different commodities are correlated; and (ii) the nonrealized trades affect the income constraint positively (if less was purchased than planned) or negatively (if less was sold than planned). If the utility function is separable then (i) does not apply: the optimal values of $x_j(t, i)$ ($j \geq i$) obtained by maximizing (4.3.1), under the constraint $\sum_{j=i}^{h} p_j(t)x(t, i) \leq$ constant, are independent of $\bar{x}_j(t)$ ($j < i$).

Four cases are distinguished, with different budget constraints according to how money and credit are treated. Again, since it is not clear a priori which version is the right one, we have looked at all versions. One might suspect that the dynamic behavior of different versions would be different, owing for example to the role of money.

Process S1: no money, no long-run credit restriction
There is no initial money holding: $M = 0$ and $m(0) = 0$. In subperiod $(t, 1)$ the consumer solves the usual optimization max $u(x(t, 1))$ under the restriction

$$\sum_{i=i}^{n} p_i(t)x_i(t, 1) \leq \sum_{i=i}^{n} p_i(t)w_i. \qquad (4.3.2)$$

This results in the following consumption plan for period t: $x_1(t, 1)$, $x_2(t, 1), ..., x_n(t, 1)$. Only demand $x_1(t, 1)$ with excess demand $z_1(t) = z_1(t, 1)$ is carried out, since $z_i(t, 1)$ $(i > 1)$ are just plans.

In subperiod (t, i) the agent has realized the trades $\bar{z}_1(t), \bar{z}_2(t), ...,$ $\bar{z}_{i-1}(t)$ and has accumulated (equation (3.3.2)) the trade surplus $s_{i-1}(t)$, which must be spent or repaid in the rest of period t. Hence the agent can spend the value of his or her remaining resources plus the surplus, provided that this sum is positive. It may be negative if (at an earlier stage) the agent was unable to sell as much as desired. For example, in a three-commodity case let resources be $(0, 6, 0)$, prices $(1, 1, 1)$, and the original consumption plan $(2, 2, 2)$. Suppose the consumer in step 1 purchased $x_1 = 2$, but in step 2 sold only 1 unit instead of 4 of good 2. This yields a deficit of 1 after step 2. The consumer can neither pay his debt nor buy good 3. Note that this case can occur only after step 2, not after step 1. We assume here that the agent cannot buy anything more in subperiod (t, i) and must offer resource w_j $(j \geq i)$ for sale completely. Because the $p_j(t)$ $(j \geq i)$ do not change in t, the agent will remain in a deficit position until the end of t, having then accumulated a debt $s(t) = s_n(t) < 0$, giving $m(t) = m(t-1) + s(t)$. Hence the consumer in stage (t, i) maximizes (4.3.1) under the budget restriction

$$p_i(t)x_i(t, i) + \cdots + p_n(t)x_n(t, i)$$
$$\leq \max\{p_i(t)w_i + \cdots + p_n(t)w_n + s_{i-1}(t), 0\}. \qquad (4.3.3)$$

In this way there are spillover effects from low-indexed goods to higher-indexed goods: If h cannot sell as much of good i as desired in stage (t, i) then h may have to reduce demand for higher-indexed goods in later stages. Thus it is assumed that the agent can borrow or lend as much as desired, provided the transaction is covered by the value of the remaining resources. However, h does not save or spend more than desired because money is not in the utility function and so h does not want to end with a positive or negative claim (nevertheless, this can occur).

In period $t+1$, the process is repeated with new prices. The deficit or surplus $m(t)$ is ignored during the process. Some agents may accumulate a debt and others a claim during the adjustment process, which is of no consequence. This treatment may be considered unsatisfactory, which motivates process S2.

Process S2: no money, no long-run debt

There is no initial money: $m^h(0) = 0$. Equation (4.3.1) is maximized as before, but in each period the budget restriction is adjusted by adding the final position of h's account $m^h(t-1)$ (positive or negative); that is, (4.3.2) in subperiod $(t, 1)$ is replaced by

$$\sum_{i=i}^{n} p_i(t)x_i(t,1) \le \max\left\{\sum_{i=i}^{n} p_i(t)w_i + m(t-1), 0\right\} \qquad (4.3.4)$$

(where $m(0) = 0$) and in subperiod (t, i) equation (4.3.3) is replaced by

$$\sum_{j=i}^{n} p_j(t)x_j(t,i) \le \max\left\{\sum_{j=i}^{n} p_j(t)w_j + m(t-1) + s_{i-1}(t), 0\right\}, \qquad (4.3.5)$$

where $s_{i-1}(t) + m(t-1) = m_{i-1}(t)$. The agent desires to end with a zero account value, but lends or borrows within the period.

Indeed, in S1 and S2, p^* with $m^{h*} = 0$ is a fixed point of this process because all markets clear ($z_i(t) = 0$) and $\bar{z}_i^h(t) = z_i^h(t)$. There cannot exist a fixed point that is not an equilibrium: Suppose all markets would clear at $p(t)$ with $m^h(t) \ne 0$; then $p(t+1) = p(t)$ but $m^h(t+1) = 0$.

Processes S3 and S4 focus on the cash-in-advance equilibrium.

Process S3: money, with short-run credit
Each agent h has an initial amount of (fiat) money $m^h(0) \ge 0$, with $M = \sum^h m^h(0) > 0$. Initially h only holds cash, but may run out of cash and acquire debt during the period. Hence $m_i^h(t)$ may become negative for $i \ge 1$ and $t > 0$. For some agents $m_i(t)$ represents a debt and for others it represents cash plus claims. Clearly $\sum_h m_i^h(t) = M$. The right-hand side of (4.3.3) is increased (cf. (3.3.9)) by the minimum position $\mu^h(t-1) = m^h(t-2) + \sigma^h(t-1)$ of the preceding period (which is set to zero in the first round in the simulations), giving the budget constraint

$$p_i(t)x_i(t,i) + \cdots + p_n(t)x_n(t,i)$$
$$\le \max\{p_i(t)w_i + \cdots + p_n(t)w_n + \mu(t-1) + s_{i-1}(t), 0\}. \qquad (4.3.6)$$

In other words, the consumer plans to decrease or increase money holdings at the end of the period by his or her minimum position in the previous period. That $\mu^h(t)$ becomes negative (out of equilibrium) is not excluded but in that case it will be repaid (if possible) during the next period.

A cash-in-advance equilibrium is a fixed point of the process. If $p(t) = p^*$ is an equilibrium price and if, for all h, $m_i^h(t) \ge 0$ for all $i = 1, 2, ..., n$ and $m_i^h(t) = 0$ for some i (and hence $\mu^h(t) = 0$), then markets clear in each subperiod and $p(t+1) = p(t) = p^*$.

Process S4: money, but no short-run credit
The budget restriction is (4.3.6), as in S3, giving the same planned demand $z_i(t)$. But this need not be the demand that is exercised: the demand is reduced by the available amount of money; that is, the agent goes to the market with demand $\hat{z}_i(t)$, defined by

$$\hat{z}_i(t) = \min\{z_i(t), m_{i-1}(t)/p_i(t)\}. \tag{4.3.7}$$

Cash cannot become negative out of equilibrium as in S3. In a cash-in-advance equilibrium, the constraint is not binding. Note that $\hat{z}$ is defined from z, not from $\bar{z}$. A cash-in-advance equilibrium is a fixed point of this process, and a fixed point is a cash-in-advance equilibrium.

In processes S1 and S2, a numéraire must be chosen. The value of p_n equals 1, and is not adjusted if the market for good n is not in equilibrium. Adjusting p_n might generate an exploding or an imploding price path. This cannot occur if the remaining wealth of each consumer in all subperiods remains nonnegative and if good n is desired by all agents. The market for good n clears, because each agent spends his or her remaining wealth on good n; p_n is not adjusted in (t, n) and $m^h(t+1) = 0$ for all h. With or without a numéraire the paths are the same, and the difference between S1 and S2 disappears. In S3 and S4, p_n cannot be a numéraire: The total amount of money determines the price level, and the process redistributes the total amount of cash in the necessary proportion (such that $\mu^h(t)$ becomes 0 and hence $m^h(t-1) = -\sigma^h(t)$). A fixed point of S3 or S4 with numéraire p_n would not be a Walrasian equilibrium of the economy. In this fixed point, some consumers are permanently short of cash, which permanently reduces their demand.

4.4   Gliding-period processes

Again we have different models, two for a Walrasian equilibrium with numéraire and two for the cash-in-advance equilibrium. In each case, the agent maximizes in (t, i) as follows:

$$u(z_1(t, i), ..., z_{i-1}(t, i), z_i(t, i), z_{i+1}(t, i), ..., z_n(t, i)), \tag{4.4.1}$$

under a budget constraint that remains to be specified. The demand to be exercised is $z_i(t) = z_i(t, i)$, whereas $z_{i+1}(t, i), ..., z_n(t, i)$ is a plan for the rest of period t and $z_1(t, i), ..., z_{i-1}(t, i)$ is the plan for the first $i-1$ stages of period $t+1$. Since $\bar{z}_j(t)$ ($j < i$) does not occur, spillovers are generated only by changes in wealth due to the monetary variables.

Process G1: no money, no long-run credit restriction
In this case $m(0) = 0$. The budget constraint is the usual one, but with new prices for goods on the $t+1$ markets:

$$p_i(t)z_i(t, i) + p_{i+1}(t)z_{i+1}(t, i) + \cdots + p_n(t)z_n(t, i) + p_1(t+1)z_1(t, i)$$
$$+ \cdots + p_{i-1}(t+1)z_{i-1}(t, i) \leq 0. \tag{4.4.2}$$

The Walrasian equilibrium is a fixed point. Some consumers may accumulate huge debts and claims and the accumulation, if it does not converge, can go on indefinitely. Out of equilibrium, there are no spillovers. This is a kind of tâtonnement, but with only one price adjusted at a time.

Process G2: no money, no long-run debt

This is similar to process S2: $m(0) = 0$, and the right-hand side of the budget restriction (4.4.2) is increased during period t with the surplus of period $t-1$, $m(t-1)$:

$$p_i(t)z_i(t,i) + p_{i+1}(t)z_{i+1}(t,i) + \cdots + p_n(t)z_n(t,i) + p_1(t+1)z_1(t,i)$$
$$+ \cdots + p_{i-1}(t+1)z_{i-1}(t,i) \le m(t-1). \tag{4.4.3}$$

The agent tries to end the period with a zero account. (In this respect the period is retained. A "gliding" analogy would be rather complex; $m(t-1)$ cannot be replaced by $m_i(t)$, for then a fixed point is not a Walrasian equilibrium.)

Process G3: money, with short-run credit

This is similar to S3. Agents have initial cash holdings $m^h(0) \ge 0$. The budget (4.4.2) is, during period t, increased by the minimal cash (see (3.3.9) and (3.3.6)) in the preceding full period $t-1$:

$$p_i(t)z_i(t,i) + p_{i+1}(t)z_{i+1}(t,i) + \cdots + p_n(t)z_n(t,i) + p_1(t+1)z_1(t,i)$$
$$+ \cdots + p_{i-1}(t+1)z_{i-1}(t,i) \le \mu^h(t-1) = m^h(t-2) + \sigma^h(t-1). \tag{4.4.4}$$

The cash-in-advance equilibrium is a fixed point of the process, with $\mu^h = 0$ and $m^h = -\sigma^h$ for all h.

Process G4: money, but no short-run credit

This process is similar to S4. Initial money and the budget are as in G3, with cash-in-advance restriction (4.3.7) for each trade as in S4. The cash-in-advance equilibrium is a fixed point of the process.

5   The simulation models

The simulations, executed for all eight variants and for each subperiod (t,i) $(t = 1, 2, \ldots, T, i = 1, 2, \ldots, n)$, run as follows.

(i)   The excess demands $z_i^h(t)$ and $z_i(t)$ are computed as described in Sections 4.3 and 4.4 (and also $\hat{z}_i^h(t)$ and $\hat{z}_i(t)$ for S4 and G4).

(ii) The new price $p_i(t+1)$ is computed by (4.1.5) from $z_i(t)$ or $\hat{z}_i^h(t)$.

(iii)   The trades $\bar{z}_i^h(t)$ are computed by (4.2.1) and (4.2.2) from $z_i^h(t)$ or $\hat{z}_i^h(t)$.

(iv)   The monetary variables $s_i^h(t)$ $(i < n)$ and $s^h(t)$, $m^h(t)$, $\sigma^h(t)$, and $\mu^h(t)$ are computed (where needed) as described in Section 3.3.

The following variables are necessary data in step (t, i):

(a) $p_i(t), p_{i+1}(t), ..., p_n(t)$ and (for the G processes) also $p_1(t+1)$, ..., $p_{i-1}(t+1)$;

(b) $m^h(t-1), \sigma^h(t-1), \mu^h(t-1)$, and $s_{i-1}^h(t)$ $(\sigma^h(0), \mu^h(0)$, and $s^h(0)$ are set to zero);

(c)   for the S processes the trades $\bar{z}_j^h(t)$ $(j < i)$ if the utility functions are not separable (although in our simulations separable functions have been used).

Clearly, if $p(t) = p^*$ (and, where necessary, $m^h(t-1) = m^{h*}$) then $p(t+1) = p^*$, since $z_i(t) = 0$ for all i. These are complicated processes that cannot be written down as a simple system of difference equations, as could be done for the tâtonnement process by which they were inspired.

A simulation of the tâtonnement process runs as follows. Given $p_1(t-1), ..., p_n(t-1)$ for $t = 1, 2, ...$:

(1)   compute $z_i^h(t)$ and $z_i(t)$ for $i = 1, 2, ..., n-1$;

(2)   compute $p_i(t+1)$ from $z_i(t)$ for $i = 1, 2, ..., n-1$ by (4.1.5).

This simulation can be written down as the system of difference equations

$$p_i(t+1) = \min\{1 + r_+, \max\{1 - r_-, 1 + \lambda z_i(p(t))\}\} p_i(t),$$
$$i = 1, 2, ..., n-1, \tag{5.1}$$

which is (4.1.5) with $z_i(t)$ replaced by $z_i(p(t))$. For this tâtonnement process, some analysis of the system out of equilibrium is possible and can explain the occurrence of erratic dynamics. The stability of (5.1) at p^* depends on the eigenvalues of the matrix with components

$$\frac{\partial p_i(t+1)}{\partial p_j} = \delta_{ij}(1 + \lambda z_i(p^*)) + \lambda p_i \frac{\partial z_i(p^*)}{\partial p_j}, \quad j = 1, 2, ..., n-1,$$

where $\delta_{ii} = 1$ and $\delta_{ij} = 0$ if $i \neq j$. If all eigenvalues are smaller than 1 in absolute value, then the system is (locally) stable. It is known that systems of the type (5.1) can show erratic dynamics (see Day and Pianigiani 1991). Without the restrictions r_- and r_+, the price paths can explode or make big jumps up and down. As mentioned previously, the restrictions guarantee that the path approaches equilibrium without converging, which is confirmed in simulations. In examples with three goods (with numéraire) and for λ sufficiently large, periodic orbits and chaos around

Table 1. *Process G1: price and credit position,*
$\lambda = 3.1$

t	p_1	p_2	p_3	m^1	m^2	m^3
0	0.50	3.00	1.00	0.00	0.00	0.00
1	0.63	2.50	1.00	−0.01	−0.29	0.30
2	0.78	2.08	1.00	−0.04	−0.30	0.33
3	0.98	1.74	1.00	−0.07	−0.19	0.26
4	1.22	1.45	1.00	−0.09	−0.05	0.15
5	1.28	1.21	1.00	0.03	−0.04	0.01
6	1.07	1.00	1.00	0.03	−0.03	−0.00
7	0.89	0.88	1.00	0.08	0.01	−0.09
8	0.96	1.10	1.00	0.01	−0.05	0.05
9	1.18	1.11	1.00	−0.12	0.08	0.04
10	0.98	0.92	1.00	0.08	−0.03	−0.05
11	0.88	0.99	1.00	0.06	−0.03	−0.03
12	1.10	1.16	1.00	−0.09	0.03	0.06
13	1.10	0.96	1.00	0.00	−0.00	0.00
14	0.92	0.96	1.00	0.05	0.00	−0.05
15	1.03	1.11	1.00	−0.03	−0.01	0.04
16	1.10	0.97	1.00	−0.04	0.03	0.01
17	0.92	0.92	1.00	0.06	0.00	−0.07
18	0.98	1.09	1.00	0.00	−0.04	0.04
19	1.15	1.07	1.00	−0.09	0.07	0.03
20	0.95	0.89	1.00	0.08	−0.01	−0.07
21	0.88	1.02	1.00	0.06	−0.05	−0.00
22	1.10	1.12	1.00	−0.11	0.05	0.06
23	1.07	0.93	1.00	0.01	−0.00	−0.01
24	0.90	0.97	1.00	0.06	−0.01	−0.05
25	1.08	1.15	1.00	−0.06	0.01	0.06
26	1.11	0.96	1.00	−0.02	0.01	0.01
27	0.93	0.96	1.00	0.05	−0.00	−0.05
28	1.03	1.10	1.00	−0.03	−0.01	0.04
29	1.09	0.98	1.00	−0.04	0.03	0.01
30	0.91	0.91	1.00	0.07	0.01	−0.07
31	0.97	1.10	1.00	0.01	−0.04	0.04
32	1.16	1.08	1.00	−0.10	0.07	0.03
33	0.97	0.90	1.00	0.08	−0.02	−0.06
34	0.87	1.00	1.00	0.06	−0.04	−0.02
35	1.09	1.13	1.00	−0.10	0.04	0.06
36	1.09	0.94	1.00	0.00	−0.00	0.00
37	0.91	0.97	1.00	0.05	−0.01	−0.04
38	1.06	1.13	1.00	−0.05	0.00	0.05
39	1.10	0.94	1.00	−0.02	0.02	0.01
40	0.91	0.97	1.00	0.05	−0.01	−0.04
41	1.06	1.12	1.00	−0.05	0.00	0.05
42	1.10	0.94	1.00	−0.03	0.02	0.01
43	0.91	0.97	1.00	0.05	−0.01	−0.04

t	p_1	p_2	p_3	m^1	m^2	m^3
44	1.06	1.12	1.00	−0.05	0.00	0.05
45	1.09	0.94	1.00	−0.03	0.02	0.01
46	0.91	0.97	1.00	0.06	−0.01	−0.04
47	1.06	1.13	1.00	−0.05	0.00	0.05
Equilibrium	1.00	1.00	1.00	0.00	0.00	0.00

the equilibrium price are obtained. The restrictions can be rationalized by assuming that the agents who adjust prices have learned that, with λ too high, high price changes tend to be followed by opposite price changes.

The Cobb–Douglas utility function is the most "regular" of all known utility functions, yet even for this function erratic dynamics can appear in a discrete tâtonnement process, as shown in Day and Pianigiani (1991), although convergence is ensured in the continuous time tâtonnement process because gross substitutability holds. Suppose that all consumers have Cobb–Douglas utilities with exponents $\alpha_i^h > 0$ and with $\sum_h \alpha_i^h = 1$. Then total excess demand of good i becomes

$$z_i = -\sum_h (1-\alpha_i^h)w_i^h + \frac{\sum_h \sum_{j \neq i} \alpha_j^h p_j w_j^h}{p_i} \equiv -A_i + \frac{\sum_{j \neq i} B_{ij} p_j}{p_i}. \qquad (5.2)$$

Inserting (5.2) in the adjustment rule (5.1) yields

$$p_i(t+1) = \min\Bigg\{(1+r_+)p_i(t),$$

$$\max\bigg\{(1-r_-)p_i(t), \bigg(1-\lambda A_i p_i(t) + \lambda \sum_{j \neq i} B_{ij} p_j(t)\bigg)\bigg\}\Bigg\},$$

$$i = 1, 2, ..., n-1, \qquad (5.3)$$

which is a piecewise linear function in $p_i(t)$, decreasing near p_i^*. The Jacobian of the system of difference equations (5.3) becomes larger than 1 in absolute value at p^* for λ sufficiently high. This indicates that the equilibrium is not stable.

A mathematical analysis of the disequilibrium models is not given, but only simulations of their different versions. They differ from tâtonnement models in that their dependence of demand on prices is far more complex and their adjustments are not simultaneous. However, the Jacobians of the difference equations of the disequilibrium models at p^* are related to the ones of the tâtonnement model. The precise relationship requires further research, but near p^* the eigenvalues cannot differ by much. This probably explains why we see roughly the same type of behavior as in the

Table 2. *Process S3: price and cash position
path*, $\lambda = 1.2$

t	p_1	p_2	p_3	m^1	m^2	m^3
0	0.50	3.00	1.00	1.20	0.00	0.00
1	0.62	2.50	1.25	1.34	0.86	−1.00
2	0.78	2.08	1.04	0.00	1.10	0.10
3	0.98	1.74	0.87	0.00	0.53	0.67
4	1.22	1.45	1.09	0.18	0.38	0.64
5	1.29	1.27	1.26	0.08	0.48	0.64
6	1.11	1.08	1.05	0.00	0.63	0.57
7	0.99	0.93	0.87	0.00	0.60	0.60
8	0.94	0.90	0.96	0.03	0.45	0.71
9	1.00	1.03	1.17	0.09	0.39	0.72
10	1.16	1.23	1.37	0.09	0.41	0.70
11	1.27	1.31	1.35	0.00	0.40	0.80
12	1.19	1.14	1.13	0.00	0.44	0.76
13	1.05	1.02	0.94	0.00	0.55	0.65
14	0.96	0.92	0.88	0.00	0.52	0.68
15	0.94	0.92	0.99	0.04	0.44	0.72
16	1.02	1.05	1.17	0.08	0.41	0.71
17	1.15	1.20	1.32	0.06	0.41	0.72
18	1.22	1.24	1.27	0.00	0.39	0.81
19	1.13	1.09	1.06	0.00	0.44	0.76
20	1.01	0.99	0.90	0.00	0.52	0.68
21	0.94	0.91	0.88	0.00	0.49	0.71
22	0.95	0.94	1.01	0.05	0.43	0.72
23	1.04	1.08	1.20	0.08	0.42	0.69
24	1.17	1.22	1.32	0.05	0.42	0.73
25	1.21	1.22	1.22	0.00	0.39	0.81
26	1.10	1.05	1.02	0.00	0.45	0.75
27	1.00	0.98	0.91	0.00	0.52	0.68
28	0.95	0.92	0.92	0.00	0.47	0.73
29	0.97	0.97	1.04	0.05	0.41	0.74
30	1.05	1.10	1.20	0.07	0.41	0.72
31	1.16	1.20	1.28	0.03	0.41	0.76
32	1.17	1.17	1.14	0.00	0.41	0.79
33	1.05	1.01	0.95	0.00	0.47	0.73
34	0.96	0.95	0.90	0.00	0.51	0.69
35	0.95	0.93	0.97	0.03	0.45	0.72
36	1.00	1.01	1.11	0.06	0.42	0.73
37	1.10	1.14	1.24	0.06	0.41	0.73
38	1.17	1.20	1.24	0.00	0.38	0.82
39	1.13	1.10	1.03	0.00	0.41	0.79
40	1.01	0.98	0.87	0.00	0.49	0.71
41	0.93	0.90	0.88	0.00	0.50	0.70
42	0.95	0.94	1.01	0.06	0.45	0.69
43	1.04	1.08	1.21	0.08	0.43	0.68

t	p_1	p_2	p_3	m^1	m^2	m^3
44	1.18	1.23	1.34	0.05	0.41	0.73
45	1.23	1.24	1.24	0.00	0.39	0.81
46	1.11	1.07	1.03	0.00	0.45	0.75
47	1.00	0.99	0.91	0.00	0.54	0.66
Equilibrium	1.00	1.00	1.00	0.00	0.40	0.80

tâtonnement model. For parameter values where tâtonnement is unstable, the simulations made with processes S and G show adjustment paths similar to those of tâtonnement, at least for the (very regular) cases studied.

6   Simulations

The economy is a three-goods, three-consumer economy. Consumers have Cobb–Douglas utility functions with exponents (0.2, 0.4, 0.4), (0.4, 0.2, 0.4), and (0.4, 0.4, 0.2) and with resources $w^1 = (1, 0, 0)$, $w^2 = (0, 1, 0)$, and $w^3 = (0, 0, 1)$. Clearly the equilibrium price is $p^* = (1, 1, 1)$ with numéraire $p_3 = 1$. In the cash-in-advance equilibrium with $M = 1.2$, p^* is the same, $m^{1*} = 0$, $m^{2*} = 0.4$, and $m^{3*} = 0.8$ (because consumer 3 must pay 0.4 for good 1 and 0.4 for good 2 before receiving 0.8 from selling good 3). The maximum adjustment rates are $1 + r_+ = 1.25$ and $1 - r_- = 1/1.2$.

Simulations have been performed with all eight models introduced in Section 4. In all models, the behavior depends heavily on the value of the adjustment parameter λ. It should be noted that no a priori arguments are known for the value of this parameter. A selection of the results of the simulations with the parameters just described is given in Tables 1 and 2 and in Figures 1–7. Each figure consists of two parts as follows.

> *Right:* time paths of the prices p_1, p_2, and p_3; p_3 remains constant if it is the numéraire.
>
> *Left:* the values of the pair p_1, p_2, from step 1001 onward; this set is the attractor of the process.

In the tables also the movement of m^h is given. Figures representing converging paths have not been printed. They would show a single point in the (p_1, p_2) plane, and quick convergence to horizontal lines.

For all models, we obtained the following results.

(1)   For small values of λ (the adjustment parameter in the price adjustment function), each process converges to its equilibrium.

(2)   If λ becomes larger than some critical value, which is of the same order of magnitude in all eight models, first cyclic paths (where p

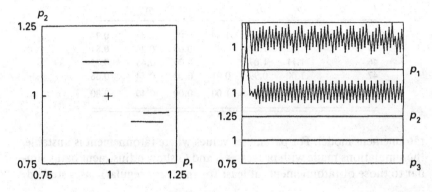

Figure 1. Process S1, $\lambda = 3.7$.

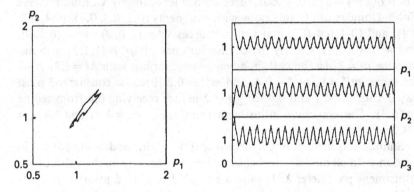

Figure 2. Process S2, $\lambda = 1.3$.

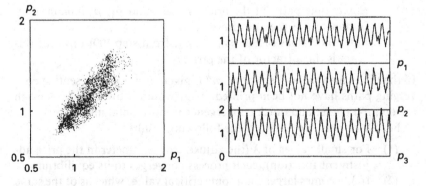

Figure 3. Process S3, $\lambda = 2.8$.

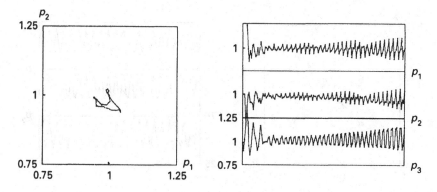

Figure 4. Process S4, $\lambda = 1.8$.

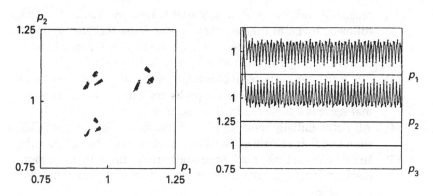

Figure 5. Process G1, $\lambda = 2.8$.

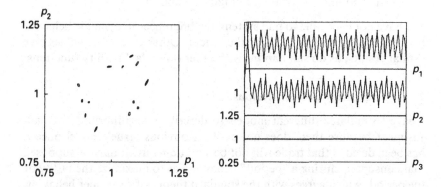

Figure 6. Process G2, $\lambda = 2.8$.

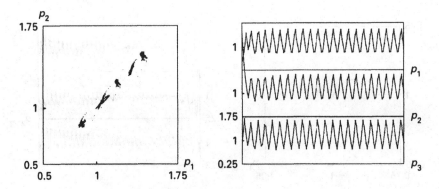

Figure 7. Process G3, $\lambda = 2.0$.

repeatedly takes on 2, 4, ... different values; see Table 1) appear, followed by paths that are cyclic in the sense that they follow a sequence through a number of disjoint sets (see Figures 5 and 6) or have "strange attractors" (see Figures 2 and 4).

(3) For high λ the paths seem chaotic, as is suggested for example by Figure 3. Proving whether the paths are indeed chaotic in a formal sense is a topic for further research.

(4) All paths initially move quickly in the direction of the equilibrium and then remain within a neighborhood of the equilibrium.

(5) In cases with a cash-in-advance equilibrium, the path of the monetary variable quickly moves in the direction of the equilibrium (see Table 2).

(6) Paths in monetary models sometimes show periods of inflation followed by periods of deflation, while the price ratios are near the equilibrium ratio (see Figures 3 and 7).

I have not been able to find systematic differences in dynamic behavior between the various versions of the model. Other parameter values give similar results, as do simulations with other ("regular") utility functions.

7   Summary and conclusions

I have formulated different models to describe disequilibrium price adjustment because there does not exist an obvious "true" model once it has been decided that trade will not be simultaneous. It may be supposed that consumers during a "period" behave so as to maximize the utility of the period, which agrees with the standard theory of consumer behavior, but it seems equally reasonable that they rather look at their consumption bundle in the near future. It seemed impossible to construct the model without some short-run store of value, and some kind of money had to be introduced in order to obtain correct budget constraints at each moment of decision. The simulations show that all these nearly related models (or, rather, different versions of the same model) give similar results, so the precise modeling seems not to affect the stability of the system. Obviously our simulations are only a case study, but since the utility functions are very "regular" there is no reason to believe that other specifications would give other results, which was confirmed by some experiments.

REFERENCES

Bela, V., and M. Majumdar (1992), "Chaotic Tâtonnement," *Economic Theory* 2: 437–45.

Benassy, J. P. (1975), "Neo-Keynesian Disequilibrium in a Monetary Economy," *Review of Economic Studies* 42: 503–23.

Clower, R. W. (1967), "A Reconsideration of the Microfoundations of Monetary Theory," *Western Economic Journal* 6: 1–9.

Day, R. H., and G. Pianigiani (1991), "Statistical Dynamics and Economics," *Journal of Economic Behavior and Organization* 16: 37–83.

Drèze, J. H. (1975), "Existence of Exchange Equilibrium under Price Rigidities," *International Economic Review* 16: 301–20.

Hahn, F. H., and T. Negishi (1962), "A Theorem on Non-tâtonnement Stability," *Econometrica* 30: 463–9.

Laroque, G. (1981), "A Comment on 'Stable Spillovers among Substitutes'," *Review of Economic Studies* 48: 355–61.

Saari, D. G. (1985), "Iterative Price Mechanisms," *Econometrica* 53: 1117–31.

Veendorp, E. (1975), "Stable Spillovers among Substitutes," *Review of Economic Studies* 42: 445–56.

Weddepohl, C. (1994), "Erratic Dynamics in a Restricted Tâtonnement Process with Two and Three Goods," in J. Grasman and G. van Straten (eds.), *Predictability and Nonlinear Modelling in Natural Sciences and Economics*. Dordrecht: Kluwer, pp. 610–21.

  (1995), "A Cautious Price Adjustment Mechanism: Chaotic Behavior," *Journal of Economic Behavior and Organization* 27: 293–300.

PART VI

Demographic and international applications

CHAPTER 16

Disequilibrium in the Canadian population distribution

William P. Anderson & Yorgos Y. Papageorgiou

1   Introduction

In this paper we study the recent evolution of the Canadian population
system at the scale of six broad regions (Figure 1), with particular emphasis on the disequilibrium characteristics of this evolution.[1] Change
in such a system stems from individual moves, so we must connect the
corresponding aggregate dynamics with a behavioral framework of migration decisions. This requires two models, one about how the system
evolves at the macro level and the other about how the decision to migrate is taken at the micro level, together with an explicit link between
the two.

We model aggregate dynamics in Section 2. The explicit link between
the macro level of regional population change and the micro level of individual migration decisions is provided by the *migration rates*. On the one
hand, migration rates serve as building blocks for the adjustment process. On the other, those rates can be derived from *migration probabilities,* which have a clear connection with the decision to migrate and which
are modeled in Section 3. We determine migration rates from migration

Author names are listed in alphabetical order. Research was supported by the Social Sciences and Humanities Research Council of Canada grants 410-87-0725 and 410-91-0906. A
more detailed review of the empirical methodology used in this paper can be found in Anderson and Papageorgiou (1994a,b). We thank Michael Atkinson, Frank Denton, Jochen
Jungeilges, Bruce Newbold, James Simmons, and the participants of the Conference on
Dynamic Disequilibrium Modelling for their help and comments.

[1] In order to avoid the extreme size variation of Canada's provinces, we combine Newfoundland, Prince Edward Island, Nova Scotia, and New Brunswick into a single region,
"Atlantic Canada," and we do the same for Manitoba and Saskatchewan, the "central
Prairies." We do not include Yukon and the Northwest Territories because they make
little difference in the population distribution of Canada, and because their migration
flows often behave too erratically over the period of our data.

1 Atlantic   4 Prairies
2 Quebec   5 Alberta
3 Ontario   6 B. Columbia

Figure 1. Canada.

probabilities in Section 4, which completely specifies the aggregate dynamics. We then move to an empirical analysis of migration probabilities in Sections 5 and 6. Using the estimated migration probabilities, we can derive the empirical form of the aggregate dynamics. We use this description in Section 7, together with a definition of *equilibrium,* in order to calculate how disequilibrium evolved in the Canadian regional population system over the study period.

Our observations extend over one of the most interesting periods in the demographic, economic, and political history of Canada. Because our data have been shaped by those events, so too is our analysis. Thus, the recent history of Canada must, to some extent, be reflected in our results. To us, this relationship is fundamental. However, since the connections are both complex and obstructed by the aggregate nature of our data, we collect our remarks on the subject in an appendix, and we ask the reader to take them only as suggestive.

2   Most probable states

We consider a population of total size $N(t)$ at time $t \in T$ distributed within a regional system $\mathfrak{R}$ $(i, j \in \mathfrak{R})$ of s regions. The population distribution among the discrete geographical alternatives of that system is given by

$$\mathbf{N}(t) \equiv (N_1(t), ..., N_s(t)), \quad 0 \le N_i(t) \le N(t), \quad \sum_{i \in \mathfrak{R}} N_i(t) = N(t), \qquad (1)$$

where $N_i(t)$ is the population in region i at time t. We call $\mathbf{N}(t)$ a *state* of the system, and our problem is to describe how it evolves through time. Because such evolution is the complex outcome of many individual and public decisions that affect (and are affected by) the economic, political, social, and cultural conditions in the system, the exact way in which the system evolves cannot be determined a priori. We therefore assume that $\mathbf{N}(t)$ is the realization of random state $\mathbb{N}\langle t \rangle$ with state probability distribution $\mathbb{P}(\mathbf{N}, t)$, which incorporates all macro information relevant to our problem.

If the Markov condition holds and if migration decisions are stochastically independent, then the unfolding of the state probability distribution over time can be specified as an evolutionary model.[2] However, such specification involves a very large number of equations – one for each possible state. To fix ideas, 25 million Canadians distributed over 10 provinces give rise to about 10^{64} possible states. Out of all these, *only one* is realized. The question then arises of how we can connect the observed state with the theoretical predictions of the evolutionary model without reference to the entire state probability distribution. One possibility is to study the evolution of the most probable state in $\mathbb{P}(\mathbf{N}, t)$. If $\mathbb{P}(\mathbf{N}, t)$ is relatively "flat" then the most probable state is not a good indicator of the observed state. If, however, $\mathbb{P}(\mathbf{N}, t)$ has a single, arbitrarily high and sharp peak in the space of possible states, one would expect to observe a state – itself with high probability – arbitrarily close to the most probable state. This actually holds in an asymptotic sense: As the total population of the evolutionary model becomes arbitrarily large, the variance of the

---

[2] See e.g. de Palma and Lefèvre (1983), Haag and Weidlich (1984), Kanaroglou, Liaw, and Papageorgiou (1986a), and Weidlich and Haag (1988). We accept these standard assumptions in the literature as "necessary evils" because they allow us to employ well-developed, operational theory. In particular, stochastic independence is used both in the macrolevel framework of this section and in the microlevel framework of Section 3. For the macro level, as discussed in Kanaroglou et al. (1986a), violation of stochastic independence is not a serious problem since it serves only to approximate state transitions that may involve more than one individual into corresponding sequences of individual transitions. For the micro level, stochastic independence is violated by the inclusion of "migration channels" in our empirical specification of Section 6.

population distribution around its most probable state becomes arbitrarily small. Because such asymptotic arguments concerning the most probable state refer to an infinitely large total population, this claim holds if the evolution of the system depends only on the *relative* population distribution, which is given by

$$\mathbf{n}(t) \equiv (n_1(t), \dots, n_s(t)), \quad 0 \le n_i(t) \le 1, \quad \sum_{i \in \Re} n_i(t) = 1, \tag{2}$$

where $n_i(t)/N(t)$ is the population share of region i. Moreover, if the effect of regional variations in birth, death, and international migration rates on changes in the relative population distribution is small, then the system of equations

$$\frac{dn_i}{dt} = \sum_{j \ne i}(n_j(t)t_{j \to i}(t) - n_i(t)r_{i \to j}(t)) \tag{3}$$

specifies exactly the evolution of the most probable state for regional systems with infinitely large total population, where $r_{ij}(t)$ is the *migration rate* from region i to j at time t (Kurtz 1978). Under these conditions, if the system is large enough then we know that the evolution of its observed state is approximated by the evolution of the most probable state determined by the theoretical predictions of the evolutionary model, and we can shift our attention from an evolutionary model involving all possible states to the dynamic model (3) involving the single most probable state.

We need to specify (3) by determining the structure of migration rates within it. Toward this end, we observe that migration rates are the time derivatives of corresponding migration probabilities, so that we can determine migration rates by determining migration probabilities. We undertake this latter task in Section 3.

3   Migration probabilities

When migration within a regional system $\Re$ $(i, j, k \in \Re)$ is unrestricted and when individuals aim to use their limited resources to their best advantage, migration choices depend on the relative value of the alternatives in the system: Individuals $h \in \mathcal{K}$ migrate to what, for them, are the most advantageous places. Let $U_{i \to j}^h$ represent the benefit (or loss) that a randomly selected individual h experiences by moving from i to j. The *migration probability* from i to j is equivalent to the probability that this move gives the highest benefit:

$$\mathbb{P}_{i \to j} = \Pr(U_{i \to j}^h > \max_{k \ne j} U_{i \to k}^h). \tag{4}$$

We seek an appropriate structure for the migration probabilities. We assume that $U_{i \to j}^h$ can be partitioned into a systematic term $V_{i \to j}$ that depends on observable characteristics and a random term $\epsilon^h_{i \to j}$ that incorporates unobservable subjective differences among individuals:

$$U^h_{i \to j} = V_{i \to j} + \epsilon^h_{i \to j}. \tag{5}$$

We call $V_{i \to i}$ the *advantage to stay* and $V_{i \to j}$ ($i \neq j$) the *advantage to migrate*. We shall discuss their empirical structure in Section 5.

Under (5), migration probabilities are specified by the nature of the error terms. It can be shown (Yellott 1977) that if the random terms are stochastically independent and identically distributed (IID), and if the preference orderings of individuals are invariant under uniform expansions of their regional choice set, then the random terms must follow the Gumbel distribution.[3] It can also be shown that IID Gumbel terms give rise to multinomial logit (McFadden 1974) and to nested logit (Ben-Akiva and Lerman 1985) migration probabilities. Thus a logit specification seems appropriate for migration probabilities.

We next consider the choice between a multinomial logit (ML) and a two-stage nested logit (NL) specification. In the former case, there is no distinction between decisions to stay and to migrate. In the latter, this distinction is made by splitting the decision to migrate in two: an upper level in which the individual decides whether to stay or leave (the departure decision) and a lower level in which individuals who choose to leave decide where to go (the destination choice decision). Since the NL model contains the ML model as a special case, adoption of the two-stage NL model does not necessarily impose a two-stage structure on the decision to migrate, but rather a one- or two-stage structure depending on the values of the estimated parameters. In contrast, by adopting the ML model we impose a single stage which, if wrong, implies a specification error (Fotheringham 1986).

There are additional reasons for preferring to use the two-stage NL model in our analysis. First, in the ML model, the relative advantage to the migrant of staying in the home region i or moving to another region j depends upon the characteristics of i and j alone. In the NL model, this relative advantage depends not only on a pairwise comparison of origin

[3] At any particular time, each region contains a number of goods and services in given amounts, which – together with income, prices, quality of the environment, etc. – determine location choice in the regional system. Multiply by the same number all given amounts of goods and services in all regions, while keeping everything else exactly as before. The new choice set is a uniform expansion of the original. A preference ordering that is invariant under uniform expansions of the choice set implies that the probability of choosing a region is the same irrespective of whether the choice is made from the original or from any uniform expansion. Uniform expansions of the regional choice set, which alter neither its composition nor its complexity but only its scale, should not affect migration probabilities.

and destination characteristics, but also on regional variations in mobility that reflect the characteristics of the origin relative to all other regions in the system. In consequence, at the upper level, the two-stage NL model does not suffer from the need to assume the "independence of irrelevant alternatives" property of the ML model, although it still does at the lower level (see McFadden 1978 on this issue). Second, since the NL model distinguishes between decisions to migrate and destination choice decisions, it can better account for the observation that the effect of origin characteristics differs from the corresponding effect of destination characteristics (see e.g. Lowry 1966 and Shaw 1985). Finally, in addition to estimating the determinants of the decision to migrate, the NL model provides some information about the distribution of uncertainty between the upper and lower levels of that decision.

When migration decisions are partitioned into departure and destination choice, migration probabilities can be expressed as

$$\mathbb{P}_{i \to j} = \mathbb{P}_{i \to} \, \mathbb{P}_{j \mid i \to} \tag{6}$$

where $\mathbb{P}_{i \to}$ is the probability that a randomly selected resident h of i will decide to migrate (the *departure probability*) and $\mathbb{P}_{j \mid i \to}$ is the conditional probability that h will then choose j (the *destination choice probability*). We can derive

$$\mathbb{P}_{i \to} = \frac{\exp(\mu \mathbb{Q}_i - V_{i \to i})}{1 + \exp(\mu \mathbb{Q}_i - V_{i \to i})}, \tag{7}$$

$$\mathbb{P}_{j \mid i \to} = \exp\left(\frac{V_{i \to j}}{\mu} - \mathbb{Q}_i\right), \quad \text{and} \tag{8}$$

$$\mathbb{Q}_i \equiv \ln\left(\sum_{k \neq i} \exp\left(\frac{V_{i \to k}}{\mu}\right)\right) \tag{9}$$

(see Kanaroglou et al. 1986b for details, including a list of further technical assumptions used to derive these probabilities). Here μ, $0 \leq \mu \leq 1$, is a parameter that expresses the degree to which uncertainty in the decision to migrate can be attributed to the opportunities outside of the origin (Ben-Akiva and Lerman 1985). Thus, when $\mu = 0$, all uncertainty belongs to the departure level. As μ increases, uncertainty can increasingly be attributed to the destination choice level. At the other extreme, where $\mu = 1$, no uncertainty belongs to the departure level.[4] Furthermore, $\mathbb{Q}_i$ is

---

[4] For $\mu \to 0$, we have

$$\lim_{\mu \to 0} \mathbb{P}_{i \to} = \frac{\exp(\max_{k \neq i} V_{i \to k})}{\exp(V_{i \to i}) + \exp(\max_{k \neq i} V_{i \to k})},$$

$$\lim_{\mu \to 0} \mathbb{P}_{j \mid i \to} = \begin{cases} 1 & \text{for } V_{i \to j} = \max_{k \neq i} V_{i \to k}, \\ 0 & \text{otherwise.} \end{cases}$$

the *inclusive value,* which can be related to the quality of opportunities outside of the origin. In particular, the expression $\mu \mathbb{Q}_i$ in the departure probability (7) differs from the expected maximum utility of destinations $j \neq i$ only by constant terms.[5] Hence a change in the inclusive value is proportional to a change in the expected maximum utility away from the origin. We call (7) the *departure model* and (8) the *destination choice model.* Taken together, these two constitute the NL model.

We close this section by considering the NL model within a temporal context. This is necessary because departure probabilities must be determined with reference to some time interval Δt. For example, departure probabilities during a time interval of zero length are zero, and they must strictly increase with an increasing time interval. It follows that the departure model (7) corresponds to a particular length of time, which we define as ν: For an interval $[t, t+\nu]$, the departure probabilities are given by

$$\mathbb{P}_{i\rightarrow}(t, \nu) = \frac{\exp(\mu(t)\mathbb{Q}_i(t) - V_{i\rightarrow i}(t))}{1 + \exp(\mu(t)\mathbb{Q}_i(t) - V_{i\rightarrow i}(t))}. \tag{10}$$

Because the length of the time interval in our data is not necessarily equal to ν, we must also specify how departure probabilities change with the time interval. Toward this end, for $\mathbb{P}_{i\rightarrow} < 1$ we define the *odds of outmigration* from i during any Δt as

$$o_i(t, \Delta t) \equiv \frac{\mathbb{P}_{i\rightarrow}(t, \Delta t)}{1 - \mathbb{P}_{i\rightarrow}(t, \Delta t)}, \tag{11}$$

and we simply assume that these odds are proportional to Δt. Hence

$$\frac{o_i(t, \Delta t)}{o_i(t, \nu)} = \frac{\Delta t}{\nu}. \tag{12}$$

Substituting (11) into (12), we obtain

$$\frac{\mathbb{P}_{i\rightarrow}(t, \Delta t)}{1 - \mathbb{P}_{i\rightarrow}(t, \Delta t)} = \frac{\Delta t}{\nu} \exp(\mu(t)\mathbb{Q}_i(t) - V_{i-i}(t)) \quad \text{(by (10)).} \tag{13}$$

Therefore, when all advantages to migrate are known perfectly well, the departure probability is determined by a comparison between the advantage to stay and the advantage to migrate to the best destination. Once the decision to migrate has been made, the best destination is chosen with certainty.

When $\mu = 1$, substitution of (7)–(9) in (6) yields the ML model

$$\mathbb{P}_{i\rightarrow j} = \frac{\exp(V_{i\rightarrow j})}{\sum_{k\in\mathfrak{R}} \exp(V_{i\rightarrow k})}.$$

[5] The expected maximum utility of destinations other than j can be expressed as

$$E(\max_{j\neq i} U_{i\rightarrow j}^h) = \mu\mathbb{Q}_i + \mu\gamma,$$

where γ is Euler's number (see e.g. Leonardi and Papageorgiou 1992).

Finally, solving (13) for $\mathbb{P}_{i\rightarrow}(t, \Delta t)$, we have

$$\mathbb{P}_{i\rightarrow}(t, \Delta t) = \frac{\exp(\alpha_0 + \mu(t)\mathbb{Q}_i(t) - V_{i\rightarrow i}(t))}{1 + \exp(\alpha_0 + \mu(t)\mathbb{Q}_i(t) - V_{i\rightarrow i}(t))} \tag{14}$$

where $\alpha_0 \equiv \ln[\Delta t/\nu]$. Notice that α_0 can be estimated for any positive time interval, and that the choice of a time interval affects no other component of the departure model.

4   Migration rates

The migration rates in (3) provide an explicit link between the disaggregate framework of individual migration decisions and the aggregate dynamics of Section 2. This is so because, by definition, migration rates are derived from migration probabilities as

$$r_{i\rightarrow j}(t)$$

$$= \lim_{\Delta t \rightarrow 0} \frac{\mathbb{P}_{i\rightarrow j}(t, \Delta t)}{\Delta t}$$

$$= \mathbb{P}_{j|i\rightarrow}(t) \lim_{\Delta t \rightarrow 0} \frac{\mathbb{P}_{i\rightarrow}(t, \Delta t)}{\Delta t} \quad \text{(by (6))}$$

$$= \exp\left(\frac{V_{i\rightarrow j}(t)}{\mu(t)} - \mathbb{Q}_i(t)\right) \lim_{\Delta t \rightarrow 0} \left(\frac{(1/\nu)\exp(\mu(t)\mathbb{Q}_i(t) - V_{i\rightarrow i}(t))}{1 + (\Delta t/\nu)\exp(\mu(t)\mathbb{Q}_i(t) - V_{i\rightarrow i}(t))}\right)$$

$$\qquad\qquad\qquad\qquad\qquad\qquad\qquad \text{(by (8) and (14))} \tag{15}$$

$$= \exp\left(\frac{V_{i\rightarrow j}(t)}{\mu(t)} - \mathbb{Q}_i(t)\right)\frac{1}{\nu}\exp(\mu(t)\mathbb{Q}_i(t) - V_{i\rightarrow i}(t))$$

$$= \frac{1}{\nu}\exp\left(-\mu(t)\left(\frac{V_{i\rightarrow i}(t)}{\mu(t)} - \mathbb{Q}_i(t)\right) + \left(\frac{V_{i\rightarrow j}(t)}{\mu(t)} - \mathbb{Q}_i(t)\right)\right).$$

Notice how increasing uncertainty at the destination choice level (increasing $\mu(t)$) causes smaller migration rates. Also notice that, through the inclusive value, migration rates depend on the entire distribution of advantages in the system. This is because, as discussed in Section 3, comparing the advantages to stay in i with the advantages to migrate to j cannot be isolated from other opportunities in the regional system except when μ takes extreme values.[6]

[6] When $\mu(t) \rightarrow 0$, we have

$$\lim_{\mu \rightarrow 0} r_{i\rightarrow j}(t) = \begin{cases} (1/\nu)\exp(-V_{i\rightarrow i}(t) + V_{i\rightarrow j}(t)) & \text{for } V_{i\rightarrow j}(t) = \max_{k\neq i} V_{i\rightarrow k}(t), \\ 0 & \text{otherwise.} \end{cases}$$

On the other hand, for $\mu(t) = 1$, the migration rates are given by

$$r_{i\rightarrow j}(t) = (1/\nu)\exp(-V_{i\rightarrow i}(t) + V_{i\rightarrow j}(t)).$$

In both cases, nonzero migration rates depend on origin and destination only.

5   Empirical specification

Our analysis is based on aggregate migration flow and socioeconomic data. Since those refer to annual observations from 1952 to 1983, all variables are defined with reference to a particular year. Let $N_i^o(t)$ represent the *observed population* of region i at the beginning of year t and $M_{i \to j}^o(t, \Delta t)$ the *observed number of migrants* from i to j during the year-long interval $[t, t + \Delta t]$. For $j, k \neq i$, an observation that corresponds to the departure probability $\mathbb{P}_{i \to}(t, \Delta t)$ is given by $\sum_k M_{i \to k}^o(t, \Delta t)/N_i^o(t)$, and to the destination choice probability $\mathbb{P}_{j|i \to}(t)$ by $M_{i \to j}^o(t, \Delta t)/\sum_k M_{i \to k}^o(t, \Delta t)$.[7] Our objective is to match these observations against the predictions of the NL model. Such empirical implementation requires that the origin advantage $V_{i \to i}(t)$ and the destination advantage $V_{i \to j}(t)$ in the NL model be defined as functions of regional socioeconomic characteristics.

The basic component of an origin or destination advantage is the corresponding maximum feasible *origin utility* $\text{OUTIL}_i(t)$ or *destination utility* $\text{DUTIL}_j(t)$, which contain factors that contribute to the attractiveness of a region. However, these utilities are not enough to determine migration probabilities. For example, given any set of regional utility levels, a departure probability can increase as national economic conditions improve, while a destination choice probability can decrease as the spatial interaction between origin and destination becomes more difficult. We therefore propose as an empirical specification of the origin advantage as follows:

$$V_{i \to i}(t) = \text{OUTIL}_i(t) - \text{PRP}_i(t), \tag{16}$$

where $\text{PRP}_i(t)$, the *migration propensity* from i at t, contains factors that encourage regional mobility. The corresponding destination advantage is written as

$$V_{i \to j}(t) = \text{DUTIL}_j(t) - \text{IMP}_{i \to j}(t), \tag{17}$$

where $\text{IMP}_{i \to j}(t)$, the *migration impedance* from i to j at t, contains factors that discourage spatial interaction.

Since utilities are the maximum feasible, they must depend on per-capita real income and amenities. They can further depend on population size

---

[7] Although the observed number of migrants depends on the time interval, the observed destination choice probability does not if the observed flow $m_{i \to j}^o(t)$ at which migrants move from i to j is constant over $[t, t + \Delta t]$. Under this assumption, we have

$$M_{i \to j}^o(t, \Delta t) = \int_t^{t+\Delta t} m_{i \to j}^o(t) \, d\tau = m_{i \to j}^o(t) \int_t^{t+\Delta t} d\tau = m_{i \to j}^o(t) \Delta t,$$

so that the observed destination choice probabilities can be expressed as $m_{i \to j}^o(t)/\sum_k m_{i \to k}^o(t)$, which is independent of the time interval.

through its effect on externalities (a larger population supports greater variety of choice, but also increases the burden on the physical environment), as well as on expectations arising from past and present indicators of regional economic expansion and contraction. Migration propensity depends both on fluctuations in the national economy (hard times reduce migration flows everywhere) and on regional population characteristics that influence individual mobility, such as the proportion of recent migrants and the age structure of the population (see e.g. the microdata studies by Grant and Joseph 1983 and Newbold and Liaw 1990). Finally, migration impedance depends on distance between origin and destination and on related cultural dissimilarities (migrants prefer familiar social environments). Impedance must be adjusted to take into account that recent immigrants generate further immigration from the region they came from. This may be attributed to migration "channels" created by information being passed to potential migrants at the origin from recent migrants at the destination.

We have collected a considerable amount of such information on an annual basis, much of which contains variables that can serve as substitutes for one another. We have experimented extensively, aiming to find a theoretically sound combination of explanatory variables that provides both good fit and statistically significant parameter values.[8] Because consumer preferences can change significantly over 30 years – as can attitudes about location change and spatial interaction – we have expanded some parameters into linear functions of time (cf. Casetti 1972). We have also examined whether the population effect on the probabilities is quadratic rather than linear. Our motivation was that since population size captures the level of public goods available, as well as of agglomeration economies and diseconomies, population change must reflect corresponding returns to scale. It seems reasonable, in turn, to anticipate that such returns will eventually decrease with population size.

---

[8] Our socioeconomic data set includes about 25 variables. An exhaustive specification search was therefore impractical. We narrowed down the number of possible combinations by appealing to theory. For example, the specification of both OUTIL and DUTIL should include one variable from a menu of income variables (disposable income, weekly earnings, etc.) and one from a menu of expectations (unemployment rate, employment growth rate, etc.). To each of these combinations we added one or more measures of nonmonetary amenities. We proceeded in a similar fashion to define specifications for PRP and IMP. We obtained maximum likelihood parameter estimates for over 200 full specifications of the model. In the interest of parsimony, we eliminated all specifications which included parameters that could not be identified as significantly different from zero on the basis of the t-scores. From among the remaining specifications we chose the one that produced the highest value of the likelihood function. We can provide details upon request.

6   Estimation results for migration probabilities

We begin the description of our results with two general observations. First, we found that although income variables are consistently significant for destination utilities, they are consistently insignificant for origin utilities. We suspect that this happens because income has positive effects on both origin utility and migration propensity in the departure model, and that these two effects tend to confound one another in the parameter estimation procedure. On the other hand, destination probabilities are not influenced by mobility, since all those to whom they relate are (by definition) movers. Second, we have been unable to build an empirically convincing NL model in which one or more amenity variables enter the specification of origin and/or destination utilities. Therefore, in the context of our data base, the effect of amenities on utility is insignificant. We suspect that our result obtains because a larger population generates more public goods and services, and because a better environment attracts a larger population. Hence population size can indeed reflect amenities.

The specification of the NL model appears in Tables 1 and 2.[9] To guard against multicollinearity, only two time trends have been included in each model.[10] Logit elasticities are contained in Tables 3 and 4. Variables with time trends have two elasticities, one each at the beginning and the end of the study period. In Tables 1–4: DIS is the interregional road distance based on average road distances between major centres; EMPRATE is the employment growth rate; GNPRATE is the rate of growth in Canadian gross national product; LNGDIS is the language distance (the sum of the absolute values of the interregional differences in the shares of four basic linguistic categories); MIG is the lagged interregional migration inflow; POPSHR is the population share (regional population divided by Canadian population); POPSQR is the square of population

---

[9] Following McFadden (1974), we have employed the Newton–Raphson algorithm to obtain maximum likelihood estimates of the NL model. The parameters of the destination choice model are estimated first, as they are used to calculate the inclusive value (9), which in turn is an independent variable in the departure model. Since applications of the logit model to aggregate data tend to underestimate the standard error, we have adopted the conservative adjustment mechanism for the t-scores recommended by Liaw and Bartells (1982). Adjusted t-scores appear in parentheses underneath the corresponding parameter estimate. The high values for the goodness-of-fit statistics (ρ^2 and r^2) are to be expected, given the aggregate nature of our data. Although ρ^2 is the appropriate goodness-of-fit measure for logit models, we include r^2 because of its familiarity.

[10] We estimated the NL model with a single time trend $\beta_0 + \beta_1 t$ for each variable separately. We then ranked those time trends according to the size of the ratio β_1/β_0. Variables with stronger time trends correspond to larger ratios. In the specification of Tables 1 and 2, we included the two strongest time trends.

Table 1. *Departure model*

Constant	-6.3451 (-56.02)
Inclusive Value	$(0.9331 - 0.0080 \cdot t) \cdot \hat{Q}_i(t)$ $(21.92)\quad(-13.53)$
$\text{OUTIL}_i(t)$	$(2.7990 - 0.0166 \cdot t) \cdot \text{POPSHR}_i(t) + 1.8888 \cdot \text{EMPRATE}_i(t)$ $(17.44)\quad(-2.24)\qquad\qquad\qquad\qquad(4.57)$
$\text{PRP}_i(t)$	$0.0138 \cdot \text{GNPRATE}(t) + 13.5996 \cdot \text{TOTMIG}_i(t-1)$ $(4.64)\qquad\qquad\qquad(11.02)$

Notes: $\rho^2 = 0.9998$; $r^2 = 0.8931$.

Table 2. *Destination choice model*

$\text{DUTIL}_j(t)$	$1.5018 \cdot \text{RWKEARN}_j(t) + 4.0859 \cdot \text{POPSHR}_j(t) - 5.5572 \cdot \text{POPSQR}_j(t)$ $(17.09)\qquad\qquad\qquad\quad(4.12)\qquad\qquad\qquad(-2.48)$
	$+(-1.6310 + 0.1848 \cdot t) \cdot \text{EMPRATE}_j(t)$ $\quad(-2.40)\quad(6.17)$
$\text{IMP}_{i \to j}(t)$	$(0.0006 - 0.00001 \cdot t) \cdot \text{DIS}_{i \to j} + 0.0060 \cdot \text{LNGDIS}_{i \to j}(t)$ $(33.13)\quad(-17.45)\qquad\qquad\qquad(23.89)$
	$-0.00003 \cdot \text{MIG}_{i \to j}(t-1)$ (28.26)

Notes: $\rho^2 = 0.952$; $r^2 = 0.968$.

share; RWKEARN is the real weekly earnings deflated by the consumer price index; and TOTMIG is the lagged total migration inflow.

A quadratic population effect with decreasing returns to scale appears in the destination choice model but not in the departure model, where POPSQR is insignificant. We found that the same asymmetry persists across different specifications of the NL model. A linear population effect generates higher utility than a corresponding quadratic effect with decreasing returns to scale. Therefore, a linear specification of the origin utility must lower the population effect on departure probabilities relative to the corresponding quadratic specification. This is precisely the case when the population size effect includes the opportunities for migration within the region, which compete with outside migration opportunities. Under these circumstances, a linear population effect in the departure model may well be consistent with a quadratic population effect in the destination choice model.

Both expanded parameters in the departure model are decreasing. For the inclusive value, decreasing μ implies that the part of the uncertainty

Table 3. *Elasticities of the departure model*

$\hat{Q}_i \| t = 1952$	+2.8471
$\hat{Q}_i \| t = 1983$	+2.1148
$POPSHR_i(1952)$	−0.6472
$POPSHR_i(1983)$	−0.5320
$EMPRATE_i(t)$	−0.0237
$GNPRATE(t)$	+0.0611
$TOTMIG_i(t-1)$	+0.2140

Table 4. *Elasticities of the destination choice model*

$RWKEARN_j(t)$	+1.2220
$POPSHR_j(t)$	+0.6347
$POPSQR_j(t)$	−0.2335
$EMPRATE_j(1952)$	−0.0210
$EMPRATE_j(1983)$	+0.0504
$DIS_{i \to j} \| t = 1952$	−0.6814
$DIS_{i \to j} \| t = 1983$	−0.3407
$LNGDIS_{i \to j}(t)$	−0.2272
$MIG_{i \to j}(t-1)$	+0.4741

attributed to departure decisions increases through time. In particular, while less than 7 percent of the variance belonged to the upper (departure) level at the beginning of the study period, about 30 percent belongs to it toward the end. At the same time, the impact of the expected maximum utility of destinations on the decision to migrate declines significantly.

For the destination choice model, expectations have a rapidly increasing impact on destination utilities and this, together with the linear structure of destination advantages, must account for the wrong sign of the constant term in the expanded parameter of EMPRATE. The positive effect of economic expectations on destination choice probabilities is restored after the first few years, as indicated in Table 4. Finally, the effect of physical distance on spatial interaction declines over the study period.

7   Disequilibrium analysis

The evolution of the Canadian regional system, as described by the adjustment process (3), is driven by all those socioeconomic conditions that were found to affect individual migration decisions. Our theoretical specifications of the nested logit model in (8) and (14), and our empirical specifications in Tables 1 and 2, indicate that the migration probabilities at year t depend on the entire distribution of population among the regions of Canada in that year through the inclusive value in the departure model. Accordingly, we can express the migration rates (15) as

$$r_{i \to j}(t) = f_{i \to j}(\mathbf{n}(t), \mathbf{D}(t)),\qquad(18)$$

where $\mathbf{D}$ contains all relevant data other than the state of the system.

An *equilibrium state* at time t, $\mathbf{n}^e(t)$, is a solution to the system of equations

$$0 = \sum_{j \neq i}(n_j f_{j \to i}(\mathbf{n}, \mathbf{D}(t)) - n_i f_{i \to j}(\mathbf{n}, \mathbf{D}(t))).\qquad(19)$$

An equilibrium is thus a population distribution that, under the current socioeconomic conditions, generates balanced total migration inflows and outflows for every regional alternative in the system.

Since the migration rates depend on the state of the system, the system of equations (19) is *nonlinear* in population. Although the general solution for such nonlinear systems is unknown, it can be established that at least one equilibrium state does exist for all $t \in T$ (see Ginsburgh, Papageorgiou, and Thisse 1985 and Kanaroglou et al. 1986a). In consequence, although we cannot calculate equilibrium states directly from (19), we can seek to find equilibrium states for all $t \in T$ by using an iterative solution algorithm that takes the observed state as its initial condition. For every t, this algorithm will provide us with no, one, or more equilibrium states. Since all such equilibria are stable *by construction,* we know that the observed state interacts with the corresponding equilibrium state in a way that is generally predictable. Roughly speaking, an observed regional population consistently below the corresponding equilibrium population implies a tendency for growth, and one above the equilibrium implies a tendency for decline. Furthermore, growth or decline is stronger on average as the dissimilarity between observed and equilibrium states increases. By definition, increasing dissimilarity denotes a higher level of *disequilibrium* in the system.[11]

Introducing (16) and (17) into (15), we can obtain the estimated migration rates $\hat{f}_{i \to j}(\mathbf{n}(t), \mathbf{D}(t))$. Introducing these, in turn, into (19), we can compute the estimated equilibrium state $\hat{\mathbf{n}}^e(t)$.[12] The evolution of

---

[11] While the equilibrium state indicates the general direction in which the observed state moves, one should not think of it as a prediction of the observed state. As the socioeconomic profile of the system evolves through time, so does its equilibrium. Thus, the equilibrium and the observed state are in continuous evolution, and we do not know if they will converge or, if they do, when and at which regional population distribution.

[12] We have used the MINPACK subroutine HYBRID, which solves a nonlinear system using a modification of Powell's hybrid method.

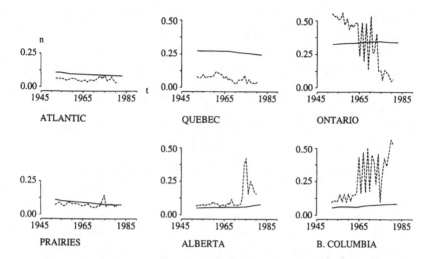

Figure 2. Population shares: solid line, observed; dashed line, estimated equilibrium.

observed and estimated equilibrium states for the Canadian regional system is shown in Figure 2.[13] Over a little less than the first half of the observation period, the disequilibrium pattern of the Canadian regional system appeared to be stable. Central Canada remained far from equilibrium, with a strong decline potential for Québec and strong growth potential for Ontario; the rest of the country was close to equilibrium, with a weak decline potential for Atlantic Canada and the Prairies, weak growth potential for Alberta, and somewhat stronger growth potential for British Columbia. In consequence, Ontario was the only region with a strong growth potential during that time. The pattern began to change abruptly around the middle 1960s. A period of instability emerged, mainly affecting Ontario and British Columbia, which lasted for about 10 years. By the end of this period, Ontario's strong growth potential had been nearly reversed and its previous place was taken by British Columbia. Notice how clearly Ontario's equilibrium state moves from a high to a low level, and how the transition is marked by strong oscillations between the old and the emerging new equilibrium trajectory for both Ontario and British Columbia. In terms of equilibrium solutions, we first observe a single equilibrium path, the emergence of a second evolving along with the original one, and the subsequent disappearance of the original equilibrium path. At the same time, Québec's equilibrium trajectory remained locked

[13] We have been unable to calculate equilibrium states for the last two years.

(1 - R)/2

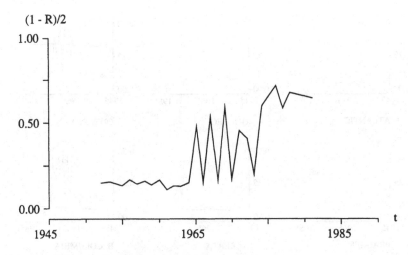

Figure 3. Disequilibrium in population shares.

at a low level so that, after the transition, the whole of central Canada exhibits a strong potential for relative decline. Toward the end of the transition, we also observe a strong temporary perturbation in Alberta's equilibrium trajectory. This perturbation seems to be correlated with a sharp temporary drop in the equilibrium trajectory of British Columbia, which blurs the transition of the latter from a low- to a high-level equilibrium. However, as Alberta's population grew, its pool of highly mobile individuals may have chosen the neighboring British Columbia, and this may have supported British Columbia's strong growth potential observed toward the end of the time series.

In order to summarize those regional deviations between observed and equilibrium states, we need an appropriate composite measure of dissimilarity. Since the correlation coefficient R indicates the degree of similarity between the observed and equilibrium states, $1 - R$ indicates their degree of dissimilarity. Thus we can use $1 - R$ directly. However, to contain our measure between zero and unity, we define $(1 - R)/2$ as the *degree of disequilibrium* in the system.[14] Figure 3 shows this measure applied to our case. In conjunction with Figure 2, we conclude that the sources of

[14] We have adopted this measure from Weidlich and Haag (1988). Zero degree of disequilibrium implies perfect positive correlation between observed and equilibrium states – hence equilibrium. As the degree of disequilibrium increases, correlation declines. When observed and equilibrium states are perfectly uncorrelated, the degree of disequilibrium in the system is 0.5. Still higher degrees of disequilibrium imply negative correlation between observed and equilibrium states.

instability and of the dramatic rise in disequilibrium are the three richest Canadian provinces: Ontario, Alberta, and British Columbia.

Appendix

A.1   *Historical background*

During our study period, the population of Canada grew from about 14 to 24 million.[15] Growth was uneven – rapid over the first half of the period, slowing down over the second half, and increasing once again toward the end of the period. The two components of such aggregate population change are natural growth and international net migration. (1) Following a long period of declining birth rates, the trend was reversed at the end of the Second World War to reach a high point at the beginning of our study period. Birth rates were stabilized around 27/1,000 for over one decade ("baby boom"), then fell precipitously to reach in 1971 the lowest level ever recorded, and were stabilized once again around 16/1,000 for the rest of our study period ("baby bust"). Throughout, death rates steadily fell as the average life expectancy grew from 68 years in 1951 to 75 in 1981. (2) The other component of aggregate population change, international net migration, was also uneven. Between 1951 and 1961, international net migration contributed 1.1 million people, who – in conjunction with the baby boom – accounted for the rapid total population growth over the first half of the period. These new immigrants reversed the existing shortage of young workers, stemming from the low prewar birth rates, and contributed significantly to the strong economic expansion of the time. Large international net migration streams were also observed toward the end of our study period, and these account for increasing total growth rates in spite of declining natural growth rates. Finally, during the middle years of our study period, there was a decline of international net migration that, together with the onset of the baby bust, slowed down aggregate population growth.

We now turn to the economic and political history of the time. Events that influenced the regional structure of the Canadian economy during our study period can be associated with two central issues: the partitioning of powers between the federal and provincial governments, and the management of policy differences (both between the two levels of government and among the provinces). From this perspective, following Simeon and Robinson (1990) (hereafter "SR") we can distinguish a stage of

---

[15] Our demographic information draws upon Denton, Feaver, and Spencer (1987) and Denton and Spencer (1991).

reconstruction that ends in 1957, a stage of *executive federalism* from 1958 to 1973, and a stage of *compound crisis* that begins in 1974.[16]

Reconstruction

Since the end of the Second World War, the federal government had pursued Keynesian macroeconomic growth policies requiring strong federal control over expenditure and taxation. This became possible because all provinces (excepting Québec, which opposed any expansion of federal powers) were convinced of the necessity of such an approach. Conflict about fiscal arrangements between the two levels of government was restrained, and the extent of their cooperation was close enough to characterize reconstruction as the "golden age" of Canadian federalism. Its highest point (in terms of popular support for a strong federal government) came at the very end of that period. Gross national product grew steadily as the employment shift out of agriculture and into the industrial and service sectors intensified.

These economic and demographic changes had important regional implications. The growth of the service sector took place in all regions, with the result that all provincial economies became more diversified. The decline of agriculture also changed the distribution of populations between country and the city in all parts of Canada . . . . (SR, p. 130)

Growth, however, was uneven: Central Canada and the west grew fast, leaving further behind the Atlantic region and the Prairies.

Executive federalism

Two events mark the beginning of decline in federal power. First, a deep recession between 1957 and 1961:

. . . weakened confidence in the capacity of the government to maintain economic growth by means of the macro-economic instruments alone. Closely related, dramatic differences in the regional impact of the recession heightened the growing recognition that even in times of rapid national economic growth, major disparities in regional income and employment would remain and could only be reduced by more focused regional policies. (SR, p. 160)

Second, the end of a long struggle in Québec brought to power a succession of reformist Québec governments increasingly bent on fiscal autonomy, jurisdictional autonomy, and the recognition of a special status for that province. In order to cope with the recession and, more significantly, with persistent regional disparities that now increasingly favored Ontario

---

[16] These correspond (respectively) to chapters 8, 9, and 10 in SR. Our discussion draws extensively from that source.

and the west, the federal government met growing demands for social programs and intensified its efforts toward regional redistribution. This accounted for the largest expansion of the welfare state in Canadian history. Furthermore, in order to avoid recognition of a special status for Québec, the federal government responded with significant concessions to *all* provinces. In turn, decentralization of federal powers, together with welfare expansion at both levels, accounted for a rapid growth of governments, especially provincial ones. Although GNP growth resumed after the recession, new threats from international economic competition brought about increasing demands for province-specific and -managed industrial diversification. Toward this end, resource-rich (producing) provinces supported stronger provincial control over resources, while resource-poor (consuming) provinces supported stronger federal redistribution powers. This conflict of interests, as well as the increasing political dependence of the federal government upon central Canada, brought about western alienation which, together with reformist Québec policies, further weakened central authority. Thus Canada moved from an era of cooperative federalism at the beginning of the period to an era of increasing conflict about jurisdiction and coordination among governments at the end.

Compound crisis

The two OPEC oil-price increases in 1973 and 1979 created massive transfers from the consuming to the producing provinces. At the same time, the adverse effects of growing international competition were strongly felt in parts of Canada, since many economic sectors still used outdated capital equipment. Deindustrialization, unemployment, and static real incomes were observed in most consuming provinces, who raised their demands for the investment necessary for modernization. Thus the conflict over resource rents – between the producing provinces on the one hand, and the federal government and the consuming provinces on the other – reached critical levels. Conditions became even more difficult for Canada after the 1976 election in Québec of the explicitly separatist Parti Québécois (PQ) government. Although all other provinces rejected the PQ proposals about sovereignty-association for Québec, they used PQ as an ally to further erode the power of the federal government. Both Québec and western alienation increased still further. When the new recession came in 1981, Canada found itself in the most difficult situation since the thirties.[17]

---

[17] The GDP growth fell from a 5.6 percent average between 1960 and 1973 to 2.0 between 1980 and 1984, while productivity (GNP/GDP) fell correspondingly from 2.7 to 0.4. Consumer inflation rose from a 2.4 percent average between 1960 and 1968 to 11.2 between 1980 and 1982 (before it was brought down once again by the recession), while unemployment rose correspondingly from 4.8 to 10.4 percent (MacDonald Commission 1985, vol. 2, pp. 48–9).

It appeared that the post-war economic order was in the midst of a fundamental mental crisis in these years and that Canada, in spite of its oil resource windfall, was in a worse position than most [OECD countries]. This extraordinary deterioration of economic performance, and the fears that it engendered, placed unprecedented strains on the political accommodations upon which the post-war order had been constructed. (SR, p. 217)

By the end of 1980, the federal government firmly believed that provincial powers had increased too much, and that decentralization should be stopped or even reversed. Its position was considerably strengthened by the defeat of a PQ referendum on sovereignty-association for Québec, which happened during the same year. Shortly afterward,

the federal government announced that it was abandoning the assumptions of co-operative federalism in favour of a new, "competitive" federalism. In the future, Ottawa would seek unilaterally to undertake constitutional reform, develop a National Energy Program, tighten the conditions governing transfers to the provinces, and establish more direct links between the federal government and Canadian citizens. (SR, p. 215)

The federal government succeeded in repatriating the Constitution (without Québec's approval), in providing Canada with an amending formula and a Charter of Rights, and in striking a new agreement on the jurisdiction over natural resources, while at the same time bitterly dividing the country. Our observation period ends just before a new federal government is elected on a platform of "national reconciliation."

The most striking correspondence between those historical events and our results is perhaps related to Figure 3, where Canada moves from a low level of disequilibrium during the stage of reconstruction to a high one during the stage of compound crisis. The transition occurs during executive federalism, the time of rapid expansion for governments, decentralization, and the welfare state. Further associations can also be obtained using the estimated trends in the NL model. Our finding – that the impact of the expected maximum utility of destinations on the decision to migrate declines significantly through time – is consistent with the rise of political decentralization in Canada. The emerging regionalism, especially Québec and western alienation, may well have blunted the perception of better opportunities elsewhere. Our finding that individuals seem to be increasingly concerned about whether employment will continue to be available at the destination is consistent with the rise of unemployment and the increasingly uncertain economic prospects for Canada. Finally, the decline of the distance effect on interaction could be related to a weakening of traditional family and community ties associated with increasing levels of urbanization and modernization during our study period.

A.2   *Regional commentary*

Atlantic

Economic and demographic decline began after the war, intensified during the 1957 recession (which was harder for peripheral areas, especially the Atlantic region), and continued throughout our observation period. Rising oil prices in 1973 and 1979 dropped revenue shares significantly. A lack of extensive natural resources (excepting oil offshore Newfoundland) and of a sound industrial basis increased the dependence of the Atlantic provinces on the federal government. In consequence, the region has strongly supported federalism and federal initiatives on redistribution – a central concern for all postwar federal governments. Federal efforts to lower the persistent regional disparities in Canada have gradually shifted from an almost exclusive reliance on federal transfers to the development of region-specific growth policies. The creation of the advisory Atlantic Development Board in 1962 marked the first step toward such policies, and its activity expanded after the change of federal government in 1963. This could be the reason why we observe (in Figure 2) a favorable change of regional demographic trends shortly thereafter, before the equilibrium population trajectory appears to relapse toward a higher potential for relative decline after the first OPEC oil-price increase.

Québec

Rising secularism, encouraged by a strong population shift from traditional rural to modern urban environments, gradually eroded the power of the conservative Québec nationalist movement in favor of reformist nationalism. The change came with the provincial elections of 1960 and marked the beginning of the "quiet revolution," which was characterized by growing demands for a special status for Québec. Special status, according to the Tremblay Report (1954), was based on

... three premises: first, that Confederation was a compact between two founding races or peoples ... ; second, that the province of Québec was the home of one of those peoples; and third, that its government was the principal defender of the rights and interests of francophones. This made the Québec government unique among the provincial governments, ... viewed as the equal of Ottawa, each representing one of the two founding peoples. (SR, p. 144)

The obvious alternative to such equality within a federation, *indépendentisme,* was expressed in 1968 by the PQ. Increasing local tensions brought the Front de Libération Québécois (FLQ) crisis of 1970, which prompted a dynamic intervention by the federal government. The resulting backlash against political violence hurt *indépendentisme,* but only for a short time: In 1973 the PQ became the official opposition and in 1976 it came to power. Over the next four years, an all-out struggle for the allegiance of the Québec electorate was fought between the federal government (proposing integration within a bilingual state) and the Québec government (proposing sovereignty-association). It ended with the defeat of a Québec referendum on sovereignty-association in 1980, the repatriation of the Constitution in 1982, and the subsequent withdrawal of an embittered Québec government from much intergovernmental activity with the rest of Canada.

The basic outlines of those remarkable political events are clearly reflected in some of our equilibrium population trajectories. The correspondence is based on the changing fortunes of *indépendentisme* during that period: As it rises, the increased net outflow of anglophones from Québec implies an increased potential for relative decline, and hence a smaller slope of the equilibrium population trajectory in Figure 2 and of other Québec trajectories strongly depending on population. Thus, in Figure 2, the beginning of the "quiet revolution" marks the beginning of a clear downward shift in the direction of the equilibrium population trajectory. The bottom is reached during the FLQ crisis, which causes an abrupt reversal of the trend corresponding to the backlash against *indépendentisme*. The downward trend is resumed once again just after the first OPEC oil-price increase. It follows that, with the exception of a brief period when federalism appeared to gain ground in Québec, the "quiet revolution" has been characterized by an increasing potential for relative decline. However, one should also take into account the adverse economic conditions of the period, such as a gradual loss of industrial base due to international competition and a drop of total revenue share due to the energy crisis. These, together with political uncertainty, weakened the Québec economy to such an extent that a staggering 44 percent of all jobs lost in Canada during the 1981 recession were in Québec (Fraser 1984, p. 322).

Ontario

At the beginning of our observation period, Ontario was the growth center of the Canadian economy. At the end, it had the strongest potential for relative decline. Nowhere is this dramatic change better shown than in the Ontario population trajectories of Figure 2. Indeed, that part of the figure may represent one of the most interesting results of our analysis – both because of the change itself and because of the clear equilibrium discontinuity it implies. An upper equilibrium population trajectory exists until the first OPEC oil-price increase of 1973. This trajectory indicates a steadily diminishing potential for relative growth. During that period, the provincial government tried to preserve and expand Ontario's industrial base in an environment of increasing national and international competition. Despite those efforts, Ontario experienced fundamental structural shifts, and its share of national GDP became smaller.

Reduced state bargaining power [across Canada] was manifested in rising budget deficits, as the capacity to tax capital while maintaining adequate levels of new private capital investment – reflected in the share of all revenues represented by corporate income taxes – declined. At the same time, the costs of economic adjustment – welfare, unemployment and re-training expenditures – increased. (SR, p. 216)

The origin and the impact of those difficulties, which become apparent in Ontario during the period of compound crisis, seems to be earlier and deeper than casual observation would indicate: As evidenced by the emergence of a lower equilibrium population trajectory, instability begins just after the 1963 federal election, which coincides with the start of the strongest public-sector expansion in Canadian history. It ends with the onset of the energy crisis, when the transition from the higher to the lower equilibrium trajectory becomes complete. By that time, Ontario had abandoned its traditional role of mediator between the two levels of government and had become instead the leader of the consuming provinces, who aimed to avoid large revenue transfers to the producing provinces by keeping oil prices well below international levels.

A 1979 Ontario government paper estimated that a $7 per barrel increase in the price of oil would add $3 billion to the coffers of the producing provinces, while adding 3.2 percent to the Ontario inflation rate and reducing its GPP by 1.5 percent (Simeon 1980, p. 1983). The revenue bonanza, Ontario argued, was creating massive inequalities in the revenues of provincial governments. (SR, p. 237)

In the end, large revenue transfers did occur and Ontario's growth rate became one of the lowest in Canada.

Prairies

The postwar shift of population away from agriculture had its strongest effect on the Prairies. After the war, many of those who left their farms resettled outside of the region, thus contributing to its relative population decline. The same trend continued within our observation period, but at a gradually lower rate – especially after 1970. In spite of declining agricultural population, the economic importance of agriculture in the region rose: From 40 percent of all Canadian farms in 1941, the Prairies (including Alberta) continued 48 percent in 1971 (Gibbins 1980, p. 78). Thus, the Prairies continued to depend heavily on agriculture and natural resources (primarily potash and some oil in Saskatchewan), while other parts of Canada diversified faster.

In 1967 the International Grain Agreement fell apart in the face of over-supply and wheat and other grain prices plummetted. Realized net farm income in Saskatchewan fell from its 1967 peak of $489 million to $202 million in 1969. . . . As the potash market was largely determined by the demand for fertilizer, the potash boom also went bust. Prices in 1969 were half of their peak value in 1965. (SR, p. 170)

The effect of those fluctuations is clearly shown in Figure 2, together with the subsequent potash boom of 1972 and the first OPEC oil-price increase of 1973. By that time, the Prairie governments came to the conclusion that balancing grain production (with potash, forestry, or even oil) was not sufficient to stabilize their economic development. Needed were industries with smaller demand fluctuations than those observed in their primary sectors. Toward this end, the Prairie governments increased public intervention by trying to expand public ownership of already developed natural resources while, at the same time, keeping associated resource rents within the region; by establishing Crown corporations for developing new resources; and by promoting industrial growth through a variety of regional programs in aid of manufacturing.

Alberta

The most important events by far in the recent history of Alberta revolve around the two OPEC oil-price increases and the subsequent battles against the federal government for the control of associated resource rents. These came just after a temporary strong decline in oil exploration in 1968 caused by the discovery of major oil fields in Alaska, which raised doubts about the future of American markets for Albertan oil and gas. Both periods, of uncertain prospects between 1968 and 1972 and of great profits between 1973 and 1981, mark the equilibrium trajectories of Figure 2. This figure provides a measure of how important the second period was for Alberta. Toward the end of that period, more than 75 percent of total revenues from oil and gas was controlled by provincial governments – 80 percent by Alberta (SR, p. 244), whose revenues from own sources was a remarkable 232 percent of the provincial average (SR, p. 237). As Alberta's windfall revenues raised the *average* provincial revenues, federal equalization payments to the poorer provinces went out of control: For every new dollar gained by Alberta, the federal government had to raise 90 cents to meet those entitlements (Courchene 1984). Thus the existing partitioning of oil revenues became unacceptable for the federal government, which claimed it needed much more in order "to support its energy initiatives and its broad management responsibilities: to cushion individual Canadians from adverse economic effects, to facilitate industrial adjustment and to see that fair play is done" (SR, pp. 243–4).

Alberta, in contrast, argued that "between 1974 and 1981 the oil [producers] had subsidized the other regions of the country . . . [by] about $40 billion" (SR, p. 237). Those resources are provincial. Because they were being depleted, Alberta had to plan for the day when they would run out, by strengthening and diversifying its economy and by trying to shift political power from its traditional Central Canadian strongholds and toward the west. Both levels of government pursued their contradictory goals, the federal government using its power to tax and the government of Alberta using royalties on production. Never before had there been such a strong intergovernmental conflict over resources. Pressure from other regions to stop that war increased, and a final agreement came in 1981.

Ironically, no sooner was agreement achieved than the price of oil and other primary commodities, which had given rise to the conflict in the first place, collapsed. Once again, Canadian domestic politics was profoundly shaped by developments outside the country. The expected benefits of massive new exploration and development did not materialize . . . . Unemployment in Alberta soared to 11 percent in 1983, four times the 1981 level . . . . The influx of new residents into the province slowed and then reversed. Far from the permanent shift in the Canadian economic balance that Ottawa's 1981 economic plans had assumed, the boom had proved temporary, as Westerners had feared all along it would. (SR, p. 248)

This is why the tremendous effect of the oil boom on Alberta seems to last for such a surprisingly short time in our figures.

British Columbia

The main industrial development policies for this region, especially between 1952 and 1972, have been resource-oriented: forestry, mining, and electrical power (which, together with that of Ontario and Québec, ranks among the cheapest in the world). After that time, development extended to manufacturing and high technology. None of this, however, is sufficient to explain why British Columbia became the rough complement of Ontario with respect to overall potential for relative population growth during our observation period. In other words, we cannot explain why the function of a growth center for Canada was transferred to British Columbia as Ontario's growth potential collapsed. We note, nevertheless, that of all Canadian regions only British Columbia has geographic advantages similar to those that led to earlier periods of growth for Ontario and Québec. First, all three have close proximity with U.S. core regions – Ontario and Québec with the largest, British Columbia with the second largest but fastest growing. On a global scale, British Columbia belongs to the Pacific Rim, now the fastest growing part of the world economy. Second, like Toronto and Montréal, Vancouver has achieved a state of rapid urban growth strong enough to generate agglomeration economies that transmit growth to the entire regional economy. One might also speculate that low regional population densities, a moderate climate, and the great beauty of the land are factors of some significance.

REFERENCES

Anderson, W. P., and Y. Y. Papageorgiou (1994a), "An Analysis of Migration Streams for the Canadian Regional System, 1952-1983: 1. Migration Probabilities," *Geographical Analysis* 26: 15-36.

(1994b), "An Analysis of Migration Streams for the Canadian Regional System, 1952-1983: 2. Disequilibrium," *Geographical Analysis* 26: 110-23.

Ben-Akiva, M., and S. R. Lerman (1985), *Discrete Choice Analysis: Theory and Application to Travel Demand.* Cambridge, MA: MIT Press.

Casetti, E. (1972), "Generating Models by the Expansion Method: Applications to Geographical Research," *Geographical Analysis* 4: 81-91.

Courchene, T. (1970), "Interprovincial Migration and Economic Adjustment," *Canadian Journal of Economics* 3: 550-76.

(1984), "Equalization Payments: Past, Present and Future," Special Report, Ontario Economic Council, Toronto.

de Palma, A., and C. Lefèvre (1983), "Individual Decision-Making in Dynamic Collective Systems," *Journal of Mathematical Sociology* 9: 103-24.

Denton, F. T., C. H. Feaver, and B. G. Spencer (1987), "The Canadian Population and Labour Force: Retrospect and Prospect," in V. W. Marshall (ed.), *Aging in Canada: Social Perspectives.* Markham, Ontario: Fidzhenry and Whiteside, pp. 11-38.

Denton, F. T., and B. G. Spencer (1991), "Some Economic and Demographic Implications of Canadian Life Cycle Changes," in E. J. McCullough and R. L. Calder (eds.), *Time as a Human Resource.* University of Calgary Press, pp. 75-101.

Fotheringham, A. S. (1986), "Modelling Hierarchical Destination Choice," *Environment and Planning A* 18: 401-18.

Fraser, G. (1984), *René Leveque and the Parti Québéqois in Power.* Toronto: Macmillan.

Gibbins, R. (1980), *Prairie Politics and Society: Regionalism in Decline.* Toronto: Butterworths.

Ginsburgh, V., Y. Y. Papageorgiou, and J.-F. Thisse (1985), "Existence and Stability of Spatial Equilibria and Steady-States," *Regional Science and Urban Economics* 15: 149-58.

Grant, E. K., and A. E. Joseph (1983), "The Spatial Aspects and Regularities of Multiple Interregional Migration within Canada: Evidence and Implications," *Canadian Journal of Regional Science* 6: 75-96.

Haag, G., and W. Weidlich (1984), "A Stochastic Theory of Interregional Migration," *Geographical Analysis* 4: 331-57.

Kanaroglou, P., K.-L. Liaw, and Y. Y. Papageorgiou (1986a), "An Analysis of Migratory Systems: 1. Theory," *Environment and Planning A* 18: 913-28.

(1986b), "An Analysis of Migratory Systems: 2. Operational Framework," *Environment and Planning A* 18: 1039-60.

Kurtz, T. (1978), "Strong Approximation Theorems for Density-Dependent Markov Chains," *Stochastic Processes and Their Applications* 6: 223-40.

Leonardi, G., and Y. Y. Papageorgiou (1992), "Conceptual Foundations of Spatial Choice Models," *Environment and Planning A* 24: 1393-1408.

Liaw, K.-L., and C. P. A. Bartells (1982), "Estimation and Interpretation of a Non-linear Migration Model," *Geographical Analysis* 14: 227-45.

Lowry, I. S. (1966), *Migration and Metropolitan Growth: Two Analytical Models*. San Francisco: Chandler.

MacDonald Commission (1985), *Report on the Economic Union and Development Prospects for Canada,* 3 vols. Ottawa: Supply and Services.

McFadden, D. (1974), "Conditional Logit Analysis of Qualitative Choice Behavior," in P. Zarembka (ed.), *Frontiers in Econometrics*. New York: Academic Press, pp. 105-42.

(1978), "Modelling the Choice of Residential Location," in A. Karlqvist, L. Lunqvist, F. Snickars, and J. W. Weibull (eds.), *Spatial Interaction Theory and Planning Models*. Amsterdam: North-Holland.

Newbold, K. B., and K.-L. Liaw (1990), "Characterization of Primary, Return, and Onward Interprovincial Migration in Canada: Overall and Age-Specific Patterns," *Canadian Journal of Regional Science* 13: 17-34.

Shaw, R. P. (1985), *Intermetropolitan Migration in Canada: Determinants over Three Decades*. Toronto: NC Press.

Simeon, R. (1980), *A Citizen's Guide to the Constitutional Issues*. Toronto: Gage.

Simeon, R., and J. Robinson (1990), *State, Society and the Development of Canadian Federalism* (The Collected Research Studies, Royal Commission on the Economic Union and Development Prospects for Canada, vol. 71). University of Toronto Press.

Tremblay Commission (1954), *Report on Inquiry on Constitutional Problems*. Editeur Officiel du Québec.

Weidlich, W., and G. Haag (eds.) (1988), *Interregional Migration: Dynamic Theory and Comparative Analysis*. Berlin: Springer-Verlag.

Yellott, J. I. (1977), "The Relationship between Luce's Choice Axiom, Thurstone's Theory of Comparative Judgement, and the Double Exponential Distribution," *Journal of Mathematical Psychology* 5: 109-44.

CHAPTER 17

Optimality of the target-zone regime

Giuseppe De Arcangelis

1   Introduction

The article by Williamson and Miller (1987) on the target-zone proposal for the reform of the international exchange-rate regime has stimulated a great deal of both theoretical and empirical work. Starting from the well-known contribution by Krugman (1991), many researchers have developed the basic flexible-price monetary model to deal with typical issues of the target-zone regime, for example, re-alignments (Bertola and Caballero 1992, Bertola and Svensson 1993), interest- versus exchange-rate variability (Svensson 1991), measures of regime credibility (Frankel and Phillips 1991, Rose and Svensson 1991), and so forth. The data source for empirical applications in the 1980s has been the European Monetary System (EMS). On the other hand, Miller and Weller (1991) and Sutherland (1992a) have studied the characteristics of a target-zone regime in a sticky-price monetary model. Svensson (1992a) and Krugman and Miller (1992) contain an excellent overview of the state of the art.

Generally, all these contributions have focused attention on the consequences of establishing a (perfectly or imperfectly credible) target zone on the exchange-rate dynamics. The main result has been the finding of a nonlinear relationship between the exchange rate and its fundamentals.

However, in all recent literature based on the Krugman (1991) model (except for Sutherland 1992b and Beetsma and van der Ploeg 1992), no contributions can be found on the comparison between the target-zone regime and the alternative perfectly flexible and perfectly fixed exchange-rate regimes. In other words, the target-zone regime is taken for granted without questioning its relative performance with respect to the other

I wish to thank Giancarlo Gandolfo, Laura Sabani, Clifford R. Wymer, and two anonymous referees for useful comments on an earlier draft of this paper. Financial support from CNR, grant no. 94.02036.10, is gratefully acknowledged. The usual disclaimers apply.

regimes. In our opinion, the lack of debate on this point is even more severe when we realize that there is no single way of designing the target-zone system, and that the different characteristics of the regime may change its relative performance.

Some recent contributions have described these advantages of the monetary independence that the target zone can offer (Svensson 1992b). This paper deals with the similar question of optimality of the target-zone regime. In particular, we design a perfectly credible target zone with finite interventions at the margin in a sticky-price model, and compare such a regime with the cases of perfectly flexible and perfectly fixed exchange rates when the official authorities can observe the movement of the foreign currency price but do not know the type of the shock (i.e., whether it is nominal, aggregate-demand type, or supply type). By computing the value of a general loss function for the official authorities, some conditions for the optimality of the target zone regime are obtained.

A similar issue is addressed in Sutherland (1992b) together with optimal bandwidth computation, but with some important differences. First, Sutherland does not consider a true sticky-price monetary model and, as a consequence, the exchange rate can be purposely described as driven by *exogenous* fundamentals in the same way as the early contributions of the most recent target-zone literature, which make use of the perfectly flexible-price exchange-rate model (i.e., no feedback from the exchange rate on the fundamentals can be included). Second, although Sutherland develops his model in a stochastic framework with Brownian motion shocks, all the innovations are permanent; the resulting extreme difficulty of the analysis brings the author to drop the supply shock in his comparison of regimes. Some of these difficulties are overcome in Beetsma and van der Ploeg (1992), where the comparison of the target-zone regime with other exchange-rate regimes is performed within a traditional sticky-price model, but at the cost of closed-form solutions obtained with numerical analysis.

In the present paper a simpler framework is considered in order to carry on the analysis inside a true sticky-price model (with both temporary and permanent shocks) and to reach open-form solutions. In addition, the paper stresses the difference between uncertainty on the shock *source* and uncertainty on the shock *intensity*. Finally, optimality conditions of the target-zone regime are also compared before and after the shock occurs, when the authorities' information set increases.

Outside the Krugman approach, there have been many empirical contributions that tried to "re-run history" under an alternative target-zone regime with world macroeconometric models (see e.g. Edison, Miller, and Williamson 1987; Currie and Wren-Lewis 1989, 1990). Although they find that a target-zone regime could have improved history, Hughes Hallet (1992) points out how this conclusion can be only a necessary condition for the target-zone optimality. In fact, a subsequent paper by Hughes Hallet (1993) obtains conditions for the optimality of the target-zone regime in a two-country model, therefore considering factors typically stressed in the traditional policy coordination literature and which could be considered as complementary to the present paper (which hinges on a one-country model).

In Section 2, the sticky-price monetary model for exchange-rate determination is reported (mainly from Miller and Weller 1991); the dynamics for the flexible and fixed exchange-rate regimes are also described. Section 3 introduces the loss function for the authorities (AA) and compares the three regimes when the three kinds of shocks occur. Sections 4 and 5 show (respectively) ex ante and posterior conditions for optimality of the target-zone regime by allowing for time inconsistency problems. Section 6 concludes by pointing out possible future developments of this approach.

2 Different exchange-rate regimes in a sticky-price model

The reference model is the standard sticky-price monetary model of exchange-rate determination, in the spirit of Dornbusch (1976) and as reconsidered by Miller and Weller (1991). In this perfect foresight version, the set-up has been enriched with the presence of three shocks:

$$m_0 - p = \kappa y - \lambda i + \nu, \tag{1}$$

$$y = \eta(s - p) - \gamma i + \epsilon, \tag{2}$$

$$ds = i - i^*, \tag{3}$$

$$dp = \varphi(y - \bar{y}) + \mu. \tag{4}$$

All the variables are expressed in log terms, and the time subscript has been omitted for simplicity. Here d must be interpreted as the derivative over time, that is, d/dt. The first equation represents the equilibrium in the money market: the real money supply on the left-hand side equals the real money demand, which depends on the current real output y and the domestic interest rate i; ν represents a nominal shock. In the second equation, real output is demand-determined and the aggregate demand (AD) depends on the real exchange rate $(s - p)$ and negatively on the domestic interest rate[1] i; ϵ is the AD shock. The nominal exchange rate s is

---

[1] As mentioned also in Miller and Weller (1991), although the AD specification requires the real interest rate, use of the nominal rate simply changes the meaning of the elasticity γ, which is equal to the corresponding real-rate elasticity divided by $(1 + \varphi)$.

expressed as the domestic currency price of the foreign currency; in this small economy, the foreign price level is set equal to unity for simplicity.

The third and the fourth equations are the dynamic equations. They respectively represent the uncovered interest-rate parity condition, where i^* is the foreign interest rate, and the determination of the inflation rate. In particular, the last equation shows that inflation depends on the excess of AD over the initial long-run output level $\bar{y}$ (at zero inflationary shock), according to the parameter φ, as well as on a supply inflationary shock μ. This latter shock can be interpreted, for instance, as the impact of increases in the costs of production (e.g. an oil shock) that have a permanent effect on the long-run output level.

In this flexible exchange-rate version, the four equations identify the following four endogenous variables: the price level p, current output y, the interest rate i, and the exchange rate[2] s. The exogenous variables are the foreign interest rate i^* and the long-run output level $\bar{y}$; the nominal money supply m_0 represents the only policy instrument available to the AA.

By obtaining y and i from the first two equations as expressions of all the other variables and then plugging them into the two dynamic equations, the model can be reduced to a system of two linear, first-order differential equations:

$$\begin{bmatrix} dp \\ ds \end{bmatrix} = \mathbf{A} \begin{bmatrix} p \\ s \end{bmatrix} + \mathbf{B} \begin{bmatrix} m_0 \\ i^* \\ \bar{y} \\ v \\ \epsilon \\ \mu \end{bmatrix}$$

where

$$\mathbf{A} \equiv \frac{1}{\Delta} \begin{bmatrix} -\varphi(\gamma + \lambda\eta) & \varphi\lambda\eta \\ 1 - \kappa\eta & \kappa\eta \end{bmatrix},$$

$$\mathbf{B} \equiv \begin{bmatrix} \varphi\gamma/\Delta & 0 & -\varphi & -\varphi\gamma/\Delta & \varphi\lambda/\Delta & 1 \\ -1/\Delta & -1 & 0 & 1/\Delta & \kappa/\Delta & 0 \end{bmatrix},$$

$$\Delta \equiv \kappa\gamma + \lambda.$$

The matrix $\mathbf{A}$ has eigenvalues with opposite sign; therefore, as is standard in perfect foresight models, the equilibrium is characterized by a saddle point (see the appendix Section A.1 for details). Figure 1 summarizes the dynamics of the system for the case of exchange-rate overshooting.

---

[2] Henceforth, "exchange rate" will mean "*nominal* exchange rate," whereas its real counterpart will be explicitly identified.

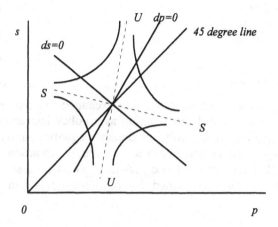

Figure 1. Model phase diagram for the flexible exchange-rate regime (overshooting case).

In the solution, the exchange rate qualifies as the forward-looking variable whereas the price level is the backward-looking variable. By applying the usual methodology for rational expectations models, the solution over time for the price level and the exchange rate can be easily obtained:

$$p(t) = H_{\text{flx}} \exp(l_s t) + p',$$

$$s(t) = \rho_s H_{\text{flx}} \exp(l_s t) + s',$$

where

$$H_{\text{flx}} = p(0) - p' = p_0 - m_0 - \lambda i^* + \kappa \bar{y} + \nu - (\kappa/\varphi)\mu.$$

In Section A.1, the long-run price level p' and the long-run exchange-rate level s' are reported, together with expressions for the stable eigenvalue l_s and the slope ρ_s of the relative stable eigenvector.

From the contemporaneous relationship between the domestic output level and the previous endogenous variables, that is,

$$y = (1/\Delta)[\gamma(m_0 - p) + \lambda\eta(s - p) - \gamma\nu + \lambda\epsilon],$$

it is possible to obtain the solution for the domestic output over time:

$$y(t) = (1/\Delta)(\lambda\eta\rho_s - \lambda\eta - \gamma)H_{\text{flx}} \exp(l_s t) + y', \tag{5}$$

where

$$y' = \bar{y} - (1/\varphi)\mu. \tag{6}$$

When the AA decide to fix the exchange rate at the value s_0, they actually fix the domestic interest rate at the foreign level. Then, a fixed exchange-rate version of the foregoing model (1)–(4) can be obtained:

$$m - p = \kappa y - \lambda i + v, \tag{7}$$

$$y = \eta(s_0 - p) - \gamma i + \epsilon, \tag{8}$$

$$i = i^*, \tag{9}$$

$$dp = \varphi(y - \bar{y}) + \mu. \tag{10}$$

The money supply m is now endogenized. The exchange-rate parity s_0 is exogenously set by the AA and can function as a policy instrument. Technically, the new regime implies only one dynamic equation, and the original system is reduced to a single first-order differential equation for p. By substituting (7) and (9) into (8) and plugging into (4), the simple first-order differential equation is obtained. Its solution for p is then

$$p(t) = H_{\text{fix}} \exp(-\varphi \eta t) + p', $$

where

$$H_{\text{fix}} \equiv p_0 - p', $$

$$p' \equiv s_0 - \frac{\gamma}{\eta} i^* - \frac{1}{\eta} \bar{y} + \frac{1}{\varphi \eta} \mu + \frac{1}{\eta} \epsilon, $$

and p_0 is the (given) initial price level.

The dynamics of the price level drives the whole system, and the other endogenous variables (i.e., m and y) present the same dynamics over time. In particular, the contemporaneous relationship between y and p is given by (8) when the domestic interest rate is equal to the foreign rate:

$$y = \eta(s_0 - p) - \gamma i^* + \epsilon. $$

It is therefore possible to obtain the solution over time of the domestic output:

$$y(t) = -\eta H_{\text{fix}} \exp(-\varphi \eta t) + y'. \tag{11}$$

Although the short-run dynamics for output is different in the two regimes, the long-run output level is the same in both the flexible and the fixed exchange-rate versions of the model:

$$y' = \bar{y} - (1/\varphi)\mu. \tag{12}$$

Equation (12) shows the *permanent* nature of the supply shock, which steadily affects the long-run output level. The other two shocks have permanent effects on the other endogenous variables in the long run, but not on the output level.

The third regime we consider is the target-zone system. In this case the AA establish a fixed band of $\pm b$ maximum magnitude around the initial equilibrium parity s_0 for the long-run exchange rate (which is supposed to be initially at the same s_0 level). However, because the AA cannot observe the long-run exchange rate, they must establish a band around the observable *short-run* exchange rate such that the long-run rate is always within the $\pm b$ band. In designing such a band, one must consider that the various shocks have different impacts on short-run versus long-run exchange rates. It is then possible to show – with some cumbersome computations about the impact of the shocks on both short-run and long-run exchange rates – that, in order to keep the *long-run* exchange rate inside the declared $\pm b$ band, the corresponding band for the observable short-run exchange rate must have magnitude $\pm[\Delta l_s/(\Delta l_s - \kappa\eta)]b = \pm\bar{s}$ (where l_s is the stable eigenvalue of matrix **A**).[3]

When the exchange rate[4] moves within the $\pm\bar{s}$ band, the AA do not intervene and the flexible exchange-rate model describes the dynamics of the system. When instead the shocks push, for instance, the exchange rate above $\bar{s}$, then the AA intervene by changing the money supply in order to offset the shock and to take back the exchange rate to the center of the band,[5] s_0. In the terminology of recent target-zone literature, this regime can be labeled the "perfectly credible target-zone system with finite interventions" (see Flood and Garber 1991 for an analytical presentation as a variant of the Krugman 1991 model).

It is important to define the AA information set in order to describe their behavior. The AA know that the economy is driven by shocks, but cannot disentangle the *source* of those shocks (i.e., whether they are nominal, AD-type, or supply-type). In fact, if they were able to recognize the shock type then the problem would be reduced to the traditional comparison of the performances of exchange-rate regimes. In particular, as the standard international economics literature has long since demonstrated, if the AA objective were to minimize short-run deviations of

---

[3] Once a b bandwidth is established around the long-run exchange rate and the different impacts of the three shocks on both the long-run and the short-run exchange rates are given, we can obtain a corresponding bandwidth for the short-run exchange rate. In particular, it is possible to obtain the impacts on the short-run exchange rate of these shocks when their magnitudes are such that the long-run exchange rate reaches the *band margin*, from which may be computed the impact of each of these shocks on the short-run exchange rate. The smallest impact is given by the supply shock, which must be of magnitude $\bar{s}$ (as just defined); hence, interventions inside the $\bar{s}$ band for the short-run exchange rate will assure that the long-run exchange rate is always inside the $(s_0 - b; s_0 + b)$ band.

[4] Henceforth, "exchange rate" will be taken to mean the "(observable) *short-run* exchange rate" unless otherwise specified.

[5] The particular type of intervention by the AA that pushes the exchange rate back to the center of the band is crucial through the analysis. Since in many observed target-zone regimes the AA do not recenter the exchange rate but simply take it inside the band (sometimes close to the margins), our centering assumption probably restricts the model to small target zones with respect to the intervention mechanism.

output from its relative long-run value[6] then they would always offset nominal shocks by changing the money supply in order to fix the exchange rate, but would not intervene when the shock is an AD- or supply-type.

In the following section we describe the loss function of the AA and compare more formally the relative performance of the three regimes.

3   Relative performance of the three regimes

The AA know that the economy is driven by the three shocks mentioned previously, but they cannot distinguish between them. The only available policy instrument is money supply, and the AA want to decide whether to adopt a money rule that follows from the fixed exchange-rate regime or (alternatively) to fix the money supply at the initial m_0 level and let the economy adjust spontaneously to the shock occurrence (flexible exchange-rate regime).

The loss function used to evaluate the relative performances of the three regimes is

$$L = \int_0^\infty \exp(-\sigma t)[y(t) - y']^2 \, dt, \tag{13}$$

where σ is the discounting rate.

In other words, the AA want to minimize the deviations of output from its long-run level.[7] Note that the long-run output level includes the effect of the supply shock (whether positive or negative). The AA can use only money supply as a policy instrument, which is not able to affect the long-run output level in order to compensate for such a μ real shock; hence a loss function like (13) is justified.

By substituting for $[y(t) - y']$ from (5) and (11), it is possible to obtain the loss functions for both the perfectly flexible and the perfectly fixed exchange-rate regimes as, respectively,

$$L_{\text{flx}} = \int_0^\infty \exp(-\sigma t)\left[\frac{1}{\Delta}(\lambda\eta\rho_s - \lambda\eta - \gamma)H_{\text{flx}}\exp(l_s t)\right]^2 dt = z_1 H_{\text{flx}}^2,$$

$$L_{\text{fix}} = \int_0^\infty \exp(-\sigma t)[-\eta H_{\text{fix}}\exp(-\varphi\eta t)]^2 dt = \eta^2 z_2 H_{\text{fix}}^2,$$

---

[6] See e.g. De Grauwe (1992, pp. 78–80) for a concise exposition of the original Poole (1970) model.

[7] It is common in the literature to include other variables, in the loss function, such as inflation. Its inclusion in our framework is very straightforward because inflation strictly depends on the output gap (see equation (4)). We reckoned that augmenting the loss function would serve only to complicate the analysis by adding a parameter of relative preference between inflation and output for the AA.

where

$$z_1 \equiv \frac{(\lambda\eta\rho_s - \lambda\eta - \gamma)^2}{(\sigma - 2l_s)(\kappa\gamma + \lambda)^2} \quad \text{and} \quad z_2 \equiv \frac{1}{\sigma + 2\varphi\eta}.$$

The value of the loss function for the target-zone regime is computed next as we present the effects of the three kinds of shocks.

3.1 The nominal shock

Let us assume that a negative nominal shock v occurs and an excess supply results in the domestic money market.

In the flexible exchange-rate regime, the forward-looking exchange rate immediately jumps up and the improvement in competitiveness of the domestic economy raises AD and output such that the equilibrium in the money market is restored. The divergence between the new output level and the relative long-run value triggers inflation. The historical variable (i.e., the price level) slowly increases, and in the long run the economy ends up with a higher price level and a higher long-run exchange rate, but with lower real money stock and unchanged long-run output level $\bar{y}$.

Hence, the impact of the negative nominal shock is an initial rise in the output level that dies out over time (see Figure 2); such an increase is proportional to the exchange-rate jump. Therefore, if we assume that the nominal shock is of size $\bar{b}$ and that initially all the endogenous variables are at their long-run levels, then the loss function for the perfectly flexible exchange-rate regime is

$$L^v_{\text{flx}} = z_1 \bar{b}^2.$$

When the fixed exchange-rate regime rule is adopted, the excess supply of money that is brought about by the negative nominal shock is immediately offset by a decrease in the endogenous money supply, with no effect on the *short-run* output level. Hence, the loss function is now equal to zero, $L^v_{\text{fix}} = 0$. Figure 2 shows the effect of the negative nominal shock on the output level.

In the target-zone regime, the value of the loss function depends on the probability that the nominal shock is so high that the exchange rate is pushed outside the $(s_0 - \bar{s}; s_0 + \bar{s})$ band. In other words, the loss function turns out to be a simple linear combination of the loss functions of the two regimes just described:

$$L^v_{tz} = p_v z_1 \bar{b}^2 + (1 - p_v)0 = p_v z_1 \bar{b}^2,$$

where

$$p_v = \Pr\{\|\bar{b}\| < b_v \,|\, \bar{b}_{\text{nominal}}\} \quad \text{and} \quad b_v \equiv \frac{\Delta l_s}{\Delta l_s - 1} b.$$

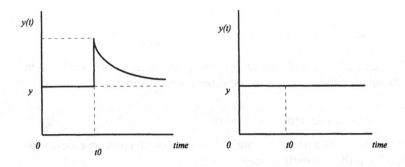

Flex. Exch. Rates   Fixed Exch. Rates

Figure 2. Output dynamics with a nominal shock.

In fact, since the impact of a unitary nominal shock on the short-run exchange rate is $(\Delta l_s - 1)/(\Delta l_s - \kappa\eta)$ (see Section A.1), smaller nominal shocks than $[\Delta l_s/(\Delta l_s - 1)]b$ will keep the short-run exchange rate within the $2\bar{s}$ band. A unitary nominal shock has a full impact on the long-run exchange rate; hence, a nominal shock of smaller magnitude than b_ν will necessarily leave the long-run exchange rate within the $2b$ band because $b_\nu < b$.

3.2   The AD shock

We consider, without loss of generality, a positive AD shock.

In the flexible exchange-rate regime, a positive AD shock has no effect on the long-run (historical) price level. Usually the forward-looking variable jumps to a value such that a spontaneous dynamic, which takes the historical variable to the new long-run value over time, is triggered. In this case, the long-run level of the backward-looking price index does not vary, and thus the exchange rate immediately jumps to its new long-run value. It is shown in Section A.1 that the magnitude of this jump is equal to

$$[s(t_0^+) - s(t_0^-)]|_\epsilon^{\text{flx}} = -\frac{1}{\eta}\epsilon.$$

From (5) it then follows that

$$[y(t_0^+) - y(t_0^-)]|_\epsilon^{\text{flx}} = \frac{\lambda\eta}{\Delta}[s(t_0^+) - s(t_0^-)]|_\epsilon^{\text{fl}} + \frac{\lambda}{\Delta}\epsilon = 0$$

and the loss function for the AA is equal to zero ($L_{\text{flx}}^\epsilon = 0$), if we still assume an initial output level equal to $\bar{y}$. In particular, the jump in the

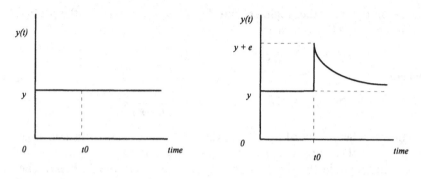

Figure 3. Output dynamics with an AD shock.

domestic price of the foreign currency is such that it entirely offsets the shock in the AD equation: the exchange rate appreciates, so that the worsening in competitiveness of the domestic economy exactly (and immediately) balances the positive AD shock.

In the fixed exchange-rate regime, the initial AD shock has a full impact on the demand-determined output level because no forward-looking variables are present and hence no corrective jumps can occur. In this case, the effect of the AD shock in the medium run is to trigger inflation, which will cause the real exchange rate to appreciate and make the effect of the AD shock die out over time. At the same time, the nominal money stock must increase in order to keep the real money stock unchanged in the long run. In fact, in the long term, output comes back to its initial level by means of the real exchange-rate appreciation, whereas the money stock must increase in the same proportion as the price level so that the long-run real money stock is unchanged and the domestic interest rate is equal to the foreign level at the initial (unchanged) long-run output level $\bar{y}$.

Therefore, unlike the case of a flexible exchange-rate regime, here the AD shock has an immediate impact on the H_{fix} component of the loss function. If we assume that the size of the shock is still $\bar{b}$ and that all the initial values of the endogenous variables are equal to the relative long-run values, then the loss function is

$$L_{\text{fix}}^{\cdot} = z_2 \bar{b}^2.$$

Figure 3 summarizes the effects of the positive AD shock on the output level.

Again, the target-zone regime is a combination of the two regimes. The loss function for the AA is a linear combination of the loss-function values in the two other regimes, and the weights are given by the probabilities of the AD shock size:

$$L_{tz}^\epsilon = p_\epsilon 0 + (1 - p_\epsilon) z_2 \tilde{b}^2 = (1 - p_\epsilon) z_2 \tilde{b}^2,$$

where

$$p_\epsilon = \Pr\{\|\tilde{b}\| < b_\epsilon \mid \tilde{b}_{AD}\} \quad \text{and} \quad b_\epsilon \equiv \frac{\Delta l_s}{\Delta l_s - \kappa\eta}\eta b.$$

In fact, the impact of a unitary AD shock on the short-run exchange rate is $1/\eta$; therefore, the size of the AD shock must be less than b_ϵ in order to maintain the short-run exchange rate within the $2\bar{s}$ band. The impact on the long-run exchange rate is still equal to $1/\eta$ times the size of the AD shock; hence, again the long-run exchange rate remains within the $2b$ band because $b_\epsilon/\eta < b$.

3.3   *The supply shock*

The supply shock μ differs from the other two shocks in that it has a *permanent* effect on the long-run output level. In other words, when such a shock occurs the dynamics of the system shows a movement of the output level toward a lower (higher) long-run value when a positive (negative) inflationary shock occurs. In this very simple model the AA have only one policy instrument (monetary policy), which does not have any permanent impact on output. Hence there is no policy instrument at their disposal that can offset the real shock on output. However, the use of monetary policy according to the different exchange-rate regimes may restrain the output's deviation from the new long-run level.

Let us consider, as an example, a positive μ shock. In the flexible exchange-rate regime, a positive supply inflationary shock has an effect on both the long-run exchange rate and the long-run price level. The discounted effect of such long-run changes makes the forward-looking variable (that is, the exchange rate) jump down. In other words, the supply shock has an inflationary effect which lowers the AD through a real appreciation of the domestic currency over time and which takes the system toward the lower long-run output level. In this perfect foresight framework, the convergence toward the new long-run value can be aided by an initial nominal appreciation.

Again, the effect on the loss function is obtained by computing the impact on the H_{flx} component:

$$L_{flx}^\mu = z_1 \left(\frac{\kappa}{\varphi}\right)^2 \tilde{b}^2,$$

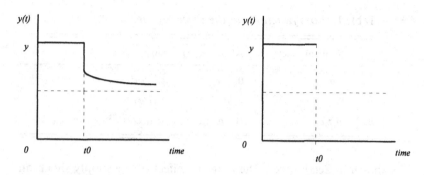

Figure 4. Output dynamics with a supply shock.

where the μ shock size is $\bar{b}$ and initially all the endogenous variables are at their long-run values.

In the fixed exchange-rate regime, the positively signed supply shock causes the price level to rise over time, the output level to slowly decrease toward the new lower long-run level, and the money supply to vary in order to keep the money market always in equilibrium at the foreign value of the interest rate. The economic system goes through a disequilibrium period, but the absence of forward-looking variables does not bring about any jump at t_0 (except for inflation).

Hence, the output level does not vary, whereas the long-run output level decreases by $-(1/\varphi)\mu$. As a consequence, by assuming $\mu = \bar{b}$, the loss function for the AA is then

$$L^{\mu}_{\text{fix}} = z_2 \left(\frac{1}{\varphi} \right)^2 \bar{b}^2.$$

The effect of the positively signed supply shock is shown in Figure 4.

Once again, the loss function for the target-zone regime is calculated as the average of the loss functions of the other two regimes weighted by the probability of shock intensity:

$$L^{\mu}_{\text{tz}} = p_{\mu} z_1 \left(\frac{\kappa}{\varphi} \right)^2 \bar{b}^2 + (1 - p_{\mu}) z_2 \left(\frac{1}{\varphi} \right)^2 \bar{b}^2,$$

where

$$p_{\mu} = \Pr\{\|\bar{b}\| < b_{\mu} \,|\, \bar{b}_{\text{supply}}\} \quad \text{and} \quad b_{\mu} \equiv \frac{\varphi\eta}{1 - \kappa\eta} b.$$

Table 1. *Loss functions in the three regimes*

	Nominal shock (ν)	AD shock (ϵ)	Supply shock (μ)
L_{flx}	$z_1 \bar{b}^2$	0	$z_1 (\kappa/\varphi)^2 \bar{b}^2$
L_{fix}	0	$z_2 \bar{b}^2$	$z_2 (1/\varphi)^2 \bar{b}^2$
L_{tz}	$p_\nu z_1 \bar{b}^2$	$(1-p_\epsilon) z_2 \bar{b}^2$	$p_\mu z_1 (\kappa/\varphi)^2 \bar{b}^2 + (1-p_\mu) z_2 (1/\varphi)^2 \bar{b}^2$

As shown in Section A.1, the long-run effect of the supply shock on the nominal exchange rate is given by $-[(1-\kappa\eta)/\varphi\eta]\mu$. Therefore, if the intensity of the supply shock is less than $[\varphi\eta/(1-\kappa\eta)]b$, then the long-run exchange rate remains in the established $2b$ band and the AA allow the price of foreign currency to fluctuate freely. At the same time, since the impact of a unitary supply shock on the short-run exchange rate is $-[\Delta l_s(1-\kappa\eta)]/[\varphi\eta(\Delta l_s-\kappa\eta)]$, a supply shock smaller than b_μ will also leave the short-run exchange rate within the established band margin.

Table 1 summarizes the results obtained so far. In particular, the better (worse) relative performance of the fixed exchange-rate regime is shown with respect to the perfectly flexible exchange-rate regime when nominal (AD) shocks occur. As already mentioned, the conclusions from Table 1 are very standard in international economics. If the AA can recognize the shock type, they will intervene with a change in the nominal money supply (fixed exchange-rate regime) when the shock is nominal, or will keep the nominal money supply unvaried and let the exchange rate adjust when the shock is AD- or supply-type.

It is more interesting to study the behavior of the AA when they are unable to disentangle the different kinds of shocks, and when their lack of knowledge concerns both the source and the intensity of the shock.

4   Ex ante conditions for optimality of the target-zone regime

In this framework, the AA are completely unaware of either the *type* or the *intensity* of the shock that hits the economy. In other words, if we assume that a $\bar{b}$ shock is expected, then the expected loss functions for the AA in the three regimes before the shock occurs can be expressed as follows:

$$EL_{\text{flx}} = \Pr\{\bar{b}_{\text{nominal}}\} z_1 \bar{b}^2 + \Pr\{\bar{b}_{\text{supply}}\} z_1 \left(\frac{\kappa}{\varphi}\right)^2 \bar{b}^2$$

$$EL_{\text{fix}} = \Pr\{\bar{b}_{\text{AD}}\} z_2 \bar{b}^2 + \Pr\{\bar{b}_{\text{supply}}\} z_2 \left(\frac{1}{\varphi}\right)^2 \bar{b}^2$$

$$EL_{tz} = \Pr\{\|\tilde{b}\| < b_\nu \,|\, \tilde{b}_{nominal}\} \Pr\{\tilde{b}_{nominal}\} z_1 \tilde{b}^2$$
$$+ \Pr\{\|\tilde{b}\| > b_\epsilon \,|\, \tilde{b}_{AD}\} \Pr\{\tilde{b}_{AD}\} z_2 \tilde{b}^2$$
$$+ \Pr\{\|\tilde{b}\| < b_\mu \,|\, \tilde{b}_{supply}\} \Pr\{\tilde{b}_{supply}\} z_1 \left(\frac{\kappa}{\varphi}\right)^2 \tilde{b}^2$$
$$+ \Pr\{\|\tilde{b}\| > b_\mu \,|\, \tilde{b}_{supply}\} \Pr\{\tilde{b}_{supply}\} z_2 \left(\frac{1}{\varphi}\right)^2 \tilde{b}^2,$$

where $\Pr\{\tilde{b}_{j\text{-type}}\}$ stands for the prior probability that the $\tilde{b}$ shock is j-type.

The framework presented heretofore clearly shows the role of the double uncertainty of the AA. In particular, the aim of this paper is to find conditions which would involve just one source of uncertainty (i.e., uncertainty about the intensity of the shocks) in order to achieve optimality of the target-zone regime, and which could neglect as much as possible the second source of uncertainty (i.e., uncertainty about the type of the shock).

It is also important to clarify explicitly the timing of the model. First, the AA declare which regime they want to join, according to the values of the ex ante expected loss functions when computed with their prior probabilities about the magnitude and the shock type. Second, the shock occurs and the exchange rate moves. Third, the AA revise their prior probabilities and recompute their expected loss functions. A time inconsistency problem arises when the initial regime choice is no longer optimal and the AA do not behave according to the initial commitment.

In the present section we consider the ex ante commitment, whereas the possibility of priors' revisions is examined in the next section. We define

$$\Pr\{\|\tilde{b}\| < b_j;\, \tilde{b}_{j\text{-type}}\} = p_j q_j$$

and

$$\Pr\{\|\tilde{b}\| < b_j \,|\, \tilde{b}_{j\text{-type}}\} = p_j,$$
$$\Pr\{\tilde{b}_{j\text{-type}}\} = q_j,$$

for $j = \nu, \epsilon, \mu$ and where the p_j and the q_j are prior probabilities. The expected ex ante loss functions can then be rewritten in the following way:

$$EL^a_{flx} = q_\mu z_1 \tilde{b}^2 + q_\mu z_1 \left(\frac{\kappa}{\varphi}\right)^2 \tilde{b}^2, \tag{14}$$

$$EL^a_{fix} = q_\epsilon z_2 \tilde{b}^2 + q_\mu z_2 \left(\frac{1}{\varphi}\right)^2 \tilde{b}^2, \tag{15}$$

$$EL^a_{tz} = p_\nu q_\nu z_1 \tilde{b}^2 + (1 - p_\epsilon) q_\epsilon z_2 \tilde{b}^2$$
$$+ p_\mu q_\mu z_1 \left(\frac{\kappa}{\varphi}\right)^2 \tilde{b}^2 + (1 - p_\mu) q_\mu z_2 \left(\frac{1}{\varphi}\right)^2 \tilde{b}^2. \tag{16}$$

Before obtaining general optimality conditions of the target-zone regime, the following proposition shows how they can be simply reduced to a system of two inequalities.

Proposition 1. *In the model* (1)–(4) *with the relative fixed exchange-rate version* (7)–(10) *and loss function* (13) *for the AA, ex ante the target-zone regime is the optimal regime if and only if the following two inequalities are contemporaneously satisfied:*

$$q_\nu + h_1 q_\epsilon > V_1, \tag{17}$$

$$q_\nu + h_2 q_\epsilon < V_2, \tag{18}$$

where

$$h_1 \equiv \frac{z(1-p_\mu)(1/\varphi)^2 - z_2(1-p_\epsilon)}{z_1(1-p_\nu) + z(1-p_\mu)(1/\varphi)^2},$$

$$V_1 \equiv \frac{z(1-p_\mu)(1/\varphi)^2}{z_1(1-p_\nu) + z(1-p_\mu)(1/\varphi)^2},$$

$$h_2 \equiv \frac{z p_\mu(1/\varphi)^2 - z_2 p_\epsilon}{z_1 p_\nu + z p_\mu(1/\varphi)^2},$$

$$V_2 \equiv \frac{z p_\mu(1/\varphi)^2}{z_1 p_\nu + z p_\mu(1/\varphi)^2},$$

$$z \equiv z_2 - z_1 \kappa^2.$$

Proof: The target-zone regime is optimal ex ante if and only if its expected performance is higher than the performance of the other two regimes:

$$EL_{tz}^a < EL_{flx}^a, \tag{19}$$

$$EL_{tz}^a < EL_{fix}^a. \tag{20}$$

Let us consider (19) first; by substituting from (14) and (16) we obtain

$$p_\nu q_\nu z_1 \bar{b}^2 + (1-p_\epsilon)q_\epsilon z_2 \bar{b}^2 + p_\mu q_\mu z_1\left(\frac{\kappa}{\varphi}\right)^2 \bar{b}^2$$

$$+ (1-p_\mu)(1-q_\nu - q_\epsilon)z_2\left(\frac{1}{\varphi}\right)^2 \bar{b}^2$$

$$< q_\nu z_1 \bar{b}^2 + (1-q_\nu - q_\epsilon)z_1\left(\frac{\kappa}{\varphi}\right)^2 \bar{b}^2$$

by using the hypothesis that three types of shocks are jointly exhaustive. The common term $\bar{b}^2$ can be eliminated and, after some algebraic manipulations, we have

$$q_\nu\left[(1-p_\nu)z_1+(1-p_\mu)(z_2-z_1\kappa^2)\left(\frac{1}{\varphi}\right)^2\right]$$

$$+q_\epsilon\left[(1-p_\mu)(z_2-z_1\kappa^2)\left(\frac{1}{\varphi}\right)^2-(1-p_\epsilon)\right]-(1-p_\mu)(z_2-z_1\kappa^2)\left(\frac{1}{\varphi}\right)^2>0.$$

We define $z\equiv z_2-z_1\kappa^2$; Section A.2 gives the parameter constraints for z to be positive. Hence, the q_ν coefficient is positive and the foregoing inequality can be rewritten as

$$q_\nu+h_1q_\epsilon>V_1,$$

where h_1 and V_1 coincide with the expressions given in the proposition statement.

Let us now plug (15) and (16) into (20):

$$p_\nu q_\nu z_1\bar{b}^2+(1-p_\epsilon)q_\epsilon z_2\bar{b}^2+p_\mu q_\mu z_1\left(\frac{\kappa}{\varphi}\right)^2\bar{b}^2+(1-p_\mu)q_\mu z_2\left(\frac{1}{\varphi}\right)^2\bar{b}^2$$

$$<q_\epsilon z_2\bar{b}^2+q_\mu z_2\left(\frac{1}{\varphi}\right)^2\bar{b}^2;$$

re-arranging, we have

$$q_\nu\left[-p_\nu z_1-p_\mu z\left(\frac{1}{\varphi}\right)^2\right]+q_\epsilon\left[p_\epsilon-p_\mu z\left(\frac{1}{\varphi}\right)^2\right]+p_\mu z\left(\frac{1}{\varphi}\right)^2>0.$$

The q_ν coefficient is now negative, whereas the q_ϵ coefficient has ambiguous sign given the condition on z. The preceding expression can be rewritten as

$$q_\nu+h_2q_\epsilon<V_2, \tag{21}$$

where h_2 and V_2 coincide with the expressions of the statement of the proposition. $\square$

By using the result of Proposition 1, the aim of this section is to find conditions on h_1, V_1, h_2, and V_2 that would imply optimality of the target zone regime. Toward this end we state the following proposition, which gives a necessary condition for target-zone regime optimality mainly in terms of restrictions on the p_j's probabilities.

Proposition 2. *Necessary conditions for the optimality of the target-zone regime in the model* (1)–(4), *with AA's loss function* (13) *and $z>0$, are:*

(a) *$p_\epsilon>p_\mu$ when $p_\nu>p_\mu$; and*
(b) *either $p_\epsilon>p_\nu$ or q_ϵ sufficiently small when $p_\mu>p_\nu$.*

Proof: If the target-zone regime is optimal, then inequalities (22) and (23) are verified as follows:

$$q_\nu + h_1 q_\epsilon > V_1, \tag{22}$$

$$q_\nu + h_2 q_\epsilon < V_2; \tag{23}$$

re-arranging yields

$$q_\nu > V_1 - h_1 q_\epsilon,$$

$$q_\nu < V_2 - h_2 q_\epsilon,$$

which necessarily implies

$$(h_1 - h_2) q_\epsilon > V_1 - V_2.$$

From the definitions of Proposition 1 we can state that

$$V_1 - V_2 = \frac{1}{D} [zz_1(p_\nu - p_\mu)] \equiv V \quad \text{and}$$

$$h_1 - h_2 = \frac{1}{D} [zz_1(p_\nu - p_\mu) + z_1 z_2 \varphi^2 (p_\epsilon - p_\nu) + zz_2(p_\epsilon - p_\mu)] \equiv V + h,$$

where

$$h \equiv \frac{1}{D} [(p_\epsilon - p_\nu) z_1 z_2 \varphi^2 + (p_\epsilon - p_\mu) z_2 z],$$

$$D \equiv \varphi^2 \left[(1 - p_\nu) z_1 + (1 - p_\mu) \left(\frac{1}{\varphi^2} \right) z \right] \left[p_\nu z_1 + p_\mu \left(\frac{1}{\varphi^2} \right) z \right],$$

and D is always positive. Hence, if the target-zone regime is optimal then the following must hold:

$$(V + h) q_\epsilon > V. \tag{24}$$

If $p_\nu > p_\mu$ then V is positive and h must be positive. In fact, suppose that $h < 0$ and distinguish two cases. If $\|h\| > V$, then $(V + h)$ is negative and (24) is never verified. If $\|h\| < V$, then $(V + h)$ is positive and (24) is equivalent to

$$q_\epsilon > \frac{V}{V + h},$$

which is also never verified since $V > (V + h)$ whereas q_ϵ must be less than unity. Because h must be positive, this means that the following must hold:

$$(p_\epsilon - p_\nu) z_1 z_2 \varphi^2 + (p_\epsilon - p_\mu) z_2 z \equiv (p_\epsilon - p_\nu) a + (p_\epsilon - p_\mu) b > 0,$$

where $a \equiv z_1 z_2 \varphi^2$ and $b \equiv z_2 z$; this is verified if and only if

$$p_\epsilon > \frac{a}{a+b} p_\nu + \frac{b}{a+b} p_\mu.$$

This inequality means that p_ϵ must be greater than a weighted average of p_ν and p_μ; therefore, necessarily:

$$p_\epsilon > p_\mu$$

given that $p_\nu > p_\mu$.

If $p_\mu > p_\nu$ then V is negative. In this case, if h is positive then the inequality (24) is always verified. In fact, if $h > \|V\|$, then $(V+h)$ is positive and (24) always holds. If $h < \|V\|$, then $(V+h)$ is negative and (24) can be rewritten as

$$q_\epsilon < \frac{V}{V+h},$$

where $\|V\| > \|V+h\|$ and the displayed inequality is always verified since q_ϵ is less than unity. Analogously to the previous case, h is positive if p_ϵ is greater than a weighted average of p_ν and p_μ; hence, necessarily, p_ϵ must be greater than p_ν.

However, if $p_\epsilon < p_\nu$ and h is negative, an alternative necessary condition for the target-zone regime optimality would involve q_ϵ. If $p_\epsilon < p_\nu < p_\mu$ then $(V+h)$ is negative and (24) is verified if q_ϵ is sufficiently small:

$$q_\epsilon < q_\epsilon^*,$$

where

$$q_\epsilon^* \equiv \frac{V}{V+h} \equiv \frac{(p_\nu - p_\mu)zz_1}{(p_\nu - p_\mu)zz_1 + (p_\epsilon - p_\nu)z_2 z_1 \varphi^2 + (p_\epsilon - p_\mu)zz_2}. \qquad \square$$

Proposition 3, which follows, is the converse of Proposition 2 and is no less important in determining sufficient conditions for the nonoptimality of the target-zone regime.

Proposition 3. *Sufficient conditions for the nonoptimality of the target-zone regime in the model (1)–(4), with AA's loss function (13) and $z > 0$, are:*

(a) $p_\epsilon < p_\mu < p_\nu$; *and*
(b) $p_\epsilon < p_\nu < p_\mu$ *and* q_ϵ *sufficiently high.*

Proof: Proposition 3 is the logical converse of Proposition 2. $\qquad \square$

Heretofore we have simply obtained a modified result of the common Poole (1970) model. Propositions 2 and 3 have given some general conditions about the optimality of the target-zone regime that are mainly based on prior probabilities about the intensity of the shock. In order to make these conditions more interpretable when stressing the importance of shock intensity versus shock source, an additional assumption on the distribution functions of the three shocks is made. In particular, in this case we assume that the three shocks have the same distribution functions, and that their impacts on the economy are different because of the different channels through which these shocks affect the endogenous variables. By doing so, we can abstain from including, for instance, different shock variances in the optimality conditions and instead consider only the restrictions on the parameters of the model that would satisfy those conditions.

As a consequence, the *intensity* and the *source* of the shock can be considered ex ante as independent events; then

$$\Pr\{\|\bar{b}\| < b_j \mid \bar{b}_{j\text{-type}}\} = \Pr\{\|\bar{b}\| < b_j\} = p_j$$

for $j = \nu, \epsilon,$ and μ. The constraints on the p_j's probabilities in our propositions thus correspond to the same constraints on the b_j's, which imply the restrictions on the parameters of the model we are looking for. In particular, the necessary conditions for target-zone optimality in the overshooting case are as follows.

(a) $b_\mu < b_\epsilon$ when $b_\mu < b_\nu$. In terms of parameters:

$$\varphi < \frac{\Delta l_s}{\Delta l_s - \kappa\eta}(1 - \kappa\eta) \quad \text{when} \quad \varphi\eta < \frac{\Delta l_s}{\Delta l_s - 1}(1 - \kappa\eta),$$

where

$$\frac{\Delta l_s}{\Delta l_s - 1}(1 - \kappa\eta) < \frac{\Delta l_s}{\Delta l_s - \kappa\eta}(1 - \kappa\eta) < 1.$$

(b) Either $b_\nu < b_\epsilon$ or q_ϵ sufficiently small if $b_\epsilon < b_\nu$ when $b_\nu < b_\mu$. In terms of parameters:

$$\eta < \frac{\Delta l_s - 1}{\Delta l_s - \kappa\eta} > 1 \quad \text{when} \quad \varphi\eta > \frac{\Delta l_s}{\Delta l_s - 1}(1 - \kappa\eta) < 1.$$

Alternatively, $q_\epsilon < q_\epsilon^*$ if η is greater than the threshold value.

In other words, the elasticity of the AD to the real exchange rate and the responsiveness of inflation to the output gap (i.e., η and φ) are the key parameters, and the conditions for optimality of the target-zone regime depend heavily on them. It is particularly important to stress the condition on the inflation parameter φ. If φ is just greater than 1 but $\varphi\eta$ is small, then the target-zone regime is *non*optimal. That is, the target-zone regime will necessarily be optimal if the dynamics for inflation is sufficiently slow (if $\varphi \ll 1$), when the dynamics under the fixed exchange-rate regime is also slow (when $\varphi\eta$ is less than the threshold value).

In conclusion, these results highlight the importance of the inflation dynamics in the ex ante choice of the optimal exchange-rate regime, even when the AA have only an estimation (i.e., big vs. small) of the shock's intensity and are completely unaware of its type. Our results show that ex ante only an economy with a high inflation dynamics (and a small η) would never decide to join a target-zone regime, since this turns out to be the worst of the three regimes when the shock source is completely unknown.

These final considerations are quite robust in that they are maintained also in the undershooting case, although they are sometimes difficult to match with the conditions for $z > 0$ (reported in Section A.2).

5 Posterior conditions for optimality of the target-zone regime

Once the shock has occurred and the exchange rate has changed, the AA can revise their priors but the previous commitment cannot yet be optimal.

Let us consider again the expected loss functions in the two cases when the exchange rate has or has not passed the relative band margin:

$$EL_{\text{flx}} = \Pr\{\tilde{b}_{\text{nominal}} \mid \|s\| < \bar{s}\} z_1 \tilde{b}^2 + \Pr\{\tilde{b}_{\text{supply}} \mid \|s\| < \bar{s}\} z_1 \left(\frac{\kappa}{\varphi}\right)^2 \tilde{b}^2,$$

$$EL_{\text{fix}} = \Pr\{\tilde{b}_{\text{AD}} \mid \|s\| < \bar{s}\} z_2 \tilde{b}^2 + \Pr\{\tilde{b}_{\text{supply}} \mid \|s\| < \bar{s}\} z_2 \left(\frac{1}{\varphi}\right)^2 \tilde{b}^2,$$

$$\begin{aligned}
EL_{\text{tz}} &= \Pr\{\|\tilde{b}\| < b_\nu \mid \tilde{b}_{\text{nominal}}; \|s\| < \bar{s}\} \Pr\{\tilde{b}_{\text{nominal}} \mid \|s\| < \bar{s}\} z_1 \tilde{b}^2 \\
&\quad + \Pr\{\|\tilde{b}\| > b_\epsilon \mid \tilde{b}_{\text{AD}}; \|s\| < \bar{s}\} \Pr\{\tilde{b}_{\text{AD}} \mid \|s\| < \bar{s}\} z_2 \tilde{b}^2 \\
&\quad + \Pr\{\|\tilde{b}\| < b_\mu \mid \tilde{b}_{\text{supply}}; \|s\| < \bar{s}\} \Pr\{\tilde{b}_{\text{supply}} \mid \|s\| < \bar{s}\} z_1 \left(\frac{\kappa}{\varphi}\right)^2 \tilde{b}^2 \\
&\quad + \Pr\{\|\tilde{b}\| > b_\mu \mid \tilde{b}_{\text{supply}}; \|s\| < \bar{s}\} \Pr\{\tilde{b}_{\text{supply}} \mid \|s\| < \bar{s}\} z_2 \left(\frac{1}{\varphi}\right)^2 \tilde{b}^2;
\end{aligned}$$

$$EL_{\text{flx}} = \Pr\{\tilde{b}_{\text{nominal}} \mid \|s\| > \bar{s}\} z_1 \tilde{b}^2 + \Pr\{\tilde{b}_{\text{supply}} \mid \|s\| > \bar{s}\} z_1 \left(\frac{\kappa}{\varphi}\right)^2 \tilde{b}^2,$$

$$EL_{\text{fix}} = \Pr\{\tilde{b}_{\text{AD}} \mid \|s\| > \bar{s}\} z_2 \tilde{b}^2 + \Pr\{\tilde{b}_{\text{supply}} \mid \|s\| > \bar{s}\} z_2 \left(\frac{1}{\varphi}\right)^2 \tilde{b}^2,$$

$$\begin{aligned}
EL_{\text{tz}} &= \Pr\{\|\tilde{b}\| < b_\nu \mid \tilde{b}_{\text{nominal}}; \|s\| > \bar{s}\} \Pr\{\tilde{b}_{\text{nominal}} \mid \|s\| > \bar{s}\} z_1 \tilde{b}^2 \\
&\quad + \Pr\{\|\tilde{b}\| > b_\epsilon \mid \tilde{b}_{\text{AD}}; \|s\| > \bar{s}\} \Pr\{\tilde{b}_{\text{AD}} \mid \|s\| > \bar{s}\} z_2 \tilde{b}^2 \\
&\quad + \Pr\{\|\tilde{b}\| < b_\mu \mid \tilde{b}_{\text{supply}}; \|s\| > \bar{s}\} \Pr\{\tilde{b}_{\text{supply}} \mid \|s\| > \bar{s}\} z_1 \left(\frac{\kappa}{\varphi}\right)^2 \tilde{b}^2 \\
&\quad + \Pr\{\|\tilde{b}\| > b_\mu \mid \tilde{b}_{\text{supply}}; \|s\| > \bar{s}\} \Pr\{\tilde{b}_{\text{supply}} \mid \|s\| > \bar{s}\} z_2 \left(\frac{1}{\varphi}\right)^2 \tilde{b}^2.
\end{aligned}$$

Prior probabilities are updated via the Bayes rule. Then we have

$$\Pr\{\bar{b}_{j\text{-type}} \mid \|s\| < \bar{s}\} = \frac{\Pr\{\|s\| < \bar{s} \mid \bar{b}_{j\text{-type}}\} \Pr\{\bar{b}_{j\text{-type}}\}}{\Pr\{\|s\| < \bar{s}\}},$$

where

$$\Pr\{\|s\| < \bar{s} \mid \bar{b}_{j\text{-type}}\} = \Pr\{\|\bar{b}\| < b_j \mid \bar{b}_{j\text{-type}}\} = \Pr\{\|\bar{b}\| < b_j\} = p_j$$

if the shock intensity and the shock source are independent events as the AA initially reckon. Therefore,

$$\Pr\{\bar{b}_{j\text{-type}} \mid \|s\| < \bar{s}\} = \frac{p_j q_j}{r},$$

where $r \equiv \Pr\{\|s\| < \bar{s}\}$. Analogously, the rule can be applied for the case $\|s\| > \bar{s}$ to yield

$$\Pr\{\bar{b}_{j\text{-type}} \mid \|s\| > \bar{s}\} = \frac{(1 - p_j)q_j}{1 - r}.$$

The conditional shock intensity probabilities may also be revised. We have

$$\Pr\{\|\bar{b}\| < b_j \mid \bar{b}_{j\text{-type}}; \|s\| < \bar{s}\} = \Pr\{\|\bar{b}\| < b_j \mid \bar{b}_{j\text{-type}}\} = p_j$$

and

$$\Pr\{\|\bar{b}\| > b_j \mid \bar{b}_{j\text{-type}}; \|s\| < \bar{s}\} = 0.$$

Analogously,

$$\Pr\{\|\bar{b}\| < b_j \mid \bar{b}_{j\text{-type}}; \|s\| < \bar{s}\} = 0,$$

$$\Pr\{\|\bar{b}\| > b_j \mid \bar{b}_{j\text{-type}}; \|s\| > \bar{s}\} = \Pr\{\|\bar{b}\| > b_j \mid \bar{b}_{j\text{-type}}\} = 1 - p_j.$$

We can now rewrite the expected loss function with the posterior probabilities in the two cases.

First, when $\|s\| < \bar{s}$,

$$EL_{\text{flx}}^p = \frac{p_\nu q_\nu}{r} z_1 \bar{b}^2 + \frac{p_\mu (1 - q_\nu + q_\epsilon)}{r} z_1 \left(\frac{\kappa}{\varphi}\right)^2 \bar{b}^2, \tag{25}$$

$$EL_{\text{fix}}^p = \frac{p_\epsilon q_\epsilon}{r} z_2 \bar{b}^2 + \frac{p_\mu (1 - q_\nu - q_\epsilon)}{r} z_2 \left(\frac{1}{\varphi}\right)^2 \bar{b}^2, \tag{26}$$

$$EL_{\text{tz}}^p = \frac{p_\nu^2 q_\nu}{r} z_1 \bar{b}^2 + \frac{p_\mu^2 (1 - q_\nu - q_\epsilon)}{r} z_1 \left(\frac{\kappa}{\varphi}\right)^2 \bar{b}^2; \tag{27}$$

when $\|s\| > \bar{s}$,

$$EL_{\text{flx}}^p = \frac{(1 - p_\nu)q_\nu}{1 - r} z_1 \bar{b}^2 + \frac{(1 - p_\mu)(1 - q_\nu - q_\epsilon)}{1 - r} z_1 \left(\frac{\kappa}{\varphi}\right)^2 \bar{b}^2, \tag{28}$$

$$EL_{\text{fix}}^p = \frac{(1-p_\epsilon)q_\epsilon}{1-r}z_2\bar{b}^2 + \frac{(1-p_\mu)(1-q_\nu-q_\epsilon)}{1-r}z_2\left(\frac{1}{\varphi}\right)^2\bar{b}^2, \qquad (29)$$

$$EL_{\text{tz}}^p = \frac{(1-p_\epsilon)^2q_\epsilon}{1-r}z_1\bar{b}^2 + \frac{(1-p_\mu)^2(1-q_\nu-q_\epsilon)}{1-r}z_1\left(\frac{\kappa}{\varphi}\right)^2\bar{b}^2. \qquad (30)$$

Conditions for the ex post target-zone regime optimality are obtained in Proposition 4.

Proposition 4. *In the model* (1)–(4) *with loss function* (13) *for the AA and parameter values such that $z > 0$, sufficient conditions for the target-zone regime optimality on the prior probabilities of the intensities and the sources of the shocks are the following two inequalities:*

$$q_\nu + h_1 q_\epsilon > V_1,$$

$$q_\nu + h_2 q_\epsilon < V_2,$$

where

$$h_1 \equiv \frac{z(1-p_\mu)(1/\varphi)^2 - (1-p_\epsilon)z_2}{(1-p_\nu)z_1 + z(1-p_\mu)(1/\varphi)^2},$$

$$V_1 \equiv \frac{z(1-p_\mu)(1/\varphi)^2}{(1-p_\nu)z_1 + z(1-p_\mu)(1/\varphi)^2},$$

$$h_2 \equiv \frac{zp_\mu(1/\varphi)^2 - z_2 p_\epsilon}{z_1 p_\nu + zp_\mu(1/\varphi)^2},$$

$$V_2 \equiv \frac{zp_\mu(1/\varphi)^2}{z_1 p_\nu + zp_\mu(1/\varphi)^2},$$

$$z \equiv z_2 - z_1\kappa^2.$$

Proof: Furnished upon request.

Proposition 4 states a particular sufficient condition for optimality of the target-zone regime; in fact, the inequalities involved are the same as the inequalities of Proposition 1, although the meaning of the probabilities (the p_j and q_j) is different because in this section they are *prior* probabilities. The other important difference is that unlike Proposition 1, Proposition 4 states only a sufficient (rather than a necessary and sufficient) condition for optimality of the target-zone regime. As a consequence, Proposition 4 simply shows the link between the two approaches in Sections 4 and 5; the resulting necessary conditions arising from Proposition 2 cannot be applied as posterior conditions on the prior probabilities. In other words, conditions that could hinge simply on the shock *intensity* probabilities are not obtainable, and additional assumptions on the shock *source* ought to be included.

6   Future research

After studying the behavior of the exchange rate when constrained to fluctuate within a given band, most literature on the target-zone system has raised the question of regime optimality. This paper presents a result in that direction. In particular, it determines necessary conditions for the optimality of the target zone regime with respect to perfectly fixed and flexible exchange-rate regimes in a sticky-price monetary model, conditions that mainly involve only one aspect of uncertainty faced by the AA (i.e., uncertainty w.r.t. shock intensity).

Some of our assumptions immediately suggest directions for further research. First, it would be desirable to investigate the optimality of the target zone regime and so find conditions that would mainly involve the second source of uncertainty (i.e., uncertainty w.r.t. shock type).

Next, it would be desirable to consider different kinds of institutional settings and design a target-zone regime for cases other than that of marginal but finite interventions.

Appendix

A.1   *Dynamics of the sticky-price monetary model*

In the flexible exchange-rate version of model (1)–(4), the four endogenous variables are the domestic interest rate i, real output y, the nominal exchange rate s, and the domestic price level p. The exogenous variables are the foreign interest rate i^*, the initial long-run output level $\bar{y}$, and the nominal money stock m_0. As shown in the text, (1)–(4) can be reduced into a system of two first-order differential equations:

$$\begin{bmatrix} dp \\ ds \end{bmatrix} = \mathbf{A} \begin{bmatrix} p \\ s \end{bmatrix} + \mathbf{B} \begin{bmatrix} m_0 \\ i^* \\ \bar{y} \\ \nu \\ \epsilon \\ \mu \end{bmatrix}, \tag{31}$$

where

$$A \equiv \frac{1}{\Delta} \begin{bmatrix} -\varphi(\gamma + \lambda\eta) & \varphi\lambda\eta \\ 1 - \kappa\eta & \kappa\eta \end{bmatrix},$$

$$B \equiv \begin{bmatrix} \varphi\gamma/\Delta & 0 & -\varphi & -\varphi\gamma/\Delta & \varphi\lambda/\Delta & 1 \\ -1/\Delta & -1 & 0 & 1/\Delta & \kappa/\Delta & 0 \end{bmatrix},$$

$$\Delta \equiv \kappa\gamma + \lambda.$$

Matrix **A** has a negative determinant. Therefore, the product of the roots of the characteristic equation is negative and the eigenvalues have opposite signs. The dynamics is then characterized by a saddle point in the phase diagram for the variables s and p.

The eigenvalues, l_u and l_s, of matrix **A** are obtained as solutions of the characteristic equation

$$l^2 - l\frac{(\kappa\eta - \varphi\gamma - \varphi\lambda\eta)}{\Delta} - \frac{\varphi\eta}{\Delta} = 0.$$

The two eigenvalues are then

$$l_u = \frac{1}{2\Delta}[(\kappa\eta - \varphi\gamma - \varphi\lambda\eta) + \sqrt{(\kappa\eta - \varphi\gamma - \varphi\lambda\eta)^2 + 4\varphi\eta\Delta}\,],$$

$$l_s = \frac{1}{2\Delta}[(\kappa\eta - \varphi\gamma - \varphi\lambda\eta) - \sqrt{(\kappa\eta - \varphi\gamma - \varphi\lambda\eta)^2 + 4\varphi\eta\Delta}\,],$$

where the subscripts u and s stand for unstable and stable.

The corresponding eigenvectors are obtained through

$$(A - l_k I)\begin{bmatrix} 1 \\ \rho_k \end{bmatrix} = 0 \quad \text{for } k = u, s.$$

Therefore, the unstable eigenvector is given by:

$$\rho_u = \frac{\Delta l_u + \varphi(\lambda\eta + \gamma)}{\varphi\lambda\eta}$$

and is unambiguously positive. The slope of the stable eigenvector is instead

$$\rho_s = \frac{1 - \kappa\eta}{\Delta l_s - \kappa\eta}.$$

This slope is negative (positive) and there is exchange-rate overshooting (undershooting) if $\kappa\eta < 1$ ($\kappa\eta > 1$). The eigenvectors ρ_u and ρ_s are shown in Figure 1 as dashed lines UU and SS, respectively. The intercept terms depend on the initial values and can be easily obtained.

The long-run loci are derived by setting the left-hand side of (31) equal to zero. The $dp = 0$ locus is

$$s = \frac{\lambda\eta+\gamma}{\lambda\eta}p - \frac{\gamma}{\lambda\eta}m_0 + \frac{\Delta}{\lambda\eta}\bar{y} + \frac{\gamma}{\lambda\eta}v - \frac{1}{\eta}\epsilon - \frac{\Delta}{\lambda\eta\varphi}\mu;$$

it is upward-sloping and steeper than the 45° line. The $ds = 0$ locus is

$$s = -\frac{1-\kappa\eta}{\kappa\eta}p + \frac{1}{\kappa\eta}m_0 + \frac{\Delta}{\kappa\eta}i^* - \frac{1}{\kappa\eta}v - \frac{1}{\eta}\epsilon;$$

its slope depends on the sign of $(1-\kappa\eta)$ and is downward (upward) sloping in case of overshooting (undershooting).

The long-run values for p and s can be obtained from the intersection of the two loci just described:

$$p^l = m_0 + \lambda i^* - \kappa\bar{y} - v + \frac{\kappa}{\varphi}\mu,$$

$$s^l = m_0 + \left(\frac{\gamma+\lambda\eta}{\eta}\right)i^* + \left(\frac{1-\kappa\eta}{\eta}\right)\bar{y} - v - \frac{1}{\eta}\epsilon - \frac{1}{\varphi}\left(\frac{1-\kappa\eta}{\eta}\right)\mu.$$

We recall also the long-run values for the other two endogenous variables:

$$y^l = \bar{y} - (1/\varphi)\mu,$$

$$i^l = i^*.$$

Comparative statics and dynamics are performed on the model always by starting at the initial long-run equilibrium; hence, both s_0 and p_0 are initially at an intersection of the two loci $ds = 0$ and $dp = 0$. When a shock occurs, this will affect the long-run values of both s and p (according to the preceding formulas) and the dynamics begins.

When a negative nominal shock v occurs, both the long-run exchange rate and price level rise by the same amount. The theory of purchasing-power parity holds for the nominal shock, and the real exchange rate remains constant in the long run. The transition toward the new equilibrium (which is aligned with the old one along the upward-sloping 45° line) includes a jump of the exchange rate up to the new stable eigenvector; this has the same slope as the stable eigenvector just obtained, but a new intercept according to the new long-run equilibrium. The size of the shift in the eigenvector gives the jump in the exchange rate, which is equal to

$$[s(t_0^+) - s(t_0^-)]|_v^{\text{flx}} = \left[-\frac{\Delta l_s - 1}{\Delta l_s - \kappa\eta}\right]v.$$

The jump always has opposite sign with respect to the nominal shock v. Its magnitude is greater or lower than unity depending on whether the system exhibits (respectively) overshooting or undershooting.

Next, an AD shock ϵ shifts both long-run loci down by the same amount, $-(1/\eta)\epsilon$. The long-run p value does not change, since ϵ does not enter the p' expression. On the other hand, the nominal exchange rate jumps directly to the new long-run value by an amount $-(1/\eta)\epsilon$. This nominal appreciation (if ϵ is positive) immediately and completely offsets the AD shock in the AD equation, and output does not vary.

Finally, the supply shock μ has an effect only on the $dp = 0$ locus, which shifts down in case of positively signed μ. Therefore, the exchange rate now appreciates in order to jump on the new stable eigenvector. Again, the magnitude of the jump is given by the shift in the eigenvector and is equal to

$$[s(t_0^+) - s(t_0^-)]\big|_\mu^{flx} = \left[-\frac{\Delta l_s(1 - \kappa\eta)}{\varphi\eta(\Delta l_s - \kappa\eta)}\right]\mu.$$

A.2   *Conditions on the sign of z*

In Proposition 1, the aggregate term $z \equiv z_2 - z_1\kappa^2$ is introduced. By substituting for the expressions of z_1 and z_2, z is positive if and only if

$$\left(\frac{\kappa}{\kappa\gamma + \lambda}\right)^2 \frac{\sigma + 2\varphi\eta}{\sigma - 2l_s}[-\lambda\eta(1 - \rho_s) - \gamma]^2 < 1. \tag{32}$$

A sufficient condition will be represented by parameter restrictions that make all three terms less than unity.

Let us start with the term in large parentheses; this is less than unity if and only if

$$\kappa(1 - \gamma) < \lambda,$$

which is always verified if $\gamma > 1$; otherwise, if $0 < \gamma < 1$ then

$$\kappa < \frac{\lambda}{1 - \gamma}.$$

We now consider the condition on the last term:

$$\lambda\eta(1 - \rho_s) + \gamma < 1$$

or

$$\lambda\eta(1 - \rho_s) < 1 - \gamma.$$

A distinction must be made between the overshooting and the undershooting case.

In the overshooting case, $\kappa\eta < 1$ and $\rho_s < 0$; therefore, $(1 - \rho_s)$ is positive and greater than unity and (32) can be verified only if $0 < \gamma < 1$. In the undershooting case, we have a condition on the product $\lambda\eta$:

$$\lambda\eta < \frac{1-\gamma}{1-\rho_s} < 1.$$

Let us still consider the overshooting case and analyze the last term:

$$\frac{\sigma+2\varphi\eta}{\sigma-2l_s} < 1. \tag{33}$$

This is verified when $\varphi\eta < \|l_s\|$. After some manipulation it can be shown that (33) is verified when $\kappa\eta < 1$; that is, it is always verified in the overshooting case. Therefore, summarizing the overshooting case, z is positive if:

    (i) $0 < \gamma < 1$,
   (ii) $\lambda\eta < (1-\gamma)/(1-\rho_s) < 1$, and
  (iii) $\kappa < \lambda/(1-\gamma)$.

In the undershooting case, the second term in (32) is never less than unity. Therefore, no clear-cut sufficient condition can be given for z to be positive. A general condition would imply that the value of the first and the third terms would be sufficiently less than unity to compensate for the second term. Therefore, in the undershooting case some general conditions are:

    (i) $0 < \gamma < 1$,
   (ii) $\lambda\eta \ll (1-\gamma)/(1-\rho_s) < 1$, and
  (iii) $\kappa \ll \lambda/(1-\gamma)$.

REFERENCES

Beetsma, R. and F. van der Ploeg (1992), "Exchange Rate Bands and Optimal Monetary Accommodation under a Dirty Float," Discussion Paper no. 725, Center for Economic and Policy Research, London.

Bertola, G., and R. J. Caballero (1992), "Target Zones and Realignments," *American Economic Review* 82: 520–36.

Bertola, G., and L. E. O. Svensson (1993), "Stochastic Devaluation Risk and the Empirical Fit of Target Zone Models," *Review of Economic Studies* 60: 689–712.

Currie, D. A., and S. Wren-Lewis (1989), "An Appraisal of Alternative Blueprints for International Policy Coordination," *European Economic Review* 33: 1769–85.

(1990), "Evaluating the Extended Target Zone Proposal for the G3," *Economic Journal* 100: 105–23.

De Grauwe, P. (1992), *The Economics of Monetary Integration.* Oxford University Press.

Dornbusch, R. (1976), "Expectations and Exchange Rate Dynamics," *Journal of Political Economy* 84: 1161–76.

Edison H., M. Miller, and J. Williamson (1987), "On Evaluating and Extending the Target Zone Proposal," *Journal of Policy Modelling* 9: 199–224.

Flood, R. P., and P. M. Garber (1991), "The Linkage between Speculative Attack and Target Zone Models of the Exchange Rate," *Quarterly Journal of Economics* 106: 1367–72.

Frankel, J., and S. Phillips (1991), "The European Monetary System: Credible at Last?" Working Paper no. 3819, National Bureau of Economic Research, Cambridge, MA.

Hughes Hallet, A. (1992), "Target Zones and International Policy Coordination," *European Economic Review* 36: 893–914.

(1993), "Exchange Rates and Asymmetric Policy Regimes: When Does Exchange Rate Targeting Pay?" *Oxford Economic Papers* 45: 191–206.

Krugman, P. R. (1991), "Target Zones and Exchange Rate Dynamics," *Quarterly Journal of Economics* 106: 669–82.

Krugman, P. R., and M. Miller (eds.) (1992), *Exchange Rate Targets and Currency Bands.* Cambridge University Press.

Miller, M., and P. Weller (1991), "Currency Bands, Target Zones and Price Flexibility," *IMF Staff Papers* 38: 184–215.

Poole, W. (1970), "Optimal Choice of Monetary Policy Instruments in a Simple Stochastic Macro Model," *Quarterly Journal of Economics* 85: 197–206.

Rose, A. K., and L. E. O. Svensson (1991), "Expected and Predicted Realignments: The FF/DM Exchange Rate During the EMS," Discussion Paper no. 552, Center for Economic and Policy Research, London.

Sutherland, M. (1992a), "Target Zone Models with Price Inertia: Some Testable Implications," Discussion Paper no. 698, Center for Economic and Policy Research, London.

(1992b), "Monetary and Real Shocks and the Optimal Target Zone," Discussion Papers in Economics no. 92/7, University of York, UK.

Svensson, L. E. O. (1991), "Target Zones and Interest Rate Variability," *Journal of International Economics* 31: 27–54.

(1992a), "An Interpretation of Recent Research on Exchange Rate Target Zones," *Journal of Economic Perspectives* 6: 119–44.

(1992b), "Why Exchange Rate Bands? Monetary Independence in Spite of Fixed Exchange Rates," Seminar Paper no. 521, Institute for International Economic Studies, Stockholm.

Williamson, J., and M. Miller (1987), "Targets and Indicators: A Blueprint for the International Coordination of Economic Policy," Institute for International Economics, Washington, DC.

CHAPTER 18

Neighborhood feedbacks, endogenous stratification, and income inequality

Steven N. Durlauf

1   Introduction

This paper illustrates how income inequality can emerge in economies through the interaction of a positive feedback structure between members of a common neighborhood with the tendency of families to stratify themselves endogenously into economically homogeneous neighborhoods. The underlying logic of the model we study is straightforward. The presence of positive feedbacks means that the income distribution of a neighborhood will strongly affect the future economic status of children within the community. Endogenous stratification, by allowing the sorting of families with like attributes into separate neighborhoods, allows children from different neighborhoods to experience very different feedback effects, so relative economic status is transmitted across generations. By focusing on the neighborhood as the primary intergenerational transmission mechanism, the model exhibits very different income distribution dynamics from those which emerge in the private-education economies originally studied by Becker and Tomes (1979) and Loury (1981).[1]

The class of models we study represents a generalization of the incomplete-market/coordination-failure models that have formed the basis of much recent work in macroeconomics. As illustrated by Cooper and John (1988), the various models in this literature possess a common positive feedback structure that creates the potential for multiple, Pareto-ranked

I thank Torben Andersen, Patrick Bolton, Suzanne Cooper, John Moore, Susan Nelson, Uday Rajan, Javier Ruiz-Castillo, Larry Samuelson, Anthony Shorrocks, two anonymous referees, and conference and seminar participants at Aarhus, Chicago, Cornell, London School of Economics, Stanford, Universidad Carlos III, UCLA, UC San Diego, Wisconsin, and York for helpful suggestions. I am especially grateful to François Laisney for providing detailed comments on an earlier draft.
[1] See Galor and Zeira (1993) for an interesting analysis of capital market imperfections as an additional source of inequality dynamics.

equilibria to exist for a given microeconomic specification. This occurs because high and low levels of activity on the part of all agents render these activity levels optimal for each individual. The macroeconomic literature on positive feedbacks and multiple equilibria has generally taken the interaction structure between agents to be exogenous. Typically, this literature has focused on economies where the spillover effects are symmetric between all agents. As such, this literature is useful in explaining how all agents in an economy can simultaneously achieve high or low incomes, but is less equipped to explain persistent income disparities within an economy.

By endogenizing the interaction sets of agents, in the sense that agents can affect the set of other agents with whom they interact, the concepts underlying incomplete-markets macroeconomics can provide a general framework for understanding how inequality can emerge within a given economy. When agents segregate themselves according to some class of attributes, we say that the economy exhibits *stratification*. If these attributes are also the source of feedback effects between members of a given interaction set, then stratification can lead to inequality. By analogy to the coordination-failure literature, high incomes and low incomes can both emerge as equilibria among subsets of families within the economy when families are stratified by income between neighborhoods. One implication of this paper is that, by endogenizing the interaction structure of agents, the macroeconomic models of positive feedbacks and multiple equilibria also provide a theory of inequality.

A body of recent theoretical research has studied the role of neighborhood influences on the distribution of income in ways related to the current paper. In Bénabou (1993), the productivity of family-specific investment in human capital is affected by the level of human capital investment among one's classmates. Rich neighborhoods are those characterized by high human capital investment by families, whereas poor neighborhoods are those with low human capital investment. Durlauf (1994) demonstrated how local financing of public education and the dependence of the productivity of human capital investment on the income distribution of a neighborhood can combine to allow permanently poor neighborhoods to emerge and coexist with permanently wealthy ones. Montgomery (1990, 1991) showed that if one's success in the labor market depends on referrals by neighborhood members, then multiple equilibria may exist in the distribution of occupations within neighborhoods. Streufert (1991) studied an economy in which the absence of role models in poor communities prevents children from accurately assessing the marginal product of effort in school. Much of this work has been stimulated by work in sociology by Wilson (1987), who documented the persistence of poverty among families trapped in inner-city ghettos. An important common feature of the role-model, tax-base, and labor-market connection effects that underlie the models in this literature is that the economic status of adults in a community will affect the economic success of the neighborhood's offspring.

Our analysis extends previous work in several respects. First, we present an analysis of how the cross-section income distribution evolves over time. Most of the models of neighborhood effects have been static. Second, we provide an analysis of how relative inequality evolves over time. The focus of models such as Bénabou (1993) and Durlauf (1994) has been on the existence of absolute low-income or poverty traps. Our analysis complements this work by showing how permanent relative inequality can emerge in an economy where the incomes of all families are growing. Third, we provide a relatively general framework that allows the study of the roles of both local financing of education and sociological feedbacks in perpetuating inequality.

This paper is related in a number of ways to Bénabou (1992), which examined the effect of stratification on economic growth.[2] That paper focused on the differences for aggregate growth dynamics in all periods in economies when the rich and poor live in separate communities versus when all families share a common community, and showed how the long-run growth rate in an economy may be augmented by economic integration even if the short-run growth rate is reduced. Our paper focuses on the role of different spillovers in sustaining relative inequality over different horizons. In addition, we show how to endogenize the neighborhood formation process. At the same time, both papers perform their analysis in the context of a constant-returns-to-scale technology, and – together with Durlauf (1994) – provide an overview of the dynamic properties of multicommunity economies for a range of microeconomic structures.

In developing the analysis, we work with a relatively tightly parameterized model in the sense that specific forms are chosen for the utility and production functions. These functional forms allow us to analyze explicitly the time-series properties of the income distribution. In the absence of such a tight parameterization, it is difficult to describe the relationship between the model's primitives and dynamics due to the complex interaction structure that links families over time. At the same time, one goal of the analysis is to indicate the extent to which our results on persistent income inequality are robust to alternative functional forms.

---

[2] deBartolome (1991) and Fernandez and Rogerson (1992) studied related models in which families stratify themselves in order to maximize education quality, although their emphasis is not on the implications of stratification for inequality. See also Lundberg and Startz (1992), who studied racial income inequality in the context of a private-education model where blacks and whites are exogenously segregated.

The empirical importance of neighborhood effects in determining economic success, even after controlling for family background, has been confirmed in a number of studies.[3] Datcher (1982) found that the mean income of a community helps to predict the years of schooling among urban males, and Corcoran et al. (1989) uncovered a similar link between the percentage of families on welfare in a community and future offspring wages. Crane (1991) demonstrated how the percentage of professional workers in a community correlates negatively with the high-school dropout rate among teenagers. Case and Katz (1991) similarly found that neighborhood characteristics help predict the incidence of many social problems among poor youths. Further, studies such as Card and Krueger (1992), which established a relationship between school quality and eventual economic success of students in combination with local financing of education, suggest a relationship between a neighborhood's income distribution and the economic status of offspring.[4]

Section 2 of the paper describes a basic model of neighborhood feedback effects. Section 3 characterizes the cross-section equilibrium in the economy, with an emphasis on the relationship between the cross-section income distribution and the equilibrium configuration of families across neighborhoods. Section 4 analyzes the dynamics of the income distribution and provides conditions under which persistent inequality will emerge. Section 5 discusses the role of various assumptions on the results, and Section 6 concludes. Appendix 1 contains proofs of all propositions, and Appendix 2 provides a housing interpretation of the endogenous stratification we study.

2   A model of family income and neighborhood spillovers

2.1   *Population structure*

The population consists of a continuum of families, indexed by i. Family i, t is composed of agent $i, t-1$, who is born at $t-1$, and i's offspring. Agents live two periods. Each agent receives education when young and has one child and works when old.

Families live in neighborhoods indexed by n. The set of families occupying neighborhood n at t is $N_{n,t}$; $\mu(N_{n,t})$ denotes the Lebesgue measure of the set of families in the neighborhood and therefore measures a community's population size. Within a neighborhood, $\hat{F}_{Y,n,t}$ is the empirical

---

[3] See Jencks and Mayer (1990) for a survey of the empirical work on neighborhood effects.
[4] Approximately 50% of all expenditures on public education between kindergarten and 12th grade in the United States are funded through locally raised revenues.

probability distribution for family incomes; $\hat{F}_{Y,n,t}(s)$ denotes the percentage of families in neighborhood n at t with incomes less than or equal to s. Finally, the average income in neighborhood n at t is $MY_{n,t}$, whereas the average income among any set of families indexed by i at t is $MY_{i,t}$. This notation is useful in distinguishing between the average income of a set of parents in a neighborhood and the average income of their descendants, who may live in several neighborhoods.

2.2   Preferences

Each agent $i, t-1$ derives utility both from i's own consumption as an adult, $C_{i,t}$, and from the expected income of i's offspring as an adult, $Y_{i,t+1}$:

$$U_{i,t-1} = \pi_1 \log(C_{i,t}) + \pi_2 \, \mathrm{E}(\log(Y_{i,t+1}) \mid \mathfrak{F}_t), \tag{1}$$

where $\mathfrak{F}_t$ denotes the complete history of the economy through t and E denotes expected value. The assumption that an adult's utility depends on the income rather than the utility of his or her offspring is common in the literature on income distribution dynamics. The assumption can be interpreted, for example, as meaning that parents care about the occupational attainment of their offspring, which is equivalent to offspring income in this model.[5] The importance of the Cobb–Douglas specification for the utility function will be discussed in Section 5.

2.3   Income determination

The realized income of each offspring in a neighborhood is determined by a constant-returns-to-scale production function that combines two factors. First, education endows each child in neighborhood n at t with a common level of human capital $H_{n,t}$; second, each offspring experiences a white-noise productivity shock $\xi_{i,t+1}$ as an adult:

$$Y_{i,t+1} = \phi H_{n,t} \xi_{i,t+1}. \tag{2}$$

The shocks $\xi_{i,t+1}$ are identically distributed across individuals and neighborhoods at all dates, and are independent across neighborhoods. Each shock has mean 1 and lies in a closed, uniformly bounded positive interval of $\mathbb{R}$. Without loss of generality, we assume that $\xi_{i,t+1}$ consists

---

[5] This assumption is also important in ensuring the existence of an equilibrium. For example, we are unaware of any proof for the existence of an equilibrium in this economy for the utility function $U_{i,t-1} = u(C_{i,t}) + \beta U_{i,t}$, given the nonconvexities in the model that derive from the neighborhood formation process.

of a neighborhoodwide component $\nu_{n,t+1}$ and an idiosyncratic component $\gamma_{i,t+1}$:

$$\xi_{i,t+1} = \nu_{n,t+1}\gamma_{i,t+1}, \tag{3}$$

where the idiosyncratic component obeys the law of large numbers in the sense that the empirical and population probability distributions of the idiosyncratic shocks are always equal. (That is, $\hat{F}_{\gamma,n,t+1}(s) = F_{\gamma,n,t+1}(s)$ for all s.)

2.4   *Budget constraint*

Agent $i, t-1$ divides income between consumption and taxes $T_{i,t}$:

$$Y_{i,t} = C_{i,t} + T_{i,t}. \tag{4}$$

2.5   *Tax determination*

Given realized family incomes at t, each neighborhood chooses a proportional income tax rate $\tau_{n,t} \in [0,1]$ whose proceeds are used to finance education. Taxes are determined by majority voting. A given $\tau_{n,t}$ is an equilibrium rate for $N_{n,t}$ if at least one half of the members of $N_{n,t}$ prefer the rate to any fixed alternative. Individual taxes therefore obey

$$T_{i,t} = \tau_{n,t}Y_{i,t} \quad \forall i \in N_{n,t}. \tag{5}$$

Following Loury (1981), neighborhoods cannot borrow in order to finance education, since there exists no mechanism to enforce repayment of such loans by offspring.

2.6   *Education investment*

All children in a neighborhood receive the same level of education investment $ED_{n,t}$, which is determined by the total tax revenues raised in the community. The level of human capital induced by this investment is characterized in what follows. The level of education expenditures within a neighborhood, $TE_{n,t}$, is assumed to have two parts: a component that increases with the level of education investment but which must be spent regardless of the number of students receiving the investment; and a component that requires spending in proportion to the total number of students. For a given population size, the fixed-cost component in spending is assumed to be a constant fraction of the total, so that

$$TE_{n,t} = \lambda_1 ED_{n,t} + \lambda_2 \mu(N_{n,t})ED_{n,t}. \tag{6}$$

Because per-capita education investment costs are decreasing in neighborhood size, there exists an incentive for wealthier families to live with poorer ones.

2.7   Sociological feedbacks and human capital formation[6]

The actual level of human capital formation induced by a given level of education investment is assumed to depend on the empirical income distribution within the neighborhood, $\hat{F}_{Y,n,t}$. This dependence is designed to reflect the influence of role-model and labor-market connection effects on the returns to schooling, and is consistent with the empirical work on neighborhood effects and economic status. We assume that this feedback takes the form

$$H_{n,t} = \Theta(\hat{F}_{Y,n,t})ED_{n,t}. \tag{7}$$

Three restrictions are placed on $\Theta(\cdot)$. First, rightward shifts in a neighborhood's income distribution increase the amount of human capital produced by a given level of education investment. If $\hat{F}_{Y,n,t}$ and $\hat{F}'_{Y,n,t}$ denote two income distributions such that $\hat{F}_{Y,n,t}(s) < \hat{F}'_{Y,n,t}(s)$ for all s, then

$$\Theta(\hat{F}'_{Y,n,t}) < \Theta(\hat{F}_{Y,n,t}). \tag{8}$$

Second, the percentage change in the marginal productivity of education investment induced by a proportional increase in the incomes of all members of a neighborhood is assumed to become nonincreasing as the minimum income in a neighborhood becomes large. This condition limits the degree of fragmentation of neighborhoods over time by ensuring that, along growing income paths, the incentive for wealthy families to segregate themselves from proportionately poorer neighborhoods is not continually growing as well. For every pair of income distributions $\hat{F}_{Y,n,t}(s)$ and $\hat{F}'_{Y,n,t}(s)$, there exists a number $\bar{Y} < \infty$ such that if $\hat{F}_{Y,n,t}(\bar{Y}) = 0$ and $\hat{F}'_{Y,n,t}(\bar{Y}) = 0$ then, for any $K > 1$,

$$|\Theta(\hat{F}_{Y,n,t}) - \Theta(\hat{F}'_{Y,n,t})| \geq |\Theta(\hat{F}_{Y,K,n,t}) - \Theta(\hat{F}'_{Y,K,n,t})|, \tag{9}$$

where, for all s, $\hat{F}_{Y,K,n,t}(Ks) = \hat{F}_{Y,n,t}(s)$ and $\hat{F}'_{Y,K,n,t}(Ks) = \hat{F}'_{Y,n,t}(s)$.

Third, $\Theta(\cdot)$ obeys a continuity restriction. For any income distribution F, let F_ϵ denote the same income distribution when the poorest $\epsilon \times 100$

---

[6] We refer to these feedbacks as sociological not only because their causes and magnitudes have been largely studied by sociologists rather than economists, but also because some aspects of these feedbacks (such as the "culture of poverty") cannot be readily derived from conventional microeconomic reasoning. However, Montgomery (1990, 1991) and Streufert (1991) have shown how these neighborhood feedbacks can emerge owing to information imperfections.

percent of families have been omitted; $\Theta(F_\epsilon)$ is assumed to be continuous in $\epsilon \in [0, 1)$. This rules out any effects from moving a measure-zero set of families between neighborhoods.

2.8   *Neighborhood formation rules*

Our notion of a neighborhood is abstract in the sense that no stock of housing is carried over across generalizations. At the beginning of each period, incomes are realized and families are free to form neighborhoods. Any group of families that forms a neighborhood may exclude any set of families it wishes. There is no limit to the number of populated neighborhoods that may be formed.

An equilibrium neighborhood configuration in this model is therefore one that lies in the core of all possible neighborhood configurations, in the sense that no positive measure of families at a given configuration wishes to withdraw and form a new neighborhood. Once all families are allocated in a core neighborhood configuration, tax rates are simultaneously chosen and children are educated given the revenues that are raised.

3   **Characterization of equilibrium**

This section describes the existence and cross-section properties of the equilibrium in the economy.

3.1   *Existence of equilibrium*

In order to establish the existence of an equilibrium in this economy, it is necessary to prove: (a) that, contingent on a fixed configuration of families, there exists a tax rate in each neighborhood supportable by majority voting; and (b) that there is a core configuration of families across neighborhoods each period.

The Cobb–Douglas preference specification not only ensures the existence of an equilibrium tax rate within a neighborhood, but also entails that the equilibrium tax rate is preferred by all families regardless of the neighborhood's empirical income distribution. To see this, observe that each agent's preferred tax rate over all possible τ will maximize

$$\pi_1 \log((1-\tau)Y_{i,t}) + \pi_2 \, \mathrm{E}(\log(\phi H_{n,t}(\tau)\xi_{i,t+1}) \,|\, \mathfrak{F}_t), \tag{10}$$

where $H_{n,t}(\tau)$ expresses the level of human capital as a function of the tax rate. By substituting in (6) and (7) to solve for $H_{n,t}(\tau)$, the preferred tax rate will maximize

$$\pi_1 \log((1-\tau)) + \pi_1 \log(Y_{i,t}) + \pi_2 \log\left(\phi\Theta(\hat{F}_{Y,n,t}) \frac{\mu(N_{n,t})}{\lambda_1 + \lambda_2 \mu(N_{n,t})}\right)$$

$$+ \pi_2 \log(\tau) + \pi_2 \log(MY_{n,t}) + \pi_2 \, \mathrm{E}(\log(\xi_{i,t+1}) \,|\, \mathcal{F}_t). \tag{11}$$

Simple algebra reveals that the most preferred tax rate for agent $i, t-1$ is $\pi_2/(\pi_1 + \pi_2)$, which is dependent on neither i's income nor the composition of i's neighborhood. This argument leads to Proposition 1.

Proposition 1 (Agreement on most preferred tax rate within a neighborhood). *For any neighborhood configuration $N_{n,t}$, the tax rate $\tau = \pi_2/(\pi_1 + \pi_2)$ is*

   (i)   *unanimously preferred to any alternative, and*
   (ii) *independent of the composition of the neighborhood.*

The Cobb–Douglas specification also implies that the economy will exhibit a positive feedback structure between families within a neighborhood, as increases in the income of one's neighbors always improve the welfare of a given family. Since all families agree on the utility maximizing tax rate within a community, rightward shifts in a neighborhood's income distribution will both increase the size of the tax base and raise the marginal product of education investment. Similarly, these effects induce a positive feedback from a neighborhood's income distribution to the expected income of offspring.

Proposition 2 (Relationship between adult expected utility, offspring expected income, and empirical income distribution in a neighborhood). *For a given population size $\mu(N_{n,t})$:*

   (i)   *the expected utility of any agent $i, t-1$ who lives in $N_{n,t}$ is increasing in monotonic rightward shifts of the empirical income distribution over all other families in the neighborhood; and*
   (ii) *the expected income of any agent i, t who lives in $N_{n,t}$ is increasing in monotonic rightward shifts of the empirical income distribution over all other families in the neighborhood.*

The neighborhood-level positive spillovers described in Proposition 2 are sufficient to prove the existence of a core configuration of families across neighborhoods. A given pair of neighborhoods is said to be *stratified* if the lowest income in one neighborhood is at least as great as the highest income in the other. Proposition 3 states not only that there exists a core configuration of families across neighborhoods in all periods, but also that all such configurations must be stratified when multiple populated neighborhoods exist.

Proposition 3 (Existence of a core neighborhood configuration).

(i) *For any cross-section income distribution, there exists a core configuration of families across neighborhoods.*

(ii) *Along any sequence of core neighborhood configurations, either all families live in a common neighborhood or all pairs of neighborhoods are stratified each period.*

Given the dependence of each i's human capital on the empirical income distribution of the neighborhood in which i grows up (as well as on the white-noise assumption on the productivity shocks), the equilibrium law of motion for individual income will have a neighborhood-based structure, as stated in Proposition 4.

Proposition 4 (Probability law for individual income). *Each family's income obeys the transition rule*

$$\mathrm{Prob}(Y_{i,t+1}\,|\,\mathfrak{F}_t) = \mathrm{Prob}(Y_{i,t+1}\,|\,\hat{F}_{Y,n,t},\,\mu(N_{n,t})).^7 \qquad (12)$$

3.2   *Stratification and the cross-section income distribution*

We now characterize the range of possible equilibrium configurations of families across neighborhoods. Proposition 3 establishes the possibility of a stratified equilibrium, but does not show that one will ever actually occur. High-income families benefit from large communities due to the decreasing average cost of human capital. On the other hand, poorer neighbors erode the tax base and reduce the marginal product of education investment through the human capital formation function. The consequences of this trade-off for the realized distribution of families across neighborhoods will depend on the empirical income distribution across the entire economy. Proposition 5 shows that stratification will always occur when the income gap between the wealthiest and poorest families in the economy is sufficiently wide. The proposition implies that a large enough degree of cross-section inequality can have strong intertemporal consequences by ensuring that the offspring of rich and poor families experience different neighborhood feedbacks.

---

[7] Throughout, $\mathrm{Prob}(x\,|\,y)$ denotes the conditional probability of x given y.

Proposition 5 (Endogenous stratification as a consequence of cross-section income distribution). *For any income level $\bar{Y}^{\text{low}}$ and population values μ_1 and μ_2, there exists an income level $\bar{Y}^{\text{high}}$ such that no neighborhood will form that contains both μ_1 families with incomes above $\bar{Y}^{\text{high}}$ and μ_2 families with incomes below $\bar{Y}^{\text{low}}$.*

At the same time, the decreasing average cost structure for human capital formation provides incentives for heterogeneous neighborhoods. Further, these incentives will become more pronounced with a smaller family population. This means that sufficiently small neighborhoods will replicate themselves over time. Specifically, one can demonstrate that once the populations of individual neighborhoods lie below a threshold μ^{thresh} (which will generally depend on $\hat{F}_{Y,n,t}$), either the neighborhood population will stabilize or offspring from different neighborhoods will begin to form joint neighborhoods as adults. Further, there will exist a uniform lower bound on this minimum size as a neighborhood becomes wealthier, so that the size of wealthy neighborhoods will eventually stabilize. These features are summarized in Proposition 6.

Proposition 6 (Self-replication or recombination of small neighborhoods). (i) *For each $\hat{F}_{Y,n,t}$ there exists a maximum value μ^{thresh} such that, if $0 < \mu(N_{n,t}) \le \mu^{\text{thresh}}$, then either*

   (a)   *all offspring in $N_{n,t}$ will form a common neighborhood at $t+1$ or*
   (b)   *some offspring in $N_{n,t}$ will combine with offspring from other neighborhoods at $t+1$.*

(ii) *There exist a $\bar{Y} < \infty$ and a $\mu^* > 0$ such that $\mu^{\text{thresh}} > \mu^*$ if $\hat{F}_{Y,n,t}(\bar{Y}) = 0$.*

Finally, we observe that Proposition 6 implies that this economy does not exhibit economywide positive feedback effects, even though (as stated in Proposition 3) the economy does exhibit positive feedback effects conditional on a neighborhood's population size. This follows from the possibility that a monotonic rightward shift in the economywide empirical income distribution can result in a re-allocation of families across neighborhoods that acts to the detriment of poorer families. In this respect, an endogenous neighborhoods model will possess a different structure from the positive feedback models conventionally studied in macroeconomics. Once agents can choose the set of other agents with whom they interact, the welfare consequences of increases in the income of other agents are very different from an economy where the interaction environment is exogenously given.

Proposition 7 (Effect of changes in economywide income distribution on expected utility of parents and expected income of offspring). *For any economywide cross-section income distribution at t, there exist some monotonic rightward shifts of the distribution, under which no family's income declines, such that the expected utility of some adults and the expected income of their offspring are both reduced.*

4   Income distribution dynamics

In this section we consider some predictions of the model for the evolution of the cross-section income distribution. Our goal is to characterize how neighborhood feedbacks and endogenous stratification can combine to generate intertemporal inequality.

4.1   *One-generation-ahead dynamics*

The role of stratification in transmitting inequality stems from the effects of higher neighborhood income on both the tax base and marginal product of educational investment. These effects increase both the total and average product of tax revenues raised within a community, which by Proposition 2(ii) means that high- and low-income communities are more likely to produce high- and low-income offspring, respectively. The dependence of the expected income of offspring on a neighborhood's income distribution holds regardless of the neighborhood formation mechanism.

Endogenous stratification of communities has an important effect on the intergenerational transmission of economic status, by allowing the rich to separate themselves from the poor. The equilibrium formation process in this economy turns out to maximize the degree of inequality between rich and poor families. Proposition 8 states that, among all possible neighborhood configurations, endogenous stratification maximizes the expected income of the offspring of the highest-income family in the economy. Similarly, endogenous stratification minimizes the expected income of the offspring of the lowest-income family among all configurations that leave the size of the poorest family's neighborhood unaffected. This latter caveat is required since, if endogenous stratification leaves the poorest family living with a positive measure of wealthier neighbors, the expected income of that family's offspring could be further reduced by isolating the poorest family from those neighbors.

Proposition 8 (Effect of endogenous stratification on expected income of offspring of highest- and lowest-income families). *Under endogenous stratification:*

(i)   *the expected offspring income of the wealthiest family in the economy is maximized relative to any other configuration of families across neighborhoods; and*

(ii)   *the expected offspring income of the poorest family in the economy is minimized relative to any other configuration of families across neighborhoods that does not reduce the size of that family's neighborhood.*

By implication, frictions in the neighborhood formation process will reduce intergenerational inequality.

Endogenous stratification not only maximizes inequality among offspring with respect to possible neighborhood configurations, but also has implications for the relationship between the income gap across parents in different neighborhoods and the income gap across their offspring. In order to see this, we consider the behavior of the expected average income–growth rate among offspring of families in neighborhood n at t:

$$g_{n,t} = \frac{E(MY_{i,t+1} \mid i \in N_{n,t}, \mathfrak{F}_t) - MY_{n,t}}{MY_{n,t}}. \tag{13}$$

When wealthy neighborhoods and poor neighborhoods invest at a common tax rate, the feedbacks that affect the marginal product of education investment imply that the wealthy neighborhood's investment will be at least as productive as the poor neighborhood's investment. As a result, the mean income gap between equal-sized rich and poor neighborhoods will grow across time, as stated in Proposition 9. The equal-size restriction is important, because for some cross-section income distributions, the higher marginal product of education investment in a high-income neighborhood is offset by a higher per-capita cost of education investment due to the small population size induced by the desire of the wealthy to isolate themselves from the poor. Conversely, the proposition indicates how the gap between a rich majority and poor minority will increase over time.

Proposition 9 (Growth in mean income differential between parents and offspring across stratified communities). *For any two neighborhoods n and n' such that $\hat{F}_{Y,n,t}(s) < \hat{F}_{Y,n',t}(s)$ for all s and $\mu(N_{n,t}) \geq \mu(N_{n',t})$, average output growth among families in n will exceed growth in n':*

$$g_{n,t} - g_{n',t} > 0. \tag{14}$$

Therefore, positive feedbacks and endogenous stratification can lead to growing inequality.

4.2   *Long-run dynamics*

The model can exhibit interesting long-run relative income dynamics when family incomes are growing across time.[8] We therefore make an assumption which ensures that the model can exhibit income growth in some neighborhoods.

Assumption 1 (Conditions for growth in family incomes across neighborhoods).   There exist numbers $\bar{Y} < \infty$ and $\bar{\mu} \leq \mu^*$ such that, if $\hat{F}_{Y,n,t}(\bar{Y}) = 0$ and $\bar{\mu} \leq \mu(N_{n,t})$, then

$$\frac{\pi_2}{\pi_1 + \pi_2} \cdot \frac{\mu(N_{n,t})}{(\lambda_1 + \lambda_2)\mu(N_{n,t})} \cdot \phi\Theta(\hat{F}_{Y,n,t}) > 1. \tag{15}$$

[9]

This cumbersome expression has a straightforward interpretation. The first term, $\pi_2/(\pi_1 + \pi_2)$, is the equilibrium tax rate and hence equals the marginal change in per-capita spending with respect to an increase in the mean income of the neighborhood. The second term, $\mu(N_{n,t})/(\lambda_1 + \lambda_2)\mu(N_{n,t})$, is the marginal change in per-capita education investment with respect to a change in per-capita spending in a neighborhood of size $\mu(N_{n,t})$. The third term, $\phi\Theta(\hat{F}_{Y,n,t})$, is the marginal product in terms of offspring income of a change in education investment. The product of the three terms therefore equals the marginal change in the mean income of offspring with respect to an increase in the mean income of parents. The proof of Proposition 6 implies that any neighborhood whose population is less than μ^* and whose income distribution is shifted far enough to the right will replicate itself over time. Assumption 1 in conjunction with Proposition 6 therefore means that sufficiently wealthy neighborhoods can stabilize in size and experience positive average income growth.

In growing economies, endogenous stratification can combine with positive feedbacks to induce long-run inequality across families in two senses. First, relative income rankings can become fixed along some sample paths

---

[8]   In general, long-run inequality can occur in an economy without growth only if one assumes that the offspring of the sufficiently wealthy (poor) cannot have lower (higher) incomes than their parents. This requires a strong set of assumptions on the joint properties of preferences, technologies, and productivity shocks. In the current model there is the additional problem that the presence of constant tax rates and constant returns to scale means that all family incomes may converge to zero in the absence of growth. This problem can be corrected, though, by assuming that each adult receives a minimum income that is linearly augmented by his or her level of human capital. See also Becker and Tomes (1979) for a discussion of inequality in a growing economy.

[9]   Proposition 6 defines μ^* as the lower bound on the population size at which all neighborhoods above some income threshold will replicate themselves. Notice that this condition will always hold for large enough ϕ.

of the economy. Second, the gap between the richest and poorest families along these paths can grow without bound. These features occur because: (a) once families are separated into distinct communities, wealthier communities can (by Proposition 9) grow faster than poorer ones; and (b) once communities separate, these growth-rate differentials can preserve the separation of families across time. As a result, if the cross-section income distribution induces a sufficiently large gap between the average incomes of rich and poor neighborhoods, then the economy can exhibit permanent inequality with positive probability. This relationship between the economywide income distribution at t and the long-run dynamics of the economy is formalized in Proposition 10.

Proposition 10 (Permanent inequality between population subgroups under some initial conditions). *There exist economywide income distributions at time t and associated population sizes such that, with positive probability, for families in some pair of neighborhoods $N_{n,t}$ and $N_{n',t}$ with $MY_{n,t}/MY_{n',t} > 1$:*

(i) *relative income differences are preserved over all future generations,*

$$\text{Prob}\left(\frac{MY_{i,t+s}}{MY_{i',t+s}} \geq \frac{MY_{n,t}}{MY_{n',t}} \; \forall s > 0 \; \middle| \; i \in N_{n,t}, \, i' \in N_{n',t}\right) > 0; \quad (16)$$

and

(ii) *the income ratio between rich and poor becomes arbitrarily large. For any $K > 1$, there exists a k such that*

$$\text{Prob}\left(\frac{MY_{i,t+s}}{MY_{i',t+s}} \geq K \; \forall s \geq k \; \middle| \; i \in N_{n,t}, \, i' \in N_{n',t}\right) > 0. \quad (17)$$

The proof of Proposition 10 requires that a small population of poor families become permanently isolated from a larger population of wealthy families, so that the lower per-capita education costs induced by fixed costs permit the income gap to be perpetuated. While it seems reasonable that the depopulation and subsequent deterioration of the tax base of poor communities such as East Saint Louis has contributed to the breakdown of such public services as education, population differences do not in general seem to be that plausible a cause of long-run inequality. Observe, however, that if $\Theta(\cdot)$ can grow without bound then it is straightforward to show that the gap between a wealthy and a poor neighborhood can – depending on the specific form of $\Theta(\cdot)$ – still obey Proposition 10, even if the poor neighborhood is larger than the wealthy one. For example, if the productivity gap between initially rich and poor neighborhoods is preserved whenever the absolute gap between the two is preserved, then one can show that the initially higher income of the wealthy neighborhood can place it on a sample path where its human capital is always more productive than that of its poor counterpart.[10]

Can the required economywide income distribution for permanent inequality occur over the sample path realization of the economy? The answer is Yes, in two senses. First, by setting $t = 0$, Proposition 10 implies that some initial conditions for the economy will induce long-run inequality. This interpretation seems appropriate for analyzing an economy such as that of the United States, where the economic status of blacks has been so strongly affected by historical factors. Second, by choosing the distribution of $\xi_{i,t}$, one can ensure that the necessary economywide income distribution can occur with positive probability even if all families start off in the same neighborhood.

A second issue relates to whether the model is path-dependent. Can two distinct sample path realizations of the economy exhibit different long-run dynamics given the same initial conditions? Again, the answer is Yes. The neighborhood-specific shocks imply that different sample realizations can exhibit different forms of limiting behavior, as can be seen through the following argument. Suppose there is a probability distribution G such that a neighborhood containing the entire population will never break up if $\hat{F}(s) \leq G(s)$ for all s. This economy will exhibit long-run equality if the economywide income distribution ever exceeds G and if all families ever occupy the same neighborhood. However, the economywide income distribution depends on the realization of the individual productivity shocks, which will not obey the law of large numbers owing to the neighborhoodwide components. One could therefore have two sample path realizations of the economy: one where, after an initial split, all neighborhoods grow over time and eventually recombine into a common community; and another where the separation is preserved as an initial income gap grows while some neighborhoods prosper and others decline. What is required for a permanent split is that the gap between rich and poor be large enough by the time the poorest community's income distribution exceeds G that the rich wish to preserve separation. This is most likely to occur when the effect on $\Theta(\cdot)$ of including very poor families is large, so that very poor families are segregated into neighborhoods with low marginal product of education investment early in the history of the economy.

---

[10] For more general specifications of $\Theta(\cdot)$ than the one we study, differences between the human capital productivity of rich and poor can be perpetuated even if Θ is bounded. For example, if the marginal product of capital depends not only on a community's absolute income distribution but also on its income distribution relative to that of the rest of society, then productivity differences can become permanent.

5   Role of assumptions

5.1   Preference restrictions

The Cobb-Douglas assumption for preferences is a strong one and plays a critical role in our results.[11] By ensuring within-neighborhood unanimity in voting over tax rates, Cobb-Douglas preferences render the core configuration of families well-defined in the sense that all members of a neighborhood agree on the set of families whom they prefer as neighbors. This agreement results because each member of a neighborhood is always the median voter. If agents disagree on the first-best tax rate then they can also disagree on the preferred population of a community, as different populations will induce different tax-rate equilibria. Consequently, the model either may not have a core neighborhood configuration or may possess multiple core configurations under alternative preferences.

In addition, the constancy of tax rates across neighborhoods is also important for the intertemporal inequality results in Section 4. If rich neighborhoods were to save a smaller fraction of their incomes than poor ones, then the relatively greater productivity of education investment in the rich community would no longer be sufficient to ensure that the relative income between the communities grows across time. In this case, Propositions 9 and 10 can still hold, although it would be necessary to place joint restrictions on the utility function and $\Theta(\cdot)$ to ensure that the sample path of each neighborhoods's tax rate is nondecreasing in mean income.

5.2   Production function restrictions

The assumptions of multiplicative productivity shocks and the linear transformation of education expenditures into human capital are important factors, both in the determination of neighborhood tax rates and for the dynamic properties of the model. The general production function

$$Y_{i,\,t+1} = f(ED_{n,\,t}, \hat{F}_{Y,\,n,\,t}, \xi_{i,\,t+1}) \tag{18}$$

can always be rewritten as

$$Y_{i,\,t+1} = \phi ED_{n,\,t}\epsilon_{i,\,t+1}(ED_{n,\,t}, \hat{F}_{Y,\,n,\,t}), \tag{19}$$

where $\epsilon_{i,\,t+1}(ED_{n,\,t}, \hat{F}_{Y,\,n,\,t})$ is a shock whose conditional distribution (at t) is a function of $ED_{n,\,t}$ and $\hat{F}_{Y,\,n,\,t}$. A modified production function has several important implications for the analysis.

---

[11] In fact, parametric specifications such as the Cobb-Douglas assumption have been used by many authors studying multicommunity/income-distribution models, in order to avoid some of the problems we describe as well as for ease of analysis. See e.g. Bénabou (1992) and Glomm and Ravikumar (1992).

First, under this more general functional form, the tax rate in a neighborhood will generally depend on the empirical income distribution. To see this, consider the new first-order condition for an agent's preferred tax rate:

$$\frac{\pi_1}{(1-\tau)} = \frac{\pi_2}{\tau} + \pi_2 \, \mathrm{E}\left[\frac{\dfrac{\partial \epsilon_{i,\,t+1}}{\partial H_{i,\,t}} \dfrac{\partial H_{i,\,t}}{\partial ED_{n,\,t}} \dfrac{\partial ED_{n,\,t}}{\partial \tau}}{\epsilon_{i,\,t+1}(H_{i,\,t}, \hat{F}_{Y,\,n,\,t})} \,\Big|\, \mathfrak{F}_t \right] = 0. \tag{20}$$

In the basic model studied here, the third term in this expression is zero since $\partial \epsilon_{i,\,t+1}/\partial H_{i,\,t}$ is zero. When this term is nonzero, differences in the third term can induce different tax rates across neighborhoods. For example, suppose that $Y_{i,\,t+1} - \mathrm{E}(f(ED_{n,\,t}, \hat{F}_{Y,\,n,\,t}, \xi_{i,\,t+1}) | \mathfrak{F}_t)$ is uniformly bounded. This would imply that the support of $\xi_{i,\,t+1}$ shrinks toward 1 as $H_{i,\,t}$ increases. In this case, higher human capital formation would provide insurance against adverse productivity shocks, so that poor neighborhoods may wish to choose higher tax rates than rich ones. Tax-rate differences can in turn allow poor communities to invest a greater percentage of their income in education than rich ones, which would mean that Proposition 9 no longer necessarily holds.

Second, under a more general production function, the model can exhibit some form of decreasing returns to scale, which would affect the relative growth rates of rich and poor communities. This would occur if

$$\frac{\partial \mathrm{E}\epsilon_{i,\,t+1}(ED_{n,\,t}, \hat{F}_{Y,\,n,\,t})}{\partial ED_{n,\,t}} < 0. \tag{21}$$

In this case, it would be possible for equal-sized poorer communities to grow faster than richer communities if the concavity of the income function offsets the higher human capital formation associated with a given level of education investment, which would again violate Proposition 9.

However, observe that tax-rate differences and concavity of production functions do not necessarily imply that the model exhibits no permanent inequality in growing economies. Specifically, if the production function becomes asymptotically linear then the tendency for poorer communities to grow faster than richer ones – owing to higher savings rates and marginal product of education investment – may not be sufficient to cause the expected income difference between any two families to converge to zero over time; that is, Proposition 10 can still hold. The reason for this is that once a poorer community's income grows, it will experience the same range of the production function experienced previously by the wealthier community. Concavity of the production function and tax-rate differences add a transition component to the growth rates of different neighborhoods that will diminish as the poorer neighborhood's income grows. This transition component has important empirical consequences: The observation that poorer families have higher growth rates than richer ones does not necessarily imply that contemporaneous inequality in an economy will disappear over time.[12]

Finally, observe that nonlinearity of the aggregate production function will permit the marginal product of education investment in a poor neighborhood to exceed that in an equal-size rich neighborhood, which cannot occur under the assumption of constant returns to scale. In this case, it could be efficient for rich neighborhoods to lend to poor ones, if such contracts were enforceable. In the current model, the marginal product of a given level of education investment in a poor neighborhood can exceed that in a rich neighborhood only if the poor neighborhood is larger.

Similarly, if the average product of education investment is increasing over some range, a transfer of tax revenues from a rich to a poor neighborhood may be output-maximizing. For example, suppose there exists a number $\bar{E}$ and a probability distribution $\bar{F}$ such that $Y_{i,t+1} = f(\alpha ED_{n,t}, \xi_{i,t+1})$ with $\alpha < 1$ if $ED_{n,t} \le \bar{E}$ and $\hat{F}_{Y,n,t}(s) < \bar{F}(s)$, and that $Y_{i,t+1} = f(ED_{n,t}, \xi_{i,t+1})$ otherwise. This means that if a poor neighborhood chooses a per-capita investment of at least $\bar{E}$ then its production function will exhibit a jump. In this case, it is easy to construct an income distribution at t such that, under internal neighborhood finance, a neighborhood may not achieve this level of education investment, whereas total output at $t+1$ would be maximized by transferring tax revenues to this neighborhood from a rich one. This type of nonlinearity will also allow the model to exhibit poverty traps, where some communities become permanently fixed below some absolute income level while others experience sustained income growth. This type of model is analyzed in Durlauf (1994).

5.3   *Neighborhood formation rules*

The use of the core as an equilibrium concept maximizes the ability of families to form exclusionary neighborhoods. It is natural to inquire as to the effects of introducing an explicit market for housing in the model. One way to do this is to assume that, at the beginning of each period, families build houses in an initial phase of neighborhood formation. Families are then allowed to sell these houses on an open market in a subsequent phase in which no further construction within existing neighborhoods can take

---

[12] A formal demonstration of this argument can be found in Bernard and Durlauf (1993). Notice that the argument implies that the negative correlation between intergenerational family income growth and initial family income found by Solon (1992) and Zimmerman (1992) is compatible with long-run inequality in relative economic status.

place. Such a setting leads to two questions. First, is the core configuration of the model supportable by house-price differences across neighborhoods? Second, do other neighborhood configurations exist which are also supportable by house prices?

As shown in Appendix 2, the core configuration of families is supportable by house prices in the following sense: If each family in a neighborhood is free to sell its house and buy in another neighborhood, then there exists a set of neighborhood house prices at the core configuration such that no family wishes to move. At the same time, the appendix shows that the existence of such prices depends critically on the preference and production function assumptions we have made. In the absence of constant tax rates across neighborhoods, it is possible to construct examples where the core configuration is not supportable. However, it is possible to add restrictions on the neighborhood formation rules in order to ensure that an equilibrium exists for more general preference and production specifications. For example, authors such as Hamilton (1975) have shown in other contexts how zoning restrictions are required to augment house-price differences in order to achieve neighborhood stratification.

As for the second question, it is generally the case that many different initial neighborhood configurations exist that are supportable by house prices. A trivial example occurs if all families have one of two incomes and the rich wish to isolate themselves from the poor. In this case, if there exist two neighborhoods with identical family compositions then a set of prices will support this configuration, just as the appendix shows that stratification can be supported. In order for noncore neighborhood configurations to be ruled out, it must be the case that a set of families can always withdraw from an extant configuration and form a new neighborhood at any time. However, in this case a problem arises with the potential for "strategic" neighborhood formation in that families may form neighborhoods with the intention of selling their houses in order to accrue capital gains. The possibility of complex within-period neighborhood dynamics due to strategic neighborhood formation is an unresolved problem in these models, and will require a richer within-generation neighborhood formation structure than that described here.

Overall, the assumptions on preferences, technology, and neighborhood formation rules clearly play an important role in establishing the existence of an equilibrium. This sensitivity is not surprising, as the existence of multicommunity equilibria has been established in the urban economics literature only for very specialized economic environments (see e.g. Westhoff 1977). Further, some aspects of the dynamic properties of the economy are strongly affected by these assumptions. At the same time, these assumptions clearly are sufficient rather than necessary, so they provide a useful benchmark for understanding what requirements exist for persistent inequality to emerge.

6   Conclusions

This paper has developed a model of the evolution of the cross-section income distribution in an economy characterized by feedbacks from a neighborhood income distribution to the economic prospects of its offspring. These feedback effects create incentives for wealthier families to isolate themselves from poorer ones, so that all equilibrium neighborhood configurations of families are stratified. Under stratification, the economy will exhibit persistent inequality in two senses. First, the differences in average income between parents across neighborhoods are shown to be transmitted to offspring. Second, for some cross-section income distributions, permanent inequality is shown to emerge with positive probability. These results collectively suggest that when agents react to positive feedbacks by choosing with whom they interact, these feedbacks can produce sustained inequality.

One important extension of our model concerns a formal analysis of the properties of the productivity shocks that augment human capital in the determination of cross-section income distribution among offspring within a neighborhood. The current model takes this distribution as exogenous. Given the implication of the analysis that a sufficiently unequal cross-section distribution will induce intertemporal inequality, it is clearly important to understand what factors determine this distribution. One likely candidate is the way in which labor markets channel workers with different skills into jobs. This process will in turn depend both on the way in which agents with different skills interact in the aggregate production function and on the mechanism by which information about job availability diffuses through the population. Bénabou (1993) and Montgomery (1990) have studied aspects of these issues in a static context. Development of a dynamic analog of their work would not only permit a better understanding of the connections between the cross-section and intertemporal spillovers, but would also be important in allowing the basic model to capture higher-frequency fluctuations in the cross-section income distribution.

Appendix 1: Proofs of the propositions

Proof of Proposition 1:   Proposition 1 follows immediately from (10) and (11) and the subsequent discussion in the text.   □

Proof of Proposition 2:   At an initial equilibrium tax rate, agent $(i, t-1)$'s utility is increasing in rightward shifts of the income distribution of his neighbors, given (6), (7), and (8). Further, by Proposition 1, the equilibrium tax rate is unaffected by a shift in the neighborhood income distribution. This proves part (i). Moreover, since the equilibrium tax rate in a neighborhood is independent of its composition, the increases in both the tax base and human capital shift factor induced by a rightward shift in the income distribution of a given family's neighbors immediately implies part (ii).   □

Proof of Proposition 3:   We prove the existence of a core configuration by describing an algorithm by which such a configuration is constructed each period. Given the realized income distribution at t, place the family with the highest income in the economy in neighborhood 1. If the range of incomes is open from above, introduce a family whose income closes the economy's income range from above into neighborhood 1. Add to that neighborhood the largest measure of families that maximizes the utility of the parent of the family initially assigned to neighborhood 1. This collection of families is defined up to a set of measure zero because $\Theta(F_\epsilon)$ is continuous in ϵ. Among the remaining families, place the highest-income family among those not assigned to neighborhood 1 into neighborhood 2; as before, if the range of incomes among the remaining families is open from above, introduce a family whose income closes the set from above and place it in neighborhood 2. Add to that neighborhood the collection of families not assigned to neighborhood 1 that will maximize the utility of the first family assigned to neighborhood 2. Repeat this procedure until all families are assigned to neighborhoods 1 to D. We claim that this algorithm produces a core configuration. To see this, observe that by Proposition 2 all members of a neighborhood wish to have the highest-income neighbors for a neighborhood of fixed size. Hence, the relative neighborhood ranking by the richest family in the population is agreed upon by all families in the neighborhood. For families in neighborhood 1, this neighborhood is utility-maximizing among all possible neighborhoods in which they could reside. Proceeding down across neighborhoods, the same argument applies, so the neighborhood configuration produced by the algorithm is in the core. To verify (ii), suppose that two neighborhoods have nonstratified income distributions. In this case there exists a re-allocation of families across neighborhoods, given Proposition 2, such that the richest member across the two neighborhoods lives in a community of equal size with a preferred income distribution; under this re-allocation, the population will now be stratified by income. All members of the now wealthier neighborhood are also better off. Hence the original neighborhood configuration could not have been a core configuration. Finally, notice that the configuration produced by the algorithm is unique except for sets of measure zero. □

Proof of Proposition 4: Proposition 4 is an immediate consequence of (8), the assumption that all financing of education is determined within a neighborhood subject to a no-borrowing constraint, and the white-noise assumption on $\xi_{i,t+1}$. □

Proof of Proposition 5: The proposition will hold for all neighborhoods if it holds for a neighborhood consisting of μ_1 families with income Y^{high} and μ_2 families with incomes Y^{low}. In this case, the high-income families will agree to live with the low-income families only if

$$\frac{\pi_2}{\pi_1+\pi_2}\mu_2 Y^{\text{low}}-\lambda_2\mu_2 ED_{n,t} > 0, \tag{A1.1}$$

where $ED_{n,t}$ is the level of per-capita education expenditure when the two groups live together. However, since the tax rate is independent of neighborhood composition, $ED_{n,t}$ increases with Y^{high} in such a way that, for a sufficiently large value of Y^{high}, (A1.1) will be violated. □

Proof of Proposition 6: Define the collection of offspring of $N_{n,t}$ as O_{t+1}, with the empirical income distribution $\hat{F}_{Y,O,t+1}$ and the associated mean income $MY_{O,t+1}$. We consider the desired neighborhood configuration of the wealthiest offspring among members of O_{t+1}, designated as agent $i, t+1$, who also resides in neighborhood n as an adult.

First, observe that if we define

$$\kappa_{i,t+1} = \frac{\phi\Theta(\hat{F}_{Y,n,t+1})\mu(N_{n,t+1})MY_{n,t+1}}{(\lambda_1+\lambda_2\mu(N_{n,t+1}))Y_{i,t+1}} \tag{A1.2}$$

then agent $(i, t+1)$'s optimal tax choice will implicitly maximize

$$\pi_1\log(Y_{i,t+1}-T_{i,t+1})+\pi_2\,\text{E}(\log(\kappa_{i,t+1}T_{i,t+1}\xi_{i,t+2}\,|\,\mathcal{F}_{t+1})), \tag{A1.3}$$

implying that the agent will choose a neighborhood that maximizes $\kappa_{i,t+1}$.

In order for agent i, t to choose $N_{n,t+1} \subset O_{t+1}$, it must be the case that dropping all families below some income threshold will make i, t better off when compared to living with all offspring in $N_{n,t}$. Let $O_{\epsilon,t+1}$ denote the population of families in O_{t+1} that remains after dropping the poorest $\epsilon \times 100$ percent of families; $\hat{F}_{Y,O,\epsilon,t+1}$ denotes the income distribution and $MY_{O,\epsilon,t+1}$ denotes the mean income after dropping the ϵ families. Without loss of generality, assume that $\Theta(\hat{F}_{O,\epsilon,t+1})$ and $MY_{O,\epsilon,t+1}$ are differentiable with respect to ϵ; in fact, continuity of the functions is sufficient.

In order for $N_{n,t+1} \subset O_{t+1}$ to denote an equilibrium or core neighborhood configuration, it must be the case that the derivative of $\kappa_{i,t+1}$ with respect to ϵ is zero or positive at some $\epsilon > 0$. This derivative is

$$\left(\frac{\phi}{Y_{i,t+1}}\right)\left(\left(\frac{\partial(\Theta(\hat{F}_{O,\epsilon,t+1})MY_{O,\epsilon,t+1})}{\partial\epsilon}\right)\left(\frac{\mu(O_{\epsilon,t+1})}{\lambda_1+\lambda_2\mu(O_{\epsilon,t+1})}\right)\right.$$
$$\left. + \Theta(\hat{F}_{O,\epsilon,t+1})MY_{O,\epsilon,t+1}\cdot\left(\frac{\lambda_1}{(\lambda_1+\lambda_2\mu(O_{\epsilon,t+1}))^2}\right)\right)\cdot\left(\frac{\partial\mu(O_{\epsilon,t+1})}{\partial\epsilon}\right).$$

$$(A1.4)$$

The variation in $\phi\Theta(\hat{F}_{O,\epsilon,t+1})MY_{O,\epsilon,t+1}/Y_{i,t+1}$ is bounded for all ϵ by (3) and (9) and by the uniform boundedness of $\xi_{i,t+1}$ (which bounds the ratio of richest to poorest offspring within a neighborhood). Further, $\partial\mu(O_{\epsilon,t+1})/\partial\epsilon = -1$. Therefore, when $\mu(O_{t+1})$ is small enough, a desired reduction in population from O_{t+1} by agent i,t requires that

$$-\frac{\phi\Theta(\hat{F}_{Y,O,\epsilon,t+1})MY_{O,\epsilon,t+1}}{Y_{i,t+1}}\cdot\frac{\lambda_1}{(\lambda_1+\lambda_2\mu(O_{\epsilon,t+1}))^2} \geq 0. \qquad (A1.5)$$

However, for $\mu(N_{n,t})$ small enough, (A1.5) can never hold because $\mu(O_{\epsilon,t+1}) < \mu(N_{n,t})$ for $\epsilon > 0$, proving part (i).

To prove part (ii), observe that if $\hat{F}_{Y,n,t}(\bar{Y}) = 0$ and $\bar{Y}$ is shifted far enough to the right then $\Theta(\hat{F}_{O,\epsilon,t+1}) - \Theta(\hat{F}_{O,t+1})$ must be nonincreasing in the lower bound on incomes in O_{t+1}, by (9). This means that changes in the largest admissible value of μ^{thresh} as the income distribution shifts to the right must eventually become negligible, which implies part (ii). $\square$

Proof of Proposition 7: Suppose that all families start with any initial income $\bar{Y}^{\text{low}}$. Under decreasing average costs, all families will inhabit the same neighborhood in this case. Now suppose that the incomes of a positive measure of families increase to $\bar{Y}^{\text{high}}$, where $\bar{Y}^{\text{high}}$ is chosen (as can always be done, by Proposition 6) so that those families with incomes greater than or equal to $\bar{Y}^{\text{high}}$ refuse to form neighborhoods with those with incomes equal to $\bar{Y}^{\text{low}}$. Clearly, those families whose incomes did not change are worse off. By extension, for any initial income distribution, there must exist some rightward shifts of the economywide income distribution, under which no family's income declines, such that a positive measure of those families who reside in the poorest neighborhood become worse off by losing their wealthier neighbors. This verifies the proposition. $\square$

Proof of Proposition 8: As discussed in the proof of Proposition 6, the wealthiest family will live in the neighborhood that maximizes $\kappa_{i,t}$ among all possible neighborhood configurations. Since $T_{i,t}$ is independent of which neighborhood the richest family resides in, this means – given (A1.2) and (A1.3) – that the human capital investment of the family's offspring is maximized, which proves part (i). For the lowest-income family, endogenous stratification means that the poorest family lives in the neighborhood with the lowest income distribution among all those of a given size. Hence, by Proposition 2(ii), this must be the neighborhood that minimizes the expected income of its offspring.   □

Proof of Proposition 9:   If two neighborhoods n and n' are of equal size at t then

$$\frac{ED_{n,t}}{MY_{n,t}} = \frac{ED_{n',t}}{MY_{n',t}}, \tag{A1.6}$$

since each will choose the same tax rate under Cobb–Douglas preferences. Furthermore, $\Theta(\hat{F}_{Y,n,t}) > \Theta(\hat{F}_{Y,n',t})$ by assumption of the proposition. Therefore, substituting (A1.6) and (2) into (13), one finds that

$$g_{n,t} = \frac{\phi\Theta(\hat{F}_{Y,n,t})ED_{n,t} - MY_{n,t}}{MY_{n,t}} > \frac{\phi\Theta(\hat{F}_{Y,n',t})ED_{n',t} - MY_{n',t}}{MY_{n',t}} = g_{n',t}. \tag{A1.7}$$

Moreover,

$$\frac{\partial(ED_{n,t}/MY_{n,t})}{\partial\mu(N_{n,t})} = \frac{\tau\lambda_1}{(\lambda_1 + \lambda_2\mu(N_{n,t}))^2} > 0, \tag{A1.8}$$

so that (A1.7) still holds if $\mu(N_{n,t}) > \mu(N_{n',t})$, proving the proposition.   □

Proof of Proposition 10:   This proposition is verified by constructing an economywide distribution of income at t and a population size that fulfill the proposition. We do this for the case where the total population of the economy lies between μ^* and $2\mu^*$, where μ^* is defined in Proposition 6; extension of the argument to a larger population is straightforward.

1. Assign a population of μ_1 families to neighborhood n and μ_2 to neighborhood n', where $\mu_1 > \mu_2$ and $\bar{\mu} \leq \mu_1 \leq \mu^*$. We designate families in $N_{n,t}$ by i and in $N_{n',t}$ by i'. By choosing a large enough minimum income for these neighborhoods at t, one can ensure that these neighborhoods are self-replicating in the sense of Proposition 6 and that the expected average growth rate in income is positive among families in $N_{n,t}$.

2. Assume that, at time t, all families have the same incomes within each of the neighborhoods that have been formed. Further, choose the incomes within each neighborhood to be far enough apart so that (a) these neighborhoods will be equilibrium configurations at t and (b) offspring

across the neighborhoods will not recombine at $t+1$ if the wealthier neighborhood's mean income grows at a faster rate than the poorer one's. This can always be done (given in Proposition 5) because, when the productivity shocks have uniformly bounded support, one can choose the population sizes in the two neighborhoods in such a way that the percentage gap between the minimum income among offspring in the wealthy neighborhood and the maximum income among offspring in the poor neighborhood grows in expected value.

3. If at $t+s$ the original neighborhoods have been preserved each period since t and if $MY_{i,t+s}/MY_{i',t+s} \geq MY_{n,t}/MY_{n',t}$, then – given the construction of the neighborhoods at t – one can always write a law of motion for $\log(MY_{i,t+s+1}/MY_{i',t+s+1})$ of the form

$$
\begin{aligned}
\log(&MY_{i,t+s+1}/MY_{i',t+s+1}) \\
&= E((\log(MY_{i,t+s+1}/MY_{i,t+s}) - \log(MY_{i',t+s+1}/MY_{i',t+s})) \,|\, \mathcal{F}_t) \\
&\quad + \log(MY_{i,t+s}/MY_{i',t+s}) + \zeta_{t+s+1},
\end{aligned} \tag{A1.9}
$$

where for some $\nu > 0$,

$$
E((\log(MY_{i,t+s+1}/MY_{i,t+s}) - \log(MY_{i',t+s+1}/MY_{i',t+s})) \,|\, \mathcal{F}_t) \geq \nu \tag{A1.10}
$$

and ζ_{t+s+1} is a martingale difference. This follows because the expected growth rate of the wealthier community must exceed that of the poorer one by some minimum amount, owing to the difference in population size. Further, ζ_{t+s+1} has uniformly bounded support, by (3).

Given (A1.9) and (A1.10), if

$$
\text{Prob}(MY_{i,t+s}/MY_{i',t+s} \geq MY_{n,t}/MY_{n',t} \; \forall s > 0) > 0 \tag{A1.11}
$$

then the log of the income gap between families i and i' will, with positive probability, behave as a random walk with drift. A random walk with a drift parameter that is bounded from below by any positive ν with uniformly bounded innovations has two important features. First, the process will diverge with probability 1. Second, following Durlauf (1994), one can show that – by the law of large numbers for uniformly bounded martingale differences (see Stout 1974 for a statement) – the set of values less than or equal to any initial value of such a process is a transient set of states for the process. This means that if (A1.11) holds, the mean incomes of the rich and poor neighborhoods will obey both parts of the proposition.

4. The probability that the income ratio between the two communities is bounded from below by $MY_{n,t}/MY_{n',t}$ can be determined by studying the auxiliary process Z_{t+s}:

$$
Z_{t+s+1} = \nu + Z_{t+s} + \zeta^*_{t+s+1}, \tag{A1.12}
$$

where ζ_{t+s}^* is a uniformly bounded martingale difference sequence such that $\zeta_{t+s}^* = \zeta_{t+s}$ if $MY_{i,\,t+r}/MY_{i',\,t+r} \geq MY_{n,\,t}/MY_{n',\,t}$ for all $r = 0, ..., s-1$, and $Z_t = \log(MY_{n,\,t}/MY_{n',\,t})$. (Recall here that we take t as fixed and let the process evolve with respect to s.)

By construction,

$$\text{Prob}(MY_{i,\,t+s}/MY_{i',\,t+s} \geq MY_{n,\,t}/MY_{n',\,t} \; \forall s > 0)$$
$$\geq \text{Prob}(Z_{t+s} \geq Z_t \; \forall s > 0). \qquad (A1.13)$$

However, the process Z_t is a random walk with constant drift and uniformly bounded increments, which means that the set of values of the support of the process that are less than or equal to its initial state is transient. That is,

$$\text{Prob}(Z_{t+s} \geq Z_t \; \forall s > 0) > 0, \qquad (A1.14)$$

which completes the proof. $\qquad\qquad\qquad\qquad\qquad\qquad\qquad\qquad\square$

Appendix 2: Supportability of neighborhood stratification with house prices

We provide an interpretation of the core configuration in this model as one that is supportable by house prices. Following the discussion in Section 5, suppose that at the beginning of every period each family is assigned to a neighborhood in which it costlessly builds a house. Once neighborhoods are initially formed, no further construction can occur.[13] However, existing houses may be sold to any family. We claim there exists a sequence of neighborhood-specific house prices $P_{d,\,t}$ such that if the initial assignment of families coincides with the core configuration described in Proposition 3, no family can improve utility by moving.

Consider first the existence of a house-price sequence that separates families assigned to neighborhoods 1 and 2 as defined in the proof of Proposition 3. In order for $P_{1,\,t}$ and $P_{2,\,t}$ to support stratification, it must be the case for any pair of agents $i, t-1 \in N_{1,\,t}$ and $i', t-1 \in N_{2,\,t}$ that if

$$\pi_1 \log((1-\tau)Y_{i,\,t}) + \pi_2 \log(\phi H_{i,\,t})$$
$$= \pi_1 \log((1-\tau)(Y_{i,\,t} + P_{1,\,t} - P_{2,\,t})) + \pi_2 \log(\phi H_{i',\,t}) \qquad (A2.1)$$

then

$$\pi_1 \log((1-\tau)(Y_{i',\,t} - P_{1,\,t} + P_{2,\,t})) + \pi_2 \log(\phi H_{i,\,t})$$
$$\leq \pi_1 \log((1-\tau)(Y_{i',\,t})) + \pi_2 \log(\phi H_{i',\,t}). \qquad (A2.2)$$

---

[13] The assumption that initial housing construction is costless has no bearing on the results. The restriction on post–neighborhood formation construction is necessary to preclude costless entry into existing neighborhoods.

Here $\tau = \pi_2/(\pi_1 + \pi_2)$ for both neighborhoods under Cobb–Douglas preferences.

Since the required price differential $P_{1,t} - P_{2,t}$ for (A2.1) to hold is increasing in $Y_{i,t}$ whereas the required range of price differentials such that (A2.2) holds is decreasing in $Y_{i',t}$, the existence of a stratifying price sequence will hold so long as (A2.1) implies (A2.2) when $Y_{i,t} = Y_{i',t}$. However, this requires that

$$\frac{Y_{i,t}}{Y_{i,t} + P_{1,t} - P_{2,t}} \leq \frac{Y_{i,t}}{Y_{i,t} - P_{1,t} + P_{2,t}}, \tag{A2.3}$$

which will always hold if $P_{1,t} - P_{2,t} > 0$. However, because all families agree on the relative ranking of neighborhoods, this last inequality must hold since the wealthiest family in neighborhood 1 prefers that neighborhood to neighborhood 2. This establishes that there exists a house-price differential between the first two neighborhoods that supports the stratification. One can proceed sequentially to construct a house-price differential between neighborhoods 2 and 3 that supports the core configuration across the first three neighborhoods, and so on until the core allocation is supported across the economy.

Notice that the constancy of tax rates across neighborhoods is essential for ensuring the existence of house prices that support the degree of stratification desired by wealthier families, given an arbitrary distribution of income. To see this, suppose that family i lives in a wealthy community w and that family i' lives in a poor community p. In a stratified equilibrium, it must be the case that if

$$\begin{aligned} u((1-\tau_w)Y_{i,t}) &+ \mathrm{E}(v(H_{w,t},\xi_{i,t}) \,|\, \mathcal{F}_t) \\ &= u((1-\tau_p)(Y_{i,t} + P_{w,t} - P_{p,t})) + \mathrm{E}(v(H_{p,t},\xi_{i,t}) \,|\, \mathcal{F}_t) \end{aligned} \tag{A2.4}$$

then

$$\begin{aligned} u((1-\tau_w)(Y_{i',t} &- P_{w,t} + P_{p,t})) + \mathrm{E}(v(H_{w,t},\xi_{i',t})) \\ &\leq u((1-\tau_p)(Y_{i',t})) + \mathrm{E}(v(H_{p,t},\xi_{i',t}) \,|\, \mathcal{F}_t); \end{aligned} \tag{A2.5}$$

(A2.4) and (A2.5) jointly require that

$$\begin{aligned} u((1-\tau_p)(Y_{i',t})) &- u((1-\tau_w)(Y_{i',t} - P_{w,t} + P_{p,t})) \\ &\geq u((1-\tau_p)(Y_{i,t} + P_{w,t} - P_{p,t})) - u((1-\tau_w)Y_{i,t}). \end{aligned} \tag{A2.6}$$

For this condition to hold for all possible income distributions, it must hold if an arbitrarily small percentage of families in neighborhood p have incomes equal to $Y_{i,t} - \epsilon$. In this case, however, (A2.6) can hold for all values of τ_p, τ_w, and $P_{w,t} - P_{p,t} > 0$ only if $\tau_w \geq \tau_p$. Otherwise, there may not be a set of prices that support stratification. Intuitively, when taxes are lower in rich neighborhoods, the cost of entry on the part of members of poorer neighborhoods is partially defrayed by the lower tax burden. Under alternative preferences, either (a) tax rates will need to increase with neighborhood size, or (b) the differences in school quality between neighborhoods will need to be large enough to ensure that the price $P_{w,t} - P_{p,t}$ which makes a rich family indifferent to moving is so high that no one in the poor neighborhood will be willing to pay it.

REFERENCES

deBartolome, C. A. M. (1991), "Equilibrium and Inefficiency in a Community Model with Peer Group Effects," *Journal of Political Economy* 98: 110–33.

Becker, G. S., and N. Tomes (1979), "An Equilibrium Theory of the Distribution of Income and Intergenerational Mobility," *Journal of Political Economy* 87: 1153–89.

Bénabou, R. (1992), "Heterogeneity, Stratification, and Growth," mimeo, Department of Economics, New York University.

(1993), "Workings of a City: Location, Education, and Production," *Quarterly Journal of Economics* 108: 619–52.

Bernard, A., and S. Durlauf (1993), "Interpreting Tests of the Convergence Hypothesis," mimeo, Department of Economics, University of Wisconsin, Madison; *Journal of Econometrics* (forthcoming).

Card, D., and A. Krueger (1992), "Does School Quality Matter? Returns to Education and the Characteristics of Public Schools in the United States," *Journal of Political Economy* 100: 1–40.

Case, A., and L. Katz (1991), "The Company You Keep: The Effects of Family and Neighborhood on Disadvantaged Families," Working Paper no. 3705, National Bureau of Economic Research, Cambridge, MA.

Cooper, R., and A. John (1988), "Coordinating Coordination Failures in Keynesian Models," *Quarterly Journal of Economics* 103: 441–64.

Corcoran, M., R. Gordon, D. Laren, and G. Solon (1989), "Effects of Family and Community Background on Men's Economic Status," Working Paper no. 2896, National Bureau of Economic Research, Cambridge, MA.

Crane, J. (1991), "The Epidemic Theory of Ghettos and Neighborhood Effects on Dropping Out and Teenage Childbearing," *American Journal of Sociology* 96: 1226–59.

Datcher, L. (1982), "Effects of Community and Family Background on Achievement," *Review of Economics and Statistics* 64: 32–41.

Durlauf, S. (1994), "A Theory of Persistent Income Inequality," mimeo, Department of Economics, University of Wisconsin, Madison; *Journal of Economic Growth* (forthcoming).

Fernandez, R., and R. Rogerson (1992), "Income Distribution, Communities, and the Quality of Public Education: A Policy Analysis," mimeo, Department of Economics, Boston University.

Galor, O., and J. Zeira (1993), "Income Distribution and Macroeconomics," *Review of Economic Studies* 60: 35–52.

Glomm, G., and B. Ravikumar (1992), "Public vs. Private Investment in Human Capital: Endogenous Growth and Income Inequality," *Journal of Political Economy* 100: 818–34.

Hamilton, B. (1975), "Zoning and Property Taxation in a System of Local Governments," *Urban Studies* 12: 205–11.

Jencks, C., and S. Mayer (1990), "The Social Consequences of Growing Up in a Poor Neighborhood," in L. E. Lynn and M. G. H. McGreary (eds.), *Inner-City Poverty in the United States*. Washington, DC: National Academy Press.

Loury, G. C. (1981), "Intergenerational Transfers and the Distribution of Earnings," *Econometrica* 49: 843–67.

Lundberg, S. and R. Startz (1992), "On the Persistence of Racial Inequality," mimeo, Department of Economics, University of Washington, Seattle.

Montgomery, J. (1990), "Social Networks and Persistent Inequality in the Labor Market," mimeo, Department of Economics, Northwestern University, Evanston, IL.

(1991), "Social Networks and Labor-Market Outcomes: Towards an Economic Analysis," *American Economic Review* 81: 1408–18.

Solon, G. (1992), "Intergenerational Income Mobility in the United States," *American Economic Review* 82: 393–408.

Stout, W. F. (1974), *Almost Sure Convergence*. New York: Academic Press.

Streufert, P. A. (1991), "The Effect of Underclass Isolation on Schooling Choice," mimeo, Department of Economics, University of Wisconsin, Madison.

Westhoff, F. (1977), "Existence of Equilibria in Economics with a Local Public Good," *Journal of Economic Theory* 14: 84–112.

Wilson, W. J. (1987), *The Truly Disadvantaged*. University of Chicago Press.

Zimmerman, D. (1992), "Regression Towards Mediocrity in Economic Stature," *American Economic Review* 82: 409–29.